The East German Social Courts

The East German Social Courts

Law and Popular Justice in a Marxist-Leninist Society

PETER W. SPERLICH

PRAEGER

Westport, Connecticut
London

Library of Congress Cataloging-in-Publication Data

Sperlich, Peter W., 1934–
The East German social courts : law and popular justice in a Marxist-Leninist society / Peter W. Sperlich.
p. cm.
Includes bibliographical references and index.
ISBN-13: 978–0–275–97564–7 (alk. paper)
ISBN-10: 0–275–97564–9 (alk. paper)
1. Municipal courts—Germany (East) 2. Lay judges—Germany, East.
3. Justice, Administration of—Germany, East. 4. Law and socialism.
5. Germany (East)—Politics and government. I. Title.
KKA3694.S64 2007
347.431′02—dc22 2006039612

British Library Cataloguing in Publication Data is available.

Library of Congress Catalog Card Number: 2006039612
ISBN-10: 0–275–97564–9
ISBN-13: 978–0–275–97564–7

First published in 2007

Praeger Publishers, 88 Post Road West, Westport, CT 06881
An imprint of Greenwood Publishing Group, Inc.
www.praeger.com

Printed in the United States of America

The paper used in this book complies with the Permanent Paper Standard issued by the National Information Standards Organization (Z39.48–1984).

10 9 8 7 6 5 4 3 2 1

This book is dedicated to my siblings
Werner M. Sperlich
and
Christa B. Schumann-Sperlich

to two very special friends
Dame Loh de Macuto
and
Siegfried E. de Cologne

and to these who have mattered
B.A., L.A., T.A., J.B., C.C., M.E., W.F., K.G.,
N.H., T.H., V.H., M.S., U.S., D.T., M.V., X.X.

Contents

Acronyms and Abbreviations

AC	Arbitration Commission
BRD	Bundesrepublik Deutschland (Federal Republic of Germany)
CDU	Christlich Demokratische Union (Christian Democratic Union)
CPSU	Communist Party of the Soviet Union
CSU	Christlich Soziale Union (Christian Social Union)
DBD	Demokratische Bauernpartei Deutschlands (Democratic Peasants Party of Germany)
DC	Dispute Commission
DDR	Deutsche Demokratische Republik (see GDR)
FDGB	Freier Deutscher Gerwerkschaftsbund (Free German Trade Union Federation)
FDJ	Freie Deutsche Jugend (Free German Youth)
FDP	Freie Demokratische Partei (Free Democratic Party)
FRG	Federal Republic of Germany
GDR	German Democratic Republic (see DDR)
KGB(NKGB)	People's Commissariat of State Security
KPD	Kommunistische Partei Deutschlands (Communist Party of Germany)
LDPD	Liberal Demokratische Partei Deutschlands (Liberal Democratic Party of Germany)
MfS	Ministerium für Staatssicherheit (Ministry for State Security)
NES	New Economic System (of Socialism)

NF	National Front
NDPD	National Democratische Partei Deutschlands (National Democratic Party of Germany)
NSDAP	Nationalsozialistische Deutsche Arbeiterpartei (National-Socialist German Workers Party)
PDS	Partei des Demokratischen Sozialimus (Party of Democratic Socialism)
SBZ	Soviet Zone of Occupation
SED	Sozialistische Einheitspartei Deutschlands (Socialist Unity Party of Germany)
SMAD	Soviet Military Administration in Germany
SPD	Sozialdemokratische Partei Deutschlands (Socialdemocratic Party of Germany)
STASI	Staatssicherheitsdienst (State Security Service)
SZ	Soviet Zone
USSR	Union of Socialist Soviet Republics

Part I

General Considerations

Chapter 1

Introduction

FAILURES AND SUCCESSES IN SOCIALIST REGIMES

This is a discussion of institutional successes that took place in the context of a comprehensive and abysmal failure. The successes are the *social courts* of the former German Democratic Republic (GDR), also know as East Germany. The failure, of course, is the GDR as such, a thoroughly rotten, shabby, and oppressive system. That there should have been an institutional success will surprise most readers. The grounds for this evaluation will appear later in the book. In the meantime, I will readily concede that the social courts were the *only* entities emerging in the GDR that were at all admirable.

The social courts were a splendid semi-innovation—"semi" because they were in part derived from Soviet models and in other part from the traditional German legal office of the *Schiedsmann* (community arbitrator). The social courts were a pure *lay* institution. They had a wide range of functions: (1) relieve the state courts of the need to deal with a variety of minor civil and criminal case, (2) give ordinary citizens an important role to play in the administration of justice, and (3) raise the citizens' legal knowledge and consciousness.[1] As will develop later, the social courts also had a large number of auxiliary functions, some relating to the administration of justice, some not. Among the most important of the auxiliary functions was to tie citizens more closely to the regime through participatory acts.[2] This, the social courts did not deliver. In most other things they were eminently successful.

To return to the failures, the *German Democratic Republic* failed as a political, economic, and social system. In addition (and closely related) *communism* failed both as an ideology and as practice.[3] Communism and its failures have been the subject of an extensive literature. Even the non-specialist public is fairly well informed abut the basic attributes and debilities of this *Weltanschauung*. The German Democratic Republic, by contrast, was not (and is not) among the well-known countries of this globe. It was a country about which the West knew very little.[4] Western writings about the GDR tended to have titles such as "Travel to an Unknown Country." Even the citizens of West Germany were but scantily informed about their brethren on the other side of the Iron Curtain.[5] As late as 1987, a West German publication reflected the situation quite correctly, when it was put forth under the title: UNKNOWN NEIGHBOR GDR.[6] Even less was known about the GDR in the other countries of Western Europe and in the United States. Indeed, the history of Central (and Eastern) Europe is barely known even among those who write about these regions.[7]

Almost nothing was (and is) known in the West about the East German social courts. Western research programs on socialist law and politics gave very little attention to these tribunals. The voluminous GDR literature on the social courts—dozens of books, hundreds of chapters, and thousands of journal and newspaper articles—has been almost entirely ignored. The legal system within which the social courts were embedded also received little attention.[8] Even scholarly volumes specifically devoted to the GDR tended to neglect the country's legal system and the organization and functioning of its courts.

The political-institutional entities that are at the core of this book (and of the two previous ones—see note 3) have, of course, disappeared. The German Democratic Republic vanished *de facto* on November 9, 1989, when the Berlin Wall was breached, and *de jure* on October 3, 1990, when the German Unification Treaty took effect. The social courts expired in stages. The factory-based dispute commissions (one of the two forms of the social courts) first fell into disuse and then became officially extinct when in 1990 the West German labor codes were extended to the territory of the former GDR. The residential-based arbitration commissions (the other form) were not formally abolished but simply evaporated when their support structures disappeared.

Communism, as ideology or practice, has not vanished entirely, of course. At this writing, there still are communist states, most prominently China (PRC), North Korea, and Cuba.[9] Communist ideology (i.e., Marxism-Leninism) has retained followers and sympathizers in the East and West. In several of the former socialist countries, socialism/communism is even making electoral comebacks. Most remarkable is the electoral success of the (East) German PDS (Party of Democratic Socialism), the direct successor to the SED (Socialist Unity Party), the official communist party of the GDR.[10] Communism, then, is by no means a dead dogma, even if its prominence and influence have drastically declined.

Why, then, write about a failed and deteriorated entity? There are several answers. First, the GDR was a country of sufficient importance to justify historical studies. Second, the ability of a political-legal investigation to produce useful[11] and interesting information does not depend on the immortality of its subject matter. Third, even system failures can teach valuable lessons—sometimes failures even more so than accomplishments. Fourth, overall failure does not necessarily bespeak failure in every detail—and, as noted, the social courts were among the more viable features of the East German system. Fifth, the experience of the social courts can convey valuable information about various aspects of lay adjudication. The social courts should not simply be consigned to oblivion.

It does seem likely, however, that in a not so distant future almost nothing will be remembered of the four-decades-plus socialist experiment on German soil. This book and its two predecessors seek to forestall the complete loss of information about a number of aspects of East German society, politics, economics, ideology, and law. The current volume, most importantly, wishes to provide a record of the structures, functions, decisions, and personnel of the social courts,[12] as well as of the interactions of these courts with other parts of the legal and political system. The analysis will include political and jurisprudential evaluations of the social courts. There will be commendations but there will also be criticisms.

COMPARATIVE LEGAL ANALYSIS

Comparative legal studies hold high promise, from a jurisprudential as well as from historical, educational, and philosophical perspectives.[13] To really understand the law and legal institutions, one cannot limit the scope of one's investigations to a single country or to a single legal tradition. Apart from the cognitive advantages, comparative explorations can also have great practical benefits. New codes and new methods of legal administration contemplated for adoption in one country may have been tried elsewhere already. It may be possible to learn how well they work, even if in a different context. It can save us the effort of "inventing the wheel all over again"; it can also save us from the harm of adopting unsound novelties.[14]

The legitimacy of comparative legal studies does not depend, of course, on the promise of practical benefits. The possibility of such benefits, however, is not to be scorned. Given the genuine need for diverting minor civil and criminal cases away from the regular courts—at least in this country, but in all likelihood also elsewhere—it would appear to be a timely undertaking to investigate systems of routinized and voluminous lay adjudication, such a the socialist social courts.[15]

In this study, the primary country of comparison will be the German Democratic Republic. The GDR provided the best example of social courts well integrated with the state courts. Also, they were extant for over 40 years—a period of sufficient length to discover the strength and weaknesses of the institution. The lay tribunals of most other socialist countries tended to be less well integrated into the country's overall administration of justice—least of all the comrades' courts of the Soviet Union[16]—which makes them less interesting for present purposes.[17]

While few will object to the study of comparative politics or comparative law as such, some may wonder about the comparability of the GDR and the United States. In many ways, they were polar opposites. Can both systems be comprehended within one analytical framework? Can anything useful be discovered in one for the other? These questions are better answered at the end than at the beginning of the comparative investigation. There seem to be good reasons, however, to make the effort.[18] As a general principle of comparative work, the more similar two systems, the easier it is to fit them into a single analytical framework, but, by the same token, the smaller will be the likely payoff. The theoretical postulates are not likely to become much enriched if the second country largely resembles the first. Comparative analysis becomes more difficult, but also potentially more fruitful, when the systems under investigation exhibit substantial differences.

Nevertheless, serious skepticism about the current enterprise must be expected. Doubts are likely to be expressed at least on these two grounds: (1) the legal systems of the GDR and the United States are too different *in practice* (even if subsumable under a highly abstract theory) to permit the incorporation of structural or functional elements of one to the other, and (2) the legal systems of the two countries are components of diametrically opposed ideologies—socialism and capitalism—representing different stages (using the marxist framework) of societal development.[19] Thus, transfers also are not possible *in principle* and any hope of utilitarian benefits is illusionary.

The first objection cannot be answered *a priori.* It seems eminently sensible to be doubtful about taking an element of one system and making part of another. Yet, it has been done—often with considerable success. The legal systems of most third-world countries are an amalgam of native traditions, civil-law codes (usually modeled on France or Germany), and common-law elements (usually modeled on the United States or Great Britain), particularly in contract law. While tensions exist among these strains, they have not generally produced chaos or breakdown. Third-world legal systems offer much support for the point of view that singularity of origin is not a requirement for a workable administration of justice. [Hirsch, 1960]

Thailand is a particularly interesting example since, in addition to the elements just discussed, its legal system also includes the traditions of ethnic-religious minorities and historically reaches back all the way to the code of Manu.[20] The Republic of China (Taiwan) also exhibits a joining of highly diverse legal traditions.[21] For a diffent type of transfer (civil law to common law) see Stepan, 1973, 181. A negative view of "alien transplants" can be found in Daniels, 1974, 106. In any case, quite obviously, a transfer must be modified. Adaptation to local circumstances, however, is generally possible.

Proponents of the second objection, of course, will have no patience with the inductive-empirical approach of answering the question of transferability by testing and by trying—though this is exactly what needs to be done. Most likely, they will insist on the impossibility of transfers on deductive-theoretical grounds. Regarding the two primary countries under discussion, it is not difficult to demonstrate truly fundamental differences, such as the conceptual frameworks of collectivism-plus-harmony on the one side against that of individualism-plus-conflict on the other.[22] Socialist philosophy takes society as the fundamental unit, views the basic relationships among persons and among societal units as naturally cooperative, regards the basic interests of all persons and societal units (excluding remnants of the "class enemy") as identical, and sees comradeship and harmony as the inherent characteristics of (advanced) socialist society.[23]

Bourgeois philosophy, by contrast, takes the individual as the fundamental unit, views the basic relationships among persons and among societal units as competitive as well as cooperative, regards the basic interests of persons and societal units as divergent as well as congruent, and sees conflict as well as harmony as an inherent characteristic of all societies. The hypothetical extremes on the cognitive level are harmony theory and conflict theory, with harmony-and-conflict theory occupying the middle ground. In fact, true conflict theory does not exist—not even with Heraclitus. The actual poles are harmony theory and harmony-and-conflict theory.[24]

At the practical level, no known society has sought to eliminate all harmony, and no known society has succeeded in eliminating all conflict, though it has not lacked in attempts. Whether the "class-less" society would be the conflict-less society (as fervently envisioned by the marxist) remains to be seen. One is justified to doubt it. It would seem that conflicts can arise not only because of the owning or not-owning of the means of production, but also because of other differences among people, not to speak of jealousy, envy, and just plain contrariness.

The doctrine of advanced socialism accepts the continued existence of "nonantagonistic" conflicts, that is, a variety of social and cultural differences among the still remaining classes and strata of society. [Autorenkollektiv, 1978b, 24–25] These differences, however, have no significant political consequences because of the (asserted) fundamental identity of interests of all classes, strata, and persons. The official pronouncements of the GDR regarding the class situation in advanced socialism read as follows:

> There are two classes in our socialist society—the working class and the class of cooperative farmers. In addition, there are various social strata, such as socialist intellectuals and professional people, craftsmen, and tradesmen. All classes and strata have an interest in constructing and strengthening socialism, because, owing to socialist property relations, there are no conflicting class interest among them. [Panorama-DDR, 1976, 58]

The relationships of the classes and strata to public policy (as was stated with great emphasis) are not based on a "pluralist compromise"[25] but are characterized by an "alliance" of forces with identical interest. The crucial point is that with the advent of socialist property relations, that is, public ownership of the means of production, all "antagonistic" conflicts vanish.[26] The key features of the advanced socialist society were (at least according to the socialists of the GDR) the comprehensive identity of interests and the equally comprehensive harmony of social relations

"Identity" and "harmony" are subject to various definitions. In the area of civil dispute resolution, it has been observed that "The socialist process of conciliation, where plaintiff and defendant together are charged with the restoration of social harmony, also subjects both to the state's definition of what harmony should look like." [Markovits, 1980] This process can be extended to all "harmonies." Not surprisingly, there was some resistance (however mild and unassertive) to the official insistence and enforcement of "harmony." Clearly, the price was a diminution of self-determination. Occasional comments in the GDR literature, as well as even casual observations of life in the GDR (particularly as it regarded the younger generation), leave little doubt about the existence of substantial needs for individual differentiation and self-assertion, departing from the binding official harmony prescriptions. [Sperlich, 2006, Chapter 7] In the context of a discussion of the work of the social courts,[27] for example, a professional judge observed that "often it is not easy to make a citizen understand, as he comes before the court, that it is a desirable good fortune to exist in peaceful harmony with one's environment. [Urban, 1981, 147]

The identity claims of advanced socialism were all-pervasive. There was, as noted, the identity of interests of the working class and all other classes and strata.[28] There was the identity of interests of individual and society,[29] of the citizen and the state,[30] of (communist party) and the people [Autorenkollektiv, 1978b, 20], of trade unions and the state [Panorama-DDR, 1975, 34], of firms and employees [Riemann, 1976, 25], and of all the members of a family. [Riemann, 1976, 26–27] If this were not yet absurd enough, Socialist theory also denied the possibility of any conflict between the dictatorship of the proletariat and personal freedoms [Zschiedrich, 1981, 293] and between different aspects of a person's life: public versus private interests and obligations, work responsibilities versus other regards, etc. [Pnorama-DDR, 1976, 57, 70]

The unity[31] and identity assertions were not limited to social, political, and economic interconnections, they were also to be found at more abstract levels. Thus, socialist theory affirmed the unity of theory and practice [Autorenkollektiv, 1978b, 18], of rights and duties [Schuessler, 1981b, 52; Seidel, 1981, 112], of discipline and democracy [Schuessler, 1980, 271], of economic and social policy,[32] of law, morality, and utility,[33] and of socialism and democracy. [Autorenkollektiv, 1978b, 74]

As long as the discussion of comparative law remains at the purely theoretical-ideological level, neither side is likely to be much interested in trying to lean from the other. Indeed, the ultra-orthodox in either camp (but particularly in the socialist domain) will regard the very idea of learning from an opponent (from the "class enemy," in GDR language) with considerably loathing. Nevertheless, there are significant similarities at the *practical* level. For example, any legal system that employs essentially unpaid[34] lay judges or jurors must address the problem of motivation. [Hastie, et al., 1983, 171–174, Sperlich, 1985b] The actual utility of any comparative study of highly diverse legal systems will not be found in the refutation of dogmatic assertions, but in the analysis of practical problems and needs. It is hoped that in the end, this volume will make a contribution to American lay adjudication by identifying certain features of the GDR social courts that can assist us to divert cases away from the regular courts to alternative forms of adjudication.

OUTLINE

The chapters of the first section of this book are broader in scope than the social courts. It seemed beneficial to place the social courts discussions into the contexts of other forms of lay adjudication (of East and West) and of socialist legal theory and legal practice in general. The specific materials on the social courts are found in the second section of the book (Chapters 6 to 10).

Chapter 2 will consider the problems that attach to doing research in a socialist system, and to using data proffered by such systems. The difficulties are considerable. First, while socialism regards itself as a science,[35] it is anything but. Worse, massive inadequacies contaminate what empirical materials are available. GDR survey research was largely incompetent, especially in the aspect of data presentation. GDR statistics tendered an even worse picture, including the non-reporting of discomforting data and outright falsifications. To do it oneself was not generally a feasible alternative. The GDR regarded Western researchers with deep suspicion—with the exception of some "useful idiots"—of which, unfortunately, there were quite a few. Reflecting its own practices, the regime was convinced that researchers with an interest in the GDR had to be CIA agents. The general climate was utterly inhospitable to Western research. There was no way of getting even simple assistance in most matters. Only in the distribution of official publications could traces of good-will and cooperation be found.

Chapter 3 shows that it was nevertheless possible to undertake a serious analysis of the social courts. Not as well as one would have wished (for example, access to social court sessions was never granted), but "good enough." Part of the reason was that the social courts were highly visible and not a great security concern. Part of the reason was that during numerous visits to the GDR, I was able to conduct a large number of citizen interviews. Finally, part of the reason was the generosity of the GDR in making available printed sources.

Chapter 4 provides an overview of the various form of lay adjudication: jurors, justices of the peace, lay assessors at the ordinary court (the "mixed tribunals"), comrades' courts, and, last but not least, the GDR's social court commissioners. This chapter also considers the pros and cons of lay adjudication, including the many scurrilous attacks on the trial jury. In my view the virtues of the jury far outweigh its weaknesses. Indeed, if we want to improve our administration of justice (particularly as it regards delay in court), greater diversion to lay adjudication seems to be the most reasonable and propitious avenue.

Chapter 5 is the final "introductory" chapter. It contains close inspections of various aspects of socialist legal theory and socialist administration of justice. It shows that the leninist legal dogmas remained effective to the very end of socialism in the GDR. It investigates the many functions of socialist law, which were much more numerous than anything in the West. It considers the general matter of citizen participation in the administration of justice. It also examines the competing criminal law approaches of punishment and rehabilitation, an area in which the GDR differed significantly from the United States. It pays particular attention to the "rule of law" in socialism (always proclaimed but seldom followed), and to the concept of "socialist legality" (developed in response to the Western conception of the *Rechtsstaat*). Finally, the chapter raises the question whether the GDR was a *Rechtsstaat* (a state of law) or its very opposite.

With Chapter 6, the book reaches the specific subject matter of the East German social courts. It explores the conceptual and historical background of these institutions. It differentiates the dispute commissions (factory based) and the arbitration commissions (residence based), and explains the common elements as well as the distinct features of these two agencies. The chapter also pays attention to the many "social forces" that could participate in social court hearings. There also is a discussion of the crucial defect in "socialist legality:" that it did not include the protection of the citizen *against the state*. An important point, however, is that the social courts were less affected by the demands for "partisan justice" than were the state courts of the GDR.

Chapter 7 focuses on the persons who staffed the social courts. It inquires how individuals came into this position, what training and assistance they received to be able to discharge their tasks, for how long they served, how much time they had to devote to these offices, and what other societal functions they also performed. The chapter also delineates the demographic characteristics of the social court members. The regime was very concerned that there would be substantial numbers of workers, women, and young people among them. Finally, the chapter explores the rewards that a social court members could hope to obtain, and raises the question of the judges' motivations to serve in this office.

Chapter 8 deals with the many obligations and responsibilities of the social court judges, which, in fact, were almost endless. There were the formal deliberations (hearings) of particular cases and the preparations for these. There were decisions to be reached, the implementation of which had to be monitored.

There were office hours to be held and informal discussions to be conducted. There was the need always to be on the lookout for incipient conflicts, which might be prevented by early intervention. There was the obligation to transmit legal education and to attend seminars and conferences. There was also the expectation that the social court judges would pay close attention to persons in danger of committing criminal offenses, as well as to help with the rehabilitation of offenders. It can fairly be said that the responsibilities of a social judge were extensive and formidable—and yet, many judges served for long periods of time. Next the chapter takes up the question of how cases reached the social courts. As will be seen, there was more than one way. The chapter finally looks into certain problems areas that impacted not only the social but all legal institutions of the GDR, above all, juvenile delinquency.

Chapter 9 explores the case loads of the social courts and the types of cases most prominently adjudicated. Some examples of particular cases are provided. The chapter also investigates what decisions and measures were available to the social courts to bring a deliberation to its conclusion. Educational measure were most prominent, but the courts could also assess fines and work obligations. The chapter also considers the obligation of the social courts to issue recommendations to third parties, with the purposes of preventing similar offenses in the future. At the end of this chapter there are brief discussions of a number of social court cases. They show that various minor criminal and civil cases can indeed be assigned to lay adjudication and need concern the regular courts only if the lay organs could not resolve them.

Finally, Chapter 10 asks how well the courts worked, from the perspectives of five crucial parties: the political leadership of the GDR, the social court judges themselves, the citizens at large, the official legal system, and the actual litigants that had to appear before the social courts. It can be said that satisfaction was generally high and that the courts enjoyed substantial respect and appreciation. The last question returns to the beginning of the inquiry: what, if anything, can we learn? The answer is: a good deal! In my view, the experience of the East German social courts is very useful for the improvement and enlargement of our system of lay adjudication and, thus, for the betterment of our administration of justice.

ACKNOWLEDGMENTS

I wish to thank my friend and colleague Steven L. Coombs for his very helpful comments on the first draft of this volume. I want thank Eugene C. Lee and Carl G. Rosberg, directors of the U.C. Berkley Institute of Government Studies and of the Institute for International Studies, respectively, who greatly assisted my research. I thank Karim Moussally and Bettina Schröder for their splendid research assistance. Thanks are also due to my brother, Werner M. Sperlich, who gathered for me various useful books and social court transcripts in the GDR, as this country came to its end, and to my sister, Christa B. Schumann-Sperlich who patiently brought order to my files. Finally, I owe a debt of gratitude to three friends who helped me through some very difficult and painful months, during which my back decided to be troublesome and vexatious: Stephen Crocker, Donald Jolly, and Tor Buck.

NOTES

1. The Soviet jurist A. Vyshinsky [1948, 506] provided a similar justification for lay adjudication in the USSR: "The participation of the people's assessors, obligatory in all courts, assures the solution of two problems: (1) to attract people into the administration of the state, into the fulfillment of the most important state functions through their participation in the decisions of [the courts]; and (2) to introduce into the functioning of justice a genuine popular principle, the people's socialist legal consciouness, conviction, and conscience."

2. There were many such participatory efforts in the GDR to secure support for the regime. They failed. See Sperlich, 2006, Chapters 4 and 8.

3. The failure of communism as an *ideology* has been detailed in my ROTTEN FOUNDATIONS: THE CONCEPTUAL BASIS OF THE MARXIST-LENINIST REGIMES OF EAST GERMANY AND OTHER COUNTRIES OF THE SOVIET BLOC (2002). The failure of communism as *practice* has been described in my OPPRESSION AND SCARCITY: THE HISTORY AND INSTITUTIONAL STRUCTURE OF THE MARXIST-LENINIST GOVERNMENT OF EAST GERMANY AND SOME PERSPECTIVES ON LIFE IN A SOCIALIST SYSTEM (2006).

4. Usually no more than that it was a communist system, part of the Soviet Bloc, and astonishingly successful in sports. (On this last topic, which is largely a story of doping, see Sperlich, 2006, 204–206.)

5. Perhaps there also was a loss of interest since reunification seemed an impossibility and since successive West German governments had made it their purpose to stabilize and strengthen the GDR—the so-called *Ostpolitik*.

6. Brigitte Deja-Loelhoeffel, UNBEKANNTER NACHBAR DDR 1987.

7. Doder [1988, 13], for example, identifies the Moscow Kremlin (The first structures of which date to 1080 and which saw many new buildings in the mid-12th century as the "ancestral home of the Romanovs," though the first Romanov Tsar did not appear until 1613. (And contrary to much learned information, the last Romanov on the Russian throne was *not* Nicholas II {1894–1917} but Elizabeth {1741–1762}.) Then there is Joffe [1987, 130], who is under the impression that "much of modern Germany east of the Elbe was *originally* settled by slavic people." (emphasis added) And NEWSWEEK magazine, at the occasion of the re-burial of *king* Frederick II of *Prussia* at Potsdam (Sans Souci), identified him as the *emperor* of *Germany*.

8. The major exception is the work of Nancy T. Wolfe. See the bibliography for her contributions.

9. Not to be overlooked are the various African experiments with socialism. See, for example, Isaacman & Isaacman, 1982.

10. In recent local and regional elections in the states (*Länder*) of the former GDR, the PDS was able to gain in excess of 20% of the popular vote and even join several governing coalitions.

11. As will be seen later, I do indeed believe that useful knowledge can emerge from a study of the GDR's social courts.

12. Some attention will also be given to the second form of lay adjudication of the GDR: the lay assessors of the state courts. There also will be a consideration of non-GDR legal institutions, especially the Soviet comrades' courts and peoples' judges.

13. As some examples, see Abraham, 1998; Becker, 1970; Ehrmann, 1976; Ingraham, 1987; Katz, 1986; Langbein, 1977; Pospisil, 1982; Rommen, 1998.

14. For discussions of the purposes of comparative legal studies see Jovanovic, 1986, 332–337; Mueller-Roemer, 1969, 1–8.

15. For some comparative literature focused specifically on lay adjudication see Abel, 1982; Casper & Zeisel, 1979; Ginsburg, 1963; Gorphe, 1936; Heinze, 1864; Jescheck, 1977; Keeney, 1949; Langbein, 1981; Moore, 1973; Petzold-Pernia, 1979; Ruggeberg, 1970; Schorn, 1955; Sperlich, 1982b.

16. The comrades' courts, however, will be given considerable attention in Chapter 4. This will provide a useful contrast to the GDR's social courts.

17. It may be noted in passing that the "integrated" courts functioned more satisfactorily than the more autonomous types. See, for example, Racz, 1979, 14; Note, 1971, 141; Boiter, 1965, 82; also see Gaul, 1965.

18. On the special suitability of the GDR, among the socialist nations, for comparative studies with Western, industrialized countries see Markovits, 1978, 612–613.

19. Most crucially from the marxist perspective the societal versus the private ownership of the means of production.

20. Engel, 1978; Thai Bar Association, 1969; Thai Bar Association, 1981.

21. U.S. Army, Judge Advocate General, 1959; Hsiung, ed., 1981 (section on law and justice); Hooker, 1978; also Beer, ed., 1979.

22. For detailed discussion of this contrast see Sperlich, 2002, 181–187.

23. The official doctrine of the GDR defined the last stage of its development as "advanced socialism." It was the product of two historical transitions: first from capitalism to rudimentary socialism, then to advanced socialism. The latter formed the basis for the anticipated "gradual transition to communism." [Panorama-DDR, 1975, 24–26]

24. On the dominant position of harmony theory (vis-a-vis harmony-and-conflict constructs) and on the absence of true conflict theory see Sperlich, 1971, 1–2, 32–38, 169–178, 215–217, et passim.

25. "Pluralist compromises" were one of the truly appalling and dreadful entities in the socialist conceptual universe. The GDR literature is rich in titles such as this: SOZIALISTISCHE BÜNDNISPOLITIK KONTRA PLURALISMUS. [Autorenkollektiv, 1980, 39–45]

26. Nevertheless, antagonistic conflicts required much attention in the GDR. Ownership of the means of production was public, but there was the existence of the "exploiter class" in other countries, and the influence of the "imperialist forces" across the wall. [Honecker, 1981, 390; Schuessler, 1981a, 434–435] These external factors were used extensively (as will be seen later) to explain away GDR problems and deficiencies.

27. As will be seen later, the conciliation process was even more strongly emphasized in the social courts than in the state courts—leading some persons to prefer to have their case heard at a state court.

28. Most other identities, unities, and harmonies derive (at least in part) from this fundamental identity. The political organization of socialist society is a direct consequence: no division of powers and no legitimate opposition. [Autorenkollektiv, 1978b, 21; Panorama-DDR, 1975, 47; Panorama-DDR, 1976, 65; Riemann, 1976, 15]

29. Autorenkollektiv, 1978b, 227; Panorama-DDR, 1976, 70; Riemann, 1976, 9.

30. Autorenkollektiv, 1978b, 225; Panorama-DDR, 1976, 57; Riemann, 1976, 11.

31. It is interesting to note in this context that the chief theoretical journal of the communist party of the GDR was called "EINHEIT" (= UNITY). The Party itself, of course, carried the label "Sozialistische Einheitspartei Deutschlands" (= Socialist Unity Party of Germany).

32. Autorenkollektiv, 1978b, 30; Panorama-DDR, 1976, 50–51; Weichelt, 1981, 338. For a detailed discussion of the interactions of social policy, law, and economics, see Heusinger, 1981b, 386.

33. E.g., Bley & Mueller, 1979, 389. There was also said to be a unity between the people of the GDR and socialist law. [Heuckendorf, 1981, 186]

34. Entirely unpaid in the GDR; meagerly paid in the United States.

35. Indeed, as THE science. See Sperlich, 2002, Chapter 3.

Chapter 2

Research and Data in Socialism

SOCIALISM AND SCIENCE

The claim that socialism is a science, indeed *The Science,* has been examined in detail in a prior book. [Sperlich, 2002, Chapter 3] It will be helpful at this point to summarize some basic points. In spite of relentless assertions about the scientific nature of socialism, inquiry reveals quite quickly that socialism is not a science, much less The Science. Many of the claims of socialism are plainly false (if empirical), or simply matters of definition and, thus, not able to generate factual assertions, and not subject to proof.

In respect to *de facto* empirical assertions, there are few efforts at empirical proof.[1] The primary operational mode of socialist thought is *deductive.* Various claims and assertions are derived from the vast compendium of Marxist-Leninist theory and, then, justified by reference to that theory. The extensive reliance on deduction and internal coherence testing, and the very limited reliance on external coherence testing, may not be troublesome to the committed socialist.[2] The non-socialist (that is, the non-believer), however, is not likely to be persuaded in this way, nor will his skepticism be assuaged by the frequent invocation of "science" and "scientific method." The conceptual apparatus of socialism is religious rather than empirical in nature: Because I strongly believe it, it *must be* true.

The following language is typical: "As a party of a new type the SED has always been guided by the universally valid teachings of Marxism-Leninism. . . . The strength and the leading role of the Socialist Unity Party of Germany, like that of any other ruling Marxist-Leninist party, arises from the fact that on the basis of a scientifically substantiated strategy and tactics it has always been able to direct social developments politically . . ." [Panorama-DDR, 1975, 20] "The working class is the driving force behind social progress . . . because Marxism-Leninism, the only scientific world outlook, is its guide to action. . . . The party's job is to give political guidance to social change on the basis of scientifically founded strategy and tactics . . ." [Panorama-DDR, 1976, 59–60]

As is true for the unproven assertions of all ideological systems, internal proclamations of veracity and validity have no hold on the outsider. Socialist announcements of "scientific substantiation" and "universal validity" are no more convincing to the non-socialist than is the doctrine of papal infallibility to the non-Catholic. The proof of the pudding is not in its proclamation, but in its eating.[3] Lack of (convincing) evidence, of course, is not the same as a demonstration of error or, indeed, of the truth of a counterclaim. The empirically oriented observer would not be justified in concluding that all of socialism's assertions are false. He is fully justified, however, to regard them as not proven.

There is a distinct difference between socialist and Western scholars in their willingness to be convinced by empirical findings produced by the other side. Given its doctrine of the materialistic base (class-base) of the "superstructure," including science, socialism has great difficulty regarding non-socialist science other than as of questionable validity.[4] The products of "bourgeois science" tended to be viewed in the GDR and other socialist countries not as "objective knowledge," but as reflections of bourgeois interests. All knowledge, according to this epistemology, is class knowledge. Only knowledge generated by socialist science escapes the blemish of subjectivity. The interests of the working class, so we were told, are not only its own subjective interests, but also the objective interests of all classes.

Neo-positivist (bourgeois) science, by contrast, is vastly more open to findings developed in the context of other philosophical systems. It does not claim absolute certainty for any of its propositions, is convinced of the presence of error in its theories, and works by falsification rather than verification. [Popper, 1963] If factual truth can be discovered in either system, socialism inflicts upon itself an intellectual blemish when it denies the validity of bourgeois science and the applicability of its findings. Needless to say, such a defect can have considerable practical consequences—to which the general backwardness of science in socialism (with the exception of certain military-technological fields) provides eloquent testimony.

REGIME PARANOIA AND PARTISAN SCIENCE

Comprehensive Suspicion

The predominant mood of GDR officialdom was one of a deep and comprehensive suspicion—of its own people as well as of foreigners—and of a paranoid and excessive craving for secrecy.[5] [Starrels and Mallinckrodt, 1975, 210]. Western scholars, of course, were particularly suspect. This in spite of the fact that some Western scholars became quasi adherents of Muscovite dicta. There was a naive acceptance of Marxism as a philosophy, parallel to the naive acceptance of the USSR as the workers' paradise. "Revived as philosophers in the 1930s and 1940s, Marx and Engels became the revered mentors of sophisticated English scientists—Joseph Needham, John Desmond Bernal, J.B.S. Haldane—who discovered in the jejune works of Engels depths of wisdom only they would fathom." [Manuel, 1995, 231] "Political enchantment" prevailed over scientific training and good sense.

The East German regime never felt bound by the ordinary norms of scholarly reciprocity. The fact that GDR researchers had ready access to Western experts, institutions, and data collections did not create any feelings of obligation.[6] [Metcalfe, 1988, 154–164] In my experience and that of others [Wechsberg, 1964, 3], scholarly inquiries from the West often did not receive the courtesy even of a *pro forma* reply, and if there was an answer, it did not usually provide the requested information or assistance. [Markovits, 1993, 12] A Swedish visitor to the GDR reported (rather plaintively) that he could not get the needed permissions "despite good references." [Holm, 1970, 6] In my case, even extended stays in the GDR and personal visits to the relevant agencies did not produce the requested help (i.e., arranging for observations of social court sessions).

Useful Idiots

As in the Soviet Union,[7] assistance was not forthcoming, unless its served the purposes of the regime. Significant aid was provided only if there was reason to believe that the visitor could be turned into a (to use Lenin's phrase) "useful idiot." There never was a dearth of "useful idiots." [Koehler, 1999, 251–257] Communist regimes "cultivate[d] these people partly because of their prestige value and partly because of their active role in the shaping of public opinion in free societies." [Counts & Lodge, 1970, 317] Thus, George Bernard Shaw, traveling in Russia in 1931, assured the West upon his return there there was no famine. [Medvedev, 1989, 243] In the 1970s, many visitors returned from China to report that "crime just isn't a problem in China today." [Cohen, 1977, 326] In fact, of course, crime was (and remained) a very important problem in China. Not all "useful idiots" were Western visitors, however. Some were homemade, for example, Maxim Gorky, who lent his name to the glorification and whitewash of Stalin's construction projects, such as the Belomor Canal, a slave labor enterprise, extremely costly in human lives. [Lewis & Whitehead, 1990, 79]

Some collaborators appear to have been simply naive, for example, the writer Lion Feuchtwanger [1937, 133–163], who observed the second series of the Moscow show trials and reached conclusions such as that the proceedings were fair, that there was nothing manufactured or artificial about them, that the accused were guilty of the charges, that there were no coerced confessions, that the accused were compelled to confess by the overwhelming evidence, that the prosecutors deliberately refrained from introducing this evidence (relying only on the confessions) in order not to confuse the ordinary Soviet citizens with unnecessary details, and that Stalin was much too modest and unambitious a person to have wrongly arranged for the destruction of his old comrades.[8] Feuchtwanger [1937, 173–174] also reported that the air "in the West is stale and foul [but hat one can breathe] again when one comes from this oppressive atmosphere of a counterfeit democracy and hypocritical humanism into the invigorating atmosphere of the Soviet Union [where] there is no hiding behind mystical, meaningless slogans."

Others gave public support to regime declarations that they knew to be false. Evangelist Billy Graham,[9] for example, when preaching in Moscow, directly witnessed suppressive measures by the secret police against citizens who protested religious persecution (silently, with a banner). Nevertheless:

> Graham publicly declared that there was freedom of religion in the USSR. Only later did he admit that his public pronouncements from Moscow were dictated by his desire not to offend his official Soviet hosts so that he could be permitted to return there in the future. [Sleeper, 1987, 344]

Harold Laski [1935, 21] visited the USSR in the mid-1930s, observing trials and interviewing Mr. Vyshinsky, all of which produced the report that he "did not observe much difference between the general character of a trial in Russia and in this country [England]."

The Webbs [S. & B. Webb, 1936, xxi] took the Stalin Constitution at face value and reported that the Soviet Union was "the most inclusive and equalized democracy in the word." Beatrice Webb wrote in 1942 that "the USSR was not only a fully fledged political democracy but also an industrial democracy with a powerful trade union and consumers cooperative movement." [Liebman, 1962, 58] D.N. Pritt (member of Parliament and president of the committee set up to investigate the proceedings the Reichstag fire trial) declared in August 1936 that "the Moscow trial was fair" and that the confessions" could not possibly have been concocted or rehearsed" and that "not even the keenest critic had been able to find a false note." His reward was an honorary Doctor of Law from Moscow University. [Dewar, 1962, 88–90]

Some journalists and scholars tended to censor themselves.[10] "The more favorable a reporter's stories are to the USSR, the more access he will be granted to senior Soviet officials . . . [and given] exclusive 'leaks' and scoops." [Sleeper, 1987, 388] When the carrot did not work, the stick was not long in coming. Malcom Muggeridge reported about the Soviet famine and promptly became *persona non grata* in the USSR. G.B. Shaw, the Webbs, Lincoln Steffens, and Walter Duranty denied the existence of the famine and retained access. [Murphy, 1992, 88–89] Most reporters "valued their continued accreditation in the Soviet Union more than the truth." [Lewis & Whitehead, 1990, 68; also see Brzezinski, 1989, 9–10]

A number of prominent West German scholars (e.g., Peter Ludz) were denied entry into the GDR after they had published reports containing some (rather mild) critical comments.[11] As Bertram Wolfe [1954, 269] noted: "Totalitarianism is painfully, morbidly distrustful. . . . Its cruelty and resolute thoroughness are based on its own inner unsureness, whence the astounding energy and hatred with which it may attack the tiniest and most neutral seeming observation." Getting Western pawns, feigning objectivity, to carry the attack was particularly effective. Feuchtwanger [1937, 10], for example, aided the attack on Andre Gide, by attributing Gide's critical comments on the Soviet Union to Gide having "his judgment warped by petty annoyances . . . [and] minor discomforts" experienced on his (Gide's) visit to Moscow. Gide's greatest offense, of course, was to recognize certain parallels in communist and fascist regimes. [Yack, 1986, 361][12] In any case, identifying flaws in the critic's character was the favored method to deal with criticism, second only to exposing the critic's inability "to think dialectically."[13]

Inhospitable to Western Research

Western GDR research was viewed by the East German regime with considerable apprehension, regarded as hostile in intent, assumed to be in the service of Western intelligence agencies, and believed to aim at the overthrow of socialism. One visitor from Princeton University was told in the GDR Foreign Ministry that they had "a great deal of trouble with visiting CIA professors." [J. Smith, 1969, 22–23] It was never possible in the GDR to call on members of agencies or institutions by simply going to their offices.[14] When I was visiting members of the faculty of East Berlin's Humboldt University, for example, *every single time* (1) I had to have a specific appointment, (2) identify myself to the uniformed guards at the entrance by showing my passport, (3) explain my business (which the guards confirmed by telephone before permitting entrance), and (4) was not permitted even then to go to the relevant office by myself (though well knowing the location), but had to be taken there by a "guide."[15] George Feifer [1976, 51–52] had similar experiences at Moscow State University:

> A crowd is bunched outside the guardhouse. Evening session is about to begin, and everyone waiting to enter the grounds is rummaging in a pocket or handbag for his pass, a little cardboard folder with a photograph of the bearer and, of course, an official stamp. The rules are universal: passes required for entrance into the University, as for every office and institution of this People's State; no citizen allowed where he does not belong;. . .[attendants] checking credentials and intentions.

GDR complaints about Western scholarship, until about 1960, were not without warrant. Since the early 1960s, however, fair standards and good will have characterized most Western inquiries.[16] Indeed, there was a tendency after 1960—but only in the West!—to overcompensate for prior animosities and to see nothing but successes and improvements.[17] [Picaper,

1982, 103–128] Among other misperceptions, this produced a massively distorted and overly positive view of the GDR economy. East German complaints, of course, continued in spite of much positive commentary—partly because of the regime's inordinate sensitivity and its dissatisfaction with anything less than total support, and partly as a preemptive tactic designed to inhibit critical assessments. [Autorenkollektiv, 1982a, 218–219] The preemptive tactic, one might note, succeeded rather well, particularly with the West German political and academic left.

The suspicions about Western scholars were less a matter of actual GDR experience than of inferences drawn from the country's own practices.[18] [Jarausch & Sabrow, 1999, 94] It was impossible for scholars from the Soviet world to travel to the West simply as a matter of curiosity or personal research interests. This applied not only to academics. No ordinary citizen of the USSR or GDR could travel to the West wholly in a private capacity (The GDR provided some exceptions for old-age pensioners.) It is testimony to the gullibility of some Western organizations and citizens that they tended to regard socialist delegates to international conferences as "average citizens."[19] The socialist citizen's activities abroad had to be useful to the regime, or they would not be allowed and supported with the necessary hard currency allocations. Those who were permitted to visit Western countries were generally required to travel in groups, at least one member of which was working for the KGB. ". . . Those who [were] allowed to travel abroad . . . are instructed what to say and what to do. Special KGB agents are placed among them to monitor their performances, while their families back home serve as hostages." [Bukosvsky, 1973, 10] Similarly, Western citizens studying in the socialist countries reported that they were assigned a native student as helper and special friend, who, in fact, was affiliated with an intelligence service and functioned as the "official stool pigeon." [Lee, 1984, 11]

The "natural" assumption prevailing in the GDR and the other Soviet bloc countries was that Western scholars worked under similar conditions and were subject to the same obligations as socialist-based scholars. Captives of the regime's unrelenting and all-inclusive demand for partisanship, GDR officials, as USSR officials, could not even imagine the pursuit of nonpartisan research.[20] "The notion of an 'objective' science of comparison, somehow divorced from the 'interests' of those undertaking the comparison, is inconsistent with Marxist-Leninist theory . . ." [Romoser, 1975, 431] As late as 1985, these were the type of *research* projects assigned to the East German political and legal sciences: to demonstrate that socialist democracy is the driving force of socialism, to prove that socialist democracy implements and actuates the interests of all of the people, to verify the increasing freedom of the citizens of the GDR, to offensively defend Marxist-Leninist positions, and to prove that democratic centralism has not become obsolete and does not hinder the development of the productive forces. [Schuessler, 1985, 19;

Wippold, 1985, 6] Given this context, it is not surprising that Western commitments to scientific objectivity and neutrality remained unconvincing to the partisan-scholars as well as to the government and Party officials of the GDR,[21] and that such commitments were mocked as devious and hypocritical.[22] [Joseph, 1975, 1051–1052]

Western Field Work and Data Access

Throughout the existence of the GDR, it was not only impossible to conduct original and systematic field research in any area of scientific enterprise,[23] it also was very difficult to obtain already existing information, other than that found in official pronouncements and publications. Typically it was not even possible to find out whether the required information existed. Not only the findings (if any) but the very fact that research had or had not been conducted was treated as a state secret. For more than ten years, I inquired at various GDR institutions (scholarly, state, and Party) whether there were any studies of any aspects of the social court system. Regardless of to whom I addressed the question , the answer invariably was: "I don't know." Translated this meant: "None of your business."

Some Western scholars thought that the GDR would be interested in the development of a "realistic" image of their country in the West and would, therefore, "act to alleviate the problem of sources and information . . ." [Burrichter and Foertsch, 1976, 107] The GDR leadership, however, knew something about the country's realities[24] and was not in the least interested in "realistic images" and "problem alleviation." Polish authorities seem to have been somewhat more relaxed about legal studies, at least domestic ones. For example, the Polish Academy of Sciences undertook a major study of lay assessors in 1964–1965.[25] There also have been studies of lay adjudicators in Hungary. [Kulcsar, 1982, 12–14; Racz, 1972]

GDR agencies conducted public opinion polls on a regular basis and on a wide variety of topics. [Niemann, 1993] They remained largely unpublished and inaccessible.[26] Not until early 1989 did a West German polling organization, INFAS, take advantage of FRG-GDR telephone connections to conduct its own telephone survey of East German citizens. The East German regime was outraged. The official Party paper characterized the poll as "a misuse of the GDR-FRG telephone agreements" and as "an attempt to manipulate the people of East Germany." [NEUES DEUTSCHLAND, April 4, 1989, p. 2] This outrage, of course, reflected the GDR practice to use polls for the manipulation, rather than the exploration, of public opinion. The vast majority of GDR polls appear to have been "in-house" undertakings, with a severely limited circulation of their findings and a similarly limited disclosure of the fact that a survey had been taken. GDR public opinion polls typically were analyzed in two stages. The poll takers performed a first, but limited, *empirical* analysis, producing basic data arrays and simple statistics.

Party experts then extended the analysis and, most important, undertook the crucial theoretical assessments, that is, the *political* analysis of the data. The complete record of data and interpretations were available only to the top Party leadership. The GDR's information policy clearly was designed to prevent anyone but the top leadership to obtain a comprehensive picture of GDR realities.[27]

Since the demise of the GDR, however, it has become evident that the leaders of the GDR either did not receive accurate and comprehensive reports about social conditions and public views, or chose to ignore them, or were unable to approach them other than through rigid ideological filters. As high-ranking East German officials now testify, for at least the last decade, Honecker et al. lived in a dreamworld, becoming ever more remote from the facts of GDR politics and economics.[28] Some, it seems, were genuinely incapable of understanding the popular dissatisfaction with the regime, which had manifested itself all along (efforts to leave the GDR, legally or illegally), but which simply exploded in 1989.

Partisan Science

The GDR's primary criterion for truth was *political,* not scientific. Truth-telling was not a principle, but a *tactic.* The truth was told when it served the regime's interest; fabrications were produced when it did not.[29] Though the high incidence of data manipulation in socialist states was well known, some Western visitors exhibited an astonishing degree of trust and naivete. "It is truly remarkable how many people, some of whom ought to know better, or do know better, take no notice of the fact that the great bulk of our information about the Soviet Union has been passed through a filter which is designed and inserted by the Soviet Union itself." [Hutchings, 1987, 1][30] Having deactivated, seemingly, their critical facilities, they returned to tell the most extraordinary tales.[31] Szajkowski [1982, 77–78], for example, declared without elaboration or comment that in 1945 the four licensed political parties of the Soviet Zone "agreed to establish a bloc of anti-fascist democratic parties," and that early in 1946 "the KPD and SPD merged their organizations." This is an account very much in line with official GDR history. It fails to reveal that "bloc" and "merger" processes were largely communist imposed and that the "bloc" was entirely under communist control.

The Soviet Union and the People's Republic of China have been particularly well known for their ability to pull the wool over the eyes of visitors. Richard Walker [1972, 162–165] recounts how visitors—from Edgar Snow to Andre Malraux—carried the Maoist hagiography to the West, apparently persuaded of the Chairman's "superhuman infallibility" and "scientific genius." At a more modest level, some Western observers accepted without question PRAVDA reports such as that "at the pre-election meetings for the nomination of candidates for deputy, 3,980,372 candidates were discussed." [J. Hahn, 1988, 440–441] One would have expected at least some suspicion about the very precision of that figure.

Foreign scholars often also tried to preserve access by avoiding any critical comments that might give offense. John Hazard, for example, writing the Introduction for the translation into English of Andrei Vyshinsky's THE LAW OF THE SOVIET STATE (1948) characterizes Vyshinsky merely in these terms: ". . . he had been Prosecutor of the USSR. In this position he had supervised the preparation for, and conducted the prosecution in, the trials of Bukharin, Pyatakov, Kamenev, Radek, and their colleagues for treason against the USSR." [Hazard, 1948, ix] Hazard continues that Vyshinsky also had "evidenced qualities as a legal scholar" and that he was the "principal organizer of the new [post-Pashukanis] jurisprudence." [Hazard, 1948, ix-x]

Not a word that the trials of Bukharin and the others were barbarous show trials, condemning to death Lenin's old comrades, who certainly were largely innocent of the charges brought against them. [Hodos, 1988; Leites & Bernaut, 1954; Hermann Weber, 1990] This in spite of the fact that Vyshinsky's book is full of the vilest denounceations against these persons. Collectively Vyshinsky speaks of "the nightmarish crimes of these bandit gangs who were annihilated by the sentences of the Soviet court." Bukharin is variously labeled a traitor, an agent of fascism, an anarchist, a crude perverter of Marxism, and as a renegade committing foul, treacherous, cruel, counterrevolutionary, and filthy deeds. Kamenev, Pyatakov, Radek, Rykov, Tukhachevsky, Yagoda, Yakir, and Zinovyev are similarly branded. Hazard also identifies Vyshinsky merely as "principal organizer of post-Pashukanis jurisprudence, when the facts are that Vyshinsky was active in bringing about the downfall of Pashukanis, and when Vyshinsky's book includes incessant denounceations of Pashukanis as a traitor, a spy and wrecker, an apostate, and as a person with a confused mind producing pseudo-scientific rubbish. Stuchka and other early Soviet jurist, such as Krylenko, Reisner, and Volkov fare no better.[32]

The GDR was no less capable to persuade its guests to accept appearances for reality.[33] James Wolfe [1971, 458], for example, attributed real political influence to the GDR's minor parties on the grounds that the Christian Democrats (CDU) and Liberal Democrats (LDPD) held ministerial posts. At the time, Kurt Wuensche (LDPD) was Minister of Justice and Heinrich Toeplitz (CDU) was President of the Supreme Court. Their actions and public statements never differed in any essentials from the Communist Party line; in fact, these functionaries were particularly ruthless enforcers of "political justice." One might note at this point that one of the reasons that Modrow's post-GDR (but still East German) government lacked support and credibility was the unfortunate re-appointment of Kurt Wuensche as minister of justice in January 1990.[34] It was, of course, in the interest of the regime to pretend that the minor parties had real influence. Hermann Matern [1959, 30], one of the early USSR-trained leaders of the Communist Party of East Germany (SED), tried to persuade Western audiences of this by reporting in an international journal that the GDR's National Democrats (NDPD) "called for the further development of the producer co-operatives. . . . This proposal was accepted [by the SED] and found reflection in the [5th SED] congress resolutions. Many examples of this kind could be cited." What Matern failed to reveal, of course, was that the NDPD never would have put forth the proposal unless it had prior SED clearance. In fact, it is most likely that the NDPD proposal was put forth on the directive of the SED. It is amusing that the task to deceive Western audiences about the nature of the GDR multiparty system would be given to Matern. It was the very comrade Matern who controlled and directed the "bloc parties" during the early years of the GDR.

The GDR guides and officials, who were the Western visitors' primary contacts, were "superbly trained dialecticians, able to out-argue the 'naive' Westerner. . ." [Wechsberg, 1964, 4] They even were able to persuade some Western visitors that the communist regime was the free choice of the East Germany's population. To Jean Smith [1967, 376–380] must go the credit of having been the first to discover a "popular acceptance of the communist government" in East Germany, and that the citizens "freely obeyed" the GDR government. For Western guests, persuasion was more a matter of the carrot than of the stick. For its own people, the regime's stick was vastly more prominent. It was called *partiinost.*

Not only GDR law, but GDR legal research and scholarship had to serve the goals of Party and state. [Schuessler, 1978, 866] Their relationship to truth was purely instrumental. This was not a cause for embarrassment. From the socialist perspective, partisan science is the proper science. No one in the GDR ever sought to deny that the primary purpose of that country's social science research was the justification and legitimation of Party policy.[35] It followed, as noted, that all GDR-supplied information, including the products of its universities and academies, had to be approached with a healthy dose of skepticism. Inkeles's [1950, xii–xiii] comments, regarding USSR information sources, apply equally well to the GDR: "here is a strong possibility that published information is not accurate, but even if the published information is reliable, a great deal of equal or greater importance may be left unsaid, and much of what happens left undescribed."

The socialist partisan (*partiinost*) obligations of all fields of scholarship were explicit throughout the Soviet Bloc. The Programme of the CPSU, for example, stated: "Combating bourgeois ideology, revisionism and dogmatism has been and remains an important task of the social sciences." [Novosti Press Agency, 1986, 62] The Programme of the Communist Party (SED) of the GDR included this pronouncement:

> The marxist-leninist social sciences are the theoretical and political-ideological instrument of the working class and its revolutionary fighting party in the continuing

formation of the developed socialist society and in the dispute with imperialism and bourgeois ideology." [Sozialistische Einheitspartei Deutschlands, 1976, 46]

University and institute faculty members who attempted to work in a non-partisan, even if by no means anticommunist style, did not remain long at their posts. [Hanhardt, 1968, 18–20] An article written by GDR legal scholar Gerhard Schuessler [1978] carried the title "Political and Legal Science in the Service of Socialist Political Practice." It included the following passages:

The work of the Academy of Political and Legal Sciences has been oriented toward the requirements of political praxis for putting into effect the policies of the marxist-leninist party. [868]

The conceptual itinerary of all research and teaching of the political and legal sciences has its source in the policies of the SED. . . . The task of the Academy . . . is to contribute creatively to the realization of the policies of the marxist-leninist party. . . . The program of the SED, the resolutions of the IXth Party Congress, and the decrees of the Central Committee are the obligatory, scientifically substantiated guidelines for the work of the Academy . . . [872]

It is the most noble duty and responsibility of the Academy . . . to dedicate its total work of research, teaching, and study to the consolidation and development of the political and legal system of the GDR, and to make the largest possible contribution to the realization of the resolutions of the IXth Party Congress of the SED. [877]

These statements of abject submission of science to Party ideology and Party policy could endlessly be duplicated.[36] They were standard components of practically all scholarly pronouncements and publications. Schuessler [1981a, 437], for example, wrote elsewhere:

Research must contribute to securing the power of the working class. . . The research efforts of the political and legal sciences consciously work toward the goal of strengthening the political and organizational unity of the political organizations of our society. This research, thus, with full determination and consistent partisanship, opposes political pluralism, abstract bourgeois conceptions of state and democracy, and any distortions of the class character of socialist law. . . Political and legal research regards it as an inseparable element of its work to take the offensive in the dispute with anticommunist, bourgeois, and revisionist views of state and law. The determined fight to preserve the purity of Marxist-Leninist theory is its scientific obligation.

Any objective and independent (not-Party-controlled) investigations of the true effects of Party policies were banned. Only the Party's own research institutes could address such issues. Their findings, of course, were not published.

All scholarship[37] had to be partisan, and this was doubly true for history and the social sciences, the disciplines whose work touches most closely on the scientific claims of communism. [Benser, 2000, 324; Fulbrook, 1995, 82]

From the very beginning of the GDR, these fields were used to buttress communist ideology, to legitimate the communist regime, and to attack ideological opponents. Empirical social science (such as it was) never rose above the status of handmaiden to regime ideology and praxis.

It is worth noting that in the GDR, as in other socialist countries, *empirical* social science occupied a place distinctly inferior to that of *theoretical* (ideological) pursuits. This is not particularly surprising. Intellectual support for absolutist ideologies cannot generally be obtained through empirical research, but must be constructed via scholastic exercises that deduce "proof" from unsubstantiated premises—with dialectics as the primary tool. Except when the Party needed "real facts" to guide its actions (and not always even then), "bourgeois" concerns with epistemology and methodology received little more than ridicule and derision in the GDR.[38] Indeed, empirical social research was often regarded with considerable hostility, the "objectivity" or "inter-subjectivity" claims of such research clearly being at variance with the doctrine of the class-character of all knowledge. In the later years of the GDR, there were some developments pointing toward greater receptivity of Western science. [e.g., Fincke, 1975, n. 92, at 17] They never gained sufficient currency to help the GDR overcome its massive economic and technological problems. [Sperlich, 2006, Chapter 5]

The research in disciplines concerned with youth issues, for example, "must above all meet the needs of the *Freie Deutsche Jugend*."[39] [Friedrich & Henning, 1976, 11] Legal studies were equally subject to partisan obligations. This is how the role of the discipline of comparative law was defined:

> The [socialist] science of the public law of the bourgeois states examines the public branch of the law of the capitalist exploiter states. . . . By way of exposure and analysis of the current developments in bourgeois public law, the [socialist] science of the public law of the bourgeois states always penetrates to the aggressive, peace-threatening, and anti-human essence of imperialism, and, thus, contributes to the unmasking of its essence. [Menzel et al., 1980, 20]

All GDR intellectuals, but particularly social scientists, legal scholars, and historians, were expected to serve the Party.[40] Congruity of findings with empirical reality was vastly less important than agreement with Party doctrine. Whatever "truth" the Party wanted to assert, there could be found, without fail, a "scholar" to provide the "evidence." Much (if unintentional) humor can be found in the avowals of socialist social science. For example, at a political/legal science conference, Guenter Baranowski [1985, 16] reminded his audience that at the occasion of the 35th anniversary of the founding of the GDR, the regime had declared that socialism in the GDR was the "heir and continuator of all that is good, progressive, humane, and democratic" in German history. As if this was not yet funny enough,

Baranowski added that the regime's declaration "was based on the findings of marxist-leninist historical-scientific research, which . . . had found universal acceptance."

As another example, when the Party thought it important to depict GDR trade unions as being politically independent, one of the faithful provided this account (published in English for an international audience):

In the literature of western countries one frequently meets the allegation that "the GDR trade unions were nationalized." Just a look into trade union life exposes such allegations as pure nonsense. Out of the completely new relationship between trade unions and the State in the socialist society, the opponents of socialism construct a subordination of the trade unions to the State. In this way the relations actually existing in the socialist society between the trade unions and the socialist State are deliberately distorted. There is no capitalist country that guarantees the trade unions such a degree of political independence as the socialist order of society does. [Schuessler, 1979b, 138]

Schuessler, it is obvious, had the task of providing an academic foundation for SED general secretary Honecker's subsequent statement to the 10th Party Congress: "In accordance with the GDR Constitution and the Labor Code, the trade unions now have rights as never before in the history of the German trade union movement." The real conditions of socialist trade unions were depicted in a comparative study by Karatnycky and colleagues:

It is one of the ironies of our age that a system which claims to speak for workers' interests inevitably denies workers their rights and, indeed, in all Communist societies, we find the very legitimacy of independent trade unions and workers' rights rejected. To be sure, Communist countries include in their constitutions and labor codes stirring declarations of how the working classes and their trade union organizations are entitled to play the "leading role" in the creation of a "socialist" system which the workers presumably own.

In reality . . . the workers have no rights in societies where all power—political, social, economic—is monopolized by the Party and state.

. . . Rather, the "trade union" in the Communist world perform functions of discipline, social control, and administration as an integral part of the Party and state monopoly of power. [Karatnycky et al., 1980, 6–7; also see Panorama DDR, 1981, 22]

In the context of complete and unrelenting politicization of scholarship, different views among the GDR's historians and social scientists came to be perceived not merely as academic disagreements, to be resolved by the normal methods of science, but as much more. Differing views were assessed in terms of their closeness to the Party line. The proponents of ideas that were seen to diverge from official views did not long retain their positions. Under such conditions, obviously, there could be no flourishing of imaginative, of independent, of real scholarship. The concept of a "socialist science" has the same defect as that of a "socialist democracy." The adjective invalidates the noun.

GDR SURVEY RESEARCH

As noted little public opinion polling was done in the GDR, and even less of it saw the light of day. [Wolle, 1998, 343] But even if the results had been freely available, not all problems would have been solved. East German publications always had to be treated with caution and skepticism—and even more so when purporting to disclose survey findings. *First,* there was the issue of respondent veracity. Can the citizens of a communist police state be expected to answer survey questions truthfully. Participation in surveys usually was obligatory. Citizens selected for a survey could not simply decline to participate. Respondents, it can be assumed, were not likely to place much trust in assurances of confidentiality, even if they were given. Simple demographic items may have elicited fairly truthful responses. It seems certain, however, that questions regarding matters of social, political, and economic conditions, as well as those inquiring about policies preferences, were answered with both eyes firmly fixed on the Party line.[41] The exact degree of citizen prevarication is not known. There is little room for doubt, however, that the apprehension-based misstatements substantially reduced the information value of the survey responses for the Party leadership. This, surely, contributed to the leadership's illusion—lasting to the very end of the GDR [Honecker, 1984a, 47–51, 64–67, 158–159, 287–288, 360–366, 401–402]—about the nature and level of popular support for the monopoly-rule and the policies of the Socialist Unity Party (SED).

Veracious information gathering, however, was *only one* of the purposes (and probably not even the most important one) of the regime's polling operations. Unreliable responses were inconsequential in light of the other functions of socialist population surveys: to control, manipulate, mobilize the population, and to help the ruling Party to preserve its dominance and achieve its goals. [Ludz in Welsh, 1981; Krisch, 1985, 120–121] As noted by Ludz [1980, 198–201], survey items had teaching functions. As "pro forma" questions, they communicated prevailing Party positions. GDR interviewers also served as propagandists, who would not let "wrong" answers go uncorrected. Surveys almost invariably elicited declarations of loyalty, which, even when insincere, might have increased the probability of adaptive conduct and external conformity. Some respondents might even have been grateful that the Party "cared" about their opinions.

Survey research in the GDR was at least as much a policy tool as it was a data-gathering instrument. Its questions suggested the correct line to the respondents; its "findings" served to encourage wider audiences to adhere to the official positions. Given, for example, the low birthrate of the GDR and the extraordinary efforts of the regime to encourage marriage (or, at least, cohabitation) and to increase the number of births, it is virtually certain that the following findings were manipulated in the hope of affecting attitudes and conduct: 98% of an (unknown sample) of adolescent respondents were reported to have answered that a family isn't complete without children, and to have wanted for their own future families two (74%) or three children or more (13%). Among women belonging to the intelligentsia, the latter figure was reported to be as high as 24.7%. [Weidig et al., 1988, 266–267]

Second, there was the issue of technical competence. The few GDR polls that I have been able to see have been of exceedingly poor quality.[42] Samples tended to be small. Design problems abounded. Control (comparison) groups often were lacking. For example, a survey on the effects of female employment included only employed women. Findings about working women, however, are difficult to interpret absent the same information for non-working women (and, depending on the nature of the analysis, also for men). Target populations tended to be poorly defined, with an ideological preference for comprehensive rather than focused studies. The appropriateness of studying smaller groups, such as particular age cohorts, even became a matter of ideological dispute in the GDR. Noncomprehensive (sub-population) studies, ultimately, were found to be "un-marxist." [Ludz, 1980, 249] Systematic replication appears to have been of little interest, greatly increasing the probability of relying on atypical outcomes while at the same time reducing the ability to do longitudinal analysis and to study change.

There existed a strong taboo against "negatively formulated indicators." The descriptive content of all questions had to be positive, even if this was likely to distort the results. As Gudorf [1981, 228] pointed out, the essential point of GDR opinion research was not to discover "social truth," since officially there was no such thing as a "search for truth." Rather, the task of opinion polls, as of all other means of communication, was to impart in the respondent a "socialist consciousness." Here is how one GDR scholar justified the positive-formulation bias in a survey of delinquent youth [as quoted in Ludz, 1980, 302]:

> The questions submitted to the respondent have exclusively positive character. The question was raised whether it would be appropriate to confront the young respondents with negative opinions. This option was rejected for pedagogic reasons. 1. The educational value of the questionnaire is located primarily in confronting the young person with positive social views, and in the conflict of these views to his own. 2. The negative formulation would not have created a conflict but, possibly, an identification, and, thus, a further affirmation and strengthening of his negative views. This method, then, would run counter to the pedagogic purposes of the survey and, thus, is to be strictly rejected.

Political correctness, obviously, was more important than scientific accuracy and results correctly reflecting existing reality.

Often it was not even possible to assess the technical quality of GDR surveys because the requisite information was missing. Published reports would state that the survey was "representative," but did not provide information about such matters as sampling frame, sampling methods, sample ratios, replacement procedures, and, even, the wording of questions. For similar reasons, it was difficult to evaluate the technical adequacy of the data analysis. Typically it was not even clear what statistical tests had been applied to the data. Political criteria tended to overpower the rules of scientific analysis. When, for example, response alternatives were reported, the sequence would be in the order of regime preference rather than response frequency. This became an insurmountable handicap to interpretation when, as so often, the actual frequencies were not provided!

GDR DATA PRESENTATION

The question of veracity of GDR survey research data was but one aspect of a much larger problem: the truth value of *any* official statement or report. The repertoire of partisan science included a wide variety of deceptive techniques, from plain falsehoods, to misrepresentation, to subterfuges, to the omissions of key elements.[43] GDR publications tended to repeat endlessly a whole host of generalities, but failed to produce the particulars—with the clear intent to frustrate outside analysis and review.[44] [Drath, 1963, xi] And when specific quantitative data were provided, there never was a way to verify them independently.

Unwelcome data typically were suppressed by complete or partial omission from the public record. The advanced paranoia of the East German regime caused it to conceal even the most innocuous data. One visitor to an East German city reported as follows.[45]

> For statistical information . . . you have to apply to the District Central Bureau of Statistics . . . But at the bureau . . . you are informed that certain statistics—such as population size and profile, emigration and immigration for particular periods, average salary scales, division of work force by sex and age—do not exist for the town separately, or else that these statistics, to the extent that they do exist, cannot be divulged. [Holm, 1970, 5–6]

Statistics tended to be fertile grounds for manipulation.[46] The GDR took full advantage of all such opportunities. It was quite common for GDR publications to provide percentages or index figures without the underlying numerical base.[47] Indeed, even the actual percentages were not always supplied, but only statements that there had been "a large increase."

When data were supplied in tabular form, the tables tended to lack sufficient identification and specificity to be of much use. An example will be instructive. The subject matter is the workload of the social courts of a

Table 2.1.

As the following table shows, there have been no changes in the structure of misdemeanors and non-criminal petty offenses.

	1977	1978	1979
Offenses against personal and socialist property	56%	58%	60%
Bodily harm	24%	23%	24%
Insults, slander, and breach of peace	93%	90%	92%

particular judicial district. What follows (Table 2.1) is the set of figures reported by the editors of DER SCHÖFFE with the complete and precise text relating to these figures. [Comment, 1980b, 183]

The text above the figures states the conclusion to be drawn: there have been no changes. The tabular array that follows is impossible to interpret, however. There are no numerical base values for the percentages. Worse, it is unclear what it is that the percentages represent. They cannot be proportions of the courts' total workload since they add to more than 100%. Discussions elsewhere in the report give some reason to think that the figures may be the percentages of cases reaching the social courts by way of the police, but this interpretation conflicts with the wording of the initial text. Transfer statistics cannot reveal the *structure* of offenses. Furthermore, the offenses in the last category (insults, slander, etc.) came to the social courts directly from the offended parties, not from the police. In effect, there is no way of telling what these figures mean and whether or not they support the conclusion.

The problems of meaning and evidentiary support are not limited to socialist criminology. Table 2.2 is an example drawn from a GDR textbook on demographics and social structure [Weidig et al., 1988, 250].

This is all there is. No identification of location, time frame, size of universe, size of sample, method of sampling, the numbers on which percentages are based (one even has to guess that the figures are percentages). Nor are there any citations identifying a more complete report. The information deficit is no accident. Supplying the missing pieces might enable "unauthorized" persons to draw conclusions, identify changes over time, or determine regional variations—precisely what the Party did not want.

System-buttressing generalities without quantitative support abounded in the GDR literature, for example, that among younger citizens there had

Table 2.2. Importance of Collective Relations

Table [2.2] shows that in today's GDR the need for good collective relations is strongly developed not only among the workers, but also among other social groups. The findings are derived from a representative, written survey of one administrative region.

Major Social Groups	Good Relations in Work Collective Are		
	Very Important	Important	Less Important
Workers	63	29	8
Farmers	56	34	10
Employees	80	17	3
Intelligentsia	65	29	6
Total	67	26	7

been an increasing acceptance of the basic goals and values of the SED. [W. Friedrich, 1976, 156] More recently, one could learn that:

Sociological inquiries, that have investigated this process over many years, have confirmed time and time again, that the majority of the workers assign first place to the work collective in respect to the development of socialist work attitudes and achievement motivations . . . [Weidig et al., 1988, 242]

This "scholarly" contribution exactly duplicated form and content of SED declarations, such as that "the great majority of the workers, farmers, and working people have penetrated so deeply into the laws of our social development that they have convinced themselves of the victory of socialism in the GDR . . ." [Buettner, 1960, 139] The methodology and the (full) findings of GDR inquiries typically remained concealed, making it impossible to assess the veracity of interpretations and conclusions—which, of course, was the very point of the socialist mode of data presentation. Examples of untestable assertions are plentiful. The Soviet (English-language and Western-audience-directed) brochure THE RIGHTS AND FREEDOMS OF SOVIET CITIZENS, for instance, contains these passages:

In . . . Latvia, an industrially developed republic, during twenty years of bourgeois rule in the 1920's and 1930's, industrial output never regained the level of the prewar year of 1913. But in Soviet times, starting with 1940, industrial production has grown by 38.8 times. [Alexandrov, 1977, 46–47]

Western propaganda continues to charge that the Soviet authorities create formidable difficulties for Soviet citizens . . . who want to leave the country. . . . But there have been very few such cases [of refusing exit visas]. Between 1970 and 1975, exit visas were issued to 98.4 per cent of the total number who applied. Only 1.6 per cent were refused. These are the facts. [Alexandrov, 1977, 91–92]

Perhaps these "are the facts," but independent inquiry and judgment would have far greater credibility.

The complete suppression of unwelcome data, of course, also was available to the guardians of the GDR's image.[48] FDJ (communist youth organization) membership figures, for example, were dropped from the official statistical reports when the organization experienced a loss of members. [Richert, 1966, 59–60] Criminal recidivism statistics became unavailable when the previously declining trend reversed and recidivism (particularly multiple recidivism) started to grow. Figures on juvenile delinquency were omitted from the annual reports because delinquency had begun to increase. Ecological information was subject to the same fate. In the 1980s, the pollution of air, water, and soil had become so bad that the whole of the GDR came to be considered a disaster area. The regime did very little to improve the situation. It did, however, stop the publication of all ecological data as of 1982. And it persecuted those would would attempt their own inquiries.[49]

The GDR was not, of course, unique in its suppression undesirable data. The Soviet Union, by the mid-1980s, had not published absolute numbers for crimes and criminal sentences in more than 50 years.[50] As Conquest [1968, 132] commented, there was a "marked shying away from publicly giving any sort of statistics for crimes or criminals in the USSR. . ." In perhaps the most gigantic act of information concealment, the Soviet Union suppressed the entire 1937 census[51]—and shot its authors. [Nove, 1992, 30] In the Soviet Union of the 1930s, data such as population size, birth rate, death rate,[52] marriage and divorce rates, real wages, price levels, the number of hospital beds, and just about everything else, became state secrets.[53] Other socialist countries also were in the habit of suppressing unwelcome parts of their census data. [Hutchings, 1987, 91, 205] The Soviet Union persistently falsified and disguised economic information.[54] Soviet accounting practices did not aim to provide accurate data, but to camouflage problems. Jan Vanous [as quoted in Prybyla, 1988, 58] called these practices attempts at "economic disinformation." They often were successful. The CIA, for example, persistently overestimated Soviet GNP by about 100 percent. [Goldman, 1991, 47–48] On the basis of a detailed and thorough analysis, Judy Shelton [1989, 17–18] concluded: "Soviet financial statements contain skillful discrepancies and omissions that disguise the true condition [major deficits] of the internal budget." This conclusion applies equally to official financial and economic data of the GDR.

All research undertakings in East Germany, as well as the publication of results, required SED authorization.[55] Given the close control exercised by the Party and the general acceptance of the principle of "partisan science" by East German academics, it does not surprise to find that the scholarly literature of the GDR teemed with findings that were at the same time (a) preposterous, (b) untestable, and (c) in splendid conformity with the Party line of the day.[56] A recent volume on East Germany's social structure, for example, reported these rather unlikely but doctrine-fitting survey findings: 99% of the intellectuals stated that the collective had a strong influence on task completion, and 96% declared that the collective had a strong influence on the protection of societal (socialist) property. [Weidig et al., 1988, 253] Needless to say, the text supplied no information how these percentages had been generated.

Preventing systematic longitudinal comparisons by changing definitions also was a popular method by which to hide unfavorable or embarrassing developments. For example, while the SED continued to proclaim itself the Party of the working class, its membership increasingly was recruited from among the intellectual and technical elites. The definition of "worker," therefore, was changed. Industrial managers, university professors, and high state officials were counted as "workers" in the Party rolls if they came from working class families.[57] [Picaper, 1982, 130] One of the most extensive employments of changing definitions to prevent longitudinal comparisons can be found in the legal statistics of the GDR. In the context of a general scarcity of published information,[58] the data arrays of the GDR Statistical Yearbook have been reconstructed with amazing frequency. By my count, in 35 years of publication, legal statistics have been presented in 52 different table formats (even when not counting minor variations) utilizing 43 different data sets (sets of reporting categories). Table formats, on the average, lasted a mere five years. The effects of such instabilities are obvious and intended: (1) preventing longitudinal analysis by "unauthorized" persons, (2) facilitating the manipulation of trends, and (3) permitting the easy "improvement" of unwelcome facts.

Fortunately, the social courts of the GDR are an exception to the generally dismal picture of lacking information and data falsification. The ability to obtain reliable information about lay adjudication in the GDR (described in detail in the next chapter) made this book possible. Also, of all the GDR's legal institutions, the social courts were least affected by the relentless demand for partisanship.[59]

NOTES

1. This is tied to Lenin's rejection of empirical methods in favor of Marx's dialectical materialism. [Lynch, 1987, 111]

2. As Zeller [2000, 26] noted, "scientific socialism" served as substitute for intelligence. Or differently, it was not permissible to recognize the weaknesses and contradictions of the system. It was easier to suppress divergent views, thus, the overblown indoctrination and surveillance apparatus of the GDR. [Schabowski, 1994, 21, 42; also see Leonhard, 1992, 342; Mathiopoulos, 1994, 104–105]

3. For a thorough treatment of socialist/capitalist epistemological differences, especially of the "lawfulness" of socialist economic and social laws, from a socialist perspective, see Heuer, 1974.

4. As Marx wrote: "The mode of production of the material subsistence, conditions the social, political and spiritual life-process in general. It is not the consciousness of men which determines their existence, but on the contrary it is their social existence which determines their consciousness." Karl Marx, Introduction, CRITIQUE OF POLITICAL ECONOMY, as quoted in Max Eastman, ed., 1932, 10–11.

5. Indeed, a quest for information beyond a strict "need to know," was regarded with grave suspicion. In some circumstances, such a pursuit qualified as a criminal offense under East German law. [Gudorf, 1981, 130–147]

6. A review of the Social Science Research Council noted (without specifically naming the GDR, but clearly including it among the countries under discussion) that in relation to some countries "it may be necessary to disregard formal reciprocity altogether," if there were to be scholarly exchanges with them at all. [E. Barber, 1986, 14]

7. The customary response of Soviet officials to foreign inquiries and requests has been described as antagonistic, resentful, suspicious, and surly. [Feifer, 1976, 351] The general policy of noncooperation and widespread personal disdain for the West seem to have reinforced each other. [Mills, 1990, 3]

8. For some clear-eyed reports see Hodos, 1988; Leites & Bernaut, 1954.

9. Billy Graham, of course, was not the first cleric to value continued missionary access higher than truth-telling. The early Jesuit missionaries produced remarkably distorted, but highly idealized portraits of China. Alain Peyrefitte [1992, 27] asked whether they had been "mere dupes." He answered his own question: "No, but they felt constrained not to publish anything about China that might offend the Chinese. To do otherwise might have brought their missionary venture to an abrupt end."

10. Soviet Bloc dissidents only had scorn for Western visitors "who would hide their lack of any real knowledge of what they were dealing with behind ponderous and empty talk about a better world and mutual understanding" and urging upon the West "an enduring love" for the Soviet people without reporting, for example, about Russian nationalism and ethnic riots." [Petrov, 1989, 30]

11. Marshall Goldman [1987, xv–xvi] reported similar difficulties.

12. From the perspective of the left (including the American and German academic left) there still is no greater transgression than noting Nazi and Bolshevik parallels. Various comments on my Rotten Foundations (where parallels were drawn) made this as clear as it could possibly be. It seems that the ire and viciousness of the left has even increased since Arendt's *The Origins of Totalitarianism* (one of the scholarly books to note the many parallels), now that is become as obvious as it could possibly be, that the left's position was delusionary and starry-eyed—yet not lacking in a certain perverse (self-regarding) realism. As Zeller pointed out, none of the West German left, who never tired in praising the GDR as the better Germany, ever moved to the GDR. [Zeller, 2000, 45; also see Schabowski, 1994, 24] Marx and Engels, in any case, founded a religion, not a science. [Sperlich, 2002, Chapter 4]

13. Hook [1934, 156–158] had much fun analyzing the nature of Soviet-dialectical claims and practices—which he found to be incoherent, self-contradictory, insane, and generally absurd. Hook could not have been more right.

14. Western visitors to the GDR were told: "In our country you can't just walk into a university or a factory unannounced and ask for the man in charge." [Wechsberg, 1964, 4] Almost always, visitors had to be accompanied by an official "guide."

15. The secrecy enveloping academic institutions was also reflected in the fact that there was no course catalogue or even a publicly available faculty listing. [Mehls, 1998, 162; Wolle, 1998, 139]

16. Burrichter and Foertsch [1976, 94–103] distinguished three phases of Western (especially West German) GDR research. (1) 1949–61: a negative, strongly anticommunist, cold-war approach to the GDR, with exclusively Western standards of evaluation. (2) 1961–69: acceptance of the status quo, the use of neutral frames of analysis, and empirical rather than ideological approaches. (3) 1969–76 (and beyond): convergence theory, emphasis on the similarities rather than the differences among the systems, a shift to specialized and detailed analysis, generally avoiding overall ideological issues. GDR complaints, however, never stopped. [e.g., Thiele, 1984; Weber, 1985, 10; Winkler, A., 1982, 1002]

17. For extended discussions see Symposium: DDR-Forschung. 1 DEUTSCHLAND ARCHIV 141–150 and 255–272 (1968).

18. Generalizing from one's own practices and standards, to be fair, is not a uniquely socialist failing. Ernst Haas [1983, 106] was right to note "our tendency to analyze Soviet decision-making as the mirror image of our own." Or as Alexander Dallin [1973, 560] phrased it: "American attitudes and views . . . have often revealed more about the United States than about the USSR."

19. Bukosvsky, 1973; Hollander, 1987; Hook, 1987.

20. Until the late 1980s, for example, "Western scholarship on Soviet history was routinely dismissed as 'bourgeois falsification'." [Fitzpatrick, 1992, 87]

21. Jesse [1988, 71] comments: It appears that East German officials "simply could not imagine that the so-called 'bourgeois ideology' permitted to keep apart science and politics . . . evidently projecting the customs of their own system onto the liberal-democratic societies." This view prevented even university professors to have access to Western literature—and this included medical journals. [Braun, 1994, 15]

22. At the same time, GDR officials were pleased by what they perceived to be a growing Western interest in their country during the 1970s and 1980s. The increasing interest was interpreted as an "acknowledgment of the progressive accomplishments" of the GDR. [Romoser, 1975, 431]

23. Gohl, 1986, 11; Sandford, 1983, x; Sontheimer & Bleek, 1975, 13.

24. Apparently, however, it did not know enough, which was mostly due to (at least in the case of Erich Honecker) not wanting to know. [Krenz, 1999, 54–55, 66, 116; also see Benser, 2000, 390–391]

25. Zawadzki & Kubicki, 1970; Zawadzki & Kubicki, 1979; also see Pomorski, 1974.

26. Baylis, 1974, xv; Nawrocki, 1967, 8; Schweigler, 1975, 131, 140.

27. Often they succeeded. Many Western observers had considerable difficulty distinguishing between GDR pretensions and GDR reality. They often knew the GDR "only from official publications or conversations with functionaries, [obtaining] an intentionally manipulated picture. . ." [Herrmann, 1984, 128]

28. It is a recurrent theme in the post-GDR reminiscences of former members of the security service (*Staatssicherheitsdienst; Stasi* for short) that they send accurate information and timely warnings upward through the channels, but that their efforts were ignored. [Arnold, 1995, 79–85; Fricke, 1984, 77; Riecker, 1990, 10–12; Schell & Kalinka, 1991, 70–73; also see Dengler, 2000, 173, 181; Fulbrook, 1995, 27, 241; Krenz, 1990]

29. In a "brazen falsification of history," this included the retouching of photos to make "inconvenient" people disappear, as well as new photos created by montage to show Stalin together with Lenin. [R. Medvedev, 1989, 810–811] Socialist "scholarship," however, was willing enough to submit to Party commands. Historians in particular persuaded themselves that partisanship and objectivity could be united. [Jarausch & Sabrow, 1999, 96; Sabrow, 1999, 198] A GDR textbook proudly proclaimed the mark of socialist law is "the unity of strict scientificness and partisanship." *(Einheit von strenger Wissenschaftlichkeit und Parteilichkeit)* [Gruel et al., 1984, 39]

30. Westerners, it might be noted, have always been more likely to be taken in by left than by right totalitarians. [Taylor, 1993, 98]

31. For some examples see Hollander, 1981; C.Mills, 1994; Ulrich, 1984, 12–13.

32. Of course, Stuchka, Krylenko, and the rest, when in power and in favor, had dealt no more kindly with their opponents than they were being dealt with now. [Pipes, 1990, 798–799]

33. It should be noted, however, that some guests, especially those affiliated with left politics in West Germany, were eager to embrace GDR fictions.

34. Wuensche was best remembered as the author and supporter of *Terror-Urteile*, of vindictively punitive sentences in political trials. [Paetzold, 1991, 47]

35. Which, however, did not stop East German authors to criticize Western scholarship for being mired in error because of its "bourgeois partisanship." [Autorenkollektiv, 1982a, 6]

36. The expected submission to Party instructions encompassed even matters of approach and style: "The directive to the [GDR] Five-Year Plan for 1981–1985 includes the obligation of the social sciences to further increase their interdisciplinary character." [Buchholz, 1981, 695]

37. I retain the term to minimize terminological disputations. It is obvious, however, that nearly all of socialist scholarship was anything but scholarly.

38. See, for example, Autorenkollektiv, 1978a; Buchholz, 1981; Dzykonski & Loose, 1972.

39. "Free German Youth," the (monopoly) communist youth organization of the GDR.

40. The Party line (of the day) had absolute priority in all affairs of state and society. This included the area of foreign relations, where the diplomats of the GDR's foreign ministry had only one function: total support of the Party's policies. Critique was not needed and not wanted. [Hacker, 1986, 79]

41. Not surprisingly, the matter of politically motivated false responses received practically no attention in the socialist literature on polling methodology. It would have exposed a fundamental weakness for which there was no remedy within the GDR's "real existing" socialism. Attention was paid only to "neutral" (nonpolitical) distortions, such as positive and negative response sets, social desirability factors, and self-image effects. [Friedrich & Henning, 1976]

42. A survey of cooperative farmers, for instance, included numerous leading questions, made no provision for confidentiality, and provided little information about design, execution, and analysis. [Autorenkollektiv, 1973, 59–74] Methodological problems, it should be noted, were not the sole property of population surveys. In the GDR as in the USSR and other socialist countries, social research tended to be "methodologically unsound." [Malcolm, 1984, 8]

43. Regarding the USSR: "The written and spoken word faithfully reflected the atmosphere of Stalin's day. The purpose of public utterances was not to inform, but to instruct and edify. The Press contained only reports glorifying the Soviet system or discrediting the imperialists. The Soviet Union was immune not only from crime but from natural disasters: both were the unhappy prerogative of the imperialist countries. Virtually no statistics were published." [Kolakowski, 1981, 3:150]

44. Or as the GDR saying went: the task of our newspapers is not to inform our citizens, but to confuse the class enemy. [Kloetzer & Lokatis, 1999, 241]

45. Even GDR economists could get economic statistics (if they could get them at all) only on promise of confidentiality. The economic debates were not guided by economists but dominated by the dogmatists. In addition, the books "were cooked" by Mittag (the GDR's "economic boss"). Kopstein [1997, 95 et passim] found a large number of false economic figures in official GDR publications. Not surprising, then, that official figures were comprehensively ignored by GDR decision-makers. [Wolle, 1998, 189] The same lack of statistical data was also to be found in other areas; for example school statistics were available only in "fragmentary form." [Koehler, H., 1999, 9]

46. Lenin said: "Statistics should illustrate the social-economic relationships which have been brought to light by a comprehensive analysis, but must not turn into an end in itself." [as quoted in Conquest, 1968, 133; also see Lenin, COLLECTED WORKS, Vol.3, 506]

47. This follows the Soviet practice of publishing crime statistics only as "indices expressed in percentages"—if at all. [Conquest, 1968, 133] In fact, it was something of a sensation when IZVESTIJA published absolute crime figures, rather than percentages, in 1989. [Paetzold, 1989, 239]

48. The Polish criminologist Kubiak [1988, 174] has pointed out that the GDR published legal and criminal data very selectively, and, indeed, had not issued *any* law enforcement statistics since 1964.

49. Bailey, 1991, 488; Klessmann & Wagner, 1993, 506; Maier, 1997, 99–102.

50. Non-reporting also was true for the other socialist nations. China often boasted about its low rates of antisocial conduct. But, as Jerome Cohen [1977, 328] pointed out, "because the PRC issues no meaningful crime statistics, we have to take such assertions on faith."

51. Stalin decided that the alarming agricultural and birthrate figures were the product of "foreign sabotage." [Wolfe, 1961, 150]

52. The Soviet Union discontinued supplying life expectancy statistics to the World Health Organization when in the 1980s neonatal death increased and life expectancy decreased.

53. Increasing Soviet secretiveness can clearly be observed in the regime's Plan publications. "The first Five Year Plan contained 1747 pages; the second, 1262 pages; the third, only 238 pages; the fourth was published as a mere six pages in *Pravda*, and the fifth in three and a half pages, containing nothing but propaganda slogans and fraudulent percentages." [Wolfe, 1961, 140]

54. Soviet officials now have admitted that their statistics were unreliable. [Brzezinski, 1989, 39]

55. EINHEIT (the chief theoretical journal of the SED) reported in the most matter-of-course tone of voice: "The central research plan for 1986 to 1990 of the marxist-leninist social sciences of the GDR was ratified by the Politburo of the

Central Committee of the SED on June 18, 1986." The article then went on to state the obvious: "The tasks of the marxist-leninist social sciences of the GDR are determined by the implementation needs of the [SED] Party Programme, on the basis of the resolutions of the XI. Party Congress of the Socialist Unity Party of Germany." [Note, 1986b, 681]

56. Arch Getty [1992, 105] rightly characterized this type of literature as "liturgical."

57. Soviet sociologists did not even need the help of a proletarian background. They simply defined the intelligentsia as part of the working class—as the "intellectual branch of the working class." [R. Medvedev, 1977, 307]

58. Not all topics received meager treatment. In the 1987 *STATISTISCHES JAHRBUCH (STATISTICAL YEARBOOK)*, for example, only six pages (out of more than 500) were devoted to legal and criminal statistics. There was space in the volume, however, for the most detailed information about organizational memberships, including annual membership figures for these hobby groups: gardeners, poultry breeders, rabbit breeders, fur-animal breeders, dog breeders, bee keepers, goat and sheep breeders, and exotic bird breeders.

59. I cannot agree with Herbert Maier [1974, 240] that the social court commissioners (and the lay assessors) were an important thrusting force toward partisanship in jurisprudence.

Chapter 3

The Specific Lay Adjudication Research

FIELD WORK

The Exceptional Status of Social Court Information

The preceding chapter has presented a rather dim view of information access and scholarly research in East Germany—and it is true indeed that to do research in the GDR meant having to work in an environment of non-cooperation, distrust, and concealment. For my social court research to have any chance to succeed, some means had to be found to cut through the fog of slogans and fabrications. Fortunately this was possible. Detailed data were available for various features of the social courts and their judges. The data were credible because because of the mode of reporting and publication.[1]

Most of the information was published in a special journal for lay judges and lay assessors: DER SCHÖFFE—about which more below. Most of the information and data presented in the SCHÖFFE were generated and submitted by members of particular social courts, who also were the readers of the journal. This made "higher level" manipulation difficult, as did the fact that information was published for the same courts at various times. The repetitive and local nature of the information made it possible to examine the data longitudinally (at least to some degree), cross-check facts, and critically evaluate proffered conclusions. While I was not able to observe social courts sessions, I had extensive and direct contacts with ordinary East German citizens, in addition to the meetings with various officials.

In the period from the mid-1970s to the late 1980s, I made numerous visits to the GDR.[2] I had extensive talks about the social courts and related issues with East German jurists, state and Party officials, university professors, members of research institutes, leaders of professional organizations, and executives of various international and cultural exchange agencies. I also was able to interview a number of GDR scholars during their visits to the United States. The information conveyed seldom strayed far from the Party line, but the meetings were useful nevertheless. They offered a comprehensive view of official thinking (and variations therein), as well as advance perspectives on likely future developments. In addition, some matters not stated explicitly could be detected in the nuances of formulations. What made these talks useful was, above all, that there was not a great necessity to prevaricate on the part of GDR officials when it came to the social courts. Here was one body that functioned rather well—better in fact than most GDR institutions. It was a body that did not concern itself with military preparedness or state security issues. And while the social courts, as all institutions, had to be "transmission belts" of Party policy, they were relatively less politicized than the regular courts and most other official bodies of the GDR. There really was not much to hide. For a long time I thought that there *had to be* something that the regime was trying to conceal. This seemed to be the only possible explanation for the persistent lack of cooperation in my attempts to attend social court sessions. Interviews with GDR citizens who had participated in social court proceedings and post-GDR inquiries have persuaded me that the real causes were bureaucratic indifference and regime paranoia—pervasive factors in the GDR, as noted previously.

Studying Courts and Lay Adjudicators

Reciting the difficulties encountered in trying to do research on the East German social courts, it seems fair to acknowledge that empirical research on the American trial jury also has been exceptionally difficult—though for different reasons.[3] The most powerful obstacle to the systematic study of the deliberation and decision-making processes of the American trial jury has been the (legally desirable) secrecy of the jury room. Except for post-trial interviews of jurors willing to be questioned,[4] scholars have had to rely on substitutes, such as the comments of professional judges [Kalven & Zeisel, 1966, 33–54] and the findings of mock jury experiments [Hastie et al., 1983, 37–58]. The problems of American jury research, however, do not even come close to the number and weight of the obstacles which were lying in the path of GDR adjudicative research by Western scholars.

While the proceedings of the East German social and state courts were open to the public as a matter of law, it generally was not possible to simply walk in and observe the conduct of a trial. GDR practice, as so often, did not conform to constitutional principles and statutory requirements—specifically Article 133 of the Constitution and Paragraph 6 of the Code of the Constitution of the Courts. [also see Loewenthal & Schellbach, 1955, 685] Two methods were employed to control attendance at GDR court proceedings. One was to require spectators to identify themselves. Since it had to be assumed that attendance records would be kept, the demand for identification served to discourage GDR citizens from observing almost any trial, but particularly those in which they had "no business."[5] Ordinary citizen interest or just plain curiosity were insufficient justifications. Indeed, they were grounds for suspicion. [Lindheim, 1978, 65] The regime was eager for citizen involvement in public affairs, particularly of the ceremonial and acclamational type. It was not eager for uncontrolled participation, based on individual initiative.[6] Spontaneity and individualism arouse deep distrust in all totalitarian systems. The "Red Prussians" of the GDR, in any case, did not leave much to individual choice. As in authoritarian religions, everything was either *prohibited or compulsory.*

The second method of attendance control was the simple refusal of admission to the courtroom. It was rationalized by way of transforming the constitutional meaning of the "public" into the "relevant public." The latter consisted of those who had good reason to attend—"good reason" as defined by the authorities.[7] Visiting scholars were not seen as being part of the relevant public. Observing a trial required prior approval from state or Party authorities—not easily obtained. The observation of other governmental agencies and activities was equally difficult—in the GDR as in other socialist states.[8] George Feifer [1976, 95], for example, reported this about his attempts to observe municipal governments in the USSR:

> I'm trying to work on municipal government: the daily functions of city soviets. But I'm not permitted to observe their sessions, see their agendas, lay eyes on archives about meetings ten—or fifty—years ago. I have begged to attend five minutes of a single conference—a discussion, say, about revising a bus schedule—in order to sample Soviet democracy in action. I'm answered that this is unnecessary and even foolish. Soviet self-government, the freest and most open in the world, has been exhaustively described by Soviet professors. . . . For analysis of municipal institutions in action, they say, go to the books—the most reliable sources. . . . But the books are impossible . . . arid elaborations of a defunct illusion.

Matters were more difficult yet in respect to the social courts. To be able to observe them required not only permission but active assistance on the part of the officials. Social courts did not have regularly scheduled sessions; they met on different days and at different times, as needed. They did not assemble in the official court buildings, but made use of a variety of neighborhood and workplace facilities. They did not have published addresses at which they could be visited or to which letters of inquiry might be sent. Since the social courts did their own scheduling, authorities would have had to obtain information about the time and place of meetings and transmit it to the petitioner—a form of assistance which neither I nor other Western scholars were able to obtain.[9]

There appear to have been at least two reasons for this lack of cooperation. The first was the absence of any positive reason to help, the second the presence of a negative one. GDR functionaries had no incentive or interest to be supportive. Assisting Western researchers, unless enjoined by Party directives, was not likely to advance one's career. Second, there was a strong negative reason. The publications of Western researchers could not be controlled. Reports at variance with the official line had to be expected, given how much of GDR reality significantly diverged from it. Such reports, certainly, would reflect poorly on officials who had opened the doors. It was official and unofficial policy to prevent as much as possible any analysis of the *actual* workings of the East German legal system by researchers whose inquiries and publications the regime could not control.[10] Information about "the legal theory of advanced socialism," on the other hand, was readily and massively available.

CITIZEN INTERVIEWS

During my visits to the GDR, I was able to conduct a variety of unsupervised interviews and conversations with ordinary GDR citizens. These talks took place with persons whom I would meet by chance in public places. Parks, museums, taverns, restaurants, department stores, and subway cars provided the settings for many candid and productive conversations. All interviews were conducted in German, which is my native language. I did not identify myself as a visitor from the United States. I believe that most of the respondents regarded me as a fellow GDR citizen. Only a few of them raised the question of nationality, thinking that I might be from Western Germany. In these cases, I admitted to being a West German—which I was before moving to the United States. It did not affect their willingness to talk.

As others had found,[11] I discovered that, on a one-to-one basis, people were eager and ready to converse, and that in unmonitored settings they were quite frank (and often forceful) in expressing their views. Wechsberg [1964, 11–13] described the difference between interviewing GDR citizens in the presence of, and apart from, official guides. The first setting produced only party-line answers. The second setting, in contrast, yielded responses substantially at variance from Party positions. Twenty years later, Weymar [1985, 7] encountered the very same divergence of public and private speech. This points to the importance of language skills in comparative research—especially for work in quasi-totalitarian societies. As Goldfarb [1989, 90] found, "if one stays a while and listens to people . . . the official language of publicity and rhetoric [disappears from] interpersonal communication."

The interviewing technique was empathetic, respondent-oriented, and nondirective—with the single exception of the questions regarding *social court* matters. I stayed away from any topic related to state security. I did not ask for (though often received) comments on the acceptance of socialist ideology, the satisfaction with socialist practice, and the level of support for the socialist regime of the GDR. (Some of the more negative comments volunteered by my respondents met the definition of a high crime under the East German criminal codes.) I did not inquire about any plans to leave the country—which could (and would) have been interpreted as a criminal offense on my part: encouraging people to flee from the GDR. I did not ask for names or addresses. I merely inquired about matters of daily life and work, as strangers might do in any conversation. I gave specific direction to these talks only in that I asked about experiences with the social courts—not different from, and no more suspicious, than asking an American citizen, in the context of a general conversation, whether he/she had ever served on a jury.

I also interviewed a number of former GDR citizens who had moved to West Germany.[12] Some of them had come to the FRG illegally; others had been permitted to emigrate. These respondents were found partly through chance and partly by asking the initial contacts about other ex-citizens. A more systematic effort was not possible since neither the government of West Germany nor other FRG agencies maintained listings and addresses of former GDR citizens. I also inquired about information obtained in the debriefings of GDR refugees, expellees, and legal emigrants conducted by West German and Allied intelligence services. I was told that these interviews did not include questions related to the social courts or (rather hard to believe) to any aspect of the administration of justice in the GDR. Since the collapse of the GDR I have talked to many other East Germans, who now, of course, can speak about their experiences without fear. The new information does not differ fundamentally or significantly from the old. I also have been able to obtain a number of actual social court records (not accessible previously), generally recording the charges or complaints and the decisions of the courts.

The data obtained from the available six sources—GDR officials, GDR citizens in the GDR, GDR citizens who had left the GDR, and GDR citizens after the country's dissolution, social court records, and GDR publications—are not, unfortunately, adequate for a quantitative analysis. The numbers are too small; there was no uniformaly applied interview schedule; and the selection of respondents was haphazard. The interview data, therefore, will be used primarily to aid in the evaluation and interpretation of the published record.

PUBLICATIONS

The Key Journals

Much of the information on which this study relies was taken from published sources. Given the nature of socialist data presentation, discussed earlier, this was not a matter of simple transcription and aggregation. It required detailed and careful searches for data arrays that could be evaluated and interpreted. It also required bringing together widely dispersed items to build a reasonably comprehensive whole and to use longitudinal analysis to verify particular arrays. On the theoretical side, it required sifting through endless pages of mind-numbing slogans for the occasional bit of useful policy discussion or academic evaluation.

The key sources for the current analysis are the legal periodicals and books of the GDR. The most important among the journals is DER SCHÖFFE[13]—a monthly magazine for the lay assessors of the state courts and the lay judges of the social courts. It was published for 37 years (1954–1990) by the GDR Ministry of Justice. It was inexpensive and widely distributed. DER SCHÖFFE sought to guide the work of the lay adjudicators as well as to report about it. The journal provided assistance and gave advice in a variety of ways. It served as a serial instruction manual. It discussed and explained new legal and organizational developments. It even published law dictionaries in numerous installments and in the form of removable inserts.[14] It also sought to encourage the lay adjudicators by praising their work and commenting on its importance. Finally, it regularly and prominently reported the recognitions and awards received by distinguished and meritorious lay judges.

DER SCHÖFFE welcomed and solicited contributions from the field. These took various forms, including reports about the actual work of the courts, analyses of particular cases, profiles of lay judges, criticisms and suggestions for improvement, and letters to the editor. In addition, there were occasional discussions of Marxist legal theory and regime legal policy. Most of the contributions incorporated the mandatory panegyrics to the wisdom of the Party and the obligatory testimonials that everything, while practically perfect already, was constantly getting better.[15] This was painful to read, but did not lessen the value of the descriptive accounts, numerical arrays, and critical comments.

The descriptive and numerical materials, and particularly the occasional critical comments (even if couched in the language of the "further perfecting of the social courts"), provided significant insights into the actual working of the social courts, as well as important information about the GDR legal system in general. Even the propaganda segments were not without value. One learns quite quickly that endlessly repeated affirmations of success and perfection tend to identify precisely the truly weak points of the system. In any case, the study would not have been possible without access to all volumes of DER SCHÖFFE. The East German government was gracious to provide me with several of these.

The major focus of DER SCHÖFFE was on the lay assessors of the regular courts and the members of the arbitration commissions—one form of the GDR social courts. It gave only occasional attention to the dispute commissions—the second form of the GDR social courts. The dispute commissions (dealing primarily with labor disputes) received more extensive coverage in a journal associated with the GDR labor union: ARBEIT UND ARBEITSRECHT (Labor and Labor Law). Many volumes of this journal, fortunately, were part of the collections of the Berkeley Law Library.

Other Sources

Other GDR periodicals important for the present analysis include NEUE JUSTIZ, STAAT UND RECHT, and EINHEIT (the theoretical journal of the SED), as well as the English-language publication LAW AND LEGISLATION IN THE GERMAN DEMOCRATIC REPUBLIC. The leading general newspapers of the GDR were the NEUES DEUTSCHLAND (the official paper of the SED) and DIE TRIBÜNE (the official labor union paper). They also provided important information. GDR laws, regulations, and decrees were published in the GESETZBLATT DER DEUTSCHEN DEMOKRATISCHEN REPUBLIK. The semi-official RECHTS-LEXIKON, the last edition of which was published in 1988, also was helpful. The largest collection of GDR statistics is contained in the STATISTISCHES JAHRBUCH DER DEUTSCHEN DEMOKRATISCHEN REPUBLIK, published from 1955 to 1990. The deficiencies and paucities of GDR statistical materials were noted earlier. The JAHRBUCH was not published to provide complete and accurate information about the GDR. To a large degree, it was part of the universal GDR *Schönfärberei* (providing a pleasing gloss).

There also exist two very useful handbooks on East Germany, one published in the GDR: HANDBUCH: DEUTSCHE DEMOKRATISCHE REPUBLIK (in two editions); the other in the FRG: DDR HANDBUCH (in three editions). Among the Western periodicals, RECHT IN OST UND WEST, JAHRBUCH FÜR OSTRECHT, DEUTSCHLAND ARCHIV, and DEUTSCHE FRAGEN have been particularly valuable.

Overviews of the GDR literature can be found in two bibliographies (unfortunately not current): Gisela Hersch's A BIBLIOGRAPHY OF GERMAN STUDIES (1972), and Anna J. Merritt & Richard L. Merritt's POLITICS, ECONOMICS, AND SOCIETY IN THE TWO GERMANIES, 1945–1975 (1978). Basic GDR and FRG documents in English translation have been collected in Guenther Doeker & Jens A. Brueckner's THE FEDERAL REPUBLIC OF GERMANY AND THE GERMAN DEMOCRATIC REPUBLIC IN INTERNATIONAL RELATIONS, 3 Vols. (1979) and in Carl-Christoph Schweitzer, et al., eds.: POLITICS AND GOVERNMENT IN THE FEDERAL REPUBLIC OF GERMANY: BASIC DOCUMENTS (1984). A collection of East German views has been assembled in Arthur W. McCardle & A. Bruce Boenau, eds.: EAST GERMANY: A NEW GERMAN NATION UNDER SOCIALISM? (1984). Weidenfeld and Zimmermann's retrospective (post-GDR) DEUTSCHLAND HANDBUCH [1989] contains interesting discussions and important information. Useful also were several publications providing biographical data for a large number of important East German citizens, e.g.: Buch: NAMEN UND DATEN

[1987]; Cerny: WER WAR WER: DDR [1992]; and Frey: PROMINENTE OHNE MASKE DDR [1991]. Finally, I had access to a large set of monographs, conference papers, and GDR and FRG documents.

In exploring the work of the East German social courts, I have also examined some books and journals from and about the other socialist countries, particularly the USSR. While there were important differences among the legal systems of the socialist nations, there also were many common features. Since the GDR was self-consciously and painstakingly Moscow-oriented—at least until the Gorbachevian reforms—Soviet materials were particularly relevant. The various sources—conversations and publications, formal and informal contacts, Eastern and Western materials—provide not a perfect, but, in my judgment, adequate basis for the present endeavor. The major deficit, of course, is the lack of direct observations of the work of the social courts.

The events of 1989–90 changed this project from a contemporary into a historical undertaking. One of the consequences is, perhaps, a diminishing of the importance of direct observation—the lack of which did not, in any case, preclude the successful investigations such as of Athenian legal procedures [Dawson, 1960], Roman party politics [Taylor, 1966], early imperial public administration [Nette, 1975], and medieval parliaments [Wilkinson, 1972]. Through force of circumstance, the present study also has come to be a chronicle of past times and vanished systems.

CRITICISM AND OBJECTIVITY

The legal and political practices of the GDR are regarded critically in this book and its two predecessors. This may give the impression of one-sidedness. It is not practical, however, to attach a confession of similar Western shortcomings to each criticism of socialist practices. It seems useful, therefore, to acknowledge at the outset that socialist regimes are not the only culprits and are not only culprits. There seem to be few socialist misdeeds that cannot also be found elsewhere—albeit to a lesser degree. The (until recently) much discussed convergence of capitalist and socialist systems[16] appeared to be a confluence of negatives, adopting each other's faults rather than positive qualities. Can one tell without a programme to which country these comments refer?

> Government deception, supported by a pervasive system of official secrecy and an enormous public relations machine, has reaped a harvest of massive public distrust. . . . It has shattered the bond of confidence between the government and the people. And it has diminished our confidence in ourselves and in our ability as a people to overcome the problems that confront us. . . . there is now a tendency to disbelieve the government even when it is telling the truth. [Wise, 1973, 499–504]

The country in question is the United States. The remarks would have been equally fitting—indeed, more fitting—if applied to the German Democratic Republic and to many other countries, East and West.

Communism, it has been charged, stands for the worship of *power.* [THE NEW REPUBLIC, August 25, 1986] This is not an unreasonable assessment. But is it not, then, equally fair to assert that capitalism stands for the worship of *wealth*? And if true, is there really all that much of a difference from an ethical perspective? Wealth and power are readily convertible into each other. If it is fair to say that Leninism is opportunism raised to the level of political theory, may it not also be said that Reaganism and Bushism are greed raised to the level of political doctrine.

This book does not assume that iniquities are the sole property of socialist regimes. It is, however, a book about the former GDR and, with the exception of an occasional aside, nothing further will be said about Western problems. The standards of evaluation employed here are, in any case, not derived from specific capitalist doctrines, but from general principles, such as honest and open government, accountability of leaders, civil rights and civil liberties, respect for human dignity, legality, and fair and equitable adjudication. These principles, of course, have all been incorporated into socialist programmes. The Socialist Unity Party (Communist Party) of East Germany identified "popular government, freedom, humanism, and justice" as primary and universal values. [Wittenbeck, 1989, 216] The Party also subscribed to universalist standards, declaring that *all* systems can be evaluated by the "criteria of progress and humanity." [Stiehler, 1968, 324]

The general acknowledgment of Western inadequacies will not, of course, satisfy socialist requirements. Only paintings in black and white could be certain to meet with approval. Socialist regimes have always been remarkably sensitive to criticism.[17] In East German eyes, any criticism of Marxist-Leninist doctrine or practice was an act of hate-inspired anticommunism, aiming at the destruction of the USSR and the GDR, wishing to injure the interests of the workers in the West, and wanting to start World War III with the use of atomic weapons. [Autorenkollektiv, 1979, 621–625] Indeed, it was regarded as a sign of "militant anticommunism" to note differences between the early and the later Marx, between Marx and Engels, and between Marx and Lenin. [Autorenkollektiv, 1979, 626–630] Critical comments on the state of human rights in any of the socialist nations invariably were interpreted as imperialist attacks on socialist accomplishments.

> It is most certainly not the rights and well-being of Soviet people that are worrying the zealous Western supporters of "human rights" in the USSR; it is not the fate of our people that they are so concerned about. What they are interested in is freedom to carry out anti-Soviet activities and to attack socialism—our people's most sacred achievement, attained through heroic labor and defended from imperialist invasion at the cost of enormous sacrifices. [Alexandrov, 1977, 93]

To characterize communist rule as "despotic" was to "slander socialism in the most contemptible manner." [Elm, 1986, 37] And observers who stated that there (ever) was suppression of jewish culture in the USSR were "anti-Soviet slanderers." [Alexandrov, 1977, 49] Needless to say, socialist sensitivity to criticism when received was entirely absent when criticism about Western institutions was to be handed down. Fortunately, these matters play but a minor role in the consideration of the East German social courts and lay assessors.

NOTES

1. I should state here that I have greatly benefited from the assistance of GDR colleagues and organizations in providing me with documents and journals, difficult to obtain in the United States. My efforts of many years to obtain official permission and cooperation for an empirical study of the social courts in the GDR, however, did not succeed. For a discussion of this project's history see Sperlich, 2002, 1–4.

2. I have repeated these visits since the demise of the GDR and have obtained a variety of data previously unavailable.

3. For recent reviews of the state of jury research see Hans & Vidmar [1986] and Wishman [1986, 255–262]. The classical account remains Kalven and Zeisel [1966].

4. A willingness that appears to be increasing quite dramatically these days—not necessarily a positive development.

5. This reflected the insecurities of the citizens of a totalitarian regime. It was an important rule of survival "not to be noticed."

6. The GDR had an official and an unofficial peace movement. The former provided the bodies for stage-managed demonstrations against Western armament. The latter wanted all swords to be made into ploughshares. "The SED leadership was caught in a severe dilemma. On the one hand, it loathed any spontaneous political activities . . . On the other hand, a crackdown against the peace activists would have destroyed the credibility of the GDR's commitment to peace." [Frey, 1987, 109] They cracked down nevertheless. Unorganized (from above) activities simply were not acceptable, even if their purposes were appropriate.

7. The "relevant public" rule was used to exclude even family members and close friends of the accused.

8. Adrew Gayle [1978, 349] reports that on a visit to China, he was able to interview two judges (who fed him the usual party line), but "I was never permitted to see an actual trial, although I asked to observe one in each city visited."

9. I have been unable to identify a single Western scholar who officially succeeded to observe social court sessions. Professor Markovits [1995, 243] had the good fortune to be taken along to a dispute commission meeting by its chairman. This, of course, cannot substitute for systematic inquiries. Observations of state court proceedings by Western scholars also were exceedingly rare. Professor Nancy Wolfe of the University of South Carolina appears to have been the only Western scholar who received permission to observe the work of the lay assessors in three state courts. In a brief report published in the SCHÖFFE, Professor Wolfe pointed out, quite rightly, that the small number of observations provided no basis for systematic analysis

and generalization. [N. Wolfe, 1986, 94] Berman & Spindler [1963, 895] also were denied the opportunity to see comrades' courts in action. Of interest is also Professor Rand's [1991] report, who managed to obtain permission to observe a number of Soviet judicial proceedings, albeit after perestroika.

10. This pattern held for all socialist systems. In China in 1972, for example, "a visiting Philippine delegation was told that 'the legal organs are not for sightseeing'." [J. Cohen, 1977, 335]

11. E.g., Markovits, 1993, 12; Nawrocki, 1967, 287; Wechsberg, 1964, 25.

12. Stanley Lubman's important article about Chinese dispute resolution relied, in addition to documentary sources, "on interviews conducted . . . with fifty Chinese emigres in Hong Kong." [Lubman, 1967, 1284] Similar data about Soviet jurist who had emigrated to the West can be found in Shelley, 1984, 796.

13. The title can be translated as "The Lay Judge."

14. The major purpose of the journal was political, of course, but it did provided clear and comprehensive guidance for the GDR's lay adjudicators. The Western observer cannot help but feel envy, knowing how little instruction and assistance the typical American trial juror receives.

15. Making much use of the notorious GDR noun "Vervollkommnung." For a discussion of this linguistic monstrosity see Sperlich, 2006, 163.

16. The expectation of convergence was based on the growing functional similarities of industrial systems. [Meyer, 1970, 313; Wassmund, 1981, 323] The official socialist position on convergence theory was paranoid consternation and uncompromising rejection. The theory was regarded as a barely camouflaged species of anticommunist propaganda [Dau et al., 1986, 217; Fedoseyev, 1979, 20] and as a "terminological fraud maneuver." [Klaus & Buhr, 1985, 654] Convergence theory was said to increase the likelihood of a new World War, weaken the opposition of the working class to monopoly-capitalist imperialism, render more difficult the work of the progressive forces of the new nations, support revisionism and counterrevolution in order to restore capitalist rule, and aid imperialist sabotage of the socialist nations. [Klaus & Buhr, 1985, 655–656] If a simple theory was thought to able to cause this much damage, how confident can the regime really have been in the widely proclaimed inexorable and unrelenting march of socialism to its historical triumph?

17. For example, an East German publication characterized as "defamation" a West German scholar's description of the GDR as a "communist governmental system of the Soviet type." In another case, it was construed to be an attack on the USSR and the GDR when two West German scholars declined to subscribe to the proposition that the transition from capitalism to socialism was controlled by the laws of historical development and, thus, was inevitable. [Quilitzsch et al., 1985, 222–223]

Chapter 4

Lay Adjudication in Various Settings

HISTORY AND FORMS OF LAY ADJUDICATION

Lay and Professional Adjudicators

Lay adjudication precedes professional adjudication, and societal courts precede state courts.[1] In all societies/communities, legal decisions were originally made by persons who, in some way or other, had attained the ability (power) to direct and regulate human affairs. Initially, there was no distinction between legal, political, social, economic, or, even, religious decisions. In agricultural and hunting-and-gathering communities this "governance" typically, was exercised by a group of elders. In communities (bands) that were oriented toward conquest and military action, the "governance" more likely was in the hands of a single military leader. Power was largely undifferentiated.

It did not take long for realization to set it that the original leader(s) could not discharge all of the governing tasks. Some of the difficulties were quantitative: too many things had to be done. This would particularly be a problem when there was but a single leader. The greater difficulties, however, were qualitative. Even the earliest communities exhibited considerable complexities. It became ever more difficult for one person to master the intricacies of each of the several tasks, knowing the rules the community had developed to handle particular problems. Specialization became a necessity.

The first specialists, of course, developed in areas of particular importance to the community in question: the right time for the planting of crops, the proper rituals to gain the favor of the deities, the correct military tactics, and the most fitting rituals and observances to deal with childbirth and health. The agronomist, the general, the physician (midwife), and the priest, most likely, were among the very earliest specialists. Whereby it should be noted that the priests have not generally been satisfied to be intermediaries between the people and the deities. They have always sought to extend their control to further areas, especially politics and law. The evidence can easily be seen in the many theocracies, past and present, and in the theocratic efforts exhibited by powerful groups in this country today.

Whatever the exact sequence in which the various specialist appeared, legal specialist, most likely, were among the earliest ones. Disputes and conflicts are a part of any social grouping. When a community developed a set of rules by which things were to be done and by which disputes were to be resolved, someone was needed who had knowledge of these rules and who knew how to apply them. The early adjudicators, of course, did not have formal learning or training in the law, this would have to await the passing of many centuries. But presumably, they were wise and knowledgeable persons whom the community trusted.[2] Thus arose the ancient Germanic office of the *Schöffe* (lay judge) and the equivalent positions of other cultural traditions.

The shift from lay adjudication to professional adjudication—from the *Schöffe* to the judge—was a fairly late development, and even today, it is by no means a complete one. It resembles the shift from customary law to statutory law. The reasons for the shift to professionals are fairly obvious: the increasing complexity and technicality of the rules. The reasons for retaining some lay participation in the adjudicative process are equally clear: the desire of ordinary group members to retain some influence in legal matters and the widespread discomfort with a class of professional judges, well removed from the ordinary citizens and their concerns.

Nearly all societies that we know of have one form or the other (or several forms) of lay adjudication.[3] There are very few exceptions. Among them can be counted, in the current era, the Netherlands, Japan,[4] Israel, and Saudi Arabia. The Netherlands is a rather interesting case. Trial by jury was introduced in the Netherlands at the time of Napoleon by the occupying French forces. The Dutch, historically ill-disposed to foreign imports brought by bayonets, abolished the jury as jury soon as the last French grenadier had left the country's soil.[5] There is an irony here, the French spreading an English institution. In any case, many other European countries received trial by jury in the same way, at the same time as the Netherlands. Some of them were willing to retain it even after Napoleon had been defeated. In Germany, for example, the jury remained part of the legal system for more than a hundred years (until 1924). In Poland it lasted until 1938. [Pomorski, 1974, 199] Some countries have retained trial by jury, but have severely limited its use. Austria, for example, uses it only for the most serious cases (e.g., capital crimes).[6] On the other hand, Greenland, for the longest time, has used a judicial system based exclusively upon lay judges. [Kulcsar, 1982, 19]

Present day lay adjudication exists essentially in four forms. First, there is the form of one-person adjudication, found mostly in common-law countries, such as the U.S. justice of the peace and the U.K. magistrate.[7] These have limited importance. The deal primarily with inconsequential traffic violations,[8] trivial criminal law cases, and small civil law disputes. Of course, such minor cases also need to be properly adjudicated. Most justices of the peace seem to have done a credible job in these situations, and, after a long decline, the institution may be due for a comeback.[9]

The legal system of the German Democratic Republic made use of the second and the third forms of lay adjudicators:[10] the social court "judges" (*Mitglieder der gesellschaftlichen Gerichte*) and the lay assessors (*Schöffen*) of the regular courts. The social courts of the GDR are the *primary focus* of this volume. To better appreciate the unique features of these courts, it will be helpful to place them into the context of the other major forms of lay adjudication (as well as in the context of similar institutions in other countries—in particular, the comrades' courts of the USSR). The fourth form of lay adjudication is the Anglo-American jury (which, for comparative purpose, will also be considered below). The four forms of lay adjudication, then, in order of their independence from the professional jurist, are the socialist social and comrades' courts, the justices of the peace, the Anglo-American jury, and the lay assessors of the mixed tribunals (mixed benches).

The Lay Assessors of the Mixed Tribunals

The use of lay assessors (*Schöffen*) in the ordinary courts was not a socialist innovation.[11] Practically all of the *civil law* countries have long made use of the "mixed bench" of lay and professional judges.[12] The European Soviet Bloc countries[13] had been part of the civil law realm and as such made use of the mixed bench well before the arrival of socialism.[14] The GDR lay assessors, as the USSR lay assessors, were ordinary citizens without formal legal education—but in both countries much was done to provide the basic elements of such an education, once they had been seated. Different from American jurors, who are chosen to try one case, the lay assessors were chosen for a period of time (often one year,[15] within which they usually served for two weeks). In that time period they were likely to participate in a number of cases. They could be challenged regarding their suitability for a particular case just like the professional judges. [N. Wolfe, 1984]

The mixed-bench courts appear to give equal power to lay and professional adjudicators.[16] The lay assessors participate in all aspects of the case; each has one vote, as do the professionals.[17] The composition of the tribunals varied in the GDR, as elsewhere. In the West German courts, for example, there are tribunals of one professional and two lay members, three professionals and two lay members, and, until 1974, three professionals and six lay members. Even the administrative courts of West Germany have two lay members (plus three professional judges). [Lorch, 1975] In Sweden there still can be found a tribunal consisting of two professionals and six lay members. Socialist Poland had courts of one professional and two lay judges, and of two professional and three lay judges. [Michalski, 1980, 103] Typically there are proportionately more lay assessors in the lower courts and fewer in the upper courts.[18] In fact, the very highest courts tend to have no lay members at all. The reason is that the work of the higher courts tends to involve technical legal issues of law, for which a formal legal training is indispensable. Or, to speak with Kulcsar [1982, 39], the more administrative the nature of the organization, the more important the professional element.[19]

While the GDR social court judges performed their tasks without interacting with trained jurists, the lay assessors were in constant interaction with the professional judges. They heard the cases together, they deliberated together, and they decided together on verdict and penalty (on decision and award). It should also be noted that they lay assessors participated in the adjudication of vastly more consequential criminal and civil cases than the social courts judges. On the other hand, the lay assessors were significantly more subject to direction and control by the professionals.[20]

Though equal rights and powers of the lay assessors are typically guaranteed (often by constitutional provisions), the professional judges tend to have considerably greater influence.[21] [Hastrich, 1965, 464] They have the technical knowledge the lay persons are lacking. If nothing else, they can bring pressure on the lay assessors by asserting "that this is the way it is always done"—an argument difficult to counter by the lay person.[22] [Conquest, 1969, 31; Racz, 1972, 410] There are other advantages on the professional side. Only a professional judge can preside over and direct the hearing, and only a professional judge can author the (mandatory) written decision of the court. In this respect, my interviews with members of mixed tribunals in West Germany unearthed an interesting way in which the professional member, if outvoted, by the lay members, can nevertheless affect the ultimate outcome of the case: He/she would write the decision in such a way that it could not survive scrutiny on appeal, most likely being returned for a new trial.[23] In general, the relative influence of the lay assessors depends largely on the professional judge's attitudes and on the way in which he conducts the trial.[24]

The Trial Jury

The trial jury, an English invention, but with a variety of precedents in other countries,[25] is one of but few truly democratic features in the administration of justice. [Nejelski, 1977] It was an important aspect in the reforms of autocratic systems. Regarding Russia, Kucherov [1953, 51] writes: "The introduction of the institution of the jury was one of the most outstanding features of the Reform of 1864." According to Atwell [1975]: "The heart of [the 1864] reform was the jury system." Not surprisingly, the First Decree on the Courts of November 1917 abolished trial by jury. This, notwithstanding the fact, that Lenin, as a young lawyer had spoken in highly complimentary terms of the jury. [Kuchrov, 1970, 341]

A number of ordinary citizen (usually between six and twelve[26]) are entrusted with determining the facts of the case and with arriving at the proper verdict in the case. The jurors also deliberate without the presence of the professional judge, which gives them considerable independence. But the hearings are, in effect, conducted by the attorneys and controlled by the professional judge. The jurors have essentially no influence in the courtroom. There have been, it should be noted, a number of fierce attacks on trial by jury [e.g., Frank, 1949 and the various comments by former Chief Justice Burger] because of supposed juror incompetence to understand the facts or the law. [also see Friloux, 1975] These accusation are vastly exaggerated.[27] It would be much better to provide the jurors with the assistance they need to do a good job, for example, various procedural explanations and comprehensible instructions from the bench,[28] as well as jury rooms that meet minimum standard of human comfort [DiPerna, 1984, 40; Wishman, 1986, 123], and (this is no minor matter) adequate parking spaces for jurors. [Kennebeck, 1975, 237]

The decision-making power of the jurors is limited in a number of ways. Typically, they can decide only on questions of fact, not of law (which they are supposed to take from the judge).[29] In many jurisdictions, furthermore, they can decide only on the verdict, not (in the case of a criminal conviction) on the penalty. An exception to this is the state of Texas, where juries also determine the penalty. Another partial exception (in many states) are death penalty cases, where "death qualified" jurors also decide on the penalty. [Glenn, 1964] ("Death qualified" jurors are those who not in principle oppose the death penalty. This can have important consequences for the verdict. "Death qualified" jurors are more likely to return a "guilty" verdict.)[30] A jury conviction can be appealed; a jury acquittal stands.[31] A further discussion of the strength and weaknesses of lay adjudication, primarily as it regards the trial jury, but applicable also to other forms, will be found below. Finally, it is of some interest to note that various jurisdictions in the United States make use of a grand jury to authorize a criminal trial. This method is in decline, being replaced by a hearing before a magistrate or judge.[32] The literature on the grand jury, in any case, is vast.[33]

The Comrades' Courts

In addition to using lay assessors in the ordinary (state) courts, the socialist countries also employed pure lay courts.[34] These were variously known as comrades' courts (USSR), social courts (GDR), mediation committees (PRC), and reconciliation boards (Yugoslavia). There were yet other manifestations. They differed by more than name in the several socialist countries. There were considerable differences in organization, membership, competence, and retribution ability.[35] [Racz, 1979, 23] The social courts of the GDR are, of course, the main topic of this volume. It may be useful, however, to provide some details for at least one of the alternative forms: the comrades' courts (*tovarishcheskii sud*) of the Soviet Union,[36] particularly since these were the first *socialist* lay courts. Together with the new Peoples' Courts (also largely lay organs), they became a necessity, since the Bolshevik Decree Nr. 1 (February 16, 1918) had abolished all existing courts, replacing the rule of law with "revolutionary legal consciousness," by which the new non-jurist judges were to decide the cases before them. Only in 1922 was there a revival of courts in the ordinary sense of that term. [Kabes, 1961, 81–82]

It should be noted that contrary to soviet claims, the comrades' courts were not the first manifestation of non-state (societal) tribunals. There were many antecedents, reaching back at least to 1775 and the rule of Catherine II, when special occupational courts (*Standesgerichte*) were created for the peasants. Catherine's son, Paul I, however abolished them in 1796. In 1838, there was a provision for village courts for the state-peasants. General peasants' courts emerged in 1861 under Alexander II. However, they lost their judicial independence under Alexander III in 1889. But following the judicial reforms of 1864 (and later) in Tsarist Russia, "the vast majority of disputes among peasants, who composed the bulk of the population, were settled on the basis of local customary rules in informal community councils or peasant *volost* courts." [Butler, 1972, 201] There even were industrial social courts before the revolution, for example, the 1905 "colleges" courts and the enterprise mediation chambers of (pre-soviet) 1917. Even in the military, there developed a variety of organs to settle disputes among the soldiers before the October Revolution. [H.T. Schmidt, 1969, 11–27]

The comrades' courts went through a number of organizational forms and official sentiments. [Schroeder, 1967, 89–96] However, the basic point of a pure lay tribunal, staffed by co-workers or neighbors, remained firm.[37] The first statements about these courts speak of them as "production-educational institutions." [Bilinsky, 1962, 306] Toward the end of the USSR, a Guide to Soviet Legal and Political Terms defined the comrades' court as an "extra-judicial group composed of 'peers' at the workplace or place of residence and assembled under Party direction to discipline those accused of deviant social behavior that falls short of criminality."[38] [SOVIET LAW AND GOVERNMENT, 1987, 113] The Chinese view of these procedures is that "the masses are thereby educated, and the dictatorship of the proletariat is strengthened." [Gayle, 1978, 351]

The (Soviet) comrades' courts were first formed in the military region of Petrograd in November and December 1917 and extended to the other units in July 1918. In their first materialization they were strictly military organs, established to deal with violations of military order. The possible punishments were fairly severe, including fines up to 300 rubles and sentences to compulsory labor. [Berman & Spindler, 1963, 850] These military comrades' courts were institutionalized by law in November 1919.[39] At about this time comrades' courts also made their emergence as labor courts in the enterprises. They were set up by the enterprise labor unions. The prime purpose was to strengthen labor discipline and to punish violations thereof.[40] The secondary purpose was prevent offenses from ever taking place. In the words of Khrushchev:

> It will be possible to discern . . . an offender not only when he has already committed a misdemeanor or crime but also when these comes to light a deviation by him from standards of social conduct, which can lead him to antisocial acts. The people can in good time bring pressure to bear upon him, so as suppress his wicked inclinations." [Report to the 21st Party Congress in 1959, as quoted in Berman & Spindler, 1963, 855]

Or, as phrased by Grzybowski [1962, 257]:

> The main task of the comradely courts is to prevent violations of the law and all actions which harm society, education of the people by means of crime prevention and social influence, creation of an atmosphere of intolerance for anti-social behavior of any kind.

The third purpose was to ease the work of the People's Courts. A 1961 estimate states that, because of the revitalization of the comrades' courts, there had been a reduction of about 25% of the number of cases before the ordinary state courts. [As reported in Berman & Spindler, 1963, 896]

The comrades' courts had fairly broad sentencing powers, including the imprisonment of offenders (deleted in later developments). In 1921, the jurisdiction of the industrial comrades courts was expanded to include hooliganism, indecent conduct, and other minor offenses. Sentencing powers, however, were somewhat reduced. Membership in the industrial comrades' courts consisted of management and trade union representatives, as well as ordinary trade union members (workers).

The comrades' courts had a rather motley history in the USSR.[41] In the early 1920s, they went into a steep decline (which coincided with the rise of the New Economic Policy). They were terminated in 1923, but resurrected in 1928/1929. Their jurisdiction was expanded and comrades' courts were authorized in residential and rural areas.[42] "In 1938 some 45,000 comrades' courts were reputed to exist in the R.S.F.S.R. alone," [Butler, 1972, 2] with a membership of about 60,000 persons. [Berman & Spindler, 1963, 852] There were at that time about 5,000 comrades' courts in Moscow alone, and more than 300,000 in the USSR. Shortly thereafter, however, they went into dramatic decline.[43] They fell largely into non-use during Stalin's time, a period of re-emphasis of state courts and the rather curious notion that the state must get stronger in order to wither away. The post-Stalinist era saw widespread discussions regarding the restoration of comrades' courts. It was with Khruschev's stress on greater popular participation in ensuring public order (and on the withering away of the state again) that the comrades' courts could blossom again.[44] [Kabes, 1961, 78–80; Racz, 1979, 10–13] A new Draft Statute on the Comrades' Courts was published in October 1959.[45] In 1961 it was approved for the R.S.F.S.R.[46] The other union republics followed suit. [Butler, 1972, 203–204]

Theoretically, the first comrades' court period lasted until 1961, when Khrushchev declared that the USSR had evolved into a "state of the whole people," characterized by the absence of class oppression, the participation of all people in the administration of society, and the gradual transference of state functions to public and social organizations in preparation for the final transition to full communism. In reality, of course, the "whole people" (as in the "state of the whole people") had no more real power than had the "proletariat" (as in the "dictatorship of the proletariat"). Throughout the existence of the Soviet Union, the Party and the state apparatus ruled, and not some social organizations. Soviet textbooks "affirm that 'the CP not only plays a decisive role in the preparation and adoption of decisions by the Soviet state organs, but systematically controls the fulfillment of these decisions . . . Finally, every state organ is guided by the directives of the Party when planning its work.'" [Feldbrugge, 1973, 633–634] It was by no means out of the question that the Party could "exert pressure on the Comrades' Courts to condemn persons for acts which [were] neither immoral nor illegal—such as criticizing Party policies or Party leaders."[47] [Berman & Spindler, 1963, 845–846] As Lipson [1968, 109] rightly noted:

> Within the party, to be sure, there is a system . . . intended to correct certain kinds of abuses. The details of its operation are not public, it would be reasonable to suppose that values protected by the system are in the first instance the power . . . of the party itself rather than the rights of the people.

One of the first thing to notice about the comrades' courts is that they were not courts in the ordinary meaning of that term. This is particularly obvious when the question of punishment is considered. Their key function was not punish miscreants, but to educate citizens in the spirit of communism and socialist community life. The 1961 statute allowed the formation of comrades' courts in a great variety of settings: enterprises and sub-units of enterprises, educational and other institutions, all kinds of organizations, collective farms, residential areas, rural population centers. These settings should be comprised of at least 50 persons, but exceptions for less than 50 persons could be made. The members of the comrades' courts (from 5 to 20, or even more) were elected by the members of the collective for a two-year term—in the 1960s and 1970s. At various times, other durations were in effect, for example one-year terms. [Bilinsky, 1962, 309].

The 1961 statute provided for an expansive jurisdiction. It included breaches of labor discipline (absenteeism, tardiness, violation of safety rules, poor quality of work, etc.), public drunkenness and other public improprieties, insulting behavior, swearing, circulating false rumors about a member of the collective, damaging communal equipment and dwelling units, failure to observe apartment house regulations, disputes regarding payment of rents or services, property disputes up to fifty rubles,[48] anti-social acts that are not classified as crimes, failure to aid an ill person, the illegal practice of medicine, and many other transgressions. In 1963, the jurisdiction of the comrades' courts was expanded to include a variety of (mostly economic) offenses: petty theft of state or social property, petty speculation,[49] unwarranted use of means of transport, and petty hooliganism.

Cases could reach the comrades' courts by a number of avenues: on the court's own initiative, by a citizen's complaint, by state agencies, local Soviets and commissions, by directors of enterprises and collective farms, by trade union committees, by the voluntary people's patrols[50] and the regular police, by the state courts and the procurators, by citizens meetings, and by a variety of other paths. There was essentially no restriction on the ability to bring charges against an individual to the comrades' courts. Together with the amorphous jurisdiction of these courts, the capability of so many persons and institutions to bring charges, made "the rule of law" rather uncertain and haphazard. Luckily, the available penalties were not harsh—except, possibly, for the issue of shame and embarrassment (see later).

As a matter of principle, comrades' courts did not issue "punishments." With the exception of modest fines (maximally fifty rubles[51]) and certain enterprise related measures (see later), the courts merely applied "social pressures." This was to accentuate the persuasive-educational approach of the comrades' courts, as against the coercive-penal approach of the state courts. The social pressures included apologies to injured parties, a comradely warning, a social censure, and a social reprimand (with or without publicity). In work-related cases there was also the possibility of demotion to a lower rank (lower pay), extra labor to pay for committing certain actions, eviction from one's apartment, and even dismissal.

The cases submitted to comrades' courts had to be clear and uncomplicated regarding the facts and the rules (law) to be applied. Complex cases had to be transferred to the state courts. The decisions[52] of the comrades' courts were final. A lack of compliance (in theory voluntary) could activate state agencies. The decisions could not be appealed as a matter of due process of law. Also absent from comrades' court proceedings were presumption of innocence, right to counsel, precise definitions of issues and offenses, and evidentiary standards of relevance and materiality. [Berman & Spindler, 1963, 903] There also was a potential violation of the anti-analogy principle[53] "*nulla poena sine lege*" (no penalty without law) since the courts were given jurisdiction over "other antisocial acts not involving criminal liability." [Berman, 1963, 290] These "other antisocial acts" are bound to be in the eyes of the beholder. Or technically speaking, they constitute criminalization by analogy—a favorite method of dictatorial regimes.[54] In these ways, the comrades' courts did not contribute to legal security (*Rechtssicherheit*) but insecurity of law.

To return to the matter of appeals, it was possible to lodge complaints against decisions with the trade union committee or the executive committee of the local soviet, depending on the organizational framework of the court. While the former were (in the main) social agencies, the latter clearly were state agencies, raising questions about the social or state nature of the courts (below). Since 1977, the role of the state has been strengthened by the creation of Social Councils for the Work of Comrades' Courts attached to the local soviets (though some of these Councils were attached to local trade union committees). [Butler, 1977, 330; Gorle, 1982, 173–174] The text of the 1961 Statute (Article 18) provided that these organizations "shall have the right to suggest that the Comrades' Court reconsider the case." This could lead to a reopening of the case. An early report of one such "appeals" agency noted that over one-half of the complaints were justified. [Friedgut, 1979, 255] In fact, these procedures were not really "appeals" (re-examination of the case on its merits) but instances of "cassation" (a higher court reversing a case that has become legally binding already—more on this later). [Feldbrugge, 1973, 100]

One of the dangers of comrades' courts was a massive invasion of the citizens private[55] affairs. "if petty misdeeds become the business of the whole community, to be criticized in public, there is a serious danger that no aspect of life will remain personal."[56] [Berman & Spindler, 1963, 847] These courts might "pry into the personal affairs of Soviet citizens and . . . be an instrument for imposing conformity of thought and behavior in all spheres of life." [Berman & Spindler, 1963, 905; also see Rogovin, 1961, 303] Not surprisingly, it was part of the obligation of the comrades' courts to deal with issues of the peoples "morality." [Kabes, 1961, 87] Further, the personal dignity of individuals was likely to be impaired by the need for public apology and expressions of repentance. Indeed, a number of cases are known,[57] where the offenders pleaded (unsuccessfully) to have their case transferred to the regular courts, in spite of the fact that they would have to expect more severe penalties. [Friedgut, 1979, 250–251] A concern on the part of the offender about personal prejudice among his co-workers and neighbors is likely to also have played a role in the preference for the regular courts. The communal pillory seemed the worse punishment. [Niedermeier, 1961, 277]

The procedures of the comrades' courts were unceremonious to encourage the greatest possible audience participation. Organizationally, each court had to have a chairman as well as a secretary to keep official protocols of the sessions. Cases had to be heard publicly by at least three members. The chairman of the court had limited powers of pre-trial investigation. Offenders, victims, and witnesses had to be listened to. However, there did not seem to be a remedy for most violations of these (rather minimal) procedural rules. The conduct of the hearings were extremely informal. Essentially anyone could speak to any point, ask questions, and to put forward motions. Basically, there were no rules of evidence. Lawyers and prosecutors were not used. The court reached its decision by majority vote.

There was a considerable amount of concern about comrades' court weaknesses and abuses. Among them were improper procedures in the selection of the members of the court, lack of member competence and attentiveness, toleration of irrelevant remarks from the audience, wrong decisions, imposing penalties not authorized, taking cases that should have gone to the regular courts, slow to respond, and failure to function when they should. [Berman & Spindler, 1963, 896–899] In recognition of these difficulties, at least since 1979, there has been a great emphasis on the education of the members of the comrades' courts. "Countless numbers hear lectures on law at local technical colleges and regularly read legal literature." There also was a strong stress on improved juridical assistance. Even "faculties for comrades' courts" were set up at some colleges. [Gorle, 1982, 174, 176]

To point briefly to some of the differences between the USSR comrades' courts (predating the social courts by nearly 40 years) and the GDR social courts, it is important to note that the social courts were marked as a part of the regular court system, and that they were responsible to the state courts.[58] Comrades' courts typically were not part of an integrated court system, but were guided by and responsible to other societal organs, that is, labor unions.[59] Systematic comparative studies are lacking, but there is some evidence that the legally integrated social courts performed more satisfactorily than the non-integrated comrades' courts.[60]

It might also be noted here that the socialist countries had innumerable ways to involve citizens in state and social functions. This had a number of advantages for the regime.[61] Participation was thought to tie the citizen more closely to the state. [Herlemann, 1984; Little, 1976] Participation was generally unpaid, saving the state the cost of professionals. To take two participation examples from the GDR:[62] The country had a system of Workers' and Farmers' Inspections, which had significant economic control functions.[63] Erich Honecker [1984a, 120] was well pleased with their work, writing: ". . . already . . . inspections by the Workers' and Farmers' Inspectorate uncovered usable reserves of materials and secondary raw materials worth almost a billion marks." Then there were the Voluntary Helpers of the Police[64] (*Freiwillige Helfer der Volkspolizei*). The only categorical qualification was that the Helpers had to be at least 18 years of age. The later years of the GDR saw about 170,000 such Helpers. Here are some of their powers and control functions: They could receive citizens' suggestions and information for transmission to the police. They could introduce immediate counter-measures if there was a danger to public order or security. They could instruct and advise citizens who were committing offenses against the public order. They could demand that citizens identify themselves, particularly if there was a suspicion of an offense; and they could take citizens in temporary arrest to escort them to the police. They could take into temporary custody physical items that might constitute a danger to public order and security. There were many more such enabling formulas. *AND* the director of the local police could authorize the Helpers to engage in a large number of additional activities, as these might be helpful in particular situations. [Meininger et al., 1988, 88–103]

The activities of the USSR comrades' courts (and most other participatory organs) took place outside regular working hours (thus, production was not affected). While there was no routine monetary remuneration, there were provisions in the Code to reward members of comrades' courts. These rewards could take the form of an announcement of gratitude, a certificate of honor, a valuable gift or cash bonus, granting of additional paid leave for a period not exceeding three days, and a preferential admission to a sanatorium or rest home. [Butler, 1983, 246]

As a final consideration, it seems that the USSR comrades' courts were not truly part of the state apparatus. According to Kerimow und Schargoroskij [as quoted in Bilinsky, 1962, 325], these courts had two sources of competencies: (1) matters not regulated by the state, and (2) matters the regulation of which the state delegated to the comrades' courts. Only the second source can be viewed as a transfer of functions from state to social organs. Regarding the first matter, it is doubtful that there were many instances where the state renounced regulation. Totalitarian dictatorships are characterized by their mania to regulate and control everything. [Sperlich, 2002, Chapter 6][65] What began, in effect as an instrument to improve military discipline, work discipline, and productivity expanded both territorially (beyond the factory) and jurisdictionally (not only violations of labor discipline but many forms of personal misconduct). There is no question that Soviet officialdom, since the re-activation of the comrades' courts after 1959, has been well pleased with the results. [Berman & Spindler, 1963, 907]

Were the comrades' courts truly *societal* institutions, or were they "hybrid" organizations, such as the GDR's social courts (as will be seen)? According to most Soviet theorists, the comrades' courts were a societal organization, not part of the *state* apparatus. They had their organizational basis in the Soviet labor unions, which elected the members of the comrades' courts. They functioned independently of the state courts. Some doubts, however, are appropriate regarding their purely societal nature. The comrades' courts came into being through state laws; elections and procedures were regulated by state laws; they were subject to the supervision of state administrative agencies (local Soviets) as well as subject to the supervision of the labor unions. Bilinsky [1962, 329–330] views the comrades' courts as *state* agencies that were independent of the state courts. In that they differed from the GDR social courts, which were coordinated with the state courts.

The USSR comrades' courts, then, it seems fair to say, were to some degree more "societal" than the GDR social courts. In the last analysis, however, they were *hybrid* institutions.

Trial Juries and Social Courts

The social courts of the GDR (and some of the other socialist countries) and the trial juries of the United States constitute the two most extensive lay adjudication endeavors ever attempted. There are similar problems and challenges in recruiting, managing, and remunerating lay judges and jurors, though these problems tend to be more severe with U.S. jurors. Recruitment is an exacting problem in the case of U.S. juries. [National Center for State Courts, 1976a] The frequent reluctance of U.S. citizens to serve as jurors is well known.[66] East German citizens, however, were not altogether strangers to such reluctance. From all appearances, (no systematic surveys available) the GDR had fewer problems with recruitment. Political, social, and legal participation were understood to be an obligation of citizenship. Refusal to participate could be expected to have negative consequences of various types. [Sperlich, 2006, Chapter 4] As Hastie et al. [1983, 1] point out: "To the typical American citizen, participation in government is represented by voting and jury service." To the typical East German citizen, participation in government, of course, was vastly more extensive.

Managing the jury system also has been a much greater problem in the United States than organizing the social courts of the GDR. Complaints about juror waiting time, for example, are strictly an American property: potential jurors being asked to present themselves at court, only to sit around in the court's basement for days on end, without ever being seated as jurors. It has been estimated that 40% of the jurors' time is spent waiting to be used. [DiPerna, 1984, 225] In a large part, this is a function of the "voir dire" screening of the potential jurors—a cumbersome but essential and beneficial matter. [Babcock, 1975] But it is also a function of the court's jury administrator's preference to have too many potential jurors at the courthouse rather than too few. Many courts have now instituted procedures to reduce or eliminate juror waiting, such as the "one day/one trial" rule, and the juror telephone standby. One of the earliest efforts in this direction was Kandt, 1971. Also see Carlson, 1977.

Juror remuneration is thoroughly inadequate in most jurisdictions: five dollars per day and one-way (!) mileage (as in California) cannot be regarded as adequate compensation, particularly for higher earners and for persons whose salary is not continued during jury service time (for civil servants, it generally is). It can be argued, of course, that jury service is a form of citizenship obligation and should be performed regardless of remuneration, even at no pay. This argument is reasonable for a few days of jury duty at multi-year intervals. But for jury service that extends for several weeks, or even several months, the argument is no longer rational and better arrangements are needed. GDR social court judges received no remuneration at all. This service, however, did not affect working time and normal salaries. Almost without exception, the social courts met outside of regular working time, most often in the evening hours. Regarding the GDR lay assessors, the Code of the Constitution of the Courts (III, 51) provided that normal salaries would be continued and that all expenses would be reimbursed. One anti-jury argument, however, is simple nonsense: that we should not have jury trials because they are too costly (more below). [James, 1971, 194–195; Sperlich, 1980a, 275–277]

It is also necessary to deal with the often negative attitudes of this country's legal professionals toward the lay adjudicators.[67] [DiPerna, 1984, 2] This problem was by no means unknown in the GDR, in spite of the persistent lip-service regarding the glories of citizen participation in all aspects of governance. One cause of professional suspicion is the occasional "run-away" decisions of the lay adjudicators, generally matters of "nullification." For one reason or another, the jury does not apply the law (as given by the judge) to the case. It may be because the jury feels that the law is out-of-date, social developments having moved beyond (imagine a current prosecution for "blasphemy"). Or it may be that the jury feel the threatened penalty is too severe (such as long prison terms for the possession of a small amount of marijuana). Jury nullification appears to be a highly desirable process, as long as its use remains occasional.[68] There also is the jury's not infrequent inability to understand the judge's "jury instructions," but this is not necessarily the fault of the jurors.[69] Finally, it is well worth considering the "legislative function" of juries. [Levine, 1984] When legislatures fail to act (as is so frequently the case), judicial bodies, including in a minor way juries, need to fill the gaps and/or respond to societal changes, even if jury verdicts carry no effect beyond the case at hand. As in the case of "nullification," the jury can send an important message about the need for legal changes.

LAY ADJUDICATION AND THE JURY: PROS AND CONS

Delay and Cost

Justice delayed is justice denied. Few are likely to disagree with this judgment. The *delay* in our courts has become extraordinarily great and has become a primary focus of court criticism, even if often exaggerated.[70] That there is criticism of the U.S. courts is not exactly news. Criticism of the country's legal institutions and processes, often harsh, has been a persistent feature in the history of the United States. The critics have been a diverse group. Among them can be found not only judges, attorneys, and academic legal experts,[71] but also scholars from a variety of other fields of learning, [Nagel, 1975; Szasz, 1963; and many of the contributors to Rist & Anson, 1977] as well as journalists [Downie, Jr., 1971; and James, 1971] and concerned citizens. [Strick, 1977] And critical commentaries have been issued at the right [Wilson, 1975] as well as at the left [Lefcourt, 1971] of the political spectrum.

Voluminous and detailed criticism has emanated from the very apex of the American judiciary. A recent Chief Justice of the United States Supreme Court authored these observations:

> It is a very serious matter when whole communities become emotionally aroused—as they are these days—by a constant pattern of serious crimes. We should not be heard to complain at the loss of public confidence in our legal institutions if people come to think that government is impotent to protect its citizens.
>
> Other conditions that caused dissatisfaction . . . are still with us. Jurors, witnesses, and litigants continue to have their time squandered. They are often shuffled about courthouses in confusion caused by poor management within the courts. The delays and high costs in resolving civil disputes continue to frighten away potential litigants, and those who persist and ultimately gain a verdict often see up to half of the recovery absorbed by fees and expenses. Inordinate delay in criminal trials and our propensity for multiple trials and appeals shock lawyers, judges, and social scientists of other countries. [Burger, 1976, iii, ix]

While we should continue with native traditions of court reform (in the spirit of Roscoe Pound), the Chief Justice thought that we should also try to learn from the experiences and arrangements of other countries. For example:

> I hardly think we endanger the republic if we also make thoughtful inquiries into England's civil procedures, and their ideas of finality of judgments, short of three or four appeals and retrials. [Burger, 1976, viii]

Reforms cannot be the exclusive province of the legal experts:

> We need not rely on [public opinion polls] to know that the public is deeply aroused and disturbed about the state of justice and all its work. . . . To break out of the mold of obsolete patterns of court organization, the whole people—not just lawyers—must be drawn into the programs for change. [Burger, 1971, 776, 780]

This change will have to be more than "petty tinkering" with the administration of justice. While we should avoid "hasty and ill-considered" reforms, we must be willing to consider "major and systematic changes." [Burger, 1976, vii; also see Langbein, 1981] For the Chief Justice, the most important of these "major and systematic changes" was the curtailment or even abolition of trial by jury.

Unjust and Ineffective

Chief Justice Burger's views are shared by other observers. Downie's investigations, for example, led him to conclude that "the vast majority of Americans [find] mostly chaos, injustice, and cynical indifference in the local courthouses," and that many citizens "no longer believe that the system will eventually work for them. They no longer have faith in the rule of law." This lack of faith is not, in the greater part, a matter of misperception or of exploitative media presentations of crime and violence. "The dismaying, ugly fact is that disbelief in the efficacy of the U.S. legal system is well founded."[72] [Downie, 1971, 7, 15] The problems of the U.S. legal system are magnified in the lower courts, which, as tribunals of first instance, are called upon to try the less serious criminal cases and the less consequential civil disputes. The experience, unfortunately, "seldom is a happy one." [Robertson, 1974, vii] There exists a substantial gulf between the American ideal of justice and what the citizen is likely to observe in the lower courts:

> Other legal institutions share the lower courts' inability to conform actuality to the ideal, but few other parts of the justice system touch so many people so directly . . . the performance of the lower courts can have a powerful socializing or alienating effect, influencing the quality and extent of order found in society. [Robertson, 1974, 12]

The U.S. legal system, of course, also has its strengths and can point to important achievements.[73] An extraordinary growth of popular dissatisfaction in recent years cannot be denied. However, it must be noted that much of the popular discontent is media generated. Commentators being fixated on convictions tend to blame the jury's deficient intelligence or lack of common sense (rather than, for example, inadequate evidence or poorly performing prosecutors) when there is an acquittal. The most recent case in point was the trial of Michael Jackson. The commentators were out for blood (in fact, at least one of them had so thoroughly prejudged the case that her presentations were that of a ferocious harridan). The acquittal was a major and personal blow to these commentators—and the jury was to blame. (Also see Graham [1975] on this point.) Watts [1975] has made a search of the American literature to see what kind of picture emerges of the jury. She found that while only few works of literature deal with trial by jury at all, the evaluations are almost uniformly negative.[74]

Apart from jury dissatisfaction, discontent with our courts has moved beyond the stage of private grumbling to organized political action, such as efforts at judicial recall and proposals to reduce the substantive jurisdiction of certain courts. There is a crisis in the courts. It should not be discounted because it has been proclaimed before. Reform is necessary. It should not be disdained because past reforms did not fulfill all expectations.[75] However, it is a canard to charge the jury with general incompetence and (as a consequence thereof) with granting outrageously large monetary awards, which, in any case, U.S. courts are perfectly capable of reducing. [Litan, 1993; Vidmar, 1995]

Case Loads and Delay

Popular dissatisfaction with the administration of justice has many causes. Some of them may well be related to a lack of popular understanding of the nature of the law, the function of the courts (including the purposes of the jury), requiring an improved legal education of the citizens rather than changes in the legal system. Increased citizen participation in adjudication and better legal instruction in the schools should have very positive results. Much, perhaps most, of popular discontent, however, has its origin in actual deficiencies. Very important among them are the large amounts of congestion and delay experienced in so many American courts. While there are other factors contributing to delay, such as poor court organization [Sperlich, 1982c], the core problem is the massive case load inflicted upon the courts. Zeisel, et al. [1959, xxii-xxiii] have written emphatically about the consequences of delay:

> Delay in the courts is unqualifiedly bad. It is bad because it deprives citizens of a basic public service; it is bad because the lapse of time frequently causes deterioration of evidence and makes it less likely that justice be done when the case is finally tried; it is bad because delay may cause severe hardship to some parties and may in general affect litigants differentially; and it is bad because it brings to the entire court system a loss of public confidence, respect, and pride. . . .
>
> These are obvious evils and scarcely require a statement. But in addition, a delayed court system brings in its wake many not so obvious secondary evils. It produces an unhealthy emphasis on the desirability of settlement and on the impropriety of litigation. It creates a stimulus for major changes in substantive law and procedure, such as the abolition of jury trial in civil cases, or shifting large areas of tort law to compensation schemes. . . . Again, extended delay may result in, indeed almost compels, departure from legal ethics. . . . And a delayed calendar creates totally new issues for a court, as it seeks to determine what if any cases should be given preference and tried ahead of others.

Chief Justice Burger [1970, 32, 39] also has pointed to the deleterious effects of delay.[76] New judgeships have been created; judicial productivity has increased. [Burger, 1980a, 13] But, the constant growth in the number of filings[77] has prevented these improvements from adequately reducing delay. The greatest injuries are suffered in the civil area. While criminal cases also may not be tried as speedily as one might wish, there exist constitutional limits to delay, which, if not observed, cause the assessment of a penalty against the prosecution, such as dismissal of charge. No such limits are prescribed for civil litigation.[78] Not surprisingly, civil litigants tend to experience waiting periods measured in years, before their claims are adjudicated.[79] Quite clearly, the number of judgeships cannot be increased indefinitely. The only possible strategy is the increased use of other persons (lay persons) or other agencies (e.g., arbitration boards).

The Virtues of Lay Adjudication and the Positive Side of Juries

In spite of delivering a decision basically injurious to trial by jury, the Supreme Court was moved to include the following language in *Williams v. Florida* (1970): The chief function of the jury is to safeguard the citizen "against arbitrary law enforcement" (p. 87). It is to prevent oppression by the government and to provide the accused with "an inestimable safeguard against the corrupt or overzealous prosecutor and against the compliant, biased, or eccentric judge" (p. 100). The jury provides "the interposition between the accused and his accuser of the common sense judgment of a group of laymen" and "the community participation and shared responsibility that results from the group's determination of guilt or innocence" (p. 100). As Hastie et al. [1983, 1] rightly say: "The jury trial is the central element in the American conception of justice."

The jury as safeguard against government oppression is an idea as old (indeed, older) as this republic. This is Jefferson: "I consider trial by jury as the only anchor ever yet imagined by man, by which a government can be held to the principles of its constitution." This echoes Blackstone:

> Trial by jury is a privilege of the highest and most beneficial nature and our most important guardian both of public and private liberty. Our liberties cannot but subsist as long as this palladium remains sacred and inviolate: not only from all open attacks, but also from all secret machinations which may sap and undermine it. [as quoted in Lehman, 1997, 14]

And, of course, it also echoes de Tocqueville [1945, 295–297], who was particularly taken with the civil jury, and who thought the jury even more important politically than legally:

> The institution of the jury, if confined to criminal causes, is always in danger; but when once it is introduced into civil proceedings, it defies the aggressions of time and man. . . . In whatever manner the jury be applied, it cannot fail to exercise a powerful influence upon the national character; but the influence is prodigiously increased when it is introduced into civil causes. The jury, and more specifically the civil jury, serves to communicate the spirit of the judges to the minds of all the citizens; and this spirit, with the habits which attend it, is the soundest preparation for free institutions. It imbues all classes with a respect for the thing judged and with the notion of right. . . . The jury teaches each man not to recoil before the responsibility of his own actions and impresses him with that manly confidence without which no political virtue can exist. . . . I think that the practical intelligence and political good sense

of the Americans are mainly attributable to the long use that they have made of the jury in civil causes. . . . Thus the jury, which is the most energic means of making the people rule, is also the most efficacious means of teaching it how to rule well.

It is a sentiment one wishes American judges would take more to heart, as they undermine the jury with changes in size and decision-rule, demands for special verdicts, and opposition to all nullification. Too many seem to have forgotten the trial of William Penn (with such courageous jurors as Edward Bushnell and Thomas Veer) and of Peter Zenger (with such courageous jurors as Thomas Hunt and Harmanus Rutgers). [Hans & Vidmar, 1986, 21–35; Lehman, 1997, 35–72, 151–174] In this context, all the complaints from the bench[80] about time and cost (exaggerated as they are) must be regarded as frivolous—as least as long as the various potential remedies to congestion and cost have not been given adequate experimentations.

The cost argument against trial by jury is particularly harebrained, given the very low pay that jurors receive. Various calculations show that the abolition of the jury would but save pennies per citizen per year. [see Corboy, 1975, 185; Sperlich, 1980a, 275–277] It is a common tactic by the opponents of the jury to report how many millions of dollars could be saved if the jury were smaller or abolished. While these millions may be correct figures, they pale to insignificance in comparison to such annual U.S. expenditures as hundreds of millions (and even billions) for golf equipment, tobacco products, gambling, and cosmetics.

It should also be noted that jury trials are more important than their numbers. It has been variously pointed out that only a minority of civil and criminal cases reach a jury trial. Only 1% to 2% of civil trials come to a jury. The others are disposed of in some other fashion (mostly settlement). Only about one-third of criminal trials go to a jury. The others are "plea-bargained." These low rates are in part a reflection of the desires of the litigants/defendants (who might know that they have a weak case) to avoid the uncertainties and expenses of an actual trial, and get a better deal (reduced charge) as part of the process. But the low rates are also a reflection of judicial necessity, a reflection of how over-burdened our courts are. But, as has often been pointed out [Abraham, 1998, 6; Kalven & Zeisel, 1966, 19–21, 31–32], the influence of the jury goes far beyond the actual jury trials. ". . . it is the background existence of the right to a jury trial, and predictions about how juries would decide cases were they to get them, that motivates parties to settle or plea bargain in the first place. Those who argue that the jury is unimportant because jury trials are infrequent thus mistake the tip of the iceberg for the whole." [Abraham, 1998, 6] Or, as Kalven & Zeisel [1966, 31–2] commented: pretrial decisions "are in part informed by expectations of what the jury will do. Thus, the jury is not controlling merely the immediate case before it, but the host of cases not before it which are destined to be disposed of by the pre-trial process."

The jury—civil and criminal—is an exceedingly important legal *and* political institution. The maintenance of our liberties may well depend on its preservation. And, viewed from another perspective, because the jury facilitates the input of popular values and sentiments into the legal system, it legitimizes, in turn, the legal system of which it is part.[81] [Ehrmann, 1976, 102] Its influence and importance are vastly greater than the actual number of cases actually brought to it. Most important, as pointed out by Kalven & Zeisel [1966, 3]: "The jury . . . represents a deep commitment to *the use of laymen in the administration of justice* . . ." [my emphasis]

To preserve the use of the jury in truly consequential litigations (and to relieve the ordinary courts of some of their burdens) the employment of *alternative modes of lay adjudication* deserves serious consideration.

REMEDY: DIVERSION AND LAY ADJUDICATION

In addition to increases in judgeships and judicial productivity, both of which are not infinitely expandable, three other strategies suggest themselves for the elimination of delay: reduction in filings, diversion to other (non-court) agencies, and lay adjudication. The first—*increases in judgeships*—is the surest cure, but also the most difficult to bring about.[82] The United States is a law-oriented ("all issues turn into legal issues") and highly litigious society. It also has high rates of crime. Reducing the total number of prosecutions and litigations (without ignoring criminal acts or impeding public access to the courts) would require nothing less than societal-cultural changes of a most fundamental type. The prospects for such changes are not particularly good.

Much effort and ingenuity have been expended on *diversion*—with considerable success. Diversion has received support from nearly all interested parties,[83] from public interest advocates to the former Chief Justice, who stated: "I have a strong feeling that a great many matters traditionally handled in the court systems, both State and federal, should be diverted away from the courts entirely." [Burger, 1980a, 35] The Chief Justice has endorsed dispute resolution experiments such as "metropolitan mediation centers" and "neighborhood justice centers," as well as non-binding but mandatory pre-trial arbitration procedures.[84] [Burger, 1980a, 6–8; and Burger, 1981, 10–13] While diversion has been advocated and tried even in the criminal law area, [Davis et al., 1980; Felstiner & Williams, 1978, 223] its greatest development has been in civil disputes.[85]

Civil diversion methods and forums now include: "no-fault" provisions for (potential) tort cases and divorce actions; voluntary and mandatory, binding and non-binding arbitration; mediation sponsored by public and private parties (most recently by mass media, such as newspapers and TV stations); ombudsmen (particularly in the Scandinavian countries, typically to assist citizens in disputes with public agencies) [Brunner, 1967, 108–109];

and courts of special jurisdiction, such as small claims courts. [Johnson et al., 1977; Sander, 1995] To lighten the case load of the regular trial courts and reduce delay, there also has been the creation of a new type of judicial officer (magistrate judges, above), [Puro, 1976, 141] as well as the retention and revival of lay justices of the peace.[86]

Depending on personnel and organizational format, some of the diversion strategies may also be part of the third method: *lay adjudication*. Most arbitration is done by legal experts. Small claims courts usually are staffed by professional judges. These forms of diversion merely shift cases to different sectors of the legal community. Only by employing lay adjudicators can the case burden of the legal professionals truly be reduced. Apart from purely private dispute resolution, there are four major forms of *lay adjudication:* juries, mixed benches, lay magistrates, and social courts.[87]

Juries and mixed benches represent combined lay-professional adjudication. Sharing of the adjudicative tasks among professionals and lay persons has many virtues,[88] but reducing case loads and delays are not among them. However, the charge is false that the use of the jury substantially increases trial time and, thus, contributes to delay. [National Center for State Courts, 1988] The charge is also false that trial by jury produces a major financial burden on courts or litigants. For a discussion of these issues see Sperlich, 1980a, 262, 275–277.

The trial jury is the major Anglo-American form of judicial lay participation, though a few countries outside the common law orbit make occasional use of trial by jury.[89] Nearly all of the civil jury trials and at least 90% of all criminal jury trials now take place in the United States. England and the other countries of the British Commonwealth have greatly reduced employment of the civil and criminal trial jury. (Interestingly, the grand jury was abolished altogether in 1933 in its country of origin—England—were it had been in existence since 1166.) [Ehrmann, 1976, 97; Leach-Lewis, 1975] In the United States, the civil jury also is an endangered species. Its opponents seek to abolish it because of a presumed inability to deal with complexities. [Austin, 1984; James, 1971, 196–199; Sperlich, 1982a; Strawn & Munsterman, 1987] The mixed bench is the major form of judicial lay participation in the civil law countries of Europe.[90] It is also widely used in the socialist countries.[91] The two primary differences between the jury and the mixed bench concern range of competence and style of deliberation. The jury's competence is limited (at least in theory[92]) to questions of fact. It does not decide issues of law and may or may not (depending on the jurisdiction) determine the sentence upon a criminal conviction.[93]

The lay judges of the mixed bench rule on all issues: fact, law, and sentence. While this may seem to give the jury less power, there is the obverse fact of the jury's independent deliberation and decision-making. The professional judge may not even enter the jury room. The lay judges of mixed bench systems, however, perform all functions together with and in the presence of one or more professional judges.[94] They lack the jurors' independence and, in this sense, some of the jurors' powers. Empirical investigations have shown that, at least in West Germany, the lay judges have only a small independent effect on verdicts and a modest independent effect on sentences. [Casper & Zeisel, 1979, 80–85; Klausa, 1972, 76–79] My own investigations of West German mixed-bench adjudication agree with Klausa's finding that the influence of the lay judges is largely a function of the style and attitude of the professional judge(s).[95]

Lay magistrates, such as justices of the peace, and the social courts constitute true lay tribunals. When cases are diverted to them, courts (and/or other sectors of the legal profession) benefit from a real reduction in caseload. The justice of the peace is an ancient judicial office, dating back to fourteenth-century England. It can be found in America at the very beginning of the colonies.[96] For several centuries, the justice of the peace was the principal trial court for lesser civil actions and misdemeanor criminal cases. The justices tended to be local notables and generally did not have training in the law. They were supported by a fee system—a major point of criticism. [Lewis et al., 1978, 40–42; Vanlandingham, 1974, 40–46] In this century, the office of the justice of the peace suffered a dramatic decline. A number of states have abolished it. Other states have stopped filling existing positions. Substantive jurisdiction almost everywhere has been greatly reduced. [Lewis et al., 1978, 40; Vanlandingham, 1974, 40–42] While there also have been efforts at revival, [Brownlee, 1975] the general tendency has been to abolish the office or to change its nature by staffing it with persons trained in the law. In either case, there is a loss of lay adjudication.[97]

Social courts, as the term is used here, are collegial lay tribunals, serving as civil and criminal courts of first instance with limited jurisdiction. By their official GDR designation, the social courts were *societal* organs.[98] As was emphasized strongly in the legal literature of the GDR, the social courts were part of the uniform system of courts. [Kasper, 1980, 221] It was also emphasized, however, that the courts of this uniform system were *state* organs. The social courts, then, were *hybrid* structures, best understood, perhaps, in the context of the general socialist/communist transfer of functions from state to societal organs.[99]

The social courts can be regarded as the most recent manifestations of the earliest form of third-party adjudication: the assembly of the village or of the tribe. [Hoebel, 1954, 294 et passim; Dawson, 1960, 35–36 et passim] In recent times social courts flourished *only in the socialist countries*. They existed in two major forms: (1) lay tribunals that were substantially integrated into the total structure of state courts, such as the social courts of East Germany, and (2) lay tribunals functioning more or less exclusively as agencies of social organizations, for example, labor unions, such as the comrades' courts of the Soviet Union (see above).[100] In fact, both forms are hybrid agencies, but with different degrees of leaning toward state or society. Social court-like forums on occasion have been suggested (unsuccessfully) for the United States. [Katz, 1974, 448–464] Some neighborhood mediation centers resemble social tribunals of the second type (agencies of social organizations). Their use, however, has been intermittent and their jurisdiction haphazard. While recent years have seen an increased interest in mediation, the United States does not yet have a system of lay courts routinely adjudicating minor civil and criminal cases. Trivial civil and criminal litigation continues to occupy much of the time of the ordinary courts, greatly contributing to congestion and delay. Ordinary courts staffed by professional judges, if trial is demanded,[101] must adjudicate such matters as tenant/landlord disputes regarding small security deposits, refusals to pay debts in any amount, minor issues associated with divorce, charges of jaywalking or littering, harmless trespass, neighborly insults, small warranty matters, etc. In many such cases even a jury trial can be demanded. The exact type of case that can or must be tried to bench or jury varies among the 51 basic jurisdictions of the United States. There is no disagreement, however, that in all jurisdictions truly trivial cases absorb major portions of the courts' resources. The ordinary courts, then, should be relieved of minor cases. But even minor cases must be properly adjudicated. The social courts of the GDR (rather than the USSR) suggest themselves for serious consideration.

NOTES

1. Even when state courts have come into being, there exist a very large number of extra-state courts, ranging from military and professional courts of honor to ecclesiastic courts and commercial mediation institutions. [Schmidt, 1969, 9–10]

2. Dawson, 1968, 149–150; Hoebel, 1954, Chapter 1; Maine, 1986, Chapters 1, 2, 5.

3. For some examples of a very rich literature see Anderson, 1990; Australia, 1965; Bradley, 1975; Burns, 1973; Cheang, 1973; Dashwood, 1972; Dashwood, 1974; Duff, 1990; Gibbs, 1967; Hale, 1973; Haley, 1982; Jacobsohn, 1977; Kalven & Zeisel, 1966; Kantowsky, 1968; Koenz, 1969; Kweit & Kweit, 1981; Lubman, 1967; Mannheim, 1937; Meschievitz & Galanter, 1982; O'Brien, 1967; Parker, 1987; Robinson, 1973; Santos, 1982; Strauss, 1973; Toyama, 1977; Vallinder, 1987.

4. Japan made use of trial by jury from 1928 (Jury Law of 1923) to 1943. Recent efforts (mostly by trial attorneys) to re-introduce trial by jury have not been successful.

5. Some of the former European colonies in Africa and Asia have, upon gaining independence, reacted in a similar way to various aspects of the colonial legal system. A number of them adopted a Soviet-style legal system, particularly Mali under Keita. [Hazard, 1969, Chapter 18]

6. Austria, however, as the other civil law countries, makes use of the mixed bench. Lay participation, thus, is more substantial than it may first appear. Some jury trials can also be found in Belgium, Denmark, Greece, Norway, and some Swiss cantons. [Abraham, 1998, 109]

7. It should be noted that both of these offices sometimes are held by legal professionals. [Diamond, 1990; Parker, 1989; Provine, 1981; Provine, 1986; Silberman, 1979] The vast majority of them, however, are lay persons without legal education—except for a small number of states, such as Texas, which require some rudimentary legal training for the justices of the peace.

8. Unfortunately, they often have to rely on traffic fines for financial resources. This is an invitation to systematic corruption. See, for example, Hood, 1962; Hood, 1972; Neely, 1983, Chapter 7.

9. Brownlee, 1975; Green, 1975; Wunder, 1979.

10. It should be noted that the very first judges of the GDR (Soviet Zone) state courts were non-jurist who were trained for judgeship in six-month emergency courses. No more than an elementary school education was required for trainees. [Schoeneburg, 1984, 223–234] The first course took place from February to March 1946. [Schuessler, 1979b, 22] Not surprisingly, these new "judges" were not well accepted by the (few remaining) old-style jurists. [Helm, 1979, 30; Muehlberger, 1986, 17–22] SMAD Order Nr. 193 of August 1947 lengthened the training period to one year. It also stipulated the complete equality of the university-trained judges (*Volljuristen*) and the new "people's judges." [H. Benjamin, 1947, 13; Helm, 1979, 35; Werkentin, 1995, 19–32]

11. It appears that the mixed-bench court was a German invention. [Dawson, 1968, 148–262; Ivkovic, 1999, 17]

12. However, the Peoples' Courts (ordinary courts) of early post-revolutionary period in the USSR were entirely staffed by non-jurists. There were various configurations of one professional judge and two lay assessors, one professional judge and six lay assessors, or one professional judge and twelve lay assessors—except that the "professional judges" were not professional jurists, but were designed "professional" because they filled that position full-time, whereas the lay assessors filled their positions only part-time. Only by about 1925 do real jurist re-emerge as the professional component of the mixed bench. [Hastrich, 1969, 121–128; Hazard, 1960, 51–52, 477]

13. The mixed-benches came as a Soviet innovation to the non-European socialist countries, for example, North Korea [Cho, 1971, 1170–1171] and Cuba. [Azicri, 1980, 168–170; Berman & Whiting, 1980, ß479] The Soviet example also provided an impetus for the (re-) adoption of mixed tribunals in European socialist countries. [Racz, 1979, 3–4]

14. For discussions of mixed benches and lay assessors see Baden-Wuertemberg, 1977; Bayern, 1976; U. Benz, 1982; Buchholz, 1986a; Casper & Zeisel, 1972; Casper & Zeisel, 1979; Feuerbach, 1813; Gneist, 1976 (1849); Grabert & Zoebe, 1970; Honig, 1974; Jescheck, 1977; Klausa, 1972; Kral & Boeck, 1971; Kuehne, 1985; Liekefett, 1965; Stoffregen, 1985; N. Wolfe, 1983; ; N. Wolfe, 1984; Zeisel, 1970a; Zeisel, 1970b.

15. In the GDR lay assessors and social court judges served for the same length of time as did those who elected them (local representatives). Initially, this period was four years, more recently it was five.

16. In the GDR it was customary that to determine the court's decision or verdict, the lay assessors voted before the professional judges. This, clearly, was an attempt to preserve the influence of the lay assessors. In a related matter, the younger judges also cast their votes ahead of the older judges. [Goerner, 1978, 90]

17. The equal rights and duties of lay and professional judges were specified in the GDR Code of the Constitution of the Courts (*Gerichtsverfassungsrecht*) IV, 96 (2). This statute, it might be noticed, also provided for "social prosecutors" and "social defenders." These were lay persons, usually members of the accused's collective, who had been delegated by it to speak for or against him. These offices were also found in the USSR. [Hastrich, 1965, 464–467] The GDR's Code of Criminal Procedure (§102) required the notification of the work collective of the accused. The members of the collective conferred and delegated at least one of the colleagues to participate in the trial as their representative. [Speck, 1990, 138]

18. The number of lay assessors used by the courts differs considerably from country to country. Here are some examples (the first number refers to the total count of lay assessors per year, the second number refers to the number of lay assessors per 100,000 persons): Hungary 18,00/170; Poland 50,000/153; Yugoslavia 54,000/231; East Germany 50,000/234; West Germany 27,000/45. [Ivkovic, 1999, 19–20]

19. As a related matter, it might be noted that the socialist countries had remarkably weak administrative court structures. In fact, for most of its existence, until December 1988, the GDR had none. From the ideological perspective of socialism, that may seem to make some sense. If there can be no conflict between government and citizen, as socialism proclaims [Sperlich, 2002, Chapter 5], why then have courts designed to protect citizens' rights against state agencies? [see, for example, Krylova, 1988]

20. Interestingly, in the USSR there were many complaints about the mixed tribunals, even after they had been re-professionalized, usually regarding violations of procedural norms. It should also be noted that on the part of the courts there were frequent complaints about inadequate facilities and supplies. All in all, the position of a judge was not particularly attractive; it failed to interest the best legal minds. [Hastrich, 1969, 135–136, 142]

21. As Kulcsar [1982, 50], regarding the USSR (but also applicable elsewhere), writes, "really equal participation in court is impossible."

22. It should be noted that many civil law countries also make use of mixed tribunals in courts of specialized jurisdiction. Typical are labor and juvenile courts; there also are insurance and tenant courts. The lay members of these tribunals are not ordinary lay persons selected at random, but individuals with considerable experience in the subject matter at hand. They posses specialized expertise of a non-legal type. In these courts, the professional judge is much less able to predominate. The use of "special juries" also has long been advocated in the United States. See Thatcher, 1947.

23. Contrary to jury decisions, where only a "guilty" verdict can be appealed, in mixed-bench courts both convictions and acquittals can be appealed.

24. This also corresponds to Kalven & Zeisel's [1966, 416–427] finding about the "balance" of judge and jury power. In jury trials, it should not be overlooked, the judge can have significant influence if the jurors perceive judicial partiality. [Landwehr & Novotny, 1976]

25. Abraham, 1998, 109–110; Adler, 1994, 244–245; DiPerna, 1984, 22–26.

26. In the United States, the recent tendency has been to reduce the number of persons who form the trial jury. This is generally understood to weaken the jury. For the time being, the smallest acceptable number (to the U.S. Supreme Court)

for a criminal or civil jury is six. [Abraham, 1998, 119–121; Keele, 1995; Kerr & MacCoun, 1987; Simon, 1980, 73–106; Van Dyke, 1977, 225–251; Zeisel, 1971; Zeisel, 1972; Zeisel & Diamond, 1974] The U.S. Supreme Court further weakened the criminal trial jury by authorizing non-unanimous verdicts. [Nemeth, 1987; Saks, 1977, 1–35; Sperlich, 1980a] This can be understood as part of the power-shift from jurors to judges. [Sperlich, 1992a, 633–634] It might be remembered in this context that in the past jurors also decided issues of law. In any case, the civil jury has almost disappeared already (though not quite as drastically as in England) and the criminal jury (in spite of Constitutional provisions) is in danger of disappearing, too. [Langbein, 1995]

27. They are made wherever and whenever there is any form of lay adjudication.

28. DiPerna, 1984, 232–236; Elwork, et al., 1987; Friedman, 1973, 137; Kassin, 1995; Kassin & Wrightsman, 1988, 2–5, 65–97, 119–139, 207–216.

29. There are exceptions to this. The jury may decide (for any number of reasons) not to apply the law to the particular case. This is "jury nullification," about which more is said later.

30. For discussions see Dershowitz, 1988, 206–208; Ellsworth, 1985; Haney, 1980; Jurow, 1971.

31. Leaving aside cases of jury misconduct and similar aberrations. [Ledy & Lefkowitz, 1975]

32. Calkins, 1966; Clark, 1972; Goodell, 1973; Scigliano, 1959.

33. As some examples: Beale & Bryson, 1986; Buiteweg, 1956; Clark, 1972; Cobden, 1976; Comment, 1956a; Dession & Cohen, 1932; Frankel & Naftalis, 1977; Gelber, 1969; Hall, 1932; Kagel, 1964; Kaufman, 1962; Kranitz, 1959; Lubbers, 1973; Note, 1972; Pizzigati, 1978; Schwartz, 1972; Sperlich, 1992b; Symposium, 1984; Tigar & Levy, 1971; Van Dyke, 1976; White, 1954; Wickersham, 1965; Younger, 1963.

34. Some non-socialist countries (especially on the African continent) also make use of lay boards to settle minor disputes. They can best be characterized as mediation forums. On the general topic of mediation and arbitration as alternatives to adjudication see Eckhoff, 1966; Hill, 1976; Hofrichter, 1987; McEwen, 1982; Starr, 1982; Tomasic, 1982; Wagatsuma & Rosset, 1986.

35. In all these variations there was a common tension between being part of the state court system and being a purely societal institution—an issue that was not fully resolved in most places. Also, these courts did not all work to the same degree of success and official satisfaction. [Cismarescu, 1977; Knuesli, 1978]

36. For the interested reader there is a considerable literature about the lay courts of the other socialist countries. For example, on the Yugoslav "reconciliation boards" see Felstiner & Drew, 1978, 27; ad Hayden, 1990; and on the Chinese "mediation committees" see Clark, 1989, 61; Cohen, 1982, 171; Leng, 1977; McCabe, 1989, 63–64, 117–121; Palmer, 1988, 219; Reichel, 1994, 254. Though it should be noted that the Chinese "mediation" procedures substantially deviated from the tactics of the other lay courts and often turned into counter-productive "rituals of struggle." [Madsen, 1984, 22]

37. ". . . the basic idea of the comrades' courts as an informal, in-group trial procedure has remained unchanged over the years, [even as these courts] have varied considerably in their form, functions, punitive prerogatives." [Feldbrugge, 1973, 145]

38. "Under Khrushchev the courts' jurisdiction included cases of labor discipline, small thefts, slander, speculation, drunkenness, and civil suits, as well as more nebulous offenses such as hooliganism and infractions of 'the rules of socialist community life'." [Sypnowich, 1990, 51]

39. The military comrades' courts, however, did not survive for very long. By the end of 1919 they were largely dissolved. For general histories of the various USSR comrades' courts see Berman, 1963; Berman & Spindler, 1963; Bilinsky, 1962; Boiter, 1973; Friedgut, 1979; Gorle, 1982; Hazard, 1960; Kuchrov, 1970; Machalz-Urban, 1980; Schmidt, 1969.

40. These early manifestations of comrades' courts could impose rather harsh punishments, including incarceration and loss of job. In 1921, the maximum incarceration became limited to a period of six months.

41. As they did in some of the other socialist countries, particularly Hungary and Poland. [Butler, 1972, 207]

42. Persons in rural areas are typically subject to only one comrades' court (of the kolkhoz or the village), but urban residents are usually subject to two of them: the work-related and the residential courts.

43. However, even during Stalin's time, much lip-service was given to (Leninist) lay adjudication. [Vyshinsky, 1948, 506–518]

44. The Stalinist dualism of law and terror was replaced by the Khrushchevian dualism of law and social pressure. [Berman & Spindler, 1963, 848]

45. Apparently this statute dates back to 1951, being published only in 1959. For late developments of the comrades' courts see Grischin, 1986, 203–204.

46. For the complete text see Berman & Spindler, 1963, 857–895; Note, 1961. For the subsequent 1977 statute, with the 1982 amendments see Butler, 1983, 238–246.

47. There is a question whether such criticism were truly not illegal. In any case, the low level of offenses heard at the comrades' courts made it unlikely that the Party made these cases a prime concern.

48. If both parties agree that the case should be heard in a comrades' court.

49. For example, buying some pieces of clothing at one price and selling them again at a slightly higher one. For a description of one such case, see Juviler, 1982, 153.

50. These are the druzhiny, citizen volunteers supplementing the ordinary security forces—first seen in Leningrad in November 1958. [Kabes, 1961, 89] They also are an aspect of the shift from state to social competence. [Berman, 1963, 286–288; Friedgut, 1979, 258–262; O'Connor, 1964, 579] However, this should in no way be understood as a lessening of the comprehensive state and Party controls. [Brunner, 1967, 111; Bilinsky, 1960, 96–97] As noted in a commentary on the 21st Party Congress: "the transfer of . . . functions from state to social organs will not weaken the role of the socialist state . . . but will widen and strengthen the political foundation of socialist society and . . . socialist democracy." [Kucherov, 1970, 155]

51. Increased in 1959 to 100 rubles.

52. "Decision" was used in preference to "judgment." Similarly, there were no "penalties," but only (educational) "measures." It should also be noted that there has been a decline in formal decisions in favor of mediated outcomes. [Friedgut, 1979, 254]

53. As Lipson [1958, 25–26; also see Lipson, 1959, 16] points out, even if the analogy principle is abolished, there are many other ways by which socialist courts

can reach the same goal, that is, to penalize "acts not specifically covered by law [by applying] the punishment which the law prescribed for the most closely similar offense." In the GDR, however, the analogy principle was strongly defended as a "legitimate means to achieve socialist legality . . . though it is not needed very much because of the harmony and unity of the interest of all the people . . . and because there a very few gaps in socialist law." [Schoenrath, 1978, 5] This is also the way the national socialists saw it, as expressed in the law of June 1935 (change of the criminal code). [Heitmann, 1996; 96–97; also see Redaktion Kritische Justiz, 1984; Wagner, 1974]

54. GDR law also knew the offense of "objectively" helping the enemy, that is, giving comfort and help to the West without subjective intent. This formulation criminalized unintended consequences (say, of a letter to a friend or relative in the West), that is consequences which could not always have been anticipated, and consequences that were wholly imaginary. Needless to say, this formulation was amply employed. [Sinyavsky, 1990, 88–89]

55. The word "private" (*chastnyi*), it should be noted, was abolished in favor of "personal" *lichnyi*)—except to refer to the capitalist world.

56. Needless to say, from the official Soviet perspective, "no personal sphere" was not a danger, but a devoutly to be hoped for condition. [Sperlich, 2002, Chapter 6]

57. Since there are no relevant data, one cannot know the true number of such cases.

58. It should be noted that the Czech comrades' courts also were closely integrated with the regular state courts. [Kabes, 1961, 104–105]

59. The exception of complaints to the local Soviets has been noted. But also, in the all-Russian labor union programme of 1918, it was declared that the labor unions are "an institution of the socialist state." [Schmidt, 1969, 33]

60. Boiter, 1965, 82; Note, 1971, 141; Racz, 1979, 14.

61. For the citizen, it was generally a burden to be discharged with as little effort as possible. For the vast majority of participants (including those who became members of the Communist Party), the motivation was strictly utilitarian. It was "little more than insurance for a tolerable life." [Nelson, 1978, 16]

62. With equivalent entities in existence in practically all the socialist countries.

63. Clearly copied from the Citizen Inspectors of the Soviet Union. [Adams, 1977; Brunner, 1967, 114–118]

64. Equivalent to the Soviet druzhiny.

65. It should be noted that the competence of the comrades' courts was expanded several times. This, however, should not be seen as a diminution of state judicial monopoly [Savickij, 1983, 263]. The delegation of quasi-judicial work to the comrades' courts took place under the ever watchful eyes of Party and state. It continued as long as it was minimally successful and did not challenge or endanger the Soviet system of justice.

66. Serving as a juror, however, turns out to be a positive and motivating experience. See, for example, Allen, 1977, 246; Diamond, 1993; Doob, 1978; Flynn, 1960, 103; James, 1971, 199–202; LaTour, 1978; Kraft, 1982; Nemeth, 1981; Richert, 1977, 233; Schorr, 1976; Schott, 1977; Simon, 1975; Timothy, 1975; Sutliffe, 1922. It also would help if some unnecessary hindrances [Parry, 1974] and hardships could be eliminated from jury service, [Pabst, 1972; Pabst, 1975; Stoever, 1974] for

example, the prohibition on note-taking, still in effect in many courts. [Abraham, 1998, 133; Bromberger, 1948, 57–58; DiPerna, 1984, 230–232; Parry, 1974, 565]

67. For discussions of judge/juror interaction see Higginbotham, 1977; Kaufman, 1971; Vanderbilt, 1956.

68. For some discussions of jury nullification see Abramson, 2000, xvii–xxiii; Conrad, 1998; Friedman, 1973, 252; Gobert, 1992, 880; Green, 1985; Kadish & Kadish, 1973; Lehman, 1977; Myers, 1987; Pabst, 1985; Scheflin & Van Dyke, 1980; Scheflin & Van Dyke, 1995.

69. Elwork, 1987; Nieland, 1979; Reed, 1980; Steele & Thornburg, 1995.

70. Church, 1978a; Church, 1978b; Sipes, 1988; Zeisel, 1959.

71. Pound, 1930; Frank, 1949; Frankel, 1978; Funston, 1977; Levy, 1974; Robertson, 1974; Weinreb, 1977.

72. Also see the findings and conclusions of the President's Commission on Law Enforcement and Administration of Justice, 1967, v–xi, 1–53 et passim.

73. For balanced treatments see Abraham, 1998; Friedman, 1973.

74. Mark Twain [1913, 55–58], it might be remembered, had these choice words to describe the jury: "The jury system puts a ban upon intelligence and honesty, and a premium upon ignorance, stupidity, and perjury." One wonders how many juries he really knew, and also whether he might not have attributed, as is so often the case, some of the deficiencies of the adversarial system simply to the jury. [DiPerna, 1984, 217–218; Levine, 1974]

75. For some general treatments of trial by jury see Abramson, 2000; American Bar Association, 1982; Broeder, 1954; Brown, 1974; Cain & Kravitz, 1978; Hans & Vidmar, 1986; Kassin & Wrightsman, 1988; Lermack, 1977; Litan, 1993; National center for State Courts, 1976a; Osborne, 1937; Pabst, 1985; Penrod & Hastie, 1979; Peterson, 1986; Rembar, 1980; Saks, 1975; Selvin & Pinkus, 1987; Simon, R., 1975; Simon, R., 1980; Stalmaster, 1938; Symposium, 1979; U.S. Department of Justice, 1974; Vidmar, 1995; Williams, 1997; Winters, 1971; Wishman, 1986; Wrightsman, 1978; Wrightsman, 1987.

76. Justice Burger is not the first chief justice to complain about increasing case loads and delay. See Earl Warren, 1958.

77. The present tale of woe has the United States as its subject. While the United States often occupies an unenviable first place, other advanced societies also suffer from increases in crime rates, and their courts experience growing caseloads. See, for example, Blankenburg, 1982.

78. Amendment VI to the U.S. Constitution prescribed a "speedy trial" for all criminal prosecutions. No such language is found regarding civil jury trials.

79. There is a large literature on case load, case processing, and delay. The classical study by Zeisel et al. [1959] has been cited. The following examples offer a variety of approaches, data, and suggestions: Church, 1978; Clark & Merryman, 1976; Flanders, 1978; Galanter, 1981; Grossman et al., 1981; Hurst, 1980; Rosenberg, 1980; Mclntosh, 1980. Also of interest in the context are Curran, 1977; National Center for State Courts, 1988.

80. There are many pro-jury judges in the lower courts, actually dealing with juries. One must be very grateful to them. [See, for example, Judge Joiner, 1975; also see the views of Judge Battani, as reported in DiPerna, 1984, 222–224.] The appellate courts, especially the U.S. Supreme Court, seems to have rather little use and even less respect for trial by jury. [Sperlich, 1980a; Sperlich, 1982a]

81. Not for the maintenance of citizen liberties, but for preservation of Party power, is citizens participation regarded as extremely important in the socialist countries. "... lay participation in the administration of justice is considered, by the legal theory in socialist countries, to be one of the most fundamental features of the judicial system of these countries." [Pomorski, 1975, 199]

82. The creation of U.S. magistrate judges in 1968 (1990) was a step in this direction. But since these magistrates were not full-fledged judges (e.g., they could not try felony defendants), they have often been used a judicial assistants ("permanent law clerks") rather than as judges. [C.E. Smith, 1992]

83. A prominent exception is the opposition of segments of the organized bar to no-fault auto insurance.

84. The advocacy for "science courts," might be noted here. See Martin, 1977; Matheny & Williams, 1978; Sperlich, 1980c; Sperlich, 1983; Sperlich, 1985a. Also of interest is an expanded use of "special masters." See Aronow, 1980.

85. The literature is vast. Examples are: Abel, 1982; Fuller, 1971; Rosenberg & Schubin, 1961; Ross, 1978; Yngvesson & Hennessey, 1975; and many of the reports issued by the Disputes Processing Research Program of the University of Wisconsin-Madison, such as Landinsky & Susmilch, 1981; Tomasic, 1980; Clune & Hyde, 1981.

86. Brownlee, 1975, 372; Hoffman, 1981; Provine, 1981.

87. See, for example, Auerbach, 1983.

88. Accounts of the positive functions of judicial lay participation can be found in these papers and in the publications cited therein: Sperlich, 1982a, 394, 413–415; and Sperlich & Jaspovice, 1974, 63, 64–67.

89. Examples are Austria and Switzerland. See Jescheck, 1977, 245–246; Richert, 1979, 7; Frassine et al., 1979, 87–88.

90. Ehrmann, 1976, 101–103; Casper & Zeisel, 1979, 7, 21; Cappelletti et al., 1967, 80.

91. Kucherov, 1970, 336–372; Racz, 1979, 4–5; Versele, 1969, 27; Zawadzki & Kubicki, 1979, 125.

92. The American trial jury used to have the right to decide questions of law. While with few exceptions this right has been lost, the jury retains the *power* to nullify law. See Sperlich, 1982a, 414.

93. Civil trial juries generally determine the size of awards.

94. The lay/professional composition of the mixed bench varies greatly from country to country and within countries for different courts. Either group may constitute a majority. See note 10.

95. On the differences between civil law and common law judges see Merryman, 1969, 35–39. On the rate of agreement between professional and lay judges see Volk, 1982, 375–376.

96. With very few exceptions, the justice of the peace tries cases as single judge. [Walker, 1980, 21–22]

97. It should be noted that since 1970 the tendency in the United States also has been to weaken the civil and criminal trial jury, most importantly by changing its structure and by limiting its jurisdiction. See Hastie, et al., 1983, 2–6, 227–230; Jacobstein & Mersky, 1998; Kaye, 1980; Sperlich, 1980a, 263–264; Sperlich, 1982a, 395–399; Zeisel, 1971. The use of the "special verdict" (rather than the

"general verdict") is but one aspect of the judicial efforts to take power from the jury. [Abraham, 1998, 139–141; Lehman, 1997, 16]

98. The German term is "gesellschaftliche Gerichte"—in strict translation: "societal courts." Official East German publications in English (as well as other English-language publications), however, consistently have employed "social courts" as translation. I have adhered to this convention, even if it is misleading in some ways.

99. It is unclear what significance, if any, should be attributed to the fact that the social courts collectively were designated as "courts" ("*Gerichte*"), but separately as "commissions" ("*Kommissionen*"). Similarly, it is not clear why the justices of the social courts were styled "members" (of the commission) rather that "judges" ("*Richter*").

100. Racz, 1979, 10–13; Berman & Spindler, 1963, 842; Butler, 1972, 200.

101. Recent years have seen a strong movement towards mandatory arbitration. This, however, is not unproblematic. The arbitrators are (or, are at least perceived to be) agents of the stronger parties (banks, insurance companies, manufacturers, etc.). The ordinary citizen (consumer) is likely to be at a distinct disadvantage.

Chapter 5

Socialist Legal Theory, Laws, and Courts

SOCIALIST LEGAL THEORY

The social and political institutions of an advanced socialist society, as manifested in the GDR and many other countries, reflected substantial progress in the implementation of a single master-plan of societal organization and development: Marxism-Leninism. While there remained some remnants of prior epochs, great efforts were being made to attain unity of theory and practice, and consistency of aim and action among the organs of state and society. An accurate and complete understanding of the social courts of the German Democratic Republic requires an appreciation of the theoretical and institutional context within which they function. This context is sizable and complex. Two prior volumes have sought to lay out the context.[1]

The history of socialist legal doctrines and institutions has not, of course, been a matter of uniform and consistent development. Particularly in the Soviet Union, a series of very different legal dogmas and practices can be found.[2] The writings of Marx, Engels, and Lenin are the foundations of socialist legal theory as of all socialist theoretical constructions. While Marx and Engels were prolific and fairly detailed in respect to the state, if not very systematic,[3] they had little to say on law and the courts, or, indeed, on the (post-revolutionary) party. [Hazard, 1951, xvii; McLellan, 1981, 7–17] This is not surprising. The primary concern of Marx and Engels was with revolution and economic justice, the elimination of human exploitation by way of a total change of the existing system.[4] They were concerned with economic rules (e.g., to each according to . . .), not with the "rule of law." Marx was particularly scornful of such "bourgeois doctrines" as equality under the law, equal rights, and equal justice.[5] As Marx saw it, as long as individuals actually are unequal economically (as in capitalism), these concepts are no more than smoke-screens for exploitation.[6] There can be no equality in bourgeois society because there can be no equality between the exploiters and the exploited. Justice, said Marx, is no more than class interest raised to law. [as cited in Mollnau et al., 1976, 18] The task at hand was to change the ownership of the means of production from the private to the public mode—changes in the superstructure (e.g., law) were bound to follow. [Pospisil, 1982, 202–206]

Lenin, a lawyer himself,[7] shared in the scorn for the "rule of law."[8] Nevertheless, in the first years of the Soviet regime two lawyers tried to deal systematically with legal issues engendered by socialist ideology: P.I. Stuchka and E.B. Pashukanis.[9] They were especially concerned with the question of the predicted withering away of the law, and with the nature of the law during the transitory period. Though their thinking and way of discussing these subjects differed substantially, they did have this in common: they took (or pretended to take) for granted the final disappearance of law (including socialist law), and tried to come to terms with the fact that though communism (or, at least socialism) had been established, law and crime[10] did not show any signs of withering away.[11] Both were holding fast to the axiom that law and crime were class-based. [Makepeace, 1980, 170]

Pashukanis, who in his early teaching (*The General Theory of Law and Marxism*) had identified all law with bourgeois law,[12] spoke of the continued existence of bourgeois law without the bourgeois.[13] He also thought that there could never be a true proletarian or socialist law. In socialism, technical rules (particularly as it related to the economy and the need for greater contractual discipline) would displace legal norms.[14] [Redhead in Beirne & Quinney, 1982, 21; Makepeace, 1980, 96–97] These notions became increasingly incompatible with the NEP and Stalinist[15] strong-state views. Stuchka, one of the early Soviet Commissars of Justice, author of the Decree No. 1 on the Soviet Court, and since 1923 chairman of the Supreme Court of the Russian Republic (and very critical of Pashukanis), however, proclaimed the notion of proletarian law (*The Revolutionary Role of Law and State*), and thought possible a socialist construction of law.[16] The key concept, however, remained the withering away of the law. [Beirne & Sharlett, 1982, 313–319] This concern was not in line with NEP and Stalinism either. Both Stuchka and Pashukanis (who succeeded Stuchka), however, noticed a new phenomenon: the intense interference of the state in economic matters. To deal with this the concept of economic laws was introduced.

As noted, the idea of the withering away of the law did not fit into Stalin's despotic system and the requirements of the new economy (NEP), thus these legal philosophies came under attack from 1930 on. Stuchka died before the purges (in 1932); Pashukanis, after several useless attempts at "self-criticism," was liquidated in 1937. [Beirne & Sharlett, 1982, 309] Vyshinsky,[17] who succeeded Pashukanis as the leading Soviet legal theorist, declared him a "wrecker" and an "enemy of the people."[18] He used the same terminology to describe (Stuchka)[19] [Stuchka, 1988, xi] The theory of the withering away of state and law was replaced by the doctrine of the required maximum strength of these while "capitalist encirclement" lasted.

> . . . it was probably Khrushchev's personal concern in the theory of the withering away of state and law which made him drop the notion of the dictatorship of the proletariat . . . at the 22nd Party Congress in 1961 and replace it by the concept of the state of the entire people,[20] as according to the official view there are in the Soviet Union no more antagonistic classes . . . This theory was then implemented by certain measures which transferred activities [from state organs] to social organizations (leaving open the question of whether there is a difference between a state organ and a so-called social organization fulfilling the same functions). Instances of such transfers were the resurrection of the comrades' courts and the setting up of units of the voluntary militia. [Feldbrugge, 1973, 351–352]

The basic positions of socialist legal thought are quite clear: The courts are organs of the state; the state is the instrument of the ruling class, and, at least for the time being, the working class needs the state to consolidate and preserve its revolutionary successes.[21] Laws are the expression of the interests of the ruling class.[22] All law is class-law.[23] Its content is determined by the productive relations of the society. [Autorenkollektiv, 1985a, 7] However, according to socialist doctrine, socialist law is unique in being formulated and exercised not solely for the benefit of the ruling class (the proletariat),[24] but for the benefit of *all working people,*[25] including such classes and strata as farmers, managers, administrators, and intellectuals.[26] As expressed by a GDR commentator (but forgetting "all the working people"): "At every stage of development, human society produces a particular kind of law and legal concepts, determined by the interest of the ruling class." [Riemann, 1976, 8] Legal thought in the GDR followed these narrower perspectives quite faithfully: "Legal questions are power questions. Thus, our law, in whole and in part, is the expression of the power of the working class." [Tisch, 1982, 114] Law-making is a function of power-holding. "Law is an instrument of direction and education of the socialist state." [Kern, 1981, 138] Constitutional questions are always power questions. [Weichelt, 1976, 116] Which is a reminder that Soviet legal theory, which clearly guided early GDR legal thought [Mahlmann, 2002, 8–9], has always placed great emphasis upon the educational role of law.[27] [Riedel, 1973, 3–9] This role of the law is stressed, as noted earlier, in the adjudicative activity of social organizations such as the comrades' courts.

> Theoretically, the educational role of Soviet law is intended to facilitate the internalization of legal norms and procedures and ultimately the dying out of official law and its replacement by social consciousness. Practically, the educational role of law is intended to implement Soviet legal policies by the exertion of social influence and social pressure upon Soviet citizens in order to guide and train them to conform to the standards of communist morality. [Feldbrugge, 1973, 387]

Or, to speak with Vyshinsky [1948, 640]:

> Soviet laws, the only laws in the world truly expressing the will of the people, are directed at strengthening the socialist economy and Soviet discipline and educating

citizens in the spirit of communism, and at pitiless struggle against all the foes of the great Soviet people, against traitors, betrayers, and agents of fascist reconnaissance, and against each and every encroachment upon the interests and rights of the people. In the hands of the socialist state, they are a mighty instrument for the reorganization of society, for refashioning human consciousness, and for strengthening socialist society.

It follows that with the establishment of socialist power- and production-conditions, the working class and its allies have created their own law, and raised it to a method with which they exercise their political power, with the purpose of forging new societal conditions. [Autorenkollektiv, 1978b, 220][28]

This, of course, reflects one of two fundamental conceptions of law. These competitive conceptions are: law as the interest of the stronger party, and law as doing what is right in the interest of all. Ralf Dahrendorf [1968a, 129–150] has splendidly explicated these two conceptions in "In Praise of Thrasymachus." Socialist legal philosophy, of course, starts in the camp of Thrasymachus (law as in the interest of the working class) but ends up in the embrace of Socrates via the notion that the interest of the working class is identical with the interest of all—the eternal socialist unities. [Sperlich, 2002, Chapter 5]

The embrace of Socrates, however, was a fraudulent ploy. It did not in the least influence GDR legal theory. Thrasymachus ruled. "At every stage of development, human society produces a particular kind of law and legal concepts, determined by the interests of the ruling class." [Riemann, 1976, 8] Socialism was no exception, as GDR writers readily admitted. In socialism, of course, the *working class* is the ruling class, and its interests must be protected. When the state finally withers away, as it will, at the latest, in full-fledged communism, the courts, as state organs, also will wither away. In the meantime they are needed as instruments of the interest and power of the working class. This is classic Marxism.

As noted, Marx and Engels did not reach the point of specifying the exact nature of law and courts in socialism. It did not seem all that important, one might guess, given the ultimate withering away and the pressing economic problems of the present. Lenin endorsed the views of Marx and Engels. [Lenin, 1976, 7–24] He also added to them, particularly out of his practical experience.[29] [Connor, 1988, 7–8; Juviler, 1976, 15–19] Lenin's basic views on the nature and function of law and the courts are pure Marx-Engels:[30] law and courts are the instruments of the working class for securing the revolution and move society toward communism. [Lenin, 1976, 17] Since the (Leninist) party leads the working class, the courts must be "transmission belts" of party policy. [Lenin, 1976, 102; also see Autorenkollektiv, 1978b, 18–21; and Panorama-DDR, 1976, 59–62.] But, of course, these thoughts provided little guidance for the exact nature of post-revolutionary legal administration and on the every-day law-and-order function of the state. Lenin was forced to improvise and revise. For these tasks he drew on the only source readily available: practical experience.[31]

Organizationally, Lenin preferred simple, informal, popular, non-bureaucratic tribunals. In fact, he greatly favored lay adjudication.[32] What developed in fact, however, was a very elaborate and bureaucratic system of law and law enforcement. [Kucherov, 1970, especially Chapters 1–4.] Most important, he insisted on legal centralism and uniformity. After a short experience with revolutionary lawlessness, no doubt remained about the (continuing) need for repression and an "iron hand."[33]

Even with Lenin's contribution to the Marx-Engels base, socialist legal philosophy is far from precise, unambiguous, or complete. Socialist theorists have the tendency to present Marxism-Leninism as the complete science, ready and able to answer all practical questions and guide all societal developments.[34] A close reading of socialist legal theory, however, reveals quickly that societal development frequently precedes theoretical efforts. The task of the socialist theoretician (in the law as well as in other areas) seems to be at least as often to find theoretical justifications for actual developments, as it is to provide theoretical guidance for prospective efforts. Specifically regarding the law, one Western observer speaks of the "ideological justification of legal practices found to be workable," [Fincke, 1975, 7] Another declares quite flatly that Soviet legal reforms were based on the needs of the economy, not on Marx. [Grzybowski, 1962, 268]

"SOCIALIST LEGALITY"

Socialist legality (as defined by Soviet theoretician S.M. Strogovich) is the "strict and unflinching observance and fulfillment of Soviet laws by all organs of the socialist state and public organizations, institutions and all citizens, in all circumstances, and at all times." Since citizens, however, had no enforcement mechanism against public organizations and institutions (the state), this really means only *citizen obedience*.[35] The "new (socialist) legality, requires that all citizens, institutions, and officials observe Soviet laws precisely and without protest." [Vyshinsky, 1948, 640] A primary goal was the protection of socialist property. [Lipson, 1958, 22–23] The GDR definition (in a late law text) was that socialist legality meant that "all social relations, which need legal orderings and legal protection, are legally regulated, and these regulations are obligatory for all the organs of the state, the enterprises, and all citizens." [Autorenkollektiv, 1986b, 25]

A secondary meaning of socialist legality is that of the legislation (and other orders) *currently in force*. In other words, legality is coterminous with that which is currently legal. This is a nice play on words, but it deprives the concept of "legality" of a crucial component, namely "justice." It leaves it with merely a dry, administrative meaning. This issue will need to be visited when we consider the (quite controversial) question whether the GDR was a *Rechtsstaat* or an *Unrechtsstaat* (state of justice or state of injustice)—it was the latter. East German commentators, however, proudly assert that "justice is the realization of socialist humanism." [Buchholz, 1988, 357] The unity of GDR legality and humanism was a constant matter of great emphasis.[36]

Socialist legality in the first period of Soviet rule meant that the new judges would be guided only by their revolutionary and socialist consciousness,[37] since they did not know tsarist law (which soon was no longer to be applied in any case) and since new laws were not published until 1922–1923 (except for a Family Code). However, "law codes became indispensable when private and international trade was reinstalled by the NEP (New Economic Policy).[38] [Schroeder, 1989b, 358–362] Litigation connected with the establishment of a semi-capitalistic economy could not depend on the revolutionary, socialist consciousness of the judges." [Feldbrugge, 1973, 619–620] Lenin observed that the NEP required adhering to greater legality. Of course, Lenin, after inventing socialist legality, had no difficulty breaking socialist legality when it suited his purposes, such as the forceful dispersion of the Constituent Assembly[39] By joining the principles of class interest, party leadership, centralism, and the repressive nature of law (law as command), Lenin established the key concept and touchstone of all subsequent socialist legal theory: socialist legality. The core meaning of which was: *legal is what benefits the Party.*

It is worth noting the utilitarian nature of this touchstone. By socialist erudition, Marxism-Leninism is the one true and comprehensive science—able to correctly answer all questions and to properly guide societal developments. This, of course, is pretentious babble. Apart from the obvious failure of the communist experiment, it is perfectly clear that, for the most, societal developments were the cause rather than the effect of theoretical (re-) formulations. The primary task of the socialist theorist was to construct theoretical justifications for developments that already had taken place. Socialist legal practices—and what a wild collection of contradictory pursuits they are[40]—were grounded in necessity and utility. They were responses to the needs of the economy and/or the interests of the Party, rather than, as claimed "innovative extrapolations" from the pronouncement of Marx, Engels, and Lenin.[41]

After Lenin's death, the tension of the need for (ordinary) legality on one side and the violation of legality on the other continued. Indeed, the gap between legal theory and illegal practices was widened under Stalin. There was an increase in rhetoric of legality, but constant and numberless violations of legality in practice. There were new assertion of legality and the rule of law after Stalin's death, but violations (in various degrees) continued to the very end of communist rule. Bourgeois legality focuses on the observance of form, on procedural justice. Socialist legality focuses on the attainment of goals, on substantive justice. As will be seen later, (in socialism and other such regimes) substantive justice can be defined in no other way than that *it serves the interest of the Party.*

East German legal theorists used to proclaim fiercely and emphatically that *socialist legality* was different from and superior to the bourgeois *Rechtsstaat.* Toward the last years of the GDR, the regime sought to downplay the disparities, pointing to similarities in the rights afforded to the citizens in both systems.[42] They were right the first time when they emphasized the differences. Of course, there were similarities to be found, but this is not saying much. Any two legal systems, picked at random, will exhibit some similarities. The key issue is that the *Rechtsstaat* is a constitutional order that guarantees the supremacy of law, whereas socialist legal systems are based upon the supremacy of the Party, that is, of the Party's leaders.[43] [Bender, 1992, 29] In the GDR, as in other socialist systems, Party policy and partisanship (*Parteilichkeit*) were principles superior to any constitutional provision and to any law.[44] The Party is the core (supreme power) of state and society—which, of course, includes the law. [Schuessler, et al., 1984, 16–17] According to GDR commentators, the equality of all citizens is not affected by the supremacy of the Party. To the contrary, "the supremacy of the Party is the crucial precondition for the guaranteeing the political liberties and social rights of all persons." [Schuessler, 1979c, 54] Needless to say, the people had unlimited confidence in the Party and "on the basis of the indestructible fundament actualizes the Party its leading role." [Schuessler, 1979c, 83]

At least three features clearly and unbridgeably separate socialist legality and the *Rechtsstaat.* Socialist legality (1) does not recognize legally enforceable citizens' rights against the state and its agencies,[45] (2) does not include truly independent judges and courts [Wentker, 2001, Chapter 3–5], and (3) emphasizes outcomes rather than procedures.[46] These differentiating characteristics emanate directly from the key doctrines of Marxism-Leninism, as well as, in a way, from Hegel and the Hegelian dialectic. [Gregor, 1968, 24–57; Schoeneburg, 1976, 105] The *first* difference derives from the principles of the unity of Party policy and the popular will, and of the identity of the interest of citizens and the state.[47] The activities of the state, as directed by the Party, cannot be in conflict with the interests of the citizens.[48] As an obvious institutional consequence, there cannot be administrative courts or courts empowered to review the constitutional adequacy of legislative acts and executive decrees. [Wentker, 2001, 190–196]

The *second* difference follows from the doctrines of partisan justice and unitary power. All branches of government are subject to a single will and direction—that of the Party. Judges were explicitly enjoined to practice partisan justice. [Strempel, 2000, 27; Timmermann, 2000, 23] If they did not, they were removed from their positions.[49] [Wentker, 2001, 560–561; Werkentin, 1995, 184, 272] Further, one branch of government cannot act against another. This would constitute a separation of powers, an arrangement not only rejected but relentlessly ridiculed by socialist writers.

The *third* difference reflects the requirement that all outcomes conform to Party policy. It matters not how the result is reached, but that it is reached. The just and proper verdict is that which serves the interests of the Party.[50] The benchmark of bourgeois legality is the observance of form. Legality is assessed in *procedural* terms. A trial will be deemed to have been fair if it followed the established rules of procedure. The benchmark of socialist legality is *substantive*. [Pashukanis & Gintsburg, 1980] A trial will be deemed to have been fair if its verdict is correct.[51]

Leaving aside the obvious political purposes of socialism's choice of substantive fairness, the fundamental problem with this criterion is the lack of an objective (external) benchmark. Whereas actual procedure can be compared to the procedural codes, the actual verdict lacks an objective standard of comparison. However much we desire substantive justice—the guilty convicted and the innocent acquitted—there is no clear test for having achieved it. Humans cannot know with complete certainty whether a defendant is guilty or innocent. All that can be done under the substantive fairness ordinance is to compare the actual *human* verdict to an alternative *human* verdict preference. We do, of course, quite routinely characterize some bench decisions and jury verdicts as *wrong*. All that this means, however, is that we are willing to substitute our own judgment for that of the judge or the jury. There is no doubt *in principle* that some cases are wrongly decided. The problem lies in our *practical* inability to identify these cases with confidence. To show that a verdict was wrong, we would need that which we do not have and cannot have: a transcendental perspective, an Archimedian fulcrum. The truth of guilt and innocence may be known in the heavens; on earth no adjudicator can be absolutely certain of having returned the correct verdict. No form of evidence, including the testimony of the accuser, eyewitnesses, polygraphs, and, even, the confession of the accused is entirely trustworthy. Not only are there false accusations, but there also are false confessions—some even made voluntarily. [Kassin & Wrightsman, 1985, 76–80; Sperlich, 1985a, 331–337] In the substantive realm there are only conflicting opinions and divergent preferences. Which of these will prevail is often simply a matter of who makes the decision—in socialism and equivalent regimes that will be the Party.

The great advantage of *procedural* standards, then, is that they can be tested, that it can be determined with great certitude whether the mandated procedures were followed. The so proudly advertised substantive orientation of socialist law is, in the last analysis, a confession of the practice of partisan trials with Party-directed verdicts. The GDR always was closer to the *Unrechtsstaat* than the *Rechtsstaat*—a fact still vehemently disputed by the very persons who profited from the *Unrecht*, from the system's unlawfulness and injustices. Whatever differences socialist legal theorists were willing to acknowledge between the *Rechtsstaat* and socialist legality, they invariably denied that these dissimilarities implied fewer rights and protections for the socialist than for the bourgeois citizen. Proclamations about the GDR citizen's superior legal position and about the true lawfulness of the socialist society always received a prominent place among the official slogans of Party Conferences and May Day celebrations. It was a matter of extraordinary pride among GDR legal commentators that GDR President Wilhelm Pieck proclaimed the SED to be "the party of legality" as early as 1950, at the Third Party Congress of the SED. [Kraeupl & Reuter, 1987, 23]

In later years, it became a common argument that socialist legality incorporated "the rule of law." This is not entirely wrong, but it is grossly misleading if taken to signify more than an absence of *total* arbitrariness. All systems exhibit regularities, even the most despotic and oppressive ones.[52] No regime could survive for any length of time without expansive rule-following, which must include reasonably stable modes of conduct and generally predictable decisions on the part of government officials and agencies. Stability and predictability are not, however, at the core of "the rule of law." A *predictable* legal system still is not a *Rechtsstaat.* In the liberal-democratic sense, "the rule of law" denotes a system in which the rulers as well as the ruled are bound by the law, where no one is "above the law."[53] GDR commentators, however, proudly proclaimed that every citizens was secure in his legal rights because the laws were strictly adhered to. [Mollnau et al., 1976, 118; Udke, 1988] In fact, of course, the law often was no more than an instrument of Party rule. [Kittke & Rodenbach, 1986, 119]

Marxism-Leninism clearly places the Communist Party—better: the Party Leaders—above the law.[54] The Party is the vanguard of the proletariat. It was the only institution qualified and eligible to guide society. It made all laws. And it could break all laws. Communist Party and government practices not only ignored laws that had become inconvenient, they also promulgated rules and enforced decrees which directly contradicted previous codes. In the framework of socialist legality, "the rule of law" signifies little more than the all-encompassing obligation of the citizen to obey the policies of the Party and the orders of the government, be these stable or unstable. The GDR claimed not only that it adhered to "the rule of law," but also that it complied with the principle of "equality before the law," guaranteeing all citizens the same rights and liberties. [e.g., Buchholz, 1987a, 19] This guarantee was as limited in its application in the GDR as elsewhere. Individuals (in any society) who are privileged in non-legal respects also tend to have significant legal advantages. The differences among societies are found in the *source* of high status and legal advantages and in the *degree* of inequality. The GDR differed from Western systems in both respects. The primary source of privilege in the GDR was political power (high office or connections to high office) rather than lineage or wealth.[55]

Below the level of high office and its privileges, it still made a great deal of difference whether an individual was known as a "good citizen" (i.e., a good communist and loyal supporter of the regime) or not. While entirely unwilling to admit outright that political power and connections could affect *verdicts*, East German commentators never denied that the offender's collectivist commitments and socialist consciousness were determinative factors in finding the proper *penalty:* "Equality before the law in the socialist administration of justice does not mean that equal wrongdoings should lead to equal punishments." [Daehn, 1987, 53; also see Geisler & Wagner, 1980, 64–73] In sum, the degree of extralegal influences in the East German legal system was much higher than that of comparable Western countries—as one would expect to find in a quasi-totalitarian country committed to *partiinost* principles. [Werkentin, 1995, 41] GDR commentators, however, stringently denied that the "big ones" had any advantages in the administration of the law. [Heuer, 1986, 100–106]

As noted, socialist legality did not include legally enforceable citizens' rights against the state (the rulers). Substantive and procedural laws that would protect the citizen against wrongful acts of the state did not, for all practical purposes, exist in socialist legal systems—a fact freely admitted by GDR commentators, but given the usual dialectical "spin." As expressed in an official GDR publication:

> People here do not find it necessary to seek freedom *from* or *against* the state because it is embodied *in* their state, which makes their freedom so real. The antithesis between the state and the people has been overcome. [Riemann & Schwabe, 1976, 20; also see Weichelt, 1979a, 99]

Socialist legality, then, was little else than the inflexible devotion of the strict observance of all laws and the unlimited loyalty to policies and interest of the Party (*Parteilichkeit*). [Lieser-Trebnigg, 1985, 10] "Socialist legality contributes to securing the policies of the Party, which have as their goals the comprehensive strengthening of socialism peace, and the welfare of the people. . . . Furthermore, it serves to protect the achievements of the people against the class enemy." [Moebis, 1984, 14–19; also see Autorenkollektiv, 1988, 116]

CHIEF ASPECTS OF THE EAST GERMAN LEGAL SYSTEM

Formal Structure

The ordinary (state) courts of the GDR formed a single, integrated system.[56] They were the Supreme Court, the county courts, and the district courts. In addition there was the High Court of Military Jurisdiction and the Courts-martial. [Sarge & Kalwert, 1973, 190] The military courts were under a certain supervision of the Supreme Court. The president (the presidency) of the Supreme Court could exercise cassation regarding their verdicts.[57] [Ludz, 1975, 359] The social courts were associated with the three-tier state system, but not fully incorporated in it.[58] Decisions of social courts could be reviewed by the district courts (*Kreisgerichte*), which also had the duty to provide guidance to the social courts. There were more than 200 district courts in the GDR. There were no courts of special jurisdiction, with the exception of the military courts and the patent courts.[59] The Supreme Court, however, had special chambers (*Senate*)—also found in the county courts[60]—for criminal, civil, family, labor,[61] and military law. [Code of the Constitution of the Courts § 33, § 38 (2)]

The Supreme Court had almost no original jurisdiction, in fact, the Constitution [Article 93 (2)] provided for none whatsoever.[62] This is the *full* text describing the duties of the Supreme Court in the Constitution:[63] "The Supreme Court guides the jurisdiction (*Rechtsprechung*) of the courts on the basis of the Constitution, the laws, and other legal rules (*Rechtsvorschriften*) of the German Democratic Republic. It secures the uniformity of the adjudication (*Rechtsanwendung*) of all courts." [Keppler, 1998; Lehmann, 1998] Commentaries, however, speak of the Supreme Court of assuming original jurisdiction when the case is of "exceptional importance for the development and the protection of the socialist social order of the GDR." [Autorenkollektiv, 1978b, 229] The Supreme Court did conduct any number of secret trials [Beckert, 1995]; one assumes that these were the cases of "exceptional importance."

The county courts (*Bezirksgerichte*) had original jurisdiction for serious crimes as well as for important civil, family, and labor cases. There were fifteen county courts in the GDR. Cases of lesser importance, which would normally have been adjudicated at district court level, could be moved to the county courts if the public prosecutor petitioned for this, or if the director of the county court moved it on his own initiative. [Code of the Constitution of the Courts Chapter 2, § 30 (1–2)] In addition, the county courts guided the activities of the district courts and social courts in its territory to secure the uniform and effective[64] application of the laws and the fulfillment of the guidance obligations of the district courts. [Code of the Constitution of the Courts [Chapter 2, § 29 (2)] Furthermore, the county courts also had appellate jurisdiction[65] and served as cassation authority regarding the decisions of the district courts. [Code of the Constitution of the Courts Chapter 2, § 30 (4)]

The district courts had original jurisdiction in most criminal, civil, family, and labor cases. They served as appellate courts for the decisions of the social courts. They also secured the execution of obligations imposed by the social courts, if voluntary performance was lacking. In addition, the district courts had a number of administrative tasks, such as to decide about the complaint of a citizen that he was not included in the list of voters. [Code of the Constitution of the Courts Chapter 2, § 23–24] Finally, the district courts had the responsibility to serve the legal needs of citizen by providing legal information free of charge. [Code of the Constitution of the Courts Chapter 2, § 28] The GDR literature speaks of "hundreds of thousands" who made use of this service every year. [Beyer, 1981, 19] In addition, newspapers and radio series also were reported to answer thousands of law-related inquiries every year. [Mollnau et al., 1976, 85]

All judges, lay assessors, and members of the social courts were elected.[66] They had to report on a regular basis to their electors. They could be recalled. The judges and lay assessors of the Supreme Court were nominated by the Council of State (*Staatsrat*) and elected by the national parliament (*Volkskammer*) and were responsible to it. [Luft, 1988, 279] The judges and lay assessors of the county and district courts were nominated by the minister of justice (in agreement with committees of the National Front) and elected by the county or district local assemblies. The term of office corresponded to that of the elective body, usually four or five years. It was a matter of great importance to the GDR that there was a close relationship between the working class and the administration of justice. Accordingly, there was an incessant pointing to such figures as that 71 percent of all judges were of working class background.[67] [Panorama DDR, 1976]

The Leninist Framework

In official accounts of its legal system, the GDR placed itself squarely within the framework of Lenin's socialist legality:[68]

> In the course of the revolutionary changes that have taken place in the GDR, law and justice has [sic] acquired a completely new content and function. The working people, who exercise all state power, make and administer their own law. Their legal system serves the interest of the working people, it helps to safeguard their achievements and to encourage progress in all fields of social endeavor. [Riemann, 1976, 9]

The claim of a "completely new content" was a huge exaggeration, as comparisons of Western and socialist codes will quickly demonstrate. The claim of a "completely new function" had a more solid foundation and was correct at least in part. Many of the old (bourgeois) tasks remained—from dispute resolution to criminal prosecution—but new ones were added, especially in the *economic* domain.

The "leading class" does not, of course, create the new laws and legal institutions. As Marxism-Leninism makes clear, the proletariat must exercise its legal leadership, as all other leadership functions, through its Party:

> A new, socialist type of law does not come into being spontaneously, just as the socialist state does not emerge and develop by itself. The Marxist-Leninist party is the leading and guiding force in socialist society. Its guiding hand is also felt in the development of the socialist legal system and in the administration of justice. [Riemann, 1976, 10]

To speak of the "guiding hand" of the Party in the administration of justice is merely to say that socialist law is an instrument of Party policy. [Lipson, 1958, 23] According to the Soviet scholar E.W. Nasarenko [1974, 13], "socialist law is the most important instrument . . . in the communist transformation of society." Or, as remarked elsewhere, as communist transformation strangely needed an ever stronger state, so was "the role of socialist law as society-forming state power ever increasing and growing . . . and this included, naturally, the further strengthening of democratic centralism." [Dettenborn & Mollnau, 1976, 7–9] As noted, the Party stands above the law. In the case of a conflict between Party policy and legal ordinances, the former prevails.[69] All the particulars of socialist legal policy and legal administration have always flowed from this principle.

State and Law

The doctrine of the withering away of the state was not confirmed in 70 years of communist rule. It is highly unlikely that it would have been confirmed if the USSR had lasted longer. [Holmes, 1981b] It is equally unlikely that the doctrine will be confirmed in China or Cuba. Under communist (Stalinist) tutelage, the state became stronger and its functions grew. These increases were too obvious to be denied even by the generally bald-faced socialist officials and by their apologists in the West. It was also obvious that the aggrandizing state contradicted the scriptures. But, as always in Marxism-Leninism, practical necessity produced ideological novelty—to be marketed, of course, as the purest of orthodoxies. Since the captives of absolutist ideologies have an overwhelming need to believe in the stability of doctrine, this task was not difficult.[70] Besides, the dialectically trained practitioners of the socialist theoretical ventures had been well tutored in this enterprise. In effect, the withering away of the state was postponed indefinitely, as was the arrival of communism. Socialist theoreticians were at their most creative when inventing new stages of socialist development. The number of specific way stations on the road to communism kept ever increasing, solemnized by new technical designations. The GDR moved through various steps to arrive at its last incarnation of the "advanced socialist society." Had the country lasted longer, one can be confident that more steps would have been invented—anything to avoid the arrival of communism. To proclaim the final stage had arrived would fully have exposed the errors of the theory and have would called the regime's bluff.

There were two aspects to the new exegesis. One was the simple assertion that Marx and Engels never held that there would be a gradual withering away of the state in socialism. The other was that the withering away regarded only the structure (the institutions) of the state, not its functions. One account is as fanciful as the other.[71] Lenin, quickly grasping the need to revise traditional Marxism, favored the second story-line. He asserted that the theory of the withering away of the state was never intended to mean a disappearance of the state's functions. Rather, it meant that these functions would be transferred to and exercised by all of the people. Socialism will "enable *everybody*, without exception, to perform 'state functions,' and this will lead to a *complete withering away* of every state in general." [Lenin, 1932, 99] As stated more recently: "Laws and rules will remain under communism, but they will lose their political and legal character." [Romashkin as quoted in Grzybowski, 1962, 246]

According to this line, the functions of the state, including rule-making and rule-enforcement, are indispensable even in communism. They will be exercised, however, by the people as a whole, that is, by society rather than by the state. Lenin quoted approvingly from Engel's letter to Bebel of March 28, 1875, spelling out the basic incompatibility of freedom and the state—socialist or otherwise. "As long as the proletariat still *needs* the state, it needs it, not in the interest of freedom, but for the purpose of crushing its antagonists; and as soon as it becomes possible to speak of freedom, then the state, as such, ceases to exist." [Lenin, 1932, 55; also see Kabes, 1961, 80]

There is a sleight-of-hand in this. For Marxism-Leninism the basic functions of the state are oppressive. Now, however, when these functions are transferred to society they are said to lose their oppressive character. There is neither theoretical nor practical justification for this transvaluation. Rules can be oppressive whether adopted by a legislative body or produced (in some mystical way) by "all the people." And the enforcement of rules can be oppressive whether carried out by state functionaries or societal agents.

In any case, from a practical perspective, the tortured reinterpretations of the withering-away-theory were wholly irrelevant. As long as the Communist Party tightly controlled all aspects of state and society, it made little difference whether a certain function (e.g., adjudication) had been assigned to an agency of the state or society. The oppressive character of the system remained the same. In the GDR there was a growing emphasis on the importance of the state in building socialist society[72] and on the need for a strict implementation of state discipline (*Staatsdizipline*).[73]

Law and Economics

As other socialist countries, the GDR viewed law not only as the instrument of the working class in its deliberate creation of new stages of social-economic development, but also as the primary tool to manage the (present) economy and to increase productivity:

A major function of socialist law is to provide a framework for the management and planning of the economy and other areas of national life, for the organization and management of affairs in enterprises and administrative departments and for labour relations. [Riemann, 1976, 9]

Statements such as these occurred without fail in socialist discussions of law: "Socialist law is an important instrument for the fulfillment of production goals." [Haring, 1978, 107] "Socialist law has the purpose of contributing to the solution of economic problems." [Kern, 1981, 138] It does this particularly by assuring order, discipline, and safety at the places of production and in other areas of life. [Moebis, 1978, 414; Moebis, 1984, 62–74]

Socialist legal discussions placed strong and persistent emphasis on the function of law in the improvement of "order, discipline, and safety" in the service of increased productivity—to fulfill the plan-goals.[74] The importance of order-discipline-safety was further emphasized by state-sponsored competitions among production and territorial units for the title "Area of Exemplary Order, Discipline, and Safety." [Heuckendorf, 1981, 186] Other important functions were: to motivate the political, social, and economic participation of all working people, to strengthen socialist collectivity in work-, life-, and leadership-processes, to encourage cooperation, mutual aid, respect, and trust, to develop socialist personalities and social relations, to develop and secure socialist habits of thought and behavior, to further a socialist life style, to protect the political and economic foundations of state and society, to aid the rapid development of productive forces, to protect the life and health of citizens, to ward off the attacks of the class enemy, and to guarantee legality, freedom, and human dignity.[75]

Without admitting that East German law ever had been anything less than perfectly socialist and perfectly just, the last years of the GDR saw earnest injunctions to increase the stature and value of the law and to "increase the perfection" of the administration of socialist justice. The first (and not very consequential) efforts to return some importance to the law began in about 1973. Similar attempts were made in other socialist countries at about the same time. In the PRC, as part of the Deng economic reforms "at the end of 1978, political revisions also were put into motion. In the name of socialist legalism, new legal codes were drafted, the judicial system was strengthened, and a pledge was made that henceforth Chinese citizens would not be subject to the arbitrariness of the Mao era. Rather, they would be treated in accordance with the provisions of the law." [Scalapino, 1992, 42] In the USSR, Leonid Brezhnev's new emphasis on "socialist legality" included opposition to "arbitrariness on the part of officials" and attempts on the part of officials "to evade responsiveness to public complaints." [Breslauer, 1982, 215; Note, 1982b] Needless to say, the revisions were sold as orthodox Marxism-Leninism by avowing (1) that increasing the role of the law in state and society was one of the lawful developments of post-revolutionary socialist systems, and (2) that the higher stages of socialism (now reached) required an improved and enlarged superstructure, particularly in its legal aspects.[76] [Mampel, 1985, 61] Thus the Party intelligentsia earned its pay and privileged position.

The *real* reasons for the GDR's "improved law" and "increased legality" moves were the requirements of the *Kombinate* (economic combines) and other enterprises for greater legal certainty and predictability, and for *enforceable* contracts. These needs, it turned out, could no more be ignored in planned than in free-market economies.[77] Thus, it was in the area of economic law that the first calls for more comprehensive and more dependable rules were heard.[78] [Dettenborn & Mollnau, 1976, 8–10; Heuer, 1977, 64–73] Legal discipline came to be stressed first and foremost "in the area of the economy, where it [was] feared that the disregard of legal regulations, including contracts, [would] upset the predictability and success of the Plan." [Markovitz, 1978, 629] The greater emphasis on law and legality should not be mistaken for an increased solicitude for the legal rights of citizens. The point was to improve productivity by stabilizing and making predictable the relations between the economic units of the GDR. [Mampel, 1985, 61–62]

The Many Missions of Socialist Law

The law and the legal system have more diverse and more extensive functions in socialist societies than they have in the West. Some of these functions are absent in Western jurisprudence, others have a less prominent place. The goals and objectives of socialist law are:[79]

- to secure and further the political power of the working class;
- to motivate the political, social, and economic participation of all working people;[80]
- to strengthen the spirit of socialist collectivity at work, in social life, and among leaders;
- to encourage cooperation, mutual aid, respect, and trust;
- to produce stable and permanent meldings of societal requirements, and individual and collective interests and deeds;
- to develop socialist personalities and socialist social relations;
- to form and secure socialist habits of thought and behavior;
- to promote the socialist lifestyle;
- to direct the socialist state;
- to protect the political and economic foundations of state and society;
- to aid the rapid development of productive forces;
- to protect the life and health of citizens;
- to ward off the attacks of the class enemy; and
- to guarantee legality, freedom, and human dignity.[81]

Socialist laws and courts, of course, also functioned to adjudicate civil disputes and criminal charges. These tasks, however, had a less prominent place in socialist jurisprudence than in Western legal systems.[82] Ordinary civil and criminal adjudication were not even the primary functions of socialist law. Its most important objectives were economic.[83] At the macro level, socialist law was envisioned as an instrument of the working class to organize the stages of social-economic development.

> With the establishment of socialist power- and production-conditions, and in the process of the revolutionary change of all aspects of social life, the working class and its allies have created their own law, and raised it to a method with which they exercise their political power, with the purpose of forging new societal conditions. [Autorenkollektiv, 1978a, 220]

At the micro level, the law was pictured as a mechanism to manage the economy and as an instrument to increase productivity. [Riemann, 1976, 9] Statements, such as the following, were standard fare in socialist discussions of the law: "Socialist law is an important instrument for the fulfillment of production goals." [Haring, 1978, 107] It is quite clear that the pre-eminent purpose of socialist law was contributing to the solution of economic problems.[84] [Kern, 1981, 138] Socialist law solved economic problems and increases production mainly by securing order, discipline, and safety at the places of work. The GDR literature strongly emphasized that it was a key function of the law to improve "order, discipline, and safety" in the service of increased productivity.[85] The importance of the theme of order-discipline-safety was further emphasized by state-sponsored competitions among production units and among territorial units for the title of "Area of Exemplary Order, Discipline, and Safety." [e.g., Heuckendorf, 1981, 186]

The Secondary Place of Dispute Resolution

Socialist law and courts, of course, also had the function of settling civil disputes[86] and adjudicating criminal charges. These tasks, while primary in bourgeois legal systems, had but a secondary function in socialism. Heger [1981, 196], for example, writes: "We must direct our attention to the false ideological position regarding the law that still prevails with some of our citizens. These are the fellow-citizens who view the solution of disputes as the only purpose of the law." The de-emphasis of dispute resolution may not have been unrelated to the doctrines of increasing social harmony and of the disappearance of crime. It should be noted, however, that socialist theory did not predict the complete disappearance of crimes and disputes in socialism (this claim was advanced only for the final stage of communism). For socialism a gradual, but substantial, disappearance of crime was asserted.[87] "The unity of socialist law and the people also serves as the foundation for the fact that no one needs to become a lawbreaker in the socialist society." [Heuckendorf, 1981, 186] This follows Engels [1993, 51], who said: When we eliminate the contradictions between man and society "we put the axe to the *root* of crime." More recent commentators have declared that it is no longer necessary to discuss the capitalist production of crime, because "such questions have long been settled." [Wenger & Bonomo, 1993, 674] It should be noted that other than the exploitation theory of crime, Marxism does not have a theory of deviance. [Hirst, 1972, 29]

Fundamental to these claims, of course, was the Marxist exploitation theory of crime.[88] [e.g., Juviler, 1976, 16] According to Marx (writing in *The German Ideology*), crime is rooted in the same conditions as is the governing power existing at the time. And according to Lenin, crime has its roots in the exploitation of the masses, in their needs and their privations. [As cited by Vyshinsky, 1948, 60] Crime, wrote Buchholz [1969, 162] is alien to the nature of socialism. There is an interesting question whether the exploitation theory of crime also applied to the GDR, which would then have to be categorized as an exploiter society. [Sander, 1979, 7–8, 34–35] Of course, the exploiters would not be old-style capitalist, but new-style functionaries of Party and State: the "new class." [Bender, 1992, 27] There is no doubt that many citizens of the GDR thought that they were not justly rewarded for their labors. And while the full story of the extravagant lifestyles of the "new class" did not become widely known until after 1989, most people had a strong suspicion that "those above" had considerable economic and other advantages.

While serious crime in the GDR had a lower frequency than that in most of the industrialized societies of the West, there remained substantial amounts of serious crimes, particularly bodily injuries[89] [Heuer 1986, 95], civil disputes, and petty crimes, such as traffic violations, public disorderliness, and property offenses. [Buchholz, 1987c, 33] The last type was particularly embarrassing, since offenses against property (public and private) might be expected to vanish first in a socialist society. Equally embarrassing with a steady increase of juvenile delinquency, as a result of which the GDR halted the publication of juvenile crime statistics. This however, did not stop GDR authors to claim that juvenile criminality had been reduced by a third in the last eight years [Buchholz, 1987b, 833] and also that crime in general showed large-scale decreases from the very beginning and throughout the existence of the GDR. [Buchholz, 1987c, 38–41; Harrland, 1965][90] It is interesting to note in this connection the widespread existence of neighborhood Commissions for Order and Safety (about which more later), another form of participation of ordinary citizens in the prevention of disorder and crime.

Law and Party Policy

Without exception, socialist law is an instrument of Party policy—all specifics flowed from this principle and little else mattered. The subordination of law followed naturally from the doctrine of the supremacy of the Party and the instrumental view of the law. "That the Party line stands over the law has been stated by Vyshinsky as far back as 1936. He wrote that in the case of collision between the formal requirements of law and party policy, law must be subordinated to Party policy." Vyshinsky also had a fine sense of humor, letting the world know that Soviet judges are truly independent, "subordinate only to the demands of the law." [Kucherov, 1970, 514, 704] To be fair, political justice is not the exclusive province of socialist countries. Rulers and regimes in all corners of the world tend not to take kindly to challenges. But Western democracies differ in this: it is legal to seek to replace governments by peaceful means. There are, however, no legal means to replace socialist regimes, particularly since election results are routinely falsified.[91] Necessarily, socialist countries have (definitionally) more political crimes and (behaviorally) more political criminals. For example, "intentional injury to the socialist order of state and society" mandated prison terms from three years to life and, even, capital punishment.[92] (Criminal Code of 1968, §§102–103) As another example, there was the offense of "treasonable information transmission (*Landesverräterische Nachrichtenübermittlung*), which merited prison sentences of two to twelve years for providing information to a foreign organization to the disadvantage of the GDR, even if this information was not classified as secret. In other words, talking to a foreign journalist about the scarcity of housing in the GDR constituted such an offense. [Kuhrt, 1996, 11; Wolle, 1998, 245]

There were, of course, blanket denials of the existence of political crimes, political trials, and political prisoners. In the early 1960s, Khrushchev, for example, declared that there were no political prisoners in the Soviet Union. [Wolfe, 1969, 393] "In his speech to the 21st Congress, however, the Soviet Premier went even further than claiming that 'political crimes' are no longer prosecuted: he also alleged that 'we now have no one in prison for political reasons.' This claim. . . was more mendacious than the first, for it suggested not merely a change in court practice but a fundamental change in the nature of the Soviet political system. . . . No such 'depoliticization' [of the law] has of course occurred." [Azrael, 1962, 11] Similar denials were issued by the GDR throughout, which, however, did not prevent the regime from selling more than 30,000 political prisoners to West Germany—and at a considerable profit—estimated at 3.3 billion westmark to 1989.[93] In addition, the GDR did not hesitate to send (without notification) some of its dangerous criminals by subway to West Berlin. [Werkentin, 1995, 388]

The predominant obligation of legal experts, including defense attorneys, private attorneys of any kind,[94] including in-house counsel, was to the Party and its policies. [Lieser, 1989, 48–51] Bourgeois in-house counsel will advise the enterprise executives how best to use the law, and even how to get around it. The obligation of socialist legal counsel was to advise the manager of the firm how to best implement the law and to make sure that all laws are strictly followed. Indeed, it was his duty to report violations of law and non-implementation to the authorities. Even the private attorney had important obligations to the state and could not solely consider the interests of his client.[95] Safeguarding the personal interest of the client is distinctly secondary to safeguarding the interests of Party and state. [Lieser-Triebnigg, 1985, 15; Shelley, 1984, 34] Typical is this statement, made in the context of a discussion of the role of the socialist lawyer: "I see a Jurist above all as a state functionary who—independent of his specific tasks—through his work enforces the decisions of the Party." [Schirmer, 1975, 133]

What was true for attorneys also was true for judges. The paramount obligation of the East German judges and all other legal practitioners was to the Party and its policies, not to the law, not to the litigants.[96] The primary responsibility, even of a private or in-house attorney, was to the Party and not to his client. What was true for the attorneys also was true for the judges. "[I]n totalitarian countries, whether Communist or fascist, the judiciary is emphatically political—in the partisan sense of the word—as is the intent of the law. Not only are many judges loyal members of the totalitarian party, but they affect an activist style of ideological crusading that disdains any formalism and at times even the law code." [Merkl, 1977, 175–176] Since these states reject any division of power and any arrangement of checks-and-balances, it follows that the judiciary can lay no claim to independence, but must let itself be guided and controlled by Party and/or state.[97] The first sentence of Weichelt's [1978a, 207] discussion of the organization of the GDR courts is paradigmatic: "The courts of the GDR are an inseparable component of the unitary socialist state-power." The fact that judges could be removed from office at any time did further contribute to their subordination to state and Party. [Rosenthal, 1962, 137]

GDR judges had the clear obligation to adjudicate as partisans. Any sign of non-partisanship—of the kind of judicial independence taken for granted in the West—would quickly be denounced as formalism and bureaucratism, and even as anticommunism and treason. A judge's career did not easily recover from such criticisms. However, the fact of judicial partisanship should not be overinterpreted. GDR judges were able to apply—and generally did apply—the law fairly and neutrally in cases that did not involve Party or state interests. When a case did have political aspects, of course, Party directives were issued and prevailed.

It seems useful at this point to remind oneself that *political crimes* are to *ordinary crimes* what *heresy* is to *sin*. The guardians of socialism reacted to political crimes exactly as the guardians of medieval catholicism to heresy—with unalloyed vengefulness. The reasons are not difficult to understand. Ordinary crimes and sins are merely offenses against particular commands of the system. Political crimes and heresies, however, are challenges to the system itself. They challenge the right of the rulers to rule. The rulers (beneficiaries) of a given absolutist/totalitarian system have always known were the true danger lies. Conveniently, they have discovered that God loves sinners, but not heretics, and they have acted accordingly. In political and economic trials the prosecution was harsh and vindictive. There were few acquittals. The sentences were extraordinarily severe and seldom lower than the maximum sanction available. The laws of the GDR, for example, provided penalties from three years to life in prison, and (until recently) even capital punishment for offenses such as speaking contemptuously of organs of the state (*öffentliche Herabwürdigung staatlicher Organe*), the intentional injury to the socialist order of state and society, and an intentional damage to the economy (Criminal Code of the GDR, 1968, §§ 102–110, 219–222). In these cases, humanitarianism, non-punitiveness, the observance of procedural safeguards, and the rule of law largely vanished in favor of simple vindictiveness. [Gornig, 1987, 88–89; Schroeder: 1986: 338–340]

To prevent formalism and other deviations from the Party line, reliable cadres were needed. The general threats and sanctions available to the regime did not seem enough. Judicial office would be entrusted only to Party members, that is, to individuals who were subject to Party discipline. Thus, the great majority of the professional judges of the GDR were members of the Communist Party (SED).[98] Those few who did not belong to the SED were members of one or the other of the communist-controlled "bloc parties."[99] [Rottleuthner, 1998] The occasional judge who did not belong to any of the parties was there as alibi and for the show. He was controlled no less than the other judges. The East German judges were precisely what Marxist-Leninist ideology demanded: transmission belts of Party policy.[100] This included the country's Supreme Court, which was not "an adjudicative organ with the obligation to preserve valid law, . . . but an agency with the task to manipulate the law in the interest of the maintenance and strengthening of socialist power." [Mampel, 1985, 62] GDR jurists, however, insisted that in the West, but not in the GDR, legality was routinely violated in the interest of the bourgeois ruling class. [Buchholz, 1961, 746] On the diverse relations of GDR jurists to the GDR see Fricke, 1999.

It does not require wide-ranging investigations into hidden archives to discover the partisan nature of socialist law. Socialist legal theory is entirely explicit on this point: the administration of justice in socialist society must be partisan.[101] Thus the Chief Justice (president) of the GDR Supreme Court declared:

> Socialist jurisdiction is an expression and a constituent element of the unified state power. Therefore, the court cannot act independently of the policy of the state, the will of the working class and the other working people allied with it, nor can it dissociate itself from the tasks of the further promotion of the developed socialist

society . . . The court cannot be independent of the continually developing socialist society whose instrument of power is the socialist state and whose views guide the judge in applying the law. . . . The notion of a jurisdiction independent of the state power in the sense of a third power or force supervising the remaining organs of state or balancing their influence is alien to socialism. [Toeplitz, 1971, 49]

Partisanship, of course, was the universal obligation in socialist societies—it did not exclude law any more than science:

Research must contribute to securing the power of the working class . . . The research efforts of the political and legal sciences consciously work toward the goal of strengthening the political and organizational unity of the political organizations of our society. This research, thus, with full determination and consistent partisanship, opposes political pluralism, abstract bourgeois conceptions of state and democracy, and any distortion of the class character of socialist law . . . Political and legal research regards it as an inseparable element of its work to take the offensive in the dispute with anticommunist, bourgeois, and revisionist views of state and law. The determined fight to preserve the purity of Marxist-Leninist theory is its scientific obligation. [Schuessler, 1981a, 437]

The primary consideration of the socialist judge were not the rights and interests of the litigants or defendants, nor was he expected to exhibit a western-style judicial neutrality:

A bourgeois jurist tends to approach law in terms of the rights it protects: faced with the task of solving a legal conflict, he will dissect the issue into the rights of the parties involved and then weigh those rights against each other . . . We expect from law the protection of what is our due. Hence the bourgeois fascination with procedure: since we understand a legal conflict as a match of right pitted against right, with both potentially of equal weight, we have to see to it that the rules of the match are impartial. Bourgeois law is basically a horizontal affair: it coordinates purposes, balances interests. Our figure of Justice is blindfolded and holds a scale—a neutral arbiter of rights.

In the socialist view, the bourgeois preoccupation with individual benefits veils and distorts the political character of all law. Law is important not because it confers rights but because it prescribes the behavior necessary to progress on the path to socialism. Rights as policy pronouncements are individualized means of conveying the commands of the law . . . Rather than balancing right against right, a socialist will look for the policies embedded in particular rights, then rank them according to their importance and urgency. We try, or pretend to be, neutral; socialists try, or pretend to be, partial—not to the parties to a dispute, but to the Party as the authoritative guide towards social progress. We want to be fair; socialists want to be correct. Law under socialism is a vertical affair: order, direction, discipline, command. A socialist figure of justice would not be blindfolded, but seeing, and she would show the way with outstretched arm and pointing finger. [Kucherov, 1970, 704–706]

And indeed, this became GDR practice. When "the Dresden court buildings . . . were restored in the early 1950s. . . . One of the minor, yet fundamental decisions we took was that we had the figure of Justice, formerly blindfolded, put back at the entrance of the court house, but this time without the bandage over her eyes." [Toeplitz, 1971, 43] Indeed, the bandage, so we were told, was a deliberate deception of the people by the bourgeois rulers. [Mollnau et al. 1976, 13; also see Heuer, 1986, 26–41]

The other major function of bourgeois law, the protection of the citizen against the state, for all practical purposes did not exist in socialist law. As expressed in one official publication: "People here do not find it necessary to seek freedom from or against the state because it is embodied in their state, which makes their freedom so real." Of course, "freedom" has a different meaning in socialist than in bourgeois discourse. Socialist freedom, for example, includes the duty to participate in political activities, but not the right to differ with Party policy. Socialist freedom, most fundamentally, means to endorse the policies and fulfill the commands of the Party—a construction which is not only splendidly Orwellian, but also wonderfully Hegelian: freedom as the acceptance of necessity.[102] In any case, "the antithesis between the state and the people has been overcome." [Riemann & Schwabe, 1976, 20]

Not surprisingly, there was very little administrative law and no separate system of administrative courts.[103] The citizen did have means to seek corrections to errors or illegalities committed by particular officials. He could not proceed by litigation, however. Meador [1986, 180] rightly remarks: "When [GDR citizens] do assert individual grievances, they tend to do so through an administrative complaint procedure which give them no 'rights.' [In general] law is primarily a means of social control rather than a means for effectuating individual rights and autonomy." Citizens could proceed only in these two ways: (1) by filing a *complaint* with the agency that they thought had wronged them, and (2) by submitting a *petition* to legislative or executive offices.[104] Both were remedies of dubious utility. While the utility of complaints was minimal for the complaining citizen, they functioned as an additional control method for the higher offices. Too many complaints about a particular court or agency were an indication of less than optimal functioning. [Lieser-Trebnigg, 1985, 25] Similarly, the much lauded judicial consultations (*Justizaussprachen*)—the annual public reports by the professional and lay judges of a district court, including discussions with the participating citizens—functioned not only to educate the citizens about the law and its administration, but also to give the (ever-present) state security (Stasi) an opportunity to identify critical and non-conforming citizens. [Rosenthal, n.d., 82–83]

Filing complaints was largely futile and often disadvantageous—politically rather than legally. Agencies receiving complaints were required to respond, but they did not have to feel kindly about the complainant. The mandate to respond could be satisfied with an explanation or a clarification—most often a rationalization. Restitution and relief were not mandated, but possible. [Constitution, Article 104] The citizens of East Germany also had the formal right to petition the legislature to review the constitutionality of legal codes—the same legislature that had promulgated these codes in the first instance. Notwithstanding government assurances that no one who made use of this right would suffer any disadvantages as a consequence, as of 1985 no citizen had ever made use of this right. [Mampel, 1985, 67] The citizens of the GDR knew well what such assurances were worth. The regime, for example, made ample use of §220, Section 1 of the Criminal Code, which criminalized (and severely penalized) the "disparagement of leaders and institutions" of the GDR. [also see Schroeder, 1986, 340]

The citizens of the GDR could also seek to remedy grievances by way of petitions (*Eingaben*). They could be directed to any governmental agency or economic body. By all appearances, they were taken quite seriously. Agencies, for example, had to respond within a certain period of time and were expected to give careful consideration to the complaints, suggestions, or requests.[105] It is important to recognize that these were petitions by which the citizens hoped to gain equitableness in individual cases. They were techniques operating outside normal legal procedures. [Werkentin, 1995, 335] They used methods more frequently found in older absolutist systems, where direct appeals to the ruler were the only way receive justice in a lawless system. [Wolle, 1998, 53] In any case, the petitions also did serve to inform the regime about popular dissatisfactions. This information, however, either remained largely in the Stasi offices or was not acknowledged at higher levels. Honecker and other members of the Politburo seem to have remained significantly uninformed.

Socialism and the "Rule of Law"

Bourgeois legal theory regards much of the law as a private affair: individuals invoke the law to protect their rights and interests—if they wish to do so. Socialist legal theory, by contrast, regards all legal matters as public affairs. "Socialist law, which views rights as policy pronouncements, sees the violation of a right as a threat to the policy in question and therefore as a social affair, in need of a social solution." [Markovits, 1978, 623] Socialist legality does not refer to a *Rechtsstaat*[106] in the sense of the liberal democracies. As seen earlier, Marxism-Leninism scorned the liberal "rule of law," which elevates law above state and ruler ("government of law"). The "rule of law" in socialist legality meant essentially obedience to the commands of the state and loyal support of the policies of the Party. This, however, bound not only the ordinary citizen, but also the functionaries of the state and social organs. Since it was doctrine that the current laws are the correct responses to current needs, as well as the correct guides to the communist future, no one's activities could be outside the laws. Obviously, since the Party made the laws, it could also change the laws. More important, it could also *break* the laws—and it did so as a matter of routine. "The law never stood above the state under the Soviet regime. The Communist Party and the Soviet government always were free to break the law created by themselves when they deemed it necessary in the interest of the socialist or communist experiment." [Kucherov, 1970, 703]

Law Implementation and Enforcement

In socialist systems, the benefit of rights was conditional on the fulfillment of duties. Freedom meant the ability to participate in political activities and state affairs, not to be protected from them.[107] As noted, Lenin endorsed Engels' view: "As long as the proletariat still has use for the state, it will use the state not in the interest of freedom, but for the suppression of its enemies . . ." [Lenin, 1976, 69] All of this, however, did not mean legal anarchism or indifference to law and the legal process. Quite on the contrary, enforcement and implementation of law had prime importance: "The implementation of socialist laws is . . . not the private affair of the citizen. Law implementation is putting into effect the citizen's responsibility toward state and society. It is the moral obligation of everyone who is loyal to, lives in, and benefits from the successes of socialist society." [Zschiedrich, 1981, 295]

Similarly, it was of greatest importance that all law-breaking be detected. There were frequent references in the literature of the USSR and the GDR and other socialist countries to the dictum of Lenin, that it was more important that each crime be detected and uncovered, than that it be severely punished.[108] There had to be a comprehensive unwillingness to tolerate law-breaking. This desired public intolerance received a much greater emphasis in socialist than in Western legal theory. Appeals for greater public intolerance of law-breaking and crime were constant themes in the socialist legal literature. Beyond being recruited as lay participants in the legal process and as propagandists for the country's legal order, the citizens of East Germany also were required to be law enforcement agents. To detect law-breaking and bring it to the attention of the authorities was a serious public responsibility. [Kern, 1981, 139] To act as informers was not a matter of choice. To look the other way would have been an act of disloyalty—and a punishable offense. [Autorenkollektiv, 1978a, 223; Markovits, 1978, 624–625] And, as in the USSR, "socialist intrusiveness and meddling in the affairs of others [were] encouraged." [Blaney & Gfoeller, 1993, 484]

Legal Education and Consultation

The legal education of *all* citizens was a prime goal of the GDR. As comments elsewhere will have made clear, this goal was not to better enable citizens to assert rights, but to assure a willing subordination to the law, that is, to Party policy. All societal agencies had to play a role in this effort: from schools and colleges, to labor unions, to the media, and various public organization.[109] [Panorama DDR, 1984, 20–21] Legal education was also furthered by the citizens' participation in the adjudicative process, as lay assessors or social court members, or as societal participants in actual court cases. Article 21 of the Constitution guaranteed in general terms the participation of citizens in adjudication. Paragraph 9 of the Code of the Constitution of the Courts provided specifically that citizens may participate as representatives of the collective or societal organization.[110] Paragraph 4 of the Civil Procedure Code and Paragraph 4 of the Code of Criminal Procedure contained the same provisions. The representative of the collective could participate as societal prosecutors, societal defenders, or "as guarantor for the offenders good behavior in the future."[111] There even was a call to social forces (*gesellschaftliche Kräfte*) to participate in some aspects of the investigation of crime. [Reuter, 1966] And there also was a institutionalized court critique (*Gerichtskritik* also known as *öffentliche Aussprache*), where the court gave an account of its work to a relevant collective (often a workers collective) and heard suggestions and criticism from the participants.[112]

Beyond this, there was a major involvement of citizens in the drafting of new law. Legal education, it was said, deepens the citizen's trust in his socialist state, and increases the citizen's efforts to further strengthen the power of the socialist state. [Mollnau, 1979, 338] In this connection, it was thought to be very important to demonstrate the justice and humanitarian content of socialist law, as well as its correspondence to the basic interests of the citizens. [Mollnau, 1979, 344–345] Socialist legal education must finally also lead to the rejection of outdated ways of thinking and attempts of the imperialists to undermine socialist legality. [Mollnau, 1979, 351; Schuessler, 1979c, 24–25]

> There are diverse opportunities for citizens to be involved in the legislative process, first and foremost through the elected members of the People's Chamber [national parliament]. They are required to maintain closest contact with the constituents and to take into account their voters' opinions, proposals, suggestions and hints. . . . It often happens that knowledgeable and interested citizens are drawn into the initial preparation of bills. . . . Major bills are put to public discussion prior to their adoption . . . This applied, for instance, to the draft of the Civil Code, the Labour Code and the Family Code, the Youth Act, the Act on Agricultural Production Cooperatives and, of course, the draft Constitution. Millions of people, displaying great interest and expertise, took part in these debates most of which lasted several weeks. Many proposals for amendments and comments were always submitted. They were all carefully monitored and those suited to improve the law taken into consideration in the final version. [Panorama DDR, 1984, 21–22]

Mollnau [1979, 330] formulated it as follows: The goal of socialist legal education is the formation of socialist personalities and, connected to it, the creation of a spiritual climate in society, that is intolerant of violations of the law and demands respect for the laws; such a climate is a component of the socialist life style. Socialist legal education must pay equal attention to these two components: an understanding of the legal norms and principles, and knowledge of the particular laws.[113] [Mollnau, 1979, 353] Law, in any case, is not only a matter of concern for experts, but for all citizen. [Moebis, 1984, 90]

The consultation efforts, at least by official accounts, were massive undertakings. For a number of legal codes, here are the (in sequence): (a) number of formal meetings, (b) number of participating citizens, (c) number of comments made, (d) number of proposals for changes submitted, and (e) number of actual changes made in the draft.

- Family Code of 1965: (a) not given; (b) 750,000; (c & d) 23,000; (e) 230. [Mollnau et al., 1976, 95]
- Constitution of 1968: (a) not given; (b) 11,000,000; (c & d) 12,494; (e) 118. [Mollnau et al., 1976, 95]
- Penal Code of 1968: (a) not given; (b) 50,000; (c & d) 8,141; (e) not given. [Schmidt, 1968, 68; Panorama DDR, 1984, 39]
- Youth Code of 1974: (a) not given; (b) 5,400,000; (c & d) 4,821; (e) 200. [Autorenkollektive, 1985a, 17; Mollnau et al., 1976, 95]
- Civil Code of 1975: (a) more than 8,500; (b) about 260,000; (c & d) 4,091; (e) 360. Five months of public discussion were devoted to the draft. The analysis of the proposals and comments showed a "fundamental acceptance" among the citizens. Only a few proposals could not be incorporated in the draft. [Panorama DDR, 1976, 85; Weichelt, 1975a, 13–19]
- Labor Code of 1977: (a) 292,196; (b) 5,814,325; (c) 147,806; (d) 39,533; (e) 90 (plus 144 editorial changes). [Autorenkollektive, 1985a, 17; Heusinger, 1979a, 63]

The participation figures, if correct,[114] are impressive; the effects of the participation less so. Were the numbers for the changes are provided, they range from 0.2% (Labor Code) to 1% (Constitution and Family Code) to 4% (Youth Code) and to 9% (Civil Code). Of course, no details about the changes ever were provided. It can reasonably be assumed that they did not relate to the fundamentals of Party policy or of the socialist state.

While most of the so-called "legal education" was little more than efforts to make the citizens conform to the socialist system and to obey its laws, some of the endeavors were indeed very instructive und useful, particularly the sequence of small paperbacks published by the *Staatsverlag* und the series title *Recht in unserer Zeit* (Law in Our Times). For example, the volume written by Beyer [1981] takes the citizens through all possible forms of legal disputes, explains which societal organ is answerable in each situation, expounds the organization of the different courts, shows how the different courts work, takes the citizen step by step through the legal process, deciphers the appeals procedures, and spells out how a court's decision is implemented—all of this in 120 small pages. The language was non-technical and easy to understand. In addition, the cost was minimal.[115] Each volume sold for just a fraction of a dollar.[116] One cannot help but wish U.S. citizens had available similar inexpensive and understandable guidance to the legal system.

The Rights and Duties of Citizens

An analysis of the legal rights and constitutional protections of the citizens of any country cannot limit itself to textual examinations. This is particularly true for countries such as East Germany, where legal codes and legal actuality were miles apart. The Constitutions of the German Democratic Republic granted a large number of rights, including some not generally found in bourgeois constitutions, such as: to develop his personality, to an apartment (*Wohnraum*), social security and safety, health and recreation, work and full employment, free choice of job, participation in planning, education, free exercise of religion, and old age care.[117] In GDR language, what is enumerated and advertised as a *right,* however, often turns out to be yet another *duty.* The "right to work" is a clear example—not working was a criminal offense. [Criminal Code of the GDR § 249; also see Autorenkollektiv, 1987, 520–525; Feifer, 1964, 188–199; Lipson, 1963, 2–3; Luchterhandt, 1985, 264; Thiel, 1988, 87] Political rights also are best understood in the GDR context as participatory duties. [Brugger, 1978, 102]

The key question clearly is not how many rights were enumerated in the Constitution and other legal codes, but whether and how well these rights were implemented and enforced. GDR authors, of course, insisted that in the GDR Constitutional law and Constitutional practice were one and the same. [Schulze, 1984, 374] Western observers tended to be skeptical about East German claims regarding citizens' rights. Even the limited pre-1989 evidence was enough to substantiate massive denials of constitutionally vested rights. Post-1989 information has confirmed the earlier assessments and has shown that conditions, in fact, were even worse than had been thought.[118] The enjoyment of socialist rights was conditional upon the fulfillment of socialist duties. The point of having individual rights in a socialist society was not to further personal growth, enrichment, or happiness, but to encourage the citizen to engage in activities "which will benefit the public interests and advance societal development." [Buchholz, 1987a, 21] As Schoenrath [1978, 111, 126] stated: Furnishing each member of the socialist society with rights and duties is not an end in itself, rather societal developments require them *objectively.* One of the favorite terms of GDR discourse was "objective necessity." Many things were said to be "objectively necessary," for example, "the role of socialist legal consciousness," which was said to be one of the fundaments of the socialist state. [Nasarenko, 1974, 7] Or, "socialist legality is indivisibly connected to the enforcement of the objective laws of socialism."[119] The meaning of "necessary" in this context is not that it should happen, but that it does happen without fail.

A clear and undisputed difference between bourgeois and socialist constitutional theory is where each system locates the origins of rights. In liberal-democratic societies, citizen rights reside in the individual, precede the state, and can be asserted against the state. In socialist societies, citizen rights are grants from the state to the individual; they cannot be asserted against the state. As formulated by a leading GDR authority:

> In the developed socialist society, a society free of antagonistic relationships, the rights of the citizens are not guaranteed rights that can be used *against* the state. Instead, they are put at the disposal of the individual and his collectives by the state (the combined might of workers and farmers) . . . [Buchholz, 1987, 21]

Needless to say, "the combined might of workers and farmers" was fully subject to the Party's pleasure—and what the Party puts at the citizen's disposal, it also can restrict or take away altogether.

Another important difference between socialist and bourgeois law is found in the socialist proclivity to resolve dispute in terms of the public interest rather than in terms of competing individual rights. The primary concern of the socialist administration of justice is not to uphold the rights of citizens (as criminal defendants or civil litigants), but to further of the public interest—as this is defined by the Party. [Kucherov, 1970, 704–706] The socialist judge is not expected to exhibit Western style judicial neutrality, nor is he expected to resolve the dispute through the analysis of competing rights. What socialist adjudicators need to determine is not who has the superior claim (the more fundamental right), but which claim corresponds (more closely) to Party policy. Inga Markovitz [1978, 625–626] noted:

> A bourgeois jurist tends to approach law in terms of the rights it protects: faced with the task of solving a legal conflict, he will dissect the issue into the rights of the parties involved and then weigh those rights against each other . . . We expect from law the protection of what is our due. Hence the bourgeois fascination with procedure: since we understand a legal conflict as a match of right pitted against right, with both potentially of equal weight, we have to see to it that the rules of the match are impartial. Bourgeois law is basically a horizontal affair: it coordinates purposes, balances interests. Our figure of justice is blindfolded and holds a scale—a neutral arbiter of rights.
>
> In the socialist view, the bourgeois preoccupation with individual benefits veils and distorts the political character of all law. Law is important not because it confers rights but because it prescribes the behavior necessary to progress on the path to socialism. Rights as policy pronouncements are individualized means of conveying

the commands of law . . . Rather than balancing right against right, a socialist will look for the policies embedded in particular rights, then rank them according to their importance and urgency. We try, or pretend to be, neutral; socialists try, or pretend to be, partial—not to the parties to a dispute, but to the Party as the authoritative guide towards social progress. We want to be fair; socialists want to be correct. Law under socialism is a vertical affair: order, direction, discipline, command. A socialist figure of justice would not be blindfolded, but seeing, and she would show the way with outstretched arm and pointing finger.

Bourgeois legal theory treats much of the (civil) legal process as a private affair. Individuals invoke the law and activate the legal process to protect their rights and interests—if they wish to do so. Socialist legal theory, however, regards all legal matters as public affairs. Socialist laws, above all, are policy pronouncements. A violation of the law is a menace to the Party policy in question. Therefore, it is not a private, but a social affair, and in need of a social remedy and resolution.

A further difference between Western and socialist approaches to individual rights is that in the former system rights are listed separately from duties, whereas in the latter rights and duties are tightly connected. This connection is comprehensive. It exists in the realm of the state as well as in the personal realm. It is made possible by the socialist property relations. [Mollnau et al., 1976, 77–80]

The purpose of socialist constitutional rights was not to establish and secure for the individual a realm of privacy and self-determination, but "to enhance social conformity and active participation in public affairs." [Gornig: 1987, 80] The key virtue of the "good socialist" is *participatory conformity.* Tending to one's own garden and not offending against fellow citizens or the regime is not enough. Only through active participation in officially decreed and managed public endeavors can the individual find favor and attain grace in socialist societies. As noted throughout, the GDR placed very great importance on the legal education of its citizens. A closer examination, however, reveals that the key ingredient of this "education" was a law-and-order campaign to persuade citizens to obey the commands of the Party. The point was not for the citizen to know his rights, but to know the law, which is to know the will of the Party and to comply with it.

Punishment and Rehabilitation

Socialist law (in the GDR and elsewhere) was firmly committed to the rehabilitative approach and was less punitive than most Western law, except in the area of offenses against Party and state, that is, political offenses and, interestingly, economic offenses. Vyshinsky [1948, 649] is quite clear about this: "'Persons making attempts upon socialist property are enemies of the people' (USSR Constitution, Art. 131). Precisely for this reason, the law of

August 7, 1932, established severe punishment for those guilty of this most serious crime." It is noteworthy that a 1986 catalogue of remaining, trouble-some offenses predominantly list economic misdeeds: "The Party attaches paramount importance to the steady and consistent eradication of violations of labour discipline, embezzlement and bribery, profiteering and parasitism, drunkenness and hooliganism, private-owner psychology and money-grubbing, toadyism and servility." [Congress of the CPSU, 1986, 58])

As noted, GDR law was much less concerned with retribution than with the rehabilitation, re-education, and societal reintegration of the offender, and the prevention of future offenses. [Weber, 1969] This was also true for the USSR. Soviet law "is organized not in order to punish the criminals, but rather to correct psychologically all the weaknesses inherent in what they have been taught, and which produce instability in their moral relationships with other members of society, thus strengthening the moral atmosphere." [Vyshinsky, 1951, 12; also see Lapenna, 1968, 87] In the GDR, crime prevention started with young children and was the proper concern of everybody. [Buchholz, 1987c, 37; Hinderer, 1966, 12–13] Re-socialization and re-education, particularly through work, were also strongly emphasized in the rehabilitation of incarcerated offenders. [Bruhn, 1971, 21] The point was to develop the societal sense of duty and to re-integrate him into the collective of the state. [Lieser-Trebnigg, 1985, 232] How the offender will conduct himself in the future (and how he can be helped in adopting correct behaviors) was at least of as much concern to the socialist court as was the question of what he has done.[120] Socialist law, then, was much more future-oriented than bourgeois law. The primary goal of the East German administration of justice was the prevention of future offenses. It aimed less at retribution and more at the rehabilitation, re-education, and reintegration of the offender. It was more interested in improving future conduct than in punishing past transgressions.

The GDR's sentencing process oriented itself at least as much on expectations about future deportment as on the facts of past wrongdoing. Indeed, it was an important obligation of the sentencing authorities to take into account the likely rehabilitation consequences of the different available penalties. Calls to further strengthen the future orientation of the administration of justice could be heard until the very end of the GDR. [Daehn, 1987, 53–55] As long as it did not encourage recidivism—and apparently it did not for the most—the extensive use of "educational measures" in the place of formal legal sanctions had a number of benefits. The offender had the immediate advantage of avoiding imprisonment and/or fines as well as the long-term advantage of not entering into the official police record. The state had the advantage of being able to devote fewer resources to its penal system.[121] [Lyon, 1969]

The GDR's rehabilitative approach should not be viewed as manifesting an indifference to crime or of a "coddling" of criminals. Certainly, the system did not respond kindly to failed re-educational efforts and recidivism. Lack of rehabilitative success was quickly interpreted as willful opposition to socialism and the GDR regime. When rehabilitation did not work, retribution was not long in returning to the administration of justice. Previous (and presumably non-recorded) educational measures then were viewed in the same light as prior criminal convictions. The consequences were more severe penalties and/or the denial of probation for repeat offenses even when formally these were *first* criminal convictions. [Schroeder, 1986: 339] East German sources were emphatic that crime must not be tolerated, and left no doubt that criminal sanctions remained important instruments in the fight against crime. [Heimberger, 1980, 127] Punishments, simply, were not the first or the only tool in this effort. Much of the GDR's massive "legal propaganda" was devoted to developing among its citizens an "intolerance for crime." But from the socialist perspective, even the most determined intolerance for lawbreaking did not require harsh punishments—at least not at the first transgression and not for "ordinary" offenses.

In general, criminal penalties in the GDR were not particularly severe. In addition, there was much use of probation and a variety of techniques of social diversion (some will be discussed in the context of the work of the social courts). As in all socialist countries, however, certain offenses did not benefit from the basic non-punitive orientation, particularly "political" and "economic" offenses. In fact, the penalties for these types of offenses were increased in 1979. [Gornig, 1987, 88–89] The criminal code of the GDR, for example, provided penalties from three years to life in prison, and even capital punishment, for such offenses as the intentional injury to the socialist order of state and society, and the intentional damage to the economy. See Paragraphs 102 and 103, Criminal Code of the GDR (*Strafgesetzbuch der Deutschen Demokratischen Republik*) of January 12, 1968. The maximum penalties were reserved, of course, for particularly grave cases. However, in June 1979, the penal code was changed, providing for increased penalties for "agitation against the state, establishing illegal contacts, public vilification." The law concerning "illegal contacts" with the West was extended to writers publishing anything in the West that was in any way critical of the GDR. [Childs, 1989, 13]

In general, however, GDR penalties tended to be less severe than those of many Western countries, particularly the United States. For example, East Germany abolished the death penalty in July 1987. [Buchholz, 1987b, 835; Heilmaier et al., 1988, 123] Furthermore, East Germany made extensive use of diversion alternatives and probation sentencing. [Streit, 1976, 73–77] The most remarkable aspect of GDR penology, however, was its unshakable optimism. [Mielke, 1966, 376–377] At a time when the United States and other Western countries abandoned rehabilitation and returned to retribution as the guiding principle, East Germany remained firmly committed to reforming the offender. GDR rehabilitation efforts were truly extraordinary. Socialist justice was committed very consistently to rehabilitation. In contrast, Western justice (particularly American) justice tends to swing like a pendulum between retribution and rehabilitation, depending on the most recent crime experiences and the party in power. They involved not only the various agencies of the GDR state, but societal and economic organizations as well, including the social courts.

Criminology and the "New Socialist Personality"

Marx and Engels were not interested in constructing a systematic criminology. This parallels their lack of interest in developing systematic and comprehensive theories of the law. These deficits are not accidental. They are the corollaries of certain key doctrines regarding socialist (and communist) societies: the increasing identity of all interests, steady increases in social harmony, and monumental reductions in the incidence of crime. To be sure, Marx did not predict the complete disappearance of criminal offenses and civil disputes in socialism—this would come about only with the arrival of communism. Nevertheless, there was a general expectation that the movement through the stages of socialist development would be associated with a substantial reduction in conflicts, disputes, and crimes. There would be ever fewer of these pathologies because the social conditions that brought them about would be ever more fully eliminated. It seems probable that Marx and Engels were uninterested in developing an adequate criminology, because they expected rather little crime even in the early stages of socialism. [Mayo, 1960, 240–241]

This was the key principle of GDR criminology: "The unity of socialist law and the people also serves as the foundation for the fact that *no one needs to become a lawbreaker in the socialist society.*" [Heuckendorf, 1981, 186; my emphasis; also see Buchholz, 1972, 8] East German criminology tended toward the "vulgar" branch of Marxism, including its exploitation theory of crime: all crimes (as all social pathologies) are generated by economic factors, that is, class differences. Popper [1963, 2:100–101] describes "vulgar Marxism" as follows:

> The average Vulgar Marxist believes that Marxism lays bare the sinister secrets of social life by revealing the hidden motives of greed and lust for material gain which actuate the powers behind the scenes of history; powers that cunningly and consciously create war, depression, unemployment, hunger in the midst of plenty, and all the other forms of social misery, in order to gratify their vile desires for profit." These views "have very little to do with . . . 'historical materialism'. [Marx did sometimes speak of] greed and the profit motive . . . but never in order to explain history. [They were the repercussions of the social-economic system] rather than moving forces of history."

Or, the same from a Marxist perspective:

We have to thank Marx, Engels, and Lenin for the fundamental discovery that crime is not a morbid degeneration of human beings, but a societal phenomenon. This is well proven scientific principle. It means that crime is not a constitutive element of all social systems. It is an integral component only of those social systems which are founded on class antagonism, exploitation of man by man, and the poverty and misery caused by the private ownership of the means of production. . . . Only the complete abolition of the private ownership of the means of production, that is, "the establishment of the classless, the communist society, will bring the complete abolition of crime. [Buchholz, 1972, 6]

Marxist economic determinism found a clear expression in its view of crime and capitalism: they were "twinbrothers," [Buchholz, 1972, 7; Harrland, 1956, 193] and criminality is the "lawful and inescapable product of capitalism." [Harrland, 1957, 207] There is the saying (already noted) that "crime has no cure under capitalism . . . and needs no cure under socialism." [Juviler, 1976, 16] Once classes had been abolished, there would remain no objective causes for criminal conduct.[122] "Since 1945, there has been a steady decline of criminality in the GDR. And it cannot be otherwise because the roots of crime were eliminated with the establishment of authority of the workers and farmers." [Schulz, 1957, 286]

Or rather, there would remain no (or few) objective *internal* causes for criminal conduct. Marxism, as all utopias, required and assumed full insulation from the outside influences and disturbances. [Dahrendorf, 1968b] The impossibility of complete insulation, especially for the GDR, gave officials a handy excuse for East German crime and delinquency (which were not inconsiderable): it was due to the pernicious and malignant influences of the West. The most important causes of crime were *external.*

Basically, all of the crimes in the GDR have their origin in the fight of the sinking capitalist world against the development of socialism in the GDR. . . . The most dangerous crimes . . . originate and are directed by the imperialists and their agents. . . . An additional source of crime in our country are the demoralizing influences of capitalism, largely originating in West Berlin and in West Germany . . . attempting to poison the minds of our people. . . . It is from these external sources that decay and corruption enter our state.[123] [Harrland, 1958, 207–209]

Juveniles, in particular, became susceptible to criminal conduct because of their visit to movie theaters in West Berlin,[124] where they saw "gangster movies." [Goerner, 1959, 177; also see Beyer, 1961, 83] Western radio and television, which could not be blocked by building a wall, also received their share of the blame for corrupting East German youth. [Case Report, 1960, 331]

There were some (minor) internal sources of crime, namely the former members of the bourgeoisie and the large landowners. These people were opponents of the new socialist order and sought to injure,[125] corrupt, and undermine it. [Goerner, 1959, 175, 178; Note, 1966b, 337] Crime was found in the GDR in those places where the "capitalist ideology still remains influential." [Beyer, 1960, 317] Here is another proclamation of the responsibility of the "class enemy" for crimes:

> Crime is a phenomenon that is alien to the nature of socialism; it is a remnant of the capitalist past. There are no compelling causes of crime in the GDR. The presently still active grounds for crime can be found in the direct influence of the class enemy and in the residues of the old bourgeois modes of thought and life—which, of course, constantly receive new nourishment through the efforts of the West German clerical-militarist regime.[126] In addition, there were some GDR citizens, who were not enemies of socialism, but who had not yet fully recognized their responsibilities toward society, and whose consciousness lagged behind the times. They were still under the influence of bourgeois thinking, i.e., egoism, ruthlessness, lack of self-control, neglect of duty, and alcoholism.[127] [Hiller, 1967, 230] These persons need education and help rather than harsh punishments. [Beyer, 1961, 80; also see Werkentin, 1995, 375]

This is a theme that had much currency ever since the founding of the USSR. Vyshinsky, [1951, 12] made use of it: The influence of old (capitalist, pre-socialist) "ways is seen in the fact that even now we have present in Soviet society a certain amount of criminality." In any case, regardless of the provenance of crime, the key instruments of GDR penology were "re-education" and "re-socialization." Reliance on these mechanisms followed logically from the (largely unacknowledged) failure of the basic premise of socialist criminology: the economic causality of crime—which would have called for *economic* remedies. The major recognized exceptions to the economic causality of crime were clinical insanity and subnormal intelligence. Either one prevented proper socialist socialization.[128] "In the German Democratic Republic the relations of capitalist exploitation have been eliminated, and the social and economic roots of crime thus very largely removed." [Ulbricht, 1963, 358] In any case, only "dialectical determinism correctly comprehends the relationship of causality and regularity" in law, as elsewhere. [Buchholz et al., 1974, 62]

Socialist criminology depended for its confirmation on the actualization of two miraculous expectations: the end of material scarcity and the development of a new type of human personality. Both were to be activated by the eradication of that prime cause of all exploitation, scarcity, misery, and crime: the private ownership of the means of production. Regarding the first expectation, reality clearly refused to affirm it. Even after practically all of the means of production had been placed into public ownership, scarcity persisted in the GDR—as did exploitation and misery and crime. Indeed, in many ways, these afflictions became worse. [Sperlich, 2006] Not surprisingly, it grew increasingly more difficult to attribute criminal conduct to economic causes. Deficiencies in the offender's socialist socialization (or subsequent damages to it) replaced economic explanations. The appropriate corrective measure was "resocialization." [Wolle, 2002, 21] However, with a new generation having grown up entirely within socialism, it became ever more difficult to blame misconduct on "bourgeois remnants." An important new cause was found in "corrupting Western influences," particularly Western styles of music and attire. [Sperlich, 2006, Chapter 7]—rock music being prominent among these.

"To each according to his needs" is a splendid sentiment, but it misreads reality.[129] It overlooks such important matters as the influence of the weather on harvests and commodity shipments, the effects of natural catastrophes and man-made accidents on industrial production, and the limited and finite nature of energy sources and raw materials. It also overlooks the strong tendency of "needs" to increase in step with growing satisfaction. And it ignores the strong disposition to value above all (and, perhaps, only) *that which is scarce*. If everyone received the Order of Lenin, the value of the award would be null. There must be scarcity of material and symbolic goods if these are to function as incentives for economic effort and political obedience—two forms of conduct greatly valued in socialist systems. Indeed, artificial scarcities might have to be created, should there ever be an end to the natural ones.

The second expectation also was disconfirmed.[130] Envy and greed and sloth and malice were found in the GDR as much as elsewhere. *There was no new socialist personality,* though praxis—the persistence of natural scarcity—demanded it even more than theory. Artificial scarcity also would have required the new personality. There never was, of course, a need to create artificial scarcities in the GDR. And the citizens of East Germany reacted to the many "natural" scarcities exactly as people in other types of system. Since shoes, tools, light bulbs, bricks, gasoline, and many other ordinary necessities could not be bought, they obtained them illegally. Petty theft, bartering, and "under-the-counter" trading were of epidemic proportions in the GDR, as they were in the other socialist countries.

If some individuals were made to do without scarce goods in order to preserve the ability of these entities to function as rewards for superior virtue and special efforts—to make, in other words, sure that society will indeed receive "from everyone according to his abilities"—then envy and greed must become unknown. If they are not eradicated, they will remain as causes of wrongdoing. And if life were to become so harmonious that there no longer would be real affronts and deliberate injuries, individuals might still seek revenge for *imagined* slights and insults—absent the new personality type. The new socialist personalities would appear to make fine citizens and desirable neighbors. Notwithstanding official claims, however, they were nowhere in sight in the GDR. The unrelenting governmental preaching and scolding, and the workloads of the regular and social courts made this quite evident.

It does seem fairly certain that East Germany had lower rates of serious crime than West Germany and other comparable countries. Exactly how much lower is difficult to determine, however. As noted elsewhere, GDR crime statistics were incomplete and unreliable. [Sagel-Grande, 1986, 279] A comparison of crime rates is complicated further by the lack of comparable definitions of crime as well as by the different extent of the criminalization of human behavior.[131] Countries such as the United States, with a fierce proclivity for criminalizing victimless conduct, will of necessity have higher rates of crime than less moralistic societies. The formal cause of crime, after all, *is* criminal law—which, of course, does not have to have secular origins. As Marx rightly remarked, the Catholic clergy "has created more crimes than forgiven sins." [Cain & Hunt, 1979, 189]

In a number of ways, the GDR was a leader in absolute and relative decriminalization. Acts formerly considered to be criminal offenses were removed from the criminal codes altogether. For example, the GDR abolished its laws against consensual adult homosexuality several years before West Germany reached this level of development.[132] [Heilmaier, 1988, 201; also see Nastola, 1999] This, however, should not be mistaken for a unqualified acceptance. Homosexual still merited special surveillance. [Muehlen, 2000, 157] In addition to de-criminalizing homosexuality, many former felonies were reduced to misdemeanors and many former misdemeanors were reclassified as simple public order offenses.[133] Most important, the socialist countries came to assign many forms of petty criminality to social courts and similar institutions.[134] Assigning cases to social courts is in itself a form of decriminalization. [Maier, 1974, 238; N. Wolfe, 1989, 72] It lowers the crime statistics of the country[135] and relieves the offender of the burden of a criminal record. Needless to say, the various ways of lowering crime rates in the GDR and other socialist countries make comparisons exceptionally difficult.

In spite of various forms of decriminalization and extensive data manipulation, the GDR continued to experience substantial quantities of crimes, misdemeanors, and civil disputes. Property offenses, public disorderliness, traffic violations, interpersonal altercations, and juvenile delinquency were particularly prominent among them. [Harrland, 1986a, 7] As noted, the persistently high levels of property offenses were particularly embarrassing to the regime. These should have been the very first to vanish in the developed socialist society that East Germany claimed to be. Equally embarrassing was the persistence of juvenile delinquency. The younger cohorts gave little evidence of the new socialist personality, in spite of having been raised in an exclusively socialist environment.[136] [Schroeder, 1983, 54] When GDR writers had to admit a "relatively high level of crime in the age group 14–15," the next sentence typically was: "The influence of the class enemy is obvious; especially influential in this are the Western media."[137] [Comment, 1967, 397] East German commentators, of course, proudly proclaimed that the GDR youth had entirely and comprehensively internalized the ideology and values of socialism. [Kirchhoefer & Neuner, 1988, 230]

To keep crime and delinquency rates from reaching yet higher levels, the GDR required extensive and intrusive police surveillance, much of it illegal, even by GDR codes. Gerig [1987, 5] reports that GDR citizens asked friends and relatives in the West not to write anymore because State Security read the letters and counted them as black marks against the recipients—even those letter having only the most innocuous content. The Constitution and the laws of the GDR, of course, guaranteed postal secrecy as well as other protections of the citizen's privacy. [Heilborn & Poppe, 1979, 105; Poppe, 1984, 169–171] Needless to say, here too practice and law did not correspond.

In addition, the GDR also required a tight net of neighborhood organizations, such as the Commissions for Safety and Order. Among the tasks of these Committees were "the prevention of dangers and disturbances by controlling whether the doors to all buildings have been locked at dusk . . . and whether all vehicles have been parked according to the regulations and have been locked." [Roesner, 1980, 225–226] Obviously, the efforts to make sure houses and cars are locked would not be required were there not significant risks of burglary and theft. The social courts, as will be seen, also were saddled with important public safety responsibilities. In any case, the "new socialist personality" remained largely invisible in the area of law as well as in the areas of work and social life. This should not come as a surprise, once it is realized that the "new socialist personality" most basically was yet another means to assure conformity and obedience. Socialist legality was one of the fundamentals "which made it possible for each individual to shape his life according to socialist principles, and to *develop his personality in accordance with the objective societal legitimate principles and conditions.*" (my emphasis) [Heilborn & Poppe, 1979, 92] To the degree that certain crime rates were comparatively low, much of it must be attributed to the effects of comprehensive surveillance[138] and considerably less to the development of new socialist personalities. It should be noted, however, that legal decisions and verdicts were closely adjusted to the perceived personality of the offender. Only in this way could one be sure that socialist justice was being wrought. [Heuer, 1986, 49, 81]

Public Participation

Citizen participation in the administration of justice was greatly valued in socialist legal theory: "The working people . . . exercise all state power, make and administer their own law." [Riemann, 1976, 9] While formal participation is not the same as real influence, East Germany, as the other socialist countries, did make extensive efforts to involve citizens in all phases of the legal process. In the GDR, as in the other socialist countries, extensive efforts were made to get citizens involved in all phases and aspects of the legal process.[139] Such involvement was regarded as absolutely necessary. [Heusinger, 1981a, 3–4; Ulbricht, 1970, 827] It is testimony to the seriousness with which citizen participation was regarded, that even the legal codes prominently and persistently spoke to this point,[140] that participation in the legal process was supported by a constitutional guarantee, and that a whole section of the constitution was devoted to stating the principles of citizen participation in the legal process and to providing guidelines for it.[141] To implement these participatory goals, great efforts were made to motivate citizens to participate, to develop a "socialist legal consciousness."[142] It should be noted that, unlike the conditions prevailing in the United States, the GDR made extensive efforts to educate and train citizen to be competent participants in the legal process. [Kern & Sarge, 1981, 290][143] It should also be noted that effective legal participation was thought to require political as well as professional-technical qualifications. [for example, Kern & Sarge, 1981, 290] The need for political competence, of course, is the direct product of the policy-nature of socialist law.

Ordinary citizens served not only as lay assessors (lay judges), but also as "social prosecutors," "social defenders,"[144] and representatives or special audiences drawn from the membership of the defendant's collective (Code of Criminal Procedure, 1968/1974: Section 3, Article 102 & Section 4, Article 197).[145] The citizens of the GDR also had the right and duty to participate in follow-up proceedings and in the rehabilitation of offenders. [Kern, 1982, 71; Posorski, 1982, 99] The latter most often took the form of a guarantee (*Bürgschaft*), whereby the perpetrator's collective would petition the court not to impose (or to set aside) a sentence of incarceration on the basis of the collective's pledge to ensure his re-socialization, re-education, and re-integration: (Code of Criminal Procedure, 1968/1974: Section 2, Article 57)

Among the guarantees also was the right of victims to participate actively in criminal proceedings. The victim had to be informed of the trial date: (Code of Criminal Procedure, 1968/1974: Section 1, Article 202.40) The victim had the right to request compensation for damages, the calling of specific witness and experts, the inclusion of specific types of evidence, to be informed about the court's decisions regarding these requests, and to file complaints in case of adverse decisions: (Code of Criminal Procedure, 1968/1974: Section 1, Articles 17.1, 198.1, 206.2).[146] The victim had the right to file complaints with the prosecutor regarding actions of the investigating agencies (police). The prosecutor was required to respond within five days: (Code of Criminal Procedure, 1968/1974: Section 1, Articles 91.1, 91.2). It should be noted that the office of the socialist public prosecutor was immensely more powerful than that of the Western equivalent, the district attorney. He was in effect the dominant legal authority in his territory, with the obligation to direct and oversee all law-related matters. As Vyshinsky [1948, 533] phrased it: "Supervision by the prosecutor's office is expressed, first of all, in seeing to it that not a single organ of authority, not a single state or social organization, either issues orders or puts into practice measures not in conformity with the law. It is obligated to protest each unlawful order or measure (as well as each unlawful court decision) upon its own initiative as well as upon complaint by citizens whose rights are thereby invaded." The prosecutor's authority even extended to civil cases. Again Vyshinsky [1948, 536–537]: "A special characteristic of the Soviet prosecutor's office in the sphere of court work is the extensive part taken by the prosecuting officer in civil proceedings. In capitalist countries its participation in civil proceedings is extremely limited. In the USSR, it has the right to initiate a civil court proceeding, or to intervene in one already begun, in all cases when the interests of the state or of the toilers so require." What was true of the USSR was equally true for the GDR.

The victim had the right to file a complaint against decisions of the trial court: (Code of Criminal Procedure, 1968/1974: Section 1, Article 305.2, 310.1). The victim had the right to be informed about any further court actions, such as cassation. And the victim, finally, had the right to participate in any appellate proceedings: (Code of Criminal Procedure, 1968/1974: Section 1, Article 292). According to GDR commentators, the victim's participation in all phases of the case served not only to safeguard his interests, but also to increase the effectiveness of criminal prosecutions. [Buchholz, 1987b, 22; Speck, 1990, 37] Unfortunately, the many rights and guarantees could be, and were, abrogated and nullified at any time at the Party's direction.

Civic participation, it should be noted, was substantially greater in the GDR and other socialist countries than it is in the liberal democracies. Nevertheless, low citizen interest and motivation are not the exclusive problems of the latter. Complaints about insufficient interest and participation could frequently be found in the socialist literature, leading to calls for more and better "legal propaganda."[147] [Christoph & Mollnau, 1981, 391; Heger, 1981, 196–198; and Opitz, 1980, 252] It is noteworthy that when a new edition of the civil code of the GDR appeared in 1975, two million copies were sold in the first year—in a population of about seventeen million. A Soviet expert reports that in a poll conducted by the Institute of State and Law, 80% of the respondents declared that they wanted to learn more about the current law. [Kudrjawzew, 1981, 460]

The citizens of the GDR had the right to participate and were asked to participate in the development of new legal codes,[148] in the discovery and investigation of crime, [Autorenkollektiv, 1978b, 231] in the conduct of adjudication, not only as lay judges, but also as societal prosecutors and defenders,[149] and special audiences and observers. [Autorenkollektiv, 1978b, 231–232] The citizens also were asked to participate in the follow-up of cases and the rehabilitation of offenders. [Kern, 1982, 71; and Posorski, 1982, 99] Citizens could participate in these various activities as individuals. More commonly, however, they participated as members of a collective or societal organization. [Autorenkollektiv, 1978b, 231–232; and Heimberger, 1980, 131–132] The life of the socialist citizen was a collective existence. There was very little room for purely private considerations. To ensure supervision and control, to bring help or impediments, praise or censure, were the responsibility of the individual's many collectives. [Hastrich, 1967, 97]

The increased assumption of responsibilities in the legal process on the part of collectives and societal organizations can be understood as manifestations of the shift of functions from state organs to societal organs. Regarding the reforms fostered by Khrushchev in the USSR, the interpretation was common that societal organs, such as comrades courts, "were now not only to assist regular law enforcement but even to begin supplanting it, as part of the gradual development of 'socialist statehood' into 'communist popular self-administration.'" [Juviler, 1976, 78; also see Brinkley, 1961, 623–625] The social courts of the GDR, as will be seen, existed for a variety of reasons and were said to have a number of virtues (most of them not very different from those asserted for trial by jury), but they also can be viewed from the perspective of societal progress towards communism. In the GDR they acquired a hybrid character, being simultaneously state and societal organs. They were established on a societal basis, but they also belonged to the uniform system of state courts of the GDR, with equal rights and responsibilities. The work of the social courts was based on the same principles as that of the other courts. [Kasper, 1980, 221] They were compatible, in any case, with the theory of a gradual shift of adjudication (and all other functions) from state to society.[150]

THE GDR: RECHTSSTAAT OR UNRECHTSSTAAT?

Initially, the East German socialist laid no claim to building a *Rechtsstaat,*[151] a state in which the rule of law is strictly followed and equally applied to everyone. It is, in other words, a state bound and limited by statutes promulgated by itself. It is a state bound by law *and* resting on a regime of legitimacy *and* possessing reasonably "just" laws.[152] The matter of legitimacy and just laws is important. Without it any dictatorial regime that strictly followed its own dictates would have to be considered a Rechtsstaat. This, presumably, was the point of the Minister of State Security (Stasi), Erich Mielke [1966, 376], when he declared that nobody could prove that they had ever acted illegally.[153] It appears that even in the West some agree, for example Professor Markovits, who would limit the concept of the Rechtsstaat to purely formal criteria. [DeNike, 1997, 42] It is quite astonishing to see repeated examples of Western scholars being unable to comprehend that an antifascist state *can also be* a totalitarian dictatorship.[154] In other words, the

Rechtsstaat is not only a matter of form and structures, but also of justice (*Gerechtigkeit*).[155] [Stahl as cited in Gneist, 1954, 33]

In December 1946, Karl Polak wrote an article advocating the elimination of the very concept of the Rechtsstaat.[156] He characterized the Rechtsstaat, including the concept of *Rechtssicherheit* (legal security), as a bourgeois notion, purely formal and empty of real meaning. He held that it was merely a "bombastic phrase," used by the bourgeoisie to secure its advantages and benefits and that it demonstrates a lack of understanding of the political function of law. Polak was the most influential (and Moscow-trained) jurist in East Germany at the time. [Heuer, 1989, 289–392] The SED followed his lead and eliminated the Rechtsstaat concept from the first GDR Constitution of 1949. [Sieveking, 1975, 42–47]

The anti-Rechtsstaat theories prevailed most strongly between 1945 and 1948. In the period from 1961 to 1968, the SED changed its mind,[157] [Sieveking, 1975, 126–129] partly to better meet the needs of the NEP [Heuer, 1965] and partly to placate a semi-mutinous people (the 1961 Berlin Wall). The SED Party Programme of 1963 termed the GDR the German Rechtsstaat. Indeed, the SED now discovered that only in a socialist democracy[158] is the Rechtsstaat even possible. [Sieveking, 1975 84] Or, as seen earlier: "justice is the realization of socialist humanism," [Buchholz, 1988, 357] and "the development of socialist democracy is closely connected to the methodical (*planmässige*) unfolding of the socialist Rechtsstaat." [Buchholz & Schulze, 1989, 476] At no time, however—early or late—was the GDR a Rechtsstaat, much less an improved one. [Fricke, 1995, 15]

The new claim of Rechtsstaat-GDR, of course, caused a great flurry of work among the legal theorists of East Germany.[159] As always, it was their role to provide the justification for the new line. Briefly, this is what they produced. The GDR is a (the) Rechtsstaat because it has historical legitimacy (the socialist transformation of society as historical necessity); it has legitimacy under international law because it faithfully implemented the Potsdam agreements; its law and its social life are just (because of the leading role of the working class); its state and laws are increasingly used as the instruments of social progress, the liberation of the creative energies of the people; its state and laws provide for the planned guidance of the people; its administration of laws involves the participation of all people; and, finally, it legally guarantees the rights and duties of the citizens. [Sieveking, 1975, 67–84] With the exception of the last item, it is difficult to see the relevance of this list. And the last item refers to "paper-guarantees," not to the legal practices of the GDR.

While the regime loudly proclaimed that it was a Rechtsstaat (indeed the only one on German soil), it was not truly happy with this claim. The Rechtsstaat has always included the principle that the citizen had rights vis-à-vis the state. Indeed, as late as 1985, one was able to read critiques of the Rechtsstaat concept because it construed rights against the state—not permissible, of course, under socialist legality. [Autorenkollektiv, 1985b, 154] In the GDR it was always possible to treat disagreeable citizen in wholly arbitrary and lawless ways because (given the lack of independence of the courts from the state) there was no institution that could protect the citizen against wrongdoings by the state. [Kleger, 1987, 16; Rottleuthner, 1994] As expressed by a GDR commentator: the state of the GDR worked so well "because of the uniformity, rather than division, of power in that country." [Toeplitz, 1971, 42–59] Others sought to claim that the GDR had a "better" judicial independence than the West. [Herrmann & Schuesseler, 1963] In fact, the judges were instructed as to decision verdict, and penalty. [Werkentin, 1999] "Socialist Justice" never was anything else but an instrument to achieve certain societal conditions; "just" was that which helped in this. [Renger, 1990, 14] Clearly, these are the attributes of an Unrechtsstaat.[160] And in principle, there was no case so objectively small and unimportant that the Party might not reach down and take the decision out of the court's hands. One could not know beforehand, whether one's case would attract the Party's attention.[161] It was, in the last analysis, a wholly arbitrary system, even if not each case was handle in an arbitrary manner. [Kraut, 1997; Laufs, 1998; J. Weber & Piazolo, eds., 1995] *The GDR exhibited elements both of the Rechtsstaat and its opposite; at balance, however, the system must be rated an Unrechtsstaat.*

NOTES

1. ROTTEN FOUNDATIONS: THE CONCEPTUAL BASIS OF THE MARXIST-LENINIST REGIMES OF EAST GERMANY AND OTHER COUNTRIES OF THE SOVIET BLOC. Praeger, 2002; and OPPRESSION AND SCARCITY: THE HISTORY AND INSTITUTIONAL STRUCTURE OF THE MARXIST-LENINIST GOVERNMENT OF EAST GERMANY AND SOME PERSPECTIVES ON LIFE IN A SOCIALIST SYSTEM. Praeger, 2006. The first volume dealt with the theoretical context, the second volume with the institutional and historical context of lay adjudication in the GDR and other socialist countries.

2. Grzybowski, 1962; Juviler, 1976; Kucherov, 1970.

3. However, there is no fully developed Marxist theory of the law or of the state. A step in this direction was taken by Lenin in his STATE AND REVOLUTION. [Cain and Hunt, 1979, xiii, 145–146] Stuchka's THE REVOLUTIONARY ROLE OF LAW AND STATE may also be counted as a first step toward a Marxist theory of law. [Stuchka, 1988, xv]

4. Collins, 1982, 9–16; Kelsen, 1955, 1–50; Reich, 1973; Tucker, 1961, 222–223.

5. However, equality under the law was an important principle of GDR legal theory. [Daehn, 1987, 53–55] It was actualized in practice, when the case had no political importance and when all of the parties were ordinary citizens. See also the comments on the *Rechtsstaat* at the end of this chapter.

6. For an analysis of class justice (bourgeois law) in the Weimar Republic from a Marxist perspective see Fraenkel, 1927, 40–45. Socialist law, however, is "a device to prevent the exploitation of man by man, a means of asserting the rightful equality of individuals, a weapon in the struggle for the triumph of the principle of economic equality among men . . ." [Vyshinsky, 1951, 1]

7. Since Lenin, Gorbachev was the first General Secretary who was a trained lawyer. [Schmidt, ed., 1990, 133] This might have been one of the reasons he did not scorn the rule of law, but advocated the Rechtsstaat for Russia, where nobody would be exempt from the rule of law. [Heuer, 1993, 469]

8. Kelsen, 1955, 51–61; Lenin, 1976; also Juviler, 1976, 18.

9. Also of interest are the efforts by M. A. Reisner who was strong advocate of "reliance on revolutionary legal consciousness" as the foundation of the new Soviet legal order. [Hazard, 1951, xxvi]

10. Crime with wither away just as the state will wither away—under the same conditions and for the same reasons. [Vyshinsky, 1948, 60; see also Cain & Hunt, 1979, 161–165]

11. As the experiences of the Soviet Union and the Peoples Republic of China show "the state and its legal apparatus does not wither; but rather it is the revolutionary forms and organs of popular participation which become hollow and ultimately bureaucratic." [Brady, 1982, 360] Schroeder [1981, 964] insists that there was no bureaucratism in the socialist administration of justice—because there was no social basis for it in the GDR. Wolf Biermann, on the other hand, coined the phrase "computer Stalinism" to describe the bureaucratic-technocratic state the GDR had become. [Holmes, 1981a, 126]

12. Beirne & Sharlet, 1980, 10–15; Cain & Hunt, 1979, 204; Kelsen, 1955, 89.

13. He recanted these views. In 1936, he characterized the idea that all law is bourgeois law as an error and as a "condescending attitude." It did not save him. [Redhead, 1982, 338; also see Sypnowich, 1990, 19–23]

14. "Pashukanis' work . . . represents a clear statement of the classical Marxist thesis that the political and juridical forms of capitalist relations of production will wither away in the phase of socialism, the transition period to the communist society that will no longer require them. "[Redhead, 1982, 337]

15. "Stalin, as General Secretary, in his address before the Central Committee Plenum of April 1929, warned against promoting hostile and antagonistic attitudes toward law." [Beirne & Sharlett, 1982, 321]

16. Hazard, 1951, xxiii; Kelsen, 1955, 67–71; Stuchka, 1988, 3–4, 7–21.

17. The initial attacks on Pashukanis originated with P. Yudin. [Kelsen, 1955, 112–115]

18. It is wonderfully ironic to find some 30 years later Vyshinsky's ideas described as "unmarxian and bourgeois." [Mollnau & Roeder, 1963, 580] In Haney's [1963, 124] language, the Stalin-Vyshinsky theory of law (including the notion of the increasingly sharp class conflict in socialism) was simply false. For a discussion of the damage done by Vyshinsky to Soviet jurisprudence see Tschchikwadse, 1989, 217–219.

19. The doctrines of Pashukanis and Stuchka have not gained a secure place in socialist legal thought. Their ideas have moved in and out of favor depending on the political exigencies of the day, that is, depending on the direction of the wind blowing from the Kremlin.

20. The notion of the state of the entire people was based on another one of the abundant socialist "dialectical unities," discussed in the two previous volumes (see note 1). According to Feldbrugge [1973, 639]: "The state . . . has become the state of the entire people and the ruling class is identical with the people itself." One wonders whether the people knew this.

21. The GDR was much given to the strong-state position, particularly in the interest of the "further constructing of socialism. [M. Benjamin & Loose, 1983, 3; Krenz, 1985, 688; Sorgenicht, 1969, 289; Sorgenicht & Weichelt, 1963, 47]

22. The dictatorship of the proletariat is authority unlimited by any statutes whatever. But it creates and makes use of laws and "demands that they be observed and punishes breach of them. [It] does not signify anarchy or disorder but, on the contrary, strict order and firm authority which operates upon strict principles, set out in the fundamental law of the proletarian state—the Soviet Constitution." [Vyshinsky, 1948, 48]

23. Marxism-Leninism puts "an end to the clerical-bourgeois notion of the state, and to the fiction that by nature it is superior to class and expresses and preserves the interests and the culture of all mankind alike. [Vyshinsky, 1948, 12]

24. Yet many formulations can be found that assert flatly that a just verdict is one that is in the interest of the working class.

25. The "people," however, turned out to be only that part of the population which identified with the goals of the Communist Party. [Sypnowich, 1990, 22]

26. As Erich Honecker [1984a] titled one of his books: "Working Class Power for the Welfare of All the People." In the GDR, so the GDR commentators, there is a unity of power and justice, and it is being used for the people, not against them. [Mollnau et al., 1976, 68] Unfortunately for the regime, the working class did not buy into this scenario. This became obvious in 1989; it could also be seen earlier in various ways, for example, the lack of working class support for the invasion of the CSSR in 1968. [Werkentin, 1995, 289]

27. It was said that it was possible in the GDR to give primary rank to the educational function of the law, rather than to the repressive one, because there was agreement (unity) of personal and societal interests. [Goehring & Drews, 1977, 185] In any case, there was a great concern to make legal proceedings a truly educational experience for all participants and the public at large. See, for example, Stiller, 1955.

28. Also see Greiger & Mueller, 1981, 160; Nasarow, 1980, 10. Of interest is also the statement by Weichelt [1979a, 93–94, 104] that *only* the working class is able to successfully fight for human rights. Therefore, the most basic human rights also have class character, at least as long as there are classes. For a classical negative view of class justice, see Fraenkel, 1927.

29. Contrary to socialism's claim, almost always practice determined theory, not the other way around. [Sperlich, 2002, Chapter 5]

30. For a detailed treatment of Lenin's theory of the state and of its "creative implementation" in the GDR, see Steding, 1987. Also see Kareva, 1965, 251.

31. Marxist economic determinism encompasses the criminological doctrine that "crime has no cure under capitalism . . . and needs no cure under socialism." [Juviler, 1976, 16] Whatever may be the truth of the first part of this statement, the second one is clearly contradicted by socialist experience, in the USSR, the GDR, and elsewhere. To

be fair, however, Marx and Engels were not altogether "vulgar Marxist." They accepted a "relative autonomy" of the superstructure (including law) and they went beyond the pure "class interest" view of the law. [Cain & Hunt, 1979, 50, 62, 147–151]

32. Lenin's support of the jury echoed Engels' position. [Cain & Hunt, 1979, 11, 36–37]

33. Bley & Mueller, 1979, 389; Juviler, 1976, 19, 28; Schuessler, 1980, 270.

34. As late as the end of 1989, socialist adherents still found comfort in Lenin's statement that "the teachings of Marx are all-powerful because they are true." [Opitz, 1989, 1002] A fine example of whistling in the graveyard.

35. The socialist legal order "signifies the stability of socialist social relationships and of socialist discipline, respect for the rules of socialist life, in common, respect and preservation inviolate of social, socialist property—the bases of the entire Soviet order, the observance of all Soviet laws." [Vyshinsky, 1948, 47] As Stalin pronounced in 1936 (at the period of the Great Purges): "We need stability of laws now more than ever." [as cited in Lipson, 1958, 22]

36. Poppe, 1985, 156; Sarge, 1988, 703; Schmollack 1989, 252.

37. This, seemingly, still was norm in the GDR of 1955, when Hilde Benjamin [as cited in Dettenborn, 1979, 260] declared that legal consciousness was not a matter of some general feeling for the law. Rather, legal consciousness must be rooted in class consciousness and must guide the decision of the judge. Even in the GDR of 1986, we can read that young judges and prosecutors, from day one, were educated by their socialist youth organization and by their party to perceive and conduct themselves as representatives of the working class. [Heuer, 1986, 42] Earlier, there were many complaints about the remnants of bourgeois ideas in GDR law. [e.g., Polak, 1961, 607; Weber, 1962, 376] Also, the Party admitted to having great worries about the socialist qualifications of GDR jurists. It demanded "absolute loyalty to socialism." [H. Benjamin, 1971, 559; Kittke, 1988, 363; also see Amos, 1996; Wentker, 2001, 461]

38. Friedrich [1969, 132] rightly remarks that "the appearance of additional legal rules and regulations ought not to be mistaken for the ineluctable harbingers of the advent of the rule of law."

39. The Bolsheviks had obtained only 175 of 707 seats—in an election conducted when the Bolsheviks already were in power—and had accepted these election results.

40. See, for example, Grzybowski, 1962; Juviler, 1976; Kucherov, 1970.

41. GDR authors, of course, claimed that in their country there could be no "resorting to utility in opposition to legality." [Bley & Mueller, 1979, 389]

42. The East German regime never wavered in its claim that the GDR had the more just and humane legal system, indeed, that the GDR was "the true German Rechtsstaat." [Toeplitz, 1966, 374] For a contrary documentation see Kroh, ed., 1988, 266–270.

43. This, notwithstanding the claim, that the elected parliament had the supreme power in the GDR. [Schuessler, 1979c, 93–94] The socialist regimes of the twentieth century (together with their fascist counterparts) hold the distinction of having resurrected divine kingship: the king ranking above the law.

44. Frenzke, 1977, 55; Grasemann, 1994, 38; Lieser-Trebnigg, 1985, 11; Maier, 1974, 239; Mampel, 1985, 63–65.

45. However, as the GDR prosecutor general [Streit, 1962, 758] told it: "The state protects the rights of the citizens." Yes, but even if this were true, what if, in some instance, it does not protect?

46. There are, of course, judges in Western countries who administer the law in a partisan fashion. However, in so doing they act against the spirit and purposes of the law, and are subject to sanctions. The partisan judges of the socialist countries, in contrast, act in conformity with the spirit and purposes of socialist law. In fact, after 1989 it became known that some judges were, in fact, Stasi agents (*informelle Mitarbeiter*). [Weinke, 2000, 155–160] On the general influence of the Stasi on matters of law, see Marxen, 1999.

47. Autorenkollektiv, 1978a, 225; Riemann, 1976, 11; Sperlich, 2006, Chapter 5.

48. Some remnants of the "class enemy" excepted—but these persons have no rights in any case. For a discussion of the thesis that the cause of criminality in the GDR was the continued presence of the "class enemy" or "class enemy infiltrations," see Herzog & Wagner, 1997, 74–75; Mahlmann, 2002, 151–160.

49. The regime never gave up the claim to have the authority to intervene in specific cases. [Werkentin, 1995, 280]

50. This, of course, applied only to those cases in which Party or state had an interest. I do not mean to imply that the outcome of every trial in the GDR was mandated by Party directives. [Arnold, 1995] Unfortunately, however, the regime was interested in a rather wide range of cases. [Armelin, 2000] It certainly included cases where the interests of an important functionary were affected. [Schroeder, 1986, 338] In any case, it is cold comfort to be told that the courts alone are "empowered to determine whether a person is guilty of a crime." [A. Sukharev, First Deputy Minister of Justice of the USSR, as cited in Novosti Press Agency, 1977, 51]

51. Since, in cases of state interest, the correct verdict is known before the trial, the trial itself is a sham. The proceedings, however, could serve important ritualistic and educational objectives.

52. The case of Max Fechner is instructive. This GDR minister of justice changed from perpetrator to victim. [Werkentin, 1995, 143–150]

53. It will be remembered here that some of the supporters of Richard Nixon asserted that an act (any act) becomes legal by the mere fact that the President ordered it. The difference is that in the United States such views are regarded as aberrant and, for the most part, do not prevail.

54. While this may not be the intent of socialism, it may be inevitable. "The Party," after all, is an abstraction, only its leaders are concrete entities, able to act and to command. In any case, this is in agreement with the legal traditions of Russia (except for some aspects of the judicial reforms of 1864), where the law was "largely the arbitrary work of an autocratic sovereign [who] was above the law." [David & Brierley, 1978, 153]

55. There were individuals in the GDR who had very substantial economic advantages, but these did not matter much in the courts—unless supplemented by political privilege.

56. For an official history of the beginnings of the GDR's legal system, see H. Benjamin, 1976. Also of interest are Arlt & Stiller, 1973; H. Benjamin 1960; H. Benjamin, 1969; Institut für die Theorie des Staates und des Rechts, 1984a

& 1984b; Jescheck, 1962; Kirchheimer, 1959; Mollnau & Schoeneburg, 1985; Reich & Reichel, 1975; Schuller, 1980; and Schoeneburg, 1973. For Western views see O. Schneider, 1988; and Mampel, 1966.

57. Cassation was the action by which an appellate court (generally the supreme court) could review and nullify a criminal case decision, the verdict of which has already become final (legally binding/*rechtskräftig*). The three grounds on which cassation could take place in the GDR were (1) the verdict violated the law, (2) the sentence was grossly mistaken, and (3) reasoning and rationale of the decision were incorrect: (Code of Criminal Procedure, 1968/1974: Section 1, Article 318, Section 6, Article 311). [Obserstes Gericht der DDR, 1970, 317; Janke, 1985, 322–323; Rosenthal, n.d., 86; Schroeder, 1986, 338; Wentker, 2001, 183–189, 462, 469] In fact, the instrument of cassation enabled the Party to change "politically defective" verdicts, even if they had already become legally binding. [Fricke, 1995, 14]

58. While the social courts were fully *lay* organs, the courts above them were all *mixed bench* institutions.

59. There also was a three-tiered courts of contract system, dealing with enterprise (not citizen) contract litigations. However, these courts were considered organs of economic administration not of the administration of justice. Accordingly, the contract courts were subordinated to the Council of Ministers (Ministerat) not the Supreme Court. [Lieser-Triebnigg, 1985, 13; Ludwig-Dodin, 2000]

60. The district courts also had equivalent chambers, here, however, called *Kammern*. [Autorenkollektiv, 1985a, 14]

61. The labor senate of the Supreme Court made use of lay assessors, but not the other senates.

62. For a discussion of the tasks of Supreme Court "in the building and completion of socialism in the GDR" see Oberstes Gericht der DDR, 1970, 14. Similarly, see the discussion of "the role of the Supreme Court in the strengthening and securing the power of the socialist state." [Toeplitz, 1974, 574]

63. A somewhat more extensive description can be found in the Code of the Constitution of the Courts § 37]

64. The legal theorists and administrators of the GDR were greatly concerned with the effectiveness of the law. This was an endless theme of publication, conferences, and international congresses—from the beginning to the end of the country. See, for example, the contributions in Mollnau, ed., 1977. For a small sample of the publications concerned with the effectiveness law and legal proceedings, see Bley, 1982; Buchholz, 1964; Buchholz, 1967; Buchholz, 1981; Buchholz & Mollnau, 1977; Funk, 1964; Heusinger, 1974; Hugot et al., 1971; Kermann et al., 1975; Krutzsch, 1959; Krutzsch & Hugot, 1958; Mueller & Lischke, 1976; Stiller, 1969; Streit, 1955a; Toeplitz, 1964; and Wendland, 1973.

65. The process of formal appeals against a court decision on the part of citizens was not well developed in the GDR. The supervision function of the higher courts, however, was very strong. This may have reflected the influence of Soviet law. [Valters, 1955]

66. Their social background was of great importance. The GDR literature reports that from 1974 to 1979, the backgrounds were as follows: workers, 72.3%; employees, 15.2%; collective farmers, 4.2%; intellectuals, 2.9%; other, 5.4%. [Heusinger, 1979b, 57]

67. I have pointed out elsewhere that "working class background" was an extremely flexible category, easily applied to intellectuals and high officials, when the Party needed to demonstrate its proletarian credentials. [Sperlich, 2006, Chapter 7]

68. Even changes in the administrative structure of the government needed to be justified as a "creative implementation of Lenin's state doctrine." [for example, Petzhold & Schuessler, 1972, 1840]

69. That the Party line must prevail over the law has been stated many times. It was asserted authoritatively by the leading Soviet jurist and Stalinist prosecutor Andrei Vyshinsky, who wrote in 1936 that in the case of a collision between the formal requirements of the law and Party policy, the law must yield. [Kucherov, 1970, 704]

70. It works in religion as well as in politics. For example, when speaking ex cathedra, popes have always been infallible, we are told. They just did not get around to telling this to the flock until 1870. A few Roman Catholics left the church as a consequence; the vast majority remained faithful.

71. For a discussion of the different interpretations of the "withering away" issue in socialist theory, see Grzybowski, 1962, 241–253. A discussion of Lenin's hostility toward the State (based more on Engels than Marx) can be found in D. Schroeder, 1967, 10.

72. Autorenkollektiv, 1984b; Autorenkollektiv, 1986a; Bartsch et al., 1981; Haney & Wagner, 1967; Kerimow, 1959; Reinhold, 1968; Schleifstein, 1982; Schuessler, 1974; Sorgenicht, 1982; Weichelt, 1979b; also see the various contributions in Harding, ed., 1984; and Schoeneburg, 1986, for historical treatments.

73. "State discipline" meant little more than rigorously and faithfully following the orders of the Party. [Kunz & Urban, 1971, 919] This, of course, was said to be in the interest of all citizens. [Autorenkollektiv, 1984a] Henrich's [1989] characterization is apt: the custodian state. Or, as it has also been said: to live in the GDR was as if to live under the control of an ill-tempered governess.

74. See, for example, Autorenkollektiv, 1978b, 222–227; Dettenborn & Schmidt, 1977, 147; Heger, 1981, 196; Kern, 1982, 70–72; Posorski, 1982, 95; Wittenberg, 1982, 12.

75. See, for example, Autorenkollektiv, 1978b, 31, 220; Daehn & Weber, 1981, 399; Haring, 1978, 107; Mollnau, 1988, 681.

76. It was necessary to say, of course, that the Soviet Union's superior legal scholarship had led the way toward these new discoveries and developments. A GDR legal scholar even found himself motivated to publicly regret that the reception of Soviet legal science in East Germany did not begin until the early 1950s when it should have begun in 1945. [Baranowski, 1987, 182]

77. The first contract law was promulgated in December of 1957. It was expanded and modernized in 1965, 1967, and 1982. [Pflicke, 1985, 5; Walter, 1979, 83]

78. It would be difficult to find anywhere in the Western literature the equivalents of the endless publications with titles such as these: "Socialist Law: Important Instrument in the Fulfillment of Production Tasks." [Haring, 1978, 107] "The Role of Socialist Law in the Development of the Economy of the GDR." [Walter, 1979, 79] "Law as Driving Force of Economic Growth." [Mollnau, 1983]

79. Lotze [1978, 446–449] distinguished six broad function of socialist law: organization of society, rules for society, direction of human conduct, protection of collectives and individuals, ideological education, and encouragement of socialist conduct.

80. Also see Slider [1986] about worker participation in enterprise decision-making in the USSR.

81. Autorenkollektiv, 1978a, 31, 220; Autorenkollektiv, 1985a, 11; Daehn & Weber, 1981, 399; Haring, 1978, 107; Kern, 1981, 138; Mampel: 1985: 61.

82. The primary purpose of socialist law "is not . . . to establish a rule of order by providing a principle for the solution of disputes. First and foremost it is a means of transforming and . . . guiding society towards the communist ideal . . ." [David & Brierley, 1978, 163]

83. For a detailed discussion of the interaction of law, economics, and social policy, see Heusinger, 1981a, 386.

84. Hundreds of books and thousands of articles were published in the GDR with titles such as "Law and the stimulation of scientific-technical achievements" [Dettenborn, 1986]; "Law as the causal force of economic growth" [Mollnau, 1983]; and "The task of the courts in supporting socialist housing-construction policies" [Note, 1987a].

85. Autorenkollektiv, 1978a, 222–227; Heger, 1981, 196; Kern, 1982, 70–72; Posorski, 1982, 95; Wittenberg, 1982, 12.

86. It is important to realize that civil dispute resolution was not a matter to see who prevailed. Rather plaintiff and defendant together were responsible for the restoration of social harmony. Socialist doctrine much preferred conciliation of the two parties to the victory of one. The key words for socialist dispute resolution were agreement and settlement (*Einigung*). [Kellner, 1978, 97; Oberstes Gericht der DDR, 1970, 267]

87. Thus, Kareva [1965, 251] can leave out adjudication from his list and write: the main function of the Soviet state and law include "economic, organizational, cultural, and educational activities."

88. For recent GDR statements on class conflict, private ownership of the means of production, and exploitation as the causes of crime, see Buchholz, 1974, 59; Daehn & Weber, 1981, 399; Opitz, 1980, 250; Riemann, 1976, 36–37. It was a long-standing claim that in the GDR there is no class antagonism and no exploitation. [Haney, 1967, 14]

89. In the last year of the GDR, there were more than 120,000 crimes, which is not inconsiderable for a population of about 17 million. Also, it must not be overlooked, that while the GDR had fewer crimes per capita than the FRG, imprisonment was two to three times that of the FRG. [Werkentin, 1995, 393]

90. For contrary data and views see Freiburg, 1975, 1076; Freiburg, 1984; Freiburg, 1985, 68; Friedrich-Ebert-Stiftung, 1977, 8; Schroeder, 1980 and the contributions to Helwig, ed., 1985. Some GDR authors were more cautious and merely called for the "stepwise eradication" of crime, now that there was a socialist economy. [Renneberg, 1963, 1595]

91. This in addition to the fact that the elections never were permitted to be free expressions of popular preferences in the first instance. See Sperlich, 2006, Chapter 4; also see Wolle, 1998, 307.

92. Whereby it should be noted that the imposition of capital punishment was not a legal decision (made by a court of law) but a political decision (made by the politburo of the SED). [Werkentin, 1995, 194]

93. Eppelmann, 1996, 196–200; Gatow, 1990, 204–209; also see Azrael, 1962, 10; Merkl, 1993, 59–60.

94. Since 1953—with a new law of 1980 [Schroder, 1980, 130]—most private attorneys had to be members of attorney-collectives that made controlling their "socialist working style" considerably easier. [Lorenz, 1998; Wolff, 1964, 17] The critique of the private attorneys in the first years of the GDR was that too many of them worked for the "imaginary interest" of the client and not for the interest of socialist society. [Eisenfeld, 1999; Wolff, 1979, 64–68]

95. In fact, a well-known criminal defense attorney was known to betray his clients to the State Security (Stasi). (It is unlikely that he was the only one.) From the socialist perspective, this is, of course, not in the least embarrassing. Thus, his conscience gave him no problems to actively participate in post-1989 German politics.

96. The GDR equivalent of the U.S. bar associations (*Vereinigung*) proudly proclaimed that all its members did the utmost to develop the socialist legal consciousness in themselves and in others, and to further the socialist societal and legal order. The *Vereinigung* takes its direction and instructions from the party of the working class and the socialist state. [Heinze & Kern, 1979, 149–150]

97. Maurach, n.d., 6–17; Rosenthal, n.d., 74–77; Vollnhals, 1994, 60; Zeng, 2000, 35.

98. Horstkotte, 1998; Immisch, 1997; Rottleuthner, 1994.

99. This was true not only for the judges, but also for the leaders of the administrative apparatus of the legal system. The GDR minister of justice from 1967 to 1972, Kurt Wünsche, for example, was a member of the Liberal-Democratic Party (LDPD). His tenure also coincided with the most intense legal terror inflicted on the East German population. Strangely, he was reappointed to his old post in the short-lived post-SED-regime Modrow government (1990). [Pätzold, 1991, 47]

100. There was no literature in the GDR (or other socialist countries) which examined court decisions in the light of basic legal principles and their own constitutional provisions. Law books and legal journals only infrequently published comments on the decisions of the East German appellate courts. When such comments did appear, they merely approved and applauded. [F. Schroeder: 1986: 340]

101. Not surprisingly, not much of the socialist theory of state and law has survived 1989. [Hohmann, 1995]

102. GDR authors typically describe bourgeois freedom" as but a cloak and pretense for class rule or for simple selfishness. [Klenner, 1983, 1055] Or as Weichelt [1979a, 98–100] has it elsewhere: the only freedom in bourgeois society is the freedom of the capitalists to exploit the workers. It follows that the only *real* freedom there is and can be, is the freedom from economic exploitation—the rest is details.

103. Only towards the very end of the GDR (with a law passed on December 14, 1988, and effective July 1, 1989) was there an attempt to re-introduce (rather limited but heavily controlled) administrative court procedures. [Arends, 1988, 283; Buchholz & Schulze, 1989, 478–480; Hoerschelmann, 1989, 109–110; Kittke & Lindheim, 1988, 364–365; Werkentin, 1995, 400–401; Wostry, 1989, 222] They had effectively been abolished in 1952, with attacks by Walter Ulbricht against the very concept of administrative law. [Westen, 1969, 370; Ziegler, 1974, 1037]

104. Autorenkollektiv, 1978a, 226; Lehmann & Pohl, 1986, 11; Markovits, 1978, 619–620; Ritter, 1971; Ritter, 1973; Sperlich, 2006, Chapter 4.

105. Harrland, 1986, 223; Kleinert, 1984, 393; Pohl & Schulze, 1979, 246; also see Sperlich, 2006, Chapter 4.

106. It was one of the more lunatic claims of the GDR that it was the true Rechtsstaat on German soil. This issue will be considered later.

107. See, for example, Seidel, 1981, 112; and Zschiedrich, 1981, 293–294.

108. For example, USSR: Kudrjawzew, 1981, 459; GDR: M. Benjamin, 1961, 35–51; Heimberger, 1980, 129; Streit, 1976, 70.

109. The Central Committee of the Communist Party declared at the 24th Party Congress that legal education and the fortification of socialist legality are not solely the task of the state agencies. The Party organizations, the labor unions, and the youth leagues also are obligated to do all they can to secure the strictest observance of the laws as well as to improve the education of all workers in the meaning (the ideas) of the legal order. Respect for the laws and justice must become part of the convictions of every person. [as cited in Mollnau, 1979, 335–336]

110. There was no area of human activity in the GDR that did not have a specific societal organization. All of them were official organs. Private organizations, with the partial exception of the churches, were not permitted. [Mand & Schulze, 1986]

111. Panorama DDR, 1976, 84; also see Barth & Schimansky, 1970; Bendrat, 1971; Heuer, 1986, 90, 110.

112. Comment, 1963a; Mueller & Lischke, 1976; Paul, 1963.

113. This needs, of course, some fine tuning in respect to the social situation of each citizen. Much, it seems, remained to be done. Over 50% of all labor disputes in the GDR had their origin in insufficient labor law knowledge of the administrators. [Mollnau, 1979, 356]

114. One wonders about the excessive exactness in some cases.

115. Low cost was a general characteristic of the GDR administration of justice. Litigation was either free of charge (for example, all labor disputes) or the fees were very modest. [Beyer, 1981, 77–83]

116. This, of course, is not incompatible with some legal regulations remaining unpublished, as was the case in the Soviet Union. [Ioffe & Maggs, 1983, 54]

117. Constitution, Articles 19–21; also see Buechner-Uhder, 1968; Klenner, 1978, 239; Moebis, 1984, 12–13; Poppe, 1980; Poppe, 1984.

118. For a small selection see Aretz & Stock, 1997; Arnold, 1995; Finn, 1981; Fricke, 1979; Friedrich, 1989; Fritzsch, 1994; Gatow, 1990; Grunenberg, 1990; Joas & Kohli, 1993; Klassmann & Wagner, 1993; Koehler, J.O., 1999; Lammich, 1980; Leonhard, 1990; Loeser, 1984; Maier, 1997; Menge, 1990; Mitter & Wolle, 1993; Pond, 1993; Przybylski, 1991; Rosenberg, 1995; Reissig & Glaessner, 1991; Schell & Kalinka, 1992; Villain, 1990; Weber, 1991; Weber, 1993.

119. Juristische Fakultät, 1963, 1846; also see H. Benjamin, 1956, 228; Bohndorf & Ratzel, 1969, 553; Haney, 1967, 7, 15; Schuessler, 117.

120. Buchholz & Dettenborn, 1980, 109; Daehn & Weber, 1981, 399; Juviler, 1976, 75; Streit, 1976, 20, 30; Weber, 1980a, 248.

121. Much of the rehabilitative and reintegrative work, it should be noted, was done by unpaid volunteers. [Zoch, 1964, 1399]

122. Benjamin, 1961, 71; Beyer, 1961, 80; Daehn & Weber, 1981, 399; Opitz, 1980, 250; Riemann, 1976, 36–37.

123. See also Ulricht, 1958, 27–28;

124. The district court of Königs Wusterhausen found that the juvenile culprits, who had committed a series of thefts, had come under the "pernicious influence of West Berlin movies and smut and trash literature. . . . The causes of the crimes, with-

out doubt, were visiting West Berlin movie theaters and reading Western smut." [Case Report, 1960, 330] The date is of interest. It will be remembered that the GDR built the "antifascist protection wall" in 1961. GDR propaganda declared that the wall had become necessary for a number of reason: imperialist aggression, sabotage, slave trade, and what not. The need to protect the purity of GDR youth from pernicious Western influences was simply another useful fable. In 1962, in any case, a Berlin county court found that the two defendants (rowdyism) would not have the offenses except that "West Berlin influences made them into brutal hooligans and practitioners of the American style of life." [Kern, 1962, 227] On the matter of the Berlin Wall also see Sperlich, 2006, Chapter 8.

125. The mayor of Hundisburg, Gertrud Mantwitz [1960, 310], was able to attribute her region's high cattle and hog mortality to the class enemy, who tried to keep the GDR from reaching its economic goals.

126. Beyer, 1961, 82; also see Beyer, 1966, 384; Heimberger, 1984, 277.

127. On the other hand, the GDR Council of State declared already in 1960 that "the remainders of capitalist egotistical thinking have now been overcome in the GDR." [Werkentin, 1995, 380]

128. M. Benjamin, 1962, 562–567; Hinderer, 1966, 11–12; Weber, 1964.

129. As was implicitly acknowledged in the GDR. The operating principle was *each according to his accomplishments*. This was given extensive justification under the title of socialist *Leistungsprincip* (merit system). [Heuer, 1986, 19–25] Its near identity with the capitalist reward system received no comment, however.

130. Disconfirmation does not necessarily lead to an abandonment of expectations and predictions. Indeed, there are many cases where disconfirmation produced a strengthening of faith in the prediction that had failed. [e.g., Festinger et al., 1964] Frequently these predictions are religious and regard the end of the world. Marxism fits the pattern.

131. Statements of this kind—a crime is what harms the interests of the working class; the only guide for our jurisprudence are the resolutions of the party of the working class—were not rare.

132. On the other hand, West Germany abolished the death penalty at the time of adopting its Constitution (Basic Law) in 1949 (Article 102). East Germany did not abolish the death penalty until 1987.

133. Similar reclassifications could be observed in the other socialist countries. Hiroshi Oda [1982, 189], for example, relates that in the 1970s in the Odessa province, between 40% and 70% of all minor criminal case were reclassified in this way.

134. Juviler, 1982, 153–154; Oda, 1982, 181, 186; Solomon, 1982, 123, 127.

135. Juviler [1982, 161] reports a tendency in at least some areas of the USSR "to lower criminal statistics by failing to initiate criminal cases or by improperly terminating them."

136. The same was observed in the USSR. [U.S. Department of State, 1953, 8]

137. It was particularly mortifying to the staunch dogma of the new socialist personality that more than 50% of juvenile misdeeds were property offenses. [Reuter, 1972, 85] Of the juvenile offenses, 32% were against "socialist property," 20% against personal property, 20% regarded unauthorized use of motor vehicles, 4% bodily injury, 3% fraud to the "disadvantage of Socialist property," and 21% unspecified (political?). Property offenses, thus, amount to 55% of the total, *not* counting the theft of motor vehicles. [Lungwitz, 1973, 22] Another report showed

the following figures regarding juvenile misdeeds: 40% were against "socialist property," 22% against personal property, 15.5% regarded unauthorized use of motor vehicles, 13% bodily injury, 5% damages to property, and 4.5% other. Property offenses accounted for 62% of all cases; 82.5% if property damages and vehicle taking are included. [Comment, 1976, 42]

138. And, as noted, large-scale decriminalization.

139. Socialist citizen participation was by no means limited to the legal sphere, but included all aspects of societal and political life. For an overview see Autorenkollektiv, 1978b, 35–50, 74–78; and Sperlich, 2006, Chapter 4. For a comprehensive listing of GDR societal organizations and discussions of their political, economic, and social functions, see Autorenkollektiv, 1980; and Friedrich-Ebert-Stiftung, 1987. However, much of official demands were unwelcome. "Pretending to participate" in such rituals as May Day demonstrations became a highly developed art in the GDR. [Wolle, 1998, 336] Social court participation was differently structured, of course, and few social court judges could merely "pretend."

140. For example: Civil Code (*Zivilgesetzbuch der DDR* of June 19, 1975): Preamble and Part 1, Chapter 1, Articles 1.2, 9.1, 9.2, 16. Code of Civil Procedure (*Zivilprozessordnung der DDR* of June 19, 1975): Section 1, Articles 1, 4.1, 4.2, 5.1, 5.2. Criminal Code (*Strafgesetzbuch der DDR* of January 12, 1968): Preamble and Chapter 1, Article 6. Code of Criminal Procedure (*Strafprozessordnung der DDR* of January 12, 1968): Section 1, Articles 2.1, 2.2, 4.1, 4.2, 4.3, 12, 18.1. Code of the Constitution of Courts (*Gerichtsverfassungsgesetz der DDR* of September 27, 1974): Chapter 1, Paragraph 9. Labor Code (*Arbeitsgesetzbuch der DDR* 1977): Preamble, Section 1, Articles 1.2, 8.1, 9.1, 13; Section 13, Article 256.3; Section 17, Article 296.3. Family Code (*Familiengesetzbuch der DDR* 1965/1975): Section 1, Article 4.1. Local Government Code (*Gesetz über die örtlichen Vorlksvertretungen in ihre Organe in der DDR* 1973): Preamble, Section 1, Articles 2.6, 3.2; Section 2, Article 10.3, 15.1.

141. Constitution (*Verfassung der DDR* of April 6, 1968): Section IV, Articles 87 and 90, Part 3. Several other provisions of the Constitution were devoted to the details and guidelines for the implementation of the participatory principle: for example, Section IV, Articles 94.2, 95, 96.2]

142. Socialist legal consciousness is the sum of legal knowledge, ideas, and feelings. The productive relations in society are the decisive factor in its development. It is a higher type of legal consciousness and socialist partisanship is its most basic component. [Nasarenko, 1974, 15–22, 36–39]

143. As I have shown elsewhere [Sperlich, 2006, Chapter 4], socialist participation is not identical with real political influence or power. Nonetheless, socialist commentator took the position that in capitalism the individual is merely a manipulated object, whereas in socialism he is a democratic co-ruler. [Haney, 1967, 26] In 1989, the democratic co-rulers made it quite clear that they did not wish to be manipulated, much to the shock of the Party official's. Of course, there had always been opposition in the GDR, no matter how fervently denied and no matter how fiercely suppressed. See, for example, Woods, 1986; also Sperlich, 2006.

144. Social prosecutors and social defenders were lay persons, usually chosen by the defendant's collective, to assist the official prosecutors and defense attorneys. The right and obligations of these "social participants" were detailed in *Strafprozessordnung der DDR* (Criminal Procedure), 1968/1974: Section 2, Articles 55, 56].

145. For discussions see Autorenkollektiv, 1978a, 231–232; Markovits, 1978, 623–625.

146. The prosecutor was obligated to inform the victim of these rights: (Code of Criminal Procedure, 1968/1974: Section 1, Articles 17.3, 206.1).

147. The German term is "*Rechtspropaganda.*" In East German and other socialist usage, "propaganda" did not have the negative connotation generally found in the West. In the GDR it meant to "enlighten and persuade" rather than to distort and deceive—which is not to say, of course, that duplicities were not part of the venture. For detailed discussions of the tasks and techniques of GDR legal propaganda, see Christoph & Mollnau, 1981, 391; Heger, 1981, 196–198; Opitz, 1980, 252; Markovits, 1978, 629–631. For legal propaganda in the USSR, see Juviler, 1976, 95. Great efforts, in any case, were made by Party and state officials to encourage citizens to become involved in the adjudicative process, in the drafting of statutes, and in other law-related activities. [Heintze, 1979, 286; Heuckendorf, 1981, 186; Riemann, 1976, 12, 38]

148. See Riemann, 1976, 12, 38, regarding popular participation in the development of the new civil and criminal codes of the GDR. Also see previously, as well as Heintze, 1979, 286; and Heuckendorf, 1981, 186. For a discussion of actual citizen influence in all that participation, see Sperlich, 2006, Chapter 4.

149. For the statutory basis of societal prosecutors and defenders, see Code of Criminal Procedure (*Strafprozessordnung der DDR* of January 12, 1968): Chapter 4, Paragraph 197.

150. As seen earlier, the withering away of the state in communism does not mean a disappearance of all state functions; it means that these functions will be exercised by "all the people." Compare Lenin, 1976, 125 et passim. For a discussion of the different phases in the socialist treatment of the "withering away" issue, see Grzybowski, 1962, 241–253. Laws and rules will remain under communism, but they will lose their political and legal character.

151. The term was introduced by Robert von Mohl in the mid-19th century. It lacked precision then, and it does now—which worked to the advantage of the GDR's Rechtsstaat claim.

152. The rulers of the GDR were well aware of their lack of legitimacy (as well as of the unpopularity of many of their laws), which explains the perpetual need for approval. This want of legitimacy (and of true legality), explains alike the rubber stamp parliaments, the plebiscites in which the only option was to say YES, the elections with no choice of whom to elect, and the fraudulent trials and confessions of those who are to be destroyed. Not only was there no right of opposition, of real choice, of control from below, but there was not even the right of abstention—not even the right of silence. As Stalin told it: "It may be said that silence is not criticism. But that is not true. The method of keeping silence, as a special method of ignoring things, is also a form of criticism." [Wolfe, 1961, 174–175] Totalitarian rulers demand from their subject not silence, as do autocratic rulers, but hymns of praise." [Curtis, 1969, 66–67]

153. Many of today's apologists for the GDR take the same position; since there was a constitution and since there were laws, the country was a Rechtsstaat. [e.g., Benser, 2000, 384–385] But as the exiled Wolf Biermann [2001, 51] rightly pointed out, the problem was not lack of laws; it was that the law was subject to Party policy.

154. The identity of democracy and anti-fascism was of course the GDR's party line to the very end. [Vietzke, 935–940] On the similarity of fascist and communist justice see Wentker, 2001, 573–605; Werkentin, 1995, 9–14. For a denial of com-

prehensive similarities between fascist and communist totalitarianism, see Fulbrook, 1995, 284–289.

155. An East German critique about reunification expresses (rightly or wrongly—and probably wrongly) the view of the purely formal nature of the Rechtsstaat: "We wanted justice (Recht) and we got the state of law (Rechtsstaat)." [Yoder, 1999, 83]

156. In this he was following Vyshinsky [1948, 20] who had tagged the concept of a Rechtsstaat as "narrow-minded, petty-bourgeois, sickly, sentimental, and banal."

157. Nevertheless, as late as 1961, justice minister Hilde Benjamin let it be known that the GDR had no need to pretend to be a Rechtsstaat. [Sieveking, 1975, 62] It was in 1963 at Fifth Party Congress of the SED that the concept of the Rechtsstaat was "rehabilitated." [Werkentin, 1995, 277] Of course, it quickly changed to "socialist legality," a supposedly superior form of the Rechtsstaat.

158. Of course, "socialist democracy" also is a better democracy because it is committed to do everything for the "welfare and happiness of the people." [Riemann, 1983, 978] Indeed, "socialist democracy" is a "higher form" of democracy. [Weichelt & Kintzel, 1981, 234]

159. It should be noted that at least since 1973 there has been a revaluation of law in GDR. [Mampel, 1985, 61] This resulted from the discovery (alluded to previously) that a modern state and a modern economy cannot function without some dependable legal rules. It should not be mistaken for a true commitment to a genuine Rechtsstaat. For one, the category of "political crimes" was significantly enlarged. [Fricke, 1995, 22–23; Zieger, 1986, 368]

160. Also see the analysis of Werkentin [1995, 395–404] on the same point. But there is less than full agreement: Kocka [1999, 23] is willing to concede that the GDR was a "totalitarian dictatorship," but still shies away from calling a "lawless" or "unjust" state, that is, an Unrechtsstaat. The same position has been taken by Fulbrook [1995, 21, 45, 85], who characterizes the GDR as a "police state" but not as an Unrechtsstaat. There seems to be no end of Western solicitude for the sensitivities of the former leaders of East Germany, who still manage to claim that the GDR was a Rechtsstaat. [Krenz, 1999, 41–43; Krenz, 2000, 14, 21] On the other hand, there are entrenched socialists like Bärbel Bohley, who was able to manufacture this ghastly sentence after the fall of the GDR: "We wanted justice, instead we got the Rechtsstaat. "[Mathiopoulos, 1994, 104; also see Mayer, 2002, 14, 48] Bohley, characteristically, refused even to speak with people who wanted to leave the GDR. [Muehlen, 2000, 185] These, of course, also are the people who categorized the revolution of 1989, as a "counter-revolution" that was directed by the West. [Natter, 1994, 13–31; Sabrow, 1999, 84; also see Dengler, 2000, 179] Of course, they still can spout force their nonsense in the context of a new political party, the PDS (Party of Democratic Socialism), which is the direct successor to the SED. [Koschyk & Weiss, 1996] Betts [2003, 192] rightly notes that the collapse of the GDR was a traumatic experience for the left of East and West, which they greeted with consternation.

161. The point is not that each litigation was influenced by arbitrary actions of a party functionary, but that it might. [Maier, 1974, 237] In any case, the citizens of the GDR were subject to a comprehensive and significant legal *insecurity*. [Bruce, 2003, 227–230]

Part II

The East German Social Courts and Lay Adjudication

Chapter 6

Historical Development

CONCEPTUAL BACKGROUND

Leninist Foundations

The social courts of East Germany were strongly and unequivocally based on Leninist principles.[1] It may be no more than a coincidence that the first GDR social court was founded in 1953,[2] the year of Stalin's death. It did, however, represent a turning away from Stalinist legal doctrine and a return to Leninist teachings.[3] Leninist legal doctrine required an extensive participation of non-jurists in the legal process, especially as lay judges (lay assessors) in the ordinary (state) courts. It also favored the creation of specific lay courts (comrade's courts) to adjudicate labor disputes and minor forms of law breaking. Lenin's views put greater emphasis on the *re-education* and *re-socialization* functions of the legal process than on its punitive functions. Finally, Lenin attached great importance to the *preventive* functions of the law as against the merely remedial ones. In all these respects, the GDR (that is, the SED) adhered very closely to Leninist principles. However, the social courts of the GDR were not simple carbon copies of the lay courts of the Soviet Union.[4] They differed considerably from the Soviet model.[5]

In the GDR, the right of the (lay) citizens to participate in various ways in the adjudicative process was given strong legal foundations.[6] It was guaranteed by the Constitution (1949: Article 130; 1968/74: Articles 87, 90 {3}, 94 {2}) and was restated in various codes (Criminal Code of 1968: Chapter 1, Article 6; Code of Criminal Procedures of 1968: §§ 2, 4; Code of the Constitution of the Courts of 1974: § 9; Civil Code of 1975: Part 1, Chapter 2, § 9; Code of Civil Procedure of 1975: §§ 4, 5; Labor Code of 1977: § 296 {3–4}). Regarding the social courts, participatory rights were also codified: Social Court Code of 1982: §§ 2, 3. It should be noted that the right of adjudicative participation was not merely a matter of code paragraphs. The government (the ruling party) of the GDR was genuinely interested in large-scale popular participation in the legal process, as in other societal processes. Unfortunately, most of this participation was only for show. Real citizen power and popular influence decidedly was not what was wanted. [Sperlich, 2006, Chapter 4] The East German social courts, however, were a certain exception to this. Its members had real power and influence—if, of course, at a rather low level of the system.

Participation of "Social Forces"

The key doctrine of GDR/SED legal thought was that the participation of of social forces—better: societal fores—(*Mitwirkung gesellschaftlicher Kräfte*) was indispensable, which, above all, meant the participation of *working classes* (workers and farmers). Only this participation could assure that the law would express the will and serve the interest of these classes,[7] and the establishment and furtherance of socialism. And the last point is the crucial one. Socialist law had many functions, but its primary role was always the advancement of socialism.[8] The most visible forms of participation of social forces in the legal process was the institution of the lay assessors (*Schöffen*) of the state courts and the office of the members of the social courts. But these two roles were not all.

The "social forces" (lay persons) were active in a number of other ways in the legal process. Many litigation proceedings saw a participation of "collectives' representatives" (*Vertreter gesellschaftlicher Kollektive*). Each year between 30,000 and 45,000 of such representatives participated in criminal cases. [Staatliche Zentralverwaltung für Statistik, 1987, 391] Their function was to help to clarify the nature of the act (crime), the personality of the perpetrator (especially his attitudes toward work and social obligations—in other words: was he a "good citizen"), and the extent of any damages caused. [Autorenkollektiv, 1985a, 71] Some cases also saw the participation of "social prosecutors" (*Gesellschaftliche Ankläger*) (between 5,000 and 8,000 per year) and "social defenders" (*Gesellschaftliche Verteidiger*) (between 1,000 and 3,000 per year). The function of both was much the same as that of the collectives' representatives, except that their role was to emphasize aggravating or mitigating factors, among which the collegial reputation of the defendant was of particular importance. [Hugot & Oehmke, 1983, 190–192; Michalski, 1979, 182] Finally, collectives (usually work collectives) could issue a "guarantee," a "surety" (*Bürgschaft*) for a convicted offender, guaranteeing, in fact, that the individual would not become a recidivist, but would be on his best behavior from now on. Each year between about 3,000 and 7,000 sureties were given. [Thiem, 1981, 130–131, Woelfel, 1983, 209–210] Additional data on social participants and "guaranties/sureties" will be found in Chapter 7.

HISTORY

Two Commission Types

There existed in the GDR two distinct types of social courts[9]: the *dispute commissions*[10] and the *arbitration commissions.*[11] By their official GDR designation, both social courts were *societal* organs. Yet, as emphasized strongly in the legal literature of the GDR, they were part of the uniform system of courts.[12] It is unclear what significance, if any, should be attributed to the fact that the social courts *collectively* were designated as "courts" (*Gerichte*), but *separately* as "commissions" (*Kommissionen*). It seems that the hybrid nature of the institutions affected the official name. The "court" appellation emphasized the membership in the uniform system of state courts; the "commission" appellation emphasized the societal nature of the institutions. The hybrid character of the societal courts was acknowledged by the GDR authorities. The chief judge of the East German supreme court used the phrasing of "two seemingly contradictory trends are merging into one entity." [Toeplitz, 1973, 5] Indeed, the regular courts had review, appeal, and quashing power for the decisions of the social court.[13] Professional judges had the right as well as the duty to direct the work of the societal courts and to train and assist the lay judges.[14] It seems optimal then to regard these organs as hybrid institutions, best understood, perhaps, in the context of the promised transfer of functions from state to society.[15] [Ulbricht, 1964a, 513; also see Brown, 1968, 14–15]

Both social courts had a variety of tasks in common. They also had some specialized tasks. Among the common tasks were the alleviation of disputes, providing legal advice, preventing crime and discord, mediation, arbitration, socialization and education (particularly of younger persons), and the adjudication of minor civil and criminal cases. [Ullmann, 1962, 246] As trial courts they formed the fourth and lowest rank in the court system of the GDR.[16]

The Dispute Commissions

The dispute commissions (hereafter, DC) were organized in 1953 on a work-place basis. Each firm with at least 50 workers formed its own commission. Several smaller firm could jointly form a commission. Large firms could have more than one commission. As a rule, each commission should embrace no more than 300 workers. The commissioners[17] were nominated by the labor union of the firm(s), after a discussion of candidates in a union membership meeting. The commissioners were elected by secret ballot by the membership. The term of office was two years, corresponding to term of office of the labor union officers. Each DC consisted of eight to fifteen commissioners. In firms with fewer than 100 workers the number of commissioners could be as low as six. Apart from industrial firms, DCs were also organized in agricultural collectives and in certain administrative associations.[18]

Other than membership in the organizing firm(s), the only formal requirement for election was being at least 18 years of age. There also were the requirements that the candidate had to be an "exemplary citizen" and had to have the "respect and confidence" of his/her colleagues—these, of course, were statements of principle rather than regulations that could be easily and uniformly implemented. The commissioners were responsible to their electors and had to report to them on a regular basis. [Hantsche, 1985, 25] They could be recalled by their electors. Re-election was permitted and, indeed, common. The commissioners had to resign if they changed their place of work.

The first dispute commission was established in April 1953 in Zwickau, Saxony. Formal DCs were preceded for a short time by unofficial workers' committees, which assumed adjudicative tasks in the factories. These committees exhibited strong syndicalist tendencies and were officially condemned as "false developments."[19] [Reiland, 1971, 60–62] The growth of the "official" social courts was rapid. In 1954 there existed already 5,682 DCs with 45,456 members. In that year they conducted 8,384 deliberations (*Beratungen*). [Heintze, 1978, 190] In the last full year (1988) of the DCs work, these figures were more than 28,000 commission, more than 255,000 members, and more than 16,000 formal deliberations.[20]

The Arbitration Commissions

The arbitration commissions (hereafter, AC) were first formed in 1963. By 1966 they were fully established. They were based, in part, on an earlier model, namely that of the old German tradition of the *Schiedsmänner* (community arbitrators), initially continued as such in the GDR.[21] The arbitration commissions were organized on a territorial (neighborhood) basis.[22] There were no specific regulations regarding the size of a residential area appropriate to form a commission, except that in its formation the proper number of residents (generally, no more than 8,000[23]) as well as reasonable distances and existing transportation conditions[24] were to be taken into account. Indeed, most cities had a large number of commissions within its boundaries. Given a population of about 17 1/2 million and about 5,500 commissions, mathematically, each AC would responsible for an area of about 3,000 persons. However, there existed considerable variations. Some AC territories had only 2,000 inhabitants [Kettner, 1984, 65], whereas others had a many as 14,000. [Ebner, 1980a, 114]

The AC commissioners were nominated by the political parties and mass organizations of the localities (by way of the National Front[25]); they were elected by the elected representatives of the localities (e.g., city council members). They AC commissioners were elected for the same time period as their electors held office (typically four or five years). The normal membership of the ACs was eight to fifteen commissioners. In exceptional circumstances the number of commissioners could be as low as six and as high as twenty. [In general see Decree regarding the Arbitration Commissions of the GDR of March 12, 1982 (hereafter "AC Decree").[26]

Arbitration commissions were also formed in the productive associations of farmers, gardeners, tradesmen (*Handwerker*) and fishermen.[27] The boards of directors of the productive associations nominated the candidates; the members elected the commissioners. As with the DCs, the commissioners were responsible to their electors and had to report to them on a regular basis. [Mueller, 1984a, 77] They could be recalled by their electors. Re-election were permitted.

Other than residence in the commission's territory or membership in the relevant productive association, the formal requirements for election were the same as for the DCs, as were the responsibility and recall provisions. Re-elections appear to have been frequent and multiple. In 1980, for example, when arbitration commissions had been in existence for seventeen years, there were frequent reports of "more than sixteen years of service" and "more than fifteen year of service" for AC commissioners. [Ebner, 1980a, 114; Note, 1980a, 254] Similar longevities of service appear to have prevailed among DC commissioners.

The first arbitration commissions, as noted, were established in 1963. Their formation was essentially completed by the end of 1966. The founding of the ACs reflected ten years of positive experience with the dispute commissions. By 1979 the arbitration commissions had grown to 5,237 commissions with about 55,000 commissioners, carrying out about 57,000 deliberations. [Heusinger, 1979b, 150; Kern, 1982, 69; also see Dokumentation, 1982, 130] During the the 1980s there were similar numbers. For example, the election of 1984 produced 5,552 commissions with 55,911 commissioners. In that year they carried out over 72,000 deliberations. [Note, 1984, 233]

THE POLITICAL BASIS

The social courts, as all institutions of socialist systems, were to be "transmission belts" of Marxist-Leninist party policy. As seen, the concept of "socialist legality" does not assign to the courts independent spheres of power. There was no, and there could not be, a separation of powers. The GDR was a thoroughly unitary system. Socialist legality did not incorporate the key element of the liberal *Rechtsstaat:* the protection of the citizen *against the state.* [Autorenkollektiv, 1978b, 225; Riemann, 1976, 11] Socialist legal theory is explicit: the administration of justice was not to be neutral but *partisan.* It had to serve the interest of the working class (that is to say, the interest of the communist party), not the securing of individual rights. All professional and lay judges were continuously instructed about their partisan obligations, and control was quite unrelenting.

To what extent did the members of the social courts conform to the demands for partisan justice; to what extent did they function as party-policy enforcing transmission belts? If my observations (and some parts of the literature) can be trusted, it was *not* to a very large degree. This was in part a function of the cases, most of which did not have significant political attributes. It also was function of the large number of cases, which made close control by superior agencies unfeasible. For the most, the deliberations of the commissioners did not seem to be policy-driven and partisan-tainted.

There was one aspect of the commissioners work that was more closely connected to socialist policies: the development of the "new socialist personality." The social courts were to serve an educational function: to mold good socialist citizens. The Social Courts Law [§ 3 {1}] specified as the purpose of these courts "strengthening the socialist state and the legal consciouness of the citizens, advancing the citizens' readiness to observe socialist law voluntarily, and to increase the citizens' intolerance of socially inappropriate behavior." Most commissioners, by my observations, identified with these goals—and they did so with touching faith and infinite patience, particularly visible in their treatment of juvenile offenders, which was generally gentle and almost infinitely patient.

Somewhat more questionable were the demands of party and state that the "nature" and the "personality" of the litigants should be reflected in the commission's decision, and that the decision should be "politically thought-out."[28] At the same time, however, there was a constant emphasis that a court's decision should not be based on subjective factors. Only fully established objective facts should lead to criminal convictions. Always ready to blow the own horn and to take a swipe at the class-enemy, GDR official depictions read as follows: "In the GDR it would be unthinkable for innocent people to be sentenced to lose their freedom for decades because of thin circumstantial evidence or unfounded testimonials, as is often the case in capitalist countries." [Riemann, 1976, 41] Similarly, Mollnau [1979, 259] contrast the objective jurisprudence of the GDR with the "feeling-jurisprudence" and "legal arbitrariness" of bourgeois law. It is entirely possible that in a case without any political bearing (and there were not many of those), even in the state courts, the above account was a correct description. In the low-level social courts, it seems that is was correct more often than not. But as a general portrayal of GDR criminal (or any) justice, it is pure fantasy. It is helpful, in this connection, to read the post-1989 accounts of the Stasi influence on the courts.[29] [Beyer, 1988, 153–156] I am not sure how seriously the commissioners took the partisan demand. I did not discover any cases in which the facts and the law were clearly on one side, but in which the other side—the better socialist—prevailed.[30] Even in this context, the formal deliberations and decisions of the social courts did not seem to be excessively partisan.

However, the social courts were not exempted *in principle* from serving as transmission belts. But they did have a measure of independence not available to the regular courts. This independence was not a matter of intention; it was the result of a practical problem. Comprehensive supervision was impossible. Party control of the regular courts was fairly easy. The number of civil and criminal cases to be tried in these courts was relatively small *and* practically all of the judges were subject to Party discipline. The work of the social courts was much more difficult to oversee and control. For one, there were about 300,000 social courts commissioners, conducting nearly 100,000 deliberations per annum. For another, the extent of Party membership among the social court commissioners was considerably less than among the judges of the regular courts. Thus, Party discipline was not as effective a tool to bring the social courts into conformity with the Party line. Finally, the social court cases lacked the importance of the cases of the ordinary courts: much less was at stake and much less control was needed. Within the sphere of minor cases, the social court commissioners possessed considerable more discretion and autonomy than the judges of the regular courts. The widespread and volitional support for the social courts among the GDR citizens may well be related to this (at least partial) independence from Party rule.

NOTES

1. It was impossible to find any general discussion of the social courts in the East German literature that did not evoke Lenin's teachings on socialist justice, for example, Goerner, 1979, 152; Heintze, 1978, 190; Kern, 1983, 226; Langer et al., 1984, 10–11; Seliger, 1978, 332.

2. In a way, however, this institution existed since 1945, when the Soviet enterprises in the GDR (e.g., the Wismut Corporation) made use of Soviet-style comrade's courts. [Heintze, 1978, 190]

3. Three broad periods can be discerned regarding Soviet lay adjudication: the "Leninist" (or revolutionary) period from 1917 to the early 1930s, with a variable but generally extensive use of lay courts and lay judges; the "Stalinist" period from the early 1930s to about the middle 1950s, with a return to state adjudication and a nearly complete abandonment of the social courts; and the "post-Stalinist" period since the mid-1950s, with a restoration of societal adjudication. [Juveler, 1976, Chapters 1–4; Kucherov, 1970, Chapters 1–10; Reiland, 1971, Chapters 1–3] For a discussion of Leninist and Stalinist legal doctrines see Chapter 5.

4. Beyer & Schmidt, 1960, 42; Schroeder, 1988, 1; Weiss, 1972, 266–268.

5. This comment of Feldbrugge [1973, 385] about the USSR apply equally to the GDR: ". . . the source of obedience to law in the Soviet Union is found in state coercion, on the one hand, and morality and social consciousness on the other, with first place now being assigned to morality and social consciousness while in an earlier time first place was assigned to state coercion."

6. See Benjamin, 1979, 197; Eser, 1970, Chapter 3; Heintze, 1978, 190; Reiland, 1971, Chapters 2–3; Seliger, 1978, 332.

7. Of course, except for some remnants of the "class enemy," all citizens of the GDR were supposed to have a common interest.

8. Which was by no means something that was concealed. Thousand of publications proudly proclaimed the invaluable assistance in the task of building the socialist state and society. See, for example, a GDR textbook: Autorenkollektiv, 1985c, 7–13.

9. The German term is *gesellschaftliche Gerichte*—in strict translation "societal courts." While there clearly is a difference between "social" and "societal," East German publications in English employed the translation "social courts." I adhere to this convention rather than introduce a new terminology.

10. The German term is *Konfliktkommissionen* (plural), which strictly translated should be rendered as "conflict commissions." Again, I adhere to the GDR convention.

11. The German term is *Schiedskommissionen* (plural).

12. Buchholz, 1980, 41; Eser, 1970, 38; Kasper, 1980, 221; Reiland, 1971, 96–103; Weiss, 1972, 272–273.

13. Brown, 1968, 21–22; Reiland, 1971, 151–154; Toeplitz, 1963, 25; Weiss, 1972, 273–274.

14. The key statutory provisions are: Social Courts Law, §§ 13, 22–27. Also see Kerst, 1962, 330; Knuesli, 1978, 90–91; Stricker, 1964, 56; Toeplitz, 1973, 14–15.

15. On the transfer of functions and the withering away of the state see Chapter 5.

16. For a discussion of the GDR courts see Chapter 5.

17. Another linguistic point: the term "courts" (*Gerichte*) was applied to both types of commissions (collectively). In German as in English usage, adjudicators operating in courts are called "judges" (*Richter*). The members of the social courts, however, were not identified as judges, but only as *members* (*Mitglieder*) of the courts. As noted earlier, when referred to in the singular, the social courts were termed "commissions" (*Kommissionen*). In English, the member of a commission may be called a "commissioner." Though this term did not appear in the GDR's English-language publications, I occasionally will make use of it to escape the awkwardness of repeated "member of" constructions. I will also occasionally use the term "social court judge," though this is not strictly accurate.

18. See Decree regarding the Dispute Commissions of the GDR of March 12, 1982 (hereafter "DC Decree"). Also see Hage, 2001; Heintze, 1978, 144; Riemann, 1976, 18.

19. As numerous examples throughout this book demonstrate, it was not permissible simply to follow the Party line (e.g., organizing workers adjudication), the venture also had to be firmly in Party control.

20. More numerical data will be found in Chapters 7, 8, and 9.

21. See, for example, Beyer, 1959a, 60–64; Beyer, 1959b, 228–232; Comment, 1963b, 7; Dillhoefer, 1954, 1; Morling, 1957, 50–51; Plenikowski, 1966, 373; Schoenfeldt, 2002.

22. Initially they functioned primarily as mediating agencies. [Barwinsky & Knecht, 1963, 347]

23. As noted earlier in the chapter, it was suggested that, ideally, ACs should serve between 6,000 and 8,000 residents. There were, however, substantial deviations.

For example, one AC reported 12,000 residents in its area. Also, several very small communities could join to form one common commission. This, of course, lessened its neighborhood character. There are reports that some commissions served as many as eleven different communities. [Kern, 1980, 246]

24. The rule was that the location of the commission should be easily accessible on foot or by public transportation. It should not require the use of private conveyances. [Gruenert, 1980, 35–36]

25. See Sperlich, 2006, Chapter 3; also see Panorama DDR, 1976, 68–69.

26. Also see Kern, 1982, 69; Langer, 1981, 257; Sahr, 1980, 11.

27. It appears that the residential ACs were more successful than those of the productive associations. [Plenikowski, 1966, 374]

28. See Hurlbeck & Koerner, 1985, 103; Peller, 1989, 226–227; Winkler & Matheus, 1983, 18–19. Also see Amboss, 1983a, 266; Koerner, 1987, 164, 176;

29. Arnold, 1995; Aretz & Stock, 1997; Baestlein, 2002; Beckert, 1995; Dennis, 2003; Fricke & Marquardt, 1995; Gatow, 1990; Gieseke, 2001; Haase, 2001; Henke et al., 1995; Kalinka, 1997; Koehler, 1999; Mertens & Voigt, 1998; Muehlen, 1995; Richter, 1996; Schwan, 1997; Suess, 1998; Suess, 1999; Schell & Kalinka, 1992.

30. However, the post-1989 literature contains endless examples of persons being more harshly judged and sentenced because of a "negative attitude toward our state." [Gatow, 1990, 176] In this connection, see also the discussion in Chapter 7 of the participation in a case of "societal forces."

Chapter 7

The Social Court Judges

GDR STATISTICS: ONCE AGAIN

This chapter and the next present a variety of numerical indicators regarding the work of the social courts and (to a lesser degree) the work of the lay assessors of the regular courts. As pointed out before (Chapter 2), GDR statistics are fearful to behold. There is a consistent lack of information about data sources, about the period of data collection, and other such matters, which makes it difficult to interpret the information. The presentation of data is sporadic rather than consistent. The reader will notice the many empty cells in the following tables. There are endless incongruities in the reporting. Sometimes the information for a full set of categories is presented (for example, the various types of offenses); sometimes the figures for only some of them are given. Further, sometimes absolute numbers are conveyed; sometimes percentages—but hardly ever both. Also, the percentages sometimes add to substantially more than 100%, no explanation given. Sometimes there are exact figures (say, 54, 290); sometimes there are approximations (more than 54,000). Needless to say, it often is difficult to gain a clear picture. Some of the reporting inconsistencies may be a matter of simple indifference, but a few of them might well be deliberate. Surely, the misreporting and (even) falsifying of data is a well-known socialist practice.[1] In the case of the social courts (and lay assessors), I suspect that most of the difficulties are due to indifference, carelessness, and incompetence rather than duplicity.

The information about the number of lay adjudicators, in my view, is fairly trustworthy, if only because it could be easily verified by the readers of DER SCHÖFFE and other publications. Most of these readers were members of a social court or were lay assessors and, thus, had direct knowledge of the membership figures at the local level. The various local numbers, of course, had to add to a reasonable total.

ELECTIONS

All judges in the GDR were elected, the professional and lay judges of the ordinary courts,[2] as well as the members of the social courts. The term of office corresponded to that of the electing body, usually five years.[3] The elective bodies were the popular assemblies of corresponding rank (corresponding territory). The judges of the Supreme Court, for example, were elected by the People's Chamber, the GDR national parliament. They were nominated by the Council of State, the collective Presidency of the GDR.[4] The judges of the lower courts were nominated by the minister of justice, in agreement with the territorial committees of the National Front.[5]

The members of the dispute commissions were nominated by the labor union of the firm after a discussion of candidates in a membership meeting.[6] There was only one labor union in the GDR, the Free German Labor Union (*Freier Deutscher Gewerkschaftsbund*). The formal requirements for the position were membership in the firm and being at least 18 years old. The informal requirements were being an "exemplary citizen" and having the "respect and confidence" of one's colleagues. The last two requirements, as noted earlier, were, of course, purely normative statements, difficult to define and enforce. The members of the dispute commissions were elected by their fellow-workers. The election proceeded by secret ballot, but usually there was only a single candidates list, with the number of candidates being equal to the number of positions to be filled.[7]

The judges were responsible to their constituents and could be recalled. They had to resign if they changed their place of work. The normal term of office was two years, corresponding to the term of office of the labor union officers. Re-elections were permitted (Law regarding the Social Courts of the GDR, §§ 4, 6, 7) and, in fact, frequent.

The judges of the territorial arbitration commissions were nominated by territorial committees of the National Front. The judges of the arbitration commissions of the productive association were nominated by the directors. Other than residence in the commission's territory (or membership in the productive association), the only formal elective requirement was a minimum age of eighteen years. The informal requirements were, again, "exemplary citizenship" and "respect of one's neighbors."

The judges of the arbitration commissions were elected by the members of the local representative assemblies (e.g., city councils).[8] The term of office of the judges corresponded to that of their electors, usually four years. [Heimberger & Sokolow, 1984, 232]. Change of residential territory required resigning the office; recall elections were also possible, Re-elections were permitted (Law regarding the Social Courts of the GDR, §§ 4, 6, 7) and, as with the dispute commissions, frequent.

It was suggested that each arbitration commission should serve between 6,000 and 8,000 residents [Sommer, 1980, 66]. There were, however, large deviations. A Leipzig commission, for example, reported 12,000 residents in its jurisdictional area [Scholz, 1982, 79]. The commission for Meuselwitz reported 14,000. [Ebner, 1978b, 163] On average, with a population of about 17.5 million and 5,787 commissions, the population base per commissions was about 3,000 people. It was also suggested that no one should have to travel more than five kilometers (three miles) to his arbitration commission. Only in the case of some very small communities (which had a common commission) was this distance limit exceeded. [Gruenert, 1980, 35] But the larger distances could be as large as twenty kilometers (twelve miles). [Kern, 1980, 246]

EDUCATION AND ASSISTANCE

From Lay Persons to Semi-Professionals

Lay assessors were employed in the state courts since 1945. The employment of "people's judges" and lay assessors took effect in the Soviet Zone of Occupation almost immediately after the defeat of the Third Reich and the comprehensive dismissal of all judges then in office. With the founding of the German Democratic Republic, new legislation formalized and expanded the legal participation of lay persons. [Riemann, 1976, 14–15] Particularly, it extended the initial criminal-case participation of the lay assessors to civil cases (1952). The next important steps came in 1953 (founding of the dispute commissions), 1963 (founding of the arbitration commissions), and 1982/83 (new laws expanding the competence of the social courts). [Ministerium der Justiz, 1989, 3–4.

From the very beginning, the GDR considered it extremely important that these lay persons received basic legal instruction. In fact, it would not be an exaggeration to say that the East German lay adjudicators were quickly and systematically turned into semi-professionals. The concern was that they would in fact be able to actuate the Leninist goal to serve as equals with the professional judges. Toward this end, for example, the lay assessors would read all case materials and participate in the various preparatory conferences regarding the case at hand. [e.g., Schramm, 1954, 30–31] "Nothing happens at court in which the lay assessors do not participate." [Hallervorden, 1954, 5] The equality of rights and duties of lay and professional judges was one of the key principles of East German jurisprudence. As the then minister of justice, Hilde Benjamin [1954, 1–2], stated it: "The workers in the factories also must be responsible functionaries in the offices of the state . . . The participation of the workers as lay assessors makes our courts to genuine courts of the might of the workers and farmers of our state . . . The participation of the lay assessors as equally empowered judges . . . is a manifestation of the democratic nature of our legal system."

The lay assessors served each year for twelve consecutive days. Whereas the work of the members of the social courts was done outside of normal working hours, the lay assessors participating in regular court sessions had to be available during their usual working times and free of usual work and social obligations. [Kleeis, 1955, 347] The enterprises had to exempt them from work, which they were generally not eager to do. For example, in Berlin alone, each year 4,000 workers had to be released from their regular work obligations to serve as lay assessors. [Probst, 1984, 73] There were many complaints about this. [e.g., Grass, 1954, 24–26] GDR officials did not have much sympathy for such complaints. However important economic production, lay adjudication (worker adjudication) was more important. [Grass, 1955, 43–45; Note, 1954, 29] Lenin would have been proud.

Important also was the formation of lay assessors collectives (*Schöffenkollektive*), which served to keep the lay assessors involved in and informed about legal matters beyond the twelve annual days of being at court.[9] It should also be noted that the lay assessors, just as the social court commissioners, had many obligations beyond participation in trials (deliberations).[10] They had to be available to colleagues and neighbors to answer legal questions. They also were asked to explain laws and regulations. And they had to give formal accounts of their activities to various entities. [Seidler, 1954, 20] Newly elected assessors were greeted with this motto: "Lay Assessors! Your efforts must be to educate all citizens to a conscientious and voluntary obedience of our laws." [Muehlberger, 1955, 289]

In the early 1950s, seminars were organized for lay assessors; formal lectures had been found to be unsatisfactory. [Walter, 1955, 14–18] Lectures had attracted only a few of the lay assessors.[11] Participation often was less than one-third. For example, only 17%of the lay assessors of the Suhl county court attended the lectures. Much pressure was brought to bear not only on the non-participants among the lay assessors, but also on the professional judges who presented the materials. They were directed to make their presentations more interesting and to hold them in easily accessible places. [Walter, 1955, 15–16]

In addition to lectures and seminars, DER SCHÖFFE regularly published instructional articles. For example, already in the journal's second volume, Lischak [1955, 105–109, 145–148, 271–277] contributed a detailed explanation of civil procedure in the GDR:[12] the opening of a civil case (especially the complaint); the preparations for the hearing; the hearing as such, with particular emphasis on the principles of orality (*Mündlichkeit,* firsthand presentation of evidence and witnesses (*Unmittelbarkeit*), and publicness of the proceedings (*Öffentlichkeit*); complete clarification of the facts of the case, with active participation of the judge (*Fragerecht*); efficacy (*zeitgemässer Abschluss*); the rules of evidence (*Beweisverfahren*), including eye witness testimony, documentary evidence, witness testimony, expert testimony, litigants' testimony; the question of the burden of proof; the verdict; and the possibilities of appeal (*Rechtsmittel*). In addition, it also included a discussion of a compromise (settlement) between the parties (*Vergleich*). Without patronizing the reader or condescending in any way, the writing was eminently intelligible the to non-jurist—one wishes our jurors were presented with equivalent materials.

Similar contributions could be found in most of the subsequent issues of DER SCHÖFFE. Considering only the contributions for two years, these discussions could be found: the statutes regarding the work of the public prosecutor (1956, 40–47), marriage and family law (1956, 79–85, 110–116; 1957, 102–104, 138–141), juvenile law (1956, 145–150), criminal penalties (1956, 173–179), the law of rentals and leases (1956, 208–214), the statutes of agricultural cooperatives (1956, 306–312), the law regarding the public reports of the courts (1957, 6–18), the law of evidence in criminal proceedings (1957, 38–44, 71–75), the law of inheritance and testaments (1957, 171–176, 212–215), public health law (1957, 238–245), and the law of separation and divorce (1957, 270–275). Subsequent issues of DER SCHÖFFE included a rich assortment of discussions of substantive and procedural law. I could not discover any helpful topic that was not discussed at one time or the other. The readings, as noted, were supplemented by lectures, seminars, and conferences, often dealing at about the same time with the same issues as the printed materials. The relevant journals—DER SCHÖFFE, ARBEIT UND ARBEITSRECHT, NEUE JUSTIZ—also reported regularly about cases that had been decided at the supreme court, the county courts, and the district courts. There is no doubt, the lay assessor who wanted to be informed about the law had many opportunities to become knowledgeable.

The Social Court Commissioners

As noted earlier, the members of the social courts saw service beginning in 1953 (dispute commissions) and 1963 (arbitration commissions). The social court members, of course, served independently of any professional jurists. Here the concern was not professional/lay equality, but rather that these courts would handle their litigation work in a truly proficient and lawful and socialist manner. The cases were to be decided not on the basis of the members sentiments[13] or "common sense," but strictly on the grounds of the principles and procedures of socialist law. Of course, the principles and procedures of socialist law are not inborn, but must be taught. Recognizing this, the GDR also made extensive efforts and expended substantial resources towards the training of the social court commissioners.

There were conferences (*Schulungen*) on a monthly basis. These conferences lasted for about ten hours. The participants received printed materials as well as lectures. As with the lay assessors, the conference topics included constitutional themes, explanations of various substantive laws, and instructions in procedural laws. [Pirntke, 1982, 370] Most important for the social courts were matters of procedure, particularly, of course, the procedures that the social courts were to follow. This became particularly important when the new social court laws became effective on January 1, 1983, and the competence of these courts was greatly increased. The key task at that time was to have the commissioners understand the new regulations and apply them correctly in practice. Towards this end numerous special meetings were held in all localities of the GDR. Many organizations and agencies participated in the preparatory efforts. For example, in Merseburg (just one of more than 200 districts) the participants included the director and the judges of the district court, the public prosecutor, members of the people's police, members of the city council, officials of the labor union, officials of the National Front, and local first secretary of the SED. Together with the 75 chairpersons of the local social courts, there were about 200 person attending the meeting. [Steffens, 1982, 416–417] If attendance in the other districts was similar—and most likely it was because of the direction from above—there were 40,000 persons involved in the local meetings to update the social courts late in 1982 and early in 1983.[14] Clearly, the GDR spared no efforts and exertions to make the social courts effective instruments of justice.

The plans for the regular conferences (*Schulungen*) were published in DER SCHÖFFE well ahead of time, so that the participants could properly prepare themselves. Here are some examples: These were the monthly topics for the year 1981 for the dispute commission conferences: the resolution of disputes regarding the year-end bonus;[15] the entitlements of workers under the enterprise collective contract (*Betriebskollektivvertrag*); the meaning of certain agreements in the work contract; the duties of the worker deriving from the work contract; content and purpose of the enterprise work regulation; the temporary assignment to an other type of work; the duties of the enterprise in ending an employment relationship; the solution of wage disputes, particularly of worker's claims against the enterprise; deliberations regarding misdemeanors; the obligations and activities of the dispute commission beyond formal deliberations. [Note, 1981, 28]

For the same year, these were the topics for the arbitration commissions (all page references are to volume 28 of DER SCHÖFFE): criminal penalties in traffic-law violations (21–27); the protection of the right of inventors and innovators (42–46); the deliberation regarding simple civil disputes (80–83): the compromise (settlement) in simple civil disputes (100–108a); the observance of socialist work discipline (194–197); the preventive work of the commissions beyond the formal deliberations (224–225); the contributions of service agents toward the satisfaction of the material and cultural needs of the citizens (240–256a); the prevention of law-breaking and the reeducation of law-breakers (265–270). In addition to these formal conference topics, volume 28 of DER SCHÖFFE also contained many other educational articles. Some examples are: new regulations regarding private attorneys (31–34); the legal education of juveniles (76–77); school truancy offenses (98–100); material responsibility in cases of management/administrative derelictions (133–135); the unlawful trade in precious metals (153–157); the calculation of support payments (182–183); the interest of under-age children in family actions (202); the concept of bodily harm in insurance law and in relation to claims for damages (226–227); insults and slander (247–249); the necessity of exact proofs of responsibility in criminal convictions (277–278); the necessary carefulness in the acceptance of checks in commercial transactions (296–297). The explanations and instructions found in these articles generally were short and to the point, but they were by no means simple-minded. To master the materials required a good mind and serious attentiveness. The East German officials never tired to point out that it was part of a commissioners (and lay assessors) professional and citizen duty to pay earnest attention to the educational texts and meetings. In turn, the East German government spent significant resources to staff the meetings and to produce the texts.

Finally, each issue of DER SCHÖFFE included a substantial number of case discussion. The cases were drawn from the social courts, the regular state courts, and even the GDR supreme court. These discussions had the purpose to instruct the readers about the proper application of the laws, from a procedural as well as substantive perspective. Frequently they pointed to errors social and lower state courts had made. They also congratulated those courts who done a first-rate job, both in their deliberations and in their efforts at crime prevention and securing socialist legality. It was a major concern of the discussion to convey the notion that cases should not be treated "schematically," but should be approached in a "differentiated" fashion. Once again, the East German officials made extraordinary exertions to educate in the law the lay assessors and social court commissioners. It was Leninism, of course, but it was very serious and professionally oriented Leninism. As expressed earlier, at the levels of the social courts and the state district courts—at least as far as their typical cases went—it does make sense to speak of *Rechtsstaat* features in GDR jurisprudence.

Never Alone

A great variety of state agencies and societal organizations were under constant pressure to aid the social courts in all ways possible. [Kern, 1984, 303] "To aid," of course, had the usual socialist double meaning: to assist *and* to control. The assist and control functions were not equally distributed. Some agencies were primarily oriented toward control (e.g., the office of the public prosecutor); the primary function of others was to assist (e.g., the in-house attorneys of the enterprises). [Haring & Langer, 1987, 89–90;

Maus, 1987, 38] None, however, had exclusively one function or the other. No citizens of the GDR ever was entirely alone—or was permitted to be. In whatever situation he found himself, there would be persons or organizations to assist and remedy. This principle can now be taken to a higher level. Not only were individuals embedded in a comprehensive framework of aid and control, but so were organization—of which the social courts are a case in point.

These were the primary institutions responsible to aid and control the work of the social courts: the local district courts; these also served as courts of appeal for social court decision, but their responsibilities were far greater than that;[16] the office of the public prosecutor, which had to examine all transfers of cases to the social courts whether they were correct and properly prepared, and which had to inspect all social court decisions regarding their conformity to the law (however, according to the official guidelines: "all forms of conduct must be avoided if they could give the impression that the social courts are being patronized") [Harrland, 1984, 39];[17] the city councils (or equivalent), which were to assist the social courts in the enforcement of socialist legality and in the education of the members;[18] the local offices of the National Front, which were expected to coordinate their "legal propaganda" efforts with the arbitration commissions, and to assist the commissions in matters of education, in the sharing of experiences, and to advise the commissions about the societal effectiveness of their decisions;[19] the legal committees of the labor unions, which had the duties to assist in the education of the dispute commission members, and to make sure that the commissions' decisions were in conformity with the law;[20] the workplace and residential collectives, which were to assist the dispute and arbitration commissions (respectively) in the enforcement of socialist legality in their territories [Grieger & Müller, 1981, 161]; the in-house attorneys (Justitiare) of the enterprises, who, among other obligations, were asked to ensure that the applications for dispute commission deliberations meet all legal requirements, as well as to assist in the education of commission members. [Haring & Radeck, 1983, 142; Lieser, 1989, 47–48] At each district court there was, furthermore, a special committee to assist the arbitration commissions (*Schiedskommissionsbeiräte*) whose tasks were to ensure that the decisions of the arbitration commissions were fully in conformity with the law, to warrant the legality of case transfers to the commissions, to make sure that the decisions of the commissions had the greatest social effectiveness, to increase the collective nature of the commissions' work, to make sure that the commissions were properly guided by the judges of the district court, and to ensure the fitting level of cooperation of the commissions with such organs as the city council and the National Front.[21] The work of the various assistance and control agencies was not left to personal initiative, but was explicitly specified in the appropriate legal codes, particularly: Law of the Social Courts of the GDR of 1982, §§ 22–32; Dispute Commission

Law of 1982, §§ 62–66; Arbitration Commission Law of 1982, §§ 58–61. It is quite clear that the social courts operated within a rather tight net of aid and control. There did not seem to be any particular resentment on the part of the social court members about this control. My impression is that the control functions appeared heavier on paper than they were in practice, and that the assistance functions were welcome indeed.

NUMBERS

Lay Assessors and Both Commissions: All GDR

Table 7.1 presents the number of lay assessors in the ordinary courts and the number of members of the social courts for most years of the GDR. The number of the lay assessors is provided for context and in order to fully illuminate the vast frequencies of lay persons participating in GDR adjudication. For the same reason the numbers for the other "social participants" in the deliberations of the social courts are provided later (Table 7.5).

As Table 7.1 shows, lay participation ranged from about 200,000 to about 300,00 social court members[22] and from 45,000 to 60,000 lay assessors per year—with a considerable increase in the very last years. The numbers could be quite substantial even for single jurisdictions. For example, in 1971 the county court (*Bezirksgericht*) of Schwerin had 1,878 lay assessors. [Winkler, 1971, 145] It also shows that there were about five times as many dispute commissions as arbitration commissions. The last decade saw a particularly heavy increase in lay assessors, from about 52,000 in 1980 to more than 59,000 in 1989. The reason for this is not clear. There were, in any case, more than four times as many dispute commission members as arbitration commissioners.

Both Commissions: Regional

Table 7.2 provides the information for both commissions for particular locations. It can be seen that there was considerable variation among the localities in respect to number of commissions and commissioners (which was largely a function of the size of the localities), and that these numbers tended to increase over time (which was largely a function of new arbitration commissions being organized).

The number of dispute commissions was a function of the size of the enterprise, a quantity not easily obtained. The number of arbitration commissions was a function of the population of the area, generally known. As seen in Table 7.1, the GDR, in 1989, had 5,787 arbitration commissions and a population of about 16,600,000. This means one arbitration commission per 2,765 citizens (including children). Regionally, however, there was much variation. Here are some examples (number of citizens per

Table 7.1. GDR Lay Assessors, Commissioners, and Commissions

Year	Number of Lay Assessors	Number of Arbitration Commission Members	Number of Arbitration Commissions	Number of Dispute Commission Members	Number of Dispute Commissions
1954	50,000+				
1963	55,000			190,000+	18,900
1965	45,000			160,928	
1966		55,533	5,620		
1967	49,600	55,000		190,000	
1968		56,000	5,291	190,000	21,318
1969	50,000				
1970	46,643*	55,502	5,267		
1971	47,000		[AC + DC 250,000 members]		
1974	48,104*	53,448		200,000	
1976	50,219**				
1976				217,209	24,654
1978		54,000+	5,124		
1979	49,700	54,290	5,237		
1980	52,000+	54,000+			
1982				233,365	26,282
1983			5,200		26,700
1984	50,857	55,911	5,552	250,567	27,831
1985				250,567	27,831
1987			5,552		
1987				255,000+	28,500+
1988		56,000+	5,500		
1989	59,440	56,917	5,787		

* Lay assessors of the district courts only.
** Of which 48,104 worked at the district courts, 2,069 at the county courts, and 46 at the labor senate of the supreme court.
The Data Sources are: 1954 [Benjamin, 1954, 2], 1963 [Kamin & Winkler, [1963, 51], 1965 [Hantsche, 1965, 369], 1966 [Winkler & Goerner, 1967, 204], 1967 [Hiller, 1967, 232], 1968 [Winkler & Goerner, 1968, 250–251], 1969 [Wuensche, 1969, 309], 1970 [Keil, 1970, 217], 1971 [Comment, 1971, 65], 1974 [Kern, 1975, 1], 1976 [Hantsche, 1977, 13 and Note, 1977, 245], 1978 [Note, 1978b, 95], 1979 [Note, 1979, 201], 1980 [Heusinger, 1981a, 3], 1982 [Hantsche, 1985, 200], 1983 [Comment, 1984b, 7], 1984 [Kern, 1984, 301 and Sahr, 1985, 272], 1985 [Hantsche, 1985, 200], 1987 [Matheus & Brueckner, 1987, 214 and Kaiser, 1987, 160], 1988 [Heusinger, 1988, 111], 1989 [Note, 1989a, 122 and Note, 1989b, 111].

Table 7.2. Commissioners and Commissions by Locations

Year	Location	Number of Arbitration Commission Members	Number of Arbitration Commissions	Number of Dispute Commission Members	Number of Dispute Commissions
1963	Halle				2,470
1964	Magdeburg	1,650	147		
1965	Halle				2,566
1966	Magdeburg	1,916	194		
1968	Berlin	1,200	93		
1971	Schwerin	3,496	379	5,750	696
1972	Halle			24,220	2,739
1974	Magdeburg	4,700	461		
1978	Mahlow		1		
1979	Dresden–Nord		18		
1982	Potsdam		452		
1983	Greiz	232	24		
1984	Cottbus		270		
1987	Rostock	3,000+		12,000+	
1989	Berlin	1,771	166		

Data Sources: 1963 & 1965 [Comment, 1973, 277], 1964 [Winkler & Jaenchen, 1965, 118], 1966 [Comment, 1966b, 173], 1968 [Probst, 1968, 106], 1971 [Heuckendorf & Kruse, 1972, 51], 1972 & 1974 [Comment, 1975b, 188], 1979 [Ebner, 1980b, 67], 1982 [Kermann, 1983, 81], 1983 [Comment, 1984c, 139], 1984 [Keil, 1985b, 132–137], 1987 [Kersten, 1988, 120], 1989 [Ziegler, 1989, 173].

commission; the figures are approximate): Berlin: 10,000 [Probst, 1983, 146]; Bad Tennstedt: 3,300 [Moritz, 1985, 227]; Dresden: 4,500 [Schoene, 1980a, 273]; Eisenhüttenstadt: 20,000 [Jacoby, 1985, 182]; Kröslin: 2000+ [Conradt, 1979, 116]; Leipzig-Süd: 12,000 [Scholz, 1982, 79]; Magdeburg-Süd: 21,000 [Ebner, 1978a, 90]; Naunhof: 5,665 [Zeidler, 1984, 39]; Plessa: 4,170 [Mertzig, 1985, 157]; Weisswasser: 4,957 [Kapp, 1985, 139]. In other words, there was a range from about 2,000 about 20,00—a factor of ten.

The social courts handled a very substantial proportion of the law suits in the GDR. Already in the 1960s, between 55 and 70% of minor criminal cases (mostly resulting from problems joint residency, particularly insults) were taken care of by the arbitration commissions. [Probst, 1968, 107; Winkler & Goerner, 1967, 205–206]

Even more impressive is the fact that from the 1960s to the very end of the GDR 90% and more of all labor law cases found their final determination in the dispute commissions.[23] This is particularly noteworthy as the total number of labor case increased in the later year of the GDR. For example, labor litigations increased 37.5% between 1978 and 1983. [Breitkopf, 1985, 117]

Here are some specific final determination figures for labor cases:

1954: 86% [Goerner & Sokolow, 1983, 77];
1979: 85% [Heusinger, 1981a, 2];
1983: 93% [Heusinger, 1984b, 4].

Two things need to be remembered at this point: (1) deciding particular cases was but one aspect of the duties of the social court commissioners and the lay assessors, and (2) in addition to working as lay adjudicators, they frequently participated in a variety of activities not directly related to the law. These are the numbers of members for the following organizations (not all the participatory organization are listed here) for the year 1978:

parents committees in the schools 700,000,
national front 300,000,
elected representatives 200,000,
worker and farmer inspection 200,000, and
people's solidarity (helpers of the Volkssolidarität) 130,000. [Note, 1978a, 91]

The figures for later years were even larger. East German citizens' social and political participation was truly phenomenal. Of course, there was some pressure to participate; it was the mark of a "good citizen." If participation was not entirely and fully voluntary, my interviews generated the impression that, to a large degree, it was it was genuinely voluntary—a point to be revisited when considering the participation in the arbitration commissions (later).

Dispute Commissions: GDR and Some Regions

There also are data that give the total number of dispute commissions and commissioners exclusively. They are presented in Table 7.3. There is some overlap to Table 7.1, but a substantial part is different.[24]

Arbitration Commissions: GDR and Some Regions

A similar data set is available for the arbitration commissions. The figures are given in Table 7.4.

Table 7.3. Dispute Commissions Data: GDR and Regional

Locations	Year	Number of Commissions	Number of Commissioners	Sources
GDR	1954	5,682	45,456	Heimberger,* 1984, 181
GDR	1961	14,728	116,000	Heimberger,* 1984, 212
GDR	1963	15,700	140,000	Heimberger,* 1984, 212
GDR	1965	21,000	188,000	Heimberger,* 1984, 212
GDR	1967	21,000	188,000	Goerner, 1983,** 78
GDR	1978	25,358	225,600	Heusinger, 1978, 158
GDR	1979	25,358	225,623	Winkler, 1980, 3
GDR	1982	26,085		Kern, 1982, 69
GDR	1982	26,282	233,365	Hantsche, 1985, 203
GDR	1984	26,744	237,821	STAT.JB.,*** 1985, 403
GDR	1985	27,831	250,567	Hantsche, 1985, 203
Grimma	1983	114		Comment, 1983, 202
Leipzig, SW	1983	154		Comment, 1983, 202
Poessneck	1985	102	895	Seiffert, 1985, 164

* Heimberger & Sokolow.
** Goerner & Sokolow.
*** STATISTISCHES JAHRBUCH DER DDR.

The legal minimum membership for an arbitration commission was six. As can be seen in Table 7.4, most commissions were well above the minimum, though some were rather close to the minimum:[25] Teichwolfsramsdorf (eight), and Rostock and Schwerin (nine). The preferred population base for an arbitration commission was 6,000 persons. As seen, for the GDR as a whole (1984) the average figure was slightly more than 10,000, but the regional figures varied considerably. Dresden, Rostock, Schwerin, and Suhl stand out because these are the figures for whole counties (*Bezirke*).

In general, then, it appears that the East German officials had no difficulty is staffing the thousands of arbitration commissions (and dispute commissions), in spite of the considerable burden imposed on the commissioners. In terms of the desired population/commission ratio, it would have been an advantage to a few more commissions—which might have been formed in future years, had the GDR lasted. It is unlikely, in any case, the deficit in commissions was attributable to having not enough citizen volunteers. More likely, the deficit was attributable to geographic-logistical circumstances.

Table 7.4. Arbitration Commissions Data: GDR and Regional

Locations	Year	Number of: Commissions	Number of: Commissioners	Sources
GDR	1966	5,600	55,000	Goerner, 1983, 78
GDR	1977	5,124	54,000	Note, 1978**, 95
GDR	1979	5,237	55,000	Heusinger, 1979**, 150*
GDR	1984	5,552	55,911	Note, 1984, 233**
Bad Doberan	1984	1	20	Lindau, 1985, 84
Berlin	1979	113	1,604	Probst, 1980, 192
Boizenburg	1984	3	36	Zecher, 1985, 152
Brück	1981	1	18	Ebner, 1981, 220
Calbe	1984	2	28	Zunder, 1985, 109
Crivitz	1982	1	12	Lienshoeft, 1982, 18
Dresden	1979	395	4,214	Schoene, 1980**, 273
Eisenhüttenstadt	1984	1	20	Jacoby, 1985, 182
Falkenberg	1984	1	16	Kunze, 1985, 208
Hellerau	1979	1	16	Ebner, 1980**, 67
Heringsdorf	1978	1	12	Schober, 1979, 120
Kirchberg	1980	1	12	Gruenert, 1980, 36
Leipzig Süd	1982	1	15	Scholz,1982, 79
Magdeburg Süd	1978	1	13	Ebner, 1978*, 90
Meuselwitz	1978	1	15	Ebner, 1978**, 164
Putbus	1984	1	16	Parthen, 1985, 69
Radebeul II	1964	1	12	Stuebner, 1980, 279
Rosslau I	1965	1	15	Zander, 1978, 66
Rostock	1984	360	3,323	Kersten, 1985, 42
Schwerin	1978	356	3,220	Heuckendorf, 1978, 190
Suhl	1983	174	1,840	Koch, 1983, 179
Teichwolframsdorf	1983	1	8	Kettner, 1984, 65
Torgelow	1983	1	16	Scheffler, 1984, 20
Weisswasser	1984	7	68	Kapp, 1985, 139
Wittenburg	1984	1	12	Pietz, 1985, 154

* also Kern, 1982, 69; Note, 1982a, 130.
** also STATISTISCHES JAHRBUCH DER DDR, 403.

Other Societal Court Participants

As noted earlier (Chapter 6), in addition to the commissioners, a number of other lay persons participated in the deliberations in a number of ways, particularly as social prosecutors, social defenders, representatives of the accused person's collective(s),[26] and as someone guaranteeing the accused person's future good behavior (*Bürgschaft*). Some data are available.[27] What Table 7.5 shows quite clearly is the heavy involvement of each citizen's collectives in his/her life, including litigation episodes. The social prosecutors and social defenders, without a doubt, also were delegated by a collective to participate in the deliberations. For better or worse, the GDR

Table 7.5. Societal Participation in the Social Courts

Year	Representatives of Collectives	Social Prosecutors	Social Defenders	Collective Guarantee Provisions
1964	36,550	5,589	2,492	3,794
1965	35,786	5,368	2,788	3,231
1966	39,903	8,487	3,146	2,764
1967	39,127	8,147	2,550	2,911
1968	35,679	7,803	2,208	3,161
1969	36,965	8,490	2,704	4,538
1970–74*	38,635	7,120	2,130	3,472
1975	38,478	6,245	2,027	3,921
1976	36,360	5,178	1,831	4,595
1977	36,611	5,618	1,871	5,895
1978	42,678	6,765	1,935	6,147
1979	43,894	8,557	1,912	5,800
1980	42,290	7,422	1,556	5,421
1981	40,925	6,450	1,505	6,289
1982	39,008	5,696	1,250	5,825
1983	39,126	4,642	1,198	5,679
1984	37,821	3,756	1,229	5,694
1985	34,665	3,353	1,095	5,850
1986	33,087	2,906	914	5,587

* annual average

Data Sources: STATISTISCHES JAHRBUCH DER DDR, Vols. 17–32; Hiller, 1967, 232. Earlier figures are not available. The data refer to all criminal cases heard in the state courts, regardless of verdict.

citizen was never alone. A solitary existence was not thinkable inside the socialist realm.

The data for the social prosecutors and the social defenders show a fairly steep decline, whereas the data for the representatives first rise and then decline again. The collective guarantees (*Bürgschaften*), however, increase over the years. There are no official explanations. One might speculate that enterprise co-workers were asked to do too much, as regards appearances at court hearings, and a certain resistance set in. The collective guarantees,

Table 7.6. Societal Participation in the Social Courts

Year	Total Criminal Offenses	As Percent of Criminal Offenses			
		Representatives of Collectives	Social Prosecutors	Social Defenders	Collective Guarantee Provisions
1964	138,350	26.4	4.0	1.8	2.7
1965	128,661	27.8	4.2	2.2	2.5
1966	124,524	32.0	6.8	2.5	2.2
1967	116,080	33.7	7.0	2.2	2.5
1968	100,126	35.6	7.8	2.2	3.2
1969	105,869	34.9	8.0	2.6	4.3
1970–74*	126,961	30.4	5.6	1.7	2.7
1975	117,994	32.6	5.3	1.7	3.3
1976	124,678	29.1	4.2	1.5	3.7
1977	116,170	31.5	4.8	1.6	5.1
1978	126,620	33.7	5.3	1.5	4.9
1979	129,099	34.0	6.6	1.5	4.5
1980	129,270	32.7	5.7	1.2	4.2
1981	122,221	33.4	5.3	1.2	5.1
1982	120,275	32.4	4.7	1.0	4.8
1983	122,656	31.9	3.8	1.0	4.6
1984	119,125	31.7	3.2	1.0	4.8
1985	113,363	30.6	3.0	1.0	5.2
1986	110,768	29.8	2.6	.8	5.0

* annual average

Data Source: STATISTISCHES JAHRBUCH DER DDR, Vols. 17–32. Earlier figures are not available. The data refer to all criminal cases heard in the state courts, regardless of verdict.

issued on behalf of a culpable co-worker, did not require appearing at court and, thus, were a lesser effort.

Table 7.6 provides some data. While generally skeptical of GDR crime statistics, I nevertheless divided the number of social prosecutor, social defenders, and collective guarantees into the overall number of criminal offenses published in the Statistical Yearbooks. The resulting percentages support the "too much" explanation. The figures for the social prosecutors and social defenders show a steep decline, especially after 1981. From the high point (1969) to the last year, both lose about two-thirds of their participation rates. The collective guarantees, by contrast, show increased rates, both in the 1969-last year comparison, and in the general earlier years (1964–1976) to later years (1977–1986) comparison. The participation of Representatives of the Collectives, however, does not fit the pattern. Such participation also required attending court hearings, yet a general decline cannot be discerned. There is some fluctuation, but the lowest figure (1964) is still three-fourths of the highest figures (1968), and there is no dramatic decline in the last years. Perhaps being a Representative was not as demanding as being a Prosecutor or Defender.

In any case, the participation of the societal delegates could have an important impact on the case. Courts were obligated to give serious consideration to their views. Particularly in the case of the representatives of the collectives, these views, it is likely, were not limited to matters of fact or, even, personality, but also included reflections on accused's social circumstances and conduct. Similarly, the decision of the collective to have a social prosecutor *or* a social defender participate in the proceedings, could serious influence the decisions of the court. [Speck, 1990, 144–145, 214–215]

RE-ELECTIONS AND LENGTH OF SERVICE

Many commissioners held office for long periods of time, with frequent re-elections. In 1980, for example, when arbitration commissions had been in existence for 17 years, many judges reported serving for periods of 15, 16, and 17 years—a matter of great pride to the GDR[28] Similar longevity of service prevails among the judges of the dispute commissions.[29]

In 1984, there were reports of continuous service since 1968 (Kettner, 1984, 66) and that one-half of the members of, for example, the Finsterwalde II commission "have been part of it for 20 years." (Barth, 1984, 20) As cited in Table 7.2, the following re-election rates were also reported: GDR 1985: 68 percent; Bad Doberan: 55 percent; Rostock: 72% Re-elections, of course, were permitted (Law regarding the Social Courts of the GDR, §§ 5–6) and they tended to be frequent and multiple.

MULTIPLE OFFICES AND POSITIONS

GDR commissioners tended to be busy persons. The duties of this office, which were plentiful, did not reduce the regular work obligations.

Commission work had to be discharged after regular working hours and on weekends. Not surprisingly, retired persons tend to be somewhat overrepresented as members of the social courts (as they were in other volunteer organizations). This was a matter of some concern. Accordingly, as will be seen shortly, the official reports generally listed the proportion of younger members, without supplying the same information for the older age cohorts.

The commissioners also performed many other honorary functions in party, state, and societal organizations. Reports about specific arbitration commissions noted with obvious pride that some of the judges also served as lay assessors (Schöffen) in the regular courts,[30] as members of representative assemblies,[31] as activists of the National Front, as officers of societal and cultural organizations, and, even, as members of dispute commissions.[32]

DEMOGRAPHICS

Women were strongly represented among the lay adjudicators. The elections of 1984 gave to women 47.3% of the social court memberships and 52.9% of the lay assessor positions on the mixed benches of the state courts. [Note, 1984, 233] In 1984, there also were elected 704 professional judges of the district and county courts; 51% were women and 56% were under the age of forty-one. [Note, 1979, 201] A different report gives these percentages as 55% and 60%. [Note, 1984, 233] It was of great importance to the East German officials that there would be many women, workers, and young people in the adjudicative positions.

Occasional, if unsystematic, demographic information was available for the lay adjudicators. In these reports, of course, the East German writers emphasized in particular the high proportion of workers[33] and women. As noted earlier, it was also a matter of concern to show high participation among the younger age cohorts. Again, for the discrepancy for the two 1984 workers percentages, I have no explanation; they come, of course, from different sources.

As seen in Table 7.7, women could be found among the lay assessors roughly in proportion to their share of the population.[34] Workers did less well. The rate for re-election was consistently high.

As can be seen in Table 7.8, in the last years women increased their participation roughly to the population proportion. Workers and the younger age cohorts have been doing less well in the arbitration commissions than in lay assessor category.

There is also some demographic information for the arbitration commissions of particular localities. Table 7.9 also shows that in the last years women increased their participation roughly to the population proportion. And again, workers and the younger age cohorts have been doing

Table 7.7. Demographic Characteristics of Lay Assessors: All GDR and One Regional Location

Year	Workers (%)	Age 18–30 (%)	Age 31–40 (%)	Women (%)	Repeat* (%)
1974				48.0	
1977				47.9**	
1979	52.0***				
1984	51.0			52.9	69.9
1984(x)‡	52.3	37.9†		47.3	
1986	52.5				53.0
1989	53.2	14.7	34.0	53.2	62.7

* Members who had served before.
** District courts only (47.2 at the county courts).
*** Intellectuals 8.4%. Party membership: SED 47.1%, other 15.4%, none 37.5%.
† Both age groups.
‡ District of Senftenberg.
Data Sources: 1974 [Kamin, 1975, 245], 1977 [Note, 1977, 245], 1979 [Heusinger, 1984a, 95], 1984 [Note, 1984, 233], 1984(x) [Comment, 1988, 171], 1986 [Note, 1986a, 243], 1989 [Paschke, 1989, 137].

less well in the arbitration commissions than in lay assessor category (Table 7.7).

The information for the dispute commissions is sparse. Table 7.10 presents what was obtainable. Meaningful figure were available only for the participation of women. It was rather less than for the dispute commissions than for the arbitration commissions, from the mid-1970s on. It is not clear why this should be the case. The proportion of women in the labor force was extremely high in the GDR (more than 80% full-time, plus additional part-time employment). Thus, it cannot have been a lack of women in the workplace. Rather, one might suspect that women, more than men, had other obligations after work and on weekends (household, children). The difficulty with this line of explanation lies in the fact that it should also apply to the arbitration commissions, where, as was seen, it doesn't. There is another puzzling issue here: the proportion of workers on the dispute commissions was only about 57%. This is very strange, given the fact that the dispute commission members were elected from among the workers of the enterprise. Unfortunately, only three figures are available and it is not known whether these are representative of the figures for other years. The three figures, in any case, are consistent with each other.

Table 7.8. Demographic Characteristics of Arbitration Commission Members: All GDR

Year	Workers (%)	Age 18–30 (%)	Age 31–40 (%)	Women (%)	Repeat* (%)
1966	33.0	7.1**			
1967	32.0***				
1968				35.0	
1974				40.5	
1978	56.0			41.0	
1979	38.9†	4.6		44.5	67.2
1983	39.0				
1984	38.6	3.6		47.3	69.9
1985	56.6			45.5	
1988		13.0**	22.0	50.0+	
1989		13.7**		51.8	68.3

* Members who had served before.
** Age 18–24.
*** Intellectuals 8.0%
† Intellectuals 8.3% Party membership: SED 39.0%, other 12.4%, none 48.6%.
Data Sources: 1966 [Goerner, 1966a, 357], 1967 [Winkler & Goerner, 1967, 204], 1968 + 1974 [Kamin, 1975, 245], 1978 [Heusinger, 1978, 157; Winkler, 1978, 102], 1979 [Note, 1979, 201; Dukes, 1980b, 567], 1983 [Heusinger, 1983b, 122], 1984 [Kern, 1984, 301; Note, 1984, 233], 1985 [Hantsche, 1985, 200], 1988, 111], 1989 [Note, 1989b, 164].

REWARDS AND APPRECIATION

All commissioners served in a honorary capacity. There was no payment for their services as such. Similarly, the commissions did not charge fees for their activities, but to the contrary, could request reimbursement for necessary expenses incurred by the parties or by witnesses.[35] Expenses of the commissioners could similarly be reimbursed [Decree regarding the Arbitration Commissions of the GDR, § 60; Decree regarding the Dispute Commissions of the GDR, § 64; also: Order Regarding the Compensation of Lay Assessors, Trial Participants, and Members of Arbitration Commissions, 1971]. There were provisions for the continuation of regular incomes and the protection of employment status of the commissioners. Since, however, the social courts almost always met outside the regular working hours, these were not generally very important matters. An exception were the participation of commissioners and lay assessors in educational courses, conferences, and other court-organized events.[36] [Severin & Wolter, 1980, 514]

Table 7.9. Demographic Characteristics of Arbitration Commission Members: Selected Commissions

Year	Location	Workers (%)	Age 18–30 (%)	Age 31–40 (%)	Women (%)	Repeat* (%)
1964	Magdeburg	40.0**				
1965	Kamenz	29.4	11.8	29.4	23.5	
1966	Magdeburg		9.1***		32.0	
1968	Berlin					76.5
1971	Schwerin				30.0†	
1974	Magdeburg					80.0
1978	Heringsdorf				67.0	
1979	Radebeul II					67.0
1984	Rostock					71.0
1984(x)	Weisswasser				62.0	
1989	Berlin	25.9	38.8‡		56.2	

* Members who had served before.
** Workers and cooperative farmers. Intellectuals 12.0%
*** Age 18–25.
† Both commissions
‡ Both age groups.
Data Sources: 1964 [Winkler & Jaenchen, 1965, 118], 1965 [Koerner & Hettmann, 1965a, 16], 1966 [Comment, 1966b, 173], 1968, 106], 1974 [Comment, 1975b, 188], 1971 [Heuckendorf & Kruse, 1972, 51], 1978 [Schober, 1979, 120], 1979 [Stuebner, 1980, 279], 1984 [Kersten, 1985, 42], 1984(x) [Kapp, 1985, 139], 1989 [Ziegler, 1989, 173].

Table 7.10. Demographic Characteristics of GDR Dispute Commission Members: All GDR

Year	Workers (%)	Age 18–30 (%)	Age 31–40 (%)	Women (%)	Repeat* (%)
1963				31.1	
1965		8.0**		37.0	
1968		16.0**		38.0	
1972				40.8	
1978	57.0			43.0	
1984	56.5			45.4	68.0
1985	57.0			45.0	68.0

* Members who had served before.
** Under 25 years.
Data Sources: 1963 + 1972 [Kamin, 1975, 245], 1965 + 1968 [Heimberger & Sokolow, 1984, 212], 1978 [Heusinger, 1978, 158], 1984 [Sahr, 1985, 272].

The social court commissioners appear to have been well appreciated at the higher levels of party, state, and society, but somewhat less so at the lower levels of officialdom. The complaints of the commissioners are not dissimilar to those of American jurors. Most of the difficulties seem to have had their sources in bureaucratic indifference, particularly in a lack of support from local administrative agencies, on whom the social courts had to rely for their material needs. Frequently they encountered problems in securing meeting rooms, bulletin boards, books, typewriters, office supplies, secretarial assistance, transportation, stamps, and a dependable budget. A feeling of not being appreciated could develop easily in these circumstances, adding to it the fact of generally low public attendance at the deliberations, even if there was nothing but praise from the top leadership.[37] There also was the occasional feeling that not enough of official honors and rewards were given to the commissioners—public honors being matters of great importance in countries were recognition through economic success (wealth) is not available.[38]

MOTIVATIONS

This, then, was the life of the social court judges: The burden of office was heavy. The conditions of service left much to be desired. Public interest and esteem were not very high. Only a small proportion of the commissioners did receive official recognition in the form of honors and awards. Very few of them were able (or interested) to use the social court service as a stepping stone to higher office. The job description, it cannot be denied, was not particularly enticing. Yet, the positions did get filled. What ever did persuade East German citizens to become members of a social court? And what made them continue in office for several electoral periods, serving not years, but decades?

It is likely that a full explanation would reveal various mixtures of altruistic *and* egotistical motivations. Only systematic empirical investigations could have reliably identified the various components and produced dependable estimates of their relative importance. As noted earlier, empirical research was not a GDR strong suit. The available data, such as the reports in DER SCHÖFFE about particular social courts and commissioners, do not provide an adequate base for discerning motivations. The best that can be done is to draw on DER SCHÖFFE and personal interviews for a number of tentative inferences.

One component (and, it seems to me, an important one) of the decision to serve as an unpaid commissioner was the relentless exhortation and pressure to be a "good socialist citizen." A key element of good citizenship was the extensive participation in collective undertakings—political, legal, social, cultural, and so forth. Committed socialist (yes, there were some in the GDR) may not have required much pressure to meet the participatory expectations; the ordinary citizen responded somewhat less readily.[39] Full withdrawal from public life into a predominantly private existence was not a realistic option for most citizens. "Individualism," it should be remembered, was a term of reprobation and scorn.[40] Moreover, many goods and services were available only through workplace or residential collectives, for example, vacation bookings at popular resort areas. Even in the absence of high ambition, just to get along, the citizen could not avoid volunteer public participation altogether. A certain amount of pro forma participation was expected. The "minimum-effort" participation, however, applied less to social court work than to other activities. The work of the dispute and arbitration commissioners was anything but pro forma. DER SCHÖFFE contained many admonitions to the social court members (and lay assessors) to adjudicate conscientiously, carefully, and effectively.[41] The GDR regime attached great importance to the work of its lay adjudicators. It was serious about it and missed no opportunity to communicate this seriousness to them. Whatever frustrations he or she may have encountered, the East German lay adjudicator did have the satisfaction to know that he was seen as performing a meaningful and important function.

The second likely component of the incentive structure of the commissioners is the fact that the office *did* offer a considerable amount of visibility and prominence. Neighbors and colleagues sought out the commissioners with requests for advice and with problems to be solved. Further, there were numerous opportunities for gaining public recognition, such as being invited to speak to assemblies of officials or citizens,[42] and getting one's name into print—perhaps as the author of a report for DER SCHÖFFE. In a society, such as the GDR, where achievements and recognitions were commonly stated in terms of collectives, opportunities for individual recognition might have possessed considerable attraction. It has been theorized that a part of the success of GDR athletes can be explained by the attractiveness of individual recognition in sports, not widely available in other endeavors.[43]

A third and closely related factor was the availability of public honors and rewards. The early volumes of DER SCHÖFFE carry many complaints about the lack of a gracious and dignified inaugural and retirement ceremonies, about "years of service without any expression of appreciation" from officialdom, and about the seemingly lesser valuation of social court commissioners (and lay assessors) than of other types of volunteers. [Arway, 1980, 227; Ebner, 1980b, 67] In more recent years, however, the commissioners of the social courts (as well as the lay assessors) received a fair number of public honors, such as medals, pins, certificates, and monetary prizes.[44] This, of course, also had the purpose of making them feel that they were part of the "ruling elite." [Ammer, 1994, 11]

The final factor (at least in the current array) regards the attraction of community influence and adjudicative power as such. There were at least two reasons why such power might have had considerable appeal: personal aggrandizement and community service. The former characterized the meddlesome person, for whom the office provided a welcome opportunity to snoop and interfere in the lives of neighbors and colleagues. Few other positions staffed by ordinary citizens carried with them the opportunity *and* the obligation to know most anything that was going on at the workplace and in the neighborhood (including intimate family matters). Western observers have tended to detect an intrusive quality in the socialist social courts[45]—or at least the potential for it. [Adams, 1977, 183; Schroeder, 1983, 137]

GDR officials have reacted sharply to such comments, regarding them as slanders and falsifications. [Weber, 1985, 10] My interviews in the GDR did not generate many complaints about intrusiveness—which may be because there really wasn't much of it, or (and this is quite likely) because it was a part of the general socialist lifestyle, where meddling in other persons' affairs was customary and not particularly discernible. A community service orientation characterized the person *genuinely* motivated by concerns for the public good and citizen welfare (as against disinterestedly doing only the absolutely necessary minimum). Of course, these two motivations (as well as the several other) are not mutually exclusive. The GDR literature emphasizes service orientation and good citizenship as motivations for social court participation.[46]

In sum, the incentive structure of the social court commissioners most likely was complex and multifaceted, the motives being diverse among the commissioners as well as for any particular one. From a material perspective, the cost of the office clearly exceeded the benefits. Two theories, then, offer themselves to explain why citizens served in spite of the material cost/benefit imbalance: One, there was no real choice; citizens were expected to participate; they could not avoid involvement in any and all "volunteer" efforts. Two, there were non-material satisfactions to be gained to serve as a commissioners—be they of the "good citizen" or of the "inveterate meddler" variety.

Based on my interviews in East Germany (and whatever clues the literature could provide), it is my impression that "going along with the inevitable" can explain the participation of a substantial proportion of the social court members. The true service-enthusiasts and community-oriented activists seemed to constitute the smaller group. I did not gain the impression, however, that the office of the commissioner was sought or cherished because of its meddling potential. I was impressed how often a genuine service orientation manifested itself. Perhaps in the participation in the social (and regular) courts, some elements of the greatly desired and always conjured up "new socialist personality" displayed itself. A fervent dedication to the cause of socialism—even more desired—was, unfortunately for the regime, not part of the personality development.

NOTES

1. Also see Adams, 1977, 176.
2. The election of the professional judges of the ordinary courts has been characterized as fraudulent. What mattered was not the vote of the citizens in the election, but the nomination of candidates, tightly controlled by the Party. [Werkentin, 1995, 327]
3. The earlier practice was election to shorter terms, which continued to hold for the members of the social courts.
4. For the governmental structure of East Germany see Sperlich, 2006, Chapter 2.
5. On the National Front see Sperlich, 2006, Chapter 3.
6. Most dispute commissions were based in units of production (factories). A few of them were found in other types of organization, such as administrative, educational, cultural, and medical units.
7. As noted in Chapter 6, a dispute commission could be formed if there were at least 50 workers in the firm. A single commission could serve several smaller firm, but there should no more than a total of 300 workers. Each commission was to have between 8 and 15 members (in exceptional cases as few as 6 or as many as 20). [Jacoby, 1985, 182]
8. The judges of the arbitration commissions of the productive association were elected by the members.
9. Jakob, 1955, 24–26; Ruebestahl, 1954, 27–28; Streit, 1954, 18.
10. Participation in litigation was "only one part of the duties of the lay assessors." [Streit, 1955b, 195]
11. Richterkollektiv, 1954, 14; Sobeck, 1954, 21; Thews, 1954, 11]
12. Of course, it began with a derogatory review of bourgeois civil procedure. The bourgeois comparison was a standard part of GDR legal writings. So that the glories of socialist law could be fully appreciated, it first had to be show how rotten things were in the West.
13. Though sentiments were not excluded altogether, as long as they were proper socialist sentiments.
14. In addition, there were meetings and conferences at the national level. For example, the council of state (*Staatsrat*) conducted a special session on December 9, 1982, to inform itself about the preparatory work for the implementation of the new social court laws. Erich Honecker chaired the meeting. Reports were presented by such functionaries as H. Heusinger (the minister of justice) and H. Tisch (the chairman of the GDR labor union). [Comment, 1983a, 10] Has there ever been a cabinet meeting in the United States to deal with matters of lay adjudication? The East German lay assessors and commissioners certainly could not complain about official indifference and neglect—American jurors, unfortunately, can.
15. This bonus was a customary part of industrial worker compensation.
16. They not only had the typical review functions, but also extensive duties in the education and guidance of the social court members. [Fischer, 1986, 338] Their work was supervised in turn by the next higher courts, the county courts.

17. Harrland, 1983, 11; Harrland, 1984, 38; Harrland, 1985, 4; Neubecker, 1978, 223.

18. Grieger & Mueller, 1981, 162; Laeufer, 1984, 139; Mueller, 1984b, 56–59; Posorski, 1979a, 49–50; Zunder, 1985, 109–110. Of course, the social courts, in turn, had to report to the city councils on a regular basis. Hugot, 1986, 104–108; Kirsten, 1978, 30–31; Staehr, 1982, 150–151.

19. Grabowski, 1985, 158–160; Holzendorf, 1986, 118–119; Kubitz, 1982, 55–56; Mueller, Frohmut, 1985, 395; Philip, 1978, 295–296; Steffens, 1982, 416; Zinke, 1986, 115–117.

20. Blaschek, 1984, 65–66; Buettner, 1987, 59–61; Hantsche & Kulitzscher, 1987, 181; Kind & Solger, 1987, 39–40; Langer, 1983, 98; Sahr, 1987, 86; Wappler, 1988, 157–158.

21. Dukes, 1980, 566; Epperlein, 1986, 64; Kern, 1986, 1–17. The last listed function can be understood, of course, as a supervision of the supervisors.

22. Whereby it is the dispute commissions that show a steady increase in membership. And, of course, there were always about four times as many dispute commissioners than arbitration commissioners.

23. 1968 [Wuensche, 1968, 198], 1982 [Tisch, 1982, 114], 1984 & 1985 [Hantsche, 1985, 201–203; Hurlbeck & Koerner, 1985, 106], 1987 [Harrland 1987, 126].

24. The occasional discrepancies (particularly for 1963) are due to different sources, which, of course, I cannot resolve.

25. Some arbitration commissions formed separate working groups (*Arbeitsgruppen*), who would take turns on a monthly basis. For example, the Crivitz commission formed two groups with six members each (just the legal minimum); Leipzig Süd had a similar arrangement. Forming separate working groups was not the general practice, but rather an exception.

26. For the many duties of the collective's representative in trials and in post-trial assistance see Buchholz, I., 1986a, 155–157; Buchholz, I., 1986b, 173–175; Note, 1987d, 199–201; Poepplow, 1986, 20–21; Schmidt, 1985, 127–128]

27. Lay participation in legal matters was not the only form of citizen participation. As Egon Krenz [1989, 836–837] proudly pointed out, nearly one third of the GDR citizens filled honorary positions in state or society.

28. The drop-out rate also appears to have been modest. Dannemann [1983, 159], for example, reports that in Berlin-Pankow arbitration commission 220 of the 240 members elected in 1979 were still active in 1983. [Comment, 1980b, 254; Ebner, 1980a, 114; Note, 1980a, 254]

29. Comment, 1980d, 254; Ebner, 1980a, 114; Moritz, 1985, 227]; Note, 1980a, 254.

30. Moritz [1985, 227] notes with great pride the simultaneous service as arbitration commissioner and lay assessor "for more than 20 years."

31. Wittenberg [1985, 150], for example, reports that in Schwerin 15.4% of the arbitration commissioners also served as elected representatives. See also Brendel, 1980, 278; Christoph, 1985, 222; Comment, 1980b, 254; Dannemann, 1983, 159; Gruenert, 1980, 34; Heuckendorf, 1978 190; Moritz, 1985, 227; Mueckler, 1984, 66; Neuhof, 1978, 247; Richter, 1978, 152; Stuebner, 1980, 279; Wittenberg, 1985, 150; Zander, 1978, 66.

32. Comment, 1980a, 161; Ebner, 1980b, 67; Gruenert, 1980, 34; Kettner, 1984, 65; Krueger, 1984, 93; Schoene et al., 1980, 276.

33. It will be remember that this is a very ambiguous category, the definition of which depended importantly on regime needs. See Sperlich, 2006, pp. 193–195.

34. Among the *professional judges* in 1986, women constituted 53 percent and working-class origins were present in 64%. [Heusinger, 1986, 391]

35. Decree regarding the Arbitration Commissions of the GDR, §14; Decree regarding the Dispute Commissions of the GDR, § 14; also see Severin & Wolter, 1980, 514–515.

36. Social prosecutors, social defenders, and similar litigation participants were also compensated for any loss of income. [Severin & Wolter, 1980, 514]

37. See, for example, Arway, 1980, 226–227; Branz, 1980, 283; Comment, 1980b, 253; Ebner, 1978a, 117; Ebner, 1980b, 67; Gensch, 1981, 265; Grafe, 1980, 190–191; Grieger, 1980, 41–42; Gruenert, 1980, 35; Hausding, 1980, 285; Heinig, 1980, 141; Heuckendorf, 1978, 187; Lienshoeft, 1982, 18; Schoene, 1980b, 275; Seidel, 1982, 14.

38. However, in the later years of the GDR, there was a substantial increase in public honors presented to commissioners and lay judges, including ceremonies conducted in the plenary chamber of the national parliament, with the participation of such dignitaries as the chief justice of the supreme court, the minister of justice, the chief public prosecutor, and high officials of party, state, and society. Arway, 1980, 226; Ebner, 1980b, 67; Fichtner, 1980, 287; Grafe, 1980, 191 NEUE JUSTIZ [e.g., 1978: 240] and DER SCHÖFFE [e.g., 1983, 125] also published regularly lists of honoraries.

39. Mere passive compliance, it will be remembered, was not adequate. Enthusiasm and initiative characterized the participation of the good citizen of a socialist county. [Adams, 1977, 6; Sperlich, 2004, Chapter 4]

40. See, for example, Sontheimer & Bleek, 1975, 91; Steele, 1977, 150–155; Winzer, 1984, 155; Zoch, 1964, 1409–1410.

41. See, for example, Arway, 1980, 225; Comment, 1980a, 183–185; Grieger, 1980, 41–44; Hauschild, 1980, 187; Hauschild, 1983, 6; Hauser, 1980, 280–281; Heusinger, 1984, 6; Laux, 1980, 202; Lengsfeld, 1980, 64; Nasarow, 1980, 10; Schoene, 1980a, 197; Winkler, 1980, 4–6.

42. The literature contains frequent accounts of citizens' respect for and trust in the commissioners of the social courts. [Comment, 1984a, 116; Heimberger & Sokolow, 1984, 212; Heusinger, 1983b, 123]

43. Of course, another part of the explanation was doping. See Sperlich, 2006, Chapter 7. Also see Geipel, 2002, 417–443.

44. See Arway, 1980, 226; Ebner, 1980, 67; Fichtner, 1980, 287; Grafe, 1980, 191; Hantsche, 1985, 26; Winkler, 1982, 129; Wittenberg, 1982, 11.

45. Particularly in the Chinese People's Arbitration and Conciliation Committees, which often were party control organs staffed with busybodies, enforcing the political line of the day, controlling community life, and seeking out deviation. Much like the Soviet comrades' court, the Chinese committees brought "organized peer and neighborhood pressure to bear on those who deviate from the societal norms in a minor way. Such volunteer activity in street committees and courts legitimizes peer group pressures present in all societies and elevates them to the status of enforceable community norms, in other words, law." [Merkl, 1977, 175] Certainly in the USSR, "socialist intrusiveness and meddling in the affairs of others was encouraged. . ."

Chapter 8

Tasks and Responsibilities

THE MANY DUTIES AND MISSIONS OF THE SOCIAL COURTS

Offenders, Litigants, and Deliberations

The substantive jurisdictions of the dispute commissions (DCs) and the arbitration commissions (ACs) were approximately the same. The exception was the special competence of the DCs for labor and employment disputes (more about which later). The two commissions could deal with *misdemeanors* (Vergehen), such as petty theft and minor bodily harm; *non-criminal petty offenses* (Verfehlungen), such as breach of the peace, insults, and defamations;[1] *public order offenses* (Ordnungswidrigkeiten), such as violations of currency and customs regulations; cases of persistent *school truancy;* and *simple civil disputes,* such as disagreements over small debts, rent payments, and child support. If either commission could handle the case, it largely depended on the context in which in arose (workplace or residence) to which it would go. It was possible, however, to detect a small preference for the territorial ACs.[2]

Resolving conflicts, disputes, disagreements, and quarrels of all types was the original mission of the commissions.[3] Both commissions dealt with minor civil and criminal offenses, such as petty larceny and frauds, money claims up to 500 GDR marks (and even beyond),[4] minor bodily injuries, defamation and insults, school truancy, and social parasitism (unwillingness to work).[5] The commissions served as courts of first instance. Truly minor cases could be submitted to them directly (*Antrag*), whereas more weighty (though still minor) had to reach them by transfer (*Übergabe*). The more weighty cases, particularly if they involved punishable offenses "are first investigated by the police, a public prosecutor, or a court of law. Provided that the case is a simple one and that the citizen involved admits having done wrong, it will be turned over to a social court." [Riemann, 1976, 18] The key condition for a transfer was not the formal importance or gravity of thc case, but the relative simplicity of its factual and legal aspects, as well as the acknowledgment or confession to the act or event at issue on the part of the accused person(s).[6]

The central element of the case work of the social courts was the formal deliberation (*Beratung*). The deliberations, whatever their frequencies,[7] required a considerable amount of time, particularly given the active participation of parties and audience, and given the strong desire for unanimous decisions. The chairperson of one AC proudly reported that in sixteen years of work, there were only two non-unanimous decisions. [Stuebner, 1980, 279] A collective work-style and decisional unanimity were highly regarded not only in the work of the social courts but in all areas of socialist life.[8] In fact, when Erich Honecker was deposed from his leadership positions in the politburo meeting of October 17, 1989, to preserve the customary unanimity, he himself voted for his dismissal.[9]

But there was more than the actual deliberation time. For example, the formal (direct) applications of citizens for social court deliberations had to be considered, even if they did not lead to actual deliberations. Several hours, most likely, were needed for each case to study the transfer documents or the citizen application, to meet with the parties (often in their homes), and in other pre-deliberation meetings to prepare for the public session.[10] There were a number of additional time-consuming tasks. Special invitation had to be issued to bring about the strongly desired participation of the "relevant social forces." For example, in dealing with school truancy cases, the following "social forces" needed to be invited to participate along with the delinquent student and his parents: the homeroom teacher, fellow students,[11] members of the parents' school collective, members of the parents' work collectives, members of the student's class collective, representatives of the youth welfare agency, officials of the official youth organization (FDJ),[12] members of the student's sports organization, members of any clubs that the student might belong to (e.g., stamp collecting), neighbors, and anyone of whom the commission thought to have beneficial influence on the student, even labor union officials (especially in the case of dispute commission deliberations),[13] the school superintendent and the local chief of police.[14] It was even suggested that the lay assessors, located in the culprits residential or work area, should participate in the proceedings. [Schlegel, 1977, 166] Not to be overlooked was the desire also to have present a representative of the office of "youth assistance" (*Jugendhilfe*). [Comment, 1987, 161]

However, it was not only students who were subjected to the pressure of "social forces." For example, when a butcher had to appear before an arbitration committee because of an insult, also invited (and present) were the butcher's boss and the bosses wife, the chief of the local butcher's association, a representative of the local craftsmen committee, and "other citizens."[15] In this connection, it will not be a surprise to learn that some citizens preferred to appear before a state court rather than a social court. The state courts had the legal disadvantage for the lawbreaker that his offense would become part of the official police records. The social courts had the social disadvantage of massive embarrassment and discomfiture in front of one's neighbors and work colleagues. The latter often seemed worse than the former. The regime, however, favored the social courts precisely because the embarrassments and discomfitures were seen as a powerful preventive factor to future wrong-doing. [Note, 1963, 37]

In any case, at the conclusion of the deliberations, formal recommendations regarding the sources of conflicts and disputes had to be agreed on and issued.[16] [Langanke, 1988, 110] These matters were neither obvious nor was agreement always easy to achieve. Finally, the decisions and recommendations of the courts required follow-up and control of implementations. Some of the control methods were home visits, general meetings of parties and "social forces," and receiving verified reports about the fulfillment of obligations.[17]

Other Tasks and Obligations

The official commentaries made it clear, the tasks of the social courts were not limited to legal rulings. They also had many functions in the areas of legal education and legal propaganda. In these matters they were expected to work in close collaboration with the organs of the state, societal organizations, enterprises, and other agencies. [Kasper, 1980, 223] Beyond the extra-legal responsibilities, there also were numerous other legal obligations apart from the deliberations.

The commissioners had to hold regular consultations (office hours), at least once a month, often once a week.[18] In addition, they were expected to answer citizen inquiries outside of normal office hours, even being visited in their homes.[19] The members of the social courts and particularly the collectives of the lay assessors at the regular courts also were expected to hold public meetings the explain matters of law. Here are the topics and number of meetings (in parentheses) of one lay assessors collective for one year: socialist legality (22), traffic offenses and their prevention (18), protection of socialist property (12), juvenile matters (9), fire protection (2), re-integration of delinquents (3), family law (10), labor law (13), civil law (17), legal education, for example, court organization and procedure (28). [Hackel, 1976, 63–64] They were also expected to discover incipient disputes in their area and resolve them without formal deliberations, for example, by having private talks with the parties.[20] The GDR very much favored the settlement of civil disputes without formal deliberations by state or social courts. [Kietz, 1984, 11–12]

The commissioners were also expected to help with the reintegration of former convicts, though most of the reintegration efforts lay elsewhere, for example, with the lay assessors of the state courts (see later). Furthermore, they had to meet on a regular basis with various leaders and agencies in their jurisdictional area to exchange information and experiences to alleviate problems and to prevent disputes from arising.[21] And, of course, each social court had to have regular internal business meetings to discuss and plan its work.[22] [Scholz, 1984, 143]

The members of the social courts also had extensive public (political) obligations. They were expected to assist the work of the National Front[23] and the Organization for Order, Discipline and Safety. [Arway, 1980, 224; Opitz, 1980, 252] They had to engage in "legal propaganda" in residential areas, firms, schools,[24] and other groups and assemblies.[25] They had to report periodically about their work to organizations and agencies such as the National Front, court advisory committees (*Beiräte*), local representative assemblies (e.g., city councils), party and labor union officials, and, of course, to their electors in the residential quarters or firms.[26] The commissioners also were encouraged (were required) to exchange experiences and know-how at special conferences.[27] There were frequent meetings with advisory committees and various types of officials, partly for educational purposes and partly for the supervision and control of the social court members. There appear to have been "run-away" social courts (or, at least, the fear of them), just as there always have been "run-away" juries. The GDR literature placed heavy emphasis on "the uniform application of socialist law" on part of the social courts.[28]

The members of the GDR social courts, it can fairly be concluded, led a busy life. Regarding most activities, systematic workload studies are not available. The data that are available (see Chapter 9) indicate that the conscientious member of an active commission needed at least one hour per day (five to ten hours per week) to discharge the many duties of his/her position.[29] Furthermore, many commissioners not only held the social court office for long periods of time,[30] but also performed other honorary functions in party, state, and society. Many reports about specific commissions noted with obvious pride that some of the commissioners also served as lay judges (*Schöffen*) in the regular courts, as members of representative assemblies, as activists of the National Front, as officers of societal and cultural organizations, and, even, as members of both types of commissions.[31] There can be no doubt that the extensive use of (unpaid) citizen volunteers bestowed upon the state substantial fiscal and manpower benefits. It is important in this context to keep in mind that the GDR suffered labor shortages throughout its history.

Care for Lawbreakers and Reintegration of Convicts

The social courts were not the primary agencies in the care for lawbreakers (except, perhaps, in the prophylactic sense) and the reintegration of convicts into society upon their release (and even before). The dispute commissions, however, did have a more prominent role in this than the arbitration commissions.[32] [Thiele, 1980, 52] Even if the social courts were only of secondary importance in the reintegration efforts, these efforts should be part of the present reflections on the East German justice system. In many ways these efforts were exemplary.

The reintegration endeavors included all sorts of personal and social assistance, including securing a job and finding persons who would care for them in whatever way necessary. The Council of Ministers (*Ministerrat*) issued a directive about reintegration on July 11, 1963.[33] The process was to be one of collective education and socialization. [Guenther, 1965, 385] But it must be emphasized that while these efforts indeed served to care for the person, they also were an effective control regarding his comportment.[34] For example, the collective reported regularly to the sentencing court about the person's conduct. [Barwinsky, 1969b, 351–353] In any case, it appears that truly great efforts of helping such persons were made at all levels (particularly at the enterprises and other workplaces) and that they met with considerable success.[35] Often there even was a formal reintegration-agreement between the enterprise (or the collective) and the convict. [Schmidt, 1969, 98–100]

It was an important principle of GDR jurisprudence that the responsibility of a court did not end with the pronouncement of the verdict—nor did the reintegration efforts begin only with the convict's release from prison. Court personnel (especially the lay assessors) as well as the work collectives and other social bodies were obligated to give close attention to his situation while incarcerated as well as to his post-prison development, particularly to the success of his social reintegration after having served his sentence.[36] Frequently one (or several) particular lay assessor(s) would be chosen to look after the convict. Typically, these assessors (or other social care-takers) reported about the conduct of their charges on a regular (often quarterly) basis to the state authorities.[37] Needless to say, the "care-takers" received full information about the convict in their care, including the case materials and the enterprise's personal file. [Drews, 1983, 63; Hiemann & Uhlig, 1979, 113–115] There was no concern with protecting the convict's privacy—privacy not being a matter given high priority in the GDR in any case. As always in socialist practice, care and control formed a single unit, and societal concerns trumped individual interests. It should also be noted that the "care-takers" received special training for this task. [Note, 1982c, 57–58; Winkler & Feist, 1982, 182–183] Of course, the care was heavily educational-political. Those whose offenses gave rise to doubt about their political dependability, often thanked their care-takers and the Party for having them shown the right way (the "right line")—a ritual that even the minister of justice could not avoid, confessing to too many mild penalties. [Werkentin, 1995, 348. 351]

The enterprises often formed special commissions to deal with the rehabilitation and reintegration of former convicts. Such commissions included members of the following departments and organizations: personnel, legal, safety; the labor union, the police, the work collective, the enterprise lay assessors collective, and the enterprise dispute commission. [Torzewski, 1976, 280] There can be no doubt that very little about a person's life could remain outside probationary supervision and control. [Barwinsky, 1969a, 230–233] If comprehensive disinterest and neglect regarding former convicts is the mode in the United States, the GDR mode was the exact opposite: comprehensive meddling. In respect to recidivism, it appears that meddling may have been more successful than neglect has been.[38]

East German authorities insisted that the criminal "must enter society, must be admitted by society, must be accepted by society, must be integrated into society—all of which requires the active participation of his/her fellow citizens." [Buchholz & Daehn, 1968, 267] As noted, the reintegration efforts, for example, of the convict's work collective generally did not wait until his release. He was visited by members of his collective while still being incarcerated. The message generally was that he was not simply an outcast, but that his collective cared for him and stood ready to help him find his way back into society.[39]

Of course, the criminal also had obligations. Particularly during the period of formal probation (resulting from a sentence without imprisonment or from an early release),[40] the convict had to make up for his previous misconduct through "the conscientious fulfillment of his duties at work and his personal life, the recognition and taking serious of his societal responsibilities, and warrant the societal trust regarding his future responsible conduct." [Nickus, 1975, 184] In addition to these general obligations, there frequently also were specific (case-related) duties the convict had to assume.[41] Probation generally was granted when the crime was not very serious; when the offender had rendered positive social services in the past; when the offender (after the offense) has drawn the right conclusions about it; when the offender (since the offense) has demonstrated a more positive development; when the offender confessed his offense, helped to solve the crime, and showed remorse; and when the offender himself has reported the offense to the authorities. Even when the crime was quite serious, probation could be granted when it was clear that the offender was willing to be re-educated as demonstrated by a responsible fulfillment of his duties, by superior efforts at work, by active participation in social activities, and by displaying a positive disposition regarding his duties toward the state.[42] It was also helpful if the offender was connected to a strong collective and had a collective guarantee of future proper conduct (*Bürgschaft*). The probationary period tended to vary between one and three years. [Wittenbeck, 1980, 203–205]

As a condition of probation, the offender had to assume a number of specific duties, which tended to regard the particulars of the case. For example, a person who had caused a severe traffic accident had agree to participate in a course of drivers' education,[43] to read the traffic safety literature, and to report about this to the collective. [Gierke, 1977, 158; Landmesser, 1976, 112] If the former convict did not fulfill his obligations, the care-taker would inform the responsible court, which could result in a cancellation of the grant of probation.[44] The controls of the conditions of probation were multiple and strict. They included conscientious work at his job, the realization of restitution agreements, the payment of fines, and the fulfillment of (unpaid) community work commitments. [Wittenbeck, 1980, 204–205; Wittenbeck & Schroeder, 1980, 15–18]

An important part of the granting of probation were the collective guarantees of future proper conduct (*Bürgschaft*), generally connected to accepting a specific place of work—often, but not necessarily, the previous workplace.[45] This led to the doctrine of workplace probation (*Bewährung am Arbeitsplatz*), a tenet expressly propounded by the GDR Council of State (*Staatsrat*) on April 4, 1963 (draft of December 5, 1962).[46] It was to be applied especially when the defendant received a penalty *without* imprisonment (probation)—which applied to 60 to 65% of all verdicts of the regular courts, finding increasing favor in GDR jurisprudence.[47] The social courts, of course, could not ever sentence persons to imprisonments. In any case, accounts of the great success of this procedure came quickly and regularly.[48]

THE SPECIFIC RESPONSIBILITIES OF THE DISPUTE COMMISSIONS

The unique focus of the dispute commissions were labor and employment matters. As Riemann [1976, 18] stated:

> One of the main duties of the dispute commissions is to handle and settle labour disputes. They have jurisdiction over all such cases, recourse to a regular court being possible only after a dispute commission has heard the case and given a ruling. Disputes may be over pay claims, bonuses, working hours, holiday leave or release from work, compensation for damage caused by the firm or an employee and so on.

The jurisdiction included disputes regarding employment contracts, changes made regarding them, and their dissolution.[49] It also included disagreements about pay rates, vacation time, health and safety issues, and compensations due to the enterprise for damages caused. [See Dispute Commissions Law of 1982, § 18]

In effect, the DCs served as labor courts of first instance. While they had other adjudicative responsibilities, the vast majority of their cases dealt with labor matters. The GDR literature reported that in 1978 more than 60% of the 60,000 DC deliberations treated labor disputes. To display the success of the work of the DCs, the literature also reported that only about 8% of the decisions were appealed, and that less than 4% of the decisions were changed by the higher courts.[50] In 1981, a full 75% of 65,282 DC deliberations regarded labor matters. [Sahr, 1982, 152] There also was a further decline in appeals and revisions. "On the average, the state courts had to correct only 2% of the decisions of the dispute commissions." [Hengelhaupt, 1982, 150] It appears, in any case, that in the 1980s, more than 90% of all labor disputes received final judgments from a dispute commission.[51] The appeals of the decisions of the arbitration commissions also were fairly low. In the time period of 1974 to 1984 (for all of the GDR and particular districts), the rate of appeals ranged from none to 6% The data are very meager on the success of the appeals, but they seem to have been in the three to four percent range of all cases, 1% to 2% range of the appealed cases.[52] Clearly, the relief received by the ordinary courts was considerable.

The social courts, it will have become apparent, had many tasks other than deliberations: preserving order and discipline and security in their areas, offering mediation, attending seminars and training sessions, meeting with public officials, reporting to their electors and constituents, and providing legal advice (*Rechtsauskünfte*). Information on the frequencies of legal information/advice, as on the many other matters, is scarce and nonsystematic. Only some examples can be given. For instance, the arbitration commission Wittenburg reported that, in 1984, it conducted 124 legal advisories and an additional 84 informal consultations. [Pietz, 1985, 154] The arbitration commission Bischofswerda reported that from May 1984 till February 1985, 59 applications for deliberations could be handled by way of informal consultations.[53] [Hensel, 1985, 87] To the degree that these data are representative, it can be seen that the commissions had much case work beyond and in addition to formal deliberations. The question suggests itself: Did the commissioners receive commensurate appreciation and rewards? A discussion of this matter is found in Chapter 7.

PROCEDURES

The procedures of the social courts were extremely informal. All those present, including the audience, could actively participate and have their say. There were no rules of relevance. Indeed, § 18 (5) of the Social Court Law of 1982 specified:

> Every participant (attendant) of a deliberation has the right to contribute to the resolution of the conflict through questions and suggestions. The social courts must conduct the deliberations in such a way that this right can be completely realized.

The pertinent decrees contain fairly detailed rules regarding the preparations for the meeting, conduct of the deliberations, reaching a decision, and the required follow-up. [AC Decree, §§ 2–14, 17–18, 23, 35, 41,

45–46; DC Decree, §§ 2–16, 21, 23, 28–29, 36–37, 43, 47–48, 51] The rules for the actual conduct of the deliberations, however, were matters of general principles rather than of detailed technical ordinances.

The aim of *civil* deliberations was to find an agreement acceptable to all disputants and, thereby, to remove the cause of the dispute. The aim of *criminal* deliberations was to re-educate and to re-habilitate the offender, and to discover and eliminate the causes of law-breaking. As in socialist courts in general, but still more so in the social courts of the GDR, the goal was to educate rather than to punish. As Vyshinsky [1951, 9–12] pronounced it:

> Soviet law not only coerces: it also educates the masses of the population in the spirit of socialist discipline. [It] expands the mental outlook of the masses, and elevates and enriches the conscience of the people. The [Soviet laws] arouse the socialist feeling of patriotism, of discipline, and of responsibility to the socialist state and its people.

The social courts were obligated to work expeditiously. The norm was that no more than four weeks should pass between an application for a deliberation and the final decision. It appears that most commissions kept to that schedule most of the time. Sometimes, however, several months would pass before all the work was completed and a decision could be issued. [Wittenberg, 1985, 150] This was a lapse in the eyes of the regime. In all courts, speedy justice was thought to be superior justice, being more effective as an instrument of legal education and crime prevention.[54]

EDUCATIONAL MEASURES

As in socialist courts in general, but still more so in the social courts, the focus was on education (re-socialization) rather than on punishment. The measures (*Massnahmen*) available to the social courts were *not* defined and treated as formal penalties (*Strafen*) but as "educational measures" (*Erziehungsmassnahmen*). They were not entered into a citizen's police record. The educational measures available included voluntarily assumed obligations and duties (usually some form of community service). It is noteworthy in this context that the culprit had to suggest his/her own duties; they could not simply be imposed [Buchholz, I., et al., 1988, 211; Krueger, 1966, 140]—though, of course, there could be informal pressures and well-known expectations. If the commission confirmed the self-chosen obligation, it became legally enforceable. [AC Decree, § 53; DC Decree, § 57] The available measures also included apologies to offended parties, reprimands, fines (*Geldbusse*) ranging from 10 to 500 marks, and restitution for damages. If fines were not paid (restitutions not made), courts could change the verdict to imprisonment. [Koener & Beckert, 1986, 226–227]

The key East German strategy for dealing with social problems (including crime) was education/socialization (re-education/re-socialization). In matters of "ordinary" (non-political) crime, punishment was seen as the last resort, and the need for its application was perceived as a significant social-political failure. The GDR's educational efforts were truly monumental. This was particularly true in respect to legal education[55] (*Rechtserziehung*), which primarily meant to communicate the lawful rules of socialist social life. [Wrege, 1973, 261] It was "to make young people gain an understanding of socialist law as instrument of power of the worker-and-farmer-state. . . . Legal propaganda does not simply seek to transmit legal norms. An important component of [legal propaganda] is to influence the legal consciousness of citizens and the development of socialist personalities." [Dobrawa, 1985, 14–15]

The technical aspects of the law, while by no means neglected,[56] were of lesser importance than the development of the right legal conscience—and that as early as possible. Thus, legal education was part of the high school curriculum.[57] "It was the responsibility of the schools to install a socialist legal consciousness in all students"; this was part of a "communist education." It was expected that they would gain the necessary legal learning to effectively keep the directives for "order, discipline and safety." [Jesella & Haertel, 1984, 369] The primary subjects for this purpose were history and civics. Other subjects, however, also had to do their part, including economics and (even) the natural sciences. [Arnold et al., 1982, 126] Even biology was seen to have great potentials for legal education.[58] [Hass & Hass, 1983, 119] Correspondingly, legal education also became a part of the curriculum of the engineering and natural sciences colleges. [Schulz, 1983, 286; also see Schaum & Strich, 1981, 84–85]

Legal education/propaganda also had a place in the training of apprentices.[59] It had an important slot in the occupational training institutions (*Berufsschulen*). [Michas et al., 1981, 266–268; Wiedmann & Israel, 1980, 203–205] "The legal instruction of the apprentices is an inseparable component of their communist education[60] and their development to skilled workers." [Sienkiewicz, 1981, 227; also see Zimmermann, 1985, 409–410] Legal education was not limited to the training institutions[61] but also took place in the apprentice collectives, in apprentice dormitories, in the work collectives, and in FDJ meetings. [Bossmann, 1981, 510–511; Parlow, 1984b, 260] The local FDJ organizations developed a special department for legal education, whose task it was to insure that its members formed attitudes for the proper adhering to law and morality, and for the support of socialist law and state. [Kahnt & Roehner, 1982, 407–408] It should be noted that the various collectives to which the juvenile belonged were thought to be particularly important and effective in inculcating right conduct. [Buchholz, et al., 1982, 175] The local lay assessors collectives were also recruited to further the legal consciousness of the apprentices, though that, of course, was a collective of which the juveniles were not members. [Bursztynowicz, 1984, 327]

Legal propaganda also was a part of the (controversial[62]) para-military training in the high schools.[63] There practically was no organization that did not have some responsibility for legal education and propaganda. The scientific society URANIA and the (purely social and leisure time) youth clubs [Haelbig, 1978, 268] were recruited for this task. The mass media also had the duty to provide effective legal education for their readers and listeners.[64] [Duehrsen et al., 1980, 269] Law students were given special assignments to participate in the legal education of juveniles, be they in the schools or already at a job.[65] In this, it was particularly important to explain the nature and superiority of socialist law as against the class law[66] of imperialism.[67] When they became judges or lawyers, their responsibilities for legal education increased further.[68] Thus, they were instructed to participate in relevant happenings and to help in solving problems in the enterprises, to guide the lay assessors and the social courts, to provide legal information where ever needed, to develop close personal contacts to the relevant state officials as well as to the workers in the enterprises, to try their cases before an expanded public[69] (*erweiterte Öffentlichkeit*) when ever possible, and to develop their own initiatives in the field of legal propaganda.[70]

Pedagogy students were given special responsibilities to support city councils and other agencies in taking case of juveniles who were in particular danger of committing criminal acts. Their training was thought to make them especially effective with youngsters. [Fuchs et al., 1984, 185] City councils and other representative assemblies, it should be noted, also had a fundamental duty to ensure the observance of socialist law in their territories. [Bergmann, 1981, 352; Steffens, 1985, 367] In effect, it may well be said that there was no one in the GDR who was not encouraged/required to aid in the legal education of the juveniles (and other citizens).

There were many efforts to familiarize juveniles with the workings of the courts.[71] For example, in some communities the participants in the "youth consecration" ritual (*Jugendweihe*)[72] (about age 14) would together attend court proceedings and would also receive explanations of what took place. [Kaulfuss, 1960, 186–187] In other communities the local arbitration commission organized a "youth hour" for the consecration participants, with the theme "your rights and duties in socialism." The point was (as with all these efforts) "to raise the legal consciousness" of the juveniles. [Kuehn, 1988, 100] For a time there even was a television program—"the comrades court of the youth television deliberates"—which sought to clarify questions of socialist morality and socialist law for the 14–18 year age group. [Comment, 1961, 286–288] There were other such TV programs, one, for example, dealing with the work of the prosecutor. [Rubitzsch & Christoph, 1978, 74–75] There also were newspaper series dealing with legal topics. For example, the daily *BZ am Abend* for many years had a column called "readers' court" (*Lesergerichte*), which sought to affect the legal consciousness of its readers and to generate an intolerance regarding law breaking. [Schriewer, 1980, 368]

Finally, it should be noted that the social courts also had the authority (and were strongly encouraged to use it) to issue formal recommendations (*Empfehlungen*) to firms and agencies, pertaining to the correction of conditions which may have caused or fostered the conflicts or breaches of law. [Christange, 1988, 187] The recipients of such recommendations were obligated to respond within two weeks. the social courts also had the right to control the implementation of their recommendations. [Code of the Social Courts, § 21] The powers of the social courts, then, were far from negligible. Beyond the formal powers assigned to them, the authority of the social courts was much enhanced by the fact the socialist doctrine (at least in its post-Stalinist manifestation) regarded lay adjudication as truly important and meritorious; it regularly received high praise from GDR functionaries. [Schippers, 1967, 427] In their areas of competence, the social courts were indeed a force of considerable consequence.

CASE INITIATION

Directly Initiated Cases/Applications *(Anträge)*

Cases could reach the arbitration commissions directly by way of applications of affected (involved) citizens, his/her work collective, or his/her residential collective. In the case of school truancy, the application was to be submitted by the school principal. [AC Decree, §§ 1, 19, 30, 44; DC Decree, §§ 45–49] Applications could be submitted to the dispute commissions by a member (or former member) of the firm, his/her work collective, his/her residential collective, the director of the firm, the firm's labor union, and the guardian of a juvenile member. An application could also be submitted by the school principal in truancy cases, [DC Decree, §§ 1, 19, 32 {1}] If the social court was unable to clarify the case, or if it thought that the case was more serious than its jurisdiction allowed, it could transmit the case to the state police for further review. If the police returned the case to the social court, its handling became binding upon the commission. [AC Decree, §§ 32–33; DC Decree, §§ 34–35]

When a case reached a commission by way of an application, the factual and legal clarifications had to be undertaken by itself (transfers were handled differently). There were occasional complaints that this was difficult and troublesome work. [R. Mueller, 1981, 101] However, the commissions could seek the assistance and advice of a variety of state organs, such as the state courts and the state prosecutor's office, as well as the help of societal organizations. [Neubecker, 1978, 223; Winkler, 1982, 127–128] The many forms of assistance provided for the commissions were congruent with the very strongly stressed dictum that the realization of socialist law was "the product of the close collaboration of state organs and societal forces." [Weichelt, 1981, 342; Kern, 1980, 247]

It is difficult to identify the number of direct applications. The literature contains only particular examples. For instance, in the city of Rostock in 1983, one arbitration commission received 74 applications. These led to 48 formal deliberation. The other applications could be handled by way of informal consultations. This means about six applications per month, all of which, whether they led to deliberations or not, had to be considered and discussed by the commission. [Weckert, 1985, 65; also see Stuebner, 1987, 41]

Case Transfers *(Übergaben)*

Cases also could reach the commissions by way of transfers from three state agencies: the police, the public prosecutor, or the state courts. To make a transfer legal, it had to meet the following criteria: a complete description of the factual elements of the case and of the available evidence; an estimate of the event, including an indication of the criminal law that had been violated; an estimate of the personality of the accused citizen; a statement of the reasons for a transfer; and an indication of the causes and conditions of the act (violation). If the case in question regarded a juvenile, the transfer documents also had to include an estimate of the juvenile's family relations and educational conditions, an evaluation of the juvenile's capability (capacity) for criminal responsibility (*Schuldfähigkeit*); [Autorenkollektiv, 1987, 218–220], and suggestions regarding the effective inclusion of state and societal tutoring persons and agencies. [AC Decree, § 24; DC Decree, §§ 1 {6}, 25 {2}, 26, 41, 42 {1}; Social Court Law, § 18 {1}]

The commission could decline a transfer if it thought that not all the transfer criteria had been adequately met[73]—and it appears that they were not always met. Particularly the transfer documents, it seems, were not always prepared with due care. Complaints and calls for improvement could be found with considerable frequency.[74] The commission also could decline to accept a transfer if it determined that the case did not come under its jurisdiction. [Nickel, 1969, 433–434] There were also many grumbles that not all transfer opportunities were utilized. There seems to have been a disinclination of some agencies to transfer cases to the social courts. Particularly, transfers from the police do not appear to have occurred frequently enough,[75] perhaps believing the social courts to be too "soft."

There are some data available regarding the transfer of cases to the social courts. Unfortunately, the different transferring agencies are not separately identified. Also the two commissions generally are not separately identified. There is reason to believe, however, that the transfers went somewhat more often to the dispute than to the arbitration commissions. Wittenberg [1985, 148] reports that in 1984, in the County of Schwerin, of the 23% of transfer cases, 14.5% went to the dispute commissions, and 8.5% to the arbitration commissions. Unfortunately, most reports only give the transfer to only one of the commissions, which rules out systematic comparisons. Table 8.1

presents some of the available information. While many of the specifics are lacking, it is quite obvious that the social courts dealt with a substantial proportion of the GDR's criminal cases.

Table 8.1 shows that in the 1960s (earlier data are not available), transfers reached their high point—nearly 40%.[76] Thereafter there was a fairly steady decline to 20%. The very last years for which there are data show a slight recovery to 25+%.[77] The reasons for the post-1960s decline are not clear. Perhaps the three transfer agencies—the police, the public prosecutor, and the state courts—did not have the same full measure of confidence in the social courts that was regularly proclaimed by the top leadership. The transferring agencies, this much seems to be sure, did have considerable discretion with regard to whether or not a case would go to the social courts.

Table 8.1. Transfer Percentages of Criminal Cases to the Social Courts

		Transfers*	
Year**	Location	Number	Percent
1962	GDR***	24,261	28.1
1963	GDR	23,385	30.7
1964	GDR	27,888	35.0
1965	GDR	28,050	38.5
1966	GDR	31,444	38.6
1967	GDR	30,982	37.8
1968	GDR	27,637	37.7
1970–74	GDR		27.5
1975	GDR		24.4
1976	GDR		28.0
1977	GDR		28.7
1978	GDR		24.7
1979	GDR		21.5
1980	GDR	19,442	20.4
1981	GDR	20,719	22.5
1982	GDR	18,292	20.6
1983	GDR	21,904	24.2
1984	GDR	22,732	25.4
1985	GDR		26.8
1979–84	Eisenhüttenstadt[a]		26.0

(Continued)

Table 8.1. (Continued)

Year	Location	Transfers[a] Number	Percent
1984	Berlin-Friedrichshain[b]		16.0
1984	Berlin-Koepenick[b]		27.0
1984	Berlin-Prenzlauer Berg[b]		16.0
1983	Leipzig[c]		23.0
1982–83	Magdeburg[d]		22.0
1983	Rostock[e]		24.0
1974–78	Strausberg[f]		25.0

* It should be noted that the GDR transfer data are based on somewhat questionable computations. For example, acquittals in the ordinary courts are not included in the total case base. This inflates the transfer percentages. Similarly, another (highly questionable) compilation reports the figure of transfers of criminal cases in 1982 as 73.7%. [Weber, 1984, 176]

**No data are available for the years 1953–1961, 1969, and 1986–1989. No numbers are available for the year 1969. The data for 1970–1974 are available only in aggregate form. For 1970–1987 only percentages are reported, no frequencies; also, no district data.

*** All GDR data come from the STATISTISCHE JAHRBUCH DER DDR, Vols. 13–32. The regional data come from a variety of sources.

Data Sources: a. Jacoby, 1985, 182; b. Probst, 1983, 148; c. Tischer, 1983, 281; d. Beckmann, 1983, 189; e. Kersten, 1985, 45; f. Haufe & Strohbach, 1978, 96.

As Probst points out, regarding the three areas of Berlin in Table 8.1, the reasons for the percentage differences are not to be found in differences in the areas' criminality but in the willingness of the agencies to transfer cases to the social courts.[78] Perhaps the transferring agencies found the preparatory work associated with transfers (which was extensive) too cumbersome. Official encouragement to transfer certainly was never lacking in all of the GDR's existence.

APPEALS, SUPERVISION, AND CONTROL

All parties to a social court proceeding had standing to appeal the decision to the local district court, as had the public prosecutor of the district. [Mueller, 1982, 154] Grounds for an appeal were that the decision violated basic principles of socialist law or that the parties to the dispute did not, in fact, reach an agreement. It was the key aim of the members of the social courts to get the parties to reach an agreement "based on the principles of socialist law." The social court then formally confirmed the agreement in its decision. If no agreement could be reached, the court could issue its own determination of the case. Such a determination could be appealed to the district court. [DC Decree, §§ 51–56; AC Decree, §§ 18–21, 48–52]

The district court could reject the appeal and affirm the commission's decision, or return the case to the commission for a new deliberation, with the appropriate suggestions. [AC Decree, §§ 48–52; DC Decree §§ 53–56] The decision of the district court was final.

As noted elsewhere, very few social court decision were appealed and very few of the appeals were successful.[79] [e.g., Buchholz, I., et al., 1988, 211] One possible interpretation is that the social courts decided the cases to the satisfaction of both the complainant and the respondent (as well as to the satisfaction of the public prosecutor), while fully adhering to the principles of socialist law. This, of course, was the accepted GDR interpretation. But alternative interpretations were possible: (1) that appeals were risky (socially or legally), though by law the state courts could not increase penalties in cases at appeal or (2) that, as a matter of policy the state courts sustained commission decisions unless a truly major error had occurred. The issue cannot be decided without empirical inquiries, which, of course, were not conducted. My own (non-quantitative) observation agree largely with the official GDR position. There appears to have been genuine and widespread satisfaction with the determinations of the social courts.[80]

In general, the social courts do not seem to have been wanton in the performance of their adjudicative and many other functions. While occasional decisions had to be, and were, changed, it is surprising how closely the lay members of the commission hewed to the law. There are at least four reasons for this. One, the great effort and good will on part of the commissioners. Two, as seen earlier, the extensive legal education provided for the commissioners. Three, the wide-ranging assistance available to the commissions. Four, the close observation, supervision, and control exercised by various state agencies and societal organizations.

PROBLEM AREAS

There were a number of problem areas in GDR social life and, accordingly, in GDR jurisprudence. Sometimes they were identified as such in the literature. Sometimes their problematic nature could only be discerned from the frequency (and urgency) with which the topic was discussed. What is rather extraordinary is the firm conviction of the regime that the lay adjudicators (social court members as well as lay assessors)[81] could greatly contribute to the solution of the problems—less so by way of their strictly legal work and more so by way of their educational efforts—it makes sense, thus, to consider some of these issues in the context of a discussion of lay adjudication, even if they are not exclusively social court concerns.

An example of a problem area, which was regarded as very serious,[82] and for which the help of the lay adjudicators is was sought, was the area of marriage and family relations.[83] That this was a matter of great concern to the regime, can also be seen by the various official policy statements, particularly in respect to the development of new family laws,[84] and by such matters as the formation of special "family committees" (*Eheaktiv*) among the lay assessors of enterprises. [Eberhardt, 1967, 283–291; Haupt, 1972, 169–170] Both social courts, but particularly the arbitration commissions, had a clear obligation to watch out for and to remedy deteriorating family relations.[85]

Another problem area was work discipline, also known as "dawdling at work" (*Arbeitsbummelei*). The issue of GDR work ethics has been examined in detail elsewhere [Sperlich, 2006, Chapter 5] Some additional citations will round out the picture.[86] The point simply is that a proper socialist has high work discipline and does not dawdle. The dispute commissions had an obligation to make every effort to improve the situation, if need be by way of special work obligations. [Haase, 1980, 85] A closely related (and particularly embarrassing to the regime) type of offense was theft,[87] especially offenses against *socialist property.*[88] Whereas offenses against private property were uniformly acknowledged to be theft, offenses against socialist property often were not perceived as such. The factory workers who lifted tools or raw materials often persuaded themselves that these things belonged to them anyhow since they belonged to "everybody." The absence of clearly identified private property made stealing much easier. Thus, Keil [1979, 226] speaks of the need to communicate the "political-ideological" meaning of socialist property. The regime did not approve of theft of personal property, of course, but it plainly was mortified by the high frequency of theft of public (socialist) property.

In the first instance, there should not have been *any* theft in the GDR. But more than that, offenses against socialist property were (correctly) perceived as manifestations of socialism's failure and bankruptcy. The official pleas not to offend against socialist property, and the "demonstrations" why it was (1) not necessary to do so, and (2) why it was singularly unsocialist to commit such acts, were endless.[89] Crucial to the regime efforts to lessen the frequency of offenses against socialist property was the "development of a socialist property-consciousness" (*Entwicklung des sozialistischen Eigentümerbewusstseins*) and the courts (particularly the social courts as educational institutions) were charged with a primary responsibility. If the socialization and jurisprudential quality of the works of the courts could be increased (and the regime did not doubt that it could) thievery would substantially decline.[90] There were a variety of other problem areas for which the social courts were seen to have important responsibilities; among them were neighborly disputes,[91] especially insults[92] and landlord/tenant relations,[93] and other matters.[94] There is, however, one area that deserves special attention: offenses committed by youngsters.

JUVENILE OFFENSES[95]

The Dilemma

The single most bothersome area of misconduct was, without doubt, *juvenile delinquency.*[96] As noted earlier (Chapter 5), the regime was persuaded that there could no crime in socialism, because no one needed to become a criminal. While, of course, there are substantial economic causes of crime, the regime had difficulty in fathoming that there also were non-economic ones. Only toward the end of the GDR did there emerge some more balanced treatments, (e.g., Lekschas, 1983). But even in these treatments, the causes of crime are still exclusively found in the private ownership of the means of production. There are no "new" causes of crime in a socialist society, such as the GDR. The still existing crime (though much less than in capitalism) is simply a hang-over ("a worm continuation") of the non-socialist past, or is a direct consequence of capitalist efforts to undermine the socialist system. [Buchholz, 1983, 199–200] The GDR literature contained endless proclamations to the effect that crime was deeply alien to socialism, though an inevitable ingredient of capitalist systems. [Comment, 1956c, 145] In socialism, juvenile crime was an "anomaly."[97] [Wehrstedt, 1971, 350] It was acknowledged by the regime that some older people, who had not had the advantage of a socialist socialization, were still under the sway of some bourgeois ideas and, thus, susceptible to criminal conduct. Juvenile delinquency could not be explained in this fashion.

Before the building of the Berlin Wall the regime never tired of proclaiming that its young people were corrupted by visits to West Berlin,[98] where they came into contact with "gangster movies" and "smut literature."[99] [e.g., Buchholz, 1972, 10–12; Comment, 1956c, 145–146] Occasionally the East German writers (inadvertently, one guesses) dropped the pretense of cultural purity and admitted to the real concern: "We must stop the malignant influence of Western *ideology.*" [Goerner, 1960, 100; my emphasis] Indeed, it was recommended to involve the FDJ (the official socialist youth organization) in cases where it seemed that the culprit needed "ideological work."[100]

It cannot be emphasized too strongly that the primary purpose of socialist law was always to preserve the socialist system.[101] Questions of law were questions of might, that is, of regime preservation.[102] The fight against (ordinary) crime, however important, did not have the same survival function for the regime. Thus, the regime could take a fairly relaxed attitude toward ordinary offenses, and favor re-education over punishment.

GDR courts were able to blame all sorts of juvenile crimes on the pernicious Western influence, including murder [Grube, 1959, 107], theft [Case Report, 1960, 330; Grube, 1959, 107; Rommel & Lungwitz, 1976, 249–250], and assault [Kern, 1962, 227]. "Bourgeois-imperialist influences" served as explanations for just about any kind of misdeed.[103] [Schroeder, 1978b, 199]

This, of course, was nonsense from the very beginning, but after the Wall, juvenile delinquency certainly could no longer be rationalized in this fashion; indeed, there was some decline in the number of publications blaming the West for the misdeeds of GDR juveniles. Nevertheless, half a decade after the Wall, the regime was still agitated about the influence of imperialism and of the "class enemy," leading East German youngsters[104] into a life of crime.[105] [Heldner, 1966, 99; Zeng, 2000, 47] As late as 1970, the problem of rowdyism in the GDR was still attributed to ideological interferences emanating from West Germany.[106] [Lischke & Keil, 1970, 70; also see Willamowski, 1967b, 314] And as late as 1977, a supreme court judge could still speak of the detrimental influence of imperialist propaganda and decadent Western styles of life, and of the capitalist smut literature.[107] [Schlegel, 1977, 163–164]

It is important at this point to recognize that the GDR combined two distinct offenses in the category of rowdyism. One was the near universal misbehaviors of juveniles (especially young males): misuse of alcohol, aggressiveness toward persons, damage to property, and similar forms of wrongdoing. This form of delinquency, while upsetting to the regime, could be forgiven. All the regime's rehabilitation and caring efforts here came into play. The other was political criticism and opposition. However mild that criticism might be (and generally it was very tame, not, for example, calling for an overthrow of the socialist system),[108] the regime reacted with great vengeance and massive retaliation.[109] It showed quite clearly that it could be punitive in the extreme if it felt that its right to rule in a dictatorial fashion had been called into question. [Auerbach, 2002, 201–206; also see Beyer, 2002, 157–200] There were two reasons to conjoin these different offenses: First, the regime could camouflage the rather extensive political dissent among the GDR's juveniles, and second the two misdeeds had, as far as the regime was concerned, the same source and cause: Western influence. [Wierling, 1999, 320] No one growing up in socialism could possibly manifest dissatisfaction with or, even, opposition to the socialist system. Such notions had to come from the outside—which, as has been seen, was the fundamental premise of socialist criminology.

All that was left for an increasingly desperate regime was to point to the influence of Western music and styles of dress—for which GDR youngsters, indeed, had some liking. The leadership of the GDR never seemed to realize how ridiculous they appeared in attributing juvenile crime to listening to the Beatles and to wearing blue jeans[110]—which, incidentally, very few youngsters could obtain in the GDR. They were equally ridiculous in the pre-Wall years when they attributed GDR juvenile offenses to viewing gangster movies and buying smutty novels in West Berlin. The proportion of East German youngsters who could undertake travel to West Berlin always was exceedingly small,[111] and the proportion of them with the means (Westmark) for such activities even smaller.[112]

How then could one explain delinquency among juveniles who were fully and entirely the product of a GDR upbringing? The tale of the external culprits of the West simply could not hold water—certainly not after the Wall. Internal causes, however, could not easily be acknowledged. As far as the regime was concerned there were no sources of crime to be found in socialism. For some few youngsters, individual pathologies might serve as an explanation.[113] [Comment, 1956c, 145–146; Dettenborn, 1983, 313–315] The rates of delinquency were so high,[114] however, that a general application of pathogenic cause would have assigned a large proportion of East German youngsters to mental institutions. [Comment, 1956c, 146] All that was left to say was that for some unfathomable reason, socialist socialization had not been efficacious with a large proportion of the new generation.[115] Often the parents were seen as the culprits, who had not sufficiently looked after their children. [Kraeupl, 1980, 303–306; Reuter, 1979, 18–21] However, the GDR literature strongly emphasized that education/socialization was not the sole task of the parents but was the common responsibility of the parents *and* the officials of the state and of the economy, of the directors and managers of enterprises [Nagler, 1974, 7–7; Oehmke, 1975, iii–v], of the collectives at the workplaces and in the schools, of the various societal organizations [Mand & Schulze, 1983, 184–186], and of the legal organs. [Rommel & Lungwitz, 1976, 250; Schroeder, 1970, 330][116]

All that was left to do was to emphasize importance of socialist education in crime prevention, and the need to raise GDR youth "to be class-conscious fighters for social progress.[117] As variously noted, crime prophylaxis and legal education/propaganda were important responsibilities of the social courts. Since no organization ever was left to its own devices, the commissions were required to work closely with the various agencies of youth assistance, for example, with the department of "youth help" (*Jugendhilfe*) of the city council as well as with the youth committees of the National Front.[118] There were, furthermore, constant reminders to the social courts that they should take into account the special particularities of young people. [e.g., Haberecht, 1986, 269–270; Mueller, 1987, 161]

School Truancy

Measured by the quantity of publications, truancy was one of the greatest regime concern among the various forms of juvenile misdeed. Serious complaints about truancy began in the mid-1950s [e.g., Priebke, 1955, 84–85]. They became ever more frequent and grave during the 1960s, and they never let up to the very end of the GDR. There were any number of reasons why the regime was greatly concerned with truancy: present-day and future. In many cases truancy was but the most visible manifestation of misconduct. Students who frequently missed school also tended to transgress against school regulations, showed lack of discipline in class, did not do their homework, and got into scuffles with their schoolmates. [Leymann, 1969b, 346; Siegel, 1966, 324] Frequently, there were non-school offenses associated with truancy, most importantly property offenses.[119] The issue of the unacceptability of property offense (especially public property) was explored earlier. Apart from current conduct, there was the question of the juvenile as future GDR citizen. Would the undisciplined and unruly deportment be reflected in adult conduct? At stake was nothing less than the "communist education of youth." [Brumme & Roeth, 1977, 131; Schlegel, 1977, 161–162] Quite apart from the specific issue of loyalty to socialism, East German officials (being the good Prussians that they were—which I mean quite positively) had no tolerance for unruliness, defiance of authority, and disobedience. In any case, it was pointed out that without a completed socialist education, young people would not be able "to take advantage of the many opportunities that their socialist society offers to them."[120]

One specific worry was that dawdling in school would lead to dawdling at work.[121] [Beinarowitz, 1963, 413] And there was the more general worry that school truancy was the first step in a criminal career. Truancy, in any case, was widely perceived as a sign of a defective socialization and personal endangerment. [Griesbach, 1983, 186; Leymann, 1969a, 172–173] The regime undertook major endeavors to identify early on endangered juveniles and to prevent offenses from ever taking place. Attempts were made to recruit as many persons as possible to work with the juveniles, for example, from among university students. [Gimmler, 1981, 286]

The social courts were given wide-reaching responsibility to remedy the truancy problem.[122] The community-based arbitration commission led these efforts, but the problem was seen as so serious that even the enterprise-based dispute commissions were compelled to deal with it,[123] (DC Decree, § 45 {1}).[124] The social courts did not come easily to truancy cases. There were frequent complaints in the literature that not enough reports were filed and/or that they were not filed soon enough.[125] It may well be that some school directors sought to protect students from the manipulation and embarrassment associated with being subjected to the participation of all the "relevant social forces" (see above). It has been reported that at times school officials did not act until more than one hundred school days and more had been missed by a student; only then did the school administrators report the case to a social court.[126] If some of reasons for not reporting truancy cases promptly was the desire to protect the student from the embarrassment to appear before all the "relevant social forces," this would not seem altogether unreasonable. These "forces" did not only consist of persons close to the culprit, but they also could be quite sizable. In one case in Berlin (by no means atypical) there were reported to have been 50 participants, of which 32 took an active part in the deliberations. [Oehme, 1967, 179–180][127]

Once a case reached one of the social courts, it was taken very seriously. The pressure brought to bear on the delinquents was immense. The members of the court as well as the other participant (the "relevant social forces") left no area of the juvenile's life unexamined. The inquiry concerned itself not only with what happened but *why?* Apart from the juvenile's own conduct there were searching investigation of his/her parents[128] and other relatives, as well as comrades and associates.[129] Had the parents and other relatives fully exercised their responsibilities to raise a decent and principled socialist citizen? Had the fellow-student and friends been bad influences? It is interesting to note that the deliberations of the regular courts[130] could be moved to schools or enterprises to increase participation. [Schroeder, 1978b, 199]

The parents (or guardians) often were identified as the real culprits in cases of school truancy. They were seen as having neglected their obligations to raise responsible socialist citizen. Too many parents were observed to be indifferent toward their children's education; other parents were too caught up in work and social obligations to take sufficient interest in educational performance. In such cases, it was the responsibility of the social courts to persuade the parents to better fulfill their parental obligations. [Leymann, 1969b, 346–349] Indeed, the parents often received a penalty.[131] In the case of the social courts, the parental penalty would most often be a public reproach or admonition (*Rüge*); it could also be a fine. But the major task of the social courts was the "societal persuasion." The parents as well as the children had to undertaken certain commitments and obligations (*Verpflichtungen*) regarding the improvement of future conduct. These obligations, of course, were subject to control.[132] In the case of non-fulfillment, probation could be revoked and a prison term activated. [Biebl, 1974, 379; Case Report, 1970, 323–326] However, obligations could not be *imposed* on juveniles by the social court. The court could only confirm a self-chosen obligation (*Selbstverpflichtung*).[133] Further, these obligations were not to exceed the juvenile's capacities and possibilities. [Biebl, 1974, 378; Schlegel, 1968, 226–227] Also, the juvenile should be present at the deliberations, even if their primary targets were the parents. [Winkler et al., 1982, 109]

In general, however, it is important to point out that the social court, when dealing with truancy case (as with other non-political cases), did function in a true socialist mode. The quest was not for punishments but for re-education. [Bruening & Lungwitz, 1984, 16–19] The courts earnestly sought to determine what went wrong in the socialization of the offenders and what would be the best educational measures to return the offender to a decent, virtuous, and dutiful way of life. [Hensel, 1984, 113] The aim was for a re-education that "would take." [Barth, 1984, 21; Fuhrmann, 1978, 271] Further, the regime, well aware of its oppressive nature, forever sought to persuade people to "voluntarily observe socialist law" (*freiwillige Einhaltung des sozialistischen Rechts*). [Mueller, 1983, 115]

Rowdyism and Other Misdeeds

Closely associated with school truancy were offenses that came under the generic label of rowdyism.[134] They included disregard of public order and the rules of socialist communal life, threats and molestations against persons, and malicious damage to property.[135] They were generally committed by juveniles or young adults, often banded together. A special youth criminal code applied to offenders ages 14 to 17. Beginning at age 18, the regular criminal code was applied. Children under 14 could not be charged with crimes. [Comment, 1956c, 148; Goerner, 1966b, 206] The penalty could be a prison term from three months to ten years, [Criminal Code, § 216] though there was a general disinclination to imprison juveniles (and even adults). Ten years was the maximum permissible prison term for juveniles. The maximum fine was 500 mark. There could not be life imprisonment or capital punishment for juveniles under *juvenile law.* [Kamin & Redlich, 1967, 122] Some crimes, even if committed by juveniles, were to be tried under provision of the regular criminal law (e.g., murder, sabotage, agitation against the state, endangerment of the peace), in which case life imprisonment was a permissible penalty. [DDR Handbuch, 1985, 692] It should be noted here that mere contacts to the West Berlin bureaus of the West German political parties counted as agitation against the state (GDR hostile acts). [Fricke, 1979, 256] As pointed out elsewhere, regime concern and kindness with offenders did not extent to political offenses [see, for example, the autobiographical report by Rainer Dellmuth, 1999].

Rowdyism was of great concern to the regime for at least two reasons: the crimes as such, and the manifestations of a failed socialist education. A proper socialist—the new socialist personality—did not commit crimes and did not lack in self-discipline and orderliness. It was pointed out, that already Lenin had characterized rowdyism as "a conscious negation of social discipline, which has its roots in petty-bourgeois anarchism and brutal egoism. It has to be fought with all determination and with the broadest participation of the population." [Lischke & Keil, 1970, 70–74] Surely, one could not bring about the "developed socialist society" with a bunch of rowdies. As Willamowski [1967b, 312] pointed out: "Rowdyism is a form of conduct crassly antithetical to socialist norms of comportment."

While numerous articles in the press expressed the view that the GDR was "ever more effective in reducing juvenile crime"[136] and while endless statistical arrays [e.g., Hiller, 1965, 316] were published to show how juvenile crime[137] had declined, the articles in DER SCHÖFFE painted a different picture. I have commented earlier on the unreliability of GDR statistics. As in other socialist countries, the figures were manipulated (to meet regime needs) or suppressed altogether. GDR publications took particular pleasure in pointing out (mostly correctly) that juvenile crime had not declined in West Germany and other western countries. [Buchholz & Roeder, 1982, 114–116; Grube, 1954, 12–13] What was not acknowledged in these comparisons was the different treatment of juvenile offenses in the GDR, where many juvenile (and some other) misdeeds were assigned to the social courts and, thus, did not enter into the crime statistics, which, of course, was not the case in the FRG. The GDR acknowledged occasionally that there had been a considerable amount of "de-penalizing" (*Depönalisierung*) in the socialist countries, failing, however, to draw the appropriate inferences how this would affect the crime statistics.[138] As it was, in order to call for remedies (particularly urgent and drastic ones), the regime had to admit that there was a problem. Thus, the reader was confronted with a constantly alternating series of messages: (a) what splendid socialist and flawless citizens East German youth had become, and (b) what an appallingly non-socialist conduct and what an irresponsible mode of citizenship they manifested.[139]

In general, these were the forms of misconduct of particular concern: violent and brutal altercations with bodily injuries,[140] unauthorized use of a motor vehicle,[141] damage to property.[142] An analysis of the 142 juvenile deliberations (regarding 179 culprits) of the Berlin arbitration commissions showed the following figures: offenses against socialist property: 40%; offenses against personal property: 22%; unauthorized use of motor vehicles: 15.5%; damage to property: 5%; intentional bodily injury: 13%; traffic accidents 2%; other: 2.5%. [Comment, 1976, 42]

Even in the case of clear rowdyism, the courts still sought to discover the causes for the misconduct and find the appropriate measures to correct them. As with all juveniles, a fine could be imposed only if the offender had his own income or adequate savings, typically in the case of apprentices but not in the case of students. Restitutions were thought to have a favorable educational effect, particularly leisure time community work[143] but also monetary payments, where possible. [Goerner, 1966b, 208–209] There could be (self-) commitments to improve school or work conduct; there could be restitution through work or through payment for damages [Wiegand, 1979, 117], and there could be the articulation of a formal reprimand or the imposition of a fine.[144] The formal reprimand was used most often. [Rommel & Lungwitz, 1976, 250–251] Formal reprimands were issued in three-fourths of all dispute commission cases, and in more than half of all arbitration commission cases. [Buchholz, I., et al., 1988, 211]

GDR law also knew a number of "supplementary penalties" (*Zusatzstrafen*). In addition to fines, they were a public announcement of the conviction, a restriction on mobility (limitation to a particular residential area), a revocation of the driver's license and other licenses, and a confiscation of certain possessions.[145] Before any penalties could be assessed, the courts had to determine the "guilt capability" (*Schuldfähigkeit*) of the defendant; that is, was the offender capable, at the time of his deed, to let himself be guided by the prevailing rules of social conduct?[146] They also had to determine the actual dangerousness of the conduct in question, so as not to impose a stricter punishment than necessary. [Lischke & Keil, 1970, 71] However, rowdyism was particularly susceptible to relapses and recidivism, at which point penalties could be quite harsh, often even imprisonment.[147] However, even regarding multiple recidivist, there still was a very serious effort to employ educational measures to integrate them into society,[148] even if it required some institutionalization. It was very important to identify as early as possible the juveniles at particular risk and provide early help and intervention. [Redlich, 1968, 146–150] For example, rowdyism (as well as recidivism) was frequently associated with excessive alcohol consumption. [Biebl, 1974, 376; Redlich, 1968, 148] Rowdyism and recidivism were also found to be correlated with dropping out of school, frequent changes in apprenticeships and/or employment, social inactivism, and lack of intellectual interest. [Redlich, 1968, 147]

In general, the courts were instructed to proceed in a "differentiated" fashion. Even if the offense was against socialist property.[149] [Biebl, 1984a, 375–377; Werkentin, 1995, 244–245] To find the right punishment, not only the actual misdeed was to be taken into account, but also the personality of the offender, his "developmental peculiarities," his social milieu, and other such factors—which could be to some degree exculpatory.[150] Whenever possible, generally for lesser forms of rowdyism (and lesser forms of other offenses), the courts would make use of probationary sentences or, in any case, a penalty without imprisonment.[151] Probation (*Verurteilung auf Bewährung*) was much favored by GDR jurisprudence. It provided the juvenile with the opportunity to continue his regular educational or vocational career and to demonstrate that he was willing and able to change his conduct. [Biebl, 1974, 378–379] But to receive probation, there had to be explicit probationary conditions, which had to be specifically related to the offense and the offender. They were to be so arrayed that he juvenile could recognize his social responsibilities and could identify the factors (motives), which caused him to commit the offense and also recognize how they could be overcome.[152]

It was of great importance that the juvenile offender recognized his guilt and manifested a readiness to conduct himself according to the rules of his society. [Amboss, 1983a, 265] The case should be conducted in a youth-relevant way; in no way should the juvenile come away from it with the feeling to have been misunderstood or treated unfairly. He had to perceive that he was being helped rather than being overwhelmed. [Amboss, 1983a, 266; Hennig, 1965, 309–313] He should have a feeling of trust in the court. [Goerner, 1966b, 208] It was also seen as very important that the juvenile offender would be fully rehabilitated and that no lasting disadvantages would result from his early transgression. For example, he should not lose his job because of the misdeed [Grube, 1959, 111, Rau, 1961, 412] and his criminal record was to be deleted in short order.[153] [Comment, 1956c, 148] If the offense was so serious as to require imprisonment, the regime was concerned that the period of imprisonment "did not last one instant longer than absolutely necessary to accomplish the necessary re-education." [Grube, 1954, 15] Further, instead of regular imprisonment, the juvenile offender could be confined to a special "youth home," were he could pursue an occupational apprenticeship and had many more cultural and athletic opportunities than he would have had in prison. [Niessen, 1963, 20–23]

Care and Assistance

The regime, as has already been seen, was exceedingly concerned with the welfare of its youth[154]—including the juvenile offenders (except, of course, regime critics or opponents). There was very little harshness or vengeance. There was instead an all-out care, and unending kindness and forgiveness. This stance might be explained by the quintessential humaneness of socialism (as the regime would have it); it might also be explained by the regime's recognition that it had no future if it could not bring the next generation over to its side.[155] [Krenz, 1989, 837–838] In the case of offenders—that is, a fairly large proportion of GDR youth—it meant near endless patience and all possible help.[156]

Youthful defendants could avail themselves of the aid of lawyers. More important, there were always quasi-legal assistants (*Beistände*) to aid them in any legal difficulties. There was much concern that there were not enough educators (persons with special abilities to work with juveniles) among the lay adjudicators of the courts' youth chambers [Niestroy, 1955a, 49], that is, persons who have empathy and sensitivity for juveniles, in addition to their jurisprudential capabilities. [Niestroy, 1955b, 151–152] It is interesting to the read personal reports of lay adjudicators describing their "personal efforts to bring delinquent youth back to right conduct." [e.g., Stoepper, 1957, 82–83]

Interestingly, the general public could be excluded from trials of juveniles—to save the juvenile embarrassment and additional stress. [Comment, 1956c, 149–150] This, of course, was quite contrary to the desired participation of all relevant social forces, explored previously. In any case, exclusion of the general public did not also require the exclusion of the social forces. Surely, it was more embarrassing to have to confess one's misdeed in front of one's relatives, teachers, and classmates than before an assortment of strangers. Obviously, the wish to protect the juvenile defendant and the wish to bring massive re-socialization pressures to bear on him collided. The conflict was resolved in favor of re-education. As one supreme court official put it: "There can be no giving up on the participation of the social forces."[157] [Hennig, 1965, 311; also see Goerner, 1966b, 207] The social pressure that would be brought on the offender by the social forces was but one of the reasons that their participation was considered to be important. It was also expected that these social-force participants (especially from the same age group as the offender, e.g., class mates) would be educated and immunized against future law-breaking of their own. [Wiegand, 1979, 118]

The East German care for juveniles, and particularly for juvenile offenders, was truly extraordinary. Apart from the "youth judges" (*Jugendrichter*) and the special "youth lay assessors" (*Jugendschöffen*) active in the youth chambers of the regular courts,[158] there was an additional functionary active to help juvenile offenders: the "youth assistant" (*Jugendbeistand*).[159] The role of the youth assistant was largely to help the juvenile with the events related to a formal court proceeding and subsequent rehabilitation. Often these assistants were recruited from among the lay assessors of the court. This led to some problems with overwork. [Schlegel, 1977, 165] There were many calls for pedagogically knowledgeable persons also to assume the duties of youth assistants. [Arnold, 1983, 107] Typical for the GDR—no social function without elaborate tutorials—there were special training sessions for these assistants, to fully explain to them their various rights and duties.[160] Also typical for the GDR, individuals performing the same tasks had to be united in collective or similar groupings. Thus, there were "youth assistance groups" (*Jugendbeistandsgruppen*). [Arway, 1985, 248]

The youth assistant functioned as a legal defender, particularly if the juvenile did not have his own defense attorney.[161] The youth assistant would, of course, talk to the juvenile (particularly to explain the proceedings to him, to gain his confidence, and advise him how to conduct himself during the trial[162]) and, generally, also to his parents and other relevant persons. As customary in the GDR, the relevant persons included the various school and/or work groups (including teachers and supervisors), as well as friends and neighbors. [Mueller, 1987, 161; Walter, 1976, 131]

The youth assistant had the same rights and duties as a defense attorney. [Buchholz & Schoenfeldt, 1984, 487] He could speak at the trial and fully participate in it. He could even discuss the case with the judge before the hearing, to get a better understanding of the particularities of the case and of the offender. [Arnold, 1983, 107–109; Traeger, 1985, 31] It was thought to be important for the youth assistant to be fully prepared for the case. He was to have adequate time before the trial to study all records and files—which was his right. He should be entirely familiar with the case materials *and* with the personality of the defendant, his social development, and his educational record, so that he could contribute to the deliberations in a knowledgeable way. He could ask questions of witnesses. He also had to review the articles of the criminal code relevant to the case at hand.

The task of the youth assistant was to defend the juvenile, not to accuse him. He even could demand that the prosecutor produce additional pieces of evidence. He also could deliver a closing argument, which would include an evaluation of all the trial materials and a suggestion as to the most appropriate penalty. He could also appeal the verdict—even against the wishes of the juvenile. In sum, he functions as a defense lawyer[163] and as a personal counselor.[164] The responsibilities of the youth assistant did not end with the completion of the legal proceedings. He had to follow up in various ways, including visit to the juvenile's home and control of any obligations that the juvenile had assumed. [Neumann, 1975, 72; Walter, 1976, 132]

As commented previously, no person in the GDR ever was alone. There was always a plethora of assistance and support—some of it technical, some of it ameliorative. Generally, these efforts were well-intentioned, which does not exclude, of course, the obvious political purposes of all this helpfulness. In any case, GDR politics and law never recognized a "private sphere" in the lives of its citizens. [Oberreuter, 1994, vii; Vollnhals & Weber, 2002, 15] There was no aspect of life in which the state did not snoop: from reading of mail, to the listening to telephone calls, to placing microphones in bedrooms, to getting copies of medical reports and financial transactions, and to other such observational intrusions. There simply was no legal or moral limit to the dominion of the state, which is to say, of the Party. [Vollnhals, 1994, 69; Wolle, 1998, 153] Similarly, there could not be any club—of however few people and however non-political (e.g., stamp collectors or flower-growers)—without state approval and state surveillance, usually in the form of Stasi collaborators. [Haase, 2002, 327] It can rightly be said that no other system, not even national-socialism, had such a complete and perfect system of surveillance over its own people. [Wolle, 1998, 137]

This was particularly hard on the younger people who preferred a more private life instead of the endless official regimentations. [Hoerschelmann, 1987, 131] Some individuals—and particularly some juvenile offenders—might have preferred to be left alone. This, however, was not an option in the GDR. Of course, a "middle way" between comprehensive intrusiveness and total neglect might be most salutary. Short of that, however, it appears that the GDR's meddling produced more favorable result than the American approach of ignoring the problem and neglecting the offenders. In any case, the social courts—in addition to all their other responsibilities—played an important role in the rehabilitation of youthful offenders. The dedication and the efforts of the social court commissioners were truly admirable.

NOTES

1. Commissions frequently had difficulties determining whether the offense was merely a misdemeanor or already the more serious petty offense. [Voigt, 1987, 42–43]

2. However, it should be noted that the jurisdiction of either commission was over persons rather than over (firm or neighborhood) territory. The commissions, therefore, could deal with offenses committed by workers outside the firm (DC) and with offenses committed by residents outside the residential quarters (AC).

3. Over time, however, their responsibilities grew and their competencies were significantly enlarged, reflecting the regime's satisfaction with the social courts.

4. The previous limit was 150 GDR marks.

5. For a full listing see DC Decree §§ 18, 25, 31, 40, 45, 50 and AC Decree §§ 1 {4}, 17, 19, 22, 23, 29, 39, 43.

6. More about case initiation later.

7. The frequencies of the deliberations and the other activities will be addressed later.

8. Arway, 1980, 225; Kasper, 1980, 222; Schabowski, 1994, 28–29; Starrels & Mallinckrodt, 1975, 36–37; Wranik, 1980, 200.

9. Andert & Herzberg, 1990, 32; Krenz, 1990, 144–145; Krenz, 1999, 118; also see Schalck-Golodkowski, 2000, 23, 311.

10. Arway, 1980, 224–225; Kasper, 1980, 222; Suckow, 1972, 239.

11. On occasion even the truant's complete home room participated in the deliberations. [Griesbach, 1983, 186]

12. There were occasional complaints from the basis that the FDJ did not give sufficient attention to court proceedings against juveniles. [Niestroy, 1955a, 50] In subsequent years, the FDJ gave increasing attention to the legal education and legal affairs of juveniles. [Borgwadt, 1984, 205–207; Woelfel & Kamuf, 1979, 316–317]

13. Participation of labor union officials was also very much desired when the ordinary courts (district courts) heard labor cases. [Kuckoreit, 1979, 271] The enterprise labor unions were generally very active in legal matters. They had special legal commissions (*Rechtkommissionen*) and legal working groups (*Arbeitsgruppen*), with considerable influence on the management. [Blaschek, 1984, 65–66; Buettner, 1984, 256–258; Haase, 1982, 84–85; Heintze, 1981, 246–248; Langenhahn & Tischendorf, 1982, 33–34; Langer, 1983, 98–99; Pommerening, 1981, 324; Pommerening, 1984, 199; Sahr, 1987, 86–89; Strasberg, 1982, 340–342; Wittenbeck, 1986, 270–271] There also were held labor union law conferences, on a regular basis. [Wappler, 1988, 157–158]

14. Buchholz, I., et al., 1988, 211; Case Report, 1984b, 141; Comment, 1956c, 148; Ebner, 1980a, 115; Hauser, 1980, 115; Heldner, 1966, 104; Jaeckel, 1981, 327; Kuehnau, 1986, 271–272; Lengsfeld, 1980, 63; Oehme, 1967, 179–180; Probst, 1980, 191.

15. Koerner & Hettmann, 1965b, 123; also see Fischer, 1986, 338; Schroeder, 1978a, 187.

16. In the 1980s, social courts were repeatedly called upon to issue more recommendations. [Arway, 1980, 225; Comment, 1980a, 183; Grieger, 1980, 41]

17. See, for example, Dollase, 1979, 263; Gruenert, 1980, 35; Kern, 1980, 249; Lellow, 1966, 328; Lengsfeld, 1980, 65; Sommer, 1980, 66; Surkau, 1985, 254; Winkler, 1980, 5; Zoch, 1964, 1411.

18. See Barth, 1984, 20; Ebner, 1978a, 89; Ebner, 1978b, 163; Ebner, 1980b, 68–72; Fichtner, 1980, 285; Gruenert, 1980, 35; Hauser, 1980, 279; Heinrich, 1980, 38; Hensel, 1985, 87; Kratky 1985, 226; Lindau, 1985, 85; Mammitsch, 1984, 38; Note, 1978c, 105; Parthen, 1985, 69; Schober, 1979, 120; Stuebner, 1980, 279; Wiedgrube, 1985, 68.

19. Arway, 1980, 224; Hausding, 1980, 284; Schoene, 1980b, 275.

20. Arway, 1980, 224; Comment, 1980b, 254; Fuhrmann, 1981, 169; Gilbers, 1975, 137; Hoffmann, 1973, 213; Probst, 1980, 191; Schrimpf, 1987, 88–90; Strohbach, 1974, 138–139; Werfel, 1973, 182; Winkler, 1980, 4.

21. Arway, 1980, 226; Hausding, 1980, 284; Kasper, 1980, 221; Opitz, 1980, 251–252.

22. Information on the frequency and time consumed by internal meetings is not available systematically. Only some examples can be provided. For instance, the arbitration commission Parchim II reported that it assembled once a month to consider applications, to schedule deliberations and other meetings, to discuss matters of law, and to prepare for deliberations. [Kratky, 1985, 226]

23. And conversely, the National Front was to support the social courts. [Mueller, F., 1985, 395] In general, the National Front had extensive responsibilities for the legal education (*Rechtserziehung*) and for the safeguarding of "socialist legality" in the territories. [Kirchhoff, 1981, 197; Kirchhoff, 1986, 217; Opitz, 1982, 166]

24. The schools were also employed for legal propaganda in the other socialist countries. See, for example, Katschurowski, 1984, 296–299, regarding the USSR.

25. Bornack, 1984, 258–259; Comment, 1980b, 254;Ebner, 1980a, 115; Gruenert, 1980, 34; Hausding, 1980, 285; Heinrich, 1980, 38; Kaspar, 1980, 223.

26. Grafe, 1980, 190; Pfefferkorn, 1984, 244; Schoene, 1980b, 276.

27. Arway, 1980, 227; Branz, 1980, 284; Kern, 1980, 247.

28. Heusinger, 1984, 6; Kaiser, 1980, 14; Lengsfeld, 1980, 64; Plenikowski, 1966, 374; Winkler, 1984, 262.

29. Arway, 1980, 224; Gensch, 1981, 263; Grieger, 1980, 41–45; Hauschild, 1980, 187; Krueger, 1984, 91–92; Nasarow, 1980, 10.

30. On frequency of re-election and length of service, see Chapter 7.

31. Comment, 1980c, 161; Ebner, 1980b, 67; Gruenert, 1980, 34; Kettner, 1984, 65; Krueger, 1984, 93; Schoene, 1980b, 276.

32. There was, naturally, greater interaction and cohesion in the workplace than in residential areas.

33. The reintegration efforts, particularly finding work, started much earlier, however. See, for example, Leim, 1955, 30–31.

34. See my comments in Chapter 7 on the aid to and the control of the social courts.

35. Bertuch, 1987, 114–116; Boese, 1982, 131; Drews, 1978, 169; Heinrich, 1967, 218–219; Hendel, 1967, 367; Neubecker, 1982, 85; Neuert & Loehmer, 1985, 113114; Parlow, 1983, 61–62; Petzold & Reitmann, 1983, 32–33; Schmidt, 1967, 104–105; Weber, 1980, 506–507; Zeppan, 1979, 35–36.

36. Dukes, 1980c, 23; Goethe, 1983, 146; Kraeupl & Reuter, 1984, 82; Goerner, 1963, 419.

37. Kaden, 1978, 243–244; Mewes, 1972, 122–123; Mueller, 1975, 136; Nagler, 1974, 6; Willamowski, 1982, 209–210.

38. See, for example, the data associated with the re-educational work of particular collectives of lay assessors. [Heinz, 1987, 35; Mueller, F-A., 1985, 250] Maier [1974, 243] estimates that the GDR recidivism was about one-half of that of the FRG.

39. See, for example, Deichmann, 1977, 186; Drews, 1978, 169; Krueger, 1978, 123.

40. For discussions of the possibilities and conditions of probation see Backhaus & Wolf, 1980, 58–61; Duft, 1975, 40–45; Jahn & Koerner, 1978, 338–340; Wittenbeck, 1980, 201–206.

41. Barwinsky, 1969c, 267; Kahler, 1977, 156; Willamowski, 1982, 214–216.

42. The duties toward the state, of course, were paramount. Not fulfilling them, in any circumstance, was interpreted as a willful, criminal, and punishable offense, with offender being categorized as an "asocial" person—very much as in the Third Reich. [Zeng, 2000, 25, 45]

43. It is important to point out that in the GDR this was serious schooling, not at all similar to the joke that passes for remedial drivers' education in the United States.

44. Case Report, 1984a, 52; Probst, 1967, 424; Pruss, 1982, 220.

45. Daene, 1969, 234; Duft & Gerberding, 1963, 377; Note, 1966a, 125–129; Wittenbeck, 1980, 205.

46. Schmidt & Beyer, 1963, 101; also see Biebl, 1967, 38–39; Willamowski, 1967a, 99.

47. [Beyer, 1965, 18; Beyer, 1967, 233; Case Report, 1980a, 262; Guenther, 1966, 331; Reuter, 1990, 144–146; Sagel-Grande, 1989, 1–13; Teichler, 1981, 512–513]

48. E.g., Ahnsehl, 1963, 74–75; Buchholz, I., 1987, 145–147; Wittenbeck, 1980, 201.

49. It did not include, however, disputes about inventions and copyrights. [Case Report, 1980b, 92–93]

50. Heintze, 1978, 190; Kirschner, 1979, 252; Note, 1987b, 89; Riemann, 1976, 18.

51. Heusinger, 1981a, 2; Heusinger, 1984b, 4; Heusinger, 1984c, 190; Hurlbeck & Koerner, 1985, 106; Seiffert, 1985, 165; Tisch, 1982, 114.

52. Comment, 1980a, 183; Comment, 1980b, 254; Denzin, 1985, 156; Ebner, 1979, 72; Heuckendorf, 1978, 191; Hurlbeck & Koerner, 1985, 106; Kersten, 1981, 114; Kunze, 1985, 208; Schober, 1979, 120; Wittenberg, 1985, 150; Zander, 1978, 66.

53. The arbitration commission of Schwarzbach reported in 1986 that, since 1981 it did not have to hold formal deliberations upon citizen application. The disputes could all be settled by way of informal consultations. [Teller, 1986, 42]

54. Herrmann, 1985, 292–293; Quandt, 1984, 465–466; Thiem, 1980, 373.

55. Instead of "legal education," the terminology of "legal propaganda" frequently was used. In this context, "propaganda" did not have a negative meaning—at least not to GDR ears. This is typical of totalitarian systems. In the Third Reich, Dr. Goebbels' official designation was Reichsminister for People's Enlightenment and Propaganda. In totalitarian discourse "education" and "propaganda" typically are used interchangeably. [e.g., Reuter, 1978, 267] Thus, without the least discomfort could GDR authors publish essays with titles such as "The Tasks of Legal Propaganda." [Christoph & Mollnau, 1981, 391]

56. Citizen participation (lay adjudication) was a key socialist principle ever since Lenin, emphatically endorsed by the GDR. [Heusinger, 1984c, 184–194] Actual adjudication did, of course, require some degree of technical competence; therefore the extensive tutoring of lay assessors and social court members.

57. Supplemented by legal study groups (*Arbeitsgemeinschaften*) in some communities. [Haage, 1981, 130] USSR legal school clubs were thought to be exemplary. [Chlaponin, 1981, 131–133]

58. "It is an important part of our educational work [in biology] to explain to the students the fundamental difference between the citizen's legal protections

in socialist society against [their lack] in the exploiter societies." [Hass & Hass, 1983, 119]

59. Michas & Udke, 1987, 171–172; Wiedmann & Israel, 1980, 203–205.

60. "The communist education of our youth demands the unity of ideological, political, legal, and moral schooling. [Sienkiewicz, 1981, 227]

61. After the completion of their occupational training, the legal education continued. There were regular legal education conferences for craftsmen (as for other occupational groups). [Gattermann, 1983, 333; Gattermann, 1986, 199–200]

62. Controversial because the protestant church and many parents objected to military training for high school students. [Braun, 1996, 34; Mayer, 2002, 56–60; Muehlen, 2000, 248]

63. Buschhagen, 1981, 290–291; Eppelmann, 1996, 315; Grafe, 2002, 399–404. Legal education/propaganda also was part of the instructions provided to the armed forces. [Penke, 1985, 130]

64. Journalist and jurists were strongly encouraged to work together for the purposes of an effective legal propaganda. [Lindner, 1984, 282; also see Laeuter, 1984b, 236–237]

65. Krause, 1984, 323; Poppe et al., 1982, 459–460; Poppe et al., 1984, 103.

66. This is rather strange, given that all law is class law and all rights are class rights and given that the GDR demanded of its jurists to have "a firm class position," [e.g., Toeplitz, 1979, 335–337; Weichelt, 1978c, 35] "to be a dependable functionary of the GDR" [Fricke, 1995, 13] and to have "a communist consciousness," [e.g., Koblikow, 1980, 73] and have a clear understanding of, and commitment to, the Marxist-Leninist ideology, which is the basis of the politics of the party of the working class. [e.g., Buchholz, 1978, 513] In politically important cases, the judges received not only instructions how to conduct the case and what the proper sentence was, but they received "pattern verdicts," which only required them to fill in the name of the defendant. [Werkentin, 1995, 257] None of this, of course, stopped East German officials from loudly proclaiming the independence of GDR judges. [Benjamin, 1979, 387] Of course, what was true for judges equally applied to the other state functionaries. [Leonhard, 1992, 341]

67. Buhl & Schmidt, 1978, 540–541.

68. The SED demanded that jurists should "at all times and in all circumstances . . . support the politics of the party." [Buchholz, 1985, 98]

69. Hearing cases before an "expanded public" was thought to be a particularly effective prophylactic against crime. It was thought to provide important components of socialist legal education to the general public. [e.g., Przybylski, 1980, 55–57; also see Buchholz, 1986b, 272–274; Henk, 1985, 59–60; Weber, 1980, 544–546; Werkentin, 1995, 51] On the other hand, the public could be excluded altogether in "sensitive" (= political) cases. [Wentker, 2001, 565] Alternatively, members of the police (in civilian dress) were ordered to be the public. [Werkentin, 1995, 186]

70. Hugot, 1981, 170–171; also see Kattanek, 1982, 354–355; Wittenbeck, 1985, 493.

71. The regular courts, especially the district courts, had major responsibilities for the legal education and, thus, for crime prevention among juveniles. [e.g., Christoph & Kersten, 1980, 127–129]

72. See Sperlich, 2006, Chapter 7 for a discussion of this ritual.

73. The transferring agency then had to re-evaluate its decision to transfer. If it reaffirmed the original decision, the transfer became binding upon the commission. [AC Decree, § 25; DC Decree, §§ 2 {1}, 27, 34 {3}, 35 {2}, 42 {2}]

74. For example, Ebner, 1980a, 114; Mammitzsch, 1984, 39; Seidel, 1982, 14; Zeidler, 1984, 39.

75. See, for example, Arway, 1980, 224; Beckmann, 1983, 190; Comment, 1980b, 183; Comment, 1983b, 204; Heusinger, 1984a, 5; Kasper, 1980, 223; Krueger, 1984, 93–94; Tischer, 1983, 281.

76. It can be assumed that most of the difference to 100% in each case consists of direct application. The only other way for a social court to take up a case was by its own initiative. This appears to have been an exceedingly rare event. While most reports simply were silent regarding the non-transfer percentages, occasionally both sides were given. Thus, Berlin-Lichtenberg reported that in the years 1965–1972, of all its cases, 75% reached the commission by application and 25% by transfer. [Mager & Winkler, 1973, 89] Similarly, the arbitration commission for Schleusigen reported that on the average 79 percent of its cases came to it by application and 21% by transfer. [Reuther, 1979, 296]

77. A set of data for the USSR (Saratow Region 1969) shows the following percentages for cases reaching the comrades courts: direct citizen applications: 27%, transfers from other organs: 71%, court's own initiative: 2%. [Braeuer, 1972, 409] At that time at least, and this region, transfers were substantially more common in the USSR than in the GDR.

78. There were also some differences in transfer percentages in respect to different offenses. For example, in the GDR in 1984 in the case of theft of private property 37.7% of the cases were transferred to a social court; theft of socialist property 37.0%; unauthorized used of motor vehicles 30.3%; intentional bodily injury 42.0%. [Hurlbeck & Koerner, 1985, 102] As seen in Table 8.1, the overall transfer figure was 25.4%. There is no information as to what types of cases were transferred less frequently. Given the many complaints in regard to school truancy transfers, it seems likely that truancy cases had a low percentage.

79. The arbitration commission II of Radebeul reported in 1985 that in sixteen years of work, not a single of its decisions had been reversed by a higher court. [Stuebner, 1985, 279]

80. This only means satisfaction with the results of the deliberations. The exposure of the litigants or defendants to comprehensive and embarrassing attention in these deliberations (see the earlier comments on the extensive inclusion of neighbors and colleagues in the proceedings) was received with considerably less delight.

81. Which explains why much of the concerns find reflection in DER SCHÖFFE.

82. The SED declarations about the importance of healthy families often sound as if they had been copied from the texts of the American Right.

83. Comment, 1970, 61–69; Dillhoefer, 1957, 33–44; Esdohr, 1962, 357–359; Hejhal, 1966, 82–85; Lichtenberg, 1984, 218–220; Mielich, 1988, 157–162; Ostmann, 1956, 110–116; Petrick, 1977, 39–40; Rieger, 1986, 61–63; Rohde, 1971a, 15–17; Rohde, 1971b, 293–297; Rohde, 1980, 60–62; Weise, 1965, 41–45; Wolfram, 1966, 158–162.

84. Benjamin, 1965, 163–169; Benjamin, 1966, 33; Comment, 1965, 193–194; Goeldner, 1962, 391–398; Goerner, 1954, 1–9, 9–18; Kempfer, 1957, 171, 212; Luebchen, 1956, 79–85; Marx, 1988, 80–84; Ostmann, 1955, 54–58; Pueschel,

1962b, 341–343; Seifert, 1978, 236–240; Thoms, 1965, 169–173; Wolfram, 1965, 46, 86; Wolfram, 1975, ix–xiv.

85. The divorce rate in the GDR was substantially higher than the same rate in the West. [Wolle, 1998, 172] Special attention was given to the problems of working mothers. [Renneberg, 1989, 257–258]

86. Brodführer, 1987, 233; Case Report, 1971, 253–254; Hantsche, 1988, 255–256; Kaiser, 1975, 265–270; Mett, 1987, 97–98; Note, 1989c, 88–90; Pohle, 1986, 263; Raubach, 1988, 183–185; Reichert, 1961, 180–181; Schaum & Strich, 1987, 113; Schlegel, 1977, 163; Skarabis, 1972, 94–100; Strasberg, 1987, 7–8; Udke, 1975, 57–58; Zipfel, 1987, 27–29.

87. Property crimes generally made up more than 50% of all crimes committed in the GDR, much to the chagrin of the no-GDR-citizen-needs-to-steal regime. [Maaz, 1995, 18–19]

88. Beyer et al., 1982, 62–65; Griebe, 1981, 210–212; Gruetzmacher, 1988, 282–284; Nagler, 1974, 5.

89. Biebl, 1984b, 105–110; Biebl, 1989, 36–43; Habe, 1988, 162–169; Roesner & Ruelicke, 1975, 273–276; Probst & Glueck, 1970, 16–22; Rietz, 1975, 205–210; Schlegel, 1973, 144–151;

90. Keil, 1979, 226–229; Note, 1973, 428–43; Pompoes, 1973, 401–407; Probst, 1971a, 68–74; Sack, 1974, 415–417; Stuebner, 1984, 172–173.

91. As pointed out earlier, housing was the most severe economic problem in the GDR. Too many persons had to live in apartments too small, and of very poor quality. Neighborly disputes were a natural by-product of the general housing misery. The regime was unable to build enough new housing units. It tried to paper over the great unhappiness by shuffling people around (*Wohnraumlenkung*) and by developing a "socialist housing relations"—to no avail. [Benser, 2000, 339–340; Bley & Nissel, 1984, 484; Borneleit, 1987, 20–21; Dengler, 2000, 166; Feldmann & Nissel, 1984, 64–65; Fuhr, 1983, 461; Kaden, 1983, 414; Kuhrt, 1996, 18–19; Martin & Wagner, 1985, 23; Sommer, 2002, 15–16; Strasberg, 1980, 342; Thoelken, 1982, 15; Wolle, 1998, 182–188]; see also the comments in Chapter 9).

92. Beyer, 1963, 243–245; Case Report, 1987a, 43–44; Case Report, 1987b, 131; Case Report, 1989, 243–244; Case Report, 1990a, 175; Hejhal, 1983, 224–228; Krutzsch, 1955, 133–135; Probst & Glueck (1969, 389–396).

93. Comment, 1956b, 208–214; Comment, 1972c, 63–68; England, 1975, 259–263; Gebert, 1976, 45–50; Hejhal, 1980, 207–214; Kieselbach, 1985, 127; Kraft, 1956, 48–50; Mandel, 1968, 11–12; Pruefer, 1973, 341–347; Schroeder, 1977, 89–92; Tauchnitz, 1971, 172–176; Wuestneck, 1975, 46–50; Zander, 1978, 67.

94. For example a large proportion of offenses (by one estimate 30%) involved the excessive consumption of alcoholic beverages. Beyer, 1966, 385; Hiller, 1967, 228–232; Neumann, 1983, 245–246; Schulz, 1957, 286.

95. This discussion, necessarily, will range beyond the boundaries of the social courts. Juvenile delinquency was serious enough to require substantial attention of the regular courts.

96. "Since the founding of our state, it has been our highest commandment to pay the greatest attention to the education and development of youth, the future bearers and designers of the socialist social order." [Wrege, 1973, 259] The new youth code was preceded by two prior versions, the codes of 1950 and of 1964.

Clearly, the regime did pay much attention to youth socialization—not atypical of regimes like that of the GDR.

97. The great embarrassment of the regime regarding juvenile crimes can be gauged by the fact that no meaningful juvenile crime statistics ever were published. Only in the Statistical Yearbook of 1990 (post-GDR) can a few figures be found. According to these (rather limited) data, juveniles from 14 to under 18 years of age committed roughly 15 percent of all crimes, while constituting only between 6 and 7% of the populations. If these figures anywhere near correct, the juveniles had a crime rate more than double the rest of the population, including children. In any case, it seems clear that youth criminality was steadily increasing in the GDR, as in most other countries. [Eppelmann, 1996, 315]

98. Those GDR citizens who worked in West Berlin, were classified as "parasites" and as persons who shamelessly contributed to the agitation against the GDR. [Dengler, 2000, 64]

99. "A major cause of crime in the GDR is the American smut literature radiating from the West." [Goerner, 1955, 211; Grube, 1954, 12] It was a paramount regime preoccupation "to protect youth from the corrupting influence of trashy Western novels." [Jahn, 1955, 149; Kamin, 1969, 203–204; Karnath, 1956, 152] See also Chapter 5 of this volume and Otto, 1955 185; Schellenberger, 1959, 114. It was even claimed that American "agents" sought to recruit East German juveniles to commit crimes. [Grube, 1954, 12]

100. Hennig, 1965, 313–315; also see Kamin & Redlich, 1967, 126; Schroeder, 1970, 336; also see Schlegel, 1977, 162–163.

101. For example, Schabowski, 1994, 31–35; Sorgenicht, 1979, 2; Stoph, 1983, 262; Weichelt, 1978b, 94.

102. This is not an unknown function elsewhere, of course. However, East German writers cheerfully charged that such functions of the law were present only in the United States (based in part on the writings of Quinney), but certainly not in the GDR. [Buchholz & Roeder, 1982, 114–115]

103. Not surprisingly, GDR socialist disciples also were able to perceive the events of 1989 as yet an other attempt of the bourgeois-imperialist-capitalist West to undermine the socialist system. As with crime, so revolutions must have external causes. [Reinhold, 1989a, 896; Reinhold, 1989b, 985] The prototype of this sort of an explanation for internal problems was found, of course, in the regime's struggle to deal with the workers' revolt of 1953.

104. And not only youngsters; when members of the working class (and of the SED) lost their class consciousness, it was because of the same influences. [Budde, 2002, 35]

105. In 1953, a 22-year-old member of the police was sentenced to eight years of imprisonment as punishment for critical statements about the GDR. The court stated that while the offender had had the advantage of a progressive socialist education, he frequently listened to western radio stations and, thus, became an enemy of the state and the working class. [Grasemann, 1994, 25] A seventeen year student received fifteen years of imprisonment for distributing critical leaflets. [Beyer, 2002, 172] As noted, the regime's approach to political criticism was punitive rather than educational. [Wolle, 1998, 128] For additional political cases, see Fricke, 1995, 16–19; Heyme, 1991.

106. One could also learn at times, that rowdyism was a remnant of fascism.

107. In 1971, GDR judges could still talk about the dangers to East German youth represented by the "anticommunist and antimoral broadcasts of West German radio and television." [Wehrstedt, 1971, 351]

108. For example, a juvenile protests against the stage ban of a popular GDR disco band (by way of signing a letter of objection) quickly involved the Stasi apparatus. [Haase, 2002, 337; also see Wierling, 1999, 319]

109. The retaliation included the parents of the offender. Juveniles were (inter alia) under great pressure to conform, so as not to jeopardize their parents' careers. [Kupferberg, 2002, 76] Parents were also put under pressure at their place of work to remove their children from religious instruction. [Braun 1996, 30]

110. It was a genuine sensation in the GDR, when Erich Honecker's grandson appeared at his "Jugendweihe" with an earring. Honecker, it appears, doted on his grandson and was unable to deny him any wishes. [Schalck-Golodkowski, 2000, 222] Of course, the offsprings of the new ruling class always had their privileges—as had their parents. [Maaz, 1990, 12; also see Dengler, 2000, 59]

111. It was made even smaller by the GDR practice to arrest East German juveniles at the border to West Berlin, which then were subjected to the indicated "educational discussions." [Maehlert, 1994, 88–89]

112. This is not to deny, however, that many GDR youngsters found Western products attractive, which, in view of the comprehensive GDR drabness, does not surprise. [Muehlen, 2000,20] The regime, of course, saw in any deviation from the ordained GDR pattern an attack on its rule and reacted accordingly—even when the divergence was more a matter of form than substance. For example, in 1988, seven high school students exhibited signs with the following words at the International Day of Remembrance for the Victims of Nazi-Terror in Berlin: "against fascist tendencies" and "neo-fascist out of here!" As a consequence, they had to endure severe disciplinary sanctions. Four of them were dismissed from the school *because of organizing a "pacifist platform."* [Muehlen, 2000, 237–238] The same fate awaited university students who did not absolutely follow the Party line. [Heinecke, 2000, 73–74; Mehls, 1998, 264]

113. Compare the general theory of crime prevailing in socialism (Chapter 5).

114. Occasionally the literature contained admissions that youth crime had not declined to the degree as adult criminality, and that the proportion of juvenile criminality had increased as part of the total criminality. [Albert, 1960, 212; Oehmke, 1965, 268] For example, persons under 25 years of age committed 50% of all crimes in the GDR. [Beyer, 1966, 385]

115. Rather late (1985), the GDR re-discovered such causes of crime as disorder, lack of watchfulness, shoddy treatment of raw materials, unlocked apartments and vehicles, and generally lack of vigilance. [Buchholz, I., 1985, 215–216] If not exactly *causes* of crime, these factors are likely to have made crime easier to perform. In socialism, however, they should not have mattered. The properly educated socialist was not to enter an apartment and pilfer things, even if that apartment was left unlocked.

116. There often was criticism of the courts that they treated matters purely as a legal job and did not sufficiently work together with the various social organs. As always in the GDR, the cooperation and partnership of the various agencies and organizations was considered to be of prime importance. [Biebl, 1974, 375; Christoph, 1986, 435–437; Hennig, 1965, 309–315; Kamin, 1969, 202; Schlegel,

1968, 222–223] The parents, in any case, should be given all possible supports in raising their children to be law-obeying citizens. [Grandke, 1984, 357–359; Kuhr, 1982, 108–111]

117. Buchholz, 1972, 9; Comment, 1956c, 146–147; Grube, 1959, 107–108; Hammer, 1957, 185–190; Schlegel, 1968, 228; Schroeder, 1970, 331; Schroeder, 1978b, 199.

118. Comment, 1975a, 140; Grube, 1959, 110; Hennig, 1965, 310; Stoessel, 1971, 200–201.

119. Bruening & Lungwitz, 1984, 14; Case Report, 1970, 323; Dreilich, 1976, 285–286; Grogorenz, 1972, 130–131; Heldner, 1966, 99–105; Hensel, 1984, 112; Knauer, 1954, 23–24; Manz, 1981, 121–122; Mueller, 1983, 115–118; Worner, 1987, 178–179.

120. Lehmann, 1981, 98; Schmidt, 1968, 21; Winkler et al., 1982, 106–108.

121. A significant problem in the GDR economy anyhow. (See Sperlich, 2006, Chapter 5.)

122. The social courts, of course, did not have sole responsibility. They were expected to work in close cooperation with the various other social and governmental agencies concerned with juvenile welfare. [Hohensee, 1979, 118–119; Leymann, 1969a, 170–173]

123. School officials could make use of the dispute commission to bring workplace pressure on a parent whose offspring did not attend school in a regular fashion. The authority of the work-collective often was seen as greater than the more lax residential groupings. [Siegel, 1966, 325–326]

124. On the question of whether the Dispute commissions should deal with truancy cases, see Kirchner, 1967, 331–332; also see Lungwitz, 1973, 24–25; Mueller, 1987, 161; Rymon, 1962, 179; Zillmer, 1986, 272–273.

125. Kurth, 1986, 184; Mager, 1974, 210; Thieme & Gerth, 1972, 18.

126. For example, Bruening & Lungwitz, 1984, 15; Ebner, 1980a, 115; J. Griesbach, 1983, 185; Hauser, 1980, 281; Heinrich, 1980, 38; Heldner, 1966, 103; Heuckendorf, 1978, 191; Kersten, 1981, 113; G.Lehmann, 1981, 98; Lengsfeld, 1980, 65; Oehme, 1968, 315; Probst, 1980, 194; Probst & Brumme, 1976, 38.

127. However, the participation of 150 citizens in a arbitration commission's deliberation was regarded as "too much." [Goerner, 1966b, 207]

128. A school truancy "always is a culpable violation of the legal duties of the parents, not of the student." [Mager, 1977, 47] The juvenile himself could be charged (be the subject of the social court deliberation) only after age 14. [Bruening & Lungwitz, 1984, 16–17; Case Report, 1990b, 176]

129. [Biebl, 1974, 377–378 Grube, 1959, 108; Heldner, 1966, 99–105; Hennig, 1965, 311] Lehmann, 1981, 99; Leymann, 1967, 327–331; Schmidt & Winkler, 1967, 283–386.

130. In the early years (youth law of 1952), the GDR had special youth courts. By the 1960s, juvenile offenses were tried in the regular court, albeit in special "youth chambers." For a discussion of the earlier format see, for example, Hammer, 1957, 185.

131. If it could be shown, however, that the parents had done everything possible, but to no effect, the juvenile could be sent to a special home. [Case Report, 1990b, 176] Short of that the juvenile could be issued a public reproach. [Case Report, 1984b, 142; Grogorenz, 1972, 130]

132. Bruening & Lungwitz, 1984, 18–19; Buchholz, et al., 1982, 174; Buchholz, I., et al., 1988, 211; Case Report, 1984b, 142–143; Comment, 1956c, 146; Griesbach,

1983, 186; Leymann, 1969c, 61–64; Schaefer, 1987, 17; Schlegel, 1979, 36–38; Schroeder, 1978b, 203–204; Winkler et al., 1982, 108; Worner, 1987, 178.

133. Bruening & Lungwitz, 1984, 15; Lehmann, 1981, 99; Note, 1980c, 39.

134. The inclusion of political criticism and oppositional conduct in this category was discussed earlier.

135. Rechtslexikon, 1988, 307–308; also see Willamowski, 1967b, 313–314; Worner, 1986, 83–84.

136. "The social courts are ever more successful to support the state's youth policies and to contribute to the development, improvement, and strengthening of a socialist state and law consciousness." [Rommel & Lungwitz, 1976, 248–249] Also see Barth, 1984, 20; Beyer, 1966, 384; Griesbach, 1983, 185; Heldner, 1966, 99; Kirchhoefer & Neuner, 1988, 230; Kremer, 1985, 153; Renneberg, 1963, 1595.

137. For some general statistical arrays, see Harrland, 1986a, 3–17; Note, 1986c, 316.

138. Buchholz & Griebe, 1987, 63–66; Reuter, 1984, 405–408; also see Teichler, 1986, 463–464.

139. General secretary Honecker as well as the GDR supreme court called attention to the problem and to the need for a remedy. [Ermisch, 1987, 161]

140. Biebl, 1974, 375; Lischke & Keil, 1970, 72; Parlow, 1984a, 126; Piekert, 1955, 85–86.

141. Biebl, 1974, 375; Lungwitz, 1973, 24; Parlow, 1984a, 127.

142. Case Report, 1986c, 274; Fuhrmann, 1978, 271; Parlow, 1984a, 127.

143. Boese, 1986, 267–268; Comment, 1956c, 146; Grube, 1959, 109; Schlegel, 1977, 164–165.

144. As noted, fines were typically quite modest. For a detailed discussion of the appropriate magnitude of fines see Lang, 1986, 160–162.

145. Comment, 1975a, 139; Ermisch, 1987, 161–163; Kamin, 1968, 235–236; Willamowski, 1967b, 314–315.

146. Buchholz, I. et al., 1988, 210; Kamin, 1968, 232–234; Schlegel, 1977, 164.

147. Laessig, 1959, 112–113; Schroeder, 1978b, 201; Schroeder, 1989a, 208.

148. There even were discussions how to get juveniles to use their leisure time in more responsible and sensible ways. [e.g., Schlegel, 1983, 32]

149. This, however, was not always the case. Particularly in respect to offenses against socialist property, early policies were to impose harsh penalties regardless of the personality of the offender. [Werkentin, 1995, 69]

150. Amboss, 1979, 39; Arnold, 1987, 100–101; Buchholz & Dettenborn, 1980, 109–111; Comment, 1966a, 8–9; Hennig, 1965, 312–313; Kamin & Redlich, 1967, 125; Kraeupl, et al., 1980, 414–416; Laessig, 1959, 112; Rommel & Lungwitz, 1976, 250–251; Schlegel, 1968, 224–225; Schroeder, 1978b, 200–203; Willamowski, 1967b, 316–317. Taking into account the personal characteristics of the offender was customary in most socialist systems. [Jakolev, 1985, 1] Of course, the cost of this personalized attention is "equality before the law."

151. Amboss, 1979, 40; Amboss, 1983a, 270–271; Buchholz et al., 1982, 173–177; Comment, 1956c, 146; Schlegel, 1979, 36–38.

152. Boese, 1981, 456–457; Buchholz, 1984, 307–309; Griebe, 1984, 460–461; Mueller, Rolf, 1983, 454–455; Schlegel, 1977, 165.

153. Also, there was no flogging or beating of juveniles in the GDR; such, we learn, was not compatible with "socialist humanism," only with the "capitalist exploitation societies." [Schroeder, 1970, 333, 336]

154. There were extensive protections of youth at work. For example, juveniles under 16 years of age could not work no between the hours of 8 p.m. and 6 a.m. Those older than 16 could be asked to work the night shift only in exceptional circumstance, but this required the prior consent of the parents, of the enterprise physician, and of the enterprise labor union. [Schroeder, 1975, vi–viii]

155. The GDR had persistent difficulties with its youth. They were much more reform-oriented than the older cohorts. Not surprisingly, those who sought to escape from the GDR, disproportionately came from the younger age groups. [Schuetzsack, 1990, 8, 17; also see Budde, 2002, 27; Eppelmann, 1996, 314; Hildebrandt, 2001, 58; Koop, 1996, 337–350; Krenz, 1999, 58–59, 98; Mayer, 2002, 77–78; Muehlen, 2000, 173–178; Neubert & Eisenfeld, 2001, 278; Schalck-Golodkowski, 2000, 222]

156. Similar concerns could also be found in the care for the families of convicts. Hilde Benjamin justified this care so that the family members did not become opponents of the regime. [Werkentin, 1995, 126]

157. However, there could be exceptions, for example, when the juvenile had a very "sensitive personality" or when the juvenile's "reputation would suffer disproportionately, in the case of a heretofore blameless conduct and a relatively minor offense." [Comment, 1975a, 142; also see Langer et al., 1984, 65–66]

158. Whose responsibilities went far beyond hearing the case and finding a verdict.

159. There also was a "youth care taker" (*Jugendbetreuer*). This person basically was an all-round social worker, seeking to assist youth (and any person) in any circumstance: crime prevention, court hearings, and rehabilitation. [e.g., Fels & Schulz, 1982, 510–511]

160. Arnold, 1983, 107; Buchholz & Schoenfeldt, 1984, 489; Dobrawa, 1982, 271–272; Schaum & Strich, 1987, 113; Schoenfeldt, 1982, 261; Schumann, 1982, 179–181.

161. Very few juvenile defendants had the services of an attorney. It was thought that juvenile cases were sufficiently uncomplicated that a defense attorney was not needed. The court, however, did usually appoint a youth assistant. [Neumann, 1975, 71] It was mandatory that the juvenile offender have a defense attorney or a youth assistant. [Buchholz & Schoenfeldt, 1984, 488; Luther, 1986, 334]

162. Whereby it should be noted that the advice included the necessity to confess and to appear repentant. [Neumann, 1975, 71]

163. It should be noted that the GDR regarded the right to a defense (including to a defense attorney in most circumstances) "as a necessary component of socialist criminal procedure." [Luther & Wolff, 1979, 308; also see Franz, 1984, 467–468; Lieser, 1989 47–52] It is also of interest to note that private attorneys were expected to provide legal advice to citizens without receiving payment for it. [Pryssok, 1982, 275]

164. "He must defend the juvenile and at the same time influence him pedagogically." [Amboss, 1983b, 276] Also see Amboss, 1983b, 272–276; Blumenthal, 1984, 216–218; Schoenfeldt, 1983, 135–138; Schoenfeldt, 1984, 81–84; Walter, 1976, 131–132.

Chapter 9

Case Loads and Cases

Chapter 7 presented the available data on the number of lay assessors in the state courts and on the number of member "judges" in the social courts, as well as some figures on the other lay participants in the courts of the German Democratic Republic. This chapter will present a variety of the available data on the workings of the social courts: the case loads, the types and frequency of offenses being litigated, the decisions reached, and the measures agreed to. At the end of the chapter there also will be some descriptions of particular cases to better illustrate the actual functioning of the social courts. As for the numerical materials, all the previous comments about GDR statistics apply; most of the figures reported in this chapter, however, are not particularly doubtful, being of an administrative rather than political nature.

These are the basic findings: The social courts engaged in a large number of formal deliberations. They relieved the state courts of very substantial burden. The dispute commissions handled as much 90% of all labor disputes; the arbitration commission as much 80% of minor "criminal" offenses.[1] There were considerable variations in the number of deliberations conducted by particular commissions. This was most likely a consequence of different transfer practices in the area rather than of difference in the number of offenses. The social courts used certain measures with considerable frequency, particularly restitutions, fines, formal reprimands, and apologies. Few of the social courts decisions were appealed to the state courts; even fewer were successful. On the civil side, in most cases, the parties to the dispute reached an "amicable agreement," which could be done without a formal deliberation and without the adoption of a particular measure by the commission.

CASE LOADS AND OFFENSES

The social court statistics leave much to desired. The most basic problem is not untrustworthiness but incompleteness. As will be seen, many of the data arrays suffer from "empty cells." There is, however, one social court task, the frequency of which has regularly been reported: the number of formal deliberations. Even here, the nature of the reporting leaves much to be desired. Data for all of East Germany were available only occasionally, but there were frequent arrays of local data. They permit fairly good estimates of the case loads of the social courts. The number of formal deliberations (roughly corresponding to trials in regular courts) is impressive. In the last year of the GDR, the (territorial) arbitration commissions (AC) appear to have conducted more than 16,000 deliberations, the (work-place) dispute commissions (DC) about 70,000. In the early to mid-1980s, the figures were quite uniform: about 90,000 deliberations per year, of which the dispute commissions handled nearly 80%.[2]

Apart from the special competence of the dispute commissions for labor and employment related disputes, both commission could deal with the following matters: *Misdemeanors* (*Vergehen*)—These were deliberate or careless anti-social criminal offenses, which harm the rights and interests of citizens, socialist property, society and state order, or other rights and interests of society. [AC Decree, § 23 {1}; DC Decree, § 25 {1}] The most important components of this category were theft and bodily harm. *Non-Criminal Petty Offenses* (*Verfehlungen*)—These were injuries of legally protected interests of society or citizens, in which the offense and culpability of the perpetrator were insignificant, which was reflected in the criminal code. [AC Decree, § 29 {1}; DC Decree, § 31 {1}] Previously they were classified among the misdemeanors. The most important components of this category were property offenses, breach of the peace, insults, and defamations. Some arbitration commissions reported that 90% of the Petty Offenses consisted of insult and defamations. [e.g., Probst, 1980, 192] *Public Order Offenses* (*Ordnungswidrigkeiten*)—These were culpable unlawful deeds, which manifested a lack of discipline, and which made more difficult the administration of public affairs or the development of socialist community life, but did not significantly injure the interest of socialist society or of its members, and, therefore, were not counted as crimes. [AC Decree, § 38 {1}; DC Decree, § 40 {1}] This was not a very clearly defined set of offenses. However, it included currency and custom violation, matters of considerable importance in the GDR. *Simple Civil Offenses* (*einfache zivilrechtliche Streitigkeiten*)—These were the types of disagreements commonly occurring between citizens, particularly if they shared an apartment or a house.[3] They included property and monetary disputes up to 1,000 marks. In the productive associations, they also included actions detrimental to socialist work discipline. In the residential units, the most important components of this category were disputes over small debts, not keeping residential agreements, and failure to pay child support. [AC Decree, § 17, 22; DC Decree, 50] *School Truancy Cases* (*Verletzung der Schulpflicht*)—These were instances in which a school-age child did not attend classes or other mandatory school events, or did not follow the school rules. It also covered instances where an apprentice did not properly discharge his/her duties. [AC Decree, § 43 {1}; DC Decree, § 45 {1}]

All GDR

The deliberation figures in Table 9.1 are listed separately for the different types of offenses.

As can be seen, at the end of the GDR, the social courts engaged in about 85,000 formal deliberations, more than 60% of which were related to labor disputes.[4]

The figures for an earlier year (1986) were somewhat higher (Table 9.2), which may be a function of the turmoil of 1989. Apart from the labor cases, which were handled only by the dispute commissions, the great majority of the cases were misdemeanors and petty offenses. The civil disputes formed a substantial bulk only with the arbitration commissions.

Table 9.2 (1986) does not differ substantially from Table 9.1 (1989).[5] The vast majority of non-labor cases were misdemeanors and petty offenses. Most "simple civil disputes," again, were dealt with by the arbitration commissions. As another example, in 1984, there were 5,560 simple civil cases, of which 94% were handled by the arbitration commissions. Further, 25% of all misdemeanors were handled by the social courts of the GDR.[6] The dispute commissions, again, handled all labor law cases.

To the degree that these data are representative, it is clear that the arbitration commissions were not yet as active in the 1970s as in the 1980s (Table 9.3). This would seem to be a function of the expansion of the jurisdictions

Table 9.1. GDR 1989: Formal Deliberations of the Social Courts

	Dispute Commissions	Arbitration Commissions	Both
Misdemeanors	10,844	4,870	15,714
Noncriminal petty offenses	3,221	6,052	9,273
Public order offenses	533	564	1,097
School truancy	63	267	330
Simple civil disputes	321	4,315	4,636
Labor law cases	54,093	–	54,093
Total	69,075	16,068	85,143

Data Source: Note, 1990, 89.

of the social courts in 1982.[7] It may also be be a function in part that the arbitration commissions still were fairly new in 1970. They were not fully established until 1966.

Comparing Table 9.4 to the data for 1986 (Table 9.2) and 1989 (Table 9.1), it may appear that there was a decline in the number of deliberations beyond what can be attributed to the revolutionary turmoil of 1989. The data are not entirely clear. In any case, fewer deliberations do not necessarily speak to a decline in the use or importance of the dispute commissions. They may indicate that there was a growing rate of success in other activities. The commissioners of both social courts always were strongly encouraged

Table 9.2. GDR 1986: Formal Deliberations of the Social Courts

	Dispute Commissions	Arbitration Commissions	Both
Misdemeanors	12,511	5,677	18,188
Noncriminal petty offenses	3,386	6,401	9,787
Public order offenses	645	614	1,259
School truancy	119	455	574
Simple civil disputes	342	5,123	5,465
Labor law cases	53,300	–	53,300
Total	70,303	18,270	88,573

Data Sources: Note, 1987c, 92a; Harrland, 1987, 127.

Table 9.3. GDR 1970 Second Half–Year: Formal Deliberations of the Arbitration Commissions

	Deliberations
Misdemeanors	3,721
Noncriminal petty offenses	7,235
Public order offenses	204
School truancy	171
Simple civil disputes	3,659
Labor law cases	—
Total	14,990

Data Source: Ministerium der Justiz, 1971a, 227.

to seek the resolution of disputes (as well as the prevention of incipient disputes) through informal, personal conversations, before they ever reached the stage of requiring a formal deliberation.[8] [Fuhrmann, 1981, 169] The prophylactic efforts on the part of the commissioners were truly extraordinary. Unfortunately, for most of them (e.g., probation supervisions) there are no data. But absent the social courts, all these activities would have had to be performed by state officials, at significant costs in time and salaries. Indeed, the GDR could be (and was) well pleased with the services of the social court commissioners.

Here are some additional data. The annual number of deliberations of the arbitration commissions were:

1972–1977 = 23,000 (per annum);
1981 = 19,164;
1982 = 19,243;
1983 = 19,834;
1984 = 19,125.[9]

These are equivalent figures for the dispute commissions:

1965 = 75,000;
1981 = more than 65,000;
1982 = 72,000;
1983 = 73,022;
1984 = 72,598.[10]

Table 9.4. GDR 1983 and 1984: Formal Deliberations of the Dispute Commissions

	1983	1984	1985	1987	1988
Misdemeanors	13,790	13,298	13,948	12,729	11,290
Petty offenses	4,218	3,527	3,604	3,466	3,279
Public order offenses	689	713	620	746	589
School truancy	172	186	147	108	77
Civil disputes	403	332	329	334	311
Labor law cases	53,750	54,547	55,317	57,107	57,240
Total	73,022	72,598	73,965	74,490	72,786

Data Sources: Note, 1989d, 112; Sahr, 1985, 273. There is further information that in the Berlin-Mitte area in the years 1966–69, 29% of all cases were of the simple civil type and 71% constituted the rest (i.e., misdemeanors, non-criminal petty offenses, public order offenses, school truancy). [Oehme, 1970, 89]

As already seen earlier, the dispute commissions conducted substantially more deliberations than the arbitration commissions.

Regional

Altogether then, the social courts handled about 100,000 formal deliberations per year—a significant figure for a country of the small size of the GDR. The reduction of the case load of the ordinary courts was quite remarkable. This can also be seen when examining the following percentages.

Arranging the data by the offenses and computing (unweighted) averages, the following percentages can be obtained from Table 9.5:

misdemeanors: 28%;
non-criminal petty: 37%;
public order 4;[11]
truancy: 4;
simple civil: 30.

Table 9.5. Proportion of Cases Treated in the Social Courts by Offenses

Year	Location	Type of Case	Type of Social Court	% in Social Court
1965–72	Berlin-Lichtenberg	misdemeanors	arbitration	22
		noncriminal petty	arbitration	39
		public order offenses	arbitration	5
		simple civil	arbitration	34
1966–69	Berlin-Mitte	simple civil	arbitration	29
		all other	arbitration	71
1969	Erfurt	misdemeanors	both	25
		noncriminal petty	both	51
		simple civil	both	24
1970	all GG	property offenses	both	50+
		traffic offenses	both	42
1971	all GDR	simple civil	arbitration	60
1971(x)	Halle	labor cases	dispute	70

(Continued)

Table 9.5. (Continued)

Year	Location	Type of Case	Type of Social Court	% in Social Court
		misdemeanors	dispute	25
		simple civil	dispute	4
		truancy	dispute	1
1972	Erfurt-Mitte	simple civil	arbitration	40
1974–79	Neustadt	criminal**	arbitration	72
		truancy	arbitration	3
		simple civil	arbitration	25
1977	Grossräschen	residential cases*	arbitration	40
1977(x)	Schwerin	criminal**	arbitration	69
		truancy	arbitration	3
		simple civil	arbitration	28
1979	Berlin	criminal**	arbitration	72
		truancy	arbitration	5
		simple civil	arbitration	23
1979(x)	Dresden	criminal**	arbitration	71
		truancy	arbitration	2
		simple civil	arbitration	27
1979(y)	Freiberg	criminal**	arbitration	40
		truancy	arbitration	15
		simple civil	arbitration	45
1979–83	Sandersdorf	criminal**	arbitration	79
		truancy	arbitration	7
		simple civil	arbitration	14
1980	Rostock	criminal**	arbitration	66
		truancy	arbitration	5
		simple civil	arbitration	29
1982	all GDR	criminal**	arbitration	68
		truancy	arbitration	3
		simple civil	arbitration	29
1982(x)	Berlin	criminal**	arbitration	71
		truancy	arbitration	6
		simple civil	arbitration	23

Table 9.5. (Continued)

Year	Location	Type of Case	Type of Social Court	% in Social Court
1982(y)	Potsdam	criminal**	arbitration	59
		truancy	arbitration	3
		simple civil	arbitration	38
1983	Berlin-Köpenick	criminal**	arbitration	78
		simple civil	arbitration	21
		truancy	arbitration	1
1983(x)	Berlin-Treptow	criminal**	arbitration	53
		simple civil	arbitration	47
1984	all GDR	misdemeanors	both	25
1987	all GDR	labor cases	dispute	92+
1987(x)	Frankfurt	misdemeanors	arbitration	34
		noncriminal petty	arbitration	30
		public order offenses	arbitration	3
		truancy	arbitration	3
		simple civil	arbitration	30
1987(y)	Rostock	misdemeanors	arbitration	34
		noncriminal petty	arbitration	27
		public order offenses	arbitration	5
		truancy	arbitration	3
		simple civil	arbitration	31

* Cases arising from residential and rental disputes.

** Misdemeanors, petty offenses, and public order offenses combined.

Data Sources: 1965–72 [Mager & Winkler, 1973, 88], 1966–69 [Oehme, 1970, 89], 1969 [Barwinsky, 1970, 167–168], 1970 [Probst, 1971b, 192], 1971 [Ministerium der Justiz, 1971b, 362], 1971(x) [Comment, 1973, 278], 1972 [Besser, 1973, 382], 1974–79 [Konrad, 1979, 217] 1977 [Comment, 1977, 99], 1977(x) [Heuckendorf, 1978, 191], 1979(x) [Schoene, 1980b, 274], 1979b [Becker, 1982, 53], 1979–83 [Comment, 1984a, 117], 1980 [Kersten, 1981, 113], 1982(x) [Probst, 1983, 145] 1982(y) [Kermann, 1983, 81], 1983 [Boerner, 1983, 176], 1983(x) [Pfefferkorn, 1984, 243], 1984 [Hantsche, 1985, 201], 1987 [Harrland 1987, 126], 1987(x) [Schilling, 1988, 114], 1987(y) [Kersten, 1988, 120].

In most places and at most times, petty offenses had the highest frequency, followed quite closely by misdemeanors, followed by much smaller frequencies by public order offenses. For example, these are the percentages (in order) for the GDR from 1973–1977: 45%, 23%, 5%. The difference to 100% is made up by simple civil cases. [Winkler, 1978, 102]

While there is considerable fluctuation among the figures (not surprising given the differences in time and location), it can be said that misdemeanors, petty offenses, and simple civil offenses on average account each for about 30% of the cases.[12] Public order and school truancy offenses account only for small proportions.

There also are available some additional percentages for the various offenses on a regional basis. As was seen in the summary figures for Table 9.5, it can also be seen in Table 9.6 that non-criminal petty offenses constitute the largest category, followed by misdemeanors and simple civil offenses.

For one commission (Lübztorf) the rank-order of the offenses is given (however, in typical GDR fashion, without numerical or percentage information). It is as follows: (1) insults and slanders; (2), offenses against property and monetary claims; (3). offenses relating to animals (pets); and (4). trespasses and disputes among tenants. [Kremer, 1985, 154]

There are yet other data arrays (Table 9.7). Some data were published numerically; others were given as percentages. The "criminal" categories are not differentiated. They include misdemeanors, non-criminal petty offenses, and public order violations. Clearly they predominate in the work of the arbitration commission. It must be kept in mind, however, that in this context "criminal" tends to refer to fairly minor misconduct.

For the GDR as a whole, the "criminal" cases can be broken down further, as can be seen in Table 9.8. The bulk of these cases consisted of petty offenses, followed by misdemeanors, followed at a great distance by public order offenses.

As can be seen in Table 9.9, the number of deliberations varied quite substantially among the arbitration commissions. As remarked elsewhere, more deliberations does not necessarily means more offenses in the territory; it may well be a function of the transfer practices of the police and the other agencies.

Annual averages of more than twenty cases do not seem to have been uncommon. Unfortunately, overall caseload figures, such as the number of annual formal deliberations of all social courts, are not available on a regular basis in the GDR literature.[13] In any case, as can be seen in Table 9.9, the number of deliberations varied quite substantially among the arbitration commissions.

Other Tasks and Appeals of Decisions

The deliberations were only one part of the work of the social courts. Quite apart from providing services for the public, there were also internal matters to be taken care of, such as discussions of applications for deliberations, preparations for deliberations, scheduling of deliberations, and making sure

Table 9.6. Proportion of Cases Treated in the Arbitration Commissions by Offenses

			Percent of				
Year	Location	Number of Deliberations	Misdemeanor	Noncriminal Petty	Public Order	Simple Civil	Other
1973	GDR	29,250	27	44	1	24	4
1977	Schwerin	980	29	38	–	27	6
1979	Dresden	1,832	25	45	–	27	3
1979(x)	Berlin	806	33	37	2	23	5
1979(y)	Eisenhüt.	–	26	56	–	16	2
1984	Wittenburg	43	–	74	–	21	5
1984(x)	Neubrand.	1,000		67*			

Neubrand. = Neubrandenburg
* = Misdemeanors and Non-criminal Petty Offenses
Data Sources: 1973 [Sharp & Hanhardt undated, 13], 1977 [Heuckendorf, 1978, 191], 1979 [Schoene, 1980a, 274], 1979(x) [Probst, 1980, 192], 1979(y) [Jacoby, 1985, 182], 1984 [Pietz, 1985, 154], 1984(x) [Moeller, 1985, 275].

Table 9.7. Proportion of Cases Treated in the Arbitration Commissions by Types of Offenses, Annually

Year	Location	Civil	Criminal	Truancy	Other
1973	GDR[a]	7,000	21,000	550	300
1982	GDR[b]	5,500	12,980	550	
1983	GDR[b]	5,500	13,880	580	
1979	Berlin[d]	186	584	36	
1982	Berlin[e]	205	629	50	
1979	Dresden[f]	494	1,303	35	
1981	Freiberg[g]	7	9	1	
1974–79	Neustadt-Sebnitz I[h]	27	76	3	
1981	Potsdam[i]	386	674	32	
1982	Potsdam[j]	422	658	44	
1980	Rostock[k]	356	820	60	5
1983	Berlin-Koepenick[l]	21%	78%	1%	
1976–80	Dresden[m]	21%	71%	2%	6%
1979–84	Eisenhüttenstadt V[n]	16%	82%	2%	
1979–83	Sandersdorf[o]	14%	79%	7%	
1977	Schwerin[p]	27%	67%	2%	4%

Data Sources: a. Sharp & Hanhardt, undated, 13; b. Winkler, 1983, 217; c. Winkler, 1984, 261; d. Probst, 1980, 192; e. Probst, 1983, 145; f. Schoene, 1980b, 274; g. Becker, 1982, 82; h. Konrad, 1979, 217; i. +j. Kermann, 1983, 81; k. Kersten, 1981, 113; l. Boerner, 1983, 176; m. Hauser, 1980, 280; n. Jacoby, 1985, 182; o. Comment, 1984a, 117; p. Heuckendorf, 1978, 191.

that the relevant legal points were comprehended. The arbitration commissions met at least once a month to deal with these matters. [e.g., Kratky, 1985, 226] Then, of course, there was the need to report about the work of the commission on a regular basis to various bodies and agencies. [e.g, Kapp, 1985, 139] Also there were frequent conferences of the arbitration commissions of a particular region,[14] to learn from each other and to exchange experiences.[15]

There have been some occasional data about other activities. They are presented in Table 9.10. It might be noted that the informal talks

Table 9.8. Arbitration Commission: Types of Criminal Cases

Year	Location	Misdemeanors	Noncriminal Petty	Public Order
1973	GDRa	37%	61%	2%
1973–77	GDRb	23%	45%	2%
1982	GDRc	27%	40%	2%

Data Sources: a. Sharp & Hanhardt, undated, 13; b. Winkler, 1978, 102; c. Winkler, 1983, 217.

Table 9.9. Number of Deliberations: Arbitration Commission

Year	Location	Number of Annual Deliberations
1965–72	Berlin-Lichtenberg	26
1974–79	Neustadt-Sebnitz I	21
1977	Dresden-Ost	23
1977(x)	Meuselwitz	50
1977(y)	Grossräschen	43
1979	Freiberg	20
1979(x)	Bad Lausick	24
1979(y)	Schleusingen	22
1981	Leipzig # 53	16
1982	Berlin, Süd	12
1983	Torgau III	10
1983(x)	Finsterwalde	32
1983(y)	Berlin-Koepenick	88
1983(z)	Torgelow I	27
1984	Grimmen Südwest	33
1984(x)	Wittenburg	43

Data Sources: 1965–72 [Mager & Winkler, 1973, 89], 1974–79 [Konrad, 1979, 217], 1977 [Streit, 1978, 196], 1977(x) [Ebner, 1978b, 164], 1977(y) [Comment, 1977, 99], 1979 [Becker, 1982, 53; 1979b], Heinig [1980, 142], 1979(y) [Reuther, 1979, 296] 1981 [Scholz, 1982, 79], 1982 [G. Richter, 1983, 182], 1983 [Mammitzsch, 1984, 39], 1983(x) [J. Barth, 1984, 20], 1983(y) [Probst, 1983, 148] 1983(z) [Scheffler, 1984, 20], 1984 [Keil, 1985, 64], 1984(x) [Pietz, 1985, 154].

(together with legal advice) served to reduce substantially the need for formal deliberations. Most commissions scheduled regular office hours (*Sprechstunden*) to which citizens could just drop in without having to make an appointment. Two office hours per month, each lasting two hours, seems to have been a fairly common arrangement. An average use by four citizens has been reported.[16] Some commissions, however, did not schedule regular office hours, but its members "were always available." [Kremer, 1985, 153] For example, the Schwerin arbitration commission reports that in 1971, 50% of all cases were solved via informal talks. [Heuckendorf & Kruse, 1972, 55] It is also of interest to note in this connection that about 75–80% of all cases reached the commission by way of a citizen application[17] and 20–25% being handed over by other agencies.[18] The data are from the 1960s and 1970s.[19] [Mager & Winkler, 1973, 89; Reuther, 1979, 296]

As noted, more than 90% of all labor cases received their final decision in the dispute commissions. These are the figures for particular years:[20]

1954: 86%;
1968: 90%;
1979: 85%;
1983: 93%;
1984: 92%;
1987: 92%.

Some further data are available for the dispute commissions, showing the number of deliberations, the percent labor cases, the percentage of appeals,[21] and the percentage of successful appeals (Table 9.11). Unfortunately, as always, the data are incomplete.

Clearly, the state courts were relieved of a great burden. The vast majority of labor disputes were assigned to the dispute commissions—between 60 and 93%—and as seen, over 90% of those received their final solution at these commissions.[22] While the state courts retained important guidance and control responsibilities, there can be no doubt about the very substantial savings in court time and personnel expenses. And, of course, there was the advantage to the litigants that the cases were handled expeditiously and in an unbureaucratic fashion. The GDR leaders could truly be pleased with the contributions of their lay adjudicators.

There are some data available showing the number or percentage of the appeals against the decisions of the arbitration commissions and the frequency of success for these appeals. An average of 6% (taking the figures of Table 9.12) of all cases were appealed. An average of 34% of the appealed cases were changed in some respect by the district courts, which is an average of 2% of all cases.[23]

Table 9.10. Selected Activities of the Social Courts

Year	Location	Type of Social Court	Formal Deliberation	Informal Talks	Legal Advice
1969	Lockwitz	arbitration	3	66	
1979	Schleusingen	arbitration	22		55
1982	Falkenberg	arbitration	5	11	
1983	Falkenberg	arbitration	14	16	
1984	Falkenberg	arbitration	15	4	
1985	Wittenburg	arbitration		84	124
1987	Eberswalde	arbitration	102	93	117
1987	Fürstenwalde	arbitration	144	122	397
1979–85	Eisenhüttenstadt	arbitration	57%	43%*	

* Informal talks and legal advice combined.

Data Sources: 1969 [Arnold, 1970, 205], 1979 [Reuther, 1979, 296], 1982–1984 [Kunze, 1985, 208], 1985 [Pietz, 1985, 154], 1987 [Schilling, 1988, 114]; 1979–85 [Jacoby, 1985, 182].

Table 9.11. Dispute Commission Decisions: Labor Cases, Appeals, and Changes

Year	Location	Number of Deliberations	Labor Cases (%)	Appealed (%)	Changed (%)
1954	GDR		86	0	
1964	GDR	65,000			
1965	GDR	75,000			
1978	GDR	60,000	60+	8	4
1979	GDR		85	0	
1981	GDR	65,282	75		
1983	GDR	72,022	93	7	
1984	GDR	72,598	75		

Data Sources: 1954 [Goerner & Sokolow, 1983, 77], 1964 + 1965 [Heimberger & Sokolow, 1984, 212], 1978 [Heintze, 1978, 190; Kirschner, 1979, 252; Riemann, 1976, 18], 1979 [Heusinger, 1981a, 2], 1981 [Sahr, 1982, 152], 1983 [Heusinger, 1984a, 4; Hurlbeck & Koerner, 1985, 101], 1984 [Hantsche, 1985 200; Hurlbeck & Koerner, 1985, 106].

Table 9.12. Social Court Decisions: Appeals and Changes

		Decicisons	Appeal of Decisions		Changes in Decisions % of		
Year	Location	*n*	*n*	(%)	*n*	Appeals	Cases
Arbitration Commissions							
1966	all GDR			1.5		33.0	
1984	Schwerin: County	807	42	5.2	18	42.8	2.2
1984(x)	Schwerin: City	157	7	4.5	3	42.9	1.9
1986	Leipzig	1,101	81	7.4	22	27.2	2.0
1986(x)	Dresden	1,577	102	6.5	23	22.5	1.5
1986(y)	Karl-Marx-Stadt			13.8			
Dispute Commissions							
1971	Schwerin			5.0		33.0	1.7
1974	Schwerin			2.7			
1986(z)	Leuna-Werke					8.0	

Data Sources: 1966 [Goerner, 1966a, 357], 1971 [Heuckendorf & Kruse, 1972, 51], 1974 [Stricker, 1975, 271], 1984 [Wittenberg, 1985, 150], 1984(x) [Denzin 1985, 156], 1986 [Matheus & Brueckner, 1987, 214], 1986(x) [Popp, 1987, 254], 1986(y) [Comment, 1986, 338], 1986(z) [Note, 1987b, 89].

Much pressure was placed on the parties to the dispute to reach an agreement, rather than countenance a court imposed decision. In the case of a decision (rather than an agreement) either party could appeal the court's decision, whereupon the case was transferred to the local district court. As seen, there was but a small number of appeals, the great majority of which did not succeed. The preferred outcome, in any case, was that both parties freely agreed to the recommendation of the court. The percentages that have been reported regarding "amicable agreements" (*gütliche Einigung*) can be found in Table 9.13.

Clearly at most times and in most places (to the degree that data are available), the percentage of agreements was extraordinarily high. One might conclude from this that the decisions of the commission were, in fact, fair and acceptable.[24] There is no explanation for the 1984 declines. The rate of agreement differed somewhat regarding the types of offenses. Goerner [1966a, 358] reports rates of 93.6% for minor criminal cases and 80% for simple civil cases (both figures: GDR 1966).

Table 9.13. Percent "Amicable Agreements" Arbitration Commissions

Year	Location	Agreement (%)
1964–66	GDR	80+
1966	Magdeburg	85
1968	Berlin	90
1977	Schwerin	98
1978	Grossoerne	98
1983	Berlin-Lichtenberg VIII	96
1984	GDR	57
1984(x)	Schwerin	60

Data Sources: 1964–66 [Winkler & Goerner, 1967, 206; Winkler, 1967, 401], 1966 [Comment, 1966a, 179], 1968 [Probst, 1968, 107], 1977 [Heuckendorf, 1978, 191], 1978 [Ermisch, 1979, 52], 1983 [Mager, 1984, 114], 1984 [Hurlbeck & Koerner, 1985, 105], 1984(x) [Wittenberg, 1985, 148].

DECISIONS AND MEASURES

Basic Measures

As pointed out earlier, the measures (*Massnahmen*) of the social courts were not defined as formal penalties. Riemann [1976, 18–19] provides a good summary:

> The measures stipulated by the social courts are not entered in the criminal records. Thus, a person having been called to account before a dispute or arbitration commission still has a clean police record. Having dealt with a case of misconduct or petty offense, a lay court may order reformatory measures. These may be in the form of an apology offered to the aggrieved person or one's fellow workers, an obligation to make amends for any damage caused, a reprimand, or a fine up to 150 marks. In the case of insulting behavior a social court will seek to bring about a reconciliation between the litigants. It is to deal with offenders in a critical but helpful way, expressing its views in no uncertain terms and encouraging them to mend their ways. Anyone taking part in the proceedings may declare their views to contribute to a correct appraisal of the situation and to help persuade wrongdoers to change their ways for the better.

It goes without saying that the social court was required to establish the facts, causes, and factors involved in a violation of the law without bias and to assess the personality of the wrongdoer and his or her behavior.[25]

Table 9.14. Measures of the Social Courts: Percentages

Year	Location	Apology	Restitution	Fine	Reprimand	Commitment	Agreement*
1984	GDR[b]	11	36	57	41	6	57
1979	Berlin[c]	29		15	34	23	
1982	Berlin[d]	22	16	18	29		15
1978	Rostock[e]			43			
1979–83	Sandersdorf[f]			21	18	11	50
1977	Schwerin[g]		64		83		
1984	Schwerin[h]						60

* The various measures are not mutually exclusive; most add to more than 100%. Also, it should not be assumed that the empty cells mean "no such measures." In most cases they simply represent a failure to report.

Data Sources: a. Hurlbeck & Koerner, 1985, 103–105; b. Probst, 1980, 192; c. Probst, 1983, 145; d. Behrends, 1979, 215; e. Comment, 1984a, 117; f. Heuckendorf, 1978, 192; g. Wittenberg, 1985, 148.

The key measures available to the social courts were (1) call for an apology (*Entschuldigung*), (2) require restitution for damages (*Schadenersatz*), (3) imposing a fine (*Geldbusse*), and (4) issuing a formal reprimand (*Rüge*). In addition the court could (5) confirm a self-chosen commitment (*Bestätigung einer Selbstverpflichtung*) of one of the parties, such as performing community-beneficial work (*gemeinnützige Arbeit*).[26] The court could also (6) confirm an agreement of both parties (*Bestätigung einer Einigung*), which could include a commitment regarding future conduct of one or both parties. [Huenich, 1987, 128] It is important to note that the various measures of the social courts (though largely voluntary agreements) could be enforced (executed) by other agencies, especially the district courts. [Note, 1967, 334–336; Richtlinie, 1965, 377–385] There are some figures on the measures arrived at in social court proceedings (Table 9.14).

It is difficult to discern any particular pattern in Table 9.14. This may be because of the fairly small number of available data; it may be because of the many empty cells. All measures, however, display considerable use, especially apologies, restitutions, fines,[27] and reprimands. It is clear that multiple measures were settled upon frequently. None of these measures, as noted earlier, were regarded to be formal penalties.

Fines

At first, fines could be levied to a maximum of 150 East German mark. Later this was increased to 500 mark. These were the maximum fines as of 1988: misdemeanors 500 mark, non-criminal petty offenses 150 mark, public order offenses 300 mark, school truancy 150 mark (parents). [RECHTSLEXIKON, 1988, 133] However, in exceptional cases (severe economic crimes) the fine could have been as much as 500,000 mark. [Matthias, 1980, 30] Hurlbeck & Koerner [1985, 103–104] report that in the 1980s, 59% of the fines were sums up to 150 mark and 41% were over 150 mark. Kersten [1985, 46] reports that even in 1984, in Rostock, only 34% of all fines were higher than 150 mark. The fines, then, generally were quite low. Thus, a Schwerin arbitration commission imposed a fine of 35 mark for theft; it also imposed a fine of 50 mark in a case of insult and assault. [Kruse, 1970, 374] Similarly, the arbitration commission for Nünchritz imposed a fine of 50 marks for the theft of a bicycle. [Grafe, 1978, 298] Another bicycle thief, who had a monthly net income of 800 mark, received a fine of 200 mark. A juvenile offender who had robbed the moneyboxes of streetcars also was given a 200 fine. [Pfefferkorn, 1983, 257–258][28]

Given an average monthly net income of about one thousand mark per household at the time [DDR HANDBUCH, 1985, 342], such fines were not particularly excessive or painful. Indeed, there was official concern that the offender should be well able to pay the fine. [Roehl, 1972, 252]

For example, fines could not be imposed on juveniles in truancy cases. [Jackwitz, 1983, 113] Along the same line, there were severe limits on to what degree wages of debtors could be garnisheed.[29] On the other hand, occasional complaints can be found in the literature that the fines tend to be too low and "seldom reach the level of the offender's monthly income."[30] In any case, in a further demonstration of regime concern, the fines could generally be paid in installments. For example, a Gero arbitration commissions imposed fines of 150, 100, and 50 mark on three juvenile offenders. Each was given the opportunity to pay these fines in five monthly installments. [Leutzsch, 1975, 256] The voluntary fulfillment of the social court measures were a matter of great importance in the GDR.[31] Kersten [1985, 47] reports that between 60 and 90% of all fines were paid voluntarily (without an order from a state court). However, if the fines were not paid voluntarily and expeditiously, political (city council) and legal (district court) agencies were called on to take action, such garnisheeing the offender's wages. [Note, 1969, 398; Winkler, 1972, 22–23]

Educational Measures and Third-Party Recommendations

There were several other acts which the social courts could and were expected to perform, especially assigning educational obligations to the offender and formal recommendations to third parties. In 1984, for example, the dispute commissions, as part of their labor deliberations, imposed 2,920 educational obligations on account of violations of work discipline (*Erzieherische Verfahren wegen Verletzung von Arbeitspflichten*). This equals only about 4% of all deliberations—not a large proportion. [Hurlbeck & Koerner, 1985, 107] The other task was to issue formal recommendations (*Empfehlungen*) to firms or agencies to eliminate the likely causes of conflicts and wrong-doings. There have been occasional reports. For example, in 1984, for all of the GDR, the social courts issued 10,924 recommendations.[32] [Hurlbeck & Koerner, 1985, 101] There are some local data for the dispute commissions separately. They show substantially higher percentages. In 1984, in the district of Poessneck, 22.7% of all deliberations resulted in formal recommendations. [Seiffert, 1985,165] In 1983, in Rostock, 19 of 48 deliberations of the arbitration commission resulted in a formal recommendation (40%).

In any case, there were constant directives to the commissions to issue more recommendations. In fact, the literature included admonitions to the effect that there should be no decisions without recommendations.[33] [Stegemann, 1976, 247] They could be issued to social organizations, enterprise managers, directors of cooperative farms, schools, state agencies, and simply any institution that might be of service in changing the conditions that led to the offense.[34] The arbitration commissions issued recommendation to all types of recipients; most of the recommendations of the dispute commissions were directed to the own firm (enterprise). [Anders, 1966, 435]

To issue a formal recommendation, of course, required that the social court undertake a comprehensive causal analysis. [Mager & Winkler, 1973, 87] The court then issued a finding regarding the conditions and circumstances that had contributed (or, even, caused) the problem or crime. For example, in the case of theft from an enterprise, the court was to inspect the system of controls and regulations which regulated the workers' access to the various tools and materials. The discovery of any deficiencies or defects would then be the object of the court's critique and of it recommendations how to improve the situation so that this type of offense was not likely to occur again.

The most important task, it was continuously emphasized, was to identify the connections between the offender and the causes of the offense. It will be remembered that the GDR regime was utterly convinced that crime was alien to socialism. If a crime occurred, something had to have gone wrong. If this something could be identified, the crime in question could be prevented in the future. [Leymann, 1967, 329] The court was to search for all types of causes: organizational, material, and derelictions of duty. All of these, of course, could be improved with the right recommendation. The offender's personal characteristics also were relevant to the degree that they manifested wrong attitudes regarding the manners and obligations of socialist living.[35]

However, the practice of some arbitration commissions (for example, in the case of neighborly disputes) to issue recommendations to both parties "to be better neighbors," were thought not to be helpful. An informal consultation was seen as more appropriate. [Matthias, 1971, 329] The use of a recommendation was more successful when it was addressed to the local housing authority, which then found a place to live for one of the hostile parties.[36] As pointed out earlier, the miserable housing situation in the GDR produced many of the conflicts with which the commissions had to deal—and which they were powerless to remedy, recommendations or not. For many commissions, about 90% of the civil disputes regarded housing matters. [Lehmann, 1974, 133] Needless to say, neighborly relations and disputes received much attention in the literature. [e.g., Walpert & Jackwitz, 1981, 212–219]

The duties of the social courts extended beyond issuing the recommendation; they also were obligated to scrutinize what happened to the recommendations. In fact, the recipient of social court recommendations had the responsibility to report back within two weeks, and to spell out in writing what they had done on the basis of the recommendation, or explain why they had not followed it.[37] If, in the later case, the court was not persuaded by the recipients explanation, it could take the matter to higher authorities, including the state courts. This procedure was adopted to give the social courts a real control function. [Anders, 1965, 135–136]

CASES

A number of actual social court cases have been discussed earlier. A few additional cases will round out the picture.[38] These cases have been reported in the GDR literature, especially in ARBEIT UND ARBEITSRECHT, regarding the dispute commissions, and in DER SCHÖFFE, regarding the arbitration commissions. Unfortunately, most of the published reports are rather condensed, usually stating the key points that were to be made, and little else. Contextual and background materials often are quite limited. Nevertheless, the materials can convey some additional understanding of the functioning and responsibilities of the social courts. They also convey, I think, the ease and utility with which these cases can be allotted to lay tribunals—and, very importantly, that if the social courts could not resolve the dispute, there were still the regular courts to take over. The social courts did not necessarily have to be the last instance and authority. The published materials will be identified as *Case Reports,* where no author is listed.

Dispute Commission Cases

Case 1: Responsibility for Loss. The enterprise (a restaurant) filed an application with the DC to hold manager V. responsible for a loss of 2,559 mark. While first working with enthusiasm and consummate attention to detail, later he became negligent and no longer controlled deliveries as to the right quantities and the correct monetary amounts. Similarly, the cashier's register was not accurately maintained. Mr. V. had been variously warned about his careless business habits, but to no effect. The DC found Mr. V. to be responsible for the loss, which he has to replace in the full amount. [Case Report, 1987c, 138]

Case 2: Dawdling at Work. The enterprise asked the DC to consider the case of the apprentice L. The issues were lack of work discipline, unexcused missing of work, and dawdling at work. His school reports also were very poor. Since Mr. L. was not yet of age, his parents were asked to be present at the deliberation. The apprentice acknowledged his misconduct; he blamed the negative influence of others as well as his own laziness. There had been a number of informal consultations with the master and the collective, which helped, but not enough. The DC issued a formal reprimand (*Rüge*) against the apprentice. It also confirmed the self-chosen commitment to improve his school reports, at least to a C, and to exhibit better work discipline. [Case Report, 1987d, 160]

Case 3: Recognition of Enterprise Membership. The worker M. applied to the DC for a formal recognition of his enterprise membership for the last two years and, accordingly, the payment of the annual bonus of 200 mark each. The facts were that in these two years Mr. M. had worked at another enterprise on the order of his own enterprise. This position was found to be in conformity with §50.3 of the GDR labor code, which states that the enterprise membership continues if an employee is ordered to perform work elsewhere for a period of time. Accordingly, the DC decided that the two bonuses must be paid. [Case Report, 1987e, 187]

Case 4: A Traffic Case. This was a case that came the the DC by way of a transfer from the Berlin police. The arraigned person, a Ms. S., was accused of having caused a grave traffic accident because she did not yield the right of way, as she was obligated to do. As a consequence, there was not only property damage, but also a severe personal injury, which left the other person unable to work. Ms. S. was a physician. She testified that the accident had made a deep impression on her. The DC saw in this an already realized needed educational effect, but decided that the payment of a fine (300 mark) would further strengthen this effect. Ms. S.'s collective gave a guarantee (*Bürgschaft*) for future blameless conduct. The police had confiscated Ms. S.'s driver's license at the scene of the accident. However, her work included home visits to to sick persons. Therefore the DC issued a recommendation to the police to return the driver's license after a period of three months. [Case Report, 1988a, 40]

Case 5: A Work Discipline Case. Worker H. (a type-setter) did not like the illumination at his place of work. Measurings, however, showed that the illumination was in conformity with the official standards. This did not satisfy Mr. H. He brought his own lamps to his workplace, where he installed them in various ways. The safety inspector of the enterprise objected to the personal lamps and asked Mr. H. to remove them, as he was entitled to do. Mr. H. lost his temper, insulted and attacked the safety inspector. From then on, he did not fulfill his work obligations. The director of the enterprise petitioned the DC to conduct a formal deliberation. At this deliberation Mr. H. showed himself entirely unreasonable. He did not see that he had done wrong and did not draw any lesson from it. The members of Mr. H.'s work collective condemned his behavior unanimously. The DC issued a formal reproach (*Rüge*) against Mr. H., it also required that he apologize to the safety inspector in the presence of his work collective. [Case Report, 1988b, 88]

Case 6: Correct Work Assignment. Ms. K. petitioned the DC because she thought that she had been asked to do work that had not been stipulated in her work contract. She had been a specialist (*Sachbearbeiter*), but now (after an illness) was asked to work at a lower skill level. The DC found that the new work assignment for Ms. K. did not conform to the regulations of the GDR labor code and the enterprise work contract. Also, the enterprise had failed to obtain the necessary agreement of the labor union for this reassignment. The DC asked the enterprise to revoke the work reassignment and to reconsider the matter. [Case Report, 1988c, 162]

Case 7: Work Dismissal. The kitchen worker P. asked the DC to look into his firing without notice, which he thought was not justified. He also asked for payment of the sum that he lost because of the dismissal. The facts were that Mr. P. had committed a number of violations against the work discipline. The enterprise conducted a disciplinary hearing against Mr. P., in which management and workers' representatives participated. The hearing decided on dismissal without notice. The DC found that the provisions of the GDR labor code had not been adequately observed. The necessary consent of the enterprise labor union also had not been obtained. The DC decided that the dismissal had not been proper and had to be revoked. The lost pay was to be disbursed. [Case Report, 1988d, 185]

Case 8: Day for Housework (Hausarbeitstag). After a period of leave, Ms. U. began to work again for the enterprise on May 4, 1988. The director denied Ms. U. the legally required off-day for homework, saying that it was due only to persons who worked all month for the enterprise. Ms. U. appealed to her DC that she be granted such a day even for May. The DC found that the legal codes of the GDR specified that the off-day is to be granted for a given month if the employees had worked for more than one-half of the workdays of that month. Accordingly, the DC decided that the enterprise had to grant retroactively the day in question to Ms. U. [Case Report, 1988e, 232]

Arbitration Commission Cases

Case 1: Dog Disturbances. The applicant asked the AC to hold a deliberation regarding the dog of a neighbor (in the same house). The dog barks and howls at all hours, day and night. Various complaints and discussions had no effect. The applicant was unable to rest and sleep. The AC found that the complaint was accurate, even though other parties, living in the same house, were not bothered by the dog and did not complain—which was essentially the defense of the dog's owner. The AC decided that the owner must within six weeks train the dog so that he no longer causes disturbance, if this is not possible the dog has to be removed from the apartment. [Case Report, 1983a, 92–93]

Case 2: Theft. Two juveniles committed a series of thefts. The police transferred the case to the AC. To increase the educational effect of the deliberation, the AC invited the participation of the parents, the homeroom teacher, the class FDJ secretary, a representative of the "youth assistance" (*Jugendhilfe*), a fellow student, and yet other citizens. The juvenile offenders freely admitted their acts. There were no previous misdeeds. They were popular among their fellow-students. Their grades in school were good. The current offenses, however, were serious. They could not be regarded as pranks. They were criminal acts against personal and socialist property, as well as damage to said property. The juveniles, however, had come to recognize the error of their acts and had taken the proper lessons from their misconduct.

They already sought to make up for the damages that they caused by way of unpaid voluntary work at the affected enterprises. They also have issued apologies to all affected parties. Given these circumstances, the AC did not impose additional educational measures. The court could only confirm the self-chosen obligation (*Selbstverpflichtung*) to work at vacation periods and use the earnings to pay for the damages. In addition, there was to be a conference of the "youth assistance" in six months to determine whether the two juveniles indeed changed their ways. [Mueller, 1983, 115–118]

Case 3: Truancy. The school applied to the AC for a deliberation regarding the continual truancy of a student. The deliberation revealed that the parents took no interest in the education of their son. They paid no attention to the messages sent by the school. The deliberation also revealed that the parents had to work at unfavorable times, which made it difficult to fulfill their parental duties. The AC arranged that there would be better cooperation between school and parents, and that the class collective took on a "guarantee" (*Bürgschaft*) for the student. The AC also issues a formal recommendation to the workplaces of the parents to arrange for better worktimes. [Weckert, 1983, 158–159]

Case 4: Truancy. Upon application of the school, the AC deliberated in the case of student W., who had frequently offended against the school regulations by not attending classes, by provocative conduct against teachers and fellow-students, and by exhibiting ill regard against teachers and fellow-students. The director of the school, the homeroom teacher, the chairman of the parent-aktiv, two FDJ representatives, and six fellow-students were present at the deliberation. Student W. was characterized as highly intelligent, yet a very poor scholar, with many Ds and Fs on his report card. Student W. told the AC that he was sorry for his irresponsible conduct. He was determined to change his behavior, and he took on the obligation to improve his scholastic performance. The AC decided to issue a formal reproach against W. It also confirmed the self-chosen obligation to obey school regulations, to improve his grades, and to participate actively in the class collective and the class's FDJ group. [Case Report, 1984b, 141–143]

Case 5: Drunk in Public. This case was transferred to the AC by the police who regarded it as a public order offense. Mr. K. had consumed great quantities of alcoholic beverages in the afternoon of the day in question. At about 7:00 pm he was discovered drunk and improperly clothed lying in the street. There was much pedestrian traffic in the area. Many persons took offense at Mr. K's condition. The police escorted him to his home. The AC decided to issue a formal reproach, assessed a fine of 300 mark, and gave him the obligation to work again on a regular basis (which he had failed to do for more than two months). [Case Report, 1985, 117]

Case 6: Disturbance of the Peace. The neighbors of Mr. X. applied to the AC to consider the matter of frequent disturbances in the apartment house at night. There was loud music and alcohol-induced noise. Investigations by the police confirmed this charge. Mr. X. apologized and promised that there would be no more disturbances. The AC decided to accept the apology and to confirm the self-chosen obligation not to cause any further disturbances. [Case Report, 1986a, 188]

Case 6: Theft of Socialist Property. Two juveniles had visited a pub; they consumed large quantities of beer. On the way to the restroom, they noticed several cases of beer in the hallway. They got the idea to steal some bottles. Accordingly, one of them went outside and the other handed him the bottles though the window. When they sought to depart with the stolen bottles, they were caught by a police patrol. The value of the bottles was about 30 mark. The juveniles recognized the wrong that they had done. It was a one-time misdeed, partly caused by excessive alcohol consumption. They stated that they had learned the necessary lessons and that it would not happen again. The AC did not impose further educational or other measures. There had been restitution. However, the AC issued two formal recommendations: one to the bureau responsible for alcohol sales, with the advice to better control the sale of alcoholic beverages to juveniles (the pub had not even tried to ascertain their ages), and one to the pub, with the advice not to store merchandise in the hallway where it can easily be pilfered. [Case Report, 1986b, 212]

Case 7: Redress of Damages. One neighbor (in an apartment house) had complained frequently about the other neighbor's loud TV reception. The complaints (to the neighbor) had no effect. Therefore, the complaining neighbor tore up the other neighbor's antenna, which ran close by the window. This ended all TV reception. The affected neighbor applied to the AC, asking for damages. The AC decided that the tearing up of the antenna was illegal and damages would have to be paid. The AC also informed the applicant about the city regulation regarding protection against noise. [Case Report, 1987f, 24]

Case 8: Deliberate Damage to Socialist Property. This case was sent by the police to the AC. A 17-year-old miscreant destroyed three windows of the local high school and entered the school though the demolished windows. However, there was no damage or theft in the interior. The police established a high level of blood alcohol. The cost of the windows was 125 mark; the expense of the blood test was 150 mark. The sums were paid by the juvenile prior to the AC deliberation. The AC found that the accused had had disciplinary problems in the past. The AC also found that he was capable of criminal responsibility (*Schuldfähig*). He knew that the deliberate destruction of socialist property was a serious crime. The accused stated that he had consumed several alcoholic beverages on the day in question. He assumed the self-chosen obligation to do 15 hours of voluntary, unpaid labor. The AC decided that he would have to pay a fine of 80 mark. The AC also confirmed the self-chosen obligation of unpaid labor. [Case Report, 1987g, 44–44a]

Case 9: Slander. The accused lived one floor below the citizen who applied to the AC to bring about an end to what she perceived to be slanderous statements. The applicant reported that the accused had stated, at various times and to various persons, that the applicant poured acid on her flowers, threw refuse on her balcony, and provoked her dog to bark. The AC found that these statements were not only not truthful but were a violation of §138 of the GDR criminal code. Furthermore, the accused had been given several opportunities to reach an agreement by way of informal consultations. She did not take advantage of chances, but continued the defamatory statements. The AC decided to issue a formal reproach against the accused. This decision was to be publicly displayed for one week in the apartment house in question. [Case Report, 1987h, 131]

NOTES

1. It should be noted that formal deliberations were but one part of the work of the commissions—and a minor part as such.
2. Heusinger, 1984b, 3; Hurlbeck & Koerner, 1985, 101; Winkler, 1984, 261.
3. As pointed out before, given the insufficient and cramped housing conditions in the GDR, frequent neighborly disputes were inevitable.
4. The high number of labor disputes in a "workers' state" is likely to be a function of the privileged position of labor in the GDR. At least since the revolt of 1953, the regime was genuinely afraid of its workers. They were given almost absolute job security, they did not have to compete for jobs, and they had virtual veto power over wages, prices, and work norms. [Sperlich, 2006, 123] Accordingly, workers were not shy to combat perceived or actual disadvantages—which could be done at little risk and low cost at the dispute commissions.
5. In addition to the data in Tables 9.1 and 9.2, the following figures are available; they represent the annual deliberations in the GDR of both commissions. Dispute commissions: 1964: 65,000; 1965: 75,000; 1981: 65,000; 1982: 68,741; 1983: 73,022; 1984: 72,598. Arbitration commissions: 1982: 19,243; 1983: 19,834; 1984: 19,125. [Heimberger, 1984, 212; Hurlbeck & Koerner, 1985, 101; Seiffert, 1985, 165]
6. Also in 1984, there were 802 monetary claims, all of which were dealt with by the arbitration commissions. [Hurlbeck & Koerner, 1985, 101] For the Berlin area in 1983, the "simple civil disputes" broke down as follows: 74% trespasses and disputes among tenants, 10% monetary claims, and 16% other disputes. [Beyer, 1983, 179]
7. For discussions of the 1982 expansion of the jurisdictions of the social courts see Beckmann, 1983, 187–190; Heusinger, 1983a, 73–75; Heusinger, 1984b, 3–6; Kern, 1982, 69–80; Pirntke, 1982, 370–371; Posorski, 1982, 95–111; Weichelt, 1982a, 93–94. The statutory changes of 1982, it should be noted, also increased the duties of the social court commissioners. [Krueger, 1984, 91–92]
8. As an example, the arbitration commission of Berlin-Lichtenberg for the years 1965–1972 reported an average of 60 *informal discussions* per year. This compares

to a yearly average of 26 *formal deliberations* for the same commission and the same period. [Mager & Winkler, 1973, 88]

9. Data sources: for 1972 [Heusinger, 1978, 159; Winkler, 1978, 102], for 1981 [Winkler & Matheus, 1983, 16], for 1982 [Heusinger, 1983b, 122], for 1983 [Winkler, 1984, 261], for 1982–1984 [Hurlbeck & Koerner, 1985, 101].

10. Data sources: for 1965 [Goerner & Sokolow, 1983, 78], for 1981 [Kern, 1982, 69], for 1982 [Heusinger, 1984b, 3], for 1983 [Hantsche, 1985b, 25], for 1984 [Hurlbeck & Koerner, 1985, 101].

11. Computing the average for the combined "criminal" category gives 67%—very close to the sum of the three separate offenses.

12. A different array provides the following social court figures for 1984 (all GDR):

offenses against socialist property: 37%;
offenses against personal property: 38%;
deliberate bodily harm: 42%;
unauthorized used of motor vehicles: 30%.
[Oberstes Gericht, 1985, 190]

13. At an earlier time, Markovits [1978, 634, n.82] could not find such data either, in her search of the GDR literature.

14. In typical socialist fashion, there also were organized competitions between the commissions. [e.g., Adler, 1986, 82–83] This followed the pattern set earlier with the lay assessors collectives at the regular courts. These collectives also had to show their merits by frequent competitive comparisons. [e.g., Schroeter, 1985, 128; Schroeter & Baufeldt, 1986, 199]

15. [e.g., Kersten, 1985, 44; Loewe, 1985, 140; Note, 1985, 147; Zecher, 1985, 152–3]

16. Ebner, 1980b, 68; Gruenert, 1980,33; Hauser, 1980, 280; Heinrich, 1980, 38; Lindau, 1985, 85; Parthen, 1985, 69.

17. In one case (1983 Rostock) there were 74 applications which resulted in 48 formal deliberations (65%). [Weckert, 1985, 65] It can be assumed that most the remaining 26 applications were handled by way of informal consultations, though some have been returned as not appropriate for a social court.

18. Some data are available regarding the number of transfers to the social courts (both types) from other agencies: 1964 = 27,888; 1965 = 28,050; 1966 = 31,444. [Hiller, 1967, 232] Assuming some 85,000 cases, the transfers constitute about one-third—somewhat higher than the one-fourth reported elsewhere.

19. Available data from the USSR (1969 Saratow Region) show the reverse picture: citizen application 27%, from other agencies 71%, self-initiated 2%. [Braeuer, 1972, 409]

20. Data sources: Goerner & Sokolow, 1983, 76; Harrland, 1987, 126; Heusinger, 1981a, 2; Heusinger, 1984b, 4; Hurlbeck & Koerner, 1985, 106; Tisch, 1982, 114; Wuensche, 1968, 198.

21. Generally less than 10%. [Gaum, 1990, 89]

22. For a detailed description of one dispute commission case see Heinecke, 2000, 81–107.

23. The arbitration commission Falkenberg/Elster reported but a single appeal of a decision. The appeal was unsuccessful. [Kunze, 1985, 208]

24. My interviews produced the same conclusion.

25. Hauschild, 1983, 6–6; Seidel & Rindert, 1987, 96; Schulz, 1980, 150–152.

26. Dietzel, 1987, 61; Plitz & Teichler, 1976, 230–235.

27. There was a consistent emphasis that even fines should be treated as an "educational measure." [Hofmann, 1989, 233; Matthias, 1980, 30; Pfefferkorn, 1983, 257; Stricker, 1976, 75]

28. Substantially higher fines, however, tended to imposed in cases of theft of socialist property and where the offender had a high income or considerable savings. [Lang, 1986, 160–162]

29. Dutschke & Wallis, 1987, 62–64; Kruschke, 1955, 233; Hauschild, 1976, 21–23.

30. Comment, 1972b, 254; Hofmann, 1989, 234–235; Reuther, 1979, 298.

31. See Haase, 1980, 85; Stricker, 1976, 78; Winkler & Goerner, 1967, 206.

32. Given nearly 90,000 deliberations, this is a larger but still fairly low amount (12%).

33. The literature also contained special instructional materials on how to work with recommendations. [Note, 1982d, 124–126; see also Anders, 1966, 434–435] Clearly, GDR officials took the matter of recommendations very seriously.

34. Luederitz, 1975, 228; Mueller, 1971, 162; Stegemann, 1969, 20.

35. Anders, 1965, 133–135; Kornetzki, 1972, 305–307; Mager, 1975, 156–159.

36. Brauner, 1975, 193; also see Luederitz, 1975, 228–229; Prueger, 1977, 10.

37. It appears that some recipients of social court recommendations saw it as a form of meddling rather than help. They did not follow the legal prescriptions to respond. [Mager & Winkler, 1973, 90–92; Voeckler, 1974, 395]

38. Of course, the cases discussed here are a very small part of an extensive array of social court cases reported in the GDR literature.

Chapter 10

Assessment and Evaluation

FIVE PERSPECTIVES

How well did the social courts work? To answer this question, the views and experiences of five East German groups should be examined first: the political leadership of the GDR, the commissioners of the social courts, the public at large, the professional jurists, and the litigants who had their cases adjudicated by social courts. Unfortunately, only the views of the members of the first two groups are available to any degree—and not in a systematic fashion. For the professional jurists one has to rely on the impressions of the social court commissioners. For the the public at large and the litigants there are only personal impressions[1] (see the data collection discussions of Chapter 3). Needless to say, my assessments and conclusions must be regarded as highly tentative.

Some of the contributions of the social courts are difficult to assess. It is quite impossible to know how many open disputes were prevented through vigilance and preventive efforts of the commissions. Only an indirect, and not very precise, indicator is available: the relative satisfaction of Party and state leadership. As will be seen later, it appears to have been extraordinarily high. Verbal expressions are lavish and glowing. The more convincing testimony, however, was leadership *behavior,* about which there was no ambiguity: the commissions' substantive competence and formal powers were increased steadily and significantly (the last time in 1982).

Political Leadership

A fairly definite conclusion can be reached for the leadership of the GDR. Party, state, and societal authorities declared themselves well satisfied with the work of the social courts. When anniversaries of the social courts were to be celebrated—and well celebrated they were—the GDR elite turned out in full force. For example, in 1983, in Berlin, at the celebration of the thirtieth anniversary of the dispute commissions, these office holders (and yet others) participated: Dr. Sorgenicht (chairman of the state and law section of the central committee of the SED, member of the council of state, and prosecutor general of the GDR), Dr. Streit (chief justice of the supreme court), Dr. Toeplitz (undersecretary of the ministry of justice), Dr. Kern (deputy minister of internal affairs), Lieutenant General Giel (of the people's army), Mr. Heintze (member of the central committee of the SED and member of the governing body of the GDR labor union), and Harry Tisch (member of the politburo of the SED and chairman of the governing body of the GDR labor union). Harry Tisch also handed out medals and awards to outstanding commission members.

Also in 1983 in Berlin, at the celebration of the twentieth anniversary of the arbitration commissions, some of the same office holders participated (Sorgenicht and Toeplitz), as well as these personalities: Dr. Heusinger (minister of justice), Dr. Harrland (deputy prosecutor general), Mr. Kirchhoff (vice president of the secretariat of the National Front), Lieutenant General Riss (deputy minister of internal affairs), Dr. Weichelt (chairman of the legal committee of the Volkskammer), and, again, many other prominent members of political and social organs. [Note, 1983, 227] Parallel celebrations took place in various localities throughout the GDR, in addition to Berlin. [e.g., Kapp, 1985, 139; Note, 1988, 138–139]

One can think of no equivalent American events which so clearly and magnanimously honored citizens who gave of their time and effort in the service of the administration of justice. For American jurors, a little recognition would go a long way. But it seems, it is not to be had.

Many of the (highly complimentary) writings cited in this volume were authored by high-level party and ministry officials, high-ranking judges, distinguished legal scholars, and prominent leaders of societal organizations. The many approving writings (and speeches) were not mere oration. The history of the GDR social courts is one of constant expansion—in numbers, responsibilities, and power (competence). Evidence of satisfaction was presented most convincingly with the adoption of new codes for the social courts in March 1982. The development of the new codes had been signaled for many years in the party programs and other statements issued by the SED. The adoption was preceded (as was nearly always the case with new laws in the GDR) by public discussions and major literary outpourings, uniformly supporting the further increases in social court responsibilities and authority.

While the tenor of GDR commentaries on the social courts had always been one of high praise, the acclamations reached new levels of applause in the discussions regarding the drafting, adoption, and implementation of the 1982 laws. The comments on the new code were uniformly favorable.[2] Official commentaries were uniformly positive.[3] Here are some examples: "The dispute commissions are part of the strong foundation of our socialist state. They are convincing examples of the development of socialist democracy . . . The commissioners have contributed—with heart, mind, and increasing legal understanding—to the development of socialist legality and its becoming an ever more stable cornerstone of socialist life . . . They have become important and influential organs of GDR justice." [Heintze, 1978, 190] "The dispute commissions have justified the high responsibility that they had been given . . . They enjoy the respect and confidence of their fellow-citizens." [Heintze, 1983, 137] "The dispute commissions have become an absolutely necessary factor in the socialist legal education of the workers." [Kamin & Sokolow, 1988, 74] "The arbitration commissions have made an essential contribution to the development of socialist justice . . . They have shown, as minister Heusinger said, that the working class is well able to administer the law in an effective and responsible way." [Seliger, 1978, 332] "The arbitration commissions have acquired a firm and respected place in the administration of justice . . . They are tried and tested organ of socialist democracy . . . The commissioners gain ever more authority because of their outstanding work and unflagging efforts." [Kern, 1983, 226] "The arbitration commissions have become an essential element in our uniform system of courts, socialist justice would be unthinkable without them. They render an indispensable contribution to the ever increasing legal security of our citizens." [Peller, 1988, 71] The arbitration commissions "have become a convincing exemplar of the development and perfection of socialist democracy and a unmistakable expression of the direct exercise of political power on part of the citizen, and thereby a clear reflection of socialist constitutional realities . . . The commissioners have rendered highly recognized contribution to the safeguarding of legality, order, and security." [Heusinger, 1988, 109–110] "The successful work of the arbitration commissions led to an ever closer connection between the people and socialist law . . . They contributed to greater adherence to the law and to the prevention of law breaking."[4] [Probst, 1968, 105]

Commissioners

The commissioners of the social courts, while also very positive about their work, nevertheless had a variety of complaints. The great majority of their published[5] views, however, express satisfaction with and support for the social court system. There was relatively little criticism of the commissions as such. Intra-organizational complaints were largely about not keeping deadlines [Arway, 1980, 225], and not adequately following up on the implementation of decisions [Gensch, 1981, 263]. Much more substantial and pervasive were the extra-organizational complaints. There were many charges of insufficient legal guidance,[6] lack of adequate educational and informative opportunities,[7] and inadequate cooperation with other judicial organs as well as with other agencies and organizations.[8] Complaints about inadequately prepared transfers were noted earlier. [Seidel, 1982, 14] Frequent complaints could also be found regarding inadequate material support, for example, finances, space, secretarial help, books, typewriters, other working materials, and dependable budgets.[9] It appears, however, that these deficiencies were largely overcome by the mid- and late-1980s, largely by making the local councils legally responsible for the material support of the commissions. [Ziegler, 1989, 173–174] Also, as noted earlier, there was unhappiness about insufficient use of the commissions, especially in truancy cases.[10] Related to this was the complaint of lack of public interest in the work of the social courts, manifested particularly in low public attendance of their deliberations.[11] And further related to this were repeated complaints about lack of public appreciation and esteem.[12]

Feelings of not being appreciated also stemmed from shortfalls in official honors and awards—public honors being matters of great importance in countries where recognition through economic success (wealth) is not available. However, there had been a substantial increase in the 1980s in the awards of public honors to lay judges and social court commissioners—including ceremonies conducted in the plenary chamber of parliament, with the participation of such dignitaries as the chief justice, the minister of justice, the chief public prosecutor, and of high officials of political and societal organizations.[13]

These, then, were the complaints. The complaints, however, were not the predominant side of the story. The positive comments were vastly more frequent than the negative ones. One could fill a whole book with them. Here are some samples of the commissioners' own commentaries: "The dispute commissions have become successful organs of societal education." [Hantzschmann, 1960, 209] There has been "substantial proof of the success of the dispute commissions in the societal education of colleagues who offended against the rules of socialist law . . . The consultations and deliberations helped them to understand that such conduct undermines our worker-and-farmer-state, which provides for them a life of prosperity and in peace." [Barth, 1960, 365; also see Jessnitzer, 1960, 367] "The dispute commissions have done exemplary work toward the realization of socialist legality . . . Their work was based on a high sense of responsibility and great expertise . . . They have been greatly successful in prevention and fight against crime, and in the development of the socialist legal consciousness among our citizens. [Hantsche, 1977, 113–116]

"The arbitration commission was able to bring all cases (direct applications as well as transfers) to a successful conclusion . . . The best educational results occurred when many citizens participated in the deliberations." [Heldner, 1965, 210–211] "The arbitration commissions performed good and effective work . . . Most of the litigants whose disputes were solved by the commissions did not return with similar problems . . . because the measures of the commissions were sound and well-regarded." [Diedrich & Kruse, 1967, 216] The arbitration commissions "contribute greatly to the prevention and solution of disputes among the citizens . . . They help to form the mode of socialist communal life." [Posorski, 1979b, 161] The work of the arbitration commissions in Neubrandenburg has been exceedingly successful, "most deliberations produced positive outcomes . . . with very high public participation." [Seidel, 1988, 79] The crucial task of social courts, it will be remembered, was educational rather than punitive. Accordingly, the literature contains continual accounts of how educational measures (usually just a good talking to) produced a real change in the offender, who recognized the error of his ways, and was not likely to repeat them.[14]

To return to the complaints, it should be noted here that American jurors frequently complain about the conditions of service, particularly about the length of time that trials sometimes take, and which can cause serious personal and employment difficulties. [Kennebeck, 1975, 236–237; Pabst & Munsterman, 1975, 496] Important issues are the lack of adequate compensation for lost wages, the extraordinary time that jurors must spend waiting. One study found that waiting takes up to 60% of the juror's time at court. [C. Simon, 1975, 208] It does not help that the waiting period is one of "utter boredom."[15] [Timothy, 1975, 18] American jurors also perceive a lack of decent respect for their contributions in juror facilities that lack the most elementary comforts—and sometimes even basic necessities.[16]

In addition, American jurors often encounter discourtesies, disrespect, and regimentation. [Kennebeck, 1975, 237; Schott, 1977, 59] One juror reflected on his service as follows: "The potential or actual juror quickly learns that he is a manipulated cog in a heavy-handed procedure. He has no say-so in a complex and vaguely comprehended machinery of rules, rituals, and arbitrary commands. If he has any questions, they are either ignored or curtly deflected not with reasoned explanations but with declarations to the effect that this is the way it will be done and you have no choice in the matter." [Kraft, 1982, 599] Whatever the problems were encountered by GDR social court judges or lay assessors in the ordinary courts, nothing in their experience would even come close to these sentences. It is not surprising that many U.S. citizens consider a call to jury a nuisance at best and that as many as one-half of the persons called seek to be excused from the honor. [Richert, 1977, 236] In this respect, we can learn a great deal from the GDR. The East German legal system was far superior in motivating and rewarding lay adjudicators.

As noted in several earlier places, empirical studies were not a GDR strong suit. Numerous inquiries on my part produced zero results. There are several possible explanation. One, empirical research on the social courts simply was not done. Two, empirical research was undertaken, but with such unfavorable result that the studies (or, at least, their publications) had be suppressed. It may have been a combination of both. I give more credence to the first. Given the low status of empirical work (as against theoretical treatises) in the GDR, simple lack of endeavor seems plausible. On the other hand, of course, the suppression of unwelcome facts was standard socialist procedure. It is not a puzzle I can solve, particularly since post-1989 efforts have been no more successful than earlier ones.

In any case, I was able to discover only a brief synopsis of one research venture. It regarded the dispute commissions and was undertaken by student of the labor union college "Fritz Heckert," apparently in 1986.[17] The results were uniformly positive: 92.3% of the respondents assigned high authoritativess to the dispute commission; 25% of the respondents had at least once approached a dispute commissioner with a legal question and 91% of those declared themselves to be well satisfied with the clarification that they received; 95.4% of the respondents thought the dispute commission to be well qualified to make legal decisions. [Hantsche & Kulitzscher, 1987, 180–181] For what it is worth, then, these data correspond entirely to my general impressions and to the result of my interviews.

Citizens

As noted, the social court commissioners did not always feel sufficiently appreciated for their work by the general public. This complaint will not shock anyone familiar with the U.S. jury system. However poorly the GDR public may have supported and appreciated the social court members, we are doing worse by a large measure. It cannot be said that the American public is particularly interested in the work of courts or juries—except when there is a sensational case or a scandalous verdict. Lack of public appreciation and esteem, if indeed widespread and deep-seated, may point to a weakness in the East German social court system. At this point the absence of systematic data regarding the views of the general public and social court litigants becomes a serious handicap to analysis. It is not my impression, given my inquiries in the GDR, that there was a serious lack of appreciation and esteem. In my conversations with East German citizens, I did *not* find a deep dissatisfaction with the work of the social courts. On the other hand, bursts of enthusiasm also were hard to find. The attitude of the general public toward the social courts can best be described, I think, as "tepid support."

Legal System

The East German leadership, in true Leninist fashion, was emphatic on this point, that the lay assessors were in every respect the equals of the professional judges. This injunction was repeated so often and so insistently that some doubts about this equality seemed well justified.[18] The commissioners of the social court were not regarded as the exact equals of the professional judges, which they did not really expect, in any case. They did see themselves, and were envisioned by the system, as competent justice professionals, deserving the respect and ungrudging cooperation of the state courts and their judges. Did they get it? As noted, there is no systematic evidence. All that is available for inspection are the (very few) occasional published comments of social court commissioners and their interview responses—which, by and large, were fairly positive, based on the perception that they and their work were given considerable respect. There was, of course, some patronizing. For the most, however, social court commissioners felt themselves to be well accepted by the professional judges.

Litigants

As one might expect, in my interviews with East German citizens, I encountered few social court litigants. Either they did not exist in great numbers, or they did not wish to reveal what most likely were embarrassing episodes of their lives. The few persons who admitted to having been before a commission were not particularly critical. The majority thought that the commission in question had genuinely tried to be fair and, in most cases, managed to be fair. It might be noted that satisfaction was somewhat higher for the dispute than for the arbitration commissions. This may have been a function of the predominant responsibility of the dispute commissions for labor disputes, which were overwhelmingly resolved in favor of the worker rather than the firm.[19] No empirical studies, or even simple opinion polls, have been published regarding the views of the litigants and the population. I do not know whether unpublished studies exist. Inquiries since the collapse of the GDR have not brought forth unpublished materials.

SUMMATION

At the risk of incurring the wrath of the more rabid partisans of the American and East German political systems, I must confess that at the level of lay adjudicative participation, I find at least as many similarities as differences. Some of the similarities can be found in the citizens' responses to the demands of their system. The U.S. trial jurors carry the lesser burden,[20] however exasperating encounters with the court bureaucracy may be. On the other hand, U.S. citizens are obligated to serve as jurors if called. Their participation is *not* voluntary.[21] The social court members clearly had the more demanding job—and it is not altogether clear that their assumption of office always was truly and fully voluntary. My impression is that, for the most part, it was.

When they entered their positions for the first time, most social court commissioners had various misgivings, particularly if they would be able to understand proceedings and evidence well enough not to appear incompetent or dimwitted. U.S. jurors share in these types of apprehension. Once they begin to serve, however, most members of both groups grow in their feeling of competence, become truly interested in the task at hand, take matters seriously, try to do as good a job as possible, respond positively to to challenges and problems, come to appreciate the experience, *and* emerge from the experience willing to serve again.[22] Indeed, multiple service is fairly common. American citizens tend not to serve at all, or do so repeatedly.[23]

While, as noted, the East German commissioners carried the much heavier burdens, they had one clear advantage over the American jurors: they could bask in practically unanimous leadership approval. Whereas a former chief justice of the United States supreme court missed few opportunities to complain about trial by jury and the jurors and to suggest the curtailment of the institution,[24] the chief justice of the East German supreme court participated in public ceremonies designed to honor the lay adjudicators. To too many American judges and public officials trial by jury seems to a relic of the past, no longer really useful or needed. To the socialist (Leninist) leadership of the GDR, by contrast, lay adjudication was the wave of the future.

Barbaric relic or harbinger of a better future, one point seems to be beyond dispute, the lay adjudicators of both countries perform (performed) invaluable services for their legal and political system. In different ways, but to much the same effect, jurors and commissioners are (were) indispensable. Through their willingness to do what is (was) asked or demanded of them, even if not enthusiastic about the task at the beginning, they become (became) the "good citizens" that every country requires. In the United States, however, they need and deserve much more esteem and appreciation.

Without the lay social courts, many of the cases (at least those that required formal deliberation) would have required the attention of the regular courts. In effect, the state received substantial amounts of free labor by shifting certain segments of dispute resolution and adjudication from *paid* professionals to *unpaid* lay adjudicators.[25] Similar efforts in the United States, though on a much smaller scale, have not been equally successful. Various types of case-diversions away from the ordinary courts have been tried in the United States and elsewhere: ombudsmen, mediation centers, mandatory pre-trial arbitration, "no-fault" provisions for tort and divorce actions, creation of lesser judicial officers (magistrates) and of lesser forums (small claims courts). Few of these, however, are free of cost to the parties and/or the state. Case-diversion, in any case, has received widespread and significant support. [For example, Burger, 1981, 10–13] Adjudicative agencies more closely resembling GDR social courts have also been suggested—unsuccessfully so far. [See for example, Katz, 1974, 448–464] Nevertheless there is no end to complaints about workload and litigation delay.[26] Certainly serious efforts are badly needed to relieve some of the burdens on the American courts.[27]

WHAT CAN WE LEARN?

What, if anything, can we learn from the East German social court experiment? The preceding pages have shown, that at least in the East German context, these institutions worked rather well. Three points are worth emphasizing: (1) they relieved the ordinary courts of a very large amount of litigation, (2) they were reasonably competent and successful in the execution of their tasks, and (3) they appear to have enjoyed general acceptance and support. There were weaknesses, of course, and there were justified criticisms. These must be viewed, however, in the context of the many and severe deficiencies of the U.S. legal system. The social courts were not perfect. If we insisted that only perfect arrangements can have something to teach us, we might just as well give up on our efforts to learn from other systems. Perfection is not of this world.

If we are serious about lay diversion of minor civil and criminal cases, in order to relieve our courts of unmanageable burdens, careful attention to the GDR social courts holds great promise. We can benefit from the East German experience to answer these types of questions:

- What type of case can be successfully adjudicated by lay persons?
- What are the maximum legal and factual complexities practicable?
- What type and amount of training should be provided to the lay judges?
- What assistance should be provided on an on-going basis?
- What procedure should be adopted; how formal or informal should they be?
- What measures—punitive, social, and educational—should be available?
- On what grounds should decisions be appealable?
- What is a reasonable length of service?
- What is a reasonable workload?
- Should these courts have obligations other than formal deliberations?
- Should these courts meet only after normal working hours? If not, what employment protections will be needed, and how can they be arranged?
- What remuneration would be appropriate?
- What will motivate citizens to serve as lay judges?

The fact that the GDR was a socialist country should not deter us from learning from its experience. Contrary to the claims of committed ideologists in East and West, many of the ordinary problems of legal systems are *not* dependent on the ideological superstructure—and neither are the solutions to them. Legal administration can to a large degree be separated from political ideology, and inter-system transfers are imaginable and feasible. We are used to looking to England and the other countries of Western Europe for advice and directions. It is the argument of this book that we would do well to broaden our scope.

American lay adjudicators, of course, cannot be expected to carry all the burdens and perform all of the tasks of their East German counterparts. It should be possible, however, to have minor criminal and civil cases be resolved through "social court" deliberations. This would make a significant contribution to our administration of justice. The potential savings in (regular) court time and cost are substantial and significant.

There are two fundamental questions: *Can?* and *Will?* Can American citizens do what the East German citizens did? There is no reason to think that the answer can be anything but YES. Will they do it? I believe the answer has to be NO—at least under current conditions. There were some signs (though by no means conclusive) that even the highly motivated East Germans grew tired of their many communal and civic obligations. It seems highly unlikely that Americans would be willing to endure anywhere near the burden that the East Germans carried. But, for one, it is clear that American citizens often give freely of their time for the common good; for the other, this is not what is being advocated. Nor is it advocated that American adjudicators—lay or professional—embrace the same intrusiveness that characterized the GDR. It is not likely that Americans, being used to a free and individualistic society, would want to be as intrusive as the East Germans; nor is it likely that the objects of that attention (also being Americans) would stand for it.

The role of "American social court judges" would strictly be the resolution of minor and uncomplicated criminal and civil cases.[28] They certainly would not be burdened by the many additional functions (even the non-intrusive ones) that the East German social court commissioners had to perform: giving legal advice, holding office hours, being available for private consultations, finding the right educational measures,[29] caring for endangered juveniles, assisting convicts to find their way back into society, making formal recommendations to third parties, seeking to prevent disputes from arising, providing legal education-propaganda, recruiting special audiences to the hearings, controlling the implementation of decisions, and meeting with various officials and functionaries to give accounts of their work. The one added matter that should be adopted from GDR practices is the education and training of the lay judges, including the participation in occasional conferences and seminars. Not, of course, to the same extent as it was done in the GDR, where lay judges were transformed into semi-professionals, but to some level of minimal conceptual-logical-legal competence.[30] Of course, if one expects a lack of motivation to perform the adjudicative task, one must expect an even greater lack of motivation to undertake the learning effort.

Either way, there are two remedies to the dilemma of lack of motivation. First, the burden can be *lessened*. As just noted, no one in his right mind could possibly suggest that American citizens assume the full burden of East German civic—or just legal—obligations. While lay adjudication could be greatly expanded in this country, the burden to be carried by each lay adjudicator could be held to a bearable amount. Such matters as frequency and length of service, proper remuneration, adequate support and assistance, and even the amount of learning provided are not difficult to adjust.[31] This is the easier part.

The second part is more difficult: to *amplify* willingness. An increase in motivation, in part, will be a function of the reward. But this will be the smaller and much less significant part. What will be crucially needed is an increase in the feeling of *civic obligation*—citizen duty,[32] in an older language. [Campbell et al., 1960, 105–107] No one, surely, wants American individualism replaced by socialist collectivism. But Marxism-Leninism is not the only tradition emphasizing communal obligations. There are any number of *Weltanschauungen* that include in their teachings a decent concern for the common welfare and the well-being of others—some religious, some not. The only means available to promote and expand the sense of civic obligation, it seems to me, is education—in families, in the schools, in social organizations, and, last but not least, in uncorrupted and unsullied politics. I can't agree that this is asking for too much.

NOTES

1. No empirical studies, not even simple opinion polls, have been published regarding the views of any of these groups. When the GDR was still in existence, I explored the feasibility of such research with various officials. To no effect: they *would* not, and I could not (on the general hostility toward research by Western scholars see Chapter 2).

2. For example, Dukes, 1980a, 260; Grieger & Mueller, 1981, 160; Gruenert, 1980, 33; Heintze, 1983, 137; Hengelhaupt, 1982, 149; Heusinger, 1982, 173; Heusinger, 1983a, 73; Kern, 1982, 69; Kern, 1983, 226; Langer, 1982, 214; Loehn, 1982, 150; Posorski, 1982, 95; Steffens, 1979, 25; Winkler, 1980, 3; Toeplitz, 1982, 98; Weichelt, 1982a, 93; Weichelt, 1982b, 148.

3. It must be noted, however, that the criteria employed in official reviews of the work of the social courts sometimes were rather relaxed. Thus, for example, an inquiry into the work of 32 dispute commissions and 26 arbitration commissions was based on a "detailed questionnaire" and on "wide-ranging personal conversations." It is likely that a more objective and scientific investigation might have produced results that were not quite so excessively glowing. [Buchholz, I. et al., 1988, 210]

4. Also see Dietzel, 1989, 49–53; Froehlich, 1970, 238–250; Gerth & Duttig, 1973, 96; Goerner & Sokolow, 1983, 76; Heuckendorf & Kruse, 1972, 50; Kaiser, 1973, 274–276; Kersten, 1988, 120; Kruse, 1969, 43; Neuschl, 1970, 51; Peller, 1988, 69–71; Probst, 1977, 223–227; Tischer, 1983, 277.

5. It should be noted here that negative views were not simply suppressed, though, of course, there may have been more than were published.

6. Arway, 1980, 225; Gensch, 1981, 264; Henselin, 1981, 148; Kern, 1980, 247; Kersten, 1981, 114–115; Schoene, 1980, 276.

7. Arway, 1980, 227; Gensch, 1981, 264; Kersten, 1981, 113.

8. Arway, 1980, 226; Ebner, 1980a, 113; Grieger, 1980, 41; Kern, 1980, 247; Kunkel, 1982, 17; Urban, 1981, 145.

9. Arway, 1980, 226; Branz, 1980, 283; Comment, 1980d, 253; Ebner, 1980a, 114–117; Ebner, 1980b, 67; Grafe, 1980, 190; Gruenert, 1980, 35; Hausding, 1980, 285; Lienshoeft, 1982, 18.

10. Hauser, 1980, 281; Heinrich, 1980, 38; Kersten, 1981, 113; Lehmann, 1981, 98; Mager & Winkler, 1973, 89.

11. Gensch, 1981, 265; Grieger, 1980, 42; Heuckendorf, 1981, 187; Schoene, 1980b, 275.

12. For example, Arway, 1980, 226–227; Ebner, 1980b, 67; Gensch, 1981, 265; Grafe, 1980, 191; Lienshoeft, 1982, 18; Seidel, 1982, 14; Urban, 1981, 147.

13. For example, Arway, 1980, 226; Ebner, 1980a, 114; Ebner, 1980b, 67; Fichtner, 1980, 287; Gensch, 1981, 265; Grafe, 1980, 191; Heusinger, 1978, 157; Heusinger, 1983b, 121; Lienshoeft, 1982, 18; Seidel, 1982, 14; Urban, 1981, 147. DER SCHOEFFE and NEUE JUSTIZ also frequently listed the recipients of honors by name and position.

14. See, for example, Ammann, 1962, 359–361; Bels, 1963, 254; Bremer & Mandel, 1961, 124; Conradt, 1979, 116; Dietrich, 1965, 132; Doberenz, 1965, 50; Draeger, 1961, 182; Grosse, 1975, 281; Helm, 1972, 351; Kliemke & Tarruhn, 1961, 409; Knoesel, 1970, 86–88; Mierow, 1973, 131; Mueller, 1962, 14; Nagler, 1973, 118; Richter, 1961, 386; Sembnista, 1971, 171; Stegemann, 1965, 100; Struch, 1970, 127; Wunderlich, 1976, 245–247.

15. The citizens who have been called for jury service but who were not chosen for a trial tend to feel that their time has been wasted altogether. One study has shown that in the federal court system, 44% of the citizens called were not selected for service, and 28% never even were sent to a courtroom for voir dire. [Van Dyke, 1977, 115] Such a waste of citizen time is eminently avoidable and is caused not by necessity but by thoughtlessness and inefficiency. [Pabst, 1972, 277]

16. Healy, 1976, 460–461; Kennebeck, 1975, 237; C. Simon, 1975, 209.

17. I am compelled to say "apparently" because this account, as well as practically all GDR research reports, lacks identifying information. We are not told the year of the undertaking, the number of dispute commissions studied, the number of commission members surveyed, or who directed the research. The text contains only percentages; a numerical base is entirely lacking.

18. See, for example, Beyer, U., 1981, 191; Brachmann, 1990, 70; Burchert, 1979, 187; Burkert, 1990, 103; Comment, 1972a, 197; Comment, 1981, 128; Deschle, 1990, 67; Hess, 1974, 20; Kirchner, 1988, 123; Kornetzki, 1971, 337; Kraushaar, 1955, 355; Lenhart, 1979, 67; Loof, 1989, 168; Matheus, 1988, 52; Meyer, 1988, 56; Parlow & Gessner, 1986, 119; Pueschel, 1962a, 252; Richter, 1980, 18; Schoenfeldt & Schoenfeldt, 1979, 101; Schubert, 1984, 119; Toeplitz, 1954, 5; Toeplitz, 1976, 110.

19. On the privileged position of workers in the GDR see Sperlich, 2006, Chapter 5.

20. The exception would be sequestered jurors in a trial lasting for weeks or months.

21. Of course, there are ways to avoid jury service—from not registering to vote, not returning the juror questionnaire, to declaring oneself to unable to give a fair hearing of the case. The success of these attempts to avoid jury service varies with place

and time, but a truly unwilling citizen is likely to achieve his/her purpose. [Richert, 1977, 243–244; Timothy, 1975, 18–20; Van Dyke, 1977, 119–134] The only exception will be found with courts so desperate for jurors that they resort to "kidnaping" citizens off the street and pressing them into service. [Abraham, 1998, 126]

22. In an early juror survey, Flynn [1960, 103] reported these finding: " . . . two-thirds of all jurors had an unmixed positive reaction as to the usefulness of their service, while only one-tenth of the responses were definitely negative. Seventy-four per cent were unconditionally willing to serve again." [Also see Allen, 1977, 250–251; Broeder, 1959, 751–752; Durand et al., 1978a, 211–212; Durand et al., 1978b, 568–570; C. Simon, 1975, 211; Timothy, 1975, 301–302] Positive action to service have also been found in other settings, for example, for West German lay assessors. [Klausa, 1972, 74–76, 213–214]

23. The University of Chicago Jury Project found the remarkably low figure of 6% as the proportion of the general population that had ever seen jury service. [Broeder, 1959, 751] On the other hand, one study found 63% prior service. [Durand et al., 1978b, 569] Another investigation found that fewer than one-fourth of the jurors were serving for the first time, and that 70% had seen prior service within the last five years. [C. Simon, 1975, 208; also see Pabst & Munsterman, 1975, 499–500]

24. See Sperlich, 1980a, 262 and Sperlich, 1982a, 394.

25. The large-scale reliance on citizen volunteers to provide the state with vast amounts of free labor is typical for socialist system, and it is not limited to adjudicative services. [Adams, 1977]

26. Burger, 1980b, 39; Church, 1978, 166; Warren, 1958, 6.

27. Also see the last section of Chapter 4.

28. Simple labor cases may be added to this repertoire.

29. As it was with the East German social courts, the primary emphasis of these institutions should not be punitive, but educational.

30. Procedures should be kept as informal as possible. The lay judges should not be encumbered with complex procedural rules. Appeals to the regular courts should be possible, of course.

31. The GDR social court commissioners spent on the average about one to two hours per day on their various duties. With greatly reduced obligation, it would seem that the American counterparts could take care of their tasks with perhaps one hour per day on the average. Surely, the work day of most Americans is not so demanding that this would be an unbearable cost. Of course, the actual service would most likely be bunched, just as jury service, and some short period of time may have to be freed from the usual work obligations.

32. Americans are by no means bereft of it, but an expanded lay adjudication will require additional commitments.

Bibliography

Abbott, Walter F. (1990): SURROGATE JURIES. American Law Institute.

Abel, Richard L., ed. (1982): THE POLITICS OF INFORMAL JUSTICE: THE AMERICAN EXPERIENCE. 2 Vls. Academic Press.

Abraham, Henry J. (1998): THE JUDICIAL PROCESS, 7th ed. Oxford University Press.

Abramson, Jeffrey (2000): WE, THE JURY: THE JURY SYSTEM AND THE IDEAL OF DEMOCRACY. Harvard University Press.

AC Decree—see Decree regarding the Arbitration Commissions of the GDR.

Adams, Jan S. (1977): CITIZEN INSPECTORS IN THE SOVIET UNION. Praeger.

Adler, Stephen J. (1994): THE JURY. Doubleday.

Adler, Werner (1986): Eine erste Bilanz im Leistungsvergleich der Schiedskommissionen. 33 DER SCHÖFFE 82–83.

Ahnsehl, Ulrich (1963): Ein Kollektiv übernahm die Bürgschaft. 10 DER SCHÖFFE 74–75.

Albert, Horst (1960): Wie können wir Schöffen die Jugendkriminalität bekämpfen? 7 DER SCHÖFFE 212–213.

Alexandrov, I. (1977): THE RIGHTS AND FREEDOMS OF SOVIET CITIZENS. Novosti Press Agency.

Allen, James L. (1977): Attitude Change Following Jury Duty. 2 JUSTICE SYSTEM JOURNAL 246.

Amboss, Margot (1979): Die Bedeutung entwicklungsbedingter Besonderheiten und der Tatmotive für die strafrechtliche Verantwortlichkeit Jugendlicher. 26 DER SCHÖFFE 39–42.

Amboss, Margot (1983a): Zur Gestaltung der Hauptverhandlung und Festlegung von Massnahmen strafrechtlicher Verantwortlichkeit in Jugendstrafverfahren. 30 DER SCHÖFFE 265–271.

Amboss, Margot (1983b): Die Mitwirkung des Jugendbeistandes an der Hauptverhandlung. 30 DER SCHÖFE 272–276.

American Bar Association (1982): STANDARDS RELATING TO JUROR USE AND MANAGEMENT. American Bar Association Publcations.

Ammann, Herbert (1962): Zur Arbeit der Konfliktkommissionen. 9 DER SCHÖFFE 359–361.

Ammer, Thomas (1994): Strukture der Macht: Die Funktionäre im SED-Staat. Juergen Weber, ed.: DER SED-STAAT. Olzog Verlag.

Amos, Heike (1996): JUSTIZVERWALTUNG IN DER SBZ/DDR: PERSONAL-POLITIK 1945 BIS ANFANG DER 50er JAHRE. Böhlau Verlag.

Anders, Walter (1965): Empfehlungen an Dritte—ein wichtiges Mittel. 12 DER SCHÖFFE 133–136.

Anders, Walter (1966): Einige Bemerkungen zur Arbeit der gesellschaftlichen Rechtpflegeorgane mit Empfehlungen. 13 DER SCHÖFFE 434–437.

Anderson, Stanley (1990): Lay Judges and Jurors in Denmark. 38 AMERICAN JOURNAL OF COMPARATIVE LAW 839–864.

Anderson, Stanley (1992): The Transition from Inquisitorial to Adversarial Criminal Procedure in Denmark. 64 SCANDINAVIAN STUDIES 181–198.

Andert, Reinhold & Wolfgang Herzberg (1990): DER STURZ: ERICH HONECKER IM KREUZVERHÖR. Aufbau-Verlag.

Arends, Petra, et al. (1988): Die Rechtsentwicklung in der DDR. 32 RECHT IN OST UND WEST 282–289.

Arendt, Hannah (1958): THE ORIGINS OF TOTALITARIANISM. 2nd ed. Meridian.

Aretz, Juergen & Wolfgang Stock (1997): DIE VERGESSENEN OPFER DER DDR. Bastei Lübbe.

Arlt, Reiner & Gerhard Stiller (1973): ENTWICKLUNG DER SOZIALISTISCHEN RECHTSORDNUNG IN DER DDR. Staatsverlag.

Armelin, Annette (2000): Die Einflussnahme der Kreis- und Bezirksleitungen der SED auf die Zivil-, Familien- und Arbeitsrechtsverfahren der Kreis- und Bezirksgerichte. Rainer Schroeder, ed.: ZIVILRECHTSKULTUR DER DDR. Duncker & Humblot.

Arnold, Herbert (1970): Sprechstunde nicht unterschätzen! 17 DER SCHÖFFE 205–206.

Arnold, Joerg (1983): Weitere Überlegungen zur Rolle des Jugendbeistandes. 30 DER SCHÖFFE 106–109.

Arnold, Joerg (1987): Zur Strafzumessung bei jugendlichen Tätern. 41 NEUE JUSTIZ 100–101.

Arnold, Joerg (1995): DIE NORMALITÄT DES STRAFRECHTS DER DDR. Edition Iuscrim.

Arnold, Karl-Heinz (1995): SCHILD UND SCHWERT. Edition Ost.

Arnold, Wolfgang, et al. (1982): Rechtsausbildung und Rechtserziehung in technischen Studienrichtungen. 36 NEUE JUSTIZ 126–127.

Aronow, Geoffrey F. (1980): The Special Master in School Desegregation Cases: The Evolution of Roles in the Reformation of Public Institutions Through Litigation. 7 HASTINGS CONSTITUTIONAL LAW QUARTERLY 739–775.

Arway, Hans (1980): Wirken der Schiedskommissionen von Leistungsfähigkeit geprägt. 27 DER SCHÖFFE 224.

Arway, Hans (1985): Bildung und Qualifizierung von Jugendbeistandsgruppen. 39 NEUE JUSTIZ 248–249.

Atwell, John W., Jr. (1975): The Russian Jury. 53 SLAVONIC AND EAST EUROPEAN REVIEW 44–61.

Auerbach, Jerold S. (1983): JUSTICE WITHOUT LAW? RESOLVING DISPUTES WITHOUT LAWYERS. Oxford University Press.

Auerbach, Thomas (2002): Jugend im Blickfeld der Staatssicherheit. Clemens Vollnhals & Juegen Weber, eds.: DER SCHEIN DER NORMALITÄT. Olzog Verlag.
Austin, Arthur D. (1984): COMPLEX LITIGATION CONFRONTS THE JURY SYSTEM. University Publications of America.
Australia, Bar Council of New South Wales (1965): YOUR RIGHT TO A JURY TRIAL. M.J. Seymour.
Autorenkollektiv (1973): KLEINES POITISCHES WÖRTERBUCH. Dietz Verlag.
Autorenkollektiv (1978a): MARXISTISCH-LENINISTISCHE PARTEI UND SOZIALISTISCHER STAAT. Dietz Verlag.
Autorenkollektiv (1978b): DDR, GESELLSCHAFT, STAAT, BÜRGER. Sec. rev. ed. Staatsverlag.
Autorenkollektiv (1980): DIE GESELLSCHAFTLICHEN ORGANIZATIONEN IN DER DDR. Staatsverlag.
Autorenkollektiv (1982a): ZEITALTER IM WIDERSTREIT: GRUNDPROBLEME DER HISTORISCHEN EPOCHE SEIT 1917 IN DER AUSEINANDERSETZUNG MIT DER BÜRGERLICHEN GESCHICHTSSCHREIBUNG. Dietz Verlag.
Autorenkollektiv (1984a): DDR: BÜRGERINTERESSEN ALS STAATSPOLITIK. Staatsverlag.
Autorenkollektiv (1984b): STAATSRECHT DER DDR. 2d ed. Staatsverlag.
Autorenkollektiv (1985a): SOZIALISTISCHES RECHT: LEHRBUCH FÜR DAS GRUNDLAGENFACH. Verlag die Wirtschaft.
Autorenkollektiv (1985b): DIE TOTALITARISMUS-DOKTRIN IM ANTIKOMMUNISMUS. Dietz Verlag.
Autorenkollektiv (1986a): DER STAAT IM POLITISCHEN SYSTEM DER DDR. Staatsverlag.
Autorenkollektiv (1986b): GRUNDLAGEN DER RECHTSPFLEGE: LEHRBUCH. 2d ed. Staatsverlag.
Autorenkollektiv (1987): STRAFRECHT DER DEUTSCHEN DEMOKRATISCHEN REPUBLIK: KOMMENTAR ZUM STRAFGESETZBUCH. 5th ed. Staatsverlag.
Autorenkollektiv (1988): DEMOKRATIE IM ALLTAG. Dietz Verlag.
Azicri, Max (1980): Change and Institutionalization in the Revolutionary Process: The Cuban Legal System in the 1970s. 6 REVIEW OF SOCIALIST LAW 164–182.
Azrael, Jeremy R. (1962): Is Coercion Withering Away? 11 PROBLEMS OF COMMINISM 9–17.
Babcock, Barbara A. (1975): Voir Dire: Preserving "Its Wonderful Power." 27 STANFORD LAW REVIEW 545–565.
Baden-Württemberg, Justizministerium (1977): DAS AMT DES SCHÖFFEN: EIN LEITFADEN. Justizministerium.
Baestlein, Klaus (2002): DER FALL MIELKE. Nomos.
Bailey, George (1991): GERMANS: THE BIOGRAPHY OF AN OBSCESSION. Free Press.
Baranowski, Günter (1985): Aspekte des historischen Erbes und der Traditionen in der Entwicklung der sozialistischen Demokratie. Rat für staats- und rechtswissenschaftliche Forschung an der Akademie der Wissenschaften der DDR: VERVOLLKOMMNUNG DER SOZIALISTISCHEN DEMOKRATIE: TRIEBKRAFT DER SOZIALISTSICHEN GESELLSCHAFT. Staatsverlag.

Baranowski, Guenter (1987): Rechtswissenschaft im Umbruch: "Neue Justiz" im Gründungsjahr 1947. 41 NEUE JUSTIZ 182–184.
Barber, Elinor (1986): Access to Research Sites Abroad. 40:1 ITEMS 12.
Barth, Gerhard (1960): Zur Arbeit der Schöffen in den Wohnbezirken. 7 DER SCHÖFFE 365–366.
Barth, Gerhard & Guenther Schimansky (1970): Mitwirkung von Pädagogen als gesellschaftliche Ankläger in Verfahren wegen Sexualdelikten. 24 NEUE JUSTIZ 330.
Barth, Joachim (1984): Einige Erfahrungen aus Beratungen mit Jugendlichen. 31 DER SCHÖFFE 20–22.
Bartsch, Heinz et al. (1981): STAATLICHE LEITUNG BEI DER GESTALTUNG DER ENTWICKELTEN SOZIALISTISCHEN GESELLSCHAFT. Staatsverlag.
Barwinsky, Karl (1969a): Zur Mitwirkung der Schöffen bei der Verwirklichung von Urteilen auf Bewährung. 16 DER SCHÖFFE 230–233.
Barwinsky, Karl (1969b): Erfahrungen mit der kollektiven Erziehung. 16 DER SCHÖFFE 351–353.
Barwinsky, Karl (1969c): Mitwirkung der Schöffen bei Verurteilungen auf Bewährung. 16 DER SCHÖFFE 266–270.
Barwinsky, Karl (1970): Einige Ergebnisse des Jahres 1969 und erste Schlussfolgerungen vom Bezirksgericht Erfurt. 167–170.
Barwinsky, Karl & Georg Knecht (1963): Die Aufgaben der Konflikt- und Schiedskommissionen bei der Beratung zivilrechtlicher Streitigkeiten. 10 DER SCHÖFFE 344.
Bayern, Staatsministerium der Justiz (1976): DAS SCHÖFFENAMT IN BAYERN: INFORMATIONEN FÜR SCHÖFFEN. Staatsministerium.
Baylis, Thomas A. (1974): THE TECHNICAL INTELLIGENTSIA AND THE EAST GERMAN ELITE: LEGITIMACY AND SOCIAL CHANGE IN MATURE COMMUNISM. University of California Press.
Beale, Sara S. & William C. Bryson (1986): GRAND JURY LAW AND PRACTICE. Callaghan.
Becker, Herbert (1982): Bewährte Erfahrungen niemals für sich behalten. 29 DER SCHÖFFE 53.
Becker, Theodore L. (1970): COMPARATIVE JUDICAL POLITICS: THE POLITICAL FUNCTIONING OF COURTS. Rand McNally.
Beckert, Rudi (1995): DIE ERSTE UND LETZTE INSTANZ: SCHAU- UND GEHEIMPROZESSE VOR DEM OBERSTEN GERICHT DER DDR. Keip Verlag.
Beckmann, Franz (1983): Zur Anwendung der neuen Rechtsvorschriften. 30 DER SCHÖFFE 187–190.
Beer, Lawrence, ed. (1979): CONSTITUTIONALISM IN ASIA. University of California Press.
Behrends, Siegfried (1979): Wie werden Geldubssen und Ordnungsstrafen realisiert? 26 DER SCHÖFFE 215–217.
Beinarowitz, Rof (1963): Auf den Spuren eines Gerichtsverfahrens. 10 DER SCHÖFFE 411–416.
Bender, Peter (1992): UNSERE ERBSCHAFT: WAS WAR DIE DDR, WAS BLEIBT VON IHR? Luctherhand.
Benjamin, Hilde (1961): Bericht des Ministers der Justiz. 8 DER SCHÖFFE 70–75.

Benjamin, Hilde (1965): Der Entwurf eines sozialistischen Familiengesetzbuches steht zur Diskussion. 12 DER SCHÖFFE 163–169.
Benjamin, Hilde (1966): Familiengesetz beweist Lebenskraft unserer Demokrtie. 13 DER SCHÖFFE 33–35.
Benjamin, Hilde (1979): Der Sozialistische Richter. 33 NEUE JUSTIZ 387–388.
Benjamin, Hilde, et al. (1984): 35 Jahre DDR—Entwicklung und Gestaltung sozialistischer Gesetzlichkeit und Rechtspflege. 38 NEUE JUSTIZ 250–253.
Benjamin, Michael (1961): Kriminalitsbekämpfung und Absehen von Strafverfolgung. 10 STAAT UND RECHT 35–51.
Benjamin, Michael (1962): Die Persönlichkeit des Verbrechers und die Ursachen der Kriminalität in der UdSSR. 16 NEUE JUSTIZ 562–567.
Benjamin, Michael (1983): Zur Dialektik der staatlichen Leitung bei der Gestaltung des entwickelten Sozialismus. 32 STAAT UND RECHT 3–16.
Benser, Guenter (2000): DDR—GEDENKT IHRER MIT NACHSICHT. Karl Dietz Verlag.
Benz, Ulrike (1982): ZUR ROLLE DER LAIENRICHTER IM STRAFPROZESS. Schmidt-Römhild.
Bergmann, Egon (1981): Langfristige Planung der Massnahmen zur Festigung der Gesetzlichkeit im Kreise Zeitz. 35 NEUE JUSTIZ 352–354.
Berman, Harold J. (1963): JUSTICE IN THE U.S.S.R.: AN INTERPRETATION OF SOVIET LAW. Harvard University Press.
Berman, Harold J. & John W. Spindler (1963): Soviet Comrades' Courts. 14 WASHINGTON LAW REVIEW 842.
Berman, Harold J. & Van R. Whiting, Jr. (1980): Impressions of Cuban Law. 27 AMERICAN JOURNAL OF COMPARATIVE LAW 475–486.
Berman, Harold J. et al. (1982): A Comparison of the Chinese and Soviet Codes of Criminal Law and Procedure. 73 JOURNAL OF CRIMINAL LAW & CRIMINOLOGY 238–258.
Besser, Gisela (1973): Vielfältige Möglichkeiten der Anleitung werden genutzt. 20 DER SCHÖFE 382–384.
Betts, Paul (2003): Remembrance of Things Past: Nostalgia in West and East Germay, 1980–2000. Paul Betts & Greg Eghigian, eds.: PAIN AND PROSPERITY. Stanford University Press.
Beyer, Achim (2002): Die Werdauer Oberschüler. Clemens Vollnhals & Juegen Weber, eds. (2002): DER SCHEIN DER NORMALITÄT. Olzog Verlag.
Beyer, Karl-Heinz (1959a): Zur Praxis mit der neuen Schiedmannsordnung. 6 DER SCHÖFFE 60–64.
Beyer, Karl-Heinz (1959b): Neugestaltung des Ordnungsstrafrechts und Schiedsmannstätigkeit. 6 DER SCHÖFFE 228–232.
Beyer, Karl-Heinz (1960): Zur Ausgestaltung eines neuen, sozialistischen Strafgesetzbuchs. 7 DER SCHÖFFE 317–324.
Beyer, Karl-Heinz (1961): Der Staatsratsbeschluss vom 30. Januar 1961—eine Anleitung zum Handeln. 8 DER SCHÖFFE 79–86.
Beyer, Karl-Heinz (1963): Bemerkungen zur weiteren Tätigkeit des Schiedsmanns wegen Beleidigungen. 10 DER SCHÖFFE 243–245.
Beyer, Karl-Heinz (1965): Zur Übernahme von Bürgschaften. 12 DER SCHÖFFE 18–22.

Beyer, Karl-Heinz (1966): Die Zurückdrängung der Kriminalität—eine gesamtgesellschaftliche Aufgabe. 13 DER SCHÖFFE 384–388.

Beyer, Karl-Heinz (1967): Zur Verantwortung für die Verwirklichung der Strafen ohne Freiheitsentzug. 14 DER SCHÖFFE 233–236.

Beyer, Karl-Heinz (1981): WENN STREIT SICH NICHT VERMEIDEN LÄSST. Staatsverlag.

Beyer, Karl-Heinz (1983): Erste Erfahrungen aus der Beilegung zivilrechtlicher Streitigkeiten. 30 DER SCHÖFFE 179–182.

Beyer, Karl-Heinz (1988): Grundsätze der gerichtlichen Beweisführung im Strafverfahren. 35 DER SCHÖFFE 153–156.

Beyer, Karl-Heinz & Helmut Schmidt (1960): Über die Aufgaben der erweiterten Konfliktkommissionen und anderer gesellschaftlichen Organe. 7 DER SCHÖFFE 41–47.

Beyer, Karl-Heinz, et al. (1982): Vorbeugung und Bekämpfung von Straftaten gegen das sozialistische Eigentum und die Volkwirtschaft. 36 NEUE JUSTIZ 62–65.

Beyer, Ursula (1981): Verpflichtung schöpferisch verwirklichen. 28 DER SCHÖFFE 190–191.

Biebl, Rudolf (1967): Zur Auswertung des 12. Plenums des Obersten Gerichts. 14 DER SCHÖFFE 35–40.

Biebl, Rudolf (1974): Erhöhung der Wirksamkeit der Rechtsprechung in Jugendstrafsachen. 21 DER SCHÖFFE 375–381.

Biebl, Rudolf (1984a): Differenzierte Strafzumessung bei Straftaten gegen das sozialistische Eigentum. 38 NEUE JUSTIZ 375–377.

Biebl, Rudolf (1984b): Der Schutz des sozialistischen Eigentums—wichtiges Anliegen der Rechtsprechung der Gerichte. 31 DER SCHÖFFE 105–110.

Biebl, Rudolf (1989): Der wirksame Schutz des persönlichen Eigentums. 36 DER SCHÖFFE 36–43.

Biermann, Wolf et al. (2001): DIE AUSBÜRGERUNG: ANFANG VOM ENDE DER DDR. Ullstein.

Bilinsky, Andreas (1960): Die "gesellschaftliche Rechtspflege" in der Sowjetunion. 4 RECHT IN OST UND WEST 89.

Bilinsky, Andreas (1962): Kameradschaftgerichte in der UdSSR. 8 OSTEUROPA-RECHT 306–330.

Blaney, John & Mike Gfoeller (1993): Lessons from the Failure of Perestroika. 108 POLITICAL SCIENCE QUARTERLY 481–496.

Blankenburg, Erhard (1982): Legal Insurance, Litigant Decision, and the Rising Caseload of Courts: A West German Study. WORKING PAPER 1983-3, Disputes Processing Research Program, University of Wisconsin-Madison.

Blaschek, Michael (1984): Gewerkschaftliche Rechtskommission hilft Ordnung, Disziplin, und Sicherheit festigen. 38 NEUE JUSTIZ 65–66.

Bley, Gotthold & Ulrich Daehn (1982): Die Wirksamkeit der sozialistischen Gesetzlichkeit weiter erhöhen. 31 STAAT UND RECHT 99–109.

Bley, Gotthold & Frohmut Mueller (1979): Gesetzlichkeit und Leitungstätigkeit im Leninschen Sinne. 33 NEUE JUSTIZ 389.

Bley, Gotthold & Reinhard Nissel (1984): Vorbeugung von Verletzungen der Instandhaltungspflicht aus Mietverträgen. 38 NEUE JUSTIZ 484–486.

Blumenthal, Ursula (1984): Aller Anfang war einmal schwer. 31 DER SCHÖFFE 216–218.

Boerner, Charlotte (1983): Persönliches Engagement entscheidet über den Erfolg. 30 DER SCHÖFFE 176–177.

Boese, Manfred (1981): Besonderheiten bei der Bewährungsverurteilung Jugendlicher. 35 NEUE JUSTIZ 456–457.

Boese, Manfred (1982): Arbeitsmethoden und -ergebnisse bei der Erziehung kriminell gefährdeter und straffällig gewordener Bürger. 36 NEUE JUSTIZ 131–132.

Boese, Manfred (1986): Erfahrungen bei der Vorbeugung und Bekämpfung der Jugendkriminalität. 33 DER SCHÖFFE 267–269.

Bohndorf, Dieter & Hartmut Ratzel (1969): Sozialistisches Rechtsbewusstsein und rechtliche Motivation. 23 NEUE JUSTIZ 553–558.

Boiter, Albert (1965): Comradely Justice: How Durable Is It? 14 PROBLEMS OF COMMUNISM 82.

Boiter, Albert (1973): Comrades' Courts. Feldbrugge, F.J.M., ed.: ENCYCLOPEDIA OF SOVIET LAW. Oceana Publications.

Borgwadt, Karl-Heinz (1984):Rechtserziehung der Jugend aktiv unterstützen. 31 DER SCHÖFFE 205–207.

Bornack, Elisabeth (1984): Rechtserziehung der Jugend. 31 DER SCHÖFFE 258–259.

Borneleit, Peter (1987): Einfluss auf das Zusammenleben in der Haus- und Wohngemeinschaft. 34 DER SCHÖFFE 20–21.

Brachmann, Ronald (1990): Rechtliche Gleichstellung der Berufs- und ehrenamtlichen Richter. 37 DER SCHÖFFE 70–72.

Bradley, Tom (1975): A Court System in Which All the People Have a Part. 58 JUDICATURE 270–275.

Brady, James P. (1982): A Season of Startling Alliance: Chinese Law and Justice in the New Order. Piers Beirne & Richard Qinney, eds.: MARXISM AND LAW. Wiley.

Braeuer, Heidrun (1972): Tätigkeit und Wirksamkeit der Kameradschaftsgerichte in der UdSSR. 19 DER SCHÖFFE 407–413.

Branz, Herta (1980): Neue Aufgaben verantwortungsvoll gelöst. 27 DER SCHÖFFE 282.

Braun, Johannes (1994): MENSCHEN UND MÄCHTE IN DER DDR. Mecke Verlag.

Braun, Johannes (1996): MEIN LEBEN MIT DEN SOZIALISTEN. Mecke Verlag.

Brauner, Rolf (1975): Empfehlungen führten zum Erfolg. 22 DER SCHÖFFE 193–194.

Breitkopf, Stephan (1985): Zur neueren DDR-Rechtsprechung in Arbeitsrechtsachen. 29 RECHT IN OST UND WEST 117–123.

Bremer, Eberhard & Joachim Mandel (1961): Die Konfliktkommission—eine erzieherische Kraft. 8 DER SCHÖFFE 124–126.

Brendel, Kurt (1980): Koordiniertes Wirken im Wohngebiet unerlässlich. 27 DER SCHÖFFE 227–278.

Breslauer, George W. (1982): KHRUSHCHEV AND BREZHNEV AS LEADERS: BUILDING AUTHORITY IN SOVIET POLITICS. Allen & Unwin.

Brinkley, George A. (1961): Das "Absterben" des Staates. 11 OSTEUROPA 620–631.

Brodführer, Klaus (1987): Mehr Ordnung und Sicherheit durch verstärkte Kontrolltätigkeit. 42 ARBEIT UND ARBEITSRECHT 233.

Broeder, Dale W. (1954): The Functions of the Jury: Facts or Fictions? 21 UNIVERSITY OF CHICAGO LAW REVIEW 386–424.
Broeder, Dale W. (1959): The University of Chicago Jury Project. 38 NEBRASKA LAW REVIEW 744.
Bromberger, L.L. (1948): Jurors Should Be Allowed to Takes Notes. 32 JUDICATURE 57.
Brown, Douglas (1974): Some Recent Criticisms and Problems of Trial by Jury. 11 WESTERN AUSTRALIA LAW REVIEW 256–263.
Brown, Edith (1968): The Disputes and Arbitration Commission: Social Organs for the Administration of Justice in the German Democratic Republic. 1 CASE WESTERN RESERVE JOURNAL OF INTERNATIONAL LAW 5.
Brownlee, E. Gardner (1975): The Revival of the Justice of the Peace in Montana. 58 JUDICATURE 372–379.
Bruce, Gary (2003): RESISTANCE WITH THE PEOPLE. Rowman & Littlefield.
Bruening, Juergen & Ilse Lungwitz (1984): Die Beratung wegen Schulpflichtverletzung. 31 DER SCHÖFFE 14.
Brugger, Winfried (1978): Marx und das Rechtsverständnis in der DDR. 22 RECHT IN OST AND WEST 101–110.
Bruhn, Hans-Henning (1971): Das Strafvollzugs- und Wiedereingliederungsgesetz der DDR unter vergleichender Berücksichtigung der Reformtendenzen in der BDR. 15 RECHT IN OST UND WEST 14–28.
Brumme, Hans & Siegfried Roeth (1977): Kontinuität in der Anleitung. 24 DER SCHÖFFE 131–133.
Brunner, Georg (1967): Kontrollfunktion und Kontrollorgane in der USSR und in Mitteldeutschland. 13 OSTEUROPA-RECHT 108.
Brzezinski, Zbigniew (1989): Preface. Leopold Labedz: THE USE AND ABUSE OF SOVIETOLOGY. Transaction Publishers.
Buch, Guenther (1982): NAMEN UND DATEN WICHTIGER PERSONEN DER DDR. Verlag J.H.W. Dietz Nachf.
Buchholz, Erich (1961): Legalität und Gleichheit. 15 NEUE JUSTIZ 745–749.
Buchholz, Erich (1964): Die erzieherische Funktion der Strafe in der Periode des entfalteten sozialistischen Aufbaus. 18 NEUE JUSTIZ 590–595.
Buchholz, Erich (1967): Der Inhalt der gesellschaftlichen Erziehung des Strafrechts. 21 NEUE JUSTIZ 212–216.
Buchholz, Erich (1972): Wesen der Kriminalität in der DDR und Möglichkeiten ihrer Überwindung. 19 DER SCHÖFFE 6–13.
Buchholz, Erich (1978): Probleme der juristischen Ausbildung. 32 NEUE JUSTIZ 512–515.
Buchholz, Erich (1980): The Social Courts in the German Democratic Republic: Bodies of Criminal Justice. 4 INTERNATIONAL JOURNAL OF COMPARATIVE AND APPLIED CRIMINAL JUSTICE 37.
Buchholz, Erich (1981): Methodologische Probleme der Wirksamkeit der Strafe. 30 STAAT UND RECHT 692–702.
Buchholz, Erich (1982): Erzieherische Rolle und Wirksamkeit der Strafe. 36 NEUE JUSTIZ 263–267.
Buchholz, Erich (1983): Zu den Ursachen der Kriminalität in der DDR. 37 NEUE JUSTIZ 199–202.
Buchholz, Erich (1985): Weitere Qualifizierung der juristischen Ausbildung. 39 NEUE JUSTIZ 98–99.

Buchholz, Erich (1986a): The Role of Lay Assessors in the German Democratic Republic. 10 INTERNATIONAL JOURNAL OF COMPARATIVE AND APPLIED CRIMINAL JUSTICE 215–222.

Buchholz, Erich (1986b): Zum Wirkungsmechanismus des Strafrechts. 40 NEUE JUSTIZ 272–274.

Buchholz, Erich (1987a): Begründung der Strafzumessung im erstinstanzlichen Urteil. 41 NEUE JUSTIZ 218–219.

Buchholz, Erich (1987b): Humanität und Rechtssicherheit. 87 EINHEIT 833–835.

Buchholz, Erich (1987c): Reasons for the Low Rate of Crime in the German Democratic Republik. 29 CRIME AND SOCIAL JUSTICE 26–42.

Buchholz, Erich (1987d): Gerechtigkeit und Freiheit im Strafrecht der DDR. 41 NEUE JUSTIZ 19.

Buchholz, Erich (1988): Soziale Gerechtigkeit: Errungenschaft und Aufgabe. 88 EINHEIT 357–362.

Buchholz, Erich & Ullrich Daehn (1968): Die Rolle der gesellschaftlichenKräfte bei Strafen ohne Freiheitsentzug und bei der Wiedereingliederung Haftentlassener. 15 DER SCHÖFFE 267–273.

Buchholz, Erich & Walter Griebe (1987): Neue Tendenzen im Strafrecht und Ordnungswidrigkeitsrecht der europäischen sozialistischen Länder. 41 NEUE JUSTIZ 63–66.

Buchholz, Erich & Karl A. Mollnau (1977): Faktoren der Wirksamkeit des sozialistischen Rechts. 31 NEUE JUSTIZ 653–655.

Buchholz, Erich & Harry Dettenborn (1980): Berücksichtigung der Fähigkeit und Bereitschaft des Straftäters zu künftig verantwortungsbewusstem Verhalten bei der Strafzumessung. 34 NEUE JUSTIZ 109–111.

Buchholz, Erich & Karl-Heinz Roeder (1982): Bemerkenswerte Erkenntnisse eines kritischen Kriminologen aus den USA. 36 NEUE JUSTIZ 114–116.

Buchholz, Erich & Hans Schoenfeldt (1984): Mitwirkung von Jugendbeiständen im Strafverfahren. 38 NEUE JUSTIZ 487–489.

Buchholz, Erich & Gerhard Schulze (1989): Der sozialistische Rechtsstaat und die verfassungsmässigen Grundlagen der sozialistischen Gesetzlichkeit und Rechtspflege in der DDR. 38 STAAT UND RECHT 476–485.

Buchholz, Erich, et al. (1969): Zum Wesen der Kriminalität in der DDR. 23 NEUE JUSTIZ 162–168.

Buchholz, Erich et al. (1974): SOCIALIST CRIMINOLOGY. Lexington Books.

Buchholz, Erich et al. (1982): Die Verwirklichung der Strafe ohne Freiheitsentzug bei Jugendlichen. 29 DER SCHÖFFE 173–177.

Buchholz, Irmgard (1984): Effektive Ausgestaltung der Verurteilung auf Bewährung bei Jugendlichen. 38 NEUE JUSTIZ 307–309.

Buchholz, Irmgard (1985): Review: Der Kriminalität keine Chance. 32 DER SCHÖFFE 215–216.

Buchholz, Irmgard (1986a): Rechte und Pflichten des Kollektivvertreters in der Hauptverhandlung. 33 DER SCHÖFFE 155–157.

Buchholz, Irmgard (1986b): Der Beitrag des Kollektivvertreters zur Verwirklichung der Strafe, speziell der Verurteilung auf Bewährung. 33 DER SCHÖFFE 173–175.

Buchholz, Irmgard (1987): Die Verpflichtung zur Bewährung am Arbeitsplatz. 41 NEUE JUSTIZ 145–147.

Buchholz, Irmgard et al. (1988): Zur Praxis der gesellschaftlichen Gerichte bei jugendlichen Rechtsverletzern. 35 DER SCHÖFFE 210–213.

Budde, Heidrun (2002): WILLKÜR! DIE SCHATTENSEITE DER DDR. Ingo Koch Verlag.

Buechner-Uhder, Willi (1968): SOCIALIST HUMAN RIGHTS IN THE GERMAN DEMOCRATIC REPUBLIC. Verlag Zeit im Bild.

Buettner, Horst (1960): Die Durchsetzung des sozialistischen Arbeitsstils und die sozialistische Bewusstseinsbildung; Institut für Philosophie der Humboldt-Universität Berlin: DER STAAT SIND WIR: BEITRäGE ZU PROBLEMEN DER ENTWICKLUNG DES SOZIALISTISCHEN STAATSBEWUSSTSEINS IN DER DDR. Dietz Verlag.

Buettner, Wolfgang (1984): Gewerkschaftliche Rechtshilfe—wichtiger Bestandteil der Interessenvertretung der Werktätigen. 38 NEUE JUSTIZ 256–258.

Buettner, Wolfgang (1987): Gewerkschaftliche Rechtshilfe im Betrieb. 42 ARBEIT UND ARBEITSRECHT 59–61.

Buiteweg, Joannes (1956): History of Michigan's One-Man Grand Jury. 33 UNIVERSITY OF DETROIT LAW JOURNAL 399–406.

Bukosvsky, Wladimir (1973): OPPOSITION: EINE NEUE GEISTESKRANKHEIT IN DER SOWJETUNION? Deutscher Taschenbuch Verlag.

Burchert, Dietrich (1979): Bewährte Erfahrungen noch stärker in der neuen Wahlperiode nutzen. 26 DER SCHÖFFE 187.

Burger, Warren E. (1970): Interview. U.S. NEWS & WORLD REPORT. (December 14, 1970).

Burger, Warren E. (1971): Remarks before the American Bar Association, New York City, July 5, 1971, as reprinted in 6 SUFFOLK UNIV. L. REV. (1972).

Burger, Warren E. (1976): Speech before the National Conference on the Causes of Popular Dissatisfaction with the Administration of Justice, St. Paul, Minnesota, April 7, 1976, as reprinted in Howard James (1977), CRISIS IN THE COURTS. David McKay.

Burger, Warren E. (1980a): End-of-the-Year Statement. U.S. Supreme Court.

Burger, Warren E. (1980b): Interview. U.S. NEWS AND WORLD REPORT 32 (December 14, 1980).

Burger, Warren E. (1981): Year-End Report on the Judiciary. U.S. Supreme Court.

Burkert, Hans-Joachim (1990): Zur Profilierung der Rolle der Schöffen. 37 DER SCHÖFFE 103–104.

Burns, P.T. (1973): A Profile of the Jury System in New Zealand. 11 WESTERN AUSTRALIA LAW REVIEW 105–110.

Burrichter, Clemens & Eckart Foertsch (1976): Development and Present Situation of GDR Research in the FRG; Klaus v. Beyme et al., eds.: GERMAN POLITICAL SYSTEMS: THEORY AND PRACTICE IN THE TWO GERMANIES. Sage.

Bursztynowicz, Ursula (1984): Schöffenkollektiv unterstützt Rechtserziehung der Lehrlinge. 38 NEUE JUSTIZ 237.

Buschhagen, Helmut (1981): Vormilitärische Ausbildung—sozialistische Rechtspflege. 28 DER SCHÖFFE 290–291.

Butler, William E. (1972): Comradely Justice in Eastern Europe. Hampstead, Lod Lloyd & Georg Schwarzenberger, eds.: CURRENT LEGAL PROBLEMS. Stevens & Sons.

Butler, William E. (1977): Comradely Justice Revisited. 3 REVIEW OF SOCIALIST LAW 325.

Butler, William E. (1983): BASIC DOCUMENTS ON THE SOVIET LEGAL SYSTEM. Oceana Publications.

Butler, William E., ed. (1988): YEARBOOK ON SOCIALIST LEGAL SYSTEMS. Transnational Publishers.

Cain, Anthony A. & Marjorie Kravitz (1978): JURY REFORM: A SELECTED BIBLIOGRAPHY. U.S. Department of Justice.

Cain, Maureen & Alan Hunt (1979): MARX AND ENGELS ON LAW. Academic Press.

Calkins, Richard M. (1966): Abolition of the Grand Jury Indictment in Illinois. 1966 UNIVERSITY OF ILLINOIS LAW FORUM 423–445.

Campbell, Angus, et al. (1960): THE AMERICAN VOTER. John Wiley.

Cappelletti, Mauro et al. (1967): THE ITALIAN LEGAL SYSTEM. Stanford University Press.

Carlson, Kenneth et al. (1977): ONE DAY/ONE TRIAL JURY SYSTEM: AN EXEMPLARY PROJECT. UNIVERSITY OF SAN DIEGO LAW JOURNAL.

Case Report (1960): Der verderbliche Einfluss West Berlins als Ursache für Verbrechen. 7 DER SCHÖFFE 330–332.

Case Report (1970): Voraussetzungen für den Vollzug einer Freiheitsstrafe bei Jugendlichen. 17 DER SCHÖFFE 323–326.

Case Report (1971): Gefährdung der öffentlichen Ordnung durch asoziales Verhalten. 18 DER SCHÖFFE 253–254.

Case Report (1980a): Oberstes Gericht: Schadenshöhe bestimmt nicht allein die Tatschwere einer Handlung. 27 DER SCHÖFFE 262–263.

Case Report (1980b): Konfliktkommission nicht zuständig für Urheberrecht. 34 NEUE JUSTIZ 92–93.

Case Report (1983a): Konflikt wegen unzumutbarer Belästigung durch Hundehaltung ist lösbar. 39 DER SCHÖFFE 92–93.

Case Report (1984a): Oberstes Gericht: Voraussetzungen für die Anordnung des Vollzugs der mit der Verurteilung auf Bewährung angedrohten Freiheitsstrafe. 31 DER SCHÖFFE 52–52a.

Case Report (1984b): Ein aussagekräftiger und kontrollfähiger Beschluss. 31 DER SCHÖFFE 141–143.

Case Report (1985): Beratung wegen Ordnungswidrigkeit. 32 DER SCHÖFFE 117.

Case Report (1986a): Ordnungswidrigkeit ruhestörender Lärm. 33 DER SCHÖFFE 188.

Case Report (1986b): Begünstigende Bedingungen beim Diebstahl sozialistischen Eigentums. 33 DER SCHÖFFE 212.

Case Report (1986c): Differenzierte Massnahmen bei rowdyhaften Handlungen. 33 DER SCHÖFFE 274–275.

Case Report (1987a): Alter schützt vor Torheit nicht. 34 DER SCHÖFFE 43–44.

Case Report (1987b): Eine Rüge wegen Verleumdung. 34 DER SCHÖFFE 131.

Case Report (1987c): Minusdifferenz in Saisongaststätte. 42 ARBEIT UND ARBEITSRECHT 138.

Case Report (1987d): Gute Ansätze. 42 ARBEIT UND ARBEITSRECHT 160.

Case Report (1987e): Betriebszugehörigkeit anerkannt. 42 ARBEIT UND ARBEITSRECHT 187.

Case Report (1987f): Schadenersatz aus einfacher Zivilrechtsstreitigkeit. 34 DER SCHÖFFE 24.

Case Report (1987g): Vorsätzliche Beschädigung sozialistischen Eigentums. 34 DER SCHÖFFE 44–44a.
Case Report (1987h): Eine Rüge wegen Verleumdung. 34 DER SCHÖFFE 131.
Case Report (1988a): Vorfahrt nicht beachtet. 43 ARBEIT UND ARBEITSRECHT 40.
Case Report (1988b): Ins schlechte Licht gesetzt. 43 ARBEIT UND ARBEITSRECHT 88.
Case Report (1988c): Nach Krankheit versetzt. 43 ARBEIT UND ARBEITSRECHT 162.
Case Report (1988d): Fristlose Entlassung revidiert. 43 ARBEIT UND ARBEITSRECHT 185.
Case Report (1988e): Hausarbeitstag ja oder nein. 43 ARBEIT UND ARBEITSRECHT 232.
Case Report (1989): Befugnisse des Gerichts strikt beachten. 36 DER SCHÖFFE 243–244.
Case Report (1990a): Wegen Hausfriedensbruch zur Verantwortung gezogen. 37 DER SCHÖFFE 175.
Case Report (1990b): Zur Problematik der Schulpflichtverletzung. 37 DER SCHÖFFE 176–177.
Casper, Gerhard & Hans Zeisel (1972): Lay Judges in the German Criminal Courts. 1 JOURNAL OF LEGAL STUDIES 135–191.
Casper, Gerhard & Hans Zeisel (1979): Einleitung & Bundesrepublik Deutschland. In Gerhard Casper & Hans Zeisel, eds., DER LAIENRICHTER IM STRAFPROZESS. C.F. Müller Juristischer Verlag.
Cerny, Jochen (1992): WER WAR WER—DDR: EIN BIOGRAPHISCHES LEXIKON. 2d ed. CH. Links Verlag.
Cheang, Molly: Jury Trial (1973): The Singapore Experience. 11 WESTERN AUSTRALIA LAW REVIEW 120–132.
Childs, David (1989): The SED faces challenges of Ostpolitik and Glasnost. David Childs et al. eds.: EAST GERMANY IN COMPARATIVE PERSPECTIVE. Routlege.
Chiu, Hung-dah (1981): Law and Justice. James C. Hsiung, ed.: THE TAIWAN EXPERIENCE 1950–1980. American Association for Chinese Studies.
Cho, Sung Yoon (1971): The Judicial System of North Korea. 11 ASIAN SURVEY 1167–1181.
Christange, Hans (1988): Ursachenforschung nach Inventurminusdifferenzen. 43 ARBEIT UND ARBEITSRECHT 187.
Christie, George C. (1974): Lawful Departures from Legal Rules: "Jury Nullification" and Legitimated Disobedience. 62 CALIFORNIA LAW REVIEW 1289–1310.
Christoph, Karl-Heinz (1985): Die Verantwortung der örtlichen Volksvertretungen für die strikte Durchsetzung der Gesetzlichkeit, Ordnung, Disziplin und Sicherheit. 32 DER SCHÖFFE 217–222.
Christoph, Karl-Heinz (1986): Zusammenarbeit der Kreisgerichte mit den örtlichen Staatsorganen zur Festigung der Gesetzlichkeit. 40 NEUE JUSTIZ 435–437.
Christoph, Karl-Heinz & Inge Kersten (1980): Beitrag der Gerichte und staatlichen Notariate zur Rechtserziehung der Jugend. 34 NEUE JUSTIZ 127–129.
Christoph, Karl-Heinz & Karl A. Mollnau (1981): Aufgaben der Rechtspropaganda. 35 NEUE JUSTIZ 391.

Church, Thomas W., Jr. (1978a): Civil Case Delay in State Trial Courts. 4 JUSTICE SYSTEM J. (1978–79).
Church, Thomas, Jr. et al. (1978b): JUSTICE DELAYED: THE PACE OF LITIGATION IN URBAN TRIAL COURTS. National Center for State Courts.
Cismarescu, Michael (1977): Über die Entwicklung der Kameradengerichte in Rumänien. 23/24 OSTEUROPA-RECHT 129–134]
Civil Code of the GDR (*ZIVILGESETZBUCH DER DDR* of June 19, 1975). Staatsverlag, 1980.
Clark, David S. & John Merryman (1976): Measuring the Duration of Judicial and Administrative Proceedings. 75 MICHIGAN L. REV.
Clark, J.P. (1989): Conflict Management Outside the Courtrooms in China. R.J. Troyer et al., eds.: SOCIAL CONTROL IN THE PEOPLE'S REPUBLIC OF CHINA. Praeger.
Clark, LeRoy (1972): THE GRAND JURY. Quadrangle Books.
Clune, William H. III & Patrick Hyde (1981): Final Offer Interest Arbitration in Wisconsin. 64 MARQUETTE L. REV. 455.
Cobden, Lynn (1976): The Grand Jury: Use and Misuse. 22 CRIME & DELINQUENCY 149–165.
Code of the Constitution of Courts of the GDR (*GERICHTSVERFASSUNGSGESETZ DER DDR* of September 27, 1974). Staatsverlag, 1984.
Code of Criminal Procedure of the GDR (*STRAFPROZESSORDNUNG DER DDR* of January 12, 1968). Staatsverlag, 1976.
Cohen, Jerome A. (1977): Reflections on the Criminal Process in China. 68 JOURNAL OF CRIMINAL LAW & CRIMINOLOGY 323–355.
Cohen, Jerome A. (1982): The Criminal Procedure Law of the People's Republic of China. 73 JOURNAL OF CRIMINAL LAW & CRIMINOLOGY 171–203.
Collins, Hugh (1982): MARXISM AND LAW. Clarendon Press.
Comment (1956a): Some Aspects of the California Grand Jury System. 8 STANFORD LAW REVIEW 631–656.
Comment (1956b): Das Wohnungsmietverhältnis. 3 DER SCHÖFFE 208–214.
Comment (1956c): Der Jugendliche im Strafrecht. 3 DER SCHÖFFE 145–150.
Comment (1961): Das Urteil sprichst Du. 8 DER SCHÖFFE 286–288.
Comment (1963a): Die öffentliche Aussprache über die höhere Qualität der Rechtspflege hat begonnen. 17 NEUE JUSTIZ 4–14.
Comment (1963b): Grundsätze zum Erlass des Staatsrates der DDR über die grundsätzlichen Aufgaben und die Arbeitsweise der Organe der Rechtspflege. 10 DER SCHÖFFE 2–10.
Comment (1965): Der Entwurf des Familiengesetzbuches—Ausdruck des sich vollziehenden geistigen Entwicklungsprozesses in der DDR. 12 DER SCHÖFFE 193–194.
Comment (1966a): Zur einheitlichen Anwendung des § 4 JGG durch die Gerichte. 13 DER SCHÖFFE 5–10.
Comment (1966b): Die Entwicklung der Schiedskommissionen im Bezirk Magdeburg. 13 DER SCHÖFFE 173–180.
Comment (1967): Aus der Schöffenkonferenz des Bezirksgerichts Frankfurt (Oder). 14 DER SCHÖFFE 395–399.
Comment (1970): Ehescheidungen unter die Lupe genommen. 17 DER SCHÖFFE 61–69.

Comment (1971): Dem VIII. Parteitag entgegen. 18 DER SCHÖFFE 65–66.
Comment (1972a): Zur Entwicklung der Schöffentätigkeit in der DDR. 19 DER SCHÖFFE 197–206.
Comment (1972b): Zur Anwendung der Geldstrafe und des Strafbefehlsverfahrens. 19 DER SCHÖFFE 253–255.
Comment (1972c): Beschluss des Plenums des Obersten Gerichts zu Fragen des Wohnungsmietrechts. 19 DER SCHÖFFE 63–68.
Comment (1973): Aufgaben der Gerichte bei der Verbesserung der Empfehlungspraxis der Konfliktkommissionen. 20 DER SCHÖFFE 277–285.
Comment (1975a): Ziele und Grundfragen der Änderungen der StPO. 22 DER SCHÖFFE 138–144.
Comment (1975b): Zur Entwicklung der gesellschaftlichen Gerichte im Bezirk Magdeburg. 22 DER SCHÖFFE 188–191.
Comment (1976): Vergehen und Verfehlungen Jugendlicher vor Schiedskommissionen. 23 DER SCHÖFFE 42–51.
Comment (1977): In unserer Schiedskommission ist immer etwas los. 24 DER SCHÖFFE 99.
Comment (1980a): Entwicklung der Schiedskommissionen im Blickpunkt des Bezirksgerichts. 27 DER SCHÖFFE 182–186.
Comment (1980b): Konferenz vermittelte Fülle reichhaltiger Anregungen. 27 DER SCHÖFFE 253.
Comment (1980c): Bilanz im Zeichen der Vorbereitung des X. Parteitages der SED. 27 DER SCHÖFFE 161.
Comment (1980d): Konferenz vermittelte Fülle reichhaltiger Anregungen. 27 DER SCHÖFFE 253.
Comment (1981): Leitung der Schöffenarbeit—ein wichtiges Anliegen. 28 DER SCHÖFFE 127–129.
Comment (1983a): Gesellschaftliche Gerichte sind zur Anwendung neuer Bestimmungen bereit. 37 NEUE JUSTIZ 10.
Comment (1983b): Schiedskommissionen bedürfen weiterhin guter Anleitung. 30 DER SCHÖFFE 204.
Comment (1984a): Auftrag in Ehren erfüllt. 31 DER SCHÖFFE 116.
Comment (1984b): Gesetz über die gesellschaftlichen Gerichte bewährt sich in der Praxis. 38 NEUE JUSTIZ 7–8.
Comment (1984c): Für hohe Wirksamkeit der Schiedskommissionen. 38 NEUE JUSTIZ 139–140.
Comment (1986): Anleitung der Schiedskommissionen bei zivilrechtlichen Streitigkeiten. 40 NEUE JUSTIZ 338–339.
Comment (1987): Besonderheiten der KK-Beratungen mit Jugendlichen. 42 ARBEIT UND ARBEITSRECHT 161.
Comment (1988): Ergebnisse des Führungsbeispiels zur Leitung der Schöffentätigkeit am Kreisgericht Senftenberg. 35 DER SCHÖFFE 171–180.
Congress of the CPSU, 27th Congress (1986): THE PROGRAMME OF THE COMMUNIST PARTY OF THE SOVIET UNION. Novosti Press Agency.
Connor, Walter D. (1988): SOCIALISM'S DILEMMAS: STATE AND SOCIETY IN THE SOVIET BLOC. Columbia University Press.
Conquest, Robert (1968): THE GREAT TERROR: STALIN'S PURGES OF THE THIRTIES. Macmillan.

Conquest, Robert (1969): JUSTICE AND THE LEGAL SYSTEM IN THE USSR. Bodley Head Ltd.

Conrad, Clay S. (1998): JURY NULLIFICATION: THE EVOLUTION OF A DOCTRINE. Carolina Academic Press.

Conradt, Siegfried (1979): Autorität der Schiedskommission ist gestiegen. 26 DER SCHÖFFE 116–117.

Constitution of the GDR (*VERFASSUNG DER DDR* of April 6, 1968, with Supplements of October 7, 1974). Staatsverlag, 1974.

CONSTITUTION OF THE USSR (1977). Novosti Press Agency.

Corboy, Philip H. (1975): From the Bar. Rita J. Simon, ed.: THE JURY SYSTEM IN AMERICA. Sage.

Counts, George S. & Nucia Lodge (1970): THE COUNTRY OF THE BLIND. Greenwood Press.

Criminal Code of the GDR (*STRAFGESETZBUCH DER DDR* of January 12, 1968). Staatsverlag. 1979.

Curran, Barbara A. (1977): THE LEGAL NEEDS OF THE PUBLIC: THE FINAL REPORT OF A NATIONAL SURVEY. American Bar Foundation.

Curtis, Michael (1969): Retreat from Totalitarianism. Carl J. Friedrich et al.: TOTALITARIANISM IN PERSPECTIVE. Praeger.

Daehn, Ulrich (1987): Verwirklichung des Grundsatzes der Gleichheit vor dem Gesetz in der Strafrechtsprechung. 41 NEUE JUSTIZ 53–55.

Daehn, Ulrich & Hans Weber (1981): Effektivität der Strafe. 35 NEUE JUSTIZ 399.

Daene, Arno (1969): Arbeit mit gerichtlich bestraften Personen in einem Grossbetrieb. 16 DER SCHÖFFE 234–236.

Dahrendorf, Ralf (1968a): In Praise of Thrasymachus. Ralf Dahrendorf: ESSAYS IN THE THEORY OF SOCIETY. Stanford University Press.

Dahrendorf, Ralf (1968b): Out of Utopia. Ralf Dahrendorf: ESSAYS IN THE THEORY OF SOCIETY. Stanford University Press.

Dallin, Alexander (1973): Bias and Blunders in American Studies on the USSR. 3 SLAVIC REVIEW 560.

Daniels, Janet (1974): Trial by Jury: Sacred Cow or Alien Transplant? 6 REV. OF GHANA LAW 106–115.

Dannemann, H. (1983): Ergebnisse einer guten Zusammenarbeit. 30 DER SCHÖFFE 159–160.

Dashwood, Alan (1972): Juries in a Multi-racial Society. 1972 CRIMINAL LAW REVIEW 85–94.

Dashwood, Alan (1974): The Jury and the Angry Brigade. 11 WESTERN AUSTRALIA LAW REVIEW 245–255.

Dau, Rudolf et al., eds. (1986): WÖRTERBUCH DES WISSENSCHAFTLICHEN KOMMUNISMUS. Dietz Verlag.

David, Rene & John E. Brierley (1978): MAJOR LEGAL SYSTEMS IN THE WORLD TODAY. Free Press.

Davis, Robert C. et al. (1980): MEDIATION AND ARBITRATION AS ALTERNATIVES TO PROSECUTION IN FELONY ARREST CASES. Vera Institute of Justice.

Dawson, John P. (1960): A HISTORY OF LAY JUDGES. Harvard University Press.

Dawson, John P. (1969): THE ORACLES OF THE LAW. University of Michigan Law School.

DC Decree—see Decree regarding the Dispute Commissions of the GDR.

DDR HANDBUCH (1985) 3rd ed. 2 Vols. Verlag Wissenschaft und Politik.

Decree regarding the Arbitration Commissions of the GDR (*Schiedskommissionsordnung der DDR*) of March 12, 1982.

Decree regarding the Dispute Commissions of the GDR (*Konfliktkommissionsordnung der DDR*) of March 12, 1982.

Deichmann, Ruth (1977): Betreuung und Wiedereingliederung der Verurteilten. 24 DER SCHÖFFE 185–187.

Deja-Loelhoeffel, Brigitte (1987): UNBEKANNTER NACHBAR DDR. Aarau Verlag.

Dellmuth, Rainer (1999): AUSFLÜGE IM "GROTEWOHL-EXPRESS:" OPERATIV-VORGANG "LEHRLING:" EINE JUGEND WIRD ZERSTÖRT. Anita Tykve Verlag.

Dengler, Gerhard (2000): VIELE BEULEN IM HELM: MEIN LEBEN ALS SED-FUNKTIONÄR. Libri Books.

DeNike, Howard J. (1997): GERMAN UNIFICATION AND THE JURISTS OF EAST GERMANY. Forum Verlag.

Dennis, Mike (2003): THE STASI: MYTH AND REALITY. Pearson Longman, 2003.

Denzin, Ruth (1985): Arbeit im Dienste der Gesellschaft bedarf guter Unterstützung. 32 DER SCHÖFFE 156–168a.

Dershowitz, Alan M. (1988): TAKING LIBERTIES. Contemporary Books.

Deschle, Regine (1990): Schöffentätigkeit—Ausdruck echter Demokratie. 37 DER SCHÖFFE 67–68.

Dession, George H. & Isadore H. Cohen (1932): The Inquisitorial Functions of Grand Juries. 41 YALE LAW JOURNAL 687–712.

Dettenborn, Harry (1979): Zur Bedeutung einzelner Strukturbestandteile des Rechtsbewusstseins der Persönlichkeit im rechtlichen Wirkungsprozess. Mollnau, Karl A., ed.: OBJEKTIVE GESETZE: RECHT HANDELN. Staatsverlag.

Dettenborn, Harry (1983): Psychologische Probleme der Gerichtsverhandlung. 37 NEUE JUSTIZ 313–315.

Dettenborn, Harry, ed. (1986): RECHT UND STIMULIERUNG WISSENSCHAFTLICH-TECHNISCHER LEISTUNGEN. Akademie-Verlag.

Dettenborn, Harry & Karl A. Mollnau (1976): RECHTSBEWUSSTSEIN UND RECHTSERZIEHUNG. Staatsverlag.

Dettenborn, Harry & Angelika Schmidt (1977): Interessen an der Rechtsnormeinhaltung in der Bewegung Ordnung und Sicherheit als Wirkungsbedingung des sozialistischen Rechts. Karl A. Mollnau, ed.: DIE GESELLSCHAFTLICHE WIRKSAMKEIT DES SOZIALISTISCHEN RECHTS: PROBLEME IHRER BEGRIFFSBESTIMMUNG UND MESSUNG. Akademie der Wissenschaften der DDR.

Dewar, Hugo (1962): How They Saw the Moscow Trials. 41 SURVEY 87–95 (April).

Diamond, Shari S. (1990): Revising Images of Public Punitiveness: Sentencing by Lay and Professional English Magistrates. 15 LAW AND SOCIAL INQUIRY 191.

Diamond, Shari S. (1993): What Jurors Think: Expectations and Reactions of Citizens Who Serve as Jurors. Robert E. Litan, ed.: VERDICT: ASSESSING THE CIVIL JURY SYSTEM. The Brookings Institution.

Diedrich, Karl-Heinz & Rose Kruse (1967): Zur Tätigkeit der Schiedskommissionen auf zivilrechtlichem Gebiet im Bezirk Schwerin. 14 DER SCHÖFFE 212–216.

Dietrich, Wilhelm (1965): Wenn Nachbarn sich streiten. 12 DER SCHÖFFE 132–133.

Dietzel, Dirk (1989): Das Wirken der ehrenamtlichen Richter—eine Errungenschaft der sozialistischen Rechtsordnung. 36 DER SCHÖFFE 49–53.

Dillhoefer, Gerhard (1954): Das Sühneverfahren. 1:3 DER SCHÖFFE 1–9.

Dillhoefer, Gerhard (1957): Zum Verfahren in Ehesachen. 4 DER SCHÖFFE 33–44.

DiPerna, Paula (1984): JURIES ON TRIAL. Dembner Books.

Doberenz, Werner (1965): Worauf muss der Vorsitzende einer Schiedskommission achten? 12 DER SCHÖFFE 50–52.

Dobrawa, Ralph (1985): Nochmals zur Rechtserziehung. 32 DER SCHÖFFE 14–15.

Doder, Dusko (1988): SHADOWS AND WHISPERS: POWER POLITICS INSIDE THE KREMLIN FROM BREZHNEV TO GORBACHEV. Penguin.

Doeker, Guenther & Jens A. Brueckner, eds. (1979): THE FEDERAL REPUBLIC OF GERMANY AND THE GERMAN DEMOCRATIC REPUBLIC IN INTERNATIONAL RELATIONS. Oceana Publications.

Dokumentation (1982): Die Aufgaben der Ausschüsse der Nationalen Front bei der Zusammenarbeit mit den Schiedskommissionen sowie bei der Wahl ihrer Mitglieder. 29 DER SCHÖFFE 130.

Dollase, Klaus-Peter (1979): Aufgaben der Schiedskommissionen bei der Beratung einfacher zivilrechtlicher Streitigkeiten und Verfehlungen. 26 DER SCHÖFFE 259–263.

Doob, Anthony N. (1978): Canadian Jurors" View of the Criminal Jury Trial: A Report to the Law Reform Commission of Canada.

Dorber, Heide-Rose (1982): Als Jugendbeistand muss man vieles Bedenken. 29 DER SCHÖFFE 270–271.

Downie, Leonard, Jr.(1971): JUSTICE DENIED: THE CASE FOR REFORM OF THE COURTS. Penguin.

Draeger, Gerhard (1961): Die Konfliktkommission fördert die sozialistische Erziehung im Betrieb. 8 DER SCHÖFFE 182.

Drath, Martin (1963): Einleitung; Ernst Richert: MACHT OHNE MANDAT. 2d ed. Westdeutscher Verlag.

Dreilich, Herbert (1976): Erfolge in Kampf gegen Schulbummelei. 23 DER SCHÖFFE 285–286.

Drews, Traugott (1978): Wiedereingliederung—verantwortungsvolle Aufgabe für alle Beteiligten. 25 DER SCHÖFFE 169.

Drews, Traugott (1983): Bewährungskontrolle durch Schöffen. 30 DER SCHÖFFE 63.

Duff, Peter et al. (1990): The Hong Kong Jury: A Microcosm of Society? 39 INTERNATIONAL & COMPARATIVE LAW QUARTERLY 881–891.

Duft, Heinz (1975): Neue rechtliche Möglichkeiten zur effektiven Ausgestaltung der Verurteilung auf Bewährung. 22 DER SCHÖFFE 40–45.

Duft, Heinz & Rolf Gerberding (1963): Wie wird der Rechtspflegeerlass des Staatsrates in der Strafrechtsprechung des Bezirks Halle durchgesetzt? 10 DER SCHÖFFE 373–379.

Dukes, Katharina (1980a): Wirksamkeit der gesellschaftlichen Gerichte und künftige Erweiterung ihrer Rechte. 34 NEUE JUSTIZ 260.

Dukes, Katharina (1980b): Schiedskommissionskonferenz in Dresden. 34 NEUE JUSTIZ 566–568.

Dukes, Katharina (1980c): Wiedereingliederung der aus dem Strafvollzug entlassenen Bürger in das gesellschaftliche Leben. 34 NEUE JUSTIZ 23–24.

Durand, Richard M. et al. (1978a): Attitudinal and Normative Beliefs Underlying Individual Perceptions of Juror Service. 106 JOURNAL OF SOCIAL PSYCHOLOGY 207.

Durand, Richard M. et al. (1978b): Previous Jury Service as a Moderating Influence on Jurors' Beliefs and Attitudes. 42 PSYCHOLOGICAL REPORTS 567.

Dutschke, Ingrid & Peter Wallis (1987): Besonderheiten bei der Pfändung und bei der Lohnabtretung. 42 ARBEIT UND ARBEITSRECHT 62–64.

Dzykonski, Kurt & Wolfgang Loose (1972): Die marxistisch-leninistische Dialektik: Wichtigstes Instrument der wissenschaftlichen Leitung. 21 STAAT UND RECHT 193–204.

Eastman, Max, ed. (1932): CAPITAL, AND OTHER WRITINGS BY KARL MARX. Modern Library.

Eberhardt, Karl-Heinz (1967): Die Aufgaben der Schöffen im Eheverfahren. 14 DER SCHÖFFE 283–291.

Ebner, Hans-Martin (1978a): Schiedskommission Mahlow besitzt Vertrauen der Bürger. 25 DER SCHÖFE 88–91.

Ebner, Hans-Martin (1978b): Das "Stadtgericht" von Meuselwitz. 25 DER SCHÖFFE 163.

Ebner, Hans-Martin (1980a): Den passenden Schlüssel finden. 27 DER SCHÖFFE 113.

Ebner, Hans-Martin (1980b): Über den eigenen Zaun schauen. 27 DER SCHÖFFE 67.

Ebner, Hans-Martin (1981): Wie man in Brück die Brücken schlägt. 28 DER SCHÖFFE 220–222.

Eckert, Rainer & Bernd Faulenbach, eds. (1996): HALBHERZIGER REVISIONISMUS: ZUM POSTKOMMUNISTISCHEN GESCHICHTSBILD. Olzog Verlag.

Eckhoff, Torstein (1966): The Mediator, the Judge, and the Administrator in Conflict Resolution. 10 ACTA SOCIOLOGICA 148–172.

Ehrmann, Henry W. (1976): COMPARATIVE LEGAL CULTURES. Prentice-Hall.

Eisenfeld, Bernd (1999): Rolle und Stellung der Rechtsanwälte in der Ära Honecker im Spiegel kaderpolitischer Entwicklungen und Einflüsse des MfS. Roger Engelmann & Clemens Vollnhals, eds.: JUSTIZ IM DIENSTE DER PARTEIHERRSCHAFT. Ch. Linkks Verlag.

Elm, Ludwig (1986): KONSERVATISMUS HEUTE. Pahl-Rugenstein.

Ellsworth, Phoebe (1985): Juries on Trial: Can Guilt Be Judged Fairly by Jurors Who Support Capital Punishment. 19:7 PSYCHOLOGY TODAY 44–46 (July 1985).

Elwork, Amiram, et al. (1987): Toward Understandable Jury Instructions. Lawrence S. Wrightsman et al., eds.: IN THE JURY BOX. Sage.

Engel, David M. (1978): CODE AND CUSTOM IN A THAI PROVINCIAL COURT. University of Arizona Press.

Engels, Frederick (1979): Speech in Elberfeld, 1845. David F. Greenberg, ed.: CRIME AND CAPITALISM: READINGS IN MARXIST CRIMINOLOGY. Temple University Press.

England, Wolfgang (1975): Die Wohnungsmiete im ZGB. 22 DER SCHÖFFE 259–263.

Eppelmann, Rainer, et al. (1996): LEXIKON DES DDR-SOZIALISMUS. Schöningh.

Epperlein, Elfriede (1986): Erhöhte Wirksamkeit der Schiedskommissionen durch planmäsige Arbeit des Beirats. 40 NEUE JUSTIZ 64–65.

Ermisch, Hermann (1979): Streitigkeiten sachkundig lösen. 26 DER SCHÖFFE 52.

Ermisch, Joachim (1987): Zur Rechtsprechung bei rowdyhaften Handlungen gegen Personen. 34 DER SCHÖFFE 161–163.

Esdohr, Jochen (1962): Familienrechtskonflikte und Wege zu ihrer Beseitigung. 9 DER SCHÖFFE 357–359.

Eser, Albin (1970): GESELLSCHAFTSGERICHTE IN DER STRAFRECHTSPFLEGE. J.C.B. Mohr.

Fedoseyev, P. (1979): Social Science and Social Progress. 10:3 SOCIAL SCIENCES 15–32.

Feifer, George (1964): JUSTICE IN MOSCOW. Simon and Schuster.

Feifer, George (1976): MOSCOW FAREWELL. Viking Press.

Feldbrugge, F.J.M., ed. (1973): ENCYCLOPEDIA OF SOVIET LAW. Occeana Publications.

Feldbrugge, F.J.M. & William B. Simon, eds. (1982): PERSPECTIVES ON SOVIET LAW FOR THE 1980s. Martinus Nijhoff.

Feldmann, Guenter & Reinhard Nissel (1984): Mitwirkung der Bürger an der Instalthaltung von Wohnraum. 38 NEUE JUSTIZ 64–65.

Fels, Barbara & Hans Schulz (1982): Kommission zur Betreuung kriminell gefährdeter und zur Wiedereingliederung aus dem Strafvollzug entlassener Bürger bei Rat des Kreises. 36 NEUE JUSTIZ 510–511.

Felstiner, William L. F. & Lynne A. Williams (1978): Mediation as an Alternative to Criminal Prosecution: Ideology and Limitations. 2 LAW AND HUMAN BEHAVIOR 223.

Felstiner, William L.F. & A.B. Drew (1978): EUROPEAN ALTERNATIVES TO CRIMINAL TRIALS AND THEIR APPLICABILITY IN THE UNITED STATES. National Institute of Law Enforcement and Criminal Justice.

Festinger, Leon et al. (1964): WHEN PROPHECY FAILS. Harper & Row.

Feuchtwanger, Lion (1937): MOSCOW 1937. Victor Gollancz.

Feuerbach, P.J.A. (1813): BETRACHTUNGEN ÜBER DAS GESCHWORNENGERICHT. Krüll.

Fichtner, Magda (1980): In Annaberg-Buchholz vielfältige Aktivitäten. 27 DER SCHÖFFE 285–287.

Fincke, Martin (1975): Marxismus und sozialistisches Recht. 16 JAHRBUCH FÜR OSTRECHT 7.

Finn, Gerhard (1981): POLITISCHER STRAFVOLLZUG IN DER DDR. Verlag Wissenschaft und Politik.

Fischer, Ursula (1986): Anleitung der Schiedskommissionen bei zivilrechtlichen Streitigkeiten. 40 NEUE JUSTIZ 338–339.

Fitzpatrick, Sheila (1992): Constructing Stalinism: Changing Western and Soviet Perspectives; Alec Nove, ed.: THE STALIN PHENOMENON. St. Martin's Press.

Flanders, Steven (1978): Case Management in Federal Courts: Some Controversies and Some Results. 4 JUSTICE SYSTEM J. 147 (1978–79)

Flynn, William J., Jr. (1960): Public Preference for the Jury. 32 N.Y. STATE BAR BULLETIN 103.

Fraenkel, Ernst (1927): ZUR SOZIOLOGIE DER KLASSENJUSTIZ. E. Laub.

Frank, Jerome (1949): COURTS ON TRIAL: MYTH AND REALITY IN AMERICAN JUSTICE. Princeton University Press.

Frankel, Marvin E. (1978): PARTISAN JUSTICE. Hill & Wand.

Frankel, Marvin E. & Gary P. Naftalis (1977): THE GRAND JURY: AN INSTITUTION ON TRIAL. Hill & Wang.

Franz, Lothar (1984): Zur Wahrung des Rechts auf Verteidigung beim Ausbleiben des gewählten Verteidigers in der Hauptverhandlung. 38 NEUE JUSTIZ 467–468.

Frassine, Ingrid, et al. (1979): Oesterreich. In Gerhard Casper & Hans Zeisel, eds.: DER LAIENRICHTER IM STRAFPROZESS. C.F. Müller Juristischer Verlag.

Freiburg, Arnold (1975): Das Gerede von der Wohlstandskriminalität: Zur Entwicklung der Kriminalität in der DDR seit 1970. 8 DEUTSCHLAND ARCHIV 1976–1984.

Freiburg, Arnold (1981): KRIMINALITäT IN DER DDR. Westdeutscher Verlag.

Freiburg, Arnold (1984): Kriminalität und Kriminalpolitik in der DDR 1968–1983. Dieter Voigt, ed.: DIE GESELLSCHAFT DER DDR. Duncker & Humblot.

Freiburg, Arnold (1985): Eine Art Produktion und Reproduktion von Jugendkriminalität. 18 DEUTSCHLAND ARCHIV 68–74.

Frenzke, Dietrich (1977): Was ist "sozialistisches" Recht? 23 OSTEUROPA-RECHT 55–79.

Frey, Eric G. (1987): DIVISION AND DETENTE: THE GERMANIES AND THEIR ALLIANCES. Praeger.

Frey: Gerhard, ed. (1991): PROMINENTE OHNE MASKE DDR. FZ-Verlag.

Fricke, Karl Wilhelm (1979): POLITIK AND JUSTIZ IN DER DDR. Verlag Wissenschaft und Politik.

Fricke, Karl Wilhelm (1984): DIE DDR-STAATSSICHERHEIT. Verlag Wissenschaft und Politik.

Fricke, Karl Wilhelm (1995): Opposition, Widerstand und Verfolgung in der SBZ/DDR. Kaff, Brigitte, ed.: "GEFÄHRLICHE POLITISCHE GEGNER:" WIDERSTAND UND VERFOLGUNG IN DER SOWJETISCHEN ZONE/DDR. Droste.

Fricke, Karl Wilhelm (1999): DDR-Juristen im Konflikt zwischen Gehorsam, Verweigerung und Widerstand. Roger Engelmann & Clemens Vollnhals, eds.: JUSTIZ IM DIENSTE DER PARTEIHERRSCHAFT. Ch. Linkks Verlag.

Fricke, Karl Wilhelm & Bernhard Marquardt (1995): DDR STAATSSICHERHEIT. Universitätsverlag Brockmeyer.

Friedgut, Theodore H. (1979): POLITICAL PARTICIPATION IN THE USSR. Princeton University Press.

Friedman, Lawrence M. (1973): A HISTORY OF AMERICAN LAW. Simon and Schuster.

Friedrich, Carl J. (1969): The Evolving Theory and Practice of Totalitarian Regimes. Carl J. Friedrich et al., eds.: TOTALITARIANISM IN PERSPECTIVE: THREE VIEWS. Praeger.

Friedrich, Walter (1976): JUGEND UND JUGENDFORSCHUNG. VEB Deutscher Verlag der Wissenschaften.

Friedrich, Walter & Werner Henning (1976): JUGENDFORSCHUNG: METHODOLOGISCHE GRUNDLAGEN, METHODIKEN UND TECHNIKEN. VEB Deutscher Verlag der Wissenschaften.

Friedrich, Wolfgang-Uwe (1989): DDR: DEUTSCHLAND ZWISCHEN ELBE UND ODER. W. Kohlhammer.

Friedrich-Ebert-Stiftung (1977): KRIMINALITÄT, STRAFVOLLZUG UND RESOZIALISIERUNG IN DER DDR. Verlag Neue Gesellschaft.

Friedrich-Ebert-Stiftung (1987): ORGANIZATIONEN UND VERBÄNDE IN DER DDR. Verlag Neue Gesellschaft.

Friloux, C. Anthony, Jr. (1975): Another View from the Bar. Rita J. Simon, ed.: THE JURY SYSTEM IN AMERICA. Sage.

Fritzsch, Guenter (1994): GESICHT ZUR WAND: WILLKÜR UND ERPRESSUNG HINTER MIELKES MAUERN. Benno Verlag.

Froehlich, Irene (1970): Zu einigen Problemen aus der Rechtsprechung der Schiedskommissionen wegen zivilrechtlicher Streitigkeiten. 17 DER SCHÖFFE 238–250.

Fuchs, Dieter et al. (1984): Einbeziehung von Studenten in die Arbeit örtlicher Räte mit kriminell gefährdeten Jugendlichen. 38 NEUE JUSTIZ 185.

Fuhr, Regina (1983): Unterstützung der Modernisierung und Instalthaltung von Wohnraum durch das staatliche Notariat. 37 NEUE JUSTIZ 461–462.

Fuhrmann, Wilhelm (1978): Erzieherische Wirkung auf jugendliche Rechtsverletzer. 25 DER SCHÖFFE 271–272.

Fuhrmann, Wilhelm (1981): Das persönliche Gespräch mit den Bürgern. 28 DER SCHÖFFE 169.

Fulbrook, Mary (1995): ANATOMY OF A DICTATORSHIP: INSIDE THE GDR 1949–1989. Oxford University Press.

Fuller, Lon (1971): Mediation—Its Forms and Functions. 44 SOUTHERN CALIFORNIA LAW REVIEW 305.

Funk, Werner (1964): Für eine stärkere Wirksamkeit der Strafen ohne Freiheitsentzug. 18 NEUE JUSTIZ 705–708.

Funston, Richard Y. (1977): CONSTITUTIONAL COUNTER-REVOLUTION. Wiley.

Gaengel, Andreas (1995): Guter Abschied nach böser Vergangenheit: Von einem "Unrechtsstaat" und seinen "Unrechtlern." Rosemarie Will, ed.: RECHTWISSENSCHAFT IN DER DDR—WAS WIRD VON IHR BLEIBEN? Pro Universitate Verlag.

Galanter, Marc (1978): Indian Law as an Indigenous Conceptual System. 32 ITEMS 42–46.

Galanter, Marc (1981): Justice in Many Rooms: Courts, Private Ordering, and Indigenous Law. 19 JOURNAL OF LEGAL PLURALISM 1.

Gatow, Hanns-Heinz (1990): VERTUSCHTE SED-VERBRECHEN. Türmer-Verlag

Gattermann, Gerhard (1983): Rechtskonferenzen der Handwerksbetriebe. 37 NEUE JUSTIZ 333.

Gattermann, Gerhard (1986): Rechtsarbeit in Handwerksbetrieben. 40 NEUE JUSTIZ 199–200.

Gaul, Dieter (1965): "Betriebsjustiz" als zulässige Konkurrenz der Rechtspflege? 18 DER BETRIEB 665–670.

Gaum, Wilfried (1990): Die Auflösung des Arbeitsrechtsverhältnisses im Arbeitsrecht der DDR. 34 RECHT IN OST UND WEST 77–91.
Gayle, Andrew M. (1978): Law and Lawyers in China. 64 AMERICAN BAR ASSOCIATION JOURNAL 348–353.
Gebert, Ursula (1976): Zur Tätigkeit der Schiedskommissionen bei der Behandlung mietrechtlicher Streitigkeiten. 23 DER SCHÖFFE 45–50.
Geipel, Ines (2002): Das "Sportwunder" DDR und die andere Seite seiner Medaillen. Clemens Vollnhals & Juegen Weber, eds.: DER SCHEIN DER NORMALITÄT. Olzog Verlag.
Geisler, Holger & Ingo Wagner (1980): Zur Individualisierung der sozialistischen Rechtsnormen in der Rechtsverwirklichung. 24 STAAT UND RECHT 64–73.
Gelatt, Timothy A. (1982): The People's Republic of China and the Presumption of Innocence. 73 JOURNAL OF CRIMINAL LAW & CRIMINOLOGY 259–316.
Gelber, Seymour (1960): A Reappraisal of the Grand Jury Concept. 60 JOURNAL OF CRIMINAL LAW, CRIMINOLGY & POLICE SCIENCE 24–27.
Gensch, Willi (1981): Wirksamkeit der Schiedskommissionen und ihrer Anleitung. 28 DER SCHÖFFE 261.
Gerig, Uwe (1987): BRIEF KONTAKT. Anita Tykve Verlag.
Gerth, Erwin & Waltraud Duttig (1973): Gesellschaftliche Gerichte—Instrumente sozialistischer Macht. 20 DER SCHÖFFE 96–98.
Getty, J. Arch (1992): The Politics of Stalinism; Alec Nove, ed.: THE STALIN PHENOMENON. St. Martin's Press.
Gibbs, James L., Jr. (1967): The Kpelle Moot. Paul Bohannan, ed.: LAW AND WARFARE. Natural History Press.
Gierke, Erika (1977): Vielfältiger Einfluss der Schöffen. 24 DER SCHÖFFE 157–159.
Gieseke, Jens (2001): MIELKE-KONZERN: DIE GESCHICHTE DER STASI 1945–1990. Deutsche Verlags-Anstalt.
Gilbers, Lothar (1975): Erfahrungen der Schiedskommission in Raschau-Grünstädtel. 22 DER SCHÖFFE 137–138.
Gimmler, Werner (1981): New Wege in der Betreuung kriminell gefährdeter Jugendlicher. 28 DER SCHÖFFE 286–287.
Ginsburg, Ruth (1963): The Jury and the Nämnd: Some Observations on Judicial Control of Lay Triers in Civil Proceedings in the United States and Sweden. 48 CORNELL LAW QUARTERLY 253–273.
Glenn, Franklin P. (1964): The California Penalty Trial. 52 CALIFORNIA LAW REVIEW 386–407.
Glien, Irma (1982): Gute Unterstützung beflügelt die Arbeit. 29 DER SCHÖFFE 16.
Gneist, Rudolf von (1954, 1879): DER RECHTSSTAAT UND DIE VERWALTUNGSGERICHTE IN DEUTSCHLAND. Verlag Julius Springer.
Gneist, Rudolf von (1967, 1849): DIE BILDUNG DER GESCHWORENENGERICHTE IN DEUTSCHLAND. Scientia Verlag.
Gobert, James J. (1992): Trial by Jury. Kermit L. Hall, ed.: THE OXFORD COMPANION TO THE SUPREME COURT OF THE UNITED STATES. Oxford University Press.
Goehring, Joachim & Werner Drews (1977): Überlegungen zur Erforschung der Wirksamkeit des sozialistischen Zivilrechts. Karl A. Mollnau, ed.: DIE GESELLSCHAFTLICHE WIRKSAMKEIT DES SOZIALISTISCHEN RECHTS:

PROBLEME IHRER BEGRIFFSBESTIMMUNG UND MESSUNG. Akademie der Wissenschaften der DDR.

Goeldner, Elfriede (1962): Der Unterhalt nach der Ehescheidung. 9 DER SCHÖFFE 391–398.

Goerner, Kurt (1954): Um die Neuregelung des Familienrechts. 1 DER SCHÖFFE (2) 1–9, (3) 9–18.

Goerner, Kurt (1955): Strafrechtsprechung der Gerichte und Verbrechensentwicklung. 2 DER SCHÖFFE 208–216.

Goerner, Kurt (1959): Ursachen und Bekämpfung der Kriminalität in der DDR. 6 DER SCHÖFFE 172–180.

Goerner, Kurt (1960): Den verderblichen Einfluss der westlichen Ideologie eindämmen! 7 DER SCHÖFFE 100–103.

Goerner, Kurt (1963): Zu einigen Fragen der Arbeit der Schöffenkollektive. 10 DER SCHÖFFE 416–421.

Goerner, Kurt (1964): Zur Richtlinie über die Bildung und Tätigkeit von Schiedskommissionen. 11 DER SCHÖFFE 347.

Goerner, Kurt (1966a): Zur Bildung und Tätigkeit von Schiedskommissionen. 13 DER SCHÖFFE 357–359.

Goerner, Kurt (1966b): Jugendliche vor der Schiedskommission. 13 DER SCHÖFFE 206–210.

Goerner, Kurt (1978): Berufsrichter und Laien. Nationales Komitee für Rechtswissenschaft der DDR: BERICHTE ZUM X. INTERNATIONALEN KONGRESS FÜR RECHTSVERGLEICHUNG.

Goerner, Kurt (1979): 25 Jahre Anleitung und Hilfe den gesellschaftlichen Kräften. 26 DER SCHÖFFE 152–157.

Goerner, Kurt & Rita Sokolow (1983): Jahrzehnte erfolgreicher Arbeit—wachsendes Gewicht der gesellschaftlichen Gerichte. 30 DER SCHÖFFE 76–80.

Goethe, Dorothee (1983): Ehrenamtliche Mitarbeiter unterstützen die örtlichen Räte bei der Erziehung kriminell gefährdeter und strafentlassener Bürger. 37 NEUE JUSTIZ 146–147.

Gohl, Dietmar (1986): DEUTSCHE DEMOKRATISCHE REPUBLIK: EINE AKTUELLE LANDESKUNDE. Fischer.

Goldfarb, Jeffrey C. (1989): BEYOND GLASNOST: THE POST-TOTALITARIAN MIND. University of Chicago Press.

Goldman, Marshall I. (1987): GORBACHEV'S CHALLENGE. Norton.

Goldman, Marshall I. (1991): WHAT WENT WRONG WITH PERESTROIKA. Norton.

Goodell, Charles E. (1973): Where Did the Grand Jury Go? HARPER'S MAGAZINE 14–28 (May 1973).

Gorle, Frits (1982): The Latest Developments in the Area of Comradely Justice. Feldbrugge, F.J.M. & William B. Simon, eds.: PERSPECTIVES ON SOVIET LAW FOR THE 1980s. Martinus Nijhoff.

Gornig, Gilbert (1987): Meinungsäusserungsrecht und Pressefreiheit nach marxistisch-leninistischem Grundrechtsverständnis. 31 RECHT IN OST UND WEST 79–90.

Gorphe, Francois (1936): Reforms of the Jury-System in Europe: France and Other Continental Countries. 27 JOURNAL OF CRIMINAL LAW AND CRIMINOLOGY 155–168.

Grabert, Hansernst & Gerhard Zoebe (1970): SCHÖFFEN UND GESCHWORENE: EIN LEITFADEN FÜR DEN STRAFPROZESS. C. F.Mueller.

Grabowski, Gerhard (1985): Feste Zusammenarbeit zwischen Nationaler Front und Schiedskommissionen. 32 DER SCHÖFFE 158–160.

Grafe, Heinz (1978): Geldbusse differenziert und überlegt anwenden. 25 DER SCHÖFFE 298–299.

Grafe, Heinz (1980): Vertrauensvolle Zusammenarbeit fördert unsere Tätigkeit. 27 DER SCHÖFFE 190.

Grafe, Roman (2002): DIE GRENZE DURCH DEUTSCHLAND. Siedler.

Graham, Gene S. (1975): From the Press. Rita J. Simon, ed.: THE JURY SYSTEM IN AMERICA. Sage.

Graham, Loren R. (1993): SCIENCE IN RUSSIA AND THE SOVIET UNION. Cambridge University Press.

Grandke, Anita (1984): Leitungstätigkeit auf dem Gebiet der Familienförderung im Bezirk Schwerin. 38 NEUE JUSTIZ 357–359.

Grasemann, Hans-Juergen (1994): Wenn die Partei Weisung gibt, folgen die Richter. Juergen Weber, ed.: DER SED-STAAT. Olzog Verlag.

Grass, Jacob (1954): Die Unterschätzung der Schöffentätigkeit muss aufhören. 1:5 DER SCHÖFFE 24–26.

Grass, Jacob (1955): Ist für einen Richter ein Schöffenpaar erforderlich? 2 DER SCHÖFFE 43–45.

Green, Justin et al. (1975): Iowa's Magistrate System: The Aftermath of Reform. 58 JUDICATURE 380–389.

Green Thomas A. (1985): VERDICT ACCORDING TO CONSCIENCE: PERSPECTIVES ON THE ENGLISH CRIMINAL TRIAL JURY: 1200–1800. University of Chicago Press.

Gregor, A. James (1968): CONTEMPORARY RADICAL IDEOLOGIES. Random House.

Greiger, Helmut & Frohmut Müller (1981): Sozialistische Demokratie und gesellschaftliche Gerichte. 35 NEUE JUSTIZ 160.

Griebe, Walter (1981): Zum sozialen Wesen der Straftaten gegen das sozialistische Eigentum. 35 NEUE JUSTIZ 210–212.

Griebe, Walter (1984): Festellung der Tatmotive bei Eigentumsdelikten. 38 NEUE JUSTIZ 460–461.

Grieger, Helmut (1980): Wirksamere Gestaltung der Tätigkeit der Schiedskommissionen. 27 DER SCHÖFFE 41.

Grieger, Helmut & Frohmut Müller (1981): Sozialistische Demokratie und gesellschaftliche Gerichte. 35 NEUE JUSTIZ 160–162.

Griesbach, Johanna (1983): Jugendlichen gilt unsere besondere Aufmerksamkeit. 30 DER SCHÖFFE 185.

Grischin, L. (1986): Das Statut über die Kameradschaftsgerichte. 33 DER SCHÖFFE 203–204.

Grogorenz, Hans (1972): Eine Rüge für Manuel. 19 DER SCHÖFFE 130–132.

Grosse, Hans-Dieter (1975): Dieser Weg hat sich bewährt. 22 DER SCHÖFFE 281–282.

Grossman, Joel B., et al. (1981): Measuring the Pace of Civil Litigation in Federal and State Trial Courts. 65 JUDICATURE 86.

Grube, Gerda (1954): Über die Jugendgerichte in der Deutschen Demokratischen Republik und in Westdeutschland. 1 (2) DER SCHÖFFE 12–15.
Grube, Gerda (1959): Zum Jugendstrafverfahren und seiner Neugestaltung. 6 DER SCHÖFFE 106–112.
Gruel, Karl-Friedrich et al. (1984): STAATSRECHT DER DDR. Staatsverlag.
Gruenert, Peter (1980): Anregungen aus der Praxis. 27 DER SCHÖFFE 33.
Gruetzmacher, Horst (1988): Die Erhöhung der erzieherischen Wirksamkeit der Beratung zur materiellen Verantwortlichkeit der Werktätigen—bedeutsam für den Schutz des sozialistischen Eigentums. 43 ARBEIT UND ARBEITSRECHT 282–284.
Grunenberg, Antonia (1990): AUFBRUCH DER INNEREN MAUER: POLITIK UND KULTUR IN DER DDR 1971–1990. Edition Temmen.
Grzybowski, Kazimierz (1962): SOVIET LEGAL INSTITUTIONS. University of Michigan Press.
Gudorf, Odilo (1981): SPRACHE ALS POLITIK: UNTERSUCHUNG ZUR ÖFFENTLICHEN SPRACHE UND KOMMUNIKATIONSSTRUKTUR IN DER DDR. Verlag für Wirtschaft und Politik.
Guenther, Erwin (1965): Wiedereingliederung aus der Strafhaft entlassener Personen in das gesellschaftliche Leben. 12 DER SCHÖFFE 385–387.
Guenther, Erwin (1966): Einbeziehung ehrenamtlicher Mitarbeiter in die Betreuung straffällig gewordener Personen. 13 DER SCHÖFFE 331–332.
Haage, Gert (1981): Rechtserziehung in einer Gemeide. 28 DER SCHÖFFE 130.
Haas, Ernst B. (1983): On Hedging Our Bets: Selective Engagement with the Soviet Union. Aaron Wildavsky, ed.: BEYOND CONTAINMENT: ALTERNATIVE AMERICAN POLICIES TOWARD THE SOVIET UNION. ICS Press.
Haase, Baldur (2002): Volkskunst und Stasi am Beispiel des Bezirkes Gera. Clemens Vollnhals & Juegen Weber, eds.: DER SCHEIN DER NORMALITÄT. Olzog Verlag.
Haase, Heinz-Joachim (1982): Die Rolle von Arbeitsgruppen bei der Umsetzung von Rechtsvorschriften in die Leitungstätigkeit eines Kombinats. 36 NEUE JUSTIZ 84–85.
Haase, Norbert & Bert Pampel, eds. (2001): DIE WALDHEIMER PROZESSE—FÜNFZIG JAHRE DANACH. Nomos.
Haase, Reinhard (1980): Nacharbeit bei Arbeitsbummelei. 34 NEUE JUSTIZ 85.
Habe, Irina (1988): Tatbestandsanforderungen bei Straftaten gegen das sozialistische und persönliche Eigentum. 35 DER SCHÖFFE 162–169.
Haberecht, Winfried (1986): Auf die Besonderheiten Jugendlicher eingehen. 33 DER SCHÖFFE 269–270.
Hackel, Georg (1976): Eine gute Bilanz bei der Rechtserläuterung und Rechtserziehung im Kreise Stendal. 23 DER SCHÖFFE 63–67.
Hacker, Jens (1986): Die Völkerrechtslehre der DDR zwischen traditionellen Dogmatismus und aussenpolitischen Erfordernissen. 30 RECHT IN OST UND WEST 77–87.
Hage, Marion (2001): BETRIEBLICHE KONFLIKTHANDHABUNG IN DER DDR UND DER BUNDESREPUBLIK. Verlag Dr. Kovac.
Hahn, Jeffrey (1988): An Experiment in Competition: the 1987 Elections to the Local Soviet. 47 SLAVIC REVIEW 434–447.

Hale, John (1973): Juries: The West Australian Experience. 11 WESTERN AUSTRALIA LAW REVIEW 99–104.

Haley, John O. (1982): The Politics of Informal Justice: The Japanese Experience, 1922–1942. Richard L. Abel, ed.: THE POLITICS OF INFORMAL JUSTICE. Vol.2 Academic Press.

Hall, Jerome (1932): Analysis of Critism of the Grand Jury. 22 JOURNAL OF CRIMINAL LAW 692–704.

Hall, Kermit L., ed. (1999): THE OXFORD GUIDE TO UNITED STATES SUPREME COURT DECISIONS. Oxford University Press.

Hallervorden, E. (1954): Als Schöffe am Kreisgericht. 1:1 DER SCHÖFFE 4–7.

Hammer, Susanne (1957): Aus der Arbeit eines Gemeinschaftlichen Jugendgerichts. 4 DER SCHÖFFE 185–190.

HANDBUCH: DEUTSCHE DEMOKRATISCHE REPUBLIK. (1979) VEB Verlag Enzyklopädie.

Haney, Craig (1980): Juries and the Death Penalty: Readdressing the *Witherspoon* Question. 26 CRIME & DELINQUENCY 512–527.

Haney, Gerhard (1963): Zum Inhalt des sozialistischen Rechtsbegriffs. 12 STAAT UND RECHT 121–137.

Haney, Gerhard (1967): SOZIALISTISCHES RECHT UND PERSÖNLICHKEIT. Staatsverlag.

Haney, Gerhard & Ingo Wagner (1967): GRUNDLAGEN DER THEORIE DES SOZIALISTISCHEN STAATES UND RECHTS. 2 Vols. 3d ed. Institut für Theorie des Staats und des Rechts.

Hanhardt, Arthur M., Jr. (1968): THE GERMAN DEMOCRATIC REPUBLIC. Johns Hopkins Press.

Hans, Valerie P. & Neil Vidmar (1986): JUDGING THE JURY. Plenum Press.

Hantsche, Walter (1965): Die Wahlen der Konfliktkommissionen und der Schöffen. 12 DER SCHÖFFE 369–371.

Hantsche, Walter (1977): Die Konfliktkommissionen—bewährte Kraft für die Wahrung der sozialistischen Gesetzlichkeit. 24 DER SCHÖFFE 113–116.

Hantsche, Walter (1985a): Der Einfluss der Konfliktkommissionen auf die Wahrung der sozialistischen Gesetzlichkeit. 32 DER SCHÖFFE 200–203.

Hantsche, Walter (1985b): Die Konfliktkommissionswahlen: Ein weiterer Schritt zur Entfaltung der sozialistischen Demokratie. 32 DER SCHÖFFE 25.

Hantsche, Walter (1988): Aufgaben zur Erhöhung der gesellschaftlichen Wirksamkeit der Tätikeit der Konfliktkommissionen. 43 ARBEIT UND ARBEITSRECHT 255–256.

Hantsche, Walter & Werner Kulitzscher (1987): Wirksamere Arbeit der Konfliktkommissionen. 41 NEUE JUSTIZ 180–181.

Hantzschmann, Arthur (1960): Schiedskommissionen. 7 DER SCHÖFFE 207–209.

Harding, Neil, ed. (1984): THE STATE IN SOCIALIST SOCIETY. Macmillan.

Haring, Werner (1978): Sozialistisches Recht—wichtiges Instrument zur Erfüllung der Produktionsaufgaben. 25 DER SCHÖFFE 107.

Haring, Werner & Sabine Langer (1987): Arbeitsrechtlicher Einfluss der Justitiare in den Betrieben. 42 ARBEIT UND ARBEITSRECHT 89–90.

Haring, Werner & Hartmut Radeck (1983): Unterstützung der Konfliktkommissionen durch die Justitiare der Kombinate und Betriebe. 37 NEUE JUSTIZ 142–143.

Harrland, Harri (1956): Über Charakter und Ursachen der Kriminalität. 3 DER SCHÖFFE 193.
Harrland, Harri (1958): Fragen der Kriminalität und ihrer Bekämpfung. 5 DER SCHÖFFE 207–213.
Harrland, Harri (1965): Entwicklung und Bekämpfung der Kriminalität in der DDR im Spiegel der Statistik. 19 NEUE JUSTIZ 401–438.
Harrland, Harri (1983): Unterstützung der gesellschaftlichen Gerichte durch die Staatsanwaltschaft. 37 NEUE JUSTIZ 11–13.
Harrland, Harri (1984): Aufgaben der Staatsanwaltschaft zur Unterstützung der gesellschaftlichen Gerichte. 38 NEUE JUSTIZ 38–40.
Harrland, Harri (1985): Aufgaben der Staatsanwaltschaft bei der Zusammenarbeit mit den gesellschaftlichen Gerichten. 39 NEUE JUSTIZ 4–7.
Harrland, Harri (1986a): On the development of Criminality in the German Democratic Republic. 86–1 LAW AND LEGISLATION IN THE GDR 3–17.
Harrland, Harri (1986b): Die Arbeit der Staatsanwaltschaft mit den Eingaben der Bürger. 40 NEUE JUSTIZ 223–224.
Harrland, Harri (1987): Gesetzlichkeit der Arbeit der gesellschaftlichen Gerichte. 41 NEUE JUSTIZ 126–128.
Hass, Gerhard & Reinhard Hass (1983): Potenzen des Biologieunterichts für die Rechtserziehung. 37 NEUE JUSTIZ 199.
Hastie, Reid et al. (1983): INSIDE THE JURY. Harvard University Press.
Hastrich, Alois (1965): Das Laienelement in der Sowjetischen Strafrechtspflege. 15 OSTEUROPA 463–474.
Hastrich, Alois (1967): ALLTAG UND RECHT DER UdSSR IM SPIEGEL DER SOWJETPRESSE. Verlag Wissemschaft und Politik.
Hastrich, Alois (1969): Volksrichter und Volksgerichte in der UdSSR. 15 OSTEUROPA-RECHT 121–142.
Haufe, Georg & Heinz Strohbach (1978): Zielstrebige Rechtserziehung zeigt Erfolge. 25 DER SCHÖFFE 96–97.
Haupt, Guenter (1972): Zum Wirken eines Eheaktivs in einem Grossbetrieb. 19 DER SCHÖFFE 169–170.
Hauschild, Helmut (1976): Aufgaben der Betriebe bei der Pfändung von Arbeitseinkommen. 23 DER SCHÖFFE 21–23.
Hauschild, Helmut (1983): Eine neue Etappe in der Tätigkeit der gesellschaftlichen Gerichte hat begonnen. 30 DER SCHÖFFE 6–9.
Hausding, Gottfried (1980): Konflikten rechtzeitig verbeugen. 27 DER SCHÖFFE 284.
Hauser, Siegfried (1980): Erzieherisch wirksame Beratung sichern. 27 DER SCHÖFFE 280.
Hayden, Robert M. (1990): SOCIAL COURTS IN THEORY AND PRACTICE: THE YUGOSLAV WORKERS' COURTS IN COMPARATIVE PERSPECTIVE. University of Pennsylvania Press.
Hazard, John N. (1948): Introduction. Andrei Vyshinsky: THE LAW OF THE SOVIET STATE. Macmillan.
Hazard, John N. (1951): SOVIET LEGAL PHILOSOPHY. Harvard University Press.
Hazard, John N. (1960): SETTLING DISPUTES IN SOVIET SOCIETY: THE FORMATIVE YEARS OF LEGAL INSTITUTIONS. Columbia University Press.

Hazard, John N. (1969): COMMUNISTS AND THEIR LAW. University of Chicago Press.
Hearden, Arthur (1974): EDUCATION IN THE TWO GERMANIES. Basil Blackwell.
Heger, Siegfried (1981): X. Parteitag der SED setzt Generallinie zum Wohle des Volkes fort. 35 NEUE JUSTIZ 194.
Heilborn, Hans & Eberhard Poppe (1979): Die sozialistischen Menschenrechte und ihre Verwirklichung in Gesetzgebung und Rechtspflege der DDR. Vereinigung der Juristen der DDR: RECHT IM DIENST DES VOLKES. Staatsverlag.
Heilmaier, Reinhard (1988): Rechtsprechung. 32 RECHT IN OST UND WEST 193–203.
Heilmaier, Reinhard, et al. (1988): Die Rechtsentwicklung in der DDR. 32 RECHT IN OST UND WEST 112–126.
Heimberger, Frank (1980): Die Strafe—ein wichtiges Mittel im Kampf gegen Kriminalität. 27 DER SCHÖFFE 127.
Heimberger, Frank (1984): Die Strafe als Mittel der Kriminalitätsbekämpfung. 31 DER SCHÖFFE 277–284.
Heimberger, Frank & Rita Sokolow (1984): 35 Jahre Entwicklung sozialistischer Demokratie in der Rechtspflege der DDR. Part 1. 31 DER SCHÖFFE 209–214; Part 2. 31 DER SCHÖFFE 230–233.
Heinecke, Barbara (2000): GESTUTZTE FLÜGEL: GESCHICHTEN AUS DER DDR. Krämer Verlag.
Heinig, Martha (1980): Selten gleicht ein "Fall" dem anderen. 27 DER SCHÖFFE 141.
Heinrich, Guenter (1967): "Wer einmal aus dem Blechnapf frisst." 14 DER SCHÖFFE 218–219.
Heinrich, Walter (1980): Energisch gegen Schulpflichtverletzungen vorgehen. 27 DER SCHÖFFE 38.
Heintze, Horst (1978): 25 Jahre erfolgreiche Arbeit der Konfliktkommissionen. 32 NEUE JUSTIZ 190.
Heintze, Horst (1979): Unser Recht trägt die Handschrift der Arbeiterklasse. 33 NEUE JUSTIZ 286–289.
Heintze, Horst (1981): Gewerkschaftliche Rechtsarbeit—wichtige Seite der Interessenvertretung der Werktätigen. 35 NEUE JUSTIZ246–248.
Heintze, Horst (1983): 30 Jahre Konfliktkommissionen. 37 NEUE JUSTIZ 137.
Heinze, Claus & Herbert Kern (1979): Die sozialistische gesellschaftliche Organisation der Juristen der DDR. Vereinigung der Juristen der DDR: RECHT IM DIENST DES VOLKES. Staatsverlag.
Heinze, Claus et al. (1979): RECHT IM DIENST DES VOLKES. Staatsverlag.
Heinze, Rudolf (1864): PARALLELEN ZWISCHEN DER ENGLISCHEN JURY UND DEM FRANZÖSISCH-DEUTSCHEN GESCHWORNENGERICHT. Enke Verlag.
Heiz, Wolfgang (1987): Unterstützung des Erziehungs- und Vorbeugungsprozesses. 34 DER SCHÖFFE 35–36.
Hejhal, Gottfried (1966): Eigentums- und Vermögensbeziehungen der Ehegatten im neuen FGB. 13 DER SCHÖFFE 83–85.
Hejhal, Gottfried (1980): Die Unterstützung der sozialistischen Wohnungspolitik durch die Rechtsprechung. 27 DER SCHÖFFE 207–214.

Hejhal, Gottfried (1983): Die Bedeutung des Mietrechts für die Gestaltung sozialistischer Wohnbeziehungen. 30 DER SCHÖFFE 224–228.
Heldner, Willi (1965): Unsere Schiedskommission—ein wichtiges Gremium im Wohngebiet. 12 DER SCHÖFFE 210–214.
Heldner, Willi (1966): Wir leisten einen Beitrag zur weiteren Zurückdrängung der Jugendkriminalität. 13 DER SCHÖFFE 99–105.
Helm, Rolf (1972): Über Effektivität und Kontinuität. 19 DER SCHÖFFE 351–354.
Helm, Rolf (1979): Der Volksrichter: Garant für die Demokratisierung der Justiz. Vereinigung der Juristen der DDR: RECHT IM DIENST DES VOLKES. Staatsverlag.
Helwig, Gisela, ed. (1985): JUGEND-KRIMINALITÄT IN BEIDEN DEUTSCHEN STAATEN. Edition Deutschland Archiv.
Hendel, Rudolf (1967): Mitwirkung in der Kommission für gesellschaftliche Erziehung. 14 DER SCHÖFFE 367–368.
Hengelhaupt, Egon (1982): Diskussionsrede. 36 NEUE JUSTIZ 149.
Henk, Regina (1985): Wirksame Öffentlichkeitsarbeit—differenziert und organspezifisch. 39 NEUE JUSTIZ 59–60.
Henke, Klaus-Dietmar et al. (1995): ANATOMIE DER STAATSSICHERHEIT. Der Bundesbeauftragte für die Unterlagen des Staatssicherheitsdienstes der ehemaligen DDR.
Hennig, Walter (1965): Zu einigen Fragen der Jugendkriminalität. 12 DER SCHÖFFE 309–315.
Henrich, Rolf (1989): DER VORMUNDSCHAFTLICHE STAAT. Rowohlt.
Hensel, Kurt (1984): Sorgfältige Ursachenermittlung—Voraussetzung für effektive erzieherische Massnahmen. 31 DER SCHÖFFE 112–114.
Hensel, Kurt (1985): Wirksame Aussprachen erübrigen Beratungen. 32 DER SCHÖFFE 87–89.
Henselin, Horst (1981): Zusammenarbeit will richtig organisiert sein. 28 DER SCHÖFFE 148.
Herlemann, Horst (1984): Zur Frage politischer Partizipation in der Sowjetunion. 34 OSTEUROPA 318–328.
Herrmann, Arnd (1985): Zur Durchführung von beschleunigten Verfahren. 39 NEUE JUSTIZ 292–293.
Herrmann, Detlef (1984): The Bitter Pills of the Politburo; Arthur W. McCardle & A. Bruce Boenau, eds.: EAST GERMANY: A NEW GERMAN NATION UNDER SOCIALISM? University Press of America.
Herrmann, Rudolf & Rolf Schuesseler (1963): Inhalt und Bedeutung der Unabhängigkeit der Richters in der DDR. 17 NEUE JUSTIZ 129–135.
Hersch, Gisela (1972): A BIBLIOGRAPHY OF GERMAN STUDIES. Indiana University Press.
Herzog, Felix & Heike Wagner (1997): Gesellschaftliche Prävention und Sanktionierung von Alltagskriminalität in der DDR. Gerhard Dilcher, ed.: RECHTSERFAHRUNG DDR. Berlin Verlag Arno Spitz.
Hess, Georg (1974): Erfahrungen und Ergebnisse in der Leitung der Schöffentätigkeit des Bezirkes Suhl. 21 DER SCHÖFFE 20–25.
Heuckendorf, Hans-Jürgen (1978): Schiedskommissionen erfüllen wirksam den gesellschaftlichen Auftrag. 25 DER SCHÖFFE 190.

Heuckendorf, Hans-Jürgen (1981): Mit Herz und Verstand die künftigen Aufgaben meistern. 28 DER SCHÖFFE 185.

Heuckendorf, Hans-Jürgen & Rose Kruse (1972): Rückschau und Ausblick. 19 DER SCHÖFFE 50–59.

Heuer, Klaus (1986): WAS IST GERECHT, WAS UNGERECHT? Staatsverlag.

Heuer, Uwe-Jens (1965): DEMOKRATIE UND RECHT IM NEUEN ÖKONOMISCHEN SYSTEM DER PLANUNG UND LEITUNG DER VOLKSWIRTSCHAFT. Staatsverlag.

Heuer, Uwe-Jens (1967): Die Funktion des Rechts im entwickelten gesellschaftlichen System des Sozialismus. 21 NEUE JUSTIZ 656–661.

Heuer, Uwe-Jens (1974): GESELLSCHAFTLICHE GESETZE UND POLITISCHE ORGANIZATION. Dietz Verlag.

Heuer, Uwe-Jens (1977): Ergebnisse aus Untersuchungen zur Wirksamkeit des Wirtschaftsrechts: Thesen. Karl A. Mollnau, ed.: DIE GESELLSCHAFTLICHE WIRKSAMKEIT DES SOZIALISTISCHEN RECHTS: PROBLEME IHRER BEGRIFFSBESTIMMUNG UND MESSUNG. Akademie der Wissenschaften der DDR.

Heuer, Uwe-Jens (1989): MARXISMUS UND DEMOKRATIE. Nomos.

Heuer, Uwe-Jens (1995a): Vorwort. Uew-Jens Heuer: DIE RECHTSORDNUNG DER DDR. Nomos.

Heuer, Uwe-Jens (1995b): Rechtsverständnis in der DDR. Uwe-Jens Heuer: DIE RECHTSORDNUNG DER DDR. Nomos.

Heuer, Uwe-Jens & Michael Schumann (1994): Politik und Justiz in der Auseinandersetzung um die DDR-Geschichte. Lothar Bisky et al., eds.: UNRECHTSSTAAT? VSA-Verlag.

Heusinger, Hans-Joachim (1974): Die Erhöhung der Wirksamkeit der Gerichte und Staatlichen Notariate. 28 NEUE JUSTIZ 571–574.

Heusinger, Hans-Joachim (1978): Anerkennung und Verpflichtung zugleich. 25 DER SCHÖFFE 157.

Heusinger, Hans-Joachim (1979a): Die demokratische Mitwirkung der Werktätigen an der sozialistischen Rechtspflege. Vereinigung der Juristen der DDR: RECHT IM DIENST DES VOLKES. Staatsverlag.

Heusinger, Hans-Joachim (1979b): Wahl der Direktoren, Richter und Schöffen der Kreisgerichte und Mitglieder der Schiedskommissionen—ein bedeutendes gesellschaftliches Ereignis. 33 NEUE JUSTIZ 150.

Heusinger, Hans-Joachim (1981a): Mit einer guten Bilanz in das Jahr 1981. 28 DER SCHÖFFE 1.

Heusinger, Hans-Joachim (1981b): Rechtsarbeit in der Volkswirtschaft nach dem X. Parteitag der SED. 35 NEUE JUSTIZ 386.

Heusinger, Hans-Joachim (1982): Neues Gesetz über die gesellschaftlichen Gerichte. 36 NEUE JUSTIZ 146.

Heusinger, Hans-Joachim (1983a): Neue Aufgaben werden gemeistert. 30 DER SCHÖFFE 73–75.

Heusinger, Hans-Joachim (1983b): 20 Jahre Bestehen der Schiedskommissionen. 30 DER SCHÖFFE 121–125.

Heusinger, Hans-Joachim (1984a): Interview: Vorbereitung der Wahl der Richter, Schöffen und Schiedskommissionsmitglieder. 38 NEUE JUSTIZ 94–96.

Heusinger, Hans-Joachim (1984b): Gesetz über die gesellschaftlichen Gerichte bewährt sich in der Praxis. 31 DER SCHÖFFE 3–6.

Heusinger, Hans-Joachim (1984c): Recht und Gesetzlichkeit im Kampf für Sozialismus und Frieden. 31 DER SCHÖFFE 184–194.

Heusinger, Hans-Joachim (1986): Impulse für die Arbeit der Gerichte und staatlichen Notariate durch die Beschlüsse des XI. Parteitages der SED. 40 NEUE JUSTIZ 390–392.

Heusinger, Hans-Joachim (1988): 25 Jahre gesellschaftliches Wirken der Schiedskommissionen. 35 DER SCHÖFFE 109–112.

Heyme, Torsten (1991): ICH KAM MIR VOR WIE EIN TIER: KNAST IN DER DDR. BasisDruck.

Hiemann, Guenter & Alice Uhlig (1979): Gesellschaftliche Praxis gründlich studieren. 26 DER SCHÖFFE 113–115.

Higginbotham, Patrick E. (1977): Continuing the Dialogue: Civil Juries and the Allocation of Judicial Power. 56 TEXAS LAW REVIEW 47–60.

Hildebrandt, Alexandra (2001): DIE MAUER: ZAHLEN, DATEN. Verlag Haus am Checkpoint Charlie.

Hill, Larry B. (1976): THE MODEL OMBUDSMAN: INSTITUTIONALIZING NEW ZEALAND'S DEMOCRATIC EXPERIMENT. Princeton University Press.

Hiller, Rudolf (1965): Zahlen und Tatsachen zur Jugendkriminalität in der DDR. 12 DER SCHÖFFE 316.

Hiller, Rudolf (1967): Ein Blick in die Kriminalstatistik der DDR. 14 DER SCHÖFFE 228–232.

Hinderer, Hans (1966): The Fight against Criminality as a Social Responsibility. 66 LAW & LEGISLATION 9–21.

Hirsch, Ernst E. (1960): Die Rezeption fremden Rechts als socialer Prozess. Otto Stammer & Karl C. Thalheim, eds.: FESTGABE FÜR FRIEDRICH BÜLOW ZUM 70. GEBURTSTAG. Duncker & Humblot.

Hirst, Paul Q. (1972): Marx and Engels on Law, Crime, and Morality. 1 ECONOMY AND SOCIETY 28–56.

Hodos, Georg H. (1988): SCHAUPROZESSE: STALINISTISCHE SÄUBERUNGEN IN OSTEUROPA 1948–54. Campus Verlag.

Hoebel, E. Adamson (1954): THE LAW OF PRIMITIVE MAN. Harvard University Press.

Hoerschelmann, Axel von (1987): Review: Jugendprobleme im geteilten Deutschland. 31 RECHT IN OST UND WEST 131.

Hoerschelmann, Axel von, et al. (1989): Die Rechtentwicklung in der DDR. 33 RECHT IN OST UND WEST 105–113.

Hoffmann, Charlotte (1973): In Uhlstädt geniesst das gesellschaftliche Gericht Vertrauen. 20 DER SCHÖFFE 213–214.

Hoffman, Richard B. (1981): Is There a Job for the Justice of the Peace. Paper delivered at the annual meeting of the Law and Society Association, Amherst, Mass.

Hofmann, Christina (1989): Geldbusse als Erziehungsmassnahme der Schiedskommission. 36 DER SCHÖFFE 233–235.

Hofrichter, Richard (1987): NEIGHBORHOOD JUSTICE IN CAPITALIST SOCIETY: THE EXPANSION OF THE INFORMAL STATE. Greenwood Press.

Hohensee, Hans-Joachim (1979): Schulpflichtverletzungen durch gemeinsame Anstrengungen überwinden. 26 DER SCHÖFE 118–119.
Hohmann, Bernd (1995): Was bleibt von Forschung und Lehre des Staats- und Verwaltungsrecht der DDR? Rosemarie Will, ed.: RECHTWISSENSCHAFT IN DER DDR—WAS WIRD VON IHR BLEIBEN? Pro Universitate Verlag.
Hollander, Paul (1981): POLITICAL PILGRIMS: TRAVELS OF WESTERN INTELLECTUALS TO THE SOVIET UNION, CHINA, AND CUBA: 1928–1978. Oxford University Press.
Hollander, Paul (1987): Enduring Misconceptions about the Soviet Union. Sidney Hook et al.: SOVIET HYPOCRISY AND WESTERN GULLIBILITY. Ethics and Public Policy Center.
Holm, Hans A. (1970): THE OTHER GERMANS: REPORT FROM AN EAST GERMAN TOWN. Pantheon Books.
Holmes, Leslie (1981a): The GDR: 'Real Socialism' or 'Computer Stalinism'? Leslie Holmes: THE WITHERING AWAY OF THE STATE? Sage.
Holmes, Leslie (1981b): Conclusions: Wither the Party and State? Leslie Holmes: THE WITHERING AWAY OF THE STATE? Sage.
Holzendorf, Hansjoerg (1989): Der gemeinsamen Verantwortung bewusst. 33 DER SCHÖFFE 118–119.
Honecker, Erich (1981): AUS MEINEM LEBEN. Dietz Verlag.
Honecker, Erich (1984a): ARBEITERMACHT ZUM WOHLE DES VOLKES. Dietz Verlag.
Honecker, Erich (1984b): On the Economic and Social Policies of Our Party. Arthur W. McCardle & A. Bruce Boneau, eds.: EAST GERMANY: A NEW NATION UNDER SOCIALISM? University Press of America.
Honig, Richard M. (1974): Ehrenamtliche Richter im Schwurgericht. 11 MONATSSCHRIFT FÜR DEUTSCHES RECHT 898–900.
Hood, Roger (1962): SENTENCING IN MAGISTRATES' COURTS: A STUDY OF VARIATIONS IN POLICY. Stevens & Sons.
Hood, Roger (1972): SENTENCING THE MOTORING OFFENDER: A STUDY OF MAGISTRATES' VIEWS AND PRACTICES. Heinemann.
Hook, Sidney (1934): The Fallacy of the Theory of Social Fascism. 8 MODERN MONTHLY 342–352.
Hook, Sidney (1987): A History of Hypocrisy. Sidney Hook et al.: SOVIET HYPOCRISY AND WESTERN GULLIBILITY. Ethics and Public Policy Center.
Hooker, M.B. (1978): A CONCISE LEGAL HISTORY OF SOUTH-EAST ASIA. Clarendon Press.
Horowitz, Irwin A. (1985): The Effect of Jury Nullification Instruction on Verdicts and Jury Functioning in Criminal Trials. 9 LAW & HUMAN BEHAVIOR 25–36.
Horstkotte, Hartmuth (1998): Rechtsbeugung durch Richter und Staatsanwälte in der DDR. Ulrich Drobnig, ed.: DIE STRAFRECHTSJUSTIZ DER DDR IM SYSTEMWECHSEL. Duncker & Humblot.
Hsiung, James C., ed. (1981): THE TAIWAN EXPERIENCE: 1950–1980. American Association for Chinese Studies.
Huenich, Helmut (1987): Vereinbarung der Bürger in Aussprachen der Schiedskommission angeregt. 34 DER SCHÖFFE 128.

Hugot, Heinz et al. (1971): Analyse der gesellschaftlichen Wirksamkeit der nicht mit Freiheitsentzug verbundenen Massnahmen der strafrechtlichen Verantwortlichkeit. 20 STAAT UND RECHT 1206–1217.

Hugot, Heinz (1986): Berichterstattung vor der örtlichen Volksvertretung. 33 DER SCHÖFFE 104–108.

Hugot, Heinz & Karl-Heinz Oehmke (1983): Gesellschaftliche Kräfte erhöhen die Wirksamkeit der Rechtsprechung. 37 NEUE JUSTIZ 190–192.

Hurlbeck, Wilhelm & Gerhard Koerner (1985): Die Aufgaben der Rechtsprechung bei der Unterstützung der Tätigkeit der gesellschaftlichen Gerichte. 32 DER SCHÖFFE 100–107.

Hurst, Willard (1980): The Functions of the Courts in the United States: 1950–1980. 15 LAW & SOCIETY REV. 401 (1980–81).

Hutchings, Raymond (1987): SOVIET SECRECY AND NON-SECRECY. Barnes & Noble.

Immisch, Lars (1997): DER SOZIALISTISCHE RICHTER IN DER DDR UND SEINE UNABHÄNGIGKEIT. Peter Lang.

Ingraham, Barton L. (1987): THE STRUCTURE OF CRIMINAL PROCEDURE: LAWS AND PRACTICE OF FRANCE, THE SOVIET UNION, CHINA, AND THE UNITED STATES. Greenwood Press.

Inkeles, Alex (1950): PUBLIC OPINION IN SOVIET RUSSIA: A STUDY IN MASS PERSUASION. Harvard University Press.

Institut für Theorie des Staates und des Rechts (1984a): GESCHICHTE DES STAATES UND DES RECHTS DER DDR: DOKUMENTE 1945–1949. Staatsverlag.

Institut für Theorie des Staates und des Rechts (1984b): GESCHICHTE DES STAATES UND DES RECHTS DER DDR: DOKUMENTE 1949–1961. Staatsverlag.

International Congress of Judges (1960).

Ioffe, Olympiad S. & Peter B. Maggs (1983): SOVIET LAW IN THEORY AND PRACTICE. Oceana Publications.

Isaacman, Barbara & Allen Isaacman (1982): A Socialist Legal System in the Making: Mozambique before and after Independence. Richard L. Abel, ed.: THE POLITICS OF INFORMAL JUSTICE. Vol.2 Academic Press.

Ivkovic, Sanja Kutnjak (1999): LAY PARTICIPATION IN CRIMINAL TRIALS: THE CASE OF CROATIA. Austin & Winfield.

Jackwitz, Juergen (1983): Erste Erfahrungen werden verallgemeinert. 30 DER SCHÖFFE 111–114.

Jacobsohn, Gary J. (1977): Citizen Participation in Policy-Making: The Role of the Jury. 39 JOURNAL OF POLITICS 73–96.

Jacobstein, J. Myron & Roy M. Mersky, eds. (1998): JURY SIZE. Rothman.

Jacoby, Harry (1985): Vertrauen fördern und Rechtsbewusstsein festigen. 32 DER SCHÖFFE 182–183.

Jaeckel, Ruth (1981): Rechtserzieherische Wirksamkeit von Massnahmen einer Schiedskommission. 35 NEUE JUSTIZ 327.

Jahn, Hans (1955): Unsere Jugend muss vor dem zersetzenden Einfluss von Westschmökern bewahrt werden. 2 DER SCHÖFFE 149–151.

Jakob, Guenther (1955): Aus der Arbeit eines Schöffenaktivs. 2 DER SCHÖFFE 24–26.

Jakovlev, Aexander M. (1985): Das Strafgesetz: Konkretisierung der Strafe oder Gleichheit vor dem Gesetz. 29 RECHT IN OST UND WEST 1–7.

James, Howard (1971): CRISIS IN THE COURTS. David McKay.

Janke, Gerd (1985): Kassation und Wiederaufnahme zivil-, familien- und arbeitsrechtlicher Entscheidungen wegen unzureichender Aufklärung des Sachverhalts. 39 NEUE JUSTIZ 322–324.

Janos, Andrew C. (1976): Systemic Models and the Theory of Change in the Comparative Study of Communist Politics. Andrew C. Janos, ed.: AUTHORITARIAN POLITICS IN COMMUNIST EUROPE. Institute of International Studies, University of California, Berkeley.

Jarausch, Konrad H., ed. (1999): DITATORSHIP AS EXPERIENCE. Berghahn Books.

Jarausch, Konrad H. & Martin Sabrow, eds. (1999): WEG IN DEN UNTERGANG: DER INNERE ZERFALL DER DDR. Vandenhoeck & Ruprecht.

Jescheck, Hans-Heinrich (1962): STRAFRECHT UND STRAFRECHTSANWENDUNG IN DER SOWJETISCH BESETZTEN ZONE DEUTSCHLANDS. J.C.B. Mohr.

Jescheck, Hans-Heinrich (1977): Das Laienrichtertum in der Strafrechtspflege der Bundesrepublik Deutschland und der Schweiz. 94 SCHWEIZERISCHE ZEITSCHRIFT FÜR STRAFRECHT 229–251.

Jesella, Erich & Klaus Haertel (1984): Belehrung der Schüler zur Einhaltung von Ordnung, Disziplin und Sicherheit. 38 NEUE JUSTIZ 369.

Jesse, Eckhard (1988): Die "Totalitarismus-Doktrin" aus DDR-Sicht. Konrad Löw, ed.: TOTALITARISMUS. Duncker & Humblot.

Jessnitzer, Erich (1960): So arbeitet unsere Konfliktkommission. 7 DER SCHÖFFE 367–368.

Joas, Hans & Martin Kohli (1993): DER ZUSAMMENBRUCH DER DDR. Suhrkamp.

Joffe, Josef (1987): The View from Bonn: The Tacit Alliance. Lincoln Gordon, ed.: ERODING EMPIRE: WESTERN RELATIONS WITH EASTERN EUROPE. Brookings Institution.

Johnson, Earl, Jr. et al. (1977): OUTSIDE THE COURTS: A SURVEY OF DIVERSION ALTERNATIVES IN CIVIL CASES. National Center for State Courts.

Johnson, Paul (1976): A HISTORY OF CHRISTIANITY. Atheneum.

Joiner, Charles W. (1975): From the Bench. Rita J. Simon, ed.: THE JURY SYSTEM IN AMERICA. Sage.

Joseph, Detlef (1975): Bemerkungen zu einigen Publikationen bürgerlicher "Erforscher" der marxistischen Rechtstheorie. 24 STAAT UND RECHT 1051–1058.

Jovanovic, Vladimir (1986): Aufgaben, Methoden und Probleme der Rechtsvergleichung. 30 RECHT IN OST UND WEST 332–337.

Judges or Comrades? LITERATURNAIA GAZETA (March 3, 1971), as reprinted in translation in 10 SOVIET LAW AND GOVERNMENT 141 (1971).

Juristische Fakultät (1963): Thesen zum Wesen und zur Entwicklung des sozialistischen Rechts. 12 STAAT UND RECHT 1841–1850.

Jurow, George L. (1971): New Data on the Effect of a "Death Qualified" Jury on the Guilt Determination Process. 84 HARVARD LAW REVIEW 567–611.

Juviler, Peter H. (1976): REVOLUTIONARY LAW AND ORDER. Free Press.

Juviler, Peter H. (1982): Diversions from Criminal to Administrative Justice: Soviet Law, Practice, and Conflicts of Policy. F.J.M. Feldbrugge & William B. Simons, eds.: PERSPECTIVES ON SOVIET LAW FOR THE 1980s. Martinus Nijhoff.

Kabes, Vladimir M. (1961): Die Gesellschaftsgerichte in der Sowjetunion und in der Tschechoslowakei. 2 JAHRBUCH FÜR OSTRECHT 77–110.

Kaden, Bernd (1983): Das Zusammenwirken der Kreisgerichte mit den örtlichen Organen der Wohnungspolitik. 37 NEUE JUSTIZ 414–415.

Kaden, Helmut (1978): Schöffenaktiv in Bewährungskontrolle einbezogen. 25 DER SCHÖFFE 243–245.

Kadish, Mortimer R. & Sanford H. Kadish (1973): DISCRETION TO DISOBEY: A STUDY OF LAWFUL DEPARTURES FROM LEGAL RULES. Stanford University Press.

Kagel, John (1964): The California Grand Jury: Two Current Problems. 52 CALIFORNIA LAW REVIEW 116–128.

Kahler, Gerhard (1977): Trotz komplizierter Bedingungen wirksame Erziehungsarbeit. 24 DER SCHÖFFE 155–157.

Kaiser, Christoph (1973): Wirkungsvolle Arbeit der Konfliktkommissionen. 20 DER SCHÖFFE 274–277.

Kaiser, Christoph (1975): Sozialistische Arbeitsdisziplin und Tätigkeit der Gerichte. 22 DER SCHÖFFE 265–270.

Kaiser, Christoph (1980): Schöffenkonferenz beim Obersten Gericht. 27 DER SCHÖFFE 14.

Kaiser, Christoph (1987): Aufgaben der Arbeitsrechtsprechung in Auswertung des 11. FDGB-Kongresses. 34 DER SCHÖFFE 157–160.

Kalinka, Werner (1997): SCHICKSAL DDR. Ullstein.

Kalven, Harry, Jr. & Hans Zeisel (1966): THE AMERICAN JURY. Little-Brown.

Kamin, Hiltrud (1968): Die Besonderheiten der strafrechtlichen Verantwortlichkeit Jugendlicher in den neuen Strafgesetzen. 15 DER SCHÖFFE 230–236.

Kamin, Hiltrud (1969): Schutz der Kinder und Jugendlichen—untrennbarer Bestandteil der sozialistischen Jugendpolitik. 16 DER SCHÖFFE 201–207.

Kamin, Hiltrud (1975): Frauen in der Justiz. 22 DER SCHÖFFE 233–247.

Kamin, Hiltrud & Rudolf Winkler (1963): Konfliktkommissionen und Schiedskommissionen: Wichtige Formen der Teilnahme der Werktätigen an der Rechtspflege. 10 DER SCHÖFFE 51–56.

Kamin, Hiltrud & Barbara Redlich (1967): Besonderheiten bei Sraftaten Jugendlicher und Straftaten gegen Jugend und Familie. 14 DER SCHÖFFE 121–127.

Kamin, Hiltrud & Rita Sokolow (1988): Gesellschaftliche Gerichte—untrennbarer Bestandteil der Staats- und Rechtsordnung. 35 DER SCHÖFFE 72–77.

Kandt, William C. (1971): Jury Waiting Time Can Be Eliminated. 55 JUDICATURE 116–117.

Kantrowitz, Arthur (1976): The Science Court Experiment: An Interim Report. 193 SCIENCE 653–656 (August 20, 1976).

Kapp, Herbert (1985): Rat der Stadt setzt auf die Kraft der Schiedskommissionen. 32 DER SCHÖFFE 139–140.

Karatnycky, Adrian et al. (1980): WORKERS' RIGHTS, EAST AND WEST. Transaction Books.

Kareva, M.P. (1965): The Theory of Law and the State. USSR Aademy of Sciences: SOCIAL SCIENCES IN THE USSR. Mouton & Co.

Karl, Fritz & Siegfried Rau, eds. (1989): SCHWER WAR DER ANFANG: ERZÄHLT VON AKTIVISTEN DER ERSTEN STUNDE. Geschichtskommission bei der Kreisleitung der SED Sonneberg.

Karnath, Margitta (1956): Unsere Regierung schützt die Jugend. 3 DER SCHÖFFE 152–153.

Kasper, Ronald (1980): Grundsätze der Arbeit der gesellschaftlichen Gerichte. 27 DER SCHÖFFE 221–223.

Kassin, Saul M. (1995): The American Jury: Handicapped in the Pursuit of Justice. G. Larry Mays & Peter R. Gregware, eds.: COURTS AND JUSTICE. Waveland Pess.

Kassin, Saul M. & Lawrence S. Wrightsman (1988): THE AMERICAN JURY ON TRIAL: PSYCHOLOGICAL PERSPECTIVES. Hemisphere.

Kassin, Saul M. & Lawrence S. Wrightsman, eds. (1985): THE PSYCHOLOGY OF EVIDENCE AND TRIAL PROCEDURE. Sage.

Katschurowski, W. (1984): Die Rechtserziehung in der Schule. 31 DER SCHÖFFE 296–299.

Katz, Alan N., ed. (1986): LEGAL TRADITIONS AND SYSTEMS: AN INTERNATIONAL HANDBOOK. Greenwood Press.

Katz, Lewis R. (1974): The Formation of Community Councils. John A. Robertson, ROUGH JUSTICE. Little, Brown.

Kaufman, Irving R. (1962): The Grand Jury: Sword and Shield. 209:4 ATLANTIC MONTHLY 54–60 (April 1962).

Kaufman, Irving R. (1971): The Judges and Jurors. Glenn R. Winters, ed.: THE JURY: SELECTED READINGS. American Judicature Society.

Kaulfuss, Kurt (1960): Teilnehmer an der Jugendweihe besuchen das Gericht. 7 DER SCHÖFFE 186–187.

Kaye, David H. (1980): And Then There Were Twelve: Statistical Reasoning, the Supreme Court, and the Size of the Jury. 68 CALIFORNIA LAW REVIEW 1004–1043.

Kayode, Oluyemi (1975): Judicial Administration in a Changing Society: Customary Courts in Western Nigeria. 8 VR 435–446.

Keele, Lucy M. (1995): An Analysis of Six- vs. Twelve-Person Juries. G. Larry Mays & Peter R. Gregware, eds.: COURTS AND JUSTICE. Waveland Press.

Keeney, Barnaby C. (1949): Judgment by Peers in Continental Europe. Barnaby C. Keeney: JUDGMENT BY PEERS. Harvard University Press.

Keil, Helmut (1970): Eine neue Wahlperiode der Schöffen hat begonnen. 17 DER SCHÖFFE 217–224.

Keil, Helmut (1979): Den Schutz des sozialistischen Eigentums erhöhen. 26 DER SCHÖFFE 226–229.

Keil, Helmut (1985a): In enger Gemeinsamkeit mit der Nationalen Front lösen wir unsere Aufgaben. 32 DER SCHÖFFE 64–65.

Keil, Helmut (1985b): Mit Blick auf den XI. Parteitag der SED. 32 DER SCHÖFFE 132–138.

Kellner, H. (1978): Die Einigung als Instrument der Streitbeilegung. Nationales Komitee für Rechtswissenschaft der DDR: BERICHTE ZUM X. INTERNATIONALEN KONGRESS FüR RECHTSVERGLEICHUNG.

Kelsen, Hans (1955): THE COMMUNIST THEORY OF LAW. Stevens & Sons.

Kempfer, H. (1957): Fragen des Erbrechts und des Testaments. 4 DER SCHÖFFE 171–176, 212–215.
Kennebeck, Edwin (1975): From the Jury Box. Rita J. Simon, ed.: THE JURY SYSTEM IN AMERICA. Sage.
Keppler, Birte E. (1998): DIE LEITUNGSINSTRUMENTE DES OBERSTEN GERICHTS DER DDR. Edition Iuscrim.
Kerimow, D.A. (1959): STAATSLEHRE UND REVISIONISMUS. VEB Deutscher Zentralverlag.
Kermann, Ekkehard (1983): Beirat trägt eine hohe Verantwortung. 30 DER SCHÖFFE 81–83.
Kermann, Ekkehard et al. (1975): Höhere Wirksamkeit der besonderen Verfahrensarten in Strafsachen. 29 NEUE JUSTIZ 355–358.
Kern, Herbert (1962): Die Rechtspflege weiter vervollkommnen. 9 DER SCHÖFFE 227–235.
Kern, Herbert (1975): In allen Bereichen die sozialistische Gesetzlichkeit festigen. 22 DER SCHÖFFE 1–4.
Kern, Herbert (1979): Allseitige Unterstützung den Schiedskommissionen. 26 DER SCHÖFFE 293–296.
Kern, Herbert (1980): Gesellschaftliche Gerichte—ein unverzichtbarer Bestandteil sozialistischer Rechtspflege. 27 DER SCHÖFFE 245.
Kern, Herbert (1981): Weitere Festigung der sozialistischen Gesetzlichkeit. 28 DER SCHÖFFE 137.
Kern, Herbert (1982): Verantwortung und Befugnisse der gesellschaftlichen Gerichte werden erweitert. 29 DER SCHÖFFE 69–80.
Kern, Herbert (1983): Zwei Jahrzehnte erfolgreiches Wirken der Schiedskommissionen. 37 NEUE JUSTIZ 226.
Kern, Herbert (1984): Rechtsprechung im Interesse des Volkes. 38 NEUE JUSTIZ 301–303.
Kern, Herbert (1986): Zur gesellschaftlichen Wirksamkeit der Schiedskommissionen und zur Stellung und zu den Aufgaben der Beiräte für Schiedskommissionen. 33 DER SCHÖFFE 1–17.
Kern, Herbert & Günter Sarge (1981): Die Aufgaben der Gerichte nach dem X. Parteitag der SED. 35 NEUE JUSTIZ 290–292.
Kerr, Norbert L. & Robert J. MacCoun (1987): The Effects of Jury Size and Polling Method on the Process and Product of Jury Deliberation. Lawrence S. Wrightsman et al., eds.: IN THE JURY BOX. Sage.
Kerst, Heinz (1962): Die Konfliktkommissionen wirksam unterstützen. 16 NEUE JUSTIZ 330.
Kersten, Inge (1981): Für neue Aufgaben gut gerüstet. 28 DER SCHÖFFE 112.
Kersten, Inge (1985): Bilanz und Erkenntnisse. 32 DER SCHÖFFE 41–48A.
Kersten, Inge (1988): Über unsere sozialistische Demokratie in der Rechtspflege. 35 DER SCHÖFFE 120–126.
Kettner, Hans (1984): Eng mit dem Leben der Bürger verbunden. 31 DER SCHÖFFE 65.
Kieselbach, Ruth (1985): Den Mietrückständen rücken wir zu Leibe. 32 DER SCHÖFFE 127.
Kietz, Herbert (1984): Eigenverantwortliche Beilegung von Zivilrechtskonflikten. 38 NEUE JUSTIZ 11–12.

Kind, Klaus & Renate Solger (1987): Gewerkschaftliche Rechtsarbeit und KK-Tätigkeit in der vergangenen Wahlperiode. 42 ARBEIT UND ARBEITSRECHT 39–40.

Kirchheimer, Otto (1959): The Administration of Justice and the Concept of Legality in East Germany. 68 YALE LAW JOURNAL 705–749.

Kirchhoefer, Dieter & Gerhart Neuner (1988): Werte in der Erziehung unserer Jugend. 88 EINHEIT 230–235.

Kirchhoff, Wener (1981): Nationale Front und sozialistische Gesetzlichkeit. 35 NEUE JUSTIZ 197–198.

Kirchhoff, Werner (1986): Die Nationale Front trägt zur Festigung der Rechtssicherheit bei. 40 NEUE JUSTIZ 217–218.

Kirchner, Steffi (1988): Arbeitsaufgabe und gesellschaftliche Funktion produktiv verbunden. 35 DER SCHÖFFE 123–124.

Kirschner, Gerhard (1979): Konfliktkommissionen verwirklichen Gesetzlichkeit im Arbeitsrecht. 33 NEUE JUSTIZ 252.

Kirsten, Werner (1978): Abgeordnete sollen über unsere Arbeit informiert sein. 25 DER SCHÖFFE 30–31.

Kittke, Host-Dieter & Hermann-Josef Rodenbach (1986): Die Rechtsentwicklung in der DDR. 30 RECHT IN OST UND WEST 117–126.

Kittke, Horst-Dieter et al. (1988): Die Rechtsentwicklung in der DDR. 32 RECHT IN OST UND WEST 361–371.

Klaus, Georg & Manfred Buhr (1985): PHILOSOPHISCHES WÖRTERBUCH. Bibliographisches Institut Leipzig.

Klausa, Ekkehard (1972): EHRENAMTLICHE RICHTER. Athenäum Verlag.

Kleeis, Franz (1955): Zur Amtsdauer der Schöffen. 2 DER SCHÖFFE 346–348.

Kleger, Heinz (1987): Totalitarismus und Demokratie: Eine Einführung. Markus Baechler et al., eds.: TOTALITARISMUS. Universitätsverlag Freiburg, Schweiz.

Kleinert, Kurt (1984): Eingaben—Instrument der Mitarbeit der Bürger. 38 NEUE JUSTIZ 393–395.

Klenner, Hermann (1978): Grund- und Persönlichkeitsrechte in der DDR. Nationales Komitee für Rechtswissenschaft der DDR: BERICHTE ZUM X. INTERNATIONALEN KONGRESS FüR RECHTSVERGLEICHUNG.

Klenner, Hermann (1981): Freiheit und Menschenrecht. 81 EINHEIT 1055–1061.

Klenner, Hermann (1983): Der Jurist Marx auf dem Wege zum Marxismus. 37 NEUE JUSTIZ 476–480.

Klessmann, Christoph & Georg Wagner (1993): DAS GESPALTENE LAND: LEBEN IN DEUTSCHLAND 1945 BIS 1990. C.H. Beck.

Kliemke, Wilhelm & Dieter Tarruhn (1961): Aus der Arbeit einer Konfliktkommission im VEB Carl Zeiss Jena. 8 DER SCHÖFFE 409–411.

Kloetzer, Sylvia & Siegfried Lokatis (1999): Criticism and Censorship. Konrad Jarausch, ed.: DICTATORSHIP AS EXPERIENCE. Berghahn Books.

Knauer, X. (1954): Schöffen berichten über Gerichtsverhandlungen. 1 (2) DER SCHÖFFE 23–24.

Knedlik, Erika (1986): Schiedskommissionsbeirat—ein beratendes und unterstützendes Organ. 40 NEUE JUSTIZ 65.

Knoesel, Dieter (1970): Nacheifern ist erlaubt! 17 DER SCHÖFFE 86–88.

Knuesli, Walter (1978): DIE GESELLSCHAFTLICHE GERICHTSBARKEIT IN OSTEUROPA. Peter Lang.
Kocka, Juergen (1999): The GDR: A Special Kind of Modern Dictatorship. Konrad Jarausch, ed.: DICTATORSHIP AS EXPERIENCE. Berghahn Books.
Kocka, Rainer (1983): Zuwachs an Erkenntnissen. 30 DER SCHÖFFE 178–179.
Koehler, Helmut (1999): WAS DIE SCHULSTATISTIK DER SBZ/DDR ERFRAGTE. Max-Planck-Institut.
Koehler, John O. (1999): STASI: THE UNTOLD STORY OF THE EAST GERMAN SECRET POLICE. Westview.
Koenz, Peider (1969): Public Participation in the Criminal Process. 27 INTERNATIONAL REVIEW OF CRIMINAL POLICY 3–8.
Koerner, Gerhard (1987): Gerichtliche Beweisführung und Wahrheitsfindung im Strafprozess. 34 DER SCHÖFFE 163–168.
Koerner, Gerhard & Rudi Beckert (1986): Wirksame Rechtsprechung zu Verurteilungen auf Bewährung und Geldstrafen. 40 NEUE JUSTIZ 225–227.
Koerner, Gerhard & Werner Hettmann (1965a): Lebenserfahrene und angesehene Bürger wurden Mitglieder einer Schiedskommission. 12 DER SCHÖFFE 15–17.
Koerner, Gerhard & Werner Hettmann (1965b): Erste Erfahrungen in der Organisierung der Tätigkeit der Schiedskommission. 12 DER SCHÖFFE 122–125.
Kolakowski, Leszek (1981): MAIN CURRENTS OF MARXISM. Oxford University Press.
Konrad, Wolfgang (1979): Hohen Arbeitsanfall durch kollektives Handeln meistern. 26 DER SCHÖFFE 217–218.
Koop, Volker (1996): DEN GEGNER VERNICHTEN. Bouvier Verlag.
Kopstein, Jeffrey (1997): THE POLITICS OF ECONOMIC DECLINE IN EAST GERMANY, 1945–1989. Universiy of North Carolina Press.
Kornetzki, Christa (1971): Ein Gericht zog Bilanz. 18 DER SCHÖFFE 337–340.
Kornetzki, Christa (1972): Erziehungsmassnahmen sind das Spiegelbild einer guten Beratung. 19 DER SCHÖFFE 305–307.
Koschyk, Hartmut & Konrad Weiss, eds. (1996): VON ERBLASTEN UND SEILSCHAFTEN. Olzog Verlag.
Kraeupl, Guenther (1980): Familiäre Fehlerziehung und Jugendkriminalität. 34 NEUE JUSTIZ 303–306.
Kraeupl, Guenther & Lothar Reuter (1984): Wirksamkeit strafrechtlicher Wiedereingliederungsmassnahmen. 38 NEUE JUSTIZ 82–85.
Kraeupl, Guenther & Lothar Reuter (1987): Gesetzlichkeit und Strafprozessuale Tätigkeit des Staatsanwalts. 41 NEUE JUSTIZ 23–26.
Kraeupl, Guenther et al. (1980): Fähigkeit und Bereitschaft des Täters zu künftig verantwortungsbewusstem Verhalten als Strafzumessungskriterium. 34 NEUE JUSTIZ 414–416.
Kraft, Ivor (1982): Happy New Year: You're a Juror. 28 CRIME & DELINQUENCY 582–600.
Kraft, Werner (1956): Wohnraumlenkung und Mietsvertrag. 3 DER SCHÖFFE 48–50.
Kral, Herbert & Karl Böck (1971): REFORM DER LAIENGERICHTSBARKEIT IN STRAFSACHEN. Vol. 2. Manz.

Kranitz, Theodore M. (1959): The Grand Jury: Past, Present, No Future. 24 MONTANA LAW REVIEW 318–329.
Kratky, Ernst (1985): Vorbereitung und Sicherung einer hohen Qualität der komplexen Beratung. 32 DER SCHÖFFE 226–227.
Krause, Udo (1983): 30 Years of Social Courts. 83–1 LAW AND LEGISLATION IN THE GDR 34–37.
Krause, Udo (1984): Rechtspropagandistische Tätigkeit während der juristischen Ausbildung. 38 NEUE JUSTIZ 323–324.
Kraushaar, Alfred (1955): Die Mitarbeit der Schöffen. 2 DER SCHÖFFE 353–356.
Kraut, Gerald M. (1997): RECHTSBEUGUNG? DIE JUSTIZ DER DDR AUF DEM PRÜFSTAND DES RECHTSSTAATES. C.H. Beck.
Kremer, Walter (1985): Mit unserer Arbeitsweise Rechtsverletzungen zurückgedrängt. 32 DER SCHÖFFE 153–154.
Krenz, Egon (1985): Staat und Recht bei der weiteren Entfaltung der Vorzüge und Triebkräfte der sozialistischen Gesellschaft. 85 EINHEIT 688–704.
Krenz, Egon (1989): Vom Sinn unseres Kampfes. 89 EINHEIT 831–838.
Krenz, Egon (1990): WENN MAUERN FALLEN. Paul Neff Verlag.
Krenz, Egon (1999): HERBST '89. Neues Leben.
Krenz, Egon (2000): BRIEFE UND ZEUGNISSE. Neues Leben.
Krisch, Henry (1985): THE GERMAN DEMOCRATIC REPUBLIC: THE SEARCH FOR IDENTITY. Westview Press.
Krueger, Gustav (1978): Auf Rechtsverletzer erzieherisch einwirken. 25 DER SCHÖFFE 123–124.
Krueger, Helfried (1966): Das Fazit der Arbeit unserer Schiedskommission. 13 DER SCHÖFFE 138–140.
Krueger, Helfried (1984): Gesellschaftliche Gerichte in der Praxis bewährt. 31 DER SCHÖFFE 91.
Kruschke, Diethart (1955): Ein neues Lohnpfändungsrecht. 2 DER SCHÖFFE 230–236.
Kruse, Rose (1969): Die Schiedskommissionen des Bezirks Schwerin auf bestem Wege zu einer effektiven Rechtsprechung. 16 DER SCHÖFFE 42–48.
Kruse, Rose (1970): Einige Kriterien für die Auflegung der Geldbusse. 17 DER SCHÖFFE 373–375.
Krutzsch, Walter (1955): Über den Schutz der Ehre des Bürgers. 2 DER SCHÖFFE 132–135.
Krutzsch, Walter (1958): Die gesellschaftliche Erziehung bei bedingter Verurteilung und öffentlichem Tadel. 12 NEUE JUSTIZ 527–529.
Krutzsch, Walter (1959): Der neue Arbeitsstil im Strafverfahren und die Aufgaben der gesellschaftlichen Erziehung. 13 NEUE JUSTIZ 113–117.
Krylova, N.S. (1988): Appeals of Citizens Against Actions of State Agencies and Officials. Butler, William E., ed.: YEARBOOK ON SOCIALIST LEGAL SYSTEMS. Transnational Publishers.
Kubiak, Jacek R. (1988): Die Publizität von Kriminalstatistiken in den osteuropäischen Staaten. 32 RECHT IN OST UND WEST 169.
Kubitz, Waltraud (1982): Schritte zu engerer Zusammenarbeit. 29 DER SCHÖFFE 55–56.
Kucherov, Samuel (1953): COURTS, LAWYERS, AND TRIALS UNDER THE LAST THREE TSARS. Praeger.

Kucherov, Samuel (1970): THE ORGANS OF SOVIET ADMINISTRATION OF JUSTICE. E.J. Brill.

Kuckoreit, Else (1979): Gewerkschaftliche Mitwirkung in arbeitsrechtlichen Verfahren. 33 NEUE JUSTIZ 271.

Kudrjawzew, Wladimir N. (1981): Sozialistische Gesetzlichkeit und Rechtswissenschaft. Published as translation in: 35 NEUE JUSTIZ 458.

Kuehn, Heinz (1988): Jugendstunde zu Recht und Pflicht. 35 DER SCHÖFFE 100–101.

Kuehnau, Karl-Heinz (1986): Öffentlichkeit geziehlt einbeziehen. 33 DER SCHÖFFE 271–272.

Kuehne, Hans-Heiner (1985): Laienrichter im Strafprozess? 2 ZEITSCHRIFT FÜR RECHTSPOLITIK 237–239.

Kuhr, Peter (1982): Familienförderung im Territorium. 36 NEUE JUSTIZ 108–110.

Kuhrt, Eberhard (1996): Einführung. Eberhard Kuhrt: DIE SED-HERRSCHAFT UND IHR ZUSAMMENBRUCH. Leske & Budrich.

Kulcsar, Kalman (1982): PEOPLE'S ASSESSORS IN THE COURTS. Akademiai Kiado, Budapest.

Kunkel, Barbara (1982): Leitungsauftrag wird erfüllt. 29 DER SCHÖFFE 17.

Kunstler, William M. (1969): Jury Nullification in Conscience Cases. 10 VIRGINIA JOURNAL OF INTERNATIONAL LAW 71–84.

Kunz, Frithjof & Doris Urban (1971): Festigung der sozialistischen Staatsdiziplin: eine wichtige Aufgabe bei der Schaffung der entwickelten sozialistischen Gesellschaft in der DDR. 20 STAAT UND RECHT 918–932.

Kunze, Joachim (1985): Gute Bedingungen für unser Wirken. 32 DER SCHÖFFE 208–209.

Kupferberg, Feiwel (2002): THE RISE AND FALL OF THE GERMAN DEMOCRATIC REPUBLIC. Transaction Publishers.

Kurth, Heinz (1986): Alle Kompetenzen der Schiedskommission nutzen. 33 DER SCHÖFFE 183–184.

Kweit, Mary G. & Robert W. Kweit (1981): IMPLEMENTING CITIZEN PARTICIPATION IN A BUREAUCRATIC SOCIETY. Praeger.

Laessig, X. (1959): Mehr Überlegung bei der Urteilsfindung gegen Jugendliche. 6 DER SCHÖFFE 112–114.

Laeuter, Christa (1984a): Für hohe Wirksamkeit der Schiedskommissionen. 38 NEUE JUSTIZ 139–140.

Laeuter, Christa (1984b): Aktivitäten zur wirksamen Rechtspublizistik im Berzirk Frankfurt (Oder). 38 NEUE JUSTIZ 236–237.

Lammich, Siegfried (1980): Das politische Strafrecht in der DDR und den anderen sozialistischen Ländern. 13 DEUTSCHLAND ARCHIV 843–854.

Landinsky, Jack & Charles Susmilch (1981): Conceptual and Operational Issues in Measuring Consumer Disputing Behavior. WORKING PAPER 1981-3.

Landmesser, Heinz (1976): Unsere Arbeit bei der Verwirklichung von Verurteilungen auf Bewährung und der Wiedereingliederung Strafentlassener. 23 DER SCHÖFFE 112–113.

Landwehr, Lawrence J. & Ronald Novotny (1976): Juror Authoritarianism and Trial Judge Partiality. 5 EXPERIMENTAL STUDY OF POLITICS 1–26.

Lang, Harry (1986): Zur Anwendung der Geldbusse bei Vergehen gegen das sozialistische Eigentum. 33 DER SCHÖFFE 160–162.

Langanke, Annemarie (1987): KK-Beratungen in Abeitsrechtssachen. 42 ARBEIT UND ARBEITSRECHT 185–187.

Langanke, Annemarie (1988): Die Arbeit mit Empfehlungen—KK-Grundkurs fortgesetzt. 43 ARBEIT UND ARBEITSRECHT 110.

Langbein, John H. (1977): COMPARATIVE CRIMINAL PROCEDURE: GERMANY. West.

Langbein, John H. (1981): Mixed Court and Jury Court: Could the Continental Alternative Fill the American Need? 1981 AMERICAN BAR FOUNDATION RESEARCH JOURNAL 195–219.

Langbein, John H. (1995): On the Myth of Written Constitutions: The Disappearance of Criminal Jury Trial. G. Larry Mays & Peter R. Gregware, eds.: COURTS AND JUSTICE. Waveland Pess.

Langenhahn, Werner & Fred Tischendorf (1982): Rechtsarbeit im Kombinatsbetrieb. 36 NEUE JUSTIZ 33–34.

Langer, Sabine (1981): Zu den Wahlen der Konfliktkommissionen. 28 DER SCHÖFFE 257.

Langer, Sabine (1982): Erweiterung der Rechte der gesellschaftlichen Gerichte. 36 NEUE JUSTIZ 214.

Langer, Sabine (1983): Aufgaben der gewerkschaftlichen Rechtkommissionen. 37 NEUE JUSTIZ 98–99.

Langer, Sabine, et al. (1984): DIE KONFLIKTKOMMISSION HAT EINGELADEN. Staatsverlag.

Lapenna, Ivo (1968): SOVIET PENAL POLICY. The Bodley Head.

Laski, Harold J. & Virginia Woolf (1935): LAW AND JUSTICE IN SOVIET RUSSIA. Hogarth Press.

LaTour, Stephen (1978): Determinants of Participant and Observer Satisfaction with Adversary and Inquisitorial Modes of Adjudication. 36 JOURNAL OF PERSONALITY AND SOCIAL PSYCHOLOGY 1531–1545.

Laufs, Adolf (1998): RECHT UND UNRECHT DER DDR: VERSUCH EINER BILANZ. Universitätsverlag C. Winter.

Laux, Guenter (1980): In vielfältiger Weise qualifizieren. 27 DER SCHÖFFE 202.

Law regarding the Social Courts of the GDR (*Gesetz über die gesellschaftlichen Gerichte der DDR*) of March 25, 1982.

Leach-Lewis, William A. (1975): THE ABOLITION OF THE GRAND JURY IN ENGLAND. Library of Congress.

Ledy, Nancy B. & Ellen Lefkowitz (1975): Judgment by Your Peers? The Impeachment of Jury Verdicts and the Case of the Insane Juror. 21 NEW YORK LAW FORUM 57–83.

Lee, Andrea (1984): RUSSIAN JOURNAL. Vintage Books.

Lefcourt, Robert, ed. (1971): LAW AGAINST THE PEOPLE. Random House.

Lehman, Godfrey D. (1997): WE THE JURY: THE IMPACT OF JURORS ON OUR BASIC FREEDOMS. Prometheus Books.

Lehmann, Cäsar (1974): Die Arbeitsweise der Schiedskommissionen bei einfachen zivilrechtlichen Streitigkeiten. 21 DER SCHÖFFE 133–138.

Lehmann, Gisela (1981): Schulpflichtverletzung nicht unterschätzen. 28 DER SCHÖFFE 98.

Lehmann, Hans-Dietrich (1998): Leitung und Lenkung der Rechtsprechung durch das Oberste Gericht der DDR. Ulrich Drobnig, ed.: DIE STRAFRECHTSJUSTIZ DER DDR IM SYSTEMWECHSEL. Duncker & Humblot.

Lehmann, Horst & Heidrun Pohl (1986): Eingaben der Bürger und weitere Vervollkommnung der sozialistischen Demokratie. 35 STAAT UND RECHT 11–19.

Leim, Ernst (1955): Strafe und Strafvollstreckung. 2 DER SCHÖFFE 26–31.

Leites, Nathan & Elsa Bernaut (1954): RITUAL OF LIQUIDATION: THE CASE OF THE MOSCOW TRIALS. Free Press.

Lekschas, John et al. (1983): KRIMINOLOGIE: THEORETISCHE GRUNDLAGEN UND ANALYSEN. Staatsverlag.

Lellow, Hans-Friedrich (1966): Sie zog die richtigen Schlussfolgerungen. 13 DER SCHÖFFE 327–328.

Leng, Shao-Chuan (1977): The Role of Law in the People's Republic of China as Reflecting Mao Tse-Tung's Influence. 68 JOURNAL OF CRIMINAL LAW & CRIMINOLOGY 356–373.

Leng, Shao-Chuan (1982): Criminal Justice in Post-Maò China: Some Preliminary Observations. 73 JOURNAL OF CRIMINAL LAW & CRIMINOLOGY 204–237.

Lengsfeld, Jutta (1980): Begünstigende Bedingungen für Schulpflichtverletzungen konsequent beseitigen. 27 DER SCHÖFFE 63.

Lenhart, Waldemar (1979): Halbzeit bei den Schöffen der Bezirksgerichte. 26 DER SCHÖFFE 67–71.

Lenin, Vladimir I. (1932): STATE AND REVOLUTION. International Publishers.

Lenin, Vladimir I. (1960): COLLECTED WORKS. Foreign Languages Publishing House.

Lenin, Vladimir I. (1976): STAAT UND REVOLUTION. Dietz Verlag.

Leonhard, Wolfgang (1990): DAS KURZE LEBEN DER DDR. Deutsche Verlags-Anstalt.

Leonhard, Wolfgang (1992): SPURENSUCHE. Kiepenheuer & Witsch.

Lermack, Paul, ed. (1977): MATERIALS ON JURIES AND JURY RESEARCH: AN ANNOTATED BIBLIOGRAPHY. American Judicature Society.

Leutzsch, Berthold (1975): Zur Anwendung der Geldbusse. 22 DER SCHÖFFE 255–256.

Levine, James P. (1984): The Legislative Role of Juries. 1984 AMERICAN BAR FOUNDATION RESEARCH JOURNAL 605–634.

Levine, Murray (1974): Scientific Method and the Adversary Model. 29 AMERICAN PSYCHOLOGIST 661–677.

Levy, Leonard W. (1974): AGAINST THE LAW. Harper & Row.

Levy, Leonard W. (1999): THE PALLADIUM OF JUSTICE: ORIGINS OF TRIAL BY JURY. Ivan R. Dee.

Lewis, Merlin, et al. (1978): AN INTRODUCTION TO THE COURTS AND JUDICIAL PROCESS. Prentice-Hall.

Lewis, Jonathan & Phillip Whitehead (1990): STALIN: A TIME FOR JUDGEMENT. Pantheon.

Leymann, Elfriede (1967): Einige Erfahrungen der Schiedskommissionen bei der Überwindung von Schulpflichtverletzungen. 14 DER SCHÖFFE 327–331.

Leymann, Elfriede (1969a): Über die Zusammenarbeit der Schiedskommissionen mit den Organen der Jugendhilfe bei der Überwindung von Schulpflichtverletzungen. 16 DER SCHÖFFE 170–173.

Leymann, Elfriede (1969b): Die Verletzung der Schulordnung—eine Form der Schulpflichtverletzung. 16 DER SCHÖFFE 345–349.

Leymann, Elfriede (1969c): Die Schiedskommissionsordnung—eine wesentliche Grundlage für die wirksamere Überwindung von Schulpflichtverltzungen. 16 DER SCHÖFFE 59–64.

Leymann, Elfriede (1983): Der Beitrag der Schiedskommissionen zur wirksamen Bekämpfung von Ordnungswidrigkeiten im Wohngebiet. 30 DER SCHÖFFE 169.

Lichtenberg, Guenter (1984): Zu einigen Aufgaben der Schöffen im Familienrecht. 31 DER SCHÖFFE 218–220.

Liebman, Marcel (1962): The Webbs and the New Civilization. 41 SURVEY 58–74 (April).

Liekefett, Karlheinz (1965): DIE EHRENAMTLICHEN RICHTER AN DEN DEUTSCHEN GERICHTEN. Ch. Schön.

Lienshoeft, Fred (1982): Der Rat kennt seine Verantwortung. 29 DER SCHÖFFE 18.

Lieser, Joachim (1989): Der Rechtsanwalt und das Recht in der DDR. 33 RECHT IN OST UND WEST 47–52.

Lieser-Trebnigg, Erika (1985): RECHT IN DER DDR. Verlag Wissenschaft und Politik.

Lindau, Hans (1985): Eckpfeiler unserer Arbeitsweise. 32 DER SCHÖFFE 84–85.

Linder, Christa (1984): Ergebnisse der Zusammenarbeit zwischen Juristen und Journalisten im Bezirk Dresden. 38 NEUE JUSTIZ 282.

Lindheim, Thomas von (1978): Das Prinzip der öffentlichkeit des Verfahrens im Strafprozess der DDR. 22 RECHT IN OST UND WEST 65–68.

Lipson, Leon (1958): The New Face of "Socialist Legality." 7 PROBLEMS OF COMMUNISM 22–30.

Lipson, Leon (1959): Socialist Legality: The Mountain Has Labored. 8 PROBLEMS OF COMMUNISM 15–19.

Lipson, Leon (1963): The Future Belongs to Parasites? 12 PROBLEMS OF COMMUNISM 1–6.

Lipson, Leon (1968): Law and Society. A. Kassof, ed.: PROSPECTS FOR SOVIET SOCIETY. Praeger.

Lischke, Hans & Helmut Keil (1970): Den Straftatbestand des Rowdytum richtig anwenden. 17 DER SCHÖFFE 70–74.

Litan, Robert E., ed. (1993): VERDICT: ASSESSING THE CIVIL JURY SYSTEM. The Brookings Institution.

Little, D. Richard (1976): Mass Political Participation in the U.S. and the U.S.S.R. 8 COMPARATIVE POLITICAL STUDIES 437–457.

Loehn, Christa (1982): Discussionsrede. 36 NEUE JUSTIZ 150.

Loeser, Franz (1984): DIE UNGLAUBWÜRDIGE GESELLSCHAFT. Bund-Verlag.

Loewe, Helling (1985): Verbesserung der Qualität mittels Leistungsvergleichs. 32 DER SCHÖFFE 140–143.

Loewenthal, Heinrich & Herta Schellbach (1955): Bemerkungen zur Öffentlichkeit des gerichtlichen Verfahrens. 9 NEUE JUSTIZ 685–687.

Loof, Marianne (1989): Streitbar für sozialistische Gesetzlichkeit. 36 DER SCHÖFFE 168–170.

Lorch, Robert S. (1975): German Administrative Courts. 58 JUDICATURE 293–298.

Lorenz, Thomas (1998): DIE RECHTSANWALTSCHAFT IN DER DDR. Berlin Verlag Arno Spitz.

Lotze, Lothar (1978): Die Funktionen des sozialistischen Rechts. 27 STAAT UND RECHT 442–450.

Lubbers, Jeffrey, ed. (1973): ANNOTATED BIBLIOGRAPHY ON THE GRAND JURY. American Judicature Society.

Lubman, Stanley (1967): Mao and Mediation: Politics and Dispute Resolution in Communist China. 55 CALIFORNIA LAW REVIEW 1284–1359.

Luchterhandt, Otto (1985): Grundrechte und Grundpflichten in beiden deutschen Staaten. 18 DEUTSCHLAND ARCHIV 264–267.

Ludwig-Dodin, Cornelia (2000): Das Staatliche Vertragsgericht: Organ der Wirtschaftsverwaltung oder der Rechtspflege? Rainer Schroeder, ed.: ZIVILRECHTSKULTUR DER DDR. Duncker & Humblot.

Ludz, Peter C. (1980): MECHANISMEN DER HERRSCHAFTSSICHERUNG: EINE SPRACHPOLITISCHE ANALYSE GESELLSCHAFTLICHEN WANDELS IN DER DDR. Carl Hanser.

Ludz, Peter C., ed. (1975): DDR HANDBUCH. Verlag Wissenschaft und Politik.

Luebchen, G.A. (1956): Über das Familienrecht in der DDR. 3 DER SCHÖFFE 79–85.

Luebchen, G.A. (1983): Social Courts in the German Democratic Republic. 83–1 LAW AND LEGISLATION IN THE GDR 21–28.

Luederitz, Horst (1975): Erfahrungen zur Empfehlungspraxis. 22 DER SCHÖFFE 228–229.

Luft, Kathleen (1988): National Security. Stephen R. Burant, ed.: EAST GERMANY: A COUNTRY STUDY. 3d ed. Library of Congress.

Lungwitz, Ilse (1973): Einige Probleme aus der Arbeit der gesellschaftlichen Gerichte in Jugendsachen. 20 DER SCHÖFFE 22–26.

Luther, Horst (1986): Das Recht auf Verteidigung in Strafverfahren gegen Jugendliche. 40 NEUE JUSTIZ 334–335.

Luther, Horst & Friedrich Wolff (1979): Zur Frage ob die Verteidigung persönliche Dienstleistung ist. 33 NEUE JUSTIZ 308–309.

Lynch, Michael J. (1987): Quantitative Analysis and Marxist Criminology. 29 CRIME AND SOCIAL JUSTICE 110–127.

Lyon, Thea (1969): Kriminalpolitische Tendenzen und die "Massnahmen strafrechtlicher Verantwortlichkeit." 9:2 JAHRBUCH FÜR OSTRECHT 81–107.

Maaz, Hans-Joachim (1995): BEHIND THE WALL: THE INNER LIFE OF COMMUNIST GERMANY. W.W. Norton.

Machalz-Urban, Doris (1980): Das neue Gesetz über die Volkskontrolle in der UdSSR. 29 STAAT UND RECHT 314–320.

Madsen, Richard (1984): MORALITY AND POWER IN A CHINESE VILLAGE. University of California Press.

Maehlert, Ulrich (1994): Die gesamte junge Generation für den Sozialismus begeistern. Juergen Weber, ed. DER SED-STAAT. Olzog Verlag.

Mager, Wolfgang (1974): Folgen verspäteter Antragstellung bei Schulpflichtverletzungen. 21 DER SCHÖFFE 210–215.

Mager, Wolfgang (1975): Erziehung ist vor allem Überzeugung. 22 DER SCHÖFFE 156–159.

Mager, Wolfgang (1977): Die Einheit von Ziel und gesetzlichen Wegen sichern. 24 DER SCHÖFFE 47–48.

Mager, Wolfgang (1984): Hohe Erziehungswirksamkeit unseres gesellschaftlichen Gerichts. 31 DER SCHÖFFE 114.

Mager, Wolfgang & Rudolf Winkler (1973): Analyse der Arbeit einer Schiedskommission. 20 DER SCHÖFFE 87–94.

Mahlmann, Christian (2002): DIE STRAFRECHTSWISSENSCHAFT DER DDR. Peter Lang.

Maier, Charles S. (1997): DISSOLUTION: THE CRISIS OF COMMUNISM AND THE END OF EAST GERMANY. Princeton University Press.

Maier, Herbert (1974): Recht. Heinz Rausch & Theo Stammen: DDR: DAS POLITISCHE, WIRTSCHAFTLICHE UND SOZIALE SYSTEM. C.H. Beck.

Maine, Henry Sumner (1986/1861): ANCIENT LAW. Dorset Press.

Makepeace, R.W. (1980): MARXIST IDEOLOGY AND SOVIET CRIMINAL LAW. Croom Helm.

Malcolm, Neil (1984): SOVIET POLITICAL SCIENTISTS AND AMERICAN POLITICS. Macmillan.

Mammitzsch, Werner (1984): Voneinander lernen um die Wirksamkeit der Arbeit zu erhöhen. 31 DER SCHÖFFE 38.

Mampel, Siegfried (1966): DAS RECHT IN MITTELDEUTSCHLAND. Carl Heymanns Verlag.

Mampel, Siegfried (1985): Verfassungsprobleme und Verfassungsinterpretation in der DDR. 29 RECHT IN OST UND WEST 61–68.

Mand, Richard & Carola Schulze (1983): Gesellschaftliche Organisationen und Rechtsverwirklichung. 37 NEUE JUSTIZ 184–186.

Mand, Richard & Carola Schulze (1986): DER BÜRGER UND SEINE GESELLSCHAFTLICHEN ORGANISATIONEN. Staatsverlag.

Mandel, Joachim (1968): Neue Bestimmungen auf dem Gebiete der Wohnraumlenkung. 15 DER SCHÖFFE 11–12.

Mannheim, Hermann (1937): Trial by Jury in Modern Continental Criminal Law. 53 LAW QUARTERLY REVIEW 99–412.

Manuel, Frank E. (1995): A REQUIEM FOR KARL MARX. Harvard University Press.

Manz, Ruth (1981): Jugendlicher nutzte Gunst der Stunde für Diebstähle. 28 DER SCHÖFFE 121–122.

Markovits, Inga (1978): Socialist vs. Bourgeois Rights—An East-West German Comparison. 45 UNIVERSITY OF CHICAGO LAW REVIEW 612.

Markovits, Inga (1980): Owning and Sharing—The Rightholder's Relation to Society in Bourgeois and Socialist Law. Paper delivered at the annual meeting of the American Political Science Association, Washington, D.C.

Markovits, Inga (1993): DIE ABWICKLUNG: EIN TAGEBUCH ZUM ENDE DER DDR-JUSTIZ. C.H.Beck.

Martin, Iris & Ingo Wagner (1985): Zum Charakter der vertraglichen Mietermitwirkung. 39 NEUE JUSTIZ 23–25.

Martin, James A. (1977): The Proposed "Science Court." 75 MICHIGAN LAW REVIEW 1058–1091.

Marx, Wolfram (1988): Gegenstand, Aufgaben und Methoden des Familienrechts der DDR. 35 DER SCHÖFFE 80–84.

Marxen, Klaus (1999): "Recht" im Verständnis des Ministeriums für Staatssicherheit der DDR. Roger Engelmann & Clemens Vollnhals, eds.: JUSTIZ IM DIENSTE DER PARTEIHERRSCHAFT. Ch. Links Verlag.

Matern, Hermann (1959): The Multi-Party System in the GDR. 2:4 WORLD MARXIST REVIEW 26–33 (April 1959).

Matheny, Albert R. & Bruce A. Williams (1978): The Science Court in the Policy-Making Process: The Minnesota Power Line Case. Unpublished Convention Paper.

Matheus, Ingetraud (1988): Arbeitstagung zur Leitung der Schöffentätigkeit. 35 DER SCHÖFFE 52–53.

Matheus, Ingetraud & Brigitte Brueckner (1987): Die Wirksamkeit der Schiedskommissionen weiter erhöhen. 34 DER SCHÖFFE 214–219.

Mathiopoulos, Margarita (1994): RENDEZVOUS MIT DER DDR: POLITISCHE MYTHEN UND IHRE AUFKLÄRUNG. Econ Verlag.

Matthias, Heinz (1971): Empfehlungen und Hinweise—wichtige Mittel in der Hand der gesellschaftlichen Gerichte. 18 DER SCHÖFFE 328–330.

Matthias, Heinz (1980): Die Geldstrafe ist ein bewährtes Erziehungsmittel. 27 DER SCHÖFFE 30–33.

Maurach, Reinhart (no date): Die richterliche Unabhängigkeit in der UdSSR. Reinhart Maurach, et al.: FRAGEN DER GERICHTSVERFASSUNG IM OSTBLOCK. Verlag für Internationalen Kulturaustausch.

Maus, Karl-Heinz (1987): Von einer Massnahme zur Aufgabe, ja zur Herzenssache. 42 ARBEIT UND ARBEITSRECHT 38.

Mayer, Wolfgang (2002): FLUCHT UND AUSREISE. Anita Tykve Verlag.

Mayo, Henry B. (1960): INTRODUCTION TO MARXIST THEORY. Oxford University Press.

McCabe, E.J. (1989): Structural Elements of Contemporary Criminal Justice in the People's Republic of China. R.J. Troyer, et al., eds.: SOCIAL CONTROL IN THE PEOPLE'S REPUBLIC OF CHINA. Praeger.

McCardle, Arthur W. & A. Bruce Boenau, eds. (1984): EAST GERMANY: A NEW GERMAN NATION UNDER SOCIALISM? University Press of America.

McEwen, Craig A. & Richard J. Maiman (1982): Arbitration and Mediation as Alternatives to Court. 10 POLICY STUDIES JOURNAL 712–726.

McIntosh, Wayne (1980): 150 Years of Litigation and Dispute Settlement: A Court Tale. 15 LAW & SOCIETY REV. 823 (1980–81)

McLellan, David (1981): Marx, Engels and Lenin on Party and State. Leslie Holmes: THE WITHERING AWAY OF THE STATE? Sage.

Meador, Daniel J. (1986): IMPRESSIONS OF LAW IN EAST GERMANY. University Press of Virginia.

Medvedev, Roy A. (1977): ON SOCIALIST DEMOCRACY. Norton.

Medvedev, Roy A. (1989): LET HISTORY JUDGE: THE ORIGINS AND CONSEQUENCES OF STALINISM. rev.ed. Columbia University Press.

Mehls, Eckart (1998): UNZUMUTBAR: EIN LEBEN IN DER DDR. GNN Verlag.

Meininger, Helmuth, et al. (1988): VOLKSPOLIZEI UND FREIWILLIGE HELFER. Staatsverlag.

Menge, Marlies (1990): OHNE UNS LÄUFT NICHTS MEHR: DIE REVOLUTION IN DER DDR. Deutsche Verlags-Anstalt.

Menzel, Wolfgang et al., eds. (1980): STAATSRECHT BÜRGERLICHER STAATEN. Staatsverlag.

Merkl, Peter H. (1977): MODERN COMPARATIVE POLITICS. 2d ed. Dryden.

Merritt, Anna J. & Richard L. Merritt (1978): POLITICS, ECONOMICS, AND SOCIETY IN THE TWO GERMANIES, 1945–1975: A BIBLIOGRAPHY OF ENGLISH-LANGUAGE WORKS. University of Illinois Press.

Merryman, John Henry (1969): THE CIVIL LAW TRADITION. Stanford University Press.

Mertens, Lothar & Dieter Voigt, eds. (1998): OPFER UND TÄTER IM SED-STAAT. Duncker & Humblot.

Mertzig, Kurt (1985): Erfahrungen mit der Aussprache bei Verfehlungen. 32 DER SCHÖFFE 157–158.

Meschievitz, Catherine S. & Marc Galanter (1982): In Search of Nyaya Panchayats: The Politics of a Moribund Institution. Richard L. Abel, ed.: THE POLITICS OF INFORMAL JUSTICE. Vol.2 Academic Press.

Metcalfe, Robyn S. (1988): THE NEW WIZARD WAR: HOW THE SOVIETS STEAL U.S. HIGH SOVIET HYPOCRISY AND GIVE IT AWAY. Tempus.

Mett, Berthold (1987): Produktionssicherheit und verbesserte Rechtsarbeit zahlen sich aus. 34 DER SCHÖFFE 97–98.

Mewes, Werner (1972): Freuden und Sorgen eines Schöffenkollektivs. 19 DER SCHÖFFE 122–125.

Meyer, Alfred G. (1970): Theories of Convergence. Chalmers Johnson, ed.: CHANGE IN COMMUNIST SYSTEMS. Stanford University Press.

Meyer, Erna (1988): Erfahrungen weitergeben. 35 DER SCHÖFFE 56–57.

Michalski, Marga (1979): Zur Anwesenheit des gesellschaftlichen Anklägers und Verteidigers in der gerichtlichen Hauptverhandlung. 33 NEUE JUSTIZ 182.

Michalski, Wojciech (1980): The People's Participation in the Administration of Justice in Poland as a Form of Extrajudicial Control. 4 INTERNATIONAL SUMMARIES 103–109.

Michas, Joachim & Gerwin Udke (1987): 10 Jahre Rechtausbildung der Lehrlinge. 42 ARBEIT UND ARBEITSRECHT 171–172.

Mielich, Charlotte (1988): Die Aufgaben des Gerichts im Eheverfahren. 35 DER SCHÖFFE 157–162.

Mielke, Erich (1966): Die sozialistische Gesetzlichkeit dient der weiteren Entfaltung der Demokratie, der Sicherung und Festigung unserer Staatsordnung. 20 NEUE JUSTIZ 376–377.

Mierow, Edith (1973): Nicht nur ein Tapetenwechsel. 20 DER SCHÖFE 129–130.

Mills, Charles W. (1994): The Moral Epistemology of Stalinism. 22 POLITICS & SOCIETY 31–57.

Mills, Richard M. (1990): AS MOSCOW SEES US: AMERICAN POLITICS AND SOCIETY IN THE SOVIET MINDSET. Oxford University Press.

Ministerium der Justiz (1971a): Zur Einbeziehung der Schiedskommissionen in die komplexe Vorbeugung und Bekämpfung der Kriminalität und anderer Rechtsverletzungen. 18 DER SCHÖFFE 227–231.

Ministerium der Justiz (1971b): Einige Schwerpunkte in der Tätigkeit der Schiedskommissionen im 1. Halbjahr 1971. 18 DER SCHÖFFE 362–365.

Ministerium der Justiz (1989): GESELLSCHAFTLICHE GERICHTE: TEXTAUSGABE. Verlag Tribüne.

Mitter, Armin & Stefan Wolle (1993): UNTERGANG AUF RATEN. Bertelsmann.

Moebis, Harry (1978): Staatliche Leitungstätigkeit und die Bewegung für vorbildliche Ordnung, Disziplin und Sicherheit. 27 STAAT UND RECHT 414–421

Moebis, Harry (1984): ORDNUNG IST DAS HALBE LEBEN. Staatsverlag.

Moeller, Hans-Joachim (1985): Bilanz und Schlussfolgerungen. 32 DER SCHÖFFE 275–282.

Mollnau, Karl A. (1979): Einfluss der Rechtserziehung auf die gesellschaftliche Wirksamkeit des sozialistischen Rechts. Mollnau, Karl A., ed.: OBJEKTIVE GESETZE: RECHT HANDELN. Staatsverlag.

Mollnau, Karl A. (1983): VOM RECHT ALS TRIEBKRAFT WIRTSCHAFTLICHEN WACHSTUMS. Staatsverlag.

Mollnau, Karl A. (1988): Gesetzlichkeit und Freiheit. 88 EINHEIT 681–683.

Mollnau, Karl A., ed. (1977): DIE GESELLSCHAFTLICHE WIRKSAMKEIT DES SOZIALISTISCHEN RECHTS: PROBLEME IHRER BEGRIFFSBESTIMMUNG UND MESSUNG. Akademie der Wissenschaften der DDR.

Mollnau, Karl A. et al. (1976): MACHT UND RECHT: EINHEIT ODER GEGENSATZ. Staatsverlag.

Mollnau, Karl A. & Karl Heinz Roeder (1963): Kollektivität und Zwang im sozialistischen Recht. 12 STAAT UND RECHT 580–592.

Mollnau, Karl A. & Karl-Heinz Schoeneburg (1985): VIER JAHRZEHNTE MIT NEUEM RECHT. Staatsverlag.

Moore, Lloyd E. (1973): THE JURY: TOOL OF KINGS, PALLADIUM OF LIBERTY. W.H. Anderson.

Moritz, Helene (1985): Im Dienst für Recht und Gesetzlichkeit. 32 DER SCHÖFFE 227–228.

Morling, Friedrich (1957): Zur Frage einer Erweiterung der Schiedsmanntätigkeit. 4 DER SCHÖFFE 50–51.

Mueckler, Hildegard (1984): Seit vielen Jahren mit der Rechtsprechung vertraut. 31 DER SCHÖFFE 66–67.

Muehlberger, Friedrich (1986): VERBRECHEN GEGEN DAS EIGENTUM DES VOLKES. Staatsverlag.

Muehlberger, X. (1955): Drei Monate Arbeit der neuen Schöffen. 2 DER SCHÖFFE 289–293.

Muehlen, Patrik von zur (2000): AUFBRUCH UND UMBRUCH IN DER DDR. J.H.W. Dietz.

Muehlen, Patrik von zur (1995): DER EISENBERGER KREIS: JUGENDWIDERSTAND UND VERFOLGUNG IN DER DDR 1953–1958. J.H.W. Dietz Nachfolger.

Mueller, Fritz-Armin (1985): Langjährige Erfahrungen in der Wiedereingliederung Haftentlassener. 32 DER SCHÖFFE 248–251.

Mueller, Frohmut (1984a): Tätigkeit und Wahl der Schöffen und der Mitglieder der Schiedskommissionen: Ausdruck der weiteren Entfaltung der sozialistischen Demokratie. 31 DER SCHÖFFE 77.

Mueller, Frohmut (1984b): Zusammenwirken örtlicher Volksvertretungen und ihrer Organe mit gesellschaftlichen Gerichten. 38 NEUE JUSTIZ 56–59.

Mueller, Frohmut (1985): Zusammenwirken der Ausschüsse der Nationalen Front und der Schiedskommissionen bei der weiteren Festigung der Gesetzlichkeit. 39 NEUE JUSTIZ 395–397.

Mueller, Frohmut & Peter Lischke (1976): Gerichtskritiken, Hinweise und Empfehlungen: Wichtige Mittel zur Erhöhung der Wirksamkeit der Rechtssprechung und zur Festigung der Gesetzlichkeit. 30 NEUE JUSTIZ 613–619.

Mueller, Georg (1971): Das Wirken der gesellschaftlichen Gerichte im Bauwesen. 18 DER SCHÖFFE 162–169.
Mueller, Gerhart (1982): Wirksamkeit der Gesellschaftlichen Gerichte. 36 NEUE JUSTIZ 154–155.
Mueller, Gerhart (1987): Besonderheiten der KK-Beratungen mit Jugendlichen. 42 ARBEIT UND ARBEITSRECHT 161.
Mueller, Heinrich (1975): Erfolgreiche Wiedereingliederung—ein Plus im sozialistischen Wettbewerb. 22 DER SCHÖFFE 135–136.
Mueller, Joachim (1962): Erfahrungen aus der Zusammenarbeit mit den Konfliktkommissionen. 9 DER SCHÖFFE 12–19.
Mueller, Rolf (1983): Differenzierte Erfassung der Motive bei Eigentumsstraftaten. 37 NEUE JUSTIZ 454–455.
Mueller, Rüdiger (1981): Zur Einigung bei einfachen zivilrechtlichen und anderen Rechtsstreitigkeiten. 28 DER SCHÖFFE 100.
Mueller, Rüdiger (1983): Gesellschaftlicher Auftrag—Erziehung zur freiwilligen Einhaltung des sozialistischen Rechts. 30 DER SCHÖFFE 115–118.
Mueller-Roemer, Dietrich (1969): Ziele und Methoden de Rechtsvergleichung zwischen beiden Teilen Deutschlands. 13 RECHT IN OST UND WEST 1–8.
Murphy, Kenneth (1992): RETREAT FROM THE FINLAND STATION: MORAL ODYSSEYS IN THE BREAKDOWN OF COMMUNISM. Free Press.
Myers, Martha A. (1987): Rule Departures and Making Law: Juries and Their Verdicts. Lawrence S. Wrightsman et al., eds. (1987): IN THE JURY BOX. Sage.
Nagel, Stuart S. (1975): IMPROVING THE LEGAL PROCESS. Lexington.
Nagler, Heinz (1973): Eine bewährte Schiedskommission. 20 DER SCHÖFFE 118–121.
Nagler, Heinz (1974): Schöffen leisten wirkungsvolle Rechtserziehung. 21 DER SCHÖFFE 4–8.
Nasarow, Willi (1980): Das sozialistische Recht is Willensausdruck und Instrument der Arbeiterklasse. 27 DER SCHÖFFE 10.
Nastola, Edgar (1999): INDIVIDUELLE FREIHEIT UND STAATLICHE REGLEMENTIERUNG: LESBEN UND SCHWULE IN DER DDR. Tectum Verlag.
National Center for State Courts (1976a): FACETS OF THE JURY SYSTEM. National Center for State Courts Publications.
National Center for State Courts (1976b): CALIFORNIA JURY SELECTION AND MANAGEMENT SURVEY. National Center for State Courts Publications.
National Center for State Courts (1988): ON TRIAL: THE LENGTH OF CIVIL AND CRIMINAL TRIALS. National Center for State Courts Publications.
Natter, Erik (1994): DIE INNEREN URSACHEN DES UMBRUCHS IN DER DDR. Forschungsgruppe Deutschland.
Nawrocki, Joachim (1967): DAS GEPLANTE WUNDER: LEBEN UND WIRTSCHAFTEN IM ANDEREN DEUTSCHLAND.C. Wegner.
Neely, Richard (1983): WHY COURTS DON'T WORK. McGraw-Hill.
Nejelski, Paul (1977): Judging in a Democracy: The Tension of Popular Participation. 61 JUDICATURE 166–175.
Nelson, Daniel N. (1978): DEVELOPMENT AND PARTICIPATION IN A COMMUNIST SYSTEM. Paper delivered at the Annual Meeting of the American Political Science Association, New York City.

Nemeth, Charlan: Jury Trials (1981): Psychology and Law. 14 ADVANCES IN EXPERIMENTAL SOCIAL PSYCHOLOGY 309–367.
Nemeth, Charlan (1987): Interactions between Jurors as a Function of Majority vs. Unanimity Decision Rules. Lawrence S. Wrightsman et al., eds.: IN THE JURY BOX. Sage.
Nette, Herbert (1975): FRIEDRICH II VON HOHENSTAUFEN. Rowohlt.
Neubecker, Josef (1978): Unterstützung der Konfliktkommissionen durch die Staatsanwaltschaft. 32 NEUE JUSTIZ 223–224.
Neubert, Ehrhart & Bernd Eisenfeld, eds. (2001): MACHT—OHNMACHT—GEGENMACHT. Edition Temmen.
Neuhof, Werner (1978): Gemeinsames Handeln qualifiziert Rechtserziehung. 25 DER SCHÖFFE 246–247.
Neumann, Christa (1975): Jugendbeistand. 22 DER SCHÖFFE 70–72.
Neumann, Hans (1983): Massnahmen des Betriebes bei Verdacht auf Alkoholgenuss während der Arbeitszeit. 37 NEUE JUSTIZ 245–246.
Neuschl, Anton (1970): Die Verantwortung für das Ganze ist gewachsen. 17 DER SCHÖFFE 51–53.
Nickel, X. (1969): Einspruch gegen eine Übergabe. 16 DER SCHÖFFE 433–434.
Nickus, Eva (1975): Betreuung Verurteilter durch gesellschaftliche Kräfte im Betrieb. 22 DER SCHÖFFE 183–185.
Niedermeier, Hans (1961): Die Kameradschaftsgerichte in der UdSSR. 14 RECHT DER ARBEIT 275–277.
Nieland, Robert C. (1979): PATTERN JURY INSTRUCTIONS: A CRITICAL LOOK AT A MODERN MOVEMENT TO IMPROVE THE JURY SYSTEM. American Judicature Society.
Niemann, Heinz (1993): MEINUNGSFORSCHUNG IN DER DDR: DIE GEHEIMEN BERICHTE DES INSTITUTS FüR MEINUNGSFORSCHUNG AN DAS POLITBÜRO DER SED. Bund-Verlag.
Niessen, Werner (1963): Wir besuchen ein Jugendhaus. 10 DER SCHÖFFE 20–23.
Niestroy, Ingeborg (1955a): Mehr Erzieher als Jugendschöffen. 2 DER SCHÖFFE 49–50.
Niestroy, Ingeborg (1955b): Weshalb besondere Jugendschöffen? 2 DER SCHÖFFE 151–152.
Nolte, Ernst (1985): DEUTSCHLAND UND DER KALTE KRIEG. Klett-Cotta.
Nolte, Ernst (1995): DIE DEUTSCHEN UND IHRE VERGANGENHEIT. Propylen.
Note (1954): Anmerkung. 1:6 DER SCHÖFFE 29.
Note (1961): Dekret des Präsidiums des Obersten Sowjets der RSFSR. 7 OSTEUROPA-RECHT 214–218.
Note (1963): Die grosse Diskussion weiter entfalten! 10 DER SCHÖFFE 33–43.
Note (1966a): Die Bindung an den Arbeitsplatz und die Bürgschaft. 13 DER SCHÖFFE 125–129.
Note (1966b): Unser Recht dient dem Volk. 13 DER SCHÖFFE 337.
Note (1967): Zur Tätigkeit der Kreisgerichte bei Vollstreckbarkeitserklärungen der Beschlüsse der Schiedskommissionen. 14 DER SCHÖFFE 334–336.
Note (1969): Anfragen zur Tätigkeit der Schiedskommissionen. 16 DER SCHÖFFE 397–399.
Note (1971): Judges or Comrades? 10 SOVIET LAW AND GOVERNMENT 141.

Note (1972): Evaluating the Grand Jury's Role in a Dual System of Prosecution: An Iowa Case Study. 57 IOWA LAW REVIEW 1354–1375.
Note (1973): Zur Erhöhung der Wirksamkeit der Rechtsprechung bei Straftaten gegen das sozialistische Eigentum. 20 DER SCHÖFFE 428–433.
Note (1977): Im Spiegel der Statistik. 24 DER SCHÖFFE 245.
Note (1978a): Vielfalt demokratischer Mitwirkung. 25 DER SCHÖFFE 91.
Note (1978b): 5124 Schiedskommissionen wirken in den Wohngebieten. 25 DER SCHÖFFE 95.
Note (1978c): Mit Ideenreichtum und Initiativen auf Kurs 30. Jahrestag. 25 DER SCHÖFFE 104–105.
Note (1979): Im Spiegel der Statistik. 26 DER SCHÖFFE 201.
Note (1980a): Konferenz vermittelte Fülle reichhaltiger Anregungen. 27 DER SCHÖFFE 253.
Note (1980b): Entwicklung der Schiedskommissionen im Blickpunkt des Bezirksgerichts. 27 DER SCHÖFFE 182.
Note (1980c): Frage—Antwort. 27 DER SCHÖFFE 39.
Note (1981): Schulungsplan für Mitglieder der Konfliktkommissionen. 28 DER SCHÖFFE 28.
Note (1982a): Die Aufgaben der Ausschüsse der Nationalen Front bei der Zusammenarbeit mit den Schiedskommissionen sowie bei der Wahl ihrer Mitglieder. 29 DER SCHÖFFE 130–132.
Note (1982b): Sowjetunion: Angst des Dienstleistungspersonals vor dem Beschwerdebuch. 32 OSTEUROPA 628–634.
Note (1982c): Erfahrungen, Ergebuisse, Erkenntnisse. 29 DER SCHÖFFE 57–59.
Note (1982d): Zur Schulung für Schiedskommissionen: 9. Empfehlungen im Zusammenhang mit Aussprachen. 29 DER SCHÖFFE 124–126.
Note (1983): Jahrestage der gesellschaftlichen Gerichte. 37 NEUE JUSTIZ 227.
Note (1984): Im Spiegel der Statistik. 31 DER SCHÖFFE 233.
Note (1985): Ein Meilenstein auf dem Weg zum XI. Parteitag der SED. 32 DER SCHÖFFE 147.
Note (1986a): Im Spiegel der Statistik. 33 DER SCHÖFFE 243.
Note (1986b): Gesellschaftswissenschaften: Bilanz und Aufgaben. 86 EINHEIT 681.
Note (1086c): Aus der Kriminalstatistik 1985. 40 NEUE JUSTIZ 316.
Note (1987a): Aus den Orientierungen des Plenums des Obersten Gerichts zu Aufgaben der Gerichte bei der Unterstützung der sozialistischen Wohnungspolitik. 41 NEUE JUSTIZ 39–40.
Note (1987b): Eröffnung der Konfliktkommissions-Wahlen im VEB Kombinat Leuna-Werke "Walter Ulbricht." 41 NEUE JUSTIZ 89.
Note (1987c): In Spiegel der Statistik. 34 DER SCHÖFFE 92a.
Note (1987d): Anleitungsmaterial für den gewerkschaftlichen Prozessvertreter im arbeitsrechtlichen Verfahren. 42 ARBEIT UND ARBEITSRECHT 199–201.
Note (1988): Gesellschaftliches Engagement überall gewürdigt. 35 DER SCHÖFFE 138–139.
Note (1989a): Schöffenverpflichtung. 36 DER SCHÖFFE 122.
Note (1989b): Im Spiegel der Statistik. 36 DER SCHÖFFE 164.
Note (1989c): Aufgaben bei der Vorbeugung, Bekämpfung und Verhütung von Straftaten und anderen Rechtsverletzungen. 44 ARBEIT UND ARBEITSRECHT 88–90.

Note (1989d): Bilanz über die KK-Beratungstätikeit. 44 ARBEIT UND ARBEITSRECHT 112.

Note (1990): In Spiegel der Statistik. 37 DER SCHÖFFE 89.

Nove, Alec, ed. (1992): THE STALIN PHENOMENON. St. Martin's Press.

Novosti Press Agency (1977): THE RIGHTS AND FREEDOMS OF SOVIET CITIZENS.

Novosti Press Agency (1986): THE PROGRAMME OF THE COMMUNIST PARTY OF THE SOVIET UNION.

Oberreuter, Heinrich (1994): Vorwort. Juergen Weber, ed.: DER SED-STAAT. Olzog Verlag.

Oberstes Gericht der DDR (1970): OBERSTES GERICHT DER DDR: HÖCHSTES ORGAN WAHRHAFT DEMOKRATISCHER RECHTSPRECHUNG. Staatsverlag.

Oberstes Gericht der DDR (1985): Aufgaben der Rechtsprechung zur Unterstützung der Tätigkeit der gesellschaftlichen Gerichte. 39 NEUE JUSTIZ 190–193.

O'Brien, Francis W. (1967): The Jury in Switzerland. 33 BROOKLYN LAW REVIEW 58–69.

O'Connor, Dennis M. (1964): Soviet People's Guards: An Experiment with Civic Police. 39 NEW YORK UNIVERSITY LAW REVIEW 579–614.

Oda, Hiroshi (1982): The System of Administrative Sanctions in the Soviet Union. F.J.M. Feldbrugge & William B. Simons, eds.: PERSPECTIVES ON SOVIET LAW FOR THE 1980s. Martinus Nijhoff.

Oehme, Paul (1967): Nicht nur feststellen sondern helfend eingreifen! 14 DER SCHÖFFE 179–180.

Oehme, Paul (1968): Wie kann man Schulpflichtverletzungen noch wirksamer entgegentreten? 15 DER SCHÖFFE 214–215.

Oehme, Paul (1970): Beratungen wegen einfacher zivilrechtlicher und anderer Rechtsstreitigkeiten. 17 DER SCHÖFFE 89–90.

Oehmke, Erika (1965): Studien zur Jugendkriminalität. 12 DER SCHÖFFE 264–270.

Oehmke, Erika (1975): Wie verwirklichen die Leiter in den Betrieben Ziele und Aufgaben des Jugendgesetzes? 22 DER SCHÖFFE iii-v.

Opitz, Gerhard (1980): Vereint im schöpferischen Handeln. 27 DER SCHÖFFE 250.

Opitz, Gerhard (1982): Bürgersinn und Bürgerinitiative zum Nutzen aller. 36 NEUE JUSTIZ 166–167.

Opitz, Heinrich (1989): Die Kommunisten und die Wahrheit. 89 EINHEIT 1002–1008.

Order Regarding the Compensation of Lay Judges, Trial Participants, and Members of Arbitration Commissions (ANORDNUNG ÜBER DIE ENTSCHÄDIGUNG FÜR SCHÖFFEN UND BETEILIGTE AM GERICHTSVERFAHREN SOWIE FÜR MITGLIEDER DER SCHIEDSKOMMISSIONEN of October 8, 1971).

Osborn, Albert S. (1937): THE MIND OF THE JUROR AS JUDGE OF THE FACTS, OR THE LAYMAN'S VIEW OF THE LAW. Boyd.

Ostmann, X. (1955): Über die weitere Arbeit am Entwurf des Familiengesetzbuches. 2 DER SCHÖFFE 54–58.

Ostmann, X. (1956): Grundzüge des Verfahrens in Ehesachen. 3 DER SCHÖFFE 110–116.

Otto, A. (1955): Prozess gegen Schund- und Schmutzliteratur. 2 DER SCHÖFFE 185–186.

Pabst, William R., Jr. (1972): An End to Juror Waiting. 55 JUDICATURE 277–281.

Pabst, William R., Jr. (1985): JURY MANUAL: A GUIDE FOR PROSPECTIVE JURORS. 2d ed. Metro Publishing.

Pabst, William R., Jr. & G. Thomas Munsterman (1975): The Economic Hardship of Jury Duty. 58 JUDICATURE 494–501.

Paetzold, Edith (1989): De lege ferenda: Glasnost-Recht in der Sowjetunion. 33 RECHT IN OST UND WEST 239–242.

Paetzold, Rainer (1991): WENN DIKTATOREN FALLEN. Haag & Herchen.

Palmer, Michael (1988): The Revival of Mediation in the People's Republic of China: (1) Extra-Judicial Mediation. W.E. Butler, ed.: YEARBOOK ON SOCIALIST LEGAL SYSTEMS. Transnational Publishers.

Panorama DDR (1975): 100 QUESTIONS, 100 ANSWERS, GDR. Panorama DDR

Panorama DDR (1976): INTRODUCTING THE GDR. Fifth rev. ed. Panorama DDR

Panorama DDR (1981): GOVERNMENT BY THE PEOPLE: DEMOCRACY UNDER SOCIALISM. Panorama DDR

Panorama DDR (1984): LAW AND JUSTICE: THE LEGAL SYSTEM OF THE GERMAN DEMOCRATIC REPUBLIC. Panorama DDR

Parker, Graham (1987): Trial by Jury in Canada. 8 JOURNAL OF LEGAL HISTORY 178–189.

Parker, H, et al. (1989): UNMASKING THE MAGISTRATES. Open University Press.

Parlow, Wolfgang (1983): Unser "Geheimnis" in der Arbeit mit Vorbestraften. 30 DER SCHÖFFE 61–62.

Parlow, Wolfgang (1984a): Erfahrungen im Umgang mit straffällig gewordenen Jugendlichen. 31 DER SCHÖFFE 126–128.

Parlow, Wolfgang (1984b): Schöffenaktiv überzeugte sich vom Stand der Rechtserziehung im Betrieb. 31 DER SCHÖFFE 259–261.

Parlow, Wolfgang & Claus Gessner (1986): Einweisung und Abschlussgespräch zum Schöffeneinsatz. 33 DER SCHÖFFE 119–120.

Parry, Michael E. (1974): Taking Note of Note-Taking. 10 COLUMBIA JOURNAL OF LAW & SOCIAL PROBLEMS 565–606.

Parthen, Friedrich (1985): Wie wirksam ist unser Einsatz für Recht und Gesetzlichkeit? 32 DER SCHÖFFE 68–70.

Paschke, Christa (1989): Zum Auftakt einer neuen Wahlperiode. 36 DER SCHÖFFE 137.

Pashukanis & Gintsburg: A COURSE ON SOVIET ECONOMIC LAW; reprinted in Beirne & Sharlett, 1980

Paul, Christel (1981): Erzieherische Möglichkeiten noch besser nutzen. 28 DER SCHÖFFE 222.

Paul, Heinz (1963): Die Gerichtskritik im arbeitsgerichtlichen Verfahren. 17 NEUE JUSTIZ 197–199.

Pavlov, I.V. (1965): The Soviet Legal System and Its Branches. USSR Academy of Sciences: SOCIAL SCIENCES IN THE USSR. Mouton & Co.

Peiris, Newton (1985): The Impact of Citizen Participation and Social Movements on Governmental Activities with Special Reference to Sri Lanka. World Congress, International Political Science Association; Paris, France; July 1985.

Peller, Wolfgang (1988): Schiedskommissionen stellen sich den täglichen Aufgaben. 35 DER SCHÖFFE 69–71.

Peller, Wolfgang (1989): Zu den Aufgaben der Schiedskommissionen in der neuen Wahlperiode. 36 DER SCHÖFFE 225–228.

Penke, Erich (1985): Gezielte Rechtserziehung und Rechtspropaganda festigen militärische Disziplin und Ordnung im Truppenteil. 32 DER SCHÖFFE 130–132.

Penrod, Steven & Reid Hastie (1979): Models of Jury Decision Making: A Critical Review. 86 PSYCHOLOGICAL BULLETIN 462–492.

Peschel-Gutzeit, Lore M. (1998): Aufarbeitung von Systemunrecht durch die Justiz. Ulrich Drobnig, ed.: DIE STRAFRECHTSJUSTIZ DER DDR IM SYSTEMWECHSEL. Duncker & Humblot.

Peterson, Mark A. (1986): A SUMMARY OF RESEARCH RESULTS: TRENDS AND PATTERNS IN CIVIL JURY VERDICTS. Rand Corporation.

Petrick, Heiz (1977): Erfahrungen bei der Überwindung von Ehekonflikten. 24 DER SCHÖFFE 39–40.

Petrov, Sergei L. (1989): The Little Drummer Boy. THE NEW REPUBLIC 30 (August 21, 1989).

Petzold-Pernia, Hermann (1979): Lay Participation in Judicial Proceedings in Latin American Countries. World Congress, International Political Science Association; Moscow, USSR; August 1979.

Petzold, Siegfried & Gerhard Schuessler (1972): Das neue Gesetz über den Ministerrat der DDR: Schöpferische Anwendung der Leninschen Staatslehre. 21 STAAT UND RECHT 1840–1854.

Peyrefitte, Alain (1992): THE IMMOBILE EMPIRE. Knopf.

Pfefferkorn, Guenter (1983): Zur Differenzierung von Geldbussen. 30 DER SCHÖFFE 257–258.

Pfefferkorn, Guenter (1984): Im Territorium fest eingebunden. 31 DER SCHÖFFE 243.

Pflicke, Gerhard (1985): Economic Contracts Act of the German Democratic Republic. 85–1 LAW AND LEGISLATION IN THE GDR 5–16.

Philip, Michael (1978): Ortsausschuss und Schiedskommission auf gemeinsamen Weg. 25 DER SCHÖFFE 295–296.

Picaper, Jean-Paul (1982): DDR: BILD IM WANDEL. Colloquium Verlag.

Piekert, X. (1955): Ein Fall von Rowdytum. 2 DER SCHÖFFE 85–86.

Pietz, Werner (1985): Als Führungsbeispiel für die Tätigkeit der Schiedskommissionen ausgewählt. 32 DER SCHÖFFE 154–155.

Pipes, Richard (1990): THE RUSSIAN REVOLUTION. Vintage Books.

Pirntke, Gunter (1982): Qualifizierung von Konfliktkommissionen für die Lösung der neuen Aufgaben. 36 NEUE JUSTIZ 370–371.

Pizzigati, Sam (1978): The Ungrand Jury. 13 HARVARD CIVIL RIGHTS-CIVIL LIBERTIES LAW REVIEW 217–223.

Plato (B. Jowett, ed.) (1959): THE REPUBLIC. Modern Library.

Plenikowski, Anton (1966): Probleme bei der Bildung und in der Tätigkeit der Schiedskommissionen. 20 NEUE JUSTIZ 373.

Plitz, Heinz & Gert Teichler (1976): Zur Anwendung der unbezahlten gemeinnützigen Arbeit in der Freizeit. 23 DER SCHÖFFE 230–235.

Poepplow, Eckard (1986): Beitrag des Schöffenkollektivs bei der Bewährungskontrolle und Wiedereingliederung. 33 DER SCHÖFFE 20–21.

Pohl, Heidrun & Gerhard Schulze (1979): Gewährleistung der Gesetzlichkeit bei der Eingabenbearbeitung. 33 NEUE JUSTIZ 246–248.

Pohle, Guenther (1986): Gesellschaftliche Kräfte nehmen Einfluss auf die Arbeitsdisziplin. 33 DER SCHÖFFE 263.

Polak, Karl (1961): Über die weitere Entwicklung der sozialistischen Rechtspflege in der DDR. 10 STAAT UND RECHT 607–657.

Pommerening, Fritz (1981): Für eine höhere Wirksamkeit der gewerkschaftlichen Rechtskommissionen. 35 NEUE JUSTIZ 324.

Pommerening, Fritz (1984): Zusammenarbeit von Gerichten und Gewerkschaften zur weiteren Durchsetzung des Arbeitsrechts. 38 NEUE JUSTIZ 199.

Pomorski, Stanislaw (1974): Lay Judges in the Polish Criminal Courts. 7 CASE WESTERN RESERVE JOURNAL OF INTERNATIONAL LAW 198–209.

Pompoes, Herbert (1973): Wirksamer Schutz des sozialistischen Eigentums. 20 DER SCHÖFFE 401–407.

Pond, Elizabeth (1993): BEYOND THE WALL. The Brookings Institution.

Popp, Sabine (1987): Die Kraft der Schiedskommissionen stärker nutzen und ihre Entwicklung allseitig fördern. 34 DER SCHÖFFE 253–258.

Poppe, Eberhard (1980): GRUNDRECHTE DES BÜRGERS IN DER SOZIALISTISCHEN GESELLSCHAFT. Staatsverlag.

Poppe, Eberhard (1984): POLITISCHE UND PERSÖNLICHE GRUNDRECHT IN DEN KÄMPFEN UNSERER ZEIT. Staatsverlag.

Poppe, Eberhard (1985): Menschenrechte—gesicherte Soziale Tatbestände in unserem Land. 85 EINHEIT 156–162.

Poppe, Stefan et al. (1982): Beitrag der Jurastudenten zur Rechtspropaganda. 36 NEUE JUSTIZ 459–460.

Poppe, Stefan et al. (1984): Rechtspropagande der Jurastudenten. 38 NEUE JUSTIZ 103.

Popper, Karl R. (1963): THE OPEN SOCIETY AND ITS ENEMIES. 2 Vols. Harper & Row

Posorski, Felix (1979a): Zur Vertiefung der Zusammenarbeit der Schiedskommissionen mit den örtlichen Volksvertretungen. 26 DER SCHÖFFE 49–50.

Posorski, Felix (1979b): Schiedskommissionen—Organe der Erziehung und Selbsterziehung der Bürger. 26 DER SCHÖFFE 159–164.

Posorski, Felix (1982): Gesellschaftliche Grundlagen und wesentlicher Inhalt eines neuen Entwicklungsabschnitts der gesellschaftlichen Gerichte. 29 DER SCHÖFFE 95–111.

Posorski, Felix (1984): Aussprachen helfen Rechtskonflikte vermeiden und beseitigen. 31 DER SCHÖFFE 34.

Pospisil, Leopold (1982): ANTHROPOLOGIE DES RECHTS: RECHT UND GESELLSCHAFT IN ARCHAISCHEN UND MODERNEN KULTUREN. Beck.

Pound, Roscoe (1930): CRIMINAL JUSTICE IN AMERICA. Henry Holt.

President's Commission on Law Enforcement and Administration of Justice (1967): THE CHALLENGE OF CRIME IN A FREE SOCIETY. U.S. Government Printing Office.

Priebke, Jerta (1955): Für regelmässigen Schulbesuch sorgen. 2 DER SCHÖFFE 84–85.
Probst, Karl (1967): Den Anfängen arbeitsscheuen Verhaltens wehren. 14 DER SCHÖFFE 421–425.
Probst, Karl (1968): Erfogreiche Bilanz—neue Aufgaben. 15 DER SCHÖFFE 105–108.
Probst, Karl (1971a): Erhöhung der Qualität der Rechtsprechung bei Angriffen auf das gesellschaftliche Eigentum. 18 DER SCHÖFFE 68–74.
Probst, Karl (1971b): Gesellschaftliche Gerichte und Gesetzlichkeit. 18 DER SCHÖFFE 190–198.
Probst, Karl (1977): Schiedskommissionen sind an ihren Aufgaben gewachsen. 24 DER SCHÖFFE 223–227.
Probst, Karl (1980): Bewährtes mit Neuem verbunden. 27 DER SCHÖFFE 191.
Probst, Karl (1983): Wirksamkeit der Schiedskommissionen mit Umsicht fördern. 30 DER SCHÖFFE 145–151.
Probst, Karl (1984): Wachsende Ansprüche an unsere Arbeit. 31 DER SCHÖFFE 72–75.
Probst, Karl & Hans Brumme (1976): Eine positive Bilanz in der Arbeit der gesellschaftlichen Gerichte. 23 DER SCHÖFE 38–42.
Probst, Karl & Hans-Joachim Glueck (1969): Zur Rechtsprechung der gesellschaftlichen Gerichte bei Beleidigung und Verleumdung. 16 DER SCHÖFFE 389–396.
Probst, Karl & Hans-Joachim Glueck (1970): Zur Rechtsprechung der gesellschaftlichen Gerichte bei Eigentumsverfehlungen und -vergehen. 17 DER SCHÖFFE 16–22.
Provine, Doris Marie (1981): Credentials in Court: On Comparing Lawyer and Non-Lawyer Judges in American Courts. Paper delivered at the annual meeting of the Law and Soclety Association, Amherst, Mass.
Provine, Doris Marie (1986): JUDGING CREDENTIALS. University of Chicago Press.
Pruefer, Edgar (1973): Vorbeugung und Überwindung von Konflikten auf dem Gebiete des Wohnungsmietrechts. 20 DER SCHÖFFE 341–347.
Prueger, Werner (1977): Wie arbeiten wir mit Hinweisen und Empfehlungen. 24 DER SCHÖFFE 10–13.
Pruss, Ursula (1982): Erfahrungen bei der Bewährungskontrolle durch Schöffen. 29 DER SCHÖFFE 216–220.
Prybyla, Jan (1988): The Great Malaise: Economic Crisis in Eastern Europe; Nicholas N. Kittrie & Ivan Volgyes, eds.: THE UNCERTAIN FUTURE: GORBACHEV'S EASTERN BLOC. Paragon House.
Pryssok, Horst (1982): Kostenlose Rechtsauskünfte durch Rechtsanwälte helfen Rechtsbewusstsein der Bürger festigen. 36 NEUE JUSTIZ 275–276.
Przybylski, Peter (1980): Öffentlichkeitsarbeit—fester Bestandteil der Bekämpfung der Kriminalität. 34 NEUE JUSTIZ 55–57.
Przybylski, Peter (1991): TATORT POLITBÜRO: DIE AKTE HONECKER. Rowohlt.
Pueschel, Heinz (1962a): Gleichberechtigte Mitwirkung des Schöffen in der Verhandlung des neuen Zivilprozesses. 9 DER SCHÖFFE 249–255.
Pueschel, Heinz (1962b): Weitere Arbeiten am Entwurf des Familiengesetzbuches. 9 DER SCHÖFFE 341–343.

Puro, Steven (1976): United States Magistrates: A New Federal Judicial Officer. 2 JUSTICE SYSTEM J. 141.

Quandt, Victor-Paul (1984): Zusammenarbeit von Untersuchungsorgan, Staatsanwalt und Gericht zur Durchführung beschleunigter Verfahren. 38 NEUE JUSTIZ 465–466.

Quilitzsch, Siegmar et al. (1985): DIE DDR IN DER WELT DES SOZIALISMUS. Staatsverlag.

Racz, Attila (1972): People's Assessors in European Socialist Countries. 14 ACTA JURIDICA ACADEMIAE SCIENTIARUM HUNGARICAE 395–415.

Racz, Attila (1979): People's Participation in Judicial and Quasi-Judicial Proceedings in the European Socialist Countries. Paper delivered at the World Congress of the International Political Science Association, Moscow.

Rand, Robert (1991): COMRADE LAWYER: INSIDE SOVIET JUSTICE IN AN ERA OF REFORM. Westview Press.

Rau, Johanne (1961): Ein Fall aus der Arbeit eines Jugendschöffen. 8 DER SCHÖFFE 412.

Rau, Siegfried et al. (1984): CHRONIK ZUR GESCHICHTE DER KREISPARTEI-ORGANIZATION SONNEBERG DER SED 1945–1984. Part 1. Kreisleitung Sonneberg der SED.

Raubach, Hans-Rainer (1988): Der Einfluss der Konfliktkommissionen auf die Gestaltung der Arbeitsrechtsverhältnisse. 43 ARBEIT UND ARBEITSRECHT 183–185.

Readhead, Steve (1982): Marxist Theory, the Rule of Law and Socialism. Piers Beirne & Richard Qinney, eds.: MARXISM AND LAW. Wiley.

RECHTSLEXIKON (1988). Staatsverlag.

Redaktion Kritische Justiz (1984): DER UNRECHTS-STAAT (Vol. II): RECHT UND JUSTIZ IM NATIONALSOZIALISMUS. Nomos.

Redlich, Barbara (1968): Internationales Symposium über die Rückfallkrimialität Jugendlicher. 15 DER SCHÖFFE 146–150.

Reed, Robin (1980): Jury Simulation: The Impact of Judge's Instruction and Attorney Tactics on Decisionmaking. 71 JOURNAL OF CRIMINAL LAW 68–72.

Reich, Norbert (1973): MARXISTISCHE RECHTSTHEORIE. J.C.B. Mohr.

Reich, Norbert & Hans-Christian Reichel (1975): EINFüHRUNG IN DAS SOZIALISTISCHE RECHT. C.H. Beck.

Reichel, P.L. (1994): COMPARATIVE CRIMINAL JUSTICE SYSTEMS. Prentice-Hall.

Reichert, X. (1961): Die Konfliktkommission half ihm seine Arbeitsdisziplin zu verbessern. 8 DER SCHÖFFE 180–181.

Reiland, Werner (1971): DIE GESELLSCHAFTLICHEN GERICHTE DER DDR. H. Erdmann.

Reinhold, Otto (1968): Die Rolle des Staates im ökonomischen System des Sozialismus. 68 EINHEIT 153–165.

Reinhold, Otto (1989a): Die Gestaltung des entwickelten Sozialismus in Theory und Praxis. 89 EINHEIT 890–896.

Reinhold, Otto (1989b): Auf der Suche nach den besten Lösungen. 89 EINHEIT 984–989.

Reissig, Rolf & Gert-Joachim Glaessner (1991): DAS ENDE EINES EXPERIMENTES. Dietz Verlag.

Rembar, Charles (1980): THE LAW OF THE LAND: THE EVOLUTION OF OUR LEGAL SYSTEM. Simon & Schuster.

Renger, Reinhard (1990): Rechtpflege in der DDR. 34 RECHT IN OST UND WEST 12–19.

Renneberg, Gerhard (1989): Die arbeitsrechtliche Verantwortung der Betriebe zur Unterstützung werktätiger Mütter. 44 ARBEIT UND ARBEITSRECHT 257–258.

Renneberg, Joachim (1963): Die gesellschaftlichen Grundlagen der schrittweisen Zurückdrängung der Kriminalität und die Aufgaben des sozialistischen Strafgesetzbuches der DDR. 12 STAAT UND RECHT 1595–1615.

Reuter, Horst (1966): Differenzierte Mitwirkung gesellschaftlicher Kräfte im Ermittlungsverfahren. 20 NEUE JUSTIZ 708–710.

Reuter, Lothar (1972): Entwicklung, Erscheinung und Strafverfolgungspraxis der Judendkriminalität in der DDR. 19 DER SCHÖFFE 84–110.

Reuter, Lothar (1979): Zur Rolle der Eltern im Strafverfahren gegen Jugendliche. 33 NEUE JUSTIZ 18–21.

Reuter, Lothar (1983): Lenin und die sowjetische Strafgesetzgebung. 37 NEUE JUSTIZ 447–449.

Reuter, Lothar (1984): Depönalisierung im Strafrecht der europäischen sozialistischen Länder. 38 NEUE JUSTIZ 405–408.

Reuter, Lothar (1990): Die Strafen mit Freiheitsentzug in der Kritik. 34 RECHT IN OST UND WEST 144–146.

Reuther, Horst (1979): Gesellschaftliches Gericht—ein bedeutender Erziehungsfaktor. 26 DER SCHÖFFE 296–298.

Richert, Ernst (1966): DAS ZWEITE DEUTSCHLAND: EIN STAAT, DER NICHT SEIN DARF. Fischer.

Richert, John P. (1977): Jurors' Attitudes toward Jury Service. 2 JUSTICE SYSTEM JOURNAL 233.

Richert, John P. (1979): Lay Participation in Judicial Proceedings in Western European Countries. Paper delivered at the IPSA World Congress, Moscow.

Richter, Arthur (1961): Gedanken zur Tätigkeit des Schiedsmanns. 8 DER SCHÖFFE 386–387.

Richter, Else (1978): Schöffe und Mitglied der Schiedskommission—eine gute Verbindung. 25 DER SCHÖFFE 151–152.

Richter, Guenter (1983): Mut zum Risiko. 30 DER SCHÖFFE 182.

Richter, Michael (1996): DIE STAATSSICHERHEIT IM LETZTEN JAHR DER DDR. Böhlau Verlag.

Richter, Wilfried (1980): Schöffen in die Leitungsarbeit einbeziehen. 27 DER SCHÖFFE 18.

Richterkollektiv Zittau (1954): Erfahrungen in der Zusammenarbeit mit den Schöffen. 1:1 DER SCHÖFFE 1–14.

Richtlinie (1965): Verfahren über die Vollstreckbarkeitserklärung von Beschlüssen der Konfliktkommissionen. 12 DER SCHÖFFE 377–385.

Riecker, Ariane et al. (1990): STASI INTIM. Forum Verlag Leipzig.

Riedel, Ulrich (1973): DER EINFLUSS DES SOWJETRECHTS UND DER WEIMARER VERFASSUNG AUF DIE VERFASSUNG DER DDR VOM 7.10.1949. Dissertation, University of Göttingen.

Rieger, Wolfgang (1986): Zur neuen Unterhaltsrichtlinie. 33 DER SCHÖFFE 61–63.

Riemann, Tord (1976): LAW AND JUSTICE IN A SOCIALIST SOCIETY: THE LEGAL SYSTEM OF THE GERMAN DEMOCRATIC REPUBLIC. Panorama-DDR.

Riemann, Tord (1983): Die qualitativ neuen Wesenszüge der sozialistischen Demokratie. 83 EINHEIT 977–980.

Riemann, Tord & Ernst-Otto Schwabe (1976): FREEDOM, DEMOCRACY, HUMAN RIGHTS—FOR WHOM AND FOR WHAT? Panorama-DDR.

Rietz, Carmen (1975): Die Grundsätze des sozialistischen Zivilrechts und seine eigentumsrechtlichen Regelungen. 22 DER SCHÖFFE 205–210.

Rist, Ray C. & Ronald J. Anson, eds. (1977): EDUCATION, SOCIAL SCIENCE, AND THE JUDICIAL PROCESS. Teachers College Press, Columbia University.

Ritter, Gertraude (1973): Beschwerdeausschüsse. 22 STAAT UND RECHT 380–392.

Ritter, Traudel (1971): About the Decree on Petitions Procedure in the GDR. 71 LAW & LEGISLATION 7–23.

Robertson, John A. (1974): ROUGH JUSTICE. Little, Brown.

Robinson, Mary T.W. (1973): The Jury System in Ireland. 11 WESTERN AUSTRALIA LAW REVIEW 111–119.

Roehl, Ulrich (1972): Anwendung der Geldstrafe bei vorsätzlichen Körperverletzungen. 19 DER SCHÖFFE 251–252.

Roesler, Heinz (1982): Dem gesellschaftlichen Fortschritt verpflichtet. 29 DER SCHÖFFE 153.

Roesner, Heinz & Rose-Marie Ruelicke (1975): Zur Praxis der Behandlung von Eigentumsverletzungen. 22 DER SCHÖFFE 273–276.

Roesner, Heinz (1980): Rührige Kommission Ordnung und Sicherheit. 27 DER SCHÖFFE 225.

Roesner, Heinz & Ingrid Struetzel (1974): Zum Umfang und zur Wirksamkeit der Tätigkeit der Schiedskommissionen bei Schulpflichtverletzungen im Bezirk Halle. 21 DER SCHÖFFE 51–62.

Rogovin, Edith B. (1961): Social Conformity and the Comradely Courts in the Soviet Union. 7 CRIME AND DELINQUENCY 303.

Rohde, Ursula (1971a): Wirtschaftliche Selbständigkeit und Wegfall der Unterhaltsverpflichtung. 18 DER SCHÖFFE 15–17.

Rohde, Ursula (1971b): Die Rechtsprechung der Gerichte in Eheverfahren. 18 DER SCHÖFFE 293–297.

Rohde, Ursula (1980): Die Aufgaben des Gerichts in der streitigen Verhandlung bei Eheverfahren. 27 DER SCHÖFFE 60–62.

Rommel, Karl-Heinz & Ilse Lungwitz (1976): Zur Beratung von Vergehen und Verfehlungen Jugendlicher vor gesellschaftlichen Gerichten. 248–252.

Rommen, Heinrich A. (1998): THE NATURAL LAW: A STUDY IN LEGAL AND SOCIAL HISTORY AND PHILOSOPHY. Liberty Fund.

Romoser, George K. (1975): The State of the German Nation. 3 EUROPEAN JOURNAL OF POLITICAL RESEARCH 425–435.

Rosenberg, Maurice (1980): Civil Justice Research and Civil Justice Reform. 15 LAW & SOCIETY REV. 473 (1980–81)

Rosenberg, Maurice & Myra Schubin (1961): Trial by Lawyer, Compulsory Arbitration of Small Claims in Pennsylvania. 74 HARVARD LAW REV. 448.

Rosenberg, Tina (1995): THE HAUNTED LAND. Vintage Books.

Rosenthal, Walther (no date): Die Gerichtsverfassung in der SBZ. Reinhart Maurach, et al.: FRAGEN DER GERICHTSVERFASSUNG IM OSTBLOCK. Verlag für Internationalen Kulturaustausch.

Rosenthal, Walther (1962): The Powers of the Judiciary in East Germany. 4 JOURNAL OF THE INTERNATIONAL COMMISSION OF JURISTS 134–149.

Ross, H. Laurence (1978): SETTLED OUT OF COURT. Aldine.

Rottleuthner, Hubert (1994): STEUERUNG DER JUSTIZ IN DER DDR. Bundesanzeiger Verlag.

Rottleuthner, Hubert (1998): Steuerung der Justiz in der DDR. Ulrich Drobnig, ed.: DIE STRAFRECHTSJUSTIZ DER DDR IM SYSTEMWECHSEL. Duncker & Humblot.

Ruebestahl, X. (1954): Bildung eines Schöffenaktivs beim Kreisgericht Hoyerswerda. 1:6 DER SCHÖFFE 27–28.

Rueggeberg, Joerg (1970): Zur Funktion der ehrenamtlichen Richter in den öffentlichrechtlichen Gerichtsbarkeiten. 61 VERWALTUNGSARCHIV 189–218.

Rymon, Joachim (1962): Zur Behandlung Jugendlicher vor der Konfliktkommission. 9 DER SCHÖFFE 179–180.

Sabrow, Martin (1999): Dictatorship as Discourse. Konrad Jarausch, ed.: DICTATORSHIP AS EXPERIENCE. Berghahn Books.

Sack, Christa (1974): Schutz dem sozialistischen Eigentum. 21 DER SCHÖFFE 415–417.

Sagel-Grande, Irene (1986): Die Bewältigung der Kleinkriminalität in den Niederlanden und in der DDR. 30 RECHT IN OST UND WEST 278–287.

Sagel-Grande, Irene (1989): Freiheitsstrafen ohne herkömmlichen Freiheitsentzug. 33 RECHT IN OST UND WEST 1–13.

Sahr, Siegfried (1980): Wahl der Konfliktkommissionen—ein Höhepunkt gewerkschaftlicher Rechtsarbeit. 34 NEUE JUSTIZ 11.

Sahr, Siegfried (1982): Eine weitere Etappe in der Arbeit der Konfliktkommissionen. 36 NEUE JUSTIZ 151.

Sahr, Siegfried (1985): Wahl der Konfliktkommissionen. 39 NEUE JUSTIZ 272–274.

Sahr, Siegfried (1987): Aufgaben der Gewerkschaften bei der weiteren Entwicklung der sozialistischen Demokratie. 41 NEUE JUSTIZ 86–89.

Saks, Michael J. et al. (1975): The Presumption of Innocence and the American Juror. 2 JOURNAL OF CONTEMPORARY LAW 46–54.

Saks, Michael J. (1977): JURY VERDICTS: THE ROLE OF GROUP SIZE AND SOCIAL DECISION RULE. Lexington.

Sander, Frank E. A. (1995): Varieties of Dispute Processing. G. Larry Mays & Peter R. Gregware, eds.: COURTS AND JUSTICE. Waveland Press.

Sander, Guenther (1979): ABWEICHENDES VERHALTEN IN DER DDR. Campus Verlag.

Sandford, Gregory W. (1983): FROM HITLER TO ULBRICHT: THE COMMUNIST RECONSTRUCTION OF EAST GERMANY: 1945–46. Princeton University Press.

Santos, Boaventura de Sousa (1982): Law and Revolution in Portugal: The Experiences of Popular Justice after the 25th of April 1974. Richard L. Abel, ed.: 2 THE POLITICS OF INFORMAL JUSTICE. Academic Press.

Sarge, Guenter (1988): Gesetzlichkeit und Humanismus unserer Rechtspflege. 88 EINHEIT 703–708.

Sarge, Guenter & Guenter Kalwert (1973): Die Entwicklung der Militärgerichtsbarkeit in der DDR. 27 NEUE JUSTIZ 190–194.

Savickij, Valerij (1982): Die Kameradengerichte in der USSR. 24 JAHRBUCH FÜR OSTRECHT 263–273.

Scalapino, Robert A. (1992): THE LAST LENINISTS: THE UNCERTAIN FUTURE OF ASIA'S COMMUNIST STATES. Center for Strategic and International Studies.

Schabowski, Guenter (1994): ABSCHIED VON DER UTOPIE. Franz Steiner Verlag.

Schaefer, Siegfried (1987): Übereinstimmung im Ziel: Pädagoge und Schöffe. 34 DER SCHÖFFE 16–17.

Schalck-Golodkowski, Alexander (2000): DEUTSCH-DEUTSCHE ERINNERUNGEN. Rowohlt.

Schaum, Renate & Michael Strich (1981): Erfahrungen bei der Rechtsverwirklichung an einer Hochschule. 35 NEUE JUSTIZ 84–85.

Schaum, Renate & Michael Strich (1987): Erziehung der Erzieher—Kenntnisse adressatenspezifisch vermittelt. 42 ARBEIT UND ARBEITSRECHT 113.

Scheffler, Rudi (1984): Wir meistern unseren Auftrag. 31 DER SCHÖFFE 19–20.

Scheflin, Alan & Jon Van Dyke (1980): Jury Nullification: The Contours of a Controversy. 43 LAW AND CONTEMPORARY PROBLEMS 51–115.

Scheflin, Alan & Jon Van Dyke (1995): Merciful Juries: The Resilience of Jury Nullification. G. Larry Mays & Peter R. Gregware, eds.: COURTS AND JUSTICE. Waveland Press.

Schell, Manfred & Werner Kalinka (1991): STASI UND KEIN ENDE. Ullstein.

Schellenberger, Gotthard (1959): Kampf gegen Schund- und Schmutzliteratur. 6 DER SCHÖFFE 114–115.

Scherzer, Landolf (1997): MITLEID IST UMSONST, NEID MUSST DU DIR ERARBEITEN. Edition Ost.

Schilling, Renate (1988): Dem gesellschaftlichen Wirken der Schiedskommissionen alle Unterstützung geben. 35 DER SCHÖFFE 114–119.

Schippers, Karl (1967): Empfehlungen haben sich bewährt. 14 DER SCHÖFFE 427–428.

Schirmer, Gregor (1975): Sozialistische Rechtserziehung. 23 DAS HOCHSCHULWESEN 130.

Schlegel, Joachim (1968): Kampf gegen die Jugendkriminalität—eine Angelegenheit der ganzen Gesellschaft. 15 DER SCHÖFFE 222–229.

Schlegel, Joachim (1973): Der Beitrag der Gerichte zum Schutze des sozialistischen und des persönlichen Eigentums. 20 DER SCHÖFFE 144–151.

Schlegel, Joachim (1977): Zur differenzierten Anwendung von Massnahmen bei der wirksamen Bekämpfung und Verhütung der Jugendkriminalität. 24 DER SCHÖFFE 161–167.

Schlegel, Joachim (1979): Zur jugendspezifischen Ausgestaltung der Bewährungsverurteilung und zur Kontrolle des Bewährungsprozesses. 26 DER SCHÖFFE 36–38.

Schlegel, Joachim (1983): Einige Aspekte der Gestaltung der Hauptverhandlung in Jugendstrafsachen. 30 DER SCHÖFFE 30–32.

Schleifstein, Josef (1982): MARXISMUS UND STAAT. Verlag Marxistische Blätter.

Schmidt, Albert (1990): THE IMPACT OF PERESTROIKA ON SOVIET LAW. Martinus Nijhoff.

Schmidt, Guenter (1967): Wirksame gesellschaftliche Hilfe für Strafgefangene. 14 DER SCHÖFFE 104–105.
Schmidt, Guenter (1969): Wirksame und differenzierte Wiedereingliederung. 16 DER SCHÖFFE 98–100.
Schmidt, Hans-Theodor (1969): DIE SOWJETISCHEN GESELLSCHAFTSGERICHTE. Verlag Wissenschaft und Politik.
Schmidt, Helmut (1968): Die wichtigsten Ergebnisse der Diskussion über das neue Strafrecht. 22 NEUE JUSTIZ 68–74,
Schmidt, Helmut & Karl-Heinz Beyer (1963): Bewährung am Arbeitsplatz und Bürgschaft gesellschaftlicher Kollektive. 10 DER SCHÖFFE 100–105.
Schmidt, Helmut & Rudolf Winkler (1967): Die Behandlung von Ordnungswidrigkeiten durch gesellschaftliche Organe der Rechtspflege. 14 DER SCHÖFFE 380–386.
Schmidt, Karl (1968): Schulpflichtverweigerung. 15 DER SCHÖFFE 21.
Schmidt, Karlheinz (1985): Welche Aufgaben hat ein gewerkschaftlicher Prozessvertreter zu erfüllen. 32 DER SCHÖFFE 127–128.
Schmollack, Juergen (1989): Gerechtigkeit: Grundwert des Sozialismus. 89 EINHEIT 252–255.
Schneider, Otmar (1988): RECHTSGEDANKEN UND RECHTSTECHNIKEN TOTALITÄRER HERRSCHAFT. Duncker & Humblot.
Schober, Helmut (1979): Gesellschaftlicher Einfluss ist effectiver geworden. 26 DER SCHÖFFE 120–121.
Schoene, Walter (1980a): Qualifiziert Arbeit mit den Schöffen: Ausdruck sozialistischer Demokratie. 27 DER SCHÖFFE 197.
Schoene, Walter (1980b): Übertragener Verantwortung voll gerecht werden. 27 DER SCHÖFFE 273.
Schoeneburg, Karl-Heinz (1973): STAAT UND RECHT IN DER GESCHICHTE DER DDR. Staatsverlag.
Schoeneburg, Karl-Heinz (1976): Dialektik, Mensch, Staat. Schoeneburg, Karl-Heinz & W. Kuenzel: DIALEKTIK, STAAT, RECHT. Akademie-Verlag.
Schoeneburg, Karl-Heinz (1984): GESCHICHTE DES STAATES UND DES RECHTS DER DDR: DOKUMENTE 1945–1949. Staatsverlag.
Schoeneburg, Karl-Heinz (1986): KPD UND STAATSFRAGE. Staatsverlag.
Schoenfeldt, Hans (1982): Gesellschaftliche Funktion und Aufgaben des Jugendbeistandes. 29 DER SCHÖFFE 260–264.
Schoenfeldt, Hans (1983): Die Vorbereitung des Jugendbeistandes auf die Mitwirkung an der Hauptverhandlung. 30 DER SCHÖFFE 134–138.
Schoenfeldt, Hans (1984): Aufgaben des Jugendbeistandes im Rechtsmittelverfahren. 31 DER SCHÖFFE 81–84.
Schoenfeldt, Hans-Andreas (2002): VOM SCHIEDSMANN ZUR SCHIEDSKOMMISSION. Vittorio Klostermann Verlag.
Schoenfeldt, Margarete & Hans Schoenfeldt (1979): Moralische Aspekte der Beziehungen zwischen Richter und Schöffen. 26 DER SCHÖFFE 101–105.
Schoenrath, T. (1978): Der Analogieschluss als Methode der Interpretation und der Anwendung des sozialistischen Rechts in der Rechtsordnung der DDR. Nationales Komitee für Rechtswissenschaft der DDR: BERICHTE ZUM X. INTERNATIONALEN KONGRESS FüR RECHTSVERGLEICHUNG.

Scholz, Paul (1982): Optimistisch lösen wir unsere Aufgaben. 29 DER SCHÖFFE 78.

Scholz, Paul (1984): Volle Aufmerksamkeit der Festigung des Kollektivs. 31 DER SCHÖFFE 143.

Scholz, U. von (1967): Gründlich arbeiten—erfolgreich erziehen. 14 DER SCHÖFFE 333–334.

Schorn, Hubert (1955): DER LAIENRICHTER IN DER STRAFRECHTSPFLEGE. Aschendorf.

Schorr, Daniel (1976): A Newsman's Reflections on Jury Service. 2:2 LITIGATION 24–25, 52 (Winter 1976).

Schott, Richard L. (1977): Trial by Jury: Reflections of a Juror. 13:5 TRIAL 56–59 (May 1977).

Schramm, X. (1954): Zusammenarbeit mit den Schöffen im Zivilprozess. 1:2 DER SCHÖFFE 30–31.

Schrimpf, Dieter (1989): Aufgaben bei der Vorbeugubg, Bekämpfung und Verhütung von Straftaten und anderen Rechtsverletzungen. 44 ARBEIT UND ARBEITSRECHT 88–90.

Schroeder, Dieter (1967): DIE KRISE DER MARXISTISCH-LENINISTISCHEN STAATSTHEORIE. Alfred Metzner Verlag.

Schroeder, Elke (1975): Probleme des arbeitsrechtlichen Schutzes des jugendlichen Werktätigen. 22 DER SCHÖFFE vi–viii.

Schroeder, Friedrich-Christian (1967): Die Abschaffung der Gesellschaftsgerichte in der Sowjetunion und die Periodisierung der Sowjetischen Rechtsentwicklung. 13 OSTEUROPA-RECHT 89–96.

Schroeder, Friedrich-Christian (1980a): Aufwertung des Strafverteidigers in der DDR? 13 DEUTSCHLAND ARCHIV 130–132.

Schroeder, Friedrich-Christian (1980b): Zunahme der Gewaltkriminalität in der DDR. 13 DEUTSCHLAND ARCHIV 282–284.

Schroeder, Friedrich-Christian (1983): DAS STRAFRECHT DES REALEN SOZIALISMUS. Westdeutscher Verlag.

Schroeder, Friedrich-Christian (1986): Tendenzen in der Strafzumessung der DDR. 30 RECHT IN OST UND WEST 338–340.

Schroeder, Friedrich-Christian (1988): Die "gesellschaftlichen Kräfte" im Strafverfahren der DDR. 32 RECHT IN OST UND WEST 1–8.

Schroeder, Friedrich-Christian (1989a): Das 5. Strafrechtsänderungsgesetz der DDR. 33 RECHT IN OST UND WEST 201–209.

Schroeder, Friedrich-Christian (1989b): Wandlungen und Konstanten der "sozialistischen Gesetzlichkeit." 33 RECHT IN OST UND WEST 358–362.

Schroeder, Horst (1977): Zu einigen Problemen des Wohnungsmietrechts. 24 DER SCHÖFFE 89–92.

Schroeder, Horst (1978a): Schutz des sozialistischen Eigentums gebietet pflichtbewusstes Handeln. 25 DER SCHÖFFE 187–205.

Schroeder, Horst (1978b): Erfahrungen und Probleme bei der Vorbeugung und Bekämpfung der Jugendkriminalität. 25 DER SCHÖFFE 199–205.

Schroeder, Otto (1981): Die Einheit von Partei, Staat und Volk festigen. 30 STAAT UND RECHT 962–972.

Schroeder, Rolf (1970): Zur überwindung von Erziehungspflichtverletzungen und asozialem Verhalten. 17 DER SCHÖFFE 329–336.

Schroeter, Ulf & Wolfgang Baufeldt (1986): Ergebnisse aus dem Leistungsvergleich zwischen Schöffenkollektiven. 33 DER SCHÖFFE 199–201.

Schubert, Christa (1984): Engagement lohnt immer. 31 DER SCHÖFFE 119–120.

Schuessler, Gerhard (1974): STAAT, RECHT UND DEMOKRATIE BEI DER GESTALTUNG DER ENTWICKELTEN SOZIALISTISCHEN GESELLSCHAFT. Staatsverlag.

Schuessler, Gerhard (1976): Zur Entwicklung des sozialistischen Rechtsbewusstseins. 25 STAAT UND RECHT 117–132.

Schuessler, Gerhard (1978): Die Staats- und Rechtswissenschaft im Dienste der sozialistischen Staatspraxis. 27 STAAT UND RECHT 866–877.

Schuessler, Gerhard (1979a): Die Rolle der marxistisch-leninistischen Staats- und Rechtsauffassung in unserer Revolution. Vereinigung der Juristen der DDR: RECHT IM DIENST DES VOLKES. Staatsverlag.

Schuessler, Gerhard (1979b): The Development of the Political System of the Socialist Society; National Committee for Political Sciences in the GDR: POLITICAL SCIENCES IN THE GDR: CONTRIBUTIONS TO THE XI. WORLD CONGRESS OF IPSA, 12.-18. AUGUST 1979 IN MOSCOW.

Schuessler, Gerhard (1979c): ICH UND MEIN STAAT. Staatsverlag.

Schuessler, Gerhard (1980): Sozialistisches Rechtsbewusstsein und demokratischer Zentralismus. 27 DER SCHÖFFE 269.

Schuessler, Gerhard (1981a): Die Beschlüsse des X. Parteitages der SED—Richtschnur der staats- und rechtswissenschaftlichen Forschung. 35 NEUE JUSTIZ 434.

Schuessler, Gerhard (1981b): Die Rolle des sozialistischen Staates und seines Rechtes bei der weiteren Gestaltung der entwickelten sozialistischen Gesellschaft. 35 NEUE JUSTIZ 50.

Schuessler, Gerhard (1985): Der demokratische Zentralismus: Tragendes Systemelement der sozialistischen Demokratie. Rat für staats- und rechtswissenschaftliche Forschung an der Akademie der Wissenschaften der DDR: VERVOLLKOMMNUNG DER SOZIALISTISCHEN DEMOKRATIE: TRIEBKRAFT DER SOZIALISTSICHEN GESELLSCHAFT. Staatsverlag.

Schuessler, Gerhard et al. (1984): STAAT, RECHT UND POLITIK IM SOZIALISMUS. Dietz Verlag.

Schuetzsack, Axel (1990): EXODUS IN DIE EINHEIT. Ernst Knoth.

Schuller, Wolfgang (1980): GESCHICHTE UND STRUKTUR DES POLITISCHEN STRAFRECHTS DER DDR BIS 1968. Verlag Rolf Gremer.

Schulz, Detlev (1980): Grössere Aufmrksamkeit der Erziehung kriminell gefährdeter Bürger. 27 DER SCHÖFFE 149–153.

Schulz, G. (1957): Alcohol and Criminalität. 4 DER SCHÖFFE 286.

Schulz, Inge (1983): Wachsende Anforderungen an die Rechtsausbildung und Rechterziehung an den Ingenieur-und Fachschulen. 37 NEUE JUSTIZ 286–288.

Schulze, Gerhard (1984): Verfassungsrecht—Verfassungswirklichkeit. 84 EINHEIT 374–375.

Schumann, Gerd (1982): Beistand im Jugendstrafverfahren. 29 DER SCHÖFFE 179–181.

Schwan, Heribert (1997): ERICH MIELKE: DER MANN DER STASSI WAR. Droemer Knaur.

Schwartz, Helene E. (1972): Demythologizing the Historic Role of the Grand Jury. 10 AMERICAN CRIMINAL LAW REVIEW 701–770.

Schweigler, Gebhard L. (1975): NATIONAL CONSCIOUSNESS IN DIVIDED GERMANY. Sage.

Schweitzer, Carl-Christoph et al., eds. (1984): POLITICS AND GOVERNMENT IN THE FEDERAL REPUBLIC OF GERMANY: BASIC DOCUMENTS. Berg Publishers.

Scigliano, Robert G. (1959): The Grand Jury, the Information, and the Judicial Inquiry. 38 OREGON LAW REVIEW 303–315.

Seidel, Achim (1982): Gesellschaftliche Erziehung ist keine Einbahnstrasse. 29 DER SCHÖFFE 13.

Seidel, Curt (1988): Stationen der Entwicklung der Schiedskommissionen im Bezirk Neubrandenburg. 35 DER SCHÖFFE 78–84.

Seidel, Dietmar (1981): Verantwortung und ihre rechtliche Relevanz. 35 NEUE JUSTIZ 112.

Seidel, Dietmar & Rolf Rindert (1987): Bedeutung der Motive des Handelns für Art und Ausmass der Schuld im Strafrecht. 41 NEUE JUSTIZ 96–99.

Seidler, Heinz (1954): Rechenschaftslegung im Betrieb. 1:7 DER SCHÖFFE 19–20.

Seifert, Wolfgang (1978): Der Beitrag der Gerichte zur Verwirklichung staatlicher Familienpolitik. 25 DER SCHÖFFE 236–240.

Seiffert, Dieter (1985): Rechtsbewusstsein und Rechtssicherheit haben sich erhöht. 32 DER SCHÖFFE 164–165.

Seliger, Arnold (1978): 15 Jahre erfolgreiche Arbeit der Schiedskommissionen. 32 NEUE JUSTIZ 332.

Selvin, Molly & Larry Picus (1987): THE DEBATE OVER JURY PERFORMANCE. Rand Corporation.

Sembnista, Leo (1971): Ein Spiegelbild unserer Arbeit. 18 DER SCHÖFFE 170–171.

Severin, Ernst-Guenter & Erika Wolter (1980): Entschädigung für Schöffen, Beteiligte an Gerichtsverfahren und Mitglieder der Schiedskommissionen. 34 NEUE JUSTIZ 514–515.

Sharp, William & Arthur M. Hanhardt, Jr.: The Social Court System of the German Democratic Republic: A Model for Dispute Processing in the U.S. University of Oregon, undated manuscript.

Shelley, Louise (1984): Interviews mit emigrierten sowjetischen Juristen. 34 OSTEUROPA 796–803.

Shelley, Louise (1990): Democratization and Law. Albert J. Schmidt: THE IMPACT OF PERESTROIKA ON SOVIET LAW. Martinus Nijhoff.

Shelton Judy (1989): THE COMING SOVIET CRASH. Free Press.

Shevchenko, Arkady N. (1985): BREAKING WITH MOSCOW. Ballantine.

Siegel, Guenther (1966): Verletzung der Schulpflicht und ihre Beratung vor der Schiedskommission. 13 DER SCHÖFFE 324–326.

Sieveking, Klaus (1975): DIE ENTWICKLUNG DES SOZIALISTISCHEN RECHTSSTAATSBEGRIFFS IN DER DDR. Nomos Verlag.

Silberman, L. (1979): NON-ATTORNEY JUSTICE IN THE U.S.: AN EMPIRICAL STUDY. Institute of Judicial Administration (New York).

Simon, Caroline K. (1975): The Juror in New York City: Attitudes and Experiences. 61 AMERICAN BAR ASSOCIATION JOURNAL 207–211.

Simon, Rita J. (1980): THE JURY: ITS ROLE IN AMERICAN SOCIETY. Lexington.

Simon, Rita J., ed. (1975): THE JURY SYSTEM IN AMERICA: A CRITICAL OVERVIEW. Sage.

Sinyavsky, Andrei (1990): SOVIET CIVILIZATION: A CULTURAL HISTORY. Little, Brown.

Sipes, Dale A. et al. (1988): ON TRIAL: THE LENGTH OF CIVIL AND CRIMINAL TRIALS. National Center for State Courts.

Skarabis, Erich (1972): Ordnungswidrigkeiten, Schulpflichtverletzungen und arbeitsscheues Verhalten. 19 DER SCHÖFFE 94–100.

Sleeper, Raymond S., ed. (1987): MESMERIZED BY THE BEAR: THE SOVIET STRATEGY OF DECEPTION. Dodd, Mead.

Slider, Darrell (1986): Worker Participation in Socialist Systems: The Soviet Case. 18 COMPARATIVE POLITICS 401–418.

Smith, Christopher E. (1992): From U.S. Magistrates to U.S. Magistrate Judges. 75 JUDICATURE 210–215.

Smith, Duncan (1988): WALLS AND MIRRORS: WESTERN REPRESENTATIONS OF REALLY EXISTING GERMAN SOCIALISM IN THE GERMAN DEMOCRATIC REPUBLIC. University Press of America.

Smith, Jean Edward (1967): The Red Prussians of the GDR. 82 POLITICAL SCIENCE QUARTERLY 368–385.

Smith, Jean Edward (1969): GERMANY BEYOND THE WALL. Little, Brown.

Sobeck, R. (1954): Ein Wort zur Schöffenschulung. 1:7 DER SCHÖFFE 21.

Social Courts Law—see Law regarding the Social Courts of the GDR.

Solomon, Peter H., Jr. (1982): Criminalization and Decriminalization in Soviet Criminal Policy, 1917–1941. F.J.M. Feldbrugge & William B. Simons, eds.: PERSPECTIVES ON SOVIET LAW FOR THE 1980s. Martinus Nijhoff.

Sommer, Fritz (1980): Praktischen Bedürfnissen Rechnung tragen. 27 DER SCHÖFFE 66.

Sommer, Stefan (2002): DAS GROSSE LEXIKON DES DDR ALLTAGS. Schwarzkopf & Schwarzkopf.

Sontheimer, Kurt & Wilhelm Bleek (1975): THE GOVERNMENT AND POLITICS OF EAST GERMANY. Hutchinson.

Sorgenicht, Klaus (1969): Aktuelle Probleme des sozialistischen Staates in der DDR. 23 NEUE JUSTIZ 289–294.

Sorgenicht, Klaus (1979): Aktuelle Aufgaben auf dem Gebiet des States und des Rechts. 33 NEUE JUSTIZ 2–6.

Sorgenicht, Klaus (1982): Die sozialistische Staatsmacht unter Führung der marxistisch-leninistischen Partei: Grundfrage der sozialistischen Revolution. 82 EINHEIT 25–32.

Sorgenicht, Klaus & Wolfgang Weichelt (1963): Zur Entwicklung der staatlichen Tätigkeit beim umfassenden Aufbau des Sozialismus. 63 EINHEIT 47–56.

Sozialistische Einheitspartei Deutschlands (1976): PROGRAMME.

Speck, Johannes (1990): DIE RECHTSSTELLUNG DES BESCHULDIGTEN IM STRAFVERFAHREN DER DDR. Max-Planck-Institut.

Sperlich, Peter W. (1971): CONFLICT AND HARMONY IN HUMAN AFFAIRS. Rand McNally.

Sperlich, Peter W. (1979a): Trial by Jury: It May Have a Future. In Philip B. Kurland & Gerhard Casper, eds.: THE SUPREME COURT REVIEW 1978. University of Chicago Press.

Sperlich, Peter W. (1979b): Lay Participation in Judicial Proceedings in the United States. World Congress, International Political Science Association; Moscow, USSR; August 1979.

Sperlich, Peter W. (1980a): And Then There Were Six: The Decline of the American Jury. 63 JUDICATURE 262, 275–277.

Sperlich, Peter W. (1980b): Postrealism: Should Ignorance Be Elevated to a Principle of Adjudication? 64 JUDICATURE 93–98.

Sperlich, Peter W. (1980c): Social Science Evidence in the Courts: Reaching Beyond the Adversary Process. 63 JUDICATURE 280–289.

Sperlich, Peter W. (1982a): The Case for Preserving Trial by Jury in Complex Civil Litigation. 65 JUDICATURE 394, 413–415.

Sperlich, Peter W. (1982b): The Theory and Practice of Lay Adjudication: East German Commissioners and United States Jurors. World Congress, International Political Science Association; Rio de Janeiro, Brazil; August 1982

Sperlich, Peter W. (1982c): Better Judicial Management: The Best Remedy for Complex Cases. 65 JUDICATURE 415–419.

Sperlich, Peter W. (1982d): Was There a Complexity Exception to Trial by Jury in 1791? 65 JUDICATURE 396–398.

Sperlich, Peter W. (1983): Scientific Evidence in the Courts: The Disutility of Adversary Proceedings. 66 JUDICATURE 472–475.

Sperlich, Peter W. (1984): The Court, the Jury, and the Facts. 1984 AMERICAN BAR FOUNDATION RESEARCH JOURNAL 705–721.

Sperlich, Peter W. (1985a): The Evidence on Evidence: Science and Law in Conflict and Cooperation. Saul M. Kassin & Lawrence S. Wrightsman, eds.: THE PSYCHOLOGY OF EVIDENCE AND COURTROOM PROCEDURE. Sage.

Sperlich, Peter W. (1985b): The Incentive Structure of Lay Adjudicators in Two Legal Cultures. World Congress, International Political Science Association; Paris, France; July 1985.

Sperlich, Peter W. (1987): Survey Research and the Law: Interviews, Probability Samples, and Statistics. TRIAL CONSULTING NOTES (March 1987).

Sperlich, Peter W. (1988): Sample Surveys and Inferences. TRIAL CONSULTING NOTES (December 1988).

Sperlich, Peter W. (1991): Courting Social Science. 16 LAW & SOCIAL INQUIRY 419–425.

Sperlich, Peter W. (1992a): Petit Juries. Kermit L. Hall, ed.: THE OXFORD COMPANION TO THE SUPREME COURT OF THE UNITED STATES. Oxford University Press.

Sperlich, Peter W. (1992b): Grand Juries. Kermit L. Hall, ed.: THE OXFORD COMPANION TO THE SUPREME COURT OF THE UNITED STATES. Oxford University Press.

Sperlich, Peter W. (1992c): The Liability of Junk and the Junk of Liability: Evidentiary Misdeeds in the Courts. 75 JUDICATURE 273.

Sperlich, Peter W. (2002): ROTTEN FOUNDATIONS: THE CONCEPTUAL BASIS OF THE MARXIST-LENINIST REGIMES OF EAST GERMANY AND OTHER COUNTRIES OF THE SOVIET BLOC. Praeger.

Sperlich, Peter W. (2006): OPPRESSION AND SCARCITY: THE HISTORY AND INSTITUTIONAL STRUCTURE OF THE MARXIST-LENINIST

GOVERNMENT OF EAST GERMANY AND SOME PERSPECTIVES ON LIFE IN A SOCIALIST SYSTEM. Praeger.

Sperlich, Peter W. & Martin L. Jaspovice (1974): Grand Juries, Grand Jurors, and the Constitution. 1 HASTINGS CONSTITUTIONAL LAW QUARTERLY 63–95.

Sperlich, Peter W. & Martin L. Jaspovice (1975): Statistical Decision Theory and the Selection of Grand Jurors: Testing for Discrimination in a Single Panel. 2 HASTINGS CONSTITUTIONAL LAW QUARTERLY 75–112.

Sperlich, Peter W. & Martin L. Jaspovice (1979): Methods for the Analysis of Jury Panel Selections: Testing for Discrimination in a Series of Panels. 6 HASTINGS CONSTITUTIONAL LAW QUARTERLY 787–852.

Staatliche Zentralverwaltung für Statistik (1987): STATISTISCHES JAHRBUCH 1987. Staatsverlag.

Staehr, Annemarie (1982): Abgeordnetentreff. 29 DER SCHÖFFE 150–151.

Stalmaster, Irvin (1938): WHAT PRICE JURY TRIALS? Callaghan & Co.

Starr, June (1982): Mediation: Anthropological Perspectives. 6 ALSA FORUM 221–257.

Starrels, John M. & Anita M. Mallinckrodt (1975): POLITICS IN THE GERMAN DEMOCRATIC REPUBLIC. Praeger.

Steding, Rolf, ed. (1987): LENINS STAATSKONZEPTION UND IHRE SCHÖPFERISCHE ANWENDUNG IN DER DDR. Akademie für Staats- und Rechtswissenschaften.

Steele, Jonathan (1977): INSIDE EAST GERMANY. Urizen Books.

Steele, Walter W., Jr. & Elizabeth G. Thornburg (1995): Jury Instructions: A Persistent Failure to Communicate. G. Larry Mays & Peter R. Gregware, eds.: COURTS AND JUSTICE. Waveland Press.

Steffens, Gerhard (1979): Erfahrungen zur Wirksamkeit der Schiedskommissionen. 33 NEUE JUSTIZ 25.

Steffens, Gerhard (1982): Verantwortungsvolle Vorbereitung auf die Arbeit mit dem Gesetz über die gesellschaftlichen Gerichte im Kreis Merseburg. 36 NEUE JUSTIZ 416–417.

Steffens, Gerhard (1985): Bezirkstag Karl-Marx-Stadt festigt die sozialistische Rechtsordnung. 39 NEUE JUSTIZ 367–369.

Stegemann, Hans (1969): Arbeitsdisziplin und materielle Verantwortlichkeit. 16 DER SCHÖFFE 20–21.

Stegemann, Hans (1976): Kein Beschluss ohne Empfehlungen. 23 DER SCHÖFFE 247–248.

Stegemann, Hans-Juergen (1965): Die Konfliktkommission setzte sich mit falschen Auffassungen auseinander. 12 DER SCHÖFFE 99–100.

Stepan, Jan (1973): Possible Lessons from Continental Criminal Procedure. In American Enterprise Institute for Public Policy Research: THE ECONOMICS OF CRIME AND PUNISHMENT.

Stiehler, Gottfried (1968): DIALEKTIK UND PRAXIS. Akademie-Verlag.

Stiller, Gerhard (1955): Die erzieherische Wirkung des Strafverfahrens. 9 NEUE JUSTIZ 682–685.

Stiller, Gerhard (1969): Grundfragen der erzieherischen Wirksamkeit des sozialistischen Rechts bei der Gestaltung des entwickelten gesellschaftlichen Systems des Sozialismus in der DDR. 18 STAAT UND RECHT 1437–1451.

Stoepper, Clara (1957): Schöffen erziehen Jugendliche. 4 DER SCHÖFFE 82–83.

Stoessel, K. (1971): Zusammenarbeit zwischen Schiedskommission und Jugendhilfekommission. 18 DER SCHÖFFE 200–201.
Stoever, William (1974): The Expendable Resource: Studies to Improve Juror Utilization. 1 JUSTICE SYSTEM JOURNAL 39–53.
Stoffregen, Susanne (1985): Der Schöffe als 'juristischer Halblaie'? 2 ZEITSCHRIFT FüR RECHTSPOLITIK 52–53.
Stoph, Willi (1983): Sozialistische Staatsmacht—schöpferische Verwirklichung der Marxschen Staatslehre. 37 NEUE JUSTIZ 262–265.
Strasberg, Werner (1980): Aufgaben der Gerichte zur Unterstützung der sozialistischen Wohnungspolitik. 34 NEUE JUSTIZ 342–343.
Strasberg, Werner (1982): Aufgaben der Arbeitsrechtsprechung nach dem 10. FDGB-Kongress. 36 NEUE JUSTIZ 340–342.
Strasberg, Werner (1987); Kameradschaftliche Zusammenarbeit der Gerichte mit den Gewerkschaften. 42 ARBEIT UND ARBEITSRECHT 7–8.
Strauss, S. A. (1973): The Jury in South Africa. 11 WESTERN AUSTRALIA LAW REVIEW 133–139.
Strawn, David U. & G. Thomas Munsterman (1987): Helping Juries Handle Complex Cases. Lawrence S. Wrightsman et al., eds.: IN THE JURY BOX. Sage.
Streit, Josef (1954): Zur Verbesserung der Schöffenarbeit. 1:7 DER SCHÖFFE 14–19.
Streit, Josef (1955a): Die erzieherische Wirkung der Tätigkeit unserer demokratischen Gerichte erhöhen. 9 NEUE JUSTIZ 5–11.
Streit, Josef (1955b): Neue Kader sind in die Gerichte eingezogen. 2 DER SCHÖFFE 194–197.
Streit, Josef (1962): Der Staat schützt die Rechte der Bürger. 16 NEUE JUSTIZ 758–759.
Streit, Josef (1976): NUR UMS STRAFEN GEHT ES NICHT. Staatsverlag.
Streit, Ludwig (1978): Vielfaltige Fragen überzeugend klären. 25 DER SCHÖFFE 196–198.
Strempel, Dieter (2000): Politische Steuerung der Justiz in der Deutschen Demokratischen Republik. Heiner Timmermann, ed.: DIE DDR: RECHT UND JUSTIZ ALS POLITISCHES INSTRUMENT. Duncker & Humblot.
Strick, Anne (1977): INJUSTICE FOR ALL. Putnam.
Stricker, Carl-Heinz (1964): Die Gerichte unterstützen die Qualifizierung der Konfliktkommissionsmitglieder. 18 NEUE JUSTIZ 56.
Stricker, Carl-Heinz (1975): Schiedskommissionen im Erfahrungsaustausch. 22 DER SCHÖFFE 271–273.
Stricker, Carl-Heinz (1976): Zur einheitlichen und differenzierten Anwendung der Geldbusse. 23 DER SCHÖFFE 75–78.
Strohbach, Heinz (1974): Zur Erledigung einfacher zivilrechtlicher Streitigkeiten ohne Beratung. 21 DER SCHÖFFE 138–139.
Struch, Rudolf (1970): Von den Bürgern geachtet und in Anspruch genommen. 17 DER SCHÖFFE 127.
Stuchka, P.I. (1988): SELECTED WRITINGS ON SOVIET LAW AND MARXISM. Sharpe.
Stuebner, Frank (1987): Erfolge durch vorbeugendes Wirken. 42 ARBEIT UND ARBEITSRECHT 41.

Stuebner, Renate (1980): Hohe Qualität setzt Stabilität voraus. 27 DER SCHÖFFE 279.
Stuebner, Rolf (1984): Sozialistisches Eigentümerbewusstsein ausprägen helfen. 31 DER SCHÖFFE 172–173.
Sucknow, Alfred (1972): Sorgfältige Vorbereitung jeder Beratung. 19 DER SCHÖFFE 239–252.
Suess, Sonja (1998): POLITISCH MISSBRAUCHT? PSYCHIATRIE UND STAATSSICHERHEIT IN DER DDR. Ch.Links Verlag.
Suess, Walter (1999): STAATSSICHERHEIT AM ENDE. Ch.Links Verlag.
Surkau, Wolfgang (1985): Der Beitrag der Schiedskommissionen zur Durchsetzung der Stadt- und Gemeindeordnungen. 32 DER SCHÖFFE 251–255.
Sutliffe, Robert S. (1922): IMPRESSIONS OF AN AVERAGE JURYMAN. Appleton.
Symposium (1968): DDR-Forschung. I DEUTSCHLAND ARCHIV 141–150 & 255–272.
Symposium (1979): A Town Hall Report on Our Jury System. 12:3:1 TOWN HALL REPORTER 3–15 (March 1979).
Symposium (1984): The Grand Jury. 75 JOURNAL OF CRIMINAL LAW 1159–1196.
Sypnowich, Christine (1990): THE CONCEPT OF SOCIALIST LAW. Clarendon Press.
Szajkowski, Bogdan, ed. (1982): THE ESTABLISHMENT OF MARXIST REGIMES. Butterworth Scientific.
Szasz, Thomas S. (1963): LAW, LIBERTY, AND PSYCHIATRY. Macmillan.
Tauchnitz, Ingrid (1971): Probleme der Rechtsprechung auf dem Gebiet des Wohnungsmietrechts. 18 DER SCHÖFFE 172–176.
Taylor, Jay (1993): THE RISE AND FALL OF TOTALITARIANISM IN THE TWENTIETH CENTURY. Paragon House.
Taylor, Lily R. (1966): PARTY POLITICS IN THE AGE OF CAESAR. University of California Press.
Teichler, Gert (1986): Reaktion auf Rechtsverletzungen im unteren Grenzbereich des Strafrechts. 40 NEUE JUSTIZ 463–464.
Teller, Wolfgang (1986): In Dienst der Gesellschaft—zum Nutzen der Bürger. 33 DER SCHÖFFE 42.
Thai Bar Association (1969): THE ADMINISTRATION OF JUSTICE IN THAILAND.
Thai Bar Association (1981): THE LEGAL SYSTEM OF THAILAND.
Thatcher, Jeannatte E. (1947): Why Not Use the Special Jury? 31 MINNESOTA LAW REVIEW 232–262.
Thews, X. (1954): Schöffentätigkeit einst und jetzt. 1:2 DER SCHÖFFE 10–12.
Thiel, Wera (1988): On the Human Right to Work in the GDR. 88–1 LAW AND LEGISLATION IN THE GDR 83–92.
Thiel, Wera & Juergen Pawelzig (1980): Verwirklichung Leninscher Leitungsprinzipien im Arbeitsrecht. 34 NEUE JUSTIZ 297–299.
Thiele, Gisela (1984): Die Gesetzesinterpretation als Element der Ideologiefunktion in der bürgerlichen "Sozialismuskritik." 33 WISSENSCHAFTLICHE ZEITSCHRIFT (JENA) 183–202.
Thiele, Gottfried (1980): Bewährungskontrolle im Blickfeld des Schöffenaktivs. 27 DER SCHÖFFE 51–55.

Thiem, Ellinor (1980): Beschleunigtes Verfahren als wirksame Reaktion auf Straftaten. 34 NEUE JUSTIZ 373.
Thiem, Ellinor (1981): Übernahme und Ausgestaltung von Bürgschaften. 35 NEUE JUSTIZ 130–131.
Thieme, Ilse & Erwin Gerth (1972): Gesellschaftliche Gerichte—Instrumente sozialistischer Macht. 19 DER SCHÖFFE 16–19.
Thoelken, Gertrud (1982): Erziehung bei Verfehlungen. 29 DER SCHÖFFE 15–16.
Thoms, Franz (1965): Die Voraussetzungen der Eheschliessung und die Anforderungen an die Familiengemeinschaft. 12 DER SCHÖFFE 169–173.
Tiedke, Kurt (1989): Die SED—eine Partei der Neuerer. 89 EINHEIT 897–904.
Tigar, Michael & Madeline R. Levy (1971): The Grand Jury as the New Inquisition. 50 MICHIGAN STATE BAR JOURNAL 693–700.
Timmermann, Heiner (2000): Die Rechtsordnung der Bundesrepublik Deutschland und der DDR. Heiner Timmermann, ed.: DIE DDR: RECHT UND JUSTIZ ALS POLITISCHES INSTRUMENT. Duncker & Humblot.
Timothy, Mary (1975): JURY WOMAN. Emty Press.
Tisch, Harry (1982): Unser Recht—Ausdruck der Macht der Arbeiterklasse. 29 DER SCHÖFFE 113.
Tischer, Klaus (1983): Höhere Verantwortung allseitig wahrnehmen. 30 DER SCHÖFFE 276–282.
Tocqueville, Alexis de (1945): DEMOCRACY IN AMERICA. Vol. I. Vintage Books.
Toeplitz, Heinrich (1954): Die Stellung der Schöffen in der Deutschen Demokratischen Republik. 1:4 DER SCHÖFFE 1–9.
Toeplitz, Heinrich (1963): The Functions of the Courts of the German Democratic Republic on the Basis of the State Council Decree. 1 LAW & LEGISLATION IN THE GDR 19.
Toeplitz, Heinrich (1964): Grössere Wirksamkeit der gerichtlichen Verfahren. 18 NEUE JUSTIZ 321–324
Toeplitz, Heinrich (1966): Die DDR ist der wahre deutsche Rechtsstaat. 20 NEUE JUSTIZ 374–376.
Toeplitz, Heinrich (1971): Independence of the Courts: Myth or Reality? 71–2 LAW AND LEGISLATION IN THE GDR 42.
Toeplitz, Heinrich (1973): Problems of the Social Courts in the German Democratic Republic. 1 LAW & LEGISLATION IN THE GDR 5.
Toeplitz, Heinrich (1974): Der Beitrag des Obersten Gerichts zur Stärkung und Festigung der sozialistischen Staatsmacht. 28 NEUE JUSTIZ 574–577.
Toeplitz, Heinrich (1976): Schöffen sind gleichberechtigte Richter. 23 DER SCHÖFFE 109–111.
Toeplitz, Heinrich (1982): Tätigkeit der Konfliktkommissionen: Ausdruck der sozialistischen Demokratie. 36 NEUE JUSTIZ 98.
Toeplitz, Heinrich (1984): DER BÜRGER UND DAS GERICHT. Staatsverlag.
Tomasic, Roman (1980): Mediation as an Alternative to Adjudication. WORKING PAPER 1980–2.
Tomasic, Roman & Malcolm M. Feeley (1982): NEIGHBORHOOD JUSTICE: ASSESSMENT OF AN EMERGING IDEA. Longman.
Torzewski, Horst (1976): Einfluss auf eine wirkungsvolle Bewährungskontrolle. 23 DER SCHÖFFE 280–281.

Toyama Titus S. (1977): Lay Participation in the Japanese Legal System. Unpublished manuscript.
Traeger, Katja (1985): Aufgaben des Jugendbeistandes. 39 NEUE JUSTIZ 31.
Tschchikwadse, Viktor M. (1989): Über den von A. Wyschinsli der sowjetischen Rechtswissenschaft zugefügten Schaden. 33 RECHT IN OST UND WEST 217–219.
Tucker, Robert C. (1961): PHILOSOPHY AND MYTH IN KARL MARX. Cambridge University Press.
Twain, Mark (1913): ROUGHING IT. Vol.II. Harper & Brothers.
Udke, Gerwin (1987): Sozialistisches Arbeitsverhalten und Arbeitsrecht. 42 ARBEIT UND ARBEITSRECHT 57–58.
Udke, Gerwin et al. (1988): SOZIALISTISCHES RECHT: LEHRBUCH. Verlag die Wirtschaft.
Ulbricht, Walter (1958): DIE STAATSLEHRE DES MARXISMUS-LENINISMUS UND IHRE ANWENDUNG IN DEUTSCHLAND. Zentralverlag.
Ulbricht, Walter (1963): DAS PROGRAMM DES SOZIALISMUS UND DIE GESCHICHTLICHE AUFGABE DER SOZIALISTISCHEN EINHEITSPARTEI DEUTSCHLANDS. Staatsverlag.
Ulbricht, Walter (1964a): Die Bildung von Schiedskommissionen: Ein weiterer Schritt zur Einbeziehung der Bürger in die Bekämpfung und Verhütung von Rechtsverletzungen. 18 NEUE JUSTIZ 513.
Ulbricht, Walter (1964b): Schiedskommissionen fördern unsere Demokratie. 11 DER SCHÖFFE 344.
Ulbricht, Walter (1970): Die weitere Gestaltung des gesellschaftlichen Systems des Sozialismus. Lothar Lippmann & Hans D. Moschuetz, eds.: DAS SYSTEM DER SOZIALISTISCHEN GESELLSCHAFTS- UND STAATSORDNUNG IN DER DEUTSCHEN DEMOKRATISCHEN REPUBLIK: DOKUMENTE. Staatsverlag.
Ullmann, Guenther (1962): Konfliktkommission behandelt geringfügige Gesetzesverletzungen. 9 DER SCHÖFFE 246–248.
Ulrich, Peter (1984): ERFAHRUNGEN UND GEDANKEN EINES DDR-BÜRGERS. Colloquium Verlag.
United States Army, Judge Advocate General (1959): COUNTRY LAW STUDY FOR THE REPUBLIC OF CHINA.
United States Department of Justice (1974): A GUIDE TO JUROR USAGE.
United States Department of State (1953): Crime does not recede in the USSR. 143 SOVIET AFFAIRS NOTES 1–8.
United States Department of State (1960): The New "Justice" in the USSR. 239 SOVIET AFFAIRS NOTES 1–12.
Urban, Karl (1981): Effektive Zusammenarbeit erhöht den Nutzen. 28 DER SCHÖFFE 145.
Vallinder, Torbjorn (1987): The Swedish Jury System in Press Cases: An Offspring of the English Trial Jury? 8 JOURNAL OF LEGAL HISTORY 190–220.
Valters, Nikolaus (1955): Urteilsüberprüfung "im Aufsichtsverfahren" nach Sowjetrecht. 1 OSTEUROPA-RECHT 38–42.
Van Dyke, Jon (1976): The Grand Jury: Representative or Elite? 28 HASTINGS LAW JOURNAL 37–71.
Van Dyke, Jon (1977): JURY SELECTION PROCEDURES. Ballinger.

Vanderbilt, Arthur T. (1956): JUDGES AND JURORS: THEIR FUNCTIONS, QUALIFICATIONS, AND SELECTION. Boston University Press.

Vanlandingham, Kenneth E. (1974): The Decline of the Justice of the Peace. As reprinted in John A. Robertson: ROUGH JUSTICE. Little, Brown.

Verch, Irmengard (1985): Erfahrungen aus Beratungen wegen Schulpflichtverletzungen. 32 DER SCHÖFFE 86.

Vereinigung der Juristen der DDR, ed. (1979): RECHT IM DENST DES VOLKES. Staatsverlag.

Versele, Severin-Carlos (1969): Public Participation in the Administration of Justice. 27 INTERNATIONAL REVIEW OF CRIMINAL POLICY 9.

Vidmar, Neil (1995): MEDICAL MALPRACTICE AND THE AMERICAN JURY: CONFRONTING THE MYTHS ABOUT JURY INCOMPETENCE, DEEP POCKETS, AND OUTRAGEOUS DAMAGE AWARDS. University of Michgan Press.

Vietzke, Siegfried (1989): Antifaschism prägt unseren Weg, unsere Macht. 89 EINHEIT 935–940.

Villain, Jean (1990): DIE REVOLUTION VERSTÖSST IHRE VÄTER. Zytglogge Verlag.

Voeckler, Erika (1974): Ziel von Empfehlungen ist es, zur Festigung von Ordnung, Disziplin und Sicherheit beizutragen. 21 DER SCHÖFFE 394–395.

Voigt, Wlf-Dietrich (1987): Schon Straftat oder noch keine. 42 ARBEIT UND ARBEITSRECHT 42–43.

Volk, Klaus (1982): Der Laie als Strafrichter. Ernst-Walter Hanack, et al. (1982): FESTSCHRIFT FüR HANNS DUENNEBIER. Walter de Gruyter.

Vollnhals, Clemens (1994): Ausführendes Organ der Diktatur des Proletariats. Juergen Weber, ed. DER SED-STAAT. Olzog Verlag.

Vollnhals, Clemens & Jucgen Weber, eds. (2002): DER SCHEIN DER NORMALITÄT: ALLTAG UND HERRSCHAFT IN DER SED-DIKTATUR. Olzog Verlag.

Vyshinsky, Andrei Y. (1948): THE LAW OF THE SOVIET STATE. Macmillan.

Vyshinsky, Andrei Y. (1951): Soviet Socialist Law. Arthur P. Coleman, translator: GREAT SOVIET ENCYCLOPEDIA. University of Texas.

Wagner, Ingo (1994): Die DDR—ein “Unrechtsstaat”? Lothar Bisky et al., eds.: UNRECHTSSTAAT? VSA-Verlag.

Wagner, Walter (1974): DER VOLKSGERICHTSHOFF IM NATIONALSOZIALISTISCHEN STAAT. Deutsche Verlags-Anstalt.

Walker, Richard (1972): Mao as Superman. 26 JOURNAL OF INTERNATIONAL AFFAIRS 160.

Wassmund, Hans (1981): German Democratic Republic. Bogdan Szajkowski, ed.: MARXIST GOVERNMENTS. Vol. 2. Macmillan.

Weber, Hermann (1990): ‘WEISSE FLECKEN’ IN DER GESCHICHTE: DIE KPD-OPFER DER STALINSCHEN SÄUBERUNGEN UND IHRE REHABILITIERUNG. ISP-Verlag.

Weber, Hermann (1991): DDR: GRUNDRISS DER GESCHICHTE, 1945–1990. Neuauflage. Fackelträger.

Weber, Wolfgang: DDR (1993): 40 JAHRE STALINISMUS: EIN BEITRAG ZUR GESCHICHTE DER DDR. Arbeiterpresse Verlag.

Wechsberg, Joseph (1964): JOURNEY THROUGH THE LAND OF ELOQUENT SILENCE: EAST GERMANY REVISITED. Little, Brown.

Weckert, Heinz (1983): Empfehlungen erhöhen Wirksamkeit der Beratungen. 30 DER SCHÖFFE 158–159.

Weckert, Heinz (1985): Die neuen Regelungen haben sich in der Praxis bewärt. 32 DER SCHÖFFE 65–66.

Weichelt, Wolfgang (1976): Zur Dialektik zwischen Staatsverfassung und Gesellschaftsentwicklung. Schoeneburg, Karl-Heinz & W. Kuenzel: DIALEKTIK, STAAT, RECHT. Akademie- Verlag.

Weichelt, Wolfgang (1978a): Die verfassungsmässigen Grundlagen für die Gerichtsorganisation in der DDR. Nationales Komitee für Rechtswissenschaft der DDR: BERICHTE ZUM X. INTERNATIONALEN KONGRESS FÜR RECHTSVERGLEICHUNG.

Weichelt, Wolfgang (1978b): Politische Macht und Demokratie im Sozialismus. 32 NEUE JUSTIZ 94–97.

Weichelt, Wolfgang (1978c): Some Remarks on the Concept of Human Rights. 78–2 LAW AND LEGISLATION IN THE GDR 35–42.

Weichelt, Wolfgang (1979a): Bemerkungen zum Begriff der Menschenrechte. Akademie der Wissenschaften der DDR: ZUR MARXISTISCHEN RECHTSKONZEPTION.

Weichelt, Wolfgang (1979b): Zur Rolle des Staates im politischen System des Sozialismus. 28 STAAT UND RECHT 780–789.

Weichelt, Wolfgang (1981): Der X. Parteitag der SED und die weitere Festigung des sozialistischen Staates. 35 NEUE JUSTIZ 338.

Weichelt, Wolfgang (1982a): Geprüft und fur gut befunden. 29 DER SCHÖFFE 93–94.

Weichelt, Wolfgang (1982b): Stellungnahme des Verfassungs- und Rechtsauschusses der Volkskammer der DDR. 36 NEUE JUSTIZ 148.

Weichelt, Wolgang & Helmut Kintzel (1981): Beseitigung der Macht der Arbeiterklasse: Grundtendenz aller Angriffe gegen den Sozialistischen Staat. 28 DER SCHÖFFE 233–249.

Weidenfeld, Werner & Hartmut Zimmermann, eds. (1989): DEUTSCHLAND HANDBUCH: EINE DOPPELTE BILANZ 1949–1989. Carl Hanser Verlag.

Weidig, Rudi (Leiter, Autorenkollektiv) (1988): SOZIALSTRUKTUR DER DDR. Dietz Verlag.

Weinke, Annette (2000): Stasi und Strafrecht: Ein dunkles Kapitel. Heiner Timmermann, ed.: DIE DDR: RECHT UND JUSTIZ ALS POLITISCHES INSTRUMENT. Duncker & Humblot.

Weinreb, Lloyd L. (1977): DENIAL OF JUSTICE. Free Press.

Weise, Wolfgang (1965): Ehescheidung—und was dann. 12 DER SCHÖFFE 41–45.

Weiss, Edith B. (1972): The East German Social Courts: Development and Comparison with China. 20 AMERICAN JOURNAL OF COMPARATIVE LAW 266.

Weller, Steven (1978): SMALL CLAIMS COURTS: A NATIONAL EXAMINATION. National Center for State Courts.

Welsh, William A., ed. (1981): SURVEY RESEARCH AND PUBLIC ATTITUDES IN EASTERN EUROPE AND THE SOVIET UNION. Pergamon Press.

Wendland, Guenter (1973): Die gesellschaftliche Wirksamkeit des Strafverfahrens erhöhen. 27 NEUE JUSTIZ 157–160.

Wenger, Morton G. & Thomas A. Bonomo (1993): Crime, the Crisis of Capitalism, and Social Revolution. David F. Greenberg, ed.: CRIME AND CAPITALISM: READINGS IN MARXIST CRIMINOLOGY. Temple University Press.

Wentker, Hermann (2001): JUSTIZ IN DER SBZ/DDR 1945–1953. R. Oldenbourg Verlag.

Werfel, Willi (1973): Lösung von Konflikten auch ohne Beratung möglich. 20 DER SCHÖFFE 182–184.

Werkentin, Falco (1995): POLITISCHE STRAFJUSTIZ IN DER ÄRA ULBRICHT. Ch. Links Verlag.

Werkentin, Falco (1999): "Souverän ist, wer über den Tod entscheidet." Die SED-Führung als Richter und Gnadeninstanz bei Todesurteilen. Roger Engelmann & Clemens Vollnhals, eds.: JUSTIZ IM DIENSTE DER PARTEIHERRSCHAFT. Ch. Links Verlag.

Westen, Klaus (1969): Verwaltungsrechtsschutz in der Retorte. 2 DEUTSCHLAND ARCHIV 370–378.

Westen, Klaus & Joachim Schleider (1984): ZIVILRECHT IM SYSTEMVERGLEICH. Nomos.

Weymar, Thomas (1985): IM TRABI ZUR SONNE, ZUR FREIHEIT. Verlag für Wirtschaft und Politik.

White, W. Wilson (1954): In Defense of the Grand Jury. 25 PENNSYLVANIA BAR ASSOCIATION QUARTERLY 260–264.

Wickersham, Cornelius W. (1965): The Grand Jury: Weapon Against Crime and Corruption. 51 AMERICAN BAR ASSOCIATION JOURNAL 1157–1161.

Wiedgrube, Dietrich (1985): Rolle der Öffentlichkeit und zivilrechtliche Streitigkeiten. 32 DER SCHÖFFE 66–68.

Wiedmann, Mechthild & Wolfgang Israel (1980): "Sozialistisches Recht" von Schöffen gelehrt. 27 DER SCHÖFFE 203–205.

Wiegand, Georg (1979): Erzieherischer Wert von Schadenersatz und gemeinnütziger Arbeit. 26 DER SCHÖFFE 117–118.

Wierling, Dorothee (1999): The Hitler Youth Generation in the GDR. Konrad Jarausch, ed.: DICTATORSHIP AS EXPERIENCE. Berghahn Books.

Wilkinson, Bertie, ed. (1972): THE CREATION OF MEDIEVAL PARLIAMENTS. Wiley.

Willamowski, Horst (1967a): Das Recht der Bürger auf unmittelbare Mitgestaltung der sozialistische Strafrechtspflege. 14 DER SCHÖFFE 93–99.

Willamowski, Horst (1967b): Neugestaltung strafrechtlicher Bestimmungen zur Bekämpfung des Rowdytums. 14 DER SCHÖFFE 312–318.

Willamowski, Horst (1982): Anforderungen an eine wirksame Bewährungskontrolle. 29 DER SCHÖFFE 209–216.

Williams, Mary E., ed. (1997): THE JURY SYSTEM. Greenhaven Press.

Wilson, James Q. (1975): THINKING ABOUT CRIME. Basic Books.

Winkler, Arno (1982): Zur Verfälschung des Wesens der sozialistischen Staatsmacht durch die bürgerliche "DDR-Forschung." 31 STAAT UND RECHT 1002–1010.

Winkler, Rudolf (1967): Zur Wahl der Mitglieder der Schiedskommissionen. 14 DER SCHÖFFE 401–405.

Winkler, Rudolf (1971): Abgeordnete und das sozialistische Recht. 18 DER SCHÖFFE 145–156.

Winkler, Rudolf (1972): Zur Vollstreckung von Geldbussen. 19 DER SCHÖFFE 22–23.

Winkler, Rudolf (1978): 15 Jahre Schiedskommissionen—anderthalb Jahrzehnt erfolgreicher Tätigkeit. 25 DER SCHÖFFE 101–103.

Winkler, Rudolf (1980): Grössere Wirksamkeit der gesellschaftlichen Gerichte. 27 DER SCHÖFFE 3.

Winkler, Rudolf (1982): Würdigung der Tätigkeit der Schiedskommissionen. 29 DER SCHÖFFE 129.

Winkler, Rudolf (1983): Einheitliche Rechtsanwendung in der Tätigkeit der Schiedskommissionen sichern. 30 DER SCHÖFFE 217–223.

Winkler, Rudolf (1984): Hohe Wirksamkeit der Schiedskommissionen auf allen Tätigkeitsgebieten gewährleisten. 31 DER SCHÖFFE 261

Winkler, Rudolf & Kurt Goerner (1967): Vor neuen Aufgaben. 14 DER SCHÖFFE 204–212.

Winkler, Rudolf & Kurt Goerner (1968): Zur Stellung und Tätigkeit der gesellschaftlichen Gerichte im System der Staats- und Rechtsordnung der DDR. 15 DER SCHÖFFE 249–257.

Winkler, Rudolf & Sonja Jaenchen (1965): Zum Stand der Bildung und Entwicklung der Schiedskommissionen in der DDR. 12 DER SCHÖFFE 117–122.

Winkler, Rudolf & Ingetraud Matheus (1983): Zur Beratung und Entscheidung der Schiedskommissionen über Verfehlungen. 30 DER SCHÖFFE 16–20.

Winkler, Rudolf et al. (1982): Zur Schulung für Schiedskommissionen. Part 1, 29 DER SCHÖFFE 106–109; Part 2, 29 DER SCHÖFFE 118.

Winkler, Siegfried & Heinz Feist (1982): Zu einigen Erfahrungen der Bewährungskontrolle. 29 DER SCHÖFFE 181–184.

Winters, Glenn R., ed. (1971): THE JURY; SELECTED READINGS. American Judicatue Society.

Winzer, Rosemarie (1984): Aktive Lebenshaltung. 31 DER SCHÖFFE 153.

Wippold, Werner (1985): Vervollkommnung der sozialistischen Demokratie: Wichtige Triebkraft der sozialistischen Gesellschaft. Rat für staats- und rechtswissenschaftliche Forschung an der Akademie der Wissenschaften der DDR: VERVOLLKOMMNUNG DER SOZIALISTISCHEN DEMOKRATIE: TRIEBKRAFT DER SOZIALISTSICHEN GESELLSCHAFT. Staatsverlag.

Wise, David (1973): THE POLITICS OF LYING. Vintage Books.

Wishman, Seymour (1986): ANATOMY OF A JURY: THE SYSTEM ON TRIAL. Penguin Books.

Wittenbeck, Siegfried (1980): Anwendung und Ausgestaltung der Verurteilung auf Bewährung. 34 NEUE JUSTIZ 201–206.

Wittenbeck, Siegfried (1985): Aktuelle Aufgaben der Öffentlichkeitsarbeit der Richter und Notare. 39 NEUE JUSTIZ 493–495.

Wittenbeck, Siegfried (1986): Analysen der Rechtsarbeit in Kombinaten und Betrieben. 40 NEUE JUSTIZ 270–271.

Wittenbeck, Siegfried (1989): Zur Entwicklung unserer sozialistischen Rechtsordnung. 89 EINHEIT 216–221.

Wittenbeck, Siegfried & Rolf Schroeder (1980): Die Anwendung der Geldstrafe als Haupt- und Zusatzstrafe. 34 NEUE JUSTIZ 15–18.

Wittenberg, Gerhard (1982): Wirksamkeit der Schiedskommissionen im Bezirk Schwerin erhöhen. 29 DER SCHÖFFE 10.

Wittenberg, Gerhard (1985): Zur Tätigkeit der Schiedskommissionen und ihre Wirksamkeit im Bezirk Schwerin. 32 DER SCHÖFFE 148–151.

Woelfel, Winfried (1983): Arbeit mit Bürgern. 37 NEUE JUSTIZ 209–210.

Woelfel, Winfried & Siegfried Kamuf (1979): Zusammenwirken bei der Rechtserziehung der Schüler. 33 NEUE JUSTIZ 316–317.

Wolfe, Bertram D. (1954): Totalitarianism and History. Carl J. Friedrich, ed.: TOTALITARIANISM. Harvard University Press.

Wolfe, Bertram D. (1961): COMMUNIST TOTALITARIANISM: KEYS TO THE SOVIET SYSTEM. rev. ed. Beacon Press.

Wolfe, Bertram D. (1969): AN IDEOLOGY IN POWER: REFLECTIONS ON THE RUSSIAN REVOLUTION. Stein & Day.

Wolfe, James H. (1971): Minor Parties in the GDR. 4 EAST EUROPEAN QUARTERLY 457–478.

Wolfe, Nancy T. (1983): Participation in Courts: American Jurors and German Lay Judges; Israel L. Barak-Glantz & Elmer H. Johnson, eds.: COMPARATIVE CRIMINOLOGY. Sage.

Wolfe, Nancy T. (1984): Challenges to Lay Judges in Germany. 8 INTERNATIONAL JOURNAL OF COMPARATIVE AND APPLIED CRIMINAL JUSTICE 151–161.

Wolfe, Nancy T. (1986): Social Courts in the German Democratic Republic: A Comparative Perspective. Paper delivered at the Meeting of the GDR Studies Association.

Wolfe, Nancy T. (1989): Social Courts in the GDR and Comrades' Courts in the Soviet Union: A Comparison. David Childs et al., eds.: EAST GERMANY IN COMPARATIVE PERSPECTIVE. Routledge.

Wolff, Friedrich (1964): On the Office of Lawyers in the German Democratic Republic. 64 LAW & LEGISLATION 17–24.

Wolff, Friedrich (1979): Von der bürgerlichen Advokatur zur sozialistischen Rechtsanwaltschaft. Vereinigung der Juristen der DDR: RECHT IM DIENST DES VOLKES. Staatsverlag.

Wolfram, Margarete (1965): Ursachen und begünstigende Bedingungen für das Scheitern junger Ehen. 12 DER SCHÖFFE 46–49, 86–91.

Wolfram, Margarete (1966): Das elterliche Erziehungsrecht. 13 DER SCHÖFFE 158–162.

Wolfram, Margarete (1975): Die Gründung von Ehe und Familie erfordert hohe gesellschaftliche Verantwortung und menschliche Reife. 22 DER SCHÖFFE ix–xiv.

Wolle, Stefan (1998): DIE HEILE WELT DER DIKTATUR: ALLTAG UND HERRSCHAFT IN DER DDR 1971–1989. Ch. Links Verlag.

Wolle, Stefan (2002): Sehnsucht nach der Diktatur? Clemens Vollnhals & Juegen Weber, eds. (2002): DER SCHEIN DER NORMALITÄT. Olzog Verlag.

Woods, Roger (1986): OPPOSITION IN THE GDR UNDER HONECKER, 1971–85. Macmillan.

Worner, Fredo (1986): Beschlüsse und Empfehlungen durchsetzen. 33 DER SCHÖFFE 83–84.

Worner, Fredo (1987): Ursachen erforscht und wirkungsvoll beseitigt. 34 DER SCHÖFFE 178–179.

Wostry, Heiz (1989): Gerichtliche Nachprüfung von Verwaltungsentscheidungen. 89 EINHEIT 222–224.

Woywod, Georg & Eckhard Heumeyer (1986): MENSCHENRECHTE IN DER DDR UND OST-BERLIN. Internationale Gesellschaft für Menschenrechte.

Wranik, Ursula (1980): Schöffen verschiedener Betriebe bilden ein Kollektiv. 27 DER SCHÖFFE 200.

Wrege, Inge (1973): Gedanken zum Entwurf des neuen Jugendgesetzes. 20 DER SCHÖFFE 259–262.

Wrightsman, Lawrence S. (1978): The American Trial Jury on Trial: Empirical Evidence and Procedural Modifications. 34 JOURNAL OF SOCIAL ISSUES 137–164.

Wrightsman, Lawrence S. et al., eds. (1987): IN THE JURY BOX. Sage.

Wuensche, Kurt (1968): Volkskammer beschloss neue Gesetze zur Rechtspflege. 15 DER SCHÖFFE 198–202.

Wuensche, Kurt (1969): Gesetzlichkeit und Rechtspflege in der DDR. 16 DER SCHÖFFE 305–310.

Wuensche, Kurt (1983): On the Legal Nature of the Social Courts and Their Jurisdiction. 83–1 LAW AND LEGISLATION IN THE GDR 29–33.

Wuensche, Kurt (1995): Der "Unrechtsstaat" DDR und sein ausgeschlagenes Erbe. Rosemarie Will, ed.: RECHTWISSENSCHAFT IN DER DDR—WAS WIRD VON IHR BLEIBEN? Pro Universitate Verlag.

Wuestneck, Ruth (1975): Die Wohnungsmiete. 22 DER SCHÖFFE 46–50.

Wunder, John R. (1979): INFERIOR COURTS, SUPERIOR JUSTICE: A HISTORY OF THE JUSTICES OF THE PEACE ON THE NORTHWEST FRONTIER, 1853–1889. Greenwood Press.

Wunderlich, Lisbeth (1976): Mit der gesellschaftlichen Entwicklung muss man Schritt halten. 23 DER SCHÖFFE 245–247.

Yack, Bernard (1986): THE LONGING FOR TOTAL REVOLUTION. Princeton University Press.

Yngvesson, Barbara & Patricia Hennessey (1975): Small Claims, Complex Disputes: A Review of the Small Claims Literature. 9 LAW & SOCIETY REVIEW 219.

Younger, Richard D. (1963): THE PEOPLE'S PANEL: THE GRAND JURY IN THE UNITED STATES, 1634–1941. Brown University Press.

Zander, Rudolf (1978): Schiedskommission Rosslau I—festgefügtes Kollektiv. 25 DER SCHÖFFE 66–67.

Zawadzki, Sylwester & Leszek Kubicki (1970): UDZIAL LAWNIKOW W POSTEPOWANIU KARNYM OPINIE A RZECZYWISTOSC. THE PARTICIPATION OF LAY PERSONS IN CRIMINAL PROCEEDINGS: OPINION AND REALITY Polish Academy of Sciences.

Zawadzki, Sylwester & Leszek Kubicki (1979): Polen. In Gerhard Casper & Hans Zeisel, eds., DER LAIENRICHTER IM STRAFPROZESS. C.F. Müller Juristischer Verlag.

Zecher, Guenther (1985): Wie der Rat der Stadt Boizenburg die Zusammenarbeit mit seinen Schiedskommissionen fördert. 32 DER SCHÖFFE 152–153.

Zeidler, Christa (1984): Qualität der Arbeit entscheidet über Erfolg. 31 DER SCHÖFFE 39.

Zeisel, Hans (1970a): Wozu überhaupt Laienrichter. Österreichischer Juristentag, Vol. II, Part 5, pp. 23–26a.

Zeisel, Hans (1970b): Diskussionsbeitrag, REFORM DER LAIENGERICHTSBERKEIT IN STRAFSACHEN. Manzsche Verlagsbuchhandlung, pp. 71–79.

Zeisel, Hans (1971): And Then There Were None: The Diminution of the Federal Jury. 38 UNIVERSITY OF CHICAGO LAW REVIEW 710–724.
Zeisel, Hans (1972): The Waning of the American Jury. 58 AMERICAN BAR ASSOCIATION JOURNAL 367–370.
Zeisel, Hans et al. (1959): DELAY IN THE COURT. Little, Brown.
Zeisel, Hans & Shari S. Diamond (1974): "Convincing Empirical Evidence" on the Six-Member Jury. Lawrence S. Wrightsman et al., eds.: IN THE JURY BOX. Sage.
Zeller, Bernd (2000): 101 GRÜNDE KEIN OSSI ZU SEIN. Raka Verlag.
Zeng, Matthias (2000): "ASOZIALE" IN DER DDR. LIT Verlag.
Zieger, Andrea (1986): Die strafrechtliche Entwicklung in Deutschland. 30 RECHT IN OST UND WEST 368–372.
Ziegler, Karl (1989): Der Beirat für Schiedskommissionen tagte beim Stadtgericht Berlin. 36 DER SCHÖFFE 171–176.
Ziegler, Uwe (1974): Zur Diskussion um Verwaltungsrecht und Verwaltungsrechtswissenschaft in der DDR. 7 DEUTSCHLAND ARCHIV 1036–1044.
Zillmer, Heinz (1986): Konfliktkommission in der Arbeit mit Jugendlichen. 33 DER SCHÖFFE 272–273.
Zimmermann, Michael (1985): Wachsende Ansprüche an die Rechtserziehung der Lehrlinge. 39 NEUE JUSTIZ 409–410.
Zimmermann, Monika, ed. (1994): WAS MACHT EIGENTLICH? 100 DDR-PROMINENTE HEUTE. Ch.Links Verlag.
Zinke, Eberhard (1986): Zur Zusammenarbeit der Schiedskommissionen mit der Nationalen Front. 33 DER SCHÖFFE 115–117.
Zipfel, Hans-Joachim (1987): Qualität verlangt fehlerlose Arbeit. 34 DER SCHÖFFE 27–29.
Zoch, Alfred (1964): Die Mitwirkung der gesellschaftlichen Kräfte in den Wohngebieten im Strafverfahren und bei der Erziehung von Rechtsverletzern. 13 STAAT UND RECHT 1399–1413.
Zschiedrich, Angelika (1981): Sozialistischer Staat und Grundrechte der Bürger. 35 NEUE JUSTIZ 293.
Zunder, Klaus-Peter (1985): Die Verantwortung des Rates der Stadt gegenüber seinen Schiedskommissionen. 32 DER SCHÖFFE 109–110.

Index

About the Author

PETER W. SPERLICH is Professor, Department of Political Science, The University of California at Berkeley.